Annotated Instructor's Edition

Boone & Kurtz

ESSENTIALS OF CONTEMPORARY BUSINESS

WileyPLUS with ORION

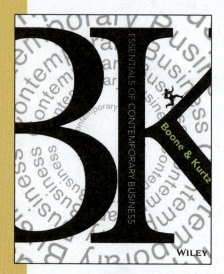

Based on cognitive science, *WileyPLUS* with ORION provides students with a personal, adaptive learning experience so they can build their proficiency on topics and use their study time most effectively.

BEGIN

Unique to ORION, students **BEGIN** by taking a quick diagnostic for any chapter. This will determine each student's baseline proficiency on each topic in the chapter. Students see their individual diagnostic report to help them decide what to do next with the help of ORION's recommendations.

PRACTICE

For each topic, students can either **STUDY**, or **PRACTICE**. Study directs students to the specific topic they choose in *WileyPLUS*, where they can read from the e-textbook or use the variety of relevant resources available there. Students can also practice, using questions and feedback powered by ORION's adaptive learning engine. Based on the results of their diagnostic and ongoing practice, ORION will present students with questions appropriate for their current level of understanding, and will continuously adapt to each student to help build proficiency.

MAINTAIN

ORION includes a number of reports and ongoing recommendations for students to help them **MAINTAIN** their proficiency over time for each topic.

Students can easily access ORION from multiple places within *WileyPLUS*. It does not require any additional registration, and there will not be any additional charge for students using this adaptive learning system.

ABOUT THE ADAPTIVE ENGINE

ORION includes a powerful algorithm that feeds questions to students based on their responses to the diagnostic and to the practice questions. Students who answer questions correctly at one difficulty level will soon be given questions at the next difficulty level. If students start to answer some of those questions incorrectly, the system will present questions of lower difficulty. The adaptive engine also takes into account other factors, such as reported confidence levels, time spent on each question, and changes in response options before submitting answers.

The questions used for the adaptive practice are numerous and are not found in the WileyPLUS assignment area. This ensures that students will not be encountering questions in ORION that they may also encounter in their WileyPLUS assessments.

ORION also offers a number of reporting options available for instructors, so that instructors can easily monitor student usage and performance.

WileyPLUS with ORION helps students learn by learning about them.™

WileyPLUS

Now with: **ORION**, An Adaptive Experience

WileyPLUS is a research-based online environment for effective teaching and learning.

WileyPLUS builds students' confidence because it takes the guesswork out of studying by providing students with a clear roadmap:

- what to do
- how to do it
- if they did it right

It offers interactive resources along with a complete digital textbook that help students learn more. With *WileyPLUS*, students take more initiative so you'll have greater impact on their achievement in the classroom and beyond.

For more information, visit www.wileyplus.com

The first edition of Essentials of Contemporary Business *is dedicated to my wife, Diane.*

She is the best thing that ever happened to me.

—Dave Kurtz

To my wife Peggy—she is and always has been the best part of me.

—John Fritschen

VICE PRESIDENT & EXECUTIVE PUBLISHER	George Hoffman
EXECUTIVE EDITOR	Lisé Johnson
SENIOR ACQUISITIONS EDITOR	Franny Kelly
PROJECT EDITOR	Brian Kamins
CONTENT MANAGER	Dorothy Sinclair
SENIOR PRODUCTION EDITOR	Valerie A. Vargas
DIRECTOR OF MARKETING	Amy Scholz
SENIOR MARKETING MANAGER	Kelly Simmons
MARKETING ASSISTANT	Juliette San Fillipo
CREATIVE DIRECTOR	Harry Nolan
SENIOR DESIGNER	Maureen Eide
COVER DESIGNER	Maureen Eide
PRODUCTION MANAGEMENT SERVICES	MPS Limited
SENIOR ILLUSTRATION EDITOR	Anna Melhorn
SENIOR PHOTO EDITOR	Mary Ann Price
PHOTO RESEARCHER	Teri Stratford
EDITORIAL ASSISTANT	Jackie Hughes
SENIOR PRODUCT DESIGNER	Allison Morris
SENIOR MEDIA SPECIALIST	Elena Santa Maria

This book was set in Janson TextLTStd-Roman 10/13 by MPS Limited, and printed and bound by R. R. Donnelley & Sons. The cover was printed by R. R. Donnelley & Sons.

This book is printed on acid free paper. ∞

Founded in 1807, John Wiley & Sons, Inc. has been a valued source of knowledge and understanding for more than 200 years, helping people around the world meet their needs and fulfill their aspirations. Our company is built on a foundation of principles that include responsibility to the communities we serve and where we live and work. In 2008, we launched a Corporate Citizenship Initiative, a global effort to address the environmental, social, economic, and ethical challenges we face in our business. Among the issues we are addressing are carbon impact, paper specifications and procurement, ethical conduct within our business and among our vendors, and community and charitable support. For more information, please visit our website: www.wiley.com/go/citizenship.

ISBN-13   978-1-118-33649-6 (BRV)

ISBN-13   978-1-118-82451-1 (AIE)

Printed in the United States of America

10 9 8 7 6 5 4 3 2 1

Boone & Kurtz
ESSENTIALS OF CONTEMPORARY BUSINESS

First Edition

David L. Kurtz
University of Arkansas

WILEY

>>> About the Author

DURING DAVE KURTZ'S high school days, no one in Salisbury, Maryland, would have mistaken him for a scholar. In fact, he was a mediocre student, so bad that his father steered him toward higher education by finding him a succession of backbreaking summer jobs. Thankfully, most of them have been erased from his memory, but a few linger, including picking peaches, loading watermelons on trucks headed for market, and working as a pipe-fitter's helper. Unfortunately, these jobs had zero impact on his academic standing. Worse yet for Dave's ego, he was no better than average as a high school athlete in football and track.

But four years at Davis & Elkins College in Elkins, West Virginia, turned him around. Excellent instructors helped get Dave on sound academic footing. His grade point average soared—enough to get him accepted by the graduate business school at the University of Arkansas, where he met Gene Boone. Gene and Dave became longtime co-authors; together they produced more than 50 books. In addition to writing, Dave and Gene were involved in various entrepreneurial ventures.

This long-term partnership ended with Gene's death a few years ago. But, this book will always be Boone & Kurtz's *Essentials of Contemporary Business*.

If you have any questions or comments about the new *Essentials* book, Dave can be reached at ProfKurtz@gmail.com.

ABOUT THE CONTRIBUTING AUTHOR

WHEN JOHN FRITSCHEN ASKED his high school guidance counselor for some career advice, she dutifully pointed him to the library and a loose-leaf binder containing a list of professions, A to Z. Opening the book, the first entry was Accountant—maybe, but no. Next up was Aerospace Engineering—now, that sounded interesting. And it was with little more thought, that his early education and career path was set. After college he went to work at Pratt & Whitney Aircraft in Florida then moved to Davis, California, to work in the wind energy field and then to Santa Rosa, California, and an optical engineering company. It was at the optics company that he was introduced to the exciting world of business, working first in technical sales, then marketing, business development, and management. Wanting to add to his practical business knowledge, he completed a Masters in Business Administration at the University of California, Berkeley. In 2002, he left the corporate world to become a full-time instructor at Santa Rosa Junior College, where he continues to teach today.

Preface

Essentials of Contemporary Business first edition represents a fresh, new approach to an introductory college business text. Like the popular *Contemporary Business*, this new book covers all the major business topics but does so in a more concise fashion. The *Essentials* version of *Contemporary Business* maintains key elements that readers have come to value, including the opening vignettes, insightful examples, charts, graphs, and figures, along with relevant photographs and current references. Adding to the concise text, *Essentials of Contemporary Business* offers readers a new look, printed in an easy-to-read, two-column format.

However, it is the content that really allows a text to connect with students and instructors, and once again *Essentials of Contemporary Business* is spot on. During the editing process, each chapter was reviewed for critical business concepts, and those parts that contributed to the understanding of the chapter concepts were retained; where appropriate, new material was incorporated into the text. Chapter 6, for instance, was updated to include examples of new ways that entrepreneurs can raise money for their ventures, including crowd funding. Other areas were expanded, such as those in Chapter 3 dealing with comparative advantage and Chapter 10 on 3D printing. Along the way, the manuscript of these newly condensed chapters were sent to our dedicated team of reviewers, and we were pleased to see from their comments that we were on the right track. The result of our collective efforts is a text that covers all the critical business concepts in a concise fashion while retaining the great traditions of *Contemporary Business*.

ACKNOWLEDGMENTS

Contemporary Business has long benefited from the instructors who have offered their time as reviewers. Comprehensive reviews of *Essentials of Contemporary Business 1e* were provided by the following colleagues:

REVIEWERS

Brenda	Anthony	Tallahassee Community College
Donna	Armelino	Red Rocks Community College
Sherrie	Bell	Monroe College
Connie	Belden	Butler Community College
Melanie	Blakely	Tidewater Community College
Ellen	Benowitz	Mercer County Community College
Patricia	Bernson	County College of Morris
Harry V	Bernstein	Essex County College
Thierry	Brusselle	Chaffey College
Thomas	Byrnes	Wake Tech Community College
Ronald	Cereola	James Madison University
Lisa	Cherivtch	Oakton Community College
David	Chittenden	Bluegrass Community & Technical College
Katherine	Clyde	Pitt Community College
Mary	Cooke	Surry Community College
Kerry	Couet	MacEwan University
Loris	Crawford	Monroe College
Dan	Creed	Normandale Community College
Helen	Davis	Jefferson Community and Technical College
Mary	Demarest	Carroll Community College
Karen	Edwards	Chemeketa Community College
Leatrice	Freer	Pitt Community College
Patrick	Greek	Macomb Community College
Mark	Gius	Quinnipiac University
Mary	Gorman	University of Cincinnati
Karen	Halpern	South Puget Sound Community College
Nathan	Himelstein	New Jersey Institute of Technology
Barbara	Hoffman	Chippewa Valley Technical College
Kimberly	Hurns	Washtenaw Community College
Steve	Janisse	St. Clair College
Martin	Karamian	Los Angeles Pierce College
Susan	Kendall	Arapahoe Community College
Joseph	Leonard	Miami University
Monty	Lynn	Abilene Christian University
Valerie	Miceli	Seneca College
Douglas	Micklich	Illinois State University
Jeanette	Milius	Iowa Western Community College
Victoria	Montanaro	Carthage College
Patrick	Nance	Butler Community College
Susan	Nealy	Baton Rouge Community College
Daniel	Nehring	Morehead State University
Lauren	Paisley	Genesee Community College
Barry	Palatnik	Burlington County College
Raymond	Paquin	JMSB-Concordia University
Sharon	Peck	Capital University
Anthony	Racka	Oakland Community College
Julie	Ranson	John Tyler Community College
Tim	Rogers	Ozarks Technical College
Michael	Rose	Butler Community College
Carol	Rowey	Community College of Rhode Island
Mark	Ryan	Hawkeye Community College
Lance	Shoemaker	West Valley College
Karl	Smart	Central Michigan University
Gail	South	Montgomery College
Yvette	Swint-Blakely	Lansing Community College
Ronald	Thomas	Oakton Community College
Valerie	Wallingford	Bemidji State University
Harold	Williamson	University of South Alabama
Doug	Wilson	University of Oregon
Kathy	Winsted	Pace University
William	Wresch	University of Wisconsin–Oshkosh
Monica	Yang	Adelphi University
Nancy	Zimmerman	Community College of Baltimore County

IN CONCLUSION

I would like to thank Ingrid Benson for her editorial efforts on behalf of *Essentials of Contemporary Business*.

Let me conclude by noting that this new edition would never have become a reality without the outstanding efforts of the Wiley editorial, production, and marketing teams. Special thanks to George Hoffman, Lisé Johnson, Franny Kelly, Kelly Simmons, Brian Kamins, Jackie Hughes, and Valerie Vargas.

Dave Kurtz

> > > **Boone & Kurtz,** *Essentials of Contemporary Business,* **1/E,** is supported by a comprehensive learning package that assists the instructor in creating a motivating and enthusiastic environment.

We are pleased to provide you with an instructor's hardback copy of *Essentials of Contemporary Business,* 1/E by Louis Boone and Dave Kurtz. Thank you for considering this text for adoption. As Wiley strives to provide products of high value and low cost to students, listed on the back cover of this book are the value-priced student versions of the text that you can select from to order for your class.

The student version of the text is in the Wiley Binder Version format; if you would like to adopt the text in another format, please contact your Wiley representative for additional ordering options. Wiley Binder Versions provide an alternative to the traditional hardback version at a lower cost. Delivered in a three-hole punched, loose-leaf format; students carry only the content they need, insert class notes and hand-outs, all in one place.

For the student-on-the-go, Wiley also offers digital textbooks allowing students to access a complete version of the text online and offline on their desktop, laptop, and mobile devices at a discounted price.

Boone & Kurtz, *Essentials of Contemporary Business,* 1/E Binder Version
ISBN for ordering: 978-1-118-33649-6

> > > Brief Contents

ix

> > > Contents

x

3

Economic Challenges Facing Contemporary Business 33

4

Competing in World Markets 51

PART 2 Starting and Growing Your Business

5

Small Business and Forms of Business Ownership 67

6

Starting Your Own Business 83

OPENING VIGNETTE:
The Marketing Zen Group:
From $1,500 to Millions in Five Years 83

PART 3 Management: Building
Organizational Capability
for Superior Performance

7

Management, Leadership, and the Internal Organization 99

OPENING VIGNETTE:
Wegmans Food Markets:
Still a Great Place to Work 99

13

Promotion and Pricing Strategies 195

PART 5 Managing Technology and Information

14

Using Technology to Manage Information 211

17

Financial Management 261

Boone & Kurtz

ESSENTIALS OF CONTEMPORARY BUSINESS

STEVE JOBS

chapter one

The Changing Face of Business

Learning Objectives

1 **Define** the term *business*.

2 **Identify** and describe the factors of production.

3 **Describe** the private enterprise system.

4 **Identify** the six eras in the history of business.

5 **Explain** how today's business workforce and the nature of work itself are changing.

6 **Identify** the skills and attributes needed for the 21st century manager.

7 **Outline** the characteristics that make a company admired.

Apple and Steve Jobs: Business Leadership as Art

When Apple's visionary founder and leader Steve Jobs passed away at the age of 56, he was widely hailed as someone whose extraordinary career had transformed the world of business. But Apple's unsurpassed string of successful technological innovations had done far more. The Apple II, the Mac, iTunes, the iPod, the iPhone, the MacBook, and the iPad have transformed the communications industry, the music industry, the entertainment industry, and even the world of print.

Despite a 12-year absence from Apple, during which he founded another successful tech firm called NeXT and built Pixar Animation Studios into an Academy Award winner, Jobs brought his revolutionary computer company from humble start-up to unheard-of success. Apple is estimated to be worth nearly $400 billion today and has become one of the most valuable brand names of all time.

Jobs was passionately committed to innovation. His ability to understand how to make technology transparently simple to use ensured the success of many of Apple's iconic products, including generations of Mac personal computers and the iPod. These achievements, and their sleek and appealing designs, led many to think of him as a great business leader.

Jobs's unrelenting attention to detail and quest for perfection could also make him a difficult boss at times, but he inspired enormous devotion and loyalty among his employees. Some say he even transformed our idea of leadership, given his ability to inspire others with the same ideals that fueled his own drive to succeed.

Thanks to Apple, products we never knew we needed have become indispensable to our lives. Nothing about the way we write, listen, speak, text, view entertainment, present information, or surf the Internet will ever be the same. How does one company achieve so much?

An extraordinary leader is an obvious advantage, and few observers expect to see another CEO like Steve Jobs any time soon. But many business leaders today are as passionate and inspired, and their firms also seek to innovate and transform. Those companies that correctly assess what customers want, that deliver it at the right time and for the right price, and that keep ahead of the wave of relentless change they face, as Apple has done, will be more likely to succeed.[1]

Overview > > >

In large part, a country depends on the wealth its businesses generate, from large enterprises like the Walt Disney Company to tiny online start-ups, and from venerable firms, like 150-year-old jeans maker Levi Strauss & Company to powerhouses like Google. What all these companies and many others like them share is the ability to meet society's needs and wants.

To succeed, business firms must know what their customers want so that they can supply it quickly and efficiently. That means they often reflect changes in consumer tastes, such as the growing preference for sports drinks and vitamin-fortified water. But firms can also *lead* in advancing technology and other changes. They have the resources, the know-how, and the financial incentive to bring about new innovations as well as the competition that inevitably follows, as in the case of Apple's iPhone and Google's Android.

You'll see throughout this book that businesses require physical inputs like auto parts, chemicals, sugar, thread, electricity, and money; the accumulated knowledge and experience of their managers and employees; and access to the latest technical innovations. Although these inputs will get an enterprise started, their long-term survivability may well depend on their ability to change with the marketplace. Flexibility is a key to long-term success—and to growth.

In short, business is at the forefront of our economy—and *Contemporary Business Essentials* is right there with it. This book explores the strategies that allow companies to grow and compete in today's interactive marketplace, along with the skills that you will need to turn ideas into action for your own success in business. This chapter sets the stage for the entire text by defining business and revealing its role in society. The chapter's discussion illustrates how the private enterprise system encourages competition and innovation while preserving business ethics.

① What Is Business?

What comes to mind when you hear the word *business?* Do you think of big corporations like ExxonMobil or Boeing? Or does the local dry cleaners or convenience store pop into your mind? Maybe you recall your first summer job. The term *business* is a broad, all-inclusive term that can be applied to many kinds of enterprises. Businesses provide the bulk of employment opportunities, as well as the products that people enjoy.

FOR-PROFIT ORGANIZATIONS

business all profit-seeking activities and enterprises that provide goods and services necessary to an economic system.

Business consists of all profit-seeking activities and enterprises. Some businesses produce tangible goods, such as automobiles, breakfast cereals, and digital music players; others provide services such as insurance, hair styling, and entertainment, ranging from the Six Flags theme parks and NFL games to concerts.

Business drives the economic pulse of a nation. It provides the means through which its citizens' standard of living improves. At the heart of every business endeavor is an exchange between a buyer and a seller. A buyer recognizes a need for a good or service and trades money with a seller to obtain that product. The seller participates in the process in hopes of gaining profits—a main ingredient in accomplishing the goals necessary for continuous improvement in the standard of living.

profits rewards earned by businesspeople who take the risks involved in blending people, technology, and information to create and market want-satisfying goods and services.

Profits represent rewards earned by businesspeople who take the risks involved in blending people, technology, and information to create and market goods and services. We often think of profits as the difference between a firm's revenues and the expenses it incurs in generating these revenues. And while this is true, it is the *opportunity* for profits that serves as incentive for people to start companies, expand them, and provide high-quality goods and services.

The quest for profits is a central focus of business, but businesspeople also recognize their social and ethical responsibilities. To succeed in the long run, companies must deal responsibly with employees, customers, suppliers, competitors, government, and the general public.

NOT-FOR-PROFIT ORGANIZATIONS

not-for-profit organization businesslike establishment that has primary objectives other than returning profits to owners.

What do a local food pantry, the U.S. Postal Service, the American Red Cross, and your local library have in common? They are all classified as **not-for-profit organizations**, businesslike establishments that have primary

objectives other than returning profits to their owners. These organizations play an important role in society. It is important to understand that these organizations need to make or raise money so that they can operate and achieve their social goals. Not-for-profit organizations operate in both the private and public sectors. Private-sector not-for-profits include museums, libraries, trade associations, and charitable and religious organizations. Government agencies, political parties, and labor unions, all of which are part of the public sector, are also classified as not-for-profit organizations.

Not-for-profit organizations are a substantial part of the U.S. economy. Currently, more than 1.5 million non-profit organizations are registered with the Internal Revenue Service in the United States, in categories ranging from arts and culture to science and technology.[2] These organizations control more than $2.6 trillion in assets and employ more people than the federal government and all 50 state governments combined.[3] In addition,

∧ This cell phone store survives through the exchange between buyer and seller—in this case, the customer and the salesperson.

∨ The Red Cross mobilizes its efforts to respond to Superstorm Sandy relief.

millions of volunteers work for them in unpaid positions. Not-for-profits secure funding from both private sources, including donations, and government sources. They are commonly exempt from federal, state, and local taxes.

> > > ## Quick Review

1 What activity lies at the heart of every business endeavor?

2 What is the primary objective of a not-for-profit organization?

2 Factors of Production

From the earliest human settlements to the modern societies of today, all economic systems require certain inputs for successful operation. Economists use the term **factors of production** to refer to the four basic inputs: natural resources, capital, human resources, and entrepreneurship. TABLE 1.1 identifies each of these inputs and the type of payment received by firms and individuals who supply them.

factors of production four basic inputs: natural resources, capital, human resources, and entrepreneurship.

natural resources all production inputs that are useful in their natural states, including agricultural land, building sites, forests, and mineral deposits.

capital an organization's technology, tools, information, and physical facilities.

Natural resources include all production inputs that are useful in their natural states, including agricultural land, building sites, forests, and mineral deposits. One of the world's largest wind farms, the Roscoe Wind Complex, generates enough power to support almost a quarter million homes. Natural resources are the basic inputs required in any economic system.

Capital, another key resource, includes technology, tools, information, and physical facilities. *Technology* is a broad term that refers to machinery and equipment such as computers and software, telecommunications, and inventions designed to improve production. Information, frequently improved by technological innovations, is another critical factor because both managers and operating employees require accurate, timely information

for effective performance of their assigned tasks. Technology plays an important role in the success of many businesses. Sometimes technology results in a new product, such as hybrid autos that run on a combination of gasoline and electricity. Most of the major car companies have introduced hybrid models in recent years.

To remain competitive, a firm needs to continually acquire, maintain, and upgrade its capital, and businesses need money for that purpose. A company's funds may come from owner-investments, profits plowed back into the business, or loans extended by others. Money then goes to work building factories; purchasing raw materials and component parts; and hiring, training, and compensating workers. People and firms that supply capital receive factor payments in the form of interest.

Human resources represent another critical input in every economic system. Human resources include anyone who works, from the chief executive officer (CEO) of a huge corporation to a self-employed writer or editor. This category encompasses both the physical labor and the intellectual inputs contributed by workers. Companies rely on their employees as a valued source of ideas and innovation as well as physical effort. Some companies solicit employee ideas through traditional means, such as an online "suggestion box" or in staff meetings. Others encourage creative thinking during company-sponsored hiking or rafting trips or during social gatherings. Effective, well-trained human resources provide a significant competitive edge because competitors cannot easily match another company's talented, motivated employees in the way they can buy the same computer system or purchase the same grade of natural resources.

human resources in an organization, anyone who works, providing either the physical labor or intellectual inputs.

Hiring and keeping the right people matter. Google employees feel they have a great place to work, partly because of the sense of mission—and the perks—the company provides.[4]

V A competent, effective workforce can be a company's best asset. Organizations strive to retain their workers by providing perks such as onsite fitness facilities.

© Plesea Petre/iStockphoto

TABLE 1.1 **What are the factors of production and their corresponding factor payments?**

Factor of Production	Corresponding Factor Payment
Natural resources	Rent
Capital	Interest
Human resources	Wages
Entrepreneurship	Profit

entrepreneurship
ability to see an opportunity and take the risks inherent in creating and operating a business.

Entrepreneurship is the ability to see an opportunity and take the risks inherent in creating and operating a business. An entrepreneur is someone who sees a potentially profitable opportunity and then devises a plan to achieve success in the marketplace and earn those profits. By age 20, Jessica Mah was CEO of inDinero, a Web site that helps small businesses keep track of their money. Mah had "noticed that anything that touches money is much harder for entrepreneurs than it should be," so she took a risk and started a firm designed to help them.[5]

U.S. businesses operate within an economic system called the *private enterprise system*. The next section looks at the private enterprise system, including competition and private property.

> ### >>> Quick Review
>
> **1** What are the four basic factors of any economic system?
>
> **2** List the four types of capital.
>
> **3** What is an entrepreneur?

3 The Private Enterprise System

No business operates in a vacuum; rather, all operate within a larger economic system that determines how goods and services are produced, distributed, and consumed in a society. The type of economic system employed in a society also determines patterns of resource use. Some economic systems, such as communism, feature strict controls on business ownership, profits, and resources to accomplish government goals.

private enterprise system economic system that rewards firms for their ability to identify and serve the needs and demands of customers.

In the United States, businesses function within the **private enterprise system**, an economic system that rewards firms for their ability to identify and serve the needs and demands of customers. The private enterprise system minimizes government interference in economic activity. Businesses that are adept at satisfying customers gain access to necessary factors of production and earn profits.

capitalism economic system that rewards firms for their ability to perceive and serve the needs and demands of consumers; also called the private enterprise system.

Another name for the private enterprise system is **capitalism**. Adam Smith, often identified as the father of capitalism, first described the concept in his book *The Wealth of Nations,* published in 1776. Smith believed that an economy is best regulated by the "invisible hand" of competition, the battle among businesses for consumer acceptance. Smith thought that competition among firms would lead to consumers' receiving the best possible products and prices because less efficient producers would gradually be driven from the marketplace.

The "invisible hand" concept is a basic premise of the private enterprise system. In the United States, competition regulates much of economic life. To compete successfully, each firm must find a basis for **competitive differentiation**, the unique combination of organizational abilities, products, and approaches that sets a company apart from competitors in the minds of customers. Businesses operating in a private enterprise system face a critical task of keeping up with changing marketplace conditions. Firms that fail to adjust to shifts in consumer preferences or ignore the actions of competitors leave themselves open to failure. Apple and Microsoft have long been known for their rivalry, despite the fact that on occasion they have teamed up. For instance, Microsoft recently partnered with Apple and Oracle in an effort to thwart Android phone makers from using patented technology.[6]

competitive differentiation
unique combination of organizational abilities, products, and approaches that sets a company apart from competitors in the minds of customers.

Throughout this book, the discussion focuses on the tools and methods that 21st century businesses apply to compete and differentiate their goods and services. The text also discusses many of the ways in which market changes will affect business and the private enterprise system in the years ahead.

BASIC RIGHTS IN THE PRIVATE ENTERPRISE SYSTEM

For capitalism to operate effectively, people living in a private enterprise economy must have certain rights. As shown in **FIGURE 1.1**, these include the rights to private property, profits, freedom of choice, and competition.

FIGURE 1.1
Basic Rights within a Private Enterprise System

private property
most basic freedom under the private enterprise system; the right to own, use, buy, sell, and bequeath land, buildings, machinery, equipment, patents, individual possessions, and various intangible kinds of property.

The right to **private property** is the most basic freedom under the private enterprise system. Every participant has the right to own, use, buy, sell, and bequeath most forms of property, including land, buildings, machinery, and equipment, patents on inventions, individual possessions, and intangible properties.

The private enterprise system also guarantees business owners the right to all profits—after taxes—they earn through their activities. Although a business is not assured of earning a profit, its owner is legally and ethically entitled to any income it generates in excess of costs.

Freedom of choice means that a private enterprise system relies on the potential for citizens to choose their own employment, purchases, and investments. They can change jobs, negotiate wages, join labor unions, and choose among many different brands of goods and services. A private enterprise economy maximizes individual prosperity by providing alternatives. Other economic systems sometimes limit freedom of choice to accomplish government goals, such as increasing industrial production of certain items or military strength.

The private enterprise system also permits fair competition by allowing the public to set rules for competitive activity. For this reason, the U.S. government has passed laws to prohibit "cutthroat" competition—excessively aggressive competitive practices designed to eliminate competition. It also has established ground rules that outlaw price discrimination, fraud in financial markets, and deceptive advertising and packaging.[7]

>>> **Quick Review**

1 What is an alternative term for *private enterprise system*?

2 What is the most basic freedom under the private enterprise system?

4 Six Eras in the History of Business

In the roughly 400 years since the first European settlements appeared on the North American continent, amazing changes have occurred in the size, focus, and goals of U.S. businesses. As **FIGURE 1.2** indicates, U.S. business history is divided into six distinct time periods: (1) the Colonial period, (2) the Industrial Revolution, (3) the age of industrial entrepreneurs, (4) the production era, (5) the marketing era, and (6) the relationship era. The following sections describe how events in each of these time periods have influenced U.S. business practices.

Era	Main Characteristics	Time Period
Colonial	Primarily agricultural	Prior to 1776
Industrial Revolution	Mass production by semiskilled workers, aided by machines	1760–1850
Industrial entrepreneurs	Advances in technology and increased demand for manufactured goods, leading to enormous entrepreneurial opportunities	Late 1800s
Production	Emphasis on producing more goods faster, leading to production innovations such as assembly lines	Through the 1920s
Marketing	Consumer orientation, seeking to understand and satisfy needs and preferences of customer groups	Since 1950s
Relationship	Benefits derived from deep, ongoing links with individual customers, employees, suppliers, and other businesses	Began in 1990s

FIGURE 1.2 Six Eras in Business History

THE COLONIAL PERIOD

Colonial society emphasized agricultural production. Colonial towns were small compared with European cities, and they functioned as marketplaces for farmers and craftspeople. The economic focus of the nation centered on rural areas because prosperity depended on the output of farms, orchards, and the like. The success or failure of crops influenced every aspect of the economy.

Colonists depended on England for manufactured items as well as financial backing for their infant industries. Even after the Revolutionary War (1775–1783), the United States maintained close economic ties with England. British investors continued to provide much of the financing for developing the U.S. business system, and this financial influence continued well into the 19th century.

THE INDUSTRIAL REVOLUTION

The Industrial Revolution began in England around 1750. It moved business operations from an emphasis on independent, skilled workers who specialized in building products one by one to a factory system that mass-produced items by bringing together large numbers of semiskilled workers. The factories profited from the savings created by large-scale production, bolstered by increasing support from machines over time. As businesses grew, they could often purchase raw materials more cheaply in larger lots than before. Specialization of labor, limiting each worker to a few specific tasks in the production process, also improved production efficiency.

Influenced by these events in England, business in the United States began a time of rapid industrialization. Agriculture became mechanized, and factories sprang up in cities. During the mid-1800s, the pace of industrialization increased as newly built railroad systems provided fast, economical transportation. In California, for example, the combination of railroad construction and the Gold Rush fueled a tremendous demand for construction.

THE AGE OF INDUSTRIAL ENTREPRENEURS

Building on the opportunities created by the Industrial Revolution, entrepreneurship increased in the United States. Henry Engelhard Steinway of Seesen, Germany, built his first piano by hand in his kitchen in 1825 as a wedding present for his bride. In 1850, the family immigrated to New York, where Henry and his sons opened their first factory in Manhattan in 1853. Over the next 30 years, they made innovations that led to the modern piano. Through an apprenticeship system, the Steinways transmitted their skills to the following generations. Steinway pianos have long been world

< Steinway pianos are world famous and are still built by hand in New York. The company is meeting the next generation's demands with iPad apps that allow users to play anywhere.

© Anatolii Babii/Alamy Limited

famous for their beautiful tone, top-quality materials and workmanship, and durability. Now known as Steinway Musical Instruments, the company still builds its pianos by hand in its factory in Astoria, New York, under the same master-apprentice system that Henry and his sons began. Building each piano takes nearly a year from start to finish. In response to 21st century demands, the company has launched Etude, an app for the iPad that displays sheet music the user can play on an on-screen piano keyboard.[8]

Inventors created a virtually endless array of commercially useful products and new production methods. Many of them are famous today:

- Eli Whitney introduced the concept of interchangeable parts, an idea that would later facilitate mass production on a previously impossible scale.

- Robert McCormick designed a horse-drawn reaper that reduced the labor involved in harvesting wheat. His son, Cyrus McCormick, saw the commercial potential of the reaper and launched a business to build and sell the machine. By 1902, the company was producing 35 percent of the nation's farm machinery.

- Cornelius Vanderbilt (railroads), J. P. Morgan (banking), and Andrew Carnegie (steel), among others, took advantage of the enormous opportunities waiting for anyone willing to take the risk of starting a new business.

The entrepreneurial spirit of this golden age in business did much to advance the U.S. business system and raise the country's overall standard of living. That market transformation, in turn, created new demand for manufactured goods.

THE PRODUCTION ERA

As demand for manufactured goods continued to increase through the 1920s, businesses focused even greater attention on the activities involved in producing those goods. Work became increasingly specialized, and huge, labor-intensive factories dominated U.S. business. Assembly lines, introduced by Henry Ford, became commonplace in major industries. Business owners turned over their responsibilities to a new class of managers trained in operating established companies. Their activities emphasized efforts to produce even more goods through quicker methods.

During the production era, business focused attention on internal processes rather than external influences. Marketing was almost an afterthought, designed solely to distribute items generated by production activities. Little attention was paid to consumer wants or needs. Instead, businesses tended to make decisions about what the market would get. If you wanted to buy a Ford Model T automobile, your color choice was black—the only color produced by the company.

THE MARKETING ERA

The Great Depression of the early 1930s changed the shape of U.S. business yet again. As incomes nosedived, businesses could no longer automatically count on selling everything they produced. Managers began to pay more attention to the markets for their goods and services, and sales and advertising took on new importance. During this period, selling was often synonymous with marketing.

Demand for all kinds of consumer goods exploded after World War II. After nearly five years of doing without new automobiles, appliances, and other items, consumers were buying again. At the same time, however, competition also heated up. Soon businesses began to think of marketing as more than just selling; they envisioned a process of first determining what consumers wanted and needed and then designing products to satisfy those needs. In short, they developed a **consumer orientation**.

Businesses began to analyze consumer desires before beginning actual production. Consumer choices skyrocketed. Car buyers, for example, could choose among a wide variety of colors and styles. Companies also discovered the need to distinguish their goods and services from those of competitors. Branding—the process of creating an identity in consumers' minds for a good, service, or company—is an important marketing tool. A **brand** can be a name, term, sign, symbol, design, or some combination that identifies the products of one firm and differentiates them from competitors' offerings.

Branding can go a long way toward creating value for a firm by providing recognition and a positive association between a company and its products. Some of the world's most famous— and enduring—brands include Coca-Cola, Apple, IBM, Google, Microsoft, GE, McDonald's, Intel, Samsung, and Toyota.[9]

The marketing era has had a tremendous effect on the way business is conducted today. Even the smallest business owners recognize the importance of understanding what customers want and the reasons they buy.

THE RELATIONSHIP ERA

As business continues in the 21st century, a significant change is taking place in the ways companies interact with customers. Since the Industrial Revolution, most businesses have concentrated on building and promoting products in the hope that enough customers will buy them to cover costs and earn acceptable profits, an approach called **transaction management**.

In contrast, in the **relationship era**, businesses are taking a different, longer-term approach to their interactions with customers. Firms now seek ways to actively nurture customer loyalty by carefully managing their interactions with buyers. They earn enormous paybacks for their efforts. A company that retains customers over the long haul reduces its advertising and sales costs. Because customer spending tends to accelerate over time, revenues also grow. Companies with long-term customers often can avoid costly reliance on price discounts to attract new business, and they find that many new buyers come from loyal customer referrals.

Business owners gain several advantages by developing ongoing relationships with customers. Because it is much less expensive to serve existing customers than to find new ones, businesses that develop long-term customer relationships can reduce their overall costs. Long-term relationships with customers enable businesses to improve their understanding of what customers want and prefer from the company. As a result, businesses enhance their chances of sustaining real advantages through competitive differentiation.

The relationship era is an age of connections—between businesses and customers, employers and employees, technology and manufacturing, and even separate companies. The world economy is increasingly interconnected as businesses expand beyond their national boundaries. In this new environment, techniques for managing networks of people, businesses, information, and technology are critically important to contemporary business success.

consumer orientation business philosophy that focuses first on determining unmet consumer wants and needs and then designing products to satisfy those needs.

branding process of creating an identity in consumers' minds for a good, service, or company; a major marketing tool in contemporary business.

brand name, term, sign, symbol, design, or some combination that identifies the products of one firm and differentiates them from competitors' offerings.

transaction management building and promoting products in the hope that enough customers will buy them to cover costs and earn profits.

relationship era business era in which firms seek ways to actively nurture customer loyalty by carefully managing their interactions with buyers.

> >> **Quick Review**

1 Describe the Industrial Revolution.

2 During which era was branding developed?

3 What is the difference between transaction management and relationship management?

5 Today's Business Workforce

A skilled and knowledgeable workforce is an essential resource for keeping pace with the accelerating rate of change in today's business world. Employers need reliable employees who are dedicated to fostering strong ties with customers and partners. They must build workforces capable of the efficient, high-quality production needed to compete in global markets. Savvy business leaders also realize that employee brainpower plays a vital role in a firm's ability to stay on top of new technologies and innovations. In short, a first-class workforce can be the foundation of a firm's competitive differentiation, providing important advantages over competing businesses.

CHANGES IN THE WORKFORCE

Companies now face several trends that challenge their skills for managing and developing human resources. Those challenges include an aging population and a shrinking labor pool, growing diversity of the workforce, the changing nature of work, the need for flexibility and mobility, and the use of collaboration to innovate.

AN AGING POPULATION AND SHRINKING LABOR POOL

By 2025, the number of U.S. workers age 65 or older will reach 64 million—double what it is today—and many of them will soon retire from the workforce, taking their experience and expertise with them. As TABLE 1.2 shows, the U.S. population as a whole is trending older. Yet today, many members of the Baby Boom generation—the huge number of people born between 1946 and 1964—are still hitting the peaks of their careers. At the same time, members of so-called Generation X (born from 1965 to 1981) and Generation Y (born from 1982 to 2005) are building their careers, so employers are finding more generations in the workforce simultaneously than ever before. This broad age diversity brings management challenges, such as accommodating a variety of work–life styles, changing expectations of work, and varying levels of technological expertise. Still, despite the widening age

TABLE 1.2 What is the trend for the U.S. population in terms of aging?

Age	2010	2020	2025
16–64	203 million	214 million	218 million
	66% of total	63% of total	61% of total
65 and older	40 million	55 million	64 million
	13% of total	16% of total	18% of total
Median	37 years	38 years	38.5 years

SOURCE: U.S. Census Bureau, "Resident Population Projections by Sex and Age: 2010 to 2050," *Statistical Abstract of the United States*, http://www.census.gov, accessed April 24, 2013.

spectrum of the workforce, some economists predict the U.S. labor pool could soon fall short by as many as 10 million people as Baby Boomers retire.

More sophisticated technology has intensified the hiring challenge by requiring workers to have ever more advanced skills. Companies are increasingly seeking—and finding—talent at the extreme ends of the working-age spectrum. Teenagers are entering the workforce sooner, and some seniors are staying longer—or seeking a new career after retiring from their primary career. Many older workers work part-time or flexible hours. Meanwhile, for older employees who do retire, employers must administer a variety of retirement planning and disability programs and insurance benefits.

INCREASINGLY DIVERSE WORKFORCE

The U.S. workforce is growing more diverse, in age and in every other way. The two fastest-growing ethnic populations in the United States are Hispanics and Asians. By the year 2060, the number of Hispanics in the United States will grow from a current 17 percent to 31 percent of the total population. The Asian population will increase from 5.1 percent to 8.2 percent of the total U.S. population.[10] Considering that minority groups are growing, managers must learn to work effectively with diverse ethnic groups, cultures, and lifestyles to develop and retain a superior workforce for their company.

Diversity—the blending of individuals of different genders, ethnic backgrounds, cultures, religions, ages, and physical and mental abilities in a workforce—can enhance a firm's chances of success. In a recent list of top companies for diversity, the top ten were also leaders and innovators in their industries:

> **diversity** in a workforce, the blending of individuals of different genders, ethnic backgrounds, cultures, religions, ages, and physical and mental abilities.

1. Sodexo
2. PricewaterhouseCoopers
3. Kaiser Permanente
4. Ernst & Young
5. MasterCard Worldwide
6. Novartis Pharmaceuticals Corporation
7. Procter & Gamble
8. Prudential Financial
9. Accenture
10. Johnson & Johnson.[11]

Several studies have shown that diverse employee teams and workforces tend to perform tasks more effectively and develop better solutions to business problems than homogeneous employee groups. This result is due in part to the varied perspectives and experiences that foster innovation and creativity in multicultural teams.

OUTSOURCING AND THE CHANGING NATURE OF WORK

Not only is the U.S. workforce changing, but so is the very nature of work. Manufacturing once accounted for most of U.S. annual output, but the balance has now shifted to services such as financial management and communications. This means firms must rely heavily on well-trained service workers with knowledge, technical skills, the ability to communicate and deal with people, and a talent for creative thinking. The Internet has made possible another business tool for staffing flexibility—**outsourcing**, or using outside vendors to produce goods or fulfill services and functions previously handled in-house. At its best, outsourcing allows a firm to reduce costs and concentrate its resources in the areas it does best while gaining access to expertise it may not have. But outsourcing also brings challenges, such as differences in language or culture.

Offshoring, the relocation of business processes to lower-cost locations overseas, can include both production and services. In recent years, China has emerged as a dominant location for production offshoring for many firms, while India has become the key player in offshoring services. Some U.S. companies are now structured so that entire divisions or functions are developed and staffed overseas. Another trend in some industries is **nearshoring**, outsourcing production or services to nations near a firm's home base. And in some cases, companies are **onshoring**—returning production to its original manufacturing location because of changes in costs or processes.

outsourcing using outside vendors to produce goods or fulfill services and functions previously handled in-house or in-country.

offshoring relocation of business processes to lower-cost locations overseas.

nearshoring outsourcing production or services to locations near a firm's home base.

onshoring returning production to its original manufacturing location because of changes in costs or processes.

10

FLEXIBILITY AND MOBILITY

Younger workers in particular are looking for something other than the work-comes-first lifestyle exemplified by the Baby Boom generation. But workers of all ages are exploring different work arrangements, such as telecommuting from remote locations and sharing jobs with two or more employees. Employers are also hiring growing numbers of temporary and part-time employees, some of whom are less interested in advancing up the career ladder and more interested in using and developing their skills. While the cubicle-filled office will likely never become entirely obsolete, technology makes productive networking and virtual team efforts possible by allowing people to work where they choose and easily share knowledge, a sense of purpose or mission, and a free flow of ideas across any geographical distance or time zone.

Managers of such far-flung workforces need to build and earn employees' trust in order to retain valued workers and to ensure that all members are acting ethically and contributing their share without the day-to-day supervision of a more conventional work environment. Managers and employees must be flexible and responsive to change while work, technology, and relationships continue to evolve.

INNOVATION THROUGH COLLABORATION

Some observers also see a trend toward more collaborative work in the future, as opposed to individuals working alone. Businesses using teamwork hope to build a creative environment where all members contribute their knowledge and skills to solve problems or seize opportunities.

The old relationship between employers and employees was pretty simple: every day, workers arrived at a certain hour, did their jobs, and departed at the same time. Companies rarely laid off workers, and employees rarely left for a job at another firm. But all that—and more—has changed. Employees are no longer likely to remain with a single company throughout their entire career and do not necessarily expect lifetime loyalty from the company they work for. They do not expect to give that loyalty, either; rather, they build their own career however and wherever they can. These changes mean that many firms now recognize the value of a partnership with employees that encourages creative thinking and problem solving and rewards risk taking and innovation.

> **>>> Quick Review**
>
> 1. Define *outsourcing*, *offshoring*, and *nearshoring*.
> 2. Describe the importance of collaboration and employee partnership.

6 The 21st Century Manager

Today's companies look for managers who are intelligent, highly motivated people with the ability to create and sustain a vision of how an organization can succeed. The 21st century manager must also apply critical-thinking skills and creativity to business challenges and lead change.

IMPORTANCE OF VISION

To thrive in the 21st century, businesspeople need **vision**, the ability to perceive marketplace needs and what an organization must do to satisfy them. Nannu Nobis, co-founder

vision the ability to perceive marketplace needs and what an organization must do to satisfy them.

Employees can be rewarded by some firms for their efforts to reduce energy use through carpooling.

© Stefanolunardi/iStockphoto

and CEO of Nobis Engineering, is recognized for his firm's environmental work as well as its efforts to convert its own business operations to the highest standards of sustainability. With only 100 employees, Nobis Engineering recently won prestigious major contracts with the U.S. Army Corps of Engineers and U.S. Environmental Protection Agency valued at $40 million. When the firm expanded to meet client needs, Nobis authorized $5 million to renovate a 20,000-square-foot historic mill building according to the U.S. Green Building Council LEED process. Nobis Engineering employees are rewarded for carpooling and reducing energy use in other ways as well. So far, Nobis Engineering has reduced its carbon emissions by more than 13,000 pounds. CEO Nobis says companies must walk the talk. "Our clients take this [sustainability] seriously and are proud to be with a firm that takes it seriously."[12]

IMPORTANCE OF CRITICAL THINKING AND CREATIVITY

Critical thinking and creativity are essential characteristics of the 21st century workforce. Today's businesspeople need to look at a wide variety of situations, draw connections between disparate information, and develop future-oriented solutions. This need applies not only to top executives but to mid-level managers and entry-level workers as well.

critical thinking ability to analyze and assess information to pinpoint problems or opportunities.

Critical thinking is the ability to analyze and assess information to pinpoint problems or opportunities. The critical-thinking process includes activities such as determining the authenticity, accuracy, and worth of information, knowledge, and arguments. It involves looking beneath the surface for deeper meaning and connections that can help identify critical issues and solutions. Without critical thinking, a firm may encounter serious problems.

creativity capacity to develop novel solutions to perceived organizational problems.

Creativity is the capacity to develop novel solutions to perceived

organizational problems. Although most people think of it in relation to writers, artists, musicians, and inventors, that is a very limited definition. In business, creativity refers to the ability to see better and different ways of operating. A computer engineer who solves a glitch in a software program is thinking creatively. Creativity and critical thinking must go beyond generating new ideas, however. They must lead to action. In addition to creating an environment in which employees can nurture ideas, managers must give them opportunities to take risks and try new solutions.

ABILITY TO LEAD CHANGE

Today's business leaders must guide their employees and organizations through the changes brought about by technology, marketplace demands, and global competition. Managers must be skilled at recognizing employee strengths and motivating people to move toward common goals as members of a team. Throughout this book, real-world examples demonstrate how companies have initiated sweeping change initiatives. Most, if not all, have been led by managers comfortable with the tough decisions that today's fluctuating conditions require.

Factors that require organizational change can come from both external and internal sources; successful managers must be aware of both. External forces might include feedback from customers, developments in the international marketplace, economic trends, and new technologies. Internal factors might arise from new company goals, emerging employee needs, labor union demands, or production problems.

>>> **Quick Review**

1. Why is vision an important managerial quality?

2. What is the difference between creativity and critical thinking?

7 What Makes a Company Admired?

Who is your hero? Is it someone who has achieved great feats in sports, government, entertainment, or business? Why do you admire the person? Does he or she lead a company, earn a lot of money, or give back to the community and society? Every year, business magazines and organizations publish lists of companies that they consider to be "most admired." Companies, like individuals, may be admired for many reasons. Most people would mention solid profits, stable growth, a safe and challenging work environment, high-quality goods and services, and business ethics and social responsibility. *Business ethics* refers to the standards of conduct and moral values involving decisions made in the work environment. *Social responsibility* is a management philosophy that includes contributing resources to the community, preserving the natural environment, and developing or participating in nonprofit programs designed to promote the well-being of the general public. You'll find business ethics and social responsibility examples throughout this book, as well as a deeper exploration of these topics in Chapter 2.

As you read this text, you'll be able to make up your mind about why companies should—or should not—be admired. *Fortune* publishes two lists of most admired companies each year, one for U.S.-based firms and one for the world. The list is compiled from surveys and other research conducted by the Hay Group, a global management consulting firm. Criteria for making the list include innovation, people management, use of corporate assets, social responsibility, quality of management, and quality of products and services.[13] TABLE 1.3 lists the top ten World's Most Admired Companies for a recent year.

TABLE 1.3 What companies are on *Fortune*'s list for top ten most admired?

1 Apple	**6** IBM
2 Google	**7** Southwest Airlines
3 Amazon.com	**8** Berkshire Hathaway
4 The Coca-Cola Company	**9** Walt Disney
5 Starbucks	**10** FedEx

SOURCE: "World's Most Admired Companies 2013," *Fortune*, http://money.cnn.com, accessed April 24, 2013. Copyright 2010 by Time, Inc. Used by permission and protected by the Copyright laws of the United States. The printing, copying, redistribution, or retransmission of the Material without express permission is prohibited.

>>> **Quick Review**

1 Define *business ethics* and *social responsibility*.

2 Name three criteria used to judge whether an organization might be considered admirable.

What's Ahead? > > >

As business speeds along in the 21st century, new technologies, population shifts, and shrinking global barriers are altering the world at a frantic pace. Businesspeople are catalysts for many of these changes, creating new opportunities for individuals who are prepared to take action. Studying contemporary business will help you prepare for the future.

Through this book, you'll gain an understanding of how marketing, production, accounting, finance, and management work together to provide competitive advantages for firms. This knowledge can help you become a more capable employee and enhance your career potential.

Now that this chapter has introduced some basic terms and issues in the business world of the 21st century, Chapter 2 takes a detailed look at the ethical and social responsibility issues facing contemporary business. Chapter 3 deals with economic challenges, and Chapter 4 focuses on the difficulties and opportunities faced by firms competing in world markets.

Weekly Updates spark classroom debate around current events that apply to your business course topics. http://www.wileybusinessupdates.com

NOTES

1. Company Web site, http://www.apple.com, accessed May 15, 2013; Katie Marsal, "Former Apple Product Manager Recounts How Jobs Motivated First iPhone Team," *Apple Insider*, February 3, 2012, www.appleinsider.com; Brian Caulfield, "The Steve Jobs Economy," *Forbes*, November 7, 2011, p. 16; Gianpiero Petriglieri, "How Steve Jobs Reinvented Leadership," *Forbes*, October 10, 2011, www.forbes.com; John Baldoni, "Learning from Steve Jobs: How to Lead with Purpose," *CNN Opinion*, October 14, 2011, www.cnn.com; John Markoff, "Apple's Visionary Redefined Digital Age," *New York Times*, October 5, 2011, www.nytimes.com; Joe Nocera, "What Makes Steve Jobs Great," *New York Times*, August 26, 2011, www.nytimes.com; David Pogue, "Steve Jobs Reshaped Industries," *New York Times*, blog post, August 25, 2011, www.nytimes.com.

2. National Center for Charitable Statistics, "Quick Facts about Nonprofits," http://nccs .urban.org/statistics, accessed April 24, 2013.

3. National Center for Charitable Statistics, "Quick Facts about Nonprofits," http://nccs .urban.org/statistics, accessed April 24, 2013; Foundation Center, Grant Space, http:// grantspace.org/, accessed April 24, 2013; Bureau of Labor Statistics, *Career Guide to Industries, 2010–11 Edition*, http://www.bls .gov, accessed April 24, 2013.

4. "100 Best Companies to Work For (2013)," CNNMoney.com, http://money.cnn.com, accessed April 24, 2013.

5. Grace Austin, "inDinero: Helping Businesses Keep Tabs on Money," *Profiles in Diversity Journal*, July 16, 2012, http://www .diversityjournal.com/9603-indinero-helping -businesses-keep-tabs-on-money/.

6. Brad Reed, "Apple Loses Latest Round in Android Patent Fight," *Network World*, January 24, 2012, http://www.networkworld .com; Wayne Rash, "Apple, Microsoft, Oracle Lead Unholy Patent Alliance against Android," July 11, 2011, http:// www.eweek.com.

7. Government Web site, "Welcome to the Bureau of Competition," Federal Trade Commission, http://www.ftc.gov/bc, accessed May 15, 2013.

8. Company Web site, "History," http://www .steinway.com, accessed April 24, 2013.

9. "Best Global Brands 2012," *interbrand*, http:// www.interbrand.com, accessed April 24, 2013.

10. Jennifer M. Ortman, "U.S. Population Projections: 2012 to 2060," U.S. Census Bureau, February 7, 2013, http://www.census .gov/population/projections.

11. "The 2013 DiversityInc Top 50 Companies for Diversity," DiversityInc, n.d., http://www .diversityinc.com, accessed April 24, 2013.

12. Company Web site, http://www .nobisengineering.com, accessed April 24, 2013; Matthew J. Mowry, "Celebrating Business Excellence," *Business NH Magazine*, May 2011, p. 54.

13. "World's Most Admired Companies 2013," *Fortune*, http://money.cnn.com, accessed April 24, 2013.

Summary of Learning Objectives

 Define the term *business*.

Business consists of all profit-seeking activities and enterprises. Some businesses produce tangible goods, such as automobiles, breakfast cereals, and digital music players; others provide services such as insurance, hair styling, and entertainment, ranging from Six Flags theme parks and NFL games to concerts.

business   all profit-seeking activities and enterprises that provide goods and services necessary to an economic system.

profits   rewards earned by businesspeople who take the risks involved in blending people, technology, and information to create and market goods and services.

not-for-profit organization   businesslike establishment that has primary objectives other than returning profits to owners.

 Identify and describe the factors of production.

The factors of production consist of four basic inputs: natural resources, capital, human resources, and entrepreneurship. Natural resources include all productive inputs that are useful in their natural states. Capital includes technology, tools, information, and physical facilities. Human resources include anyone who works for the firm. Entrepreneurship is the ability to see an opportunity and take the risks inherent in creating and operating a business.

factors of production   four basic inputs: natural resources, capital, human resources, and entrepreneurship.

natural resources   all production inputs that are useful in their natural states, including agricultural land, building sites, forests, and mineral deposits.

capital   an organization's technology, tools, information, and physical facilities.

human resources   in an organization, anyone who works, providing either the physical labor or intellectual inputs.

entrepreneurship   ability to see an opportunity and take the risks inherent in creating and operating a business.

Describe the private enterprise system.

The private enterprise system is an economic system that rewards firms for their ability to perceive and serve the needs and demands of consumers. Competition in the private enterprise system ensures success for firms that satisfy consumer demands. Citizens in a private enterprise economy enjoy the rights to private property, profits, freedom of choice, and competition. Entrepreneurship drives economic growth.

private enterprise system   economic system that rewards firms for their ability to identify and serve the needs and demands of customers.

capitalism   economic system that rewards firms for their ability to perceive and serve the needs and demands of consumers; also called the private enterprise system.

competitive differentiation   unique combination of organizational abilities, products, and approaches that sets a company apart from competitors in the minds of customers.

private property   most basic freedom under the private enterprise system; the right to own, use, buy, sell, and bequeath land, buildings, machinery, equipment, patents, individual possessions, and various intangible kinds of property.

 Identify the six eras in the history of business.

The six historical eras are the Colonial period, the Industrial Revolution, the age of industrial entrepreneurs, the production era, the marketing era, and the relationship era. In the Colonial period, businesses were small and rural, emphasizing agricultural production. The Industrial Revolution brought factories and mass production to business. The age of industrial entrepreneurs built on the Industrial Revolution through an expansion in the number and size of firms. The production era focused on the growth of factory operations through assembly lines and other efficient internal processes. During and following the Great Depression, businesses concentrated on finding markets for their products through advertising and selling, giving rise to the marketing era. In the relationship era, businesspeople focused on developing and sustaining long-term relationships with customers and other businesses. Technology promotes innovation and communication, while alliances create a competitive advantage through partnerships. Concern for the environment also helps build strong relationships with consumers.

consumer orientation   business philosophy that focuses first on determining unmet consumer wants and needs and then designing products to satisfy those needs.

branding   process of creating an identity in consumers' minds for a good, service, or company; a major marketing tool in contemporary business.

brand   name, term, sign, symbol, design, or some combination that identifies the products of one firm and differentiates them from competitors' offerings.

transaction management   building and promoting products in the hope that enough customers will buy them to cover costs and earn profits.

relationship era business era in which firms seek ways to actively nurture customer loyalty by carefully managing their interaction with buyers.

5 **Explain** how today's business workforce and the nature of work itself are changing.

The workforce is changing in several significant ways: (1) it is aging and the labor pool is shrinking, and (2) it is becoming increasingly diverse. The nature of work has shifted toward services and a focus on information. More firms now rely on outsourcing, offshoring, and nearshoring to produce goods or fulfill services and functions that were previously handled in-house or in-country. In addition, today's workplaces are becoming increasingly flexible, allowing employees to work from different locations. And companies are fostering innovation through teamwork and collaboration.

diversity in a workforce, the blending of individuals of different genders, ethnic backgrounds, cultures, religions, ages, and physical and mental abilities.

outsourcing using outside vendors to produce goods or fulfill services and functions previously handled in-house or in-country.

offshoring relocation of business processes to lower-cost locations overseas.

nearshoring outsourcing production or services to locations near a firm's home base.

onshoring returning production to its original manufacturing location because of changes in costs or processes.

6 **Identify** the skills and attributes needed for the 21st century manager.

Today's managers need vision, the ability to perceive marketplace needs and the way their firm can satisfy them. Critical-thinking skills and creativity allow managers to pinpoint problems and opportunities and plan novel solutions. Managers are dealing with rapid change, and they need skills to help lead their organizations through shifts in external and internal conditions.

vision the ability to perceive marketplace needs and what an organization must do to satisfy them.

critical thinking ability to analyze and assess information to pinpoint problems or opportunities.

creativity capacity to develop novel solutions to perceived organizational problems.

7 **Outline** the characteristics that make a company admired.

A company is usually admired for its solid profits, stable growth, a safe and challenging work environment, high-quality goods and services, and business ethics and social responsibility.

>>> Quick Review >>>

LO1

1 What activity lies at the heart of every business endeavor?

2 What is the primary objective of a not-for-profit organization?

LO2

1 What are the four basic factors of any economic system?

2 List the four types of capital.

3 What is an entrepreneur?

LO3

1 What is an alternative term for *private enterprise system*?

2 What is the most basic freedom under the private enterprise system?

LO4

1 Describe the Industrial Revolution.

2 During which era was branding developed?

3 What is the difference between transaction management and relationship management?

LO5

1 Define *outsourcing, offshoring,* and *nearshoring.*

2 Describe the importance of collaboration and employee partnership.

LO6

1 Why is vision an important managerial quality?

2 What is the difference between creativity and critical thinking?

LO7

1 Define *business ethics* and *social responsibility.*

2 Name three criteria used to judge whether an organization might be considered admirable.

© Izabela Habur/iStockphoto

chapter two

2

Business Ethics and Social Responsibility

Learning Objectives

1 **Explain** society's concern for ethical issues.

2 **Describe** the contemporary ethical environment.

3 **Discuss** how organizations shape ethical conduct.

4 **Describe** how businesses can act responsibly to satisfy society.

5 **Explain** the ethical responsibilities of businesses to the general public.

6 **Describe** the responsibilities to investors and the financial community.

Panera, a Bakery Café on a Mission

To be socially responsible means more than donating a few dollars to worthy causes, using recyclable packaging, or planting trees. It is really about aligning an entire organization's culture to the values of their community. Panera Bread has taken corporate social responsibility to a whole new level. Although the $3 billion company donates more than $150 million in food products each year, it wasn't enough. Co-CEO and founder Ron Shaich recently made it personal by setting up several Panera restaurants as "pay what you can" cafes. The company has just opened its fourth "Panera Cares" restaurant in Chicago.

The three restaurants already in operation in other states are even turning a profit, which the company gives to social service organizations that provide job training for at-risk youth. Taking it one step further, the company then hires those young people to work at Panera.

With "Panera Cares" and their food donation program, "Panera Bread Foundation," the company is setting a powerful example of true corporate social responsibility. For Panera, it is no longer "my sandwich is better than the guy's across the street" but rather about building a business based on living their core values. Or as their new advertising campaign states, "live consciously, eat deliciously."

Firms like Whole Foods Markets, Ben and Jerry's Ice Cream, and Levis take their corporate social responsibility seriously as well. These firms and many others like them provide consumers, employees, and all their stakeholders with products that respect the environment, and they embrace the communities they serve. Being socially responsible is just who they are. And for Panera, incorporating their core values into their organization is a lot like the yeast in their bread dough; it raises the entire organization.[1]

Overview > > >

Companies like Panera that want to prosper over the long term are smart to consider how **business ethics**—the standards of conduct and moral values governing actions and decisions in the work environment—will affect their environment, employees, and customers. All businesses must find the proper balance between doing what is right and doing what is profitable.

In business, as in life, deciding what is right or wrong in a given situation does not always involve a clear-cut choice. Firms have many responsibilities—to customers, to employees, to investors, and to society as a whole. Sometimes conflicts arise in trying to serve the different needs of these separate constituencies. The ethical values of executives and individual employees at all levels can influence the decisions and actions a business takes. Throughout your career, you will encounter many situations in which you will need to weigh right and wrong before making a decision or taking action. Our discussion begins by focusing on individual ethics.

In addition to individual ethics, business ethics are also shaped by the ethical climate within an organization. Codes of conduct and ethical standards play increasingly significant roles in businesses in which doing the right thing is both supported and applauded. This chapter demonstrates how a firm can create a framework to encourage—and even demand—high standards of ethical behavior and social responsibility from its employees. It also considers the complex question of what business owes to society and how societal forces mold the actions of businesses.

business ethics standards of conduct and moral values governing actions and decisions in the work environment.

▼ The cartoon suggests ethics are a complex part of our society.

Jon Carter/www.CartoonStock.com

❶ Ethical Challenges

In both your personal and business life, you will sometimes be called on to weigh the ethics of decisions that can affect not just your own future but possibly the future of your fellow workers, your company, and its customers. As already noted, it's not always easy to distinguish between what is right and wrong in many business situations, especially when the needs and concerns of various parties conflict.

Solving ethical dilemmas is not easy. In many cases, each possible decision can have both unpleasant consequences and positive benefits that must be evaluated. The ethical issues that confront manufacturers with unsold merchandise are just one example of many different types of ethical questions encountered in the workplace. **FIGURE 2.1** identifies the most common ethical challenges that business people face.

CONFLICT OF INTEREST

A **conflict of interest** occurs when a businessperson is faced with a situation in which an action benefiting one person or group

> **conflict of interest** occurs when a businessperson is faced with a situation in which an action benefiting one person or group has the potential to harm another.

has the potential to harm another. Conflicts of interest may pose ethical challenges when they involve the businessperson's own interests and those of someone to whom he or she has a duty or when they involve two parties to whom the businessperson has a duty. Lawyers, business consultants, or advertising agencies would face a conflict of interest if they represented two competing companies: a strategy that would benefit one of the client companies might harm the other client. A conflict of interest may also occur when one person holds two or more similar jobs in two different workplaces.

Ethical ways to handle conflicts of interest include (1) avoiding them and (2) disclosing them. Some companies have policies against taking on clients who are competitors of existing clients. Most businesses and government agencies have written policies prohibiting employees from accepting gifts or specifying a maximum gift value. Or a member of a board of directors or committee might abstain from voting on a decision in which he or she has a financial interest. In other situations, people state their potential conflict of interest so that the people affected can decide whether to get information or help they need from another source instead.

HONESTY AND INTEGRITY

Employers value honesty and integrity. An employee who is honest can be counted on to tell the truth. An employee with integrity goes beyond truthfulness. Having **integrity**

> **integrity** adhering to deeply felt ethical principles in business situations.

means adhering to deeply felt ethical principles in business situations. It includes doing what you say you will do and accepting responsibility for mistakes. Behaving with honesty and integrity inspires trust, and as a result, it can help build long-term relationships with customers, employers, suppliers, and the public. Employees, in turn, want their managers and the company as a whole to treat them honestly and with integrity.

Unfortunately, violations of honesty and integrity are all too common. Some people misrepresent their academic credentials on their résumés or job applications. Reputable organizations take these violations very seriously and often terminate employees for their actions.[2] Others steal from their employers by taking home supplies or products without permission or by carrying out personal business during the time they are being paid to work. And many employees use company computers to surf the Web for personal shopping, e-mail, gaming, and social networking. This misuse costs U.S. companies an estimated $85 billion annually in lost productivity.[3]

⌄ Employers and employees value honesty and integrity, but what should happen when employees misuse Internet privileges for personal purposes?

XiXinXing/Shutterstock

FIGURE 2.1
Common Business Ethical Challenges

LOYALTY VERSUS TRUTH

Businesspeople expect their employees to be loyal and to act in the best interests of the company. But when the truth about a company is not favorable, an ethical conflict can arise. Individuals may have to decide between loyalty to the company and truthfulness in business relationships. People resolve such dilemmas in various ways. Some place the highest value on loyalty, even at the expense of truth. Others avoid volunteering negative information but answer truthfully if someone asks them a specific question. People may emphasize truthfulness and actively disclose negative information, especially if the cost of silence is high, as in the case of operating a malfunctioning aircraft or selling tainted food items.

> >> **Quick Review**

1 To whom does a business have an ethical responsibility?

2 If a firm is meeting all of its responsibilities, why do ethical conflicts arise?

20

2 The Contemporary Ethical Environment

In today's business environment, individuals can make the difference in ethical expectations and behavior. As executives, managers, and employees demonstrate their personal ethical principles—or lack of ethical principles—the expectations and actions of those who work for and with them can change.

What is the current status of individual business ethics in the United States? Although ethical behavior can be difficult to track or define in all circumstances, evidence suggests that unfortunately some individuals act unethically or illegally on the job. And technology seems to have expanded the range and impact of unethical behavior. For example, anyone with computer access to data has the potential to steal or manipulate the data or to shut down the system, even from a remote location. Banks, insurance companies, and other financial institutions are often targeted for such attacks. Although some might shrug these occurrences away, in fact they have an impact on how investors, customers, and the general public view a firm. It is difficult to rebuild a tarnished image, and long-term customers may be lost.

Nearly every employee, at every level, wrestles with ethical questions at some point or another. Some rationalize questionable behavior by saying, "Everybody's doing it." Others act unethically because they feel pressured in their jobs or have to meet performance quotas. Yet some avoid unethical acts that don't mesh with their personal values and morals. To help you understand the differences in the ways individuals arrive at ethical choices, the next section focuses on how personal ethics and morals develop.

DEVELOPMENT OF PERSONAL ETHICS

An individual's stage in moral and ethical development is determined by a huge number of factors. Experiences help shape responses to different situations. A person's family, educational, cultural, and religious backgrounds can also play a role, as can the environment within the firm. Individuals can also have different styles of deciding ethical dilemmas, no matter what their stage of moral development.

Regardless of their ethical background, psychologist Lawrence Kohlberg identified that individuals typically develop ethical standards in the three stages shown in **FIGURE 2.2**: the pre-conventional, conventional, and post-conventional stages.[4]

In stage 1, the pre-conventional stage, individuals primarily consider their own needs and desires in making decisions. They obey external rules only because they are afraid of punishment or hope to receive rewards if they comply. For them, ethics is proscriptive in that they do not think about or evaluate unique ethical situations but rather just identify the rules and follow them (or not). A stage 1 ethical approach to taking something that doesn't belong to you—for example, food—would be saying that such an action is theft and is always wrong.

In stage 2, the conventional stage, individuals are aware of and act in response to their duty to others, including their obligations to family members, co-workers, and organizations. The expectations of these groups influence how they choose between what is acceptable and unacceptable in certain situations. In stage 2, individuals who take food without permission from a restaurant where they work could make the ethical argument that the need to feed their family was an overriding concern, and taking food in such circumstances is not unethical. Self-interest, however, continues to play a role in decisions.

Stage 3, the post-conventional stage, represents the highest level of ethical and moral behavior. Individuals are able to move beyond mere self-interest and duty and take the larger needs of society into account as well. They have developed personal ethical

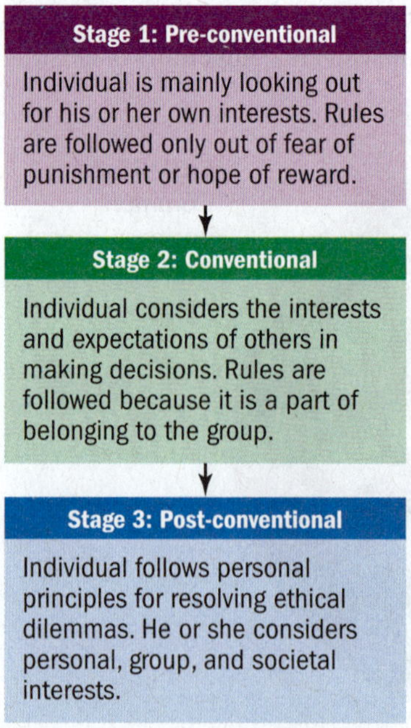

FIGURE 2.2 Stages of Moral and Ethical Development

Stage 1: Pre-conventional

Individual is mainly looking out for his or her own interests. Rules are followed only out of fear of punishment or hope of reward.

↓

Stage 2: Conventional

Individual considers the interests and expectations of others in making decisions. Rules are followed because it is a part of belonging to the group.

↓

Stage 3: Post-conventional

Individual follows personal principles for resolving ethical dilemmas. He or she considers personal, group, and societal interests.

principles for determining what is right and can apply those principles in a wide variety of situations.

FIGURE 2.3 Johnson & Johnson Credo

3 How Organizations Shape Ethical Conduct

Regardless of where a person is in terms of ethical development, it is important to remember that no one makes decisions in a vacuum. Choices are strongly influenced by the standards of conduct established within the organizations where people work. Unfortunately, not all organizations are able to build a solid framework of business ethics. Because the damage from ethical misconduct can powerfully affect a firm's **stakeholders**—customers, investors, employees, and the public—pressure is exerted on businesses to act in acceptable ways.

stakeholders
customers, investors, employees, and public affected by or with an interest in a company.

ETHICAL AWARENESS

The foundation of an ethical climate is ethical awareness. As we have already seen, ethical dilemmas occur frequently in the workplace. Employees need help identifying ethical problems when they occur and knowing how the firm expects them to respond.

code of conduct
formal statement that defines how an organization expects its employees to resolve ethical questions.

One way for a firm to provide this support is to develop a **code of conduct**, a formal statement that defines how the organization expects employees to resolve ethical questions. Johnson & Johnson's credo, shown in **FIGURE 2.3**, is such a code. Recently Johnson & Johnson's CEO, Alex Gorsky, took the time at a shareholder's meeting to review the credo, pointing out along the way how each part illustrates how current Johnson & Johnson employees put the code into action each day.[5]

At the most basic level, a code of conduct may simply specify ground rules for acceptable behavior, such as identifying the laws and regulations that employees must obey. Other companies use their codes of conduct to identify key corporate values and provide frameworks that guide employees as they resolve moral and ethical dilemmas.

ETHICAL EDUCATION

Although a code of conduct can provide an overall framework, it cannot detail a solution for every ethical situation. Some ethical questions have black-and-white answers, but others do not.

Businesses must provide employees the tools and training they need to evaluate the options and arrive at suitable decisions. Similar strategies are being used in many business school ethics programs, where case studies and practical scenarios work best. Convicted white-collar criminal Walter Pavlo, a former employee at telecommunications firm MCI, speaks at colleges and universities about his experiences in the firm and prison. Pavlo, who along with other MCI associates stashed money in offshore accounts, speaks about his actions in an effort to warn students of the consequences of cheating.[6]

ETHICAL LEADERSHIP

Executives must not only talk about ethical behavior but also demonstrate it in their actions. This requires top managers to be personally committed to the company's core values and be willing to base their actions on them. The recent recession exposed executive-level misdeeds that damaged or even destroyed entire organizations and wiped out many people's life savings. In the aftermath, some organizations and business leaders have made a commitment to demonstrate ethical leadership and increased social responsibility. It is imperative that executives demonstrate high ethical standards in their words and actions. Put another way, they must "walk the talk" when it comes to ethics. Employees and middle managers look to senior managers as examples of acceptable behavior within a company. If the bosses are less than ethical, it is likely their workers will be as well.

The current ethical environment of business also includes the appointment of new corporate officers specifically charged with deterring wrongdoing and ensuring that ethical standards are met. Ethics compliance officers, whose numbers are rapidly rising, are responsible for conducting employee training programs that help spot potential fraud and abuse within the firm, investigating sexual harassment and discrimination charges, and monitoring any potential conflicts of interest.

WHISTLE-BLOWING

When individuals encounter unethical or illegal actions at work, they must decide what action to take. Sometimes it is possible to resolve the problem by working through channels within the organization. Resolving an ethical problem within the organization can be more effective than going outside of the organization—assuming, of course, that higher-level managers cooperate with the investigation. However, sometimes ethical violations involve an organization's management team; when this is the case, managers may not investigate the wrongdoing or, in extreme cases, suppress or cover up the allegations. When this happens, the individual should consider the potential damages to the company against the needs of the stakeholders to be informed as well as the greater public good. If the damage is significant, a person may conclude that the only solution is to blow the whistle. **Whistle-blowing** is an employee's disclosure to company officials, government authorities, or the media of illegal, immoral, or unethical practices.

State and federal laws protect whistle-blowers in certain situations, such as reports of discrimination, and the **Sarbanes-Oxley Act of 2002** now requires that firms in the private sector provide procedures for anonymous reporting of accusations of fraud. Shortly after this act was passed, the wrongdoings of three high-profile organizations were exposed by internal whistle-blowers. Ethical violations as well as illegal acts at WorldCom and Enron were exposed by employees after they tried to resolve the issues internally. To encourage whistle-blowing, the Act makes it illegal for anyone to retaliate against an employee for taking concerns of unlawful conduct to a public official. In addition, whistle-blowers can seek protection under the False Claims Act, under which they can file a lawsuit on behalf of the government if they believe that a company has somehow defrauded the government. Charges against health care companies for fraudulent billing for Medicare or Medicaid are examples of this type of lawsuit.

whistle-blowing employee's disclosure to company officials, government authorities, or the media of illegal, immoral, or unethical practices committed by an organization.

Sarbanes-Oxley Act of 2002 federal legislation designed to deter and punish corporate and accounting fraud and corruption and to protect the interests of workers and shareholders through enhanced financial disclosures, criminal penalties for CEOs and CFOs who defraud investors, safeguards for whistle-blowers, and establishment of a new regulatory body for public accounting firms.

22

< Cynthia Cooper, a whistle-blower at WorldCom, has created an organization to speak to employees about ethics in the workplace.[7]

The University of Mississippi, Kevin Bain/AP

> > > **Quick Review**

1 Why is a code of conduct important to an organization's ethical standards?

2 Why is it important for senior leadership to set good examples when it comes to ethics?

4 Acting Responsibly to Satisfy Society

Companies that want to attract skilled and knowledgeable workers have wide-ranging responsibilities to their employees, both here and abroad. These include workplace safety, quality-of-life issues, ensuring equal opportunity on the job, avoiding age discrimination, and preventing sexual harassment and sexism.

WORKPLACE SAFETY

A century ago, few businesses paid much attention to the safety of their workers. In fact, most business owners viewed employees as mere cogs in the production process. Workers, some of them young children, toiled in frequently dangerous conditions. In 1911, a fire at the Triangle Shirtwaist Factory in New York City killed 146 people, mostly young girls. Contributing to the massive loss of life were the sweatshop working conditions at the factory, including overcrowding, blocked exits, and a lack of fire escapes. This tragedy forced businesses to begin to recognize their responsibility for workers' safety.

Workplace safety is now an important business responsibility. The Occupational Safety and Health Administration (OSHA) is the main federal regulatory force in setting safety and health standards. Its mandates range from broad guidelines on storing hazardous materials to specific safety standards in industries such as construction, manufacturing, and mining. OSHA tracks and investigates workplace accidents and has the authority to fine employers found liable for injuries and deaths on the job.

Although most businesses strive to make their operations safe for all employees and customers, in some cases a business's need for workplace health and safety can conflict with an individual worker's personal beliefs. Take for example the case of an Indiana hospital that fired eight workers for failing to take a flu shot. A

∧ Workplace safety is an important business responsibility. In potentially dangerous areas, workers are required to wear safety equipment, including hard hats and protective eyewear.

Oriontrail/Shutterstock

hospital spokeswoman said, "The flu has the highest death rate of any vaccine-preventable disease, and it would be irresponsible from our perspective for health care providers to ignore that." Many of the fired workers filed exemptions, claiming religious reasons for not taking the injections, but the hospital's need to provide a safe environment for their staff and patients outweighed these employees' concerns.[8]

QUALITY-OF-LIFE ISSUES

Balancing work and family is becoming harder for many employees. They find themselves squeezed between working long hours and handling child-care problems, caring for elderly parents, and solving other family crises.

family leave unpaid leave of up to 12 weeks annually for any employee for the birth or adoption of a child; to become a foster parent; or to care for a seriously ill relative, spouse, or self in the event of a serious health condition or injury; prescribed for employers with 50 or more employees by the Family and Medical Leave Act of 1993.

Many employers offer **family leave** to employees who need to deal with family matters. Under the Family and Medical Leave Act of 1993, employers with 50 or more employees must provide unpaid leave annually for any eligible employee who wants time off for the birth or adoption of a child; to become a foster parent; or to care for a seriously ill relative, spouse, or self if he or she has a serious health condition or injury. The law requires employers to grant up to 12 weeks of leave each year, and leave may be taken intermittently as medical conditions necessitate.

ENSURING EQUAL OPPORTUNITY ON THE JOB

Businesspeople also face challenges managing an increasingly diverse workforce. Technological advances are expanding the ways people with physical disabilities can contribute in the workplace. Businesses need to find ways to responsibly recruit and manage older workers and workers with varying lifestyles. In addition to their direct employees, companies may offer benefits such as health insurance to family members and unmarried domestic partners. More than half of Fortune 500 companies currently offer domestic-partner benefits to their employees.[9]

To a great extent, efforts at managing diversity are regulated by law. The Civil Rights Act (1964) outlawed many kinds of discriminatory practices, and Title VII of the act specifically prohibits **discrimination**—biased treatment of a job candidate or employee—in the workplace. As shown in TABLE 2.1, other nondiscrimination laws include the Equal Pay Act (1963), the Age Discrimination in Employment Act (1967), the Equal Employment Opportunity Act (1972), the Pregnancy Discrimination Act (1978), the Civil Rights Act of 1991, and numerous executive orders. The Americans with Disabilities Act (1990) protects the rights of physically challenged people. The Vietnam Era Veterans Readjustment Act (1974) protects the employment of veterans of the Vietnam War. The Genetic Information Nondiscrimination Act (2008) prohibits discrimination on the basis of genetic tests or the medical history of an individual or that individual's family.

The **Equal Employment Opportunity Commission (EEOC)**

discrimination biased treatment of a job candidate or employee.

Equal Employment Opportunity Commission (EEOC) government commission created to increase job opportunities for women and minorities and to help end discrimination based on race, color, religion, disability, gender, or national origin in any personnel action.

∨ The birth or adoption of a child is covered under the Family and Medical Leave Act, allowing new parents to take time off during the year.

© USGirl/iStockphoto

TABLE 2.1 What are the laws designed to ensure equal opportunity?

Law	Key Provisions
Title VII of the Civil Rights Act of 1964 (as amended by the Equal Employment Opportunity Act of 1972)	Prohibits discrimination in hiring, promotion, compensation, training, or dismissal on the basis of race, color, religion, sex, or national origin.
Age Discrimination in Employment Act of 1967 (as amended)	Prohibits discrimination in employment against anyone age 40 or older in hiring, promotion, compensation, training, or dismissal.
Equal Pay Act of 1963	Requires equal pay for men and women working for the same firm in jobs that require equal skill, effort, and responsibility.
Vocational Rehabilitation Act of 1973	Requires government contractors and subcontractors to take affirmative action to employ and promote qualified disabled workers. Coverage now extends to all federal employees. Coverage has been broadened through court rulings to include people with communicable diseases, including AIDS.
Vietnam Era Veterans Readjustment Act of 1974	Requires government contractors and subcontractors to take affirmative action to employ and retain disabled veterans. Coverage now extends to all federal employees and has been broadened by the passage of similar laws in more than 20 states.
Pregnancy Discrimination Act of 1978	Requires employers to treat pregnant women and new mothers the same as other employees for all employment-related purposes, including receipt of benefits under company benefit programs.
Americans with Disabilities Act of 1990	Makes discrimination against the disabled illegal in public accommodations, transportation, and telecommunications; stiffens employer penalties for intentional discrimination on the basis of an employee's disability.
Civil Rights Act of 1991	Makes it easier for workers to sue their employers for alleged discrimination. Enables victims of sexual discrimination to collect punitive damages; includes employment decisions and on-the-job issues such as sexual harassment, unfair promotions, and unfair dismissal. The employer must prove that it did not engage in discrimination.
Family and Medical Leave Act of 1993	Requires all businesses with 50 or more employees to provide up to 12 weeks of unpaid leave annually to employees who have had a child or are adopting a child, are becoming foster parents, are caring for a seriously ill relative or spouse, or are themselves seriously ill. Workers must meet certain eligibility requirements.
Uniformed Services Employment and Reemployment Rights Act of 1994	Prohibits employers from denying employment benefits on the basis of employees' membership in or obligation to serve in the uniformed services and protects the rights of veterans, reservists, and National Guard members to reclaim their jobs after being absent due to military service or training.
Genetic Information Nondiscrimination Act of 2008	Prohibits employers from discriminating against employees or applicants on the basis of genetic information, including genetic tests of an individual or family member or an individual's personal or family medical history.

24

was created to increase job opportunities for women and minorities and to help end discrimination based on race, color, religion, disability, gender, or national origin in any personnel action. To enforce fair-employment laws, it investigates charges of discrimination and harassment and files suit against violators. The EEOC can also help employers set up programs to increase job opportunities for women, minorities, people with disabilities, and people in other protected categories.

AGE DISCRIMINATION

With the average age of U.S. workers steadily rising, more than half of the workforce is projected to be age 40 or older in a few years. Yet some employers find it less expensive to hire and retain younger workers, who generally have lower medical bills as well as lower salary and benefits packages. At the same time, many older workers have training and skills that younger workers have yet to acquire. The Age Discrimination in Employment Act of 1967 (ADEA) protects individuals who are age 40 or older, prohibiting

discrimination on the basis of age and denial of benefits to older employees.

Legal issues aside, employers might do well to consider not only the experience that older workers bring to the

> Employees who are age 40 or older are protected from discrimination based on age by the Age Discrimination in Employment Act.

workplace but also their enthusiasm. Many surveys report that older workers who remain on the job by choice—not because they are forced to do so for economic reasons—are often happy with their employment. But other studies show that aging Baby Boomers are increasingly dissatisfied with the workplace due to the falling value of their retirement investments and diminishing options such as relocation. Still, employees with decades of work experience can be a valuable asset to any firm.[10]

SEXUAL HARASSMENT AND SEXISM

Every employer has a responsibility to ensure that all workers are treated fairly and are safe from sexual harassment. **Sexual harassment** refers to unwelcome and inappropriate actions of a sexual nature in the workplace. It is a form of sex discrimination that violates the Civil Rights Act of 1964, which gives both men and women the right to file lawsuits for intentional sexual harassment. About 11,000 sexual harassment complaints are filed with the EEOC each year, of which about 16 percent are filed by men.[11] Thousands of other cases are either handled internally by companies or never reported.

> **sexual harassment** unwelcome and inappropriate actions of a sexual nature in the workplace.

Two types of sexual harassment exist. The first type occurs when an employee is pressured to comply with unwelcome advances and requests for sexual favors in return for job security, promotions, and raises. The second type results from a hostile work environment in which an employee feels hassled or degraded because of unwelcome flirting, lewd comments, or obscene jokes. The courts have ruled that allowing sexually oriented materials in the workplace can create a hostile atmosphere that interferes with an employee's ability to do the job. Employers are also legally responsible to protect employees from sexual harassment by customers and clients. The EEOC's Web site informs employers and employees of criteria for identifying sexual harassment and how it should be handled in the workplace.

Sexual harassment is often part of the broader problem of **sexism**—discrimination against members of either sex, but primarily affecting women. One important sexism issue is equal pay for equal work.

> **sexism** discrimination against members of either sex, but primarily affecting women.

U.S. Census statistics show that, overall, women still earn 77 cents for every 1 dollar earned by men. The number drops to 68 cents for African American women and 58 cents for Hispanic women. Education, occupation, work hours, and other factors don't seem to affect the gap, which remains unexplained other than the differences by gender.[12] In some extreme cases, differences in pay and advancement can become the basis for sex discrimination suits which, like sexual harassment suits, can be costly and time-consuming to settle. As in all business practices, it is better to act legally and ethically in the first place than to attempt to resolve these issues when they become the subject of litigation.

>>> **Quick Review**

1. What is the name of the main federal regulatory force in setting safety and health standards?

2. Why was the Equal Employment Opportunity Commission (EEOC) created?

5 Ethical Responsibilities to the General Public

In a general sense, **social responsibility** is management's acceptance of the role that ethics plays in their business and their obligation to consider consumer satisfaction, and societal well-being of equal value to profit in evaluating the firm's performance. Businesses may exercise social responsibility because such behavior is required by law, because it enhances the company's image, or because management believes it is the ethical course of action.

Historically, a company's social performance has been measured by its contribution to the overall economy and the employment opportunities it provides. Variables such as total wages paid often indicate social performance. Although profits and employment remain crucial, today many factors contribute to an assessment of a firm's social performance, including providing equal employment opportunities; respecting the cultural diversity of employees; responding to environmental concerns; providing a safe, healthy workplace; and producing high-quality products that are safe to use. The responsibilities of business to the general public include dealing with public health issues, protecting the environment, and developing the quality of the workforce.

> **social responsibility** management's acceptance of the role that ethics plays in their business and their obligation to consider consumer satisfaction, and societal well-being of equal value to profit in evaluating the firm's performance.

PUBLIC-HEALTH ISSUES

One of the most complex issues facing business as it addresses its ethical and social responsibilities to the general public is public health. Central to the public-health debate is the question of what businesses should do about dangerous products such as tobacco and alcohol. Tobacco products represent a major health risk, contributing to heart disease, stroke, and cancer among smokers. Families and co-workers of smokers share this danger as well, as their exposure to secondhand smoke increases their risks for cancer, asthma, and respiratory infections. Many cities have not only banned smoking in public places but also in commercial businesses, such as restaurants. Several states, including Arkansas, California, Louisiana, and Maine, have bans on smoking in cars when children under the age of 18 are present, depending on the specific state's law.[13]

Heart disease, diabetes, and obesity have become major public health issues as the rates of these three conditions have been rising. More than 5 million American children between the ages of 6 and 17 are said to be overweight. Three-quarters of obese teenagers will become obese adults at risk for diabetes and heart disease. Jared Fogle became famous for losing 245 pounds over a two-year period through exercise and a diet that included SUBWAY sandwiches. He has since set up the Jared Foundation with the goal of fighting childhood obesity by encouraging children to develop healthy diet and exercise habits. Spreading his message through speaking tours, grants to schools, and programs for children and their families, Fogle says, "My goal is to help children avoid the physical and emotional hardships I went through living with obesity." SUBWAY's Web site lists the nutritional values of its menu items and sources of diet and nutrition advice. The Web site also features a linked page supporting the Jared Foundation and its mission.[14]

PROTECTING THE ENVIRONMENT

Businesses affect the environment in a variety of ways—through the energy they consume, the waste they produce, the natural resources they use, and more. Today, many businesses have taken significant steps toward protecting the environment. Some have even launched sustainability initiatives—operating in such a way that the firm not only minimizes its impact on the environment but actually regenerates or replaces used resources. Procter & Gamble and Kaiser Permanente maintain sustainability assessments of their suppliers, rating them on energy and water use, recycling, waste production, greenhouse gases produced, and other factors.[15]

For many managers, finding ways to minimize pollution and other environmental damage caused by their products or operating processes has become an important economic and legal issue as well as a social one. Apple is one company that is working hard to reduce the environmental impact caused

^ Restaurants can convert used restaurant oils into biodiesel fuel. This image shows used restaurant grease on the left that was processed to produce the biodiesel shown on the right.

Robert Nickelsberg/Getty Images

by the generation of energy they consume. The goal for Apple is to use renewable sources for power in their facilities—solar, wind, hydro, and geothermal. Investing in this effort is starting to pay off for the company. Apple's data centers now use 100 percent renewable energy. The corporate centers aren't far behind. They'll keep working at it until all they reach 100 percent renewable energy.[16]

Despite the efforts of companies like Procter & Gamble, Kaiser Permanente, Apple, and thousands of others, production and manufacturing methods still leave behind large quantities of waste materials that can further pollute the air, water, and soil. Some products themselves, such as electronics that contain lead and mercury, are difficult to recycle or reuse—although scientists and engineers are finding ways to do this. In other instances, the action (or lack of action) on the part of a firm results in an environmental disaster, as in the case of the explosion and large-scale spill from BP's offshore drilling rig in the Gulf of Mexico. The months-long spill not only affected the ocean and coastal environments but also the lives of residents and local economies.[17] Despite the difficulty, however, companies are finding that they can be environmentally friendly and profitable, too.

Another solution to the problems of pollutants is **recycling**—reprocessing used materials for reuse. Recycling can sometimes provide much of the raw material that manufacturers need, thereby conserving the world's natural resources and reducing

< Some businesses collaborate with urban neighborhoods to set up community gardens as a way of showing kids how to eat healthy.

Jani Bryson/iStockphoto

recycling reprocessing of materials for reuse.

the need for landfills. Robert King founded King Diesel on the island of Maui in Hawaii. The company used conventional diesel fuel to run the generators at the Central Maui Landfill. After King became concerned at the large amounts of used cooking oil being dumped, he contacted Daryl Reece at the University of Idaho. Reece helped develop a process that converts used restaurant oils into biodiesel fuel. Together they founded Pacific Biodiesel, using biodiesel to run the generators at the landfill in one of America's first commercially viable, community-based biodiesel plants. Today, Robert King and his wife Kelly manage Pacific Biodiesel and its associated companies, producing and selling biodiesel and other biofuels and designing and building similar plants around the country.[18]

CORPORATE PHILANTHROPY

As Chapter 1 pointed out, not-for-profit organizations play an important role in society by serving the public good. They provide the human resources that enhance the quality of life in communities around the world. To fulfill this mission, many not-for-profit organizations rely on financial contributions from the business community. Firms respond by donating billions of dollars each year to not-for-profit organizations. This **corporate philanthropy** includes cash contributions, donations of equipment and products, and supporting the volunteer efforts of company employees.

corporate philanthropy an organization's effort to contribute to the communities in which it earns profits through cash contributions, donations of equipment and products, and supporting the volunteer efforts of company employees.

Recipients include cultural organizations, adopt-a-school programs, neighborhood sports programs, and housing and job training programs.

Corporate philanthropy can have many positive benefits beyond purely "feel-good" rewards, such as higher employee morale, enhanced company image, and improved customer relationships. General Mills, for instance, is a major contributor to Susan G. Komen for the Cure, a foundation dedicated to curing breast cancer, through its line of yogurt products marketed under the Yoplait brand name. Yoplait's target market is health-conscious women, the same group most likely to know of or become involved with the foundation's fund-raising efforts. Through its other brands, General Mills sponsors other nationwide initiatives that support education, families, and community improvement projects.[19]

RESPONSIBILITIES TO CUSTOMERS

Businesspeople share a social and ethical responsibility to treat their customers fairly and act in a manner that is not harmful to them. **Consumerism**—the public demand that a business consider the wants and needs of its customers in making decisions—has gained widespread acceptance. Consumerism is based on the belief that consumers have certain rights. A frequently quoted statement of consumer rights was made by President John F. Kennedy in 1962. **FIGURE 2.4** summarizes these consumer rights. Numerous state and federal laws have been implemented since then to protect these rights.

consumerism public demand that a business consider the wants and needs of its customers in making decisions.

THE RIGHT TO BE SAFE

Contemporary businesspeople must recognize obligations, both moral and legal, to ensure the safe operation and sale of their products. Consumers should feel assured that the products they

▼ Through sales of its Yoplait yogurt line, General Mills contributes to Susan G. Komen for the Cure, a charity important to the health-conscious consumers who buy Yoplait.

Richard B. Levine/NewsCom

FIGURE 2.4
Consumer Rights as Proposed by President Kennedy

product liability
the responsibility of manufacturers for injuries and damages caused by their products.

purchase will not cause injuries in normal use. **Product liability** refers to the responsibility of manufacturers and sellers of those products for injuries and damages caused by their products. Items that lead to injuries, either directly or indirectly, can have disastrous consequences for the manufacturer or seller of that product.

Many companies rigorously test their products to avoid safety problems. Still, testing alone cannot foresee every eventuality. Companies must try to consider all possibilities and provide adequate warning of potential dangers. When a product does pose a threat to customer safety, a responsible manufacturer responds quickly to correct the problem or recall the product. Although we take for granted that our food and our pets' food is safe, sometimes contamination occurs, which can cause illness or even death. A recent concern about salmonella, a microorganism that produces dangerous infections, caused Natura to voluntarily recall dry pet food. No illnesses or deaths were reported, but the company wanted to be certain its products were safe for pets.[20]

THE RIGHT TO BE INFORMED

Consumers should have access to enough education and product information to make responsible buying decisions. In their efforts to promote and sell their goods and services, companies can easily neglect consumers' right to be fully informed. False or misleading advertising is a violation of the Wheeler-Lea Act, a federal law enacted in 1938. The Federal Trade Commission and other federal and state agencies have established rules and regulations that govern advertising truthfulness.

The Food and Drug Administration (FDA), which sets standards for advertising conducted by drug manufacturers, eased restrictions for prescription drug advertising on television. In print ads, drug makers are required to spell out potential side effects and the proper uses of prescription drugs. Because of the requirement to disclose this information, prescription drug television advertising was limited. Now, however, the FDA says drug ads on radio and television can directly promote a prescription drug's benefits if they provide a quick way, such as displaying a toll-free number or Internet address, for consumers to learn about side effects.

The responsibility of business to preserve consumers' right to be informed extends beyond avoiding misleading advertising. All communications with customers from salespeople's comments to warranties and invoices must be controlled to clearly and accurately inform customers. Most packaged-goods firms, personal computer makers, and makers of other products bought for personal use by consumers include toll-free customer service numbers on their product labels so that consumers can get answers to questions about a product.

THE RIGHT TO CHOOSE

Consumers should have the right to choose which goods and services they need and want to purchase. Socially responsible firms attempt to preserve this right, even if they reduce their own sales and profits in the process. Brand-name drug makers are engaged in a battle being waged by state governments, insurance companies, consumer groups, unions, and major employers such as General Motors and Verizon. These groups want to force down the rising price of prescription drugs by ensuring that consumers have the right and the opportunity to select cheaper, generic brands.

THE RIGHT TO BE HEARD

Consumers should be able to express legitimate complaints to appropriate parties. Many companies expend considerable effort to ensure full hearings for consumer complaints. Auction Web site eBay assists buyers and sellers who believe they were victimized in transactions conducted through the site, deploying employees to work with users and law enforcement agencies to combat fraud.[21]

> >>> **Quick Review**
>
> **1** To whom does an organization have ethical responsibilities?
>
> **2** What is corporate philanthropy, and what are some ways organizations practice it?
>
> **3** What are the rights of consumers as put forward by President Kennedy in 1962?

6 Responsibilities to Investors and the Financial Community

Although a fundamental goal of any business is to make a profit for its shareholders, investors and the financial community demand that businesses behave ethically and legally. When firms fail in this responsibility, thousands of investors and consumers can suffer.

RIGHT TO FAIR ACCOUNTING

State and federal government agencies are responsible for protecting investors from financial misdeeds. At the federal level, the Securities and Exchange Commission (SEC) investigates suspicions of unethical or illegal behavior by publicly traded firms. It investigates accusations that a business is using faulty accounting practices to inaccurately portray its financial resources and profits to investors. Regulation FD ("Fair Disclosure") is an SEC rule that requires publicly traded companies to announce major information to the general public, rather than first disclosing the information to selected major investors. The agency also operates an Office of Internet Enforcement to target fraud in online trading and online sales of stock by unlicensed sellers.

Although pledges and codes of conduct are common in American business, not all organizations live up to them. In addition to provisions for protecting whistle-blowing, the Sarbanes-Oxley Act of 2002 established new rules and regulations for securities trading and accounting practices. Companies are now required to publish their code of ethics, if they have one, and inform the public of any changes made to it. The law may actually motivate even

more firms to develop written codes and guidelines for ethical business behavior. The federal government also created the U.S. Sentencing Commission to institutionalize ethics compliance programs that would establish high ethical standards and end corporate misconduct.

>>> **Quick Review**

1 Why do firms need to do more than simply earn a profit?

2 Describe some of the safeguards that protect investors and the financial community.

What's Ahead? > > >

The decisions and actions of businesspeople are often influenced by outside forces such as the legal environment and society's expectations about business responsibility. Firms also are affected by the economic environments in which they operate. The next chapter discusses the broad economic issues that influence businesses around the world. Our discussion will focus on how factors such as supply and demand, unemployment, inflation, and government monetary policies pose both challenges and opportunities for firms seeking to compete in the global marketplace.

Don't miss the Weekly Updates located at http://contemporarybusinessupdates.com to help you take the first step toward success.

NOTES

1. Company website, http://www.panerabread.com, accessed April 21, 2013; Stuart Elliott, "Selling Products by Selling Shared Values," *New York Times*, February 13, 2013, http://www.nytimes.com; Kate Rogers, "Panera Opens Free-Food, Suggested-Donations-Only Cafes," *Fox Business*, January 23, 2013, http://smallbusiness.foxbusiness.com; S. W. Hartley, "Café of Sharing," July 2012, http://kerinmarketing.com.

2. Steve Strunsky, "Port Authority Manager Fired for Misrepresenting Academic Credentials," *Star-Ledger,* September 19, 2012, http://www.nj.com.

3. "Internet Abuse at Work," *Memory Spy*, January 15, 2012, http://memoryspy.com.

4. Robert N. Barger, "Summary of Lawrence Kohlberg's Stages of Moral Development," University of Notre Dame, www.library.spscc.ctc.edu, accessed January 23, 2013.

5. Company Web site, http://www.jnj.com, accessed September 13, 2013; Susan Todd, "Johnson & Johnson's New CEO Emphasizes Company Credo at Shareholder's Meeting," *The Star-Ledger,* April 27, 2012, http://blog.nj.com.

6. Walter Pavlo, "There Are No Nice Prosecutors When You Are a Defendant," Forbes, January 21, 2013, http://blogs.forbes.com.

7. Company Web site, http://www.cynthiacooper.com, accessed January 30, 2013.

8. Associated Press, "Indiana Hospital Fires 8 Workers Who Refused Flu Shot," Fox News, http://www.foxnews.com, January 1, 2013.

9. Organization Web site, Human Rights Campaign, http://www.hrc.org, accessed January 23, 2013.

10. "Conference Board Job Satisfaction Survey Finds Older Workers as Dissatisfied as Others," *Aging Workforce News*, http://www.agingworkforcenews.com, accessed January 23, 2013.

11. U.S. Equal Employment Opportunity Commission, "Sexual Harassment Charges EEOC & FEPAs Combined: FY 1997-FY 2011," http://www1.eeoc.gov, accessed January 23, 2013.

12. National Committee on Pay Equity, "Wage Gap Statistically Unchanged," http://www.pay-equity.org, accessed January 23, 2013.

13. "Many U.S. Kids Still Exposed to Smoke in Cars: Study," February 6, 2012, http://www.reuters.com.

14. Company Web site, http://www.subway.com, accessed January 23, 2013; Jared Foundation, http://www.jaredfoundation.org, accessed January 23, 2013.

15. Company Web site, http://www.pgscorecard.com, accessed March 31, 2013; Akhila Vijayaraghavan, "Kaiser Permanente Greens Its Supply Chain by Switching to Safer IV Equipment," *Triple Pundit,* January 20, 2012, http://www.triplepundit.com.

16. Company Web site, http://www.apple.com, accessed March 31, 2013.

17. Company Web site, http://www.bp.com, accessed January 21, 2013.

18. Company Web site, http://www.biodiesel.com, accessed April 23, 2013; Melanie Stephens, "Pono Biofuels Agriculture Plan for Maui Pacific Biodiesel: VP Kelly King Looks at the Possibilities," *Maui Weekly,* October 11, 2012.

19. Company Web site, "Brand Partnerships," http://www.generalmills.com, accessed January 23, 2013.

20. U.S. Food and Drug Administration, "Natura Pet Issues Voluntary Recall of Specialized Dry Pet Foods Due to Possible Health Risk," press release, March 18, 2013, http://www.fda.gov.

21. Company Web site, "Rules and Policies," http://pages.ebay.com, accessed January 23, 2013.

Summary of Learning Objectives

 Explain society's concern for ethical issues.

Business ethics refers to the standards of conduct and moral values that businesspeople rely on to guide their actions and decisions in the workplace. Businesspeople must take a wide range of social issues into account when making decisions. Social responsibility refers to management's acceptance of the obligation to place a significant value of profit, consumer satisfaction, and societal well-being in evaluating the firm's performance.

business ethics standards of conduct and moral values regarding right and wrong actions in the work environment.

conflict of interest occurs when a businessperson is faced with a situation in which an action benefiting one person or group has the potential to harm another.

integrity adhering to deeply felt ethical principles in business situations.

 Describe the contemporary ethical environment.

Among the many factors shaping individual ethics are personal experience, peer pressure, and organizational culture. Individual ethics are also influenced by family, cultural, and religious standards. Additionally, the culture of the organization where a person works can be a factor. In the pre-conventional stage, individuals primarily consider their own needs and desires in making decisions. In the conventional stage, individuals are aware of and respond to their duty to others. In the post-conventional stage, the individual can move beyond self-interest and duty to include consideration of the needs of society. Conflicts of interest occur when a businessperson is faced with a situation in which an action benefiting one person has the potential to harm another, as when the person's own interests conflict with those of a customer. Honesty and integrity are valued qualities that engender trust, but a person's immediate self-interest may seem to require violating these principles. Loyalty to an employer sometimes conflicts with truthfulness. Whistle-blowing is a possible response to misconduct in the workplace, but the personal costs of doing so may be high.

 Discuss how organizations shape ethical conduct.

Employees are strongly influenced by the standards of conduct established and supported within the organization where they work. Businesses can help shape ethical behavior by developing codes of conduct that define their expectations. Organizations can also use this training to develop employees' ethics awareness and reasoning. Executives must also demonstrate ethical behavior in their decisions and actions to provide ethical leadership.

stakeholders customers, investors, employees, and public affected by or with an interest in a company.

code of conduct formal statement that defines how an organization expects its employees to resolve ethical questions.

whistle-blowing employee's disclosure to company officials, government authorities, or the media of illegal, immoral, or unethical practices committed by an organization.

Sarbanes-Oxley Act of 2002 federal legislation designed to deter and punish corporate and accounting fraud and corruption and to protect the interests of workers and shareholders through enhanced financial disclosures, criminal penalties for CEOs and CFOs who defraud investors, safeguards for whistle-blowers, and establishment of a new regulatory body for public accounting firms.

 Describe how businesses can act responsibly to satisfy society.

Today's businesses are expected to weigh their qualitative impact on consumers and society, in addition to their quantitative economic contributions such as sales, employment levels, and profits. One measure is their compliance with labor and consumer protection laws and their charitable contributions. Another measure some businesses take is to conduct social audits. Public-interest groups also create standards and measure companies' performance relative to those standards. The responsibilities of business to the general public include protecting the public health and the environment and developing the quality of the workforce. Additionally, many would argue that businesses have a social responsibility to support charitable and social causes in the communities in which they earn profits. Businesses also must treat customers fairly and protect consumers, upholding their rights to be safe, to be informed, to choose, and to be heard. Businesses have wide-ranging responsibilities to their workers. They should make sure the workplace is safe, address quality-of-life issues, ensure equal opportunity, and prevent sexual harassment and other forms of discrimination.

family leave unpaid leave of up to 12 weeks annually for the birth or adoption of a child; to become a foster parent; or to care for a seriously ill relative, spouse, or self in the event of a serious health condition or injury; prescribed for employers with 50 or more employees by the Family and Medical Leave Act of 1993.

discrimination biased treatment of a job candidate or employee.

Equal Employment Opportunity Commission (EEOC) government commission created to increase job opportunities for women and minorities and to help end discrimination based on race, color, religion, disability, gender, or national origin in any personnel action.

sexual harassment unwelcome and inappropriate actions of a sexual nature in the workplace.

sexism discrimination against members of either sex, but primarily affecting women.

social responsibility management's acceptance of the role that ethics plays in their business and their obligation to consider consumer satisfaction and societal well-being of equal value to profit in evaluating a firm's performance.

recycling reprocessing of used materials for reuse.

corporate philanthropy an organization's effort to contribute to the communities in which it earns profits through cash contributions, donations of equipment and products, and supporting the volunteer efforts of company employees.

consumerism public demand that a business consider the wants and needs of its customers in making decisions.

product liability the responsibility of manufacturers for injuries and damages caused by their products.

5 Explain the ethical responsibilities of businesses to the general public.

Social responsibility is management's acceptance of the role that ethics plays in their business and their obligation to consider consumer satisfaction and societal well-being of equal value to profit in evaluating a firm's performance. A company's social performance has historically been measured by its contribution to the overall economy and the employment opportunities it provides. Businesses face the complex issue of public health as they address their ethical and social responsibilities to the general public. The environment is also affected by businesses.

6 Describe the responsibilities to investors and the financial community.

Investors and the financial community demand that businesses behave ethically as well as legally in handling their financial transactions. Businesses must be honest in reporting their profits and financial performance to avoid misleading investors. The Securities and Exchange Commission is the federal agency responsible for investigating suspicions that publicly traded firms have engaged in unethical or illegal financial behavior.

>>> Quick Review >>>>

LO1
1 To whom does a business have an ethical responsibility?
2 If a firm is meeting all of its responsibilities, why do ethical conflicts arise?

LO2
1 Why is it difficult to solve ethical dilemmas?
2 Describe Kohlberg's three stages of ethical development.

LO3
1 Why is a code of conduct important to an organization's ethical standards?
2 Why is it important for senior leadership to set good examples when it comes to ethics?

LO4
1 What is the name of the main federal regulatory force in setting safety and health standards?

2 Why was the Equal Employment Opportunity Commission (EEOC) created?

LO5
1 To whom does an organization have ethical responsibilities?
2 What is corporate philanthropy, and what are some ways organizations practice it?
3 What are the rights of consumers as put forward by President Kennedy in 1962?

LO6
1 Why do firms need to do more than simply earn a profit?
2 Describe some of the safeguards that protect investors and the financial community.

chapter three

Economic Challenges Facing Contemporary Business

Learning Objectives

1. **Discuss** microeconomics and explain the forces of demand and supply.

2. **Describe** macroeconomics and the issues for the entire economy.

3. **Identify** how to evaluate economic performance.

4. **Discuss** government's attempts to manage economic performance.

Kids Come Home to Roost

In the new economic reality facing U.S. workers, many parents can't afford to retire because they're unexpectedly stretching resources to support grown children forced to return home because of a lack of employment opportunities. But ironically, by staying in the workforce, these parents may be filling the jobs younger workers need.

Employment rates for young U.S. adults are so low that a record 6 million people between ages 25 and 34 now live with their parents. The National Endowment for Financial Education (NEFE) reports nearly 6 in 10 parents give financial assistance to grown non-student children. (AARP puts this figure at 7 in 10.) Fully 26 percent of parents took on extra debt in the process, and 20 percent postponed major financial events like retiring or purchasing a home.

One divorced woman in Florida is helping to support three daughters. Two are college graduates in their 20s with thousands of dollars in educational loans and only part-time employment. Because it costs her about $600 a month to support them, she cannot afford homeowners or health insurance. "If the economy remains weak," says NEFE's president, "you may see more parents sacrificing their financial health for their struggling adult offspring."

Having raised their children to believe they could achieve anything, parents living with so-called "boomerang" kids are wondering what went wrong. Was it the financial crisis, the global recession, large-scale job outsourcing, or all of the above?[1]

Overview > > >

Economics is the social science that analyzes the choices individuals, groups, and governments make in allocating scarce resources. Economics affects all of us because everyone is involved in producing, distributing, or simply consuming goods and services. Whether you buy tickets to a NASCAR race or decide to stay home and watch TV instead, you are making an economic choice. Understanding how the activities of one industry affect those of other industries, and how they relate in the overall economic status of a country, is an important part of understanding economics.

Businesses, not-for-profit organizations, and local governments also make economic decisions as they choose how to use human and natural resources and invest in equipment, machinery, and buildings. Economists refer to the study of small economic units, such as individual consumers, families, and businesses, as **microeconomics**.

The study of a country's overall economic issues is called **macroeconomics** (*macro* meaning large). Macroeconomics addresses such issues as how an economy uses its resources and how public policies affect people's standard of living. For example, the substitution of ethanol for gasoline or biodiesel for diesel fuel has macroeconomic consequences, affecting many parts of the U.S. economy and suppliers around the world. Macroeconomics examines not just the economic policies of individual nations but the ways in which those individual policies affect the overall world economy.

economics
social science that analyzes the choices individuals, groups, and governments make in allocating scarce resources.

microeconomics
study of small economic units, such as individual consumers, families, and businesses.

macroeconomics
study of a nation's overall economic issues, such as how an economy uses its resources and how national governmental policies affect people's standard of living.

1 Microeconomics: The Forces of Demand and Supply

At the heart of every business transaction is an exchange between a buyer and a seller. The buyer recognizes that he or she needs or wants a particular good or service—whether it's a hamburger or a haircut—and is willing to pay a seller for it. The seller enters into the exchange to generate revenue and earn a profit. So, the exchange process involves both demand from consumers and supply from producers. Specifically, **demand** refers to the willingness and ability of buyers to purchase goods and services at different prices. The other side of the process

demand willingness and ability of buyers to purchase goods and services at different prices.

△ Farmer's markets are just one of many places where buyers and sellers come together.

© Robert Kyllo/Shutterstock

supply amount of goods and services for sale at different prices.

is **supply**, the amount of goods and services for sale at different prices. Understanding the factors that determine demand and supply, as well as how the two interact, can help you understand many actions and decisions of individuals, businesses, and government. This section takes a closer look at these concepts.

FACTORS DRIVING DEMAND

For most of us, economics amounts to choices we make with our scarce resources, principally money and time. Each person must therefore choose how much money to save (for future consumption) and how much to spend (present consumption). If we use our money for present consumption, we must decide among all the goods and services competing for our attention. Suppose you wanted to purchase a smart phone. You'd have

▽ Prices for commodities such as gasoline and food are highly influenced by the available supply. When there are supply interruptions, wholesale and retail prices can rise sharply.

© Heather A. Craig/Shutterstock

to choose from a variety of brands and models. You'd also have to decide where you wanted to buy one. After shopping around, you might decide you didn't want a smart phone at all. Instead, you might purchase something else or save your money. All of these choices are part of the landscape that is microeconomics.

Demand for any good or service is driven by a number of factors that influence how people decide to spend their money, by outside circumstances, or larger economic events such as the recent recession. Typically, consumers will tend to purchase more of a good if the price is lower and less of a good if the price is higher (think about items on sale, where lower prices often attracts more buyers). A **demand curve** is a graph of the amount of a product that buyers will purchase at different prices. Demand curves typically slope downward, meaning that lower and lower prices attract larger and larger purchases.

demand curve graph of the amount of a product that buyers will purchase at different prices.

Gasoline provides a classic example of how demand curves work. The left side of **FIGURE 3.1** shows a possible demand curve for the total amount of gasoline that people will purchase at different prices. The prices shown may not reflect the actual price in your location at this particular time, but they still demonstrate the concept. When gasoline is priced at $3.76 a gallon, drivers may fill up their tanks once or twice a week. However, when the price of gasoline goes up—say, to $4.06 a gallon—many consumers start economizing. They may combine errands or carpool to work. So, the quantity of gasoline demanded at $4.06 a gallon is lower than the amount demanded at $3.76 a gallon. The opposite happens at $3.36 a gallon. More gasoline is sold at $3.36 a gallon than at $3.76 a gallon, as people opt to take a weekend trip.

Movement along a demand curve is caused by changes in the price of the good. However, the overall demand for a product at any price can change as well, increasing or decreasing demand at all prices. Many factors can combine to determine the overall demand for a product—that is the shape and position of the demand curve. These influences include customer preferences and income, the prices of substitute and complementary items, whether the good is a necessity or a luxury, the number of buyers in a market, and the strength of their optimism regarding the future. Changes in any of these factors produce a new demand curve. Changes in household income also change demand. As consumers have more money to spend, firms can sell more services and merchandise at every price. This means the demand curve has shifted to the right. When income shrinks, nearly everyone suffers, and the demand curve shifts to the left. TABLE 3.1 describes how a demand curve is likely to respond to each of these changes.

FACTORS DRIVING SUPPLY

As consumers are willing to buy more goods at lower prices, sellers are willing to produce more products if they can sell

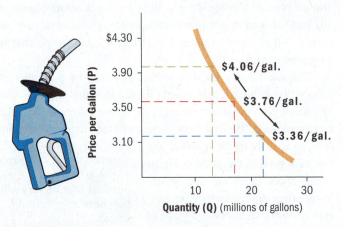

A. Demand Curve for Gasoline and Change in Quantity Demanded

Price per Gallon (P)

$4.30
3.90
3.50
3.10

$4.06/gal.
$3.76/gal.
$3.36/gal.

10   20   30
Quantity (Q) (millions of gallons)

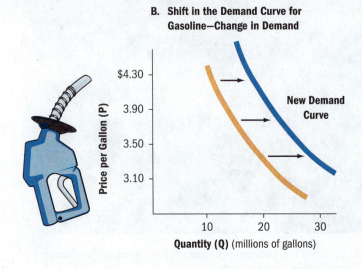

B. Shift in the Demand Curve for Gasoline—Change in Demand

Price per Gallon (P)

$4.30
3.90
3.50
3.10

New Demand Curve

10   20   30
Quantity (Q) (millions of gallons)

FIGURE 3.1 Demand Curves for Gasoline

TABLE 3.1 How does a demand curve respond to expected shifts?

	Demand Curve Shifts	
Factor	to the Right *if:*	to the Left *if:*
Customer preferences	Increase	Decrease
Number of buyers	Increase	Decrease
Buyers' incomes	Increase	Decrease
Prices of substitute goods	Increase	Decrease
Prices of complementary goods	Decrease	Increase
Future expectations become more	Optimistic	Pessimistic

contradictory pressures on prices and quantities. In other cases, the final direction of prices and quantities reflects the factor that has changed the most.

FIGURE 3.3 shows the interaction of both supply and demand curves for gasoline on a single graph. Notice that the two curves intersect at *P.* The law of supply and demand states that prices (*P*) are set by the intersection of the supply and demand curves. The point where the two curves meet identifies

supply curve
graph that shows the relationship between different prices and the quantities that sellers will offer for sale, regardless of demand.

them at higher prices. A **supply curve** shows the relationship between different prices and the quantities that sellers will offer for sale, regardless of demand. Movement along the supply curve is the opposite of movement along the demand curve. As prices rise, the quantity that sellers are willing to supply also rises. At progressively lower prices, the quantity supplied decreases. In **FIGURE 3.2**, a possible supply curve for gasoline shows that increasing prices for gasoline should bring increasing supplies to market.

TABLE 3.2 summarizes how changes in various factors can affect the supply curve. Sometimes forces of nature can affect the supply curve.

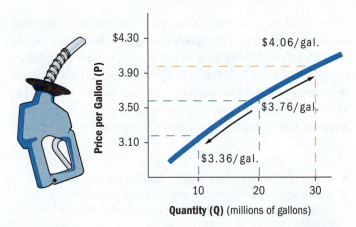

Price per Gallon (P)

$4.30
3.90
3.50
3.10

$4.06/gal.
$3.76/gal.
$3.36/gal.

10   20   30
Quantity (Q) (millions of gallons)

FIGURE 3.2 Supply Curve for Gasoline

HOW DEMAND AND SUPPLY INTERACT

Separate shifts in demand and supply have obvious effects on prices and the availability of products. In the real world, factors affecting the supply and demand often change at the same time—and they keep changing. Sometimes such changes cause

TABLE 3.2 How do changes in various factors affect the supply curve?

	Supply Curve Shifts	
Factor	to the Right *if:*	to the Left *if:*
Costs of inputs	Decrease	Increase
Costs of technologies	Decrease	Increase
Taxes	Decrease	Increase
Number of suppliers	Increase	Decrease

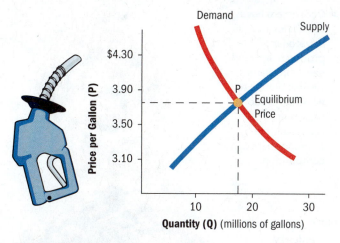

FIGURE 3.3 Law of Supply and Demand

equilibrium price
prevailing market price at which you can buy an item.

the **equilibrium price**, the prevailing market price at which you can buy an item. It is important to note that the equilibrium price is an imaginary point, as prices and quantities are constantly changing. Every purchase moves the point slightly and causes a ripple effect as both consumers and producers react to the new market prices.

As pointed out earlier, the forces of demand and supply can be affected by a variety of factors. One important variable is the larger economic environment. The next section explains how macroeconomics and economic systems influence market forces and, ultimately, demand, supply, and prices.

> > > **Quick Review**

1 Define macroeconomics and microeconomics.

2 Explain how demand and supply curves work.

② Macroeconomics: Issues for the Entire Economy

Each nation's policies and the choices their citizens make help determine its economic system, and although some are similar, no two countries have exactly the same economic system. In general, however, these systems can be classified into three categories: private enterprise systems; planned economies; or combinations of the two, referred to as mixed economies. As business becomes an increasingly global undertaking, it is important to understand the primary features of the various economic systems operating around the world.

CAPITALISM: THE PRIVATE ENTERPRISE SYSTEM AND COMPETITION

Most industrialized nations operate economies based on the *private enterprise system,* also known as *capitalism* or a *market economy.* A private enterprise system rewards businesses for meeting the needs and demands of consumers. Government tends to favor a hands-off attitude toward controlling business ownership, profits, and resource allocations. Instead, competition regulates economic life, creating opportunities and challenges that businesspeople must handle to succeed.

The relative competitiveness of a particular industry is an important consideration for every firm because it determines the ease and cost of doing business within that industry. Four basic types of competition take shape in a private enterprise system: pure competition, monopolistic competition, oligopoly, and monopoly. TABLE 3.3 highlights the main differences among these types of competition.

Pure competition is a market structure, like that of small-scale

pure competition
market structure in which large numbers of buyers and sellers exchange homogeneous products and no single participant can significantly influence price.

TABLE 3.3 What are some of the characteristics among different types of competition?

Characteristics	Types of Competition			
	Pure Competition	Monopolistic Competition	Oligopoly	Monopoly
Number of competitors	Many	Few to many	Few	No direct competition
Ease of entry into industry by new firms	Easy	Somewhat difficult	Difficult	Regulated by government
Similarity of goods or services offered by competing firms	Similar	Different	Similar or different	No directly competing products
Control over price by individual firms	None	Some	Some	Considerable in a pure monopoly; little in a regulated monopoly
Examples	Small-scale farmer in Indiana	Local fitness center	General Mills	Rawlings Sporting Goods, exclusive supplier of Major League baseballs

agriculture or fishing, in which large numbers of buyers and sellers exchange homogeneous products and no single participant can significantly influence price. Instead, prices are set by the market as the forces of supply and demand interact. Firms can easily enter or leave a purely competitive market because no single company dominates. Also, in pure competition, buyers see little difference between the goods and services offered by competitors.

The fishing industry is a good example of pure competition. The oysters, clams, and mussels that one fishing boat gathers are virtually identical to those gathered by others. In this type of market, suppliers become what is known as "price takers." The market price is set through intermediaries (for example, canneries and wholesalers), and the fishermen have to take the market price for their catch. Because they are selling nearly identical goods, they have little or no ability to influence the price of the goods. For fishermen, becoming a price taker all changes when poisonous "red tides" of algae contaminate the season's supply of shellfish. When this happens, fishermen with uncontaminated shellfish can get much higher prices for their product.

> Consumers have the choice of private-label products or brand-name products when it comes to what they feed their pets. This is an example of monopolistic competition.

© cmannphoto/iStockphoto

monopolistic competition market structure in which large numbers of buyers and sellers exchange heterogeneous products so each participant has some control over price.

Monopolistic competition is a market structure, like that of retailing, in which large numbers of buyers and sellers exchange differentiated (heterogeneous) products, so each participant has some control over price. Sellers can differentiate their products from competing offerings on the basis of price, quality, or

other features. In an industry that features monopolistic competition, it is relatively easy for a firm to begin or stop selling a good or service. The success of one seller often attracts new competitors to such a market. Individual firms also have some control over how their goods and services are priced.

One example of monopolistic competition is the market for pet food. Consumers can choose from private-label products (store brands such as Walmart's Ol'Roy) and brand-name products like Purina. Producers of pet food and the stores that sell it have wide latitude in setting prices. Consumers can choose the store or brand with the lowest prices, or sellers can convince them that a more expensive offering—for example, the Fromm brand—is worth more because it offers better nutrition or other benefits.

An **oligopoly** is a market situation in which relatively few sellers compete and high start-up costs serve as barriers to new competitors. In some oligopolistic industries, such as paper and steel, competitors offer similar products. In others, such as aircraft and automobiles, they sell different models and features. The huge investment required to enter an oligopoly market tends to discourage new competitors. The limited number of sellers also enhances the control these firms exercise over price. Competing products in an oligopoly usually sell for very similar prices because substantial price competition would reduce profits for all firms in the industry. So a price cut by one firm in an oligopoly will typically be met by its competitors. However, prices can vary from one market to another, as from one country to another.

oligopoly market situation in which relatively few sellers compete and high start-up costs serve as barriers to new competitors.

The final type of market structure is a **monopoly**, in which a single seller dominates the trade of a

monopoly market situation in which a single seller dominates trade of a good or service for which buyers can find no close substitutes.

38

ᐁ Fishing is a good example of pure competition. Because seafood gathered by one boat is virtually identical to that gathered by others, the price rises and falls with changes in supply and demand.

© mikeuk/iStockphoto

good or service for which buyers can find no close substitutes. A pure monopoly occurs when a firm possesses characteristics so important to competition in its industry that they form barriers to prevent entry by would-be competitors. In contrast to markets that are purely competitive, firms with monopoly power almost always become "price setters" as they control the supply and hence the price of products in the market. The cartel of the Organization of the Petroleum Exporting Countries (OPEC) operates in such a way, attempting to set prices for crude oil on the world market.

Because a monopoly market lacks the benefits of competition, many governments regulate monopolies. For example, the U.S. government prohibits most pure monopolies through antitrust legislation such as the Sherman Act and the Clayton Act. The government has applied these laws against monopoly behavior by Microsoft and by disallowing proposed mergers of large companies in some industries. In other cases, the government permits certain monopolies in exchange for regulating their activities.

Many firms create short-term monopolies when research breakthroughs permit them to receive exclusive patents on new products. In the pharmaceuticals industry, drug giants such as Merck and Pfizer invest billions in research and development programs. When the research leads to successful new drugs, the companies can enjoy the benefits of their patents: the ability to set prices without fear of competitors undercutting them. Once the patent expires, generic substitutes enter the market, driving down prices.

regulated monopoly market situation in which a local, state, or federal government grants exclusive rights in a certain market to a single firm.

With **regulated monopolies**, a local, state, or federal government grants exclusive rights in a certain market to a single firm. Pricing decisions—particularly rate increase requests—are subject to control by regulatory authorities such as state public service commissions. An example is the delivery of first-class mail, a monopoly held by the U.S. Postal Service (USPS). The USPS is a self-supporting corporation wholly owned by the federal government. Its postal rates are set by a postal commission and approved by a board of governors.

During the 1980s and 1990s, the U.S. government trended away from regulated monopolies and toward deregulation. Regulated monopolies that have been deregulated include long-distance and local telephone service, cable television, cell phones, airlines, and electric utilities. The idea is to improve customer service and reduce prices for customers through increased competition. In contrast, the Federal Communication Commission's (FCC's) restrictions preventing a single company from owning TV stations, newspapers, and other media in the same market continue to be challenged. When newspapers are struggling to survive, companies are asking the FCC to change their rules or grant waivers so that TV stations and newspapers can share resources under one company.[2]

PLANNED ECONOMIES: SOCIALISM AND COMMUNISM

In a **planned economy**, government controls determine business ownership, profits, and resource allocation to accomplish government goals rather than those set by individual firms. Two forms of planned economies are communism and socialism.

Socialism is characterized by government ownership and operation of major industries such as communications. Socialists argue that major industries like medical care are too important to a society to be left in private hands, and that government-owned businesses can serve the public's interest better than private firms. However, socialism allows private ownership in industries considered less crucial to social welfare, such as retail shops, restaurants, and certain types of manufacturing facilities. Scandinavian countries such as Denmark, Sweden, and Finland have many socialist features in their societies, as do some African nations—such as Tanzania, Zambia, and Namibia—and India.

The writings of Karl Marx in the mid-1800s formed the basis of communist theory. Marx believed that private enterprise economies created unfair conditions and led to worker exploitation because business owners controlled most of society's resources and reaped most of the economy's rewards. Instead, he suggested an economic system called **communism**, in which all property would be shared equally by the people of a community under the direction of a strong central government. Marx believed that elimination of private ownership of property and businesses would ensure the emergence of a classless society that would benefit all. Each individual would contribute to the nation's overall economic success, and resources would be distributed according to each person's needs. Under communism, the central government owns the means of production, and the people work for state-owned enterprises. The government determines what people can buy because it dictates what is produced in the nation's factories and farms.

Several nations adopted communist-like economic systems during the early 20th century in an effort to correct what they saw as abuses in their existing systems. In practice, however, under these new governments individuals typically found less freedom of choice in regard to jobs and purchases. Consider the former

planned economy economic system in which government controls determine business ownership, profits, and resource allocation to accomplish government goals rather than those set by individual firms.

socialism economic system characterized by government ownership and operation of major industries such as communications.

communism economic system in which all property would be shared equally by the people of a community under the direction of a strong central government.

Western products from McDonald's and Walmart are a part of Chinese consumers' lives today.

© vario images GmbH & Co.KG/Alamy

systems that mix both types of economies, to different degrees. In nations generally considered to have a private enterprise economy, government-owned firms frequently operate alongside private enterprises.

France has blended socialist and free enterprise policies for hundreds of years. The nation's energy production, public transportation, and defense industries are operated as nationalized industries, controlled by the government. Meanwhile, a market economy operates in other industries. Over the past two decades, the French government has loosened its reins on state-owned companies, inviting both competition and private investment into industries previously operated as government monopolies.

The proportions of private and public enterprise can vary widely in mixed economies, and the mix frequently changes. Dozens of countries have converted government-owned and -operated companies into privately held businesses in a trend known as **privatization**. Even the United States has seen proposals to privatize everything from the postal service to Social Security.

Governments may privatize state-owned enterprises in an effort to raise funds and improve their economy. The objective is to cut costs and run the operation more efficiently. For most of its existence, Air Canada was a state-owned airline. But in 1989 the airline became fully privatized, and in 2000 the firm acquired Canadian Airlines International, becoming the world's tenth-largest international air carrier. Air Canada now maintains an extensive global network, with destinations in the United States, Europe, the Middle East, Asia, Australia, the Caribbean, Mexico, and South America.[3] TABLE 3.4 compares the alternative economic systems on the basis of ownership and management of enterprises, rights to profits, employee rights, and worker incentives.

> **privatization**
> conversion of government-owned and -operated companies into privately held businesses.

Soviet Union, where large government bureaucracies controlled nearly every aspect of daily life. Shortages became chronic because producers had little or no incentive to satisfy customers. The quality of goods and services also suffered for the same reason. When Mikhail Gorbachev became the last president of the dying Soviet Union, he tried to improve the quality of Soviet-made products. Effectively shut out of trading in the global marketplace and caught up in a treasury-depleting arms race with the United States, the Soviet Union faced severe financial problems. Eventually, these events led to the collapse of Soviet communism and the breakup of the Soviet Union itself.

Today, communist-like systems exist in just a few countries, such as North Korea. By contrast, the People's Republic of China has shifted toward a more market-oriented economy. The national government has given local government and individual plant managers more say in business decisions and has permitted some private businesses. Households now have more control over agriculture, in contrast to the collectivized farms introduced during an earlier era. In addition, Western products such as McDonald's restaurants and Coca-Cola soft drinks are now part of Chinese consumers' lives, and Chinese workers manufacture products for export to other countries.

MIXED MARKET ECONOMIES

> **mixed market economy** economic system that mixes both private enterprise systems and planned economies.

Private enterprise systems and planned economies adopt basically opposite approaches to operating their economies. In reality though, many countries operate **mixed market economies**, economic

TABLE 3.4 What are the system features of alternative economic systems?

System Features	Capitalism (Private Enterprise)	Planned Economies		
		Communism	Socialism	Mixed Economy
Ownership of enterprises	Businesses are owned privately. Minimal government ownership leaves production in private hands.	Government owns the means of production with few exceptions, such as small plots of land.	Government owns basic industries, but private owners operate some small enterprises.	A strong private sector blends with public enterprises.
Management of enterprises	Enterprises are managed by owners or their representatives, with minimal government interference.	Centralized management controls all state enterprises in line with three- to five-year plans. Planning is being decentralized.	Significant government planning. State enterprises are managed by government bureaucrats.	Management of the private sector resembles capitalism. Professionals may also manage state enterprises.
Rights to profits	Entrepreneurs and investors are entitled to all profits (minus taxes) that their firms earn.	Profits are not allowed under communism.	Only the private sector of a socialist economy generates profits.	Entrepreneurs and investors are entitled to private-sector profits, often paying high taxes. State enterprises are also expected to produce returns.
Rights of employees	The right to choose one's occupation and to join a labor union have long been recognized.	Employee rights are limited in exchange for promised protection against unemployment.	Workers may choose their occupations and join labor unions, but government influences career decisions for many people.	Workers may choose jobs and labor union membership. Unions often become quite strong.
Worker incentives	Considerable incentives motivate people to perform at their highest levels.	Incentives are emerging in communist countries.	Incentives usually are limited in state enterprises but motivate workers in the private sector.	Capitalist-style incentives in the private sector. More limited incentives influence public-sector activities.

 Evaluating Economic Performance

Ideally, an economic system should provide two important benefits for its citizens: a stable business environment and sustained growth. In a stable business environment, the overall supply of needed goods and services is aligned with the overall demand for these items. No wild fluctuations in price or availability make economic decisions complicated. Consumers and businesses not only have access to ample supplies of desired products at affordable prices but also have money to buy the items they demand.

Growth is another important economic goal. An ideal economy incorporates steady change directed toward continually expanding the amount of goods and services produced from the nation's resources. Growth leads to expanded job opportunities, improved wages, and a rising standard of living.

FLATTENING THE BUSINESS CYCLE

A nation's economy tends to flow through various stages of a business cycle: prosperity, recession, depression, and recovery. Decisions made by businesses and consumers differ at each stage of the business cycle. In periods of economic prosperity, unemployment is typically low, confidence about the future is high, and consumers make more purchases. In response to increased demand, businesses expand—by hiring more employees, investing in new technology, and making similar purchases—to take advantage of new opportunities.

While we all enjoy times of prosperity, there comes a point in the economic cycle when consumers begin to pull back on their purchases. Either they are concerned about their rising debt level or some economic event happens to shake their confidence. When this happens, consumers begin to postpone their major purchases and shift buying patterns toward basic, low-priced products. Businesses mirror these changes by slowing production, postponing expansion plans, reducing inventories, and often cutting the size of their workforce. As economic activity slows down, the rate of economic growth is reduced. If the economic contraction lasts for six months or longer, the country is said to be in **recession**. **FIGURE 3.4** illustrates the various elements of the business cycle, showing economic recessions, expansions, recoveries, and booms.

During recessions, people facing layoffs and depletions of household savings become much more conservative in their spending, postponing luxury purchases and vacations. They often

recession cyclical economic contraction that lasts for six months or longer.

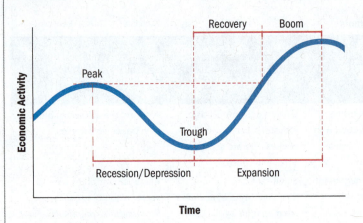

FIGURE 3.4 Phases of the Business Cycle

turn to lower-priced retailers like Dollar Tree and Dollar General for the goods they need. And they may have sold cars, jewelry, and stocks to make ends meet. They have also sold everything from old books to artwork to kitchenware on eBay.

A **depression** can occur if the economic slowdown continues for an extended period of time or is particularly severe (significant drop in gross domestic product [GDP]). Many Americans have grown up hearing stories about their great-grandparents who lived through the Great Depression of the 1930s, when food and other basic necessities were scarce and jobs were even scarcer.

depression
prolonged recession or one that causes a significant drop in GDP.

In the recovery stage of the business cycle, the economy emerges from recession and consumer spending picks up. Even though businesses often continue to rely on part-time and other temporary workers during the early stages of recovery, unemployment begins to decline as business activity accelerates and firms seek additional workers to meet growing production demands. Gradually, the concerns of recession begin to disappear, and consumers start visiting Olive Garden restaurants, booking Florida vacations, and buying new Kias.

PRODUCTIVITY AND THE NATION'S GROSS DOMESTIC PRODUCT

An important concern for every economy is **productivity**, the relationship between the goods and services produced in a nation each year and the inputs needed to produce them. In general, as productivity rises, so does an economy's growth and the wealth of its citizens. In a recession, productivity stalls or even declines.

productivity
relationship between the goods and services produced in a nation each year and the inputs needed to produce them.

Productivity describes the relationship between the number of units produced and the number of human and other production inputs necessary to produce them. Productivity is a ratio of output to input. When a constant amount of inputs generates increased outputs, an increase in productivity occurs.

Total productivity considers all inputs necessary to produce a specific amount of outputs. Stated in equation form, it can be written as follows:

$$\text{Total Productivity} = \frac{\text{Output (goods or services produced)}}{\text{Input (human/natural resources, capital)}}$$

Many productivity ratios focus on only one of the inputs in the equation: labor productivity or output per labor-hour. An increase in labor productivity means that the same amount of work produces more goods and services than before. Many of the gains in U.S. productivity can be attributed to technology.

Productivity is a widely recognized measure of a company's efficiency. In turn, the total productivity of a nation's businesses has become a measure of its economic strength and standard of living. Economists refer to this measure as a country's **gross domestic product (GDP)**—the sum of all goods and services produced within its boundaries. The GDP is based on a country's per-capita output—in other words, total national output divided by the number of citizens. As **FIGURE 3.5** shows, only the European Union—which includes 28 member nations and an estimated GDP of $15.48 trillion—has a GDP higher than that of the United States.[4] In the United States, GDP is tracked by the Bureau of Economic Analysis (BEA), a division of the U.S. Department of Commerce. Current updates and historical data on the GDP are available at the BEA's Web site (http://www.bea.gov).

gross domestic product (GDP)
sum of all goods and services produced within a country's boundaries.

PRICE LEVEL CHANGES

An important indicator of an economy's stability is the general level of prices. For the last 100 years, economic decision makers

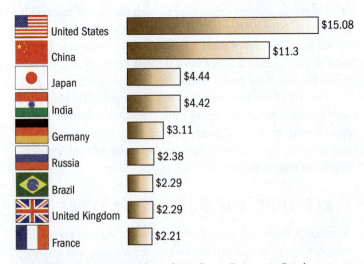

FIGURE 3.5 Nations with Highest Gross Domestic Products

SOURCE: *World Factbook,* Central Intelligence Agency, https://www.cia .gov, accessed January 31, 2013.

inflation economic situation characterized by rising prices caused by a combination of excess consumer demand and increases in the costs of raw materials, component parts, human resources, and other factors of production.

core inflation rate inflation rate of an economy after energy and food prices are removed.

hyperinflation economic situation characterized by soaring prices.

concerned themselves with **inflation**, rising prices caused by a combination of excess consumer demand and increases in the costs of raw materials, component parts, human resources, and other factors of production. The **core inflation rate** is the inflation rate of an economy after energy and food prices are removed. This measure is often an accurate prediction of the inflation rate that consumers, businesses, and other organizations can expect to experience during the near future.

America's most severe inflationary period during the last half of the 20th century peaked in 1980, when general price levels jumped almost 14 percent in a single year. In extreme cases, an economy may experience **hyperinflation**—an economic situation characterized by soaring prices. This situation has occurred in Zimbabwe, Argentina, and countries that once formed the Soviet Union (for example, Belarus).

Inflation devalues money as persistent price increases reduce the amount of goods and services people can purchase with a given amount of money. This is bad news for people whose earnings do not keep up with inflation, who live on fixed incomes, or who have most of their wealth in investments paying a fixed rate of interest. Inflation can be good news for people whose income is rising or those with debts at a fixed rate of interest.

The opposite situation—**deflation**—occurs when prices continue to fall. In Japan, where deflation has been a reality for several years, shoppers pay less for a variety of products ranging

deflation opposite of inflation; occurs when prices continue to fall.

from groceries to homes. While this situation may sound ideal to consumers, it can weaken the economy. For instance, if consumers believe that prices will be cheaper in the future, they are likely to postpone their purchases. When all consumers do this, it then becomes self-fulfilling as producers react to the lower demand by further

reducing their prices. Seeing the reduced prices, consumers are willing to postpone their purchases once again. And so the cycle goes. Without predictable prices, industries such as housing and auto manufacturing cannot operate effectively, and weak demand in these sectors tends to depress the rest of the economy.

In the United States, the government tracks changes in price levels with the **Consumer Price Index (CPI)**, which measures the monthly average change in prices of goods and services. The federal Bureau of Labor Statistics (BLS) calculates the

Consumer Price Index (CPI) measurement of the monthly average change in prices of goods and services.

CPI monthly based on prices of a "market basket," a compilation of the goods and services most commonly purchased by urban consumers. **FIGURE 3.6** shows the categories included in the CPI market basket. Each month, BLS representatives visit thousands of stores, service establishments, rental units, and doctors' offices across the United States to price the many items in the CPI market basket. From these data they create the CPI, providing a running measurement of changes in consumer prices.

EMPLOYMENT LEVELS

People need money to buy the goods and services produced in an economy. Because most consumers earn that money by working, the number of people in a nation who currently have jobs is an important indicator of how well the economy is doing. In general, employment has dropped during the recent U.S. recession, although it recently began to rebound. Areas that have seen gains include professional and technical services, as well as education, health care, and social assistance.[5]

Economists refer to a nation's unemployment rate as an indicator of its economic health. The **unemployment rate** is usually expressed as a percentage of the total workforce actively seeking work but who are currently unemployed. The total labor force includes all people who are willing and available to work at the going market wage, whether they currently have jobs or are seeking work. The U.S. Department

unemployment rate percentage of the total workforce actively seeking work but who are currently unemployed.

of Labor, which tracks unemployment rates, also measures so-called discouraged workers and "underemployed" workers. Discouraged workers are individuals who want to work but have given up looking for jobs. Underemployed workers are individuals who have taken lower-paying positions than their qualifications would suggest. Unemployment can be grouped into the four categories: frictional, seasonal, cyclical, and structural.

Frictional unemployment is experienced by members of the workforce who are temporarily not working but are looking for jobs. This pool of potential workers includes new graduates, people who have left jobs for any reason and are

frictional unemployment experienced by members of the workforce who are temporarily not working but are looking for jobs.

v During periods of hyperinflation, governments often print amazingly large currency denominations.

© Martin Shields/Alamy

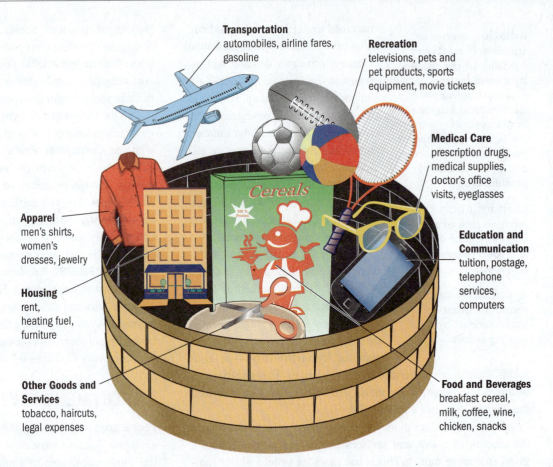

Transportation
automobiles, airline fares, gasoline

Recreation
televisions, pets and pet products, sports equipment, movie tickets

Medical Care
prescription drugs, medical supplies, doctor's office visits, eyeglasses

Apparel
men's shirts, women's dresses, jewelry

Education and Communication
tuition, postage, telephone services, computers

Housing
rent, heating fuel, furniture

Other Goods and Services
tobacco, haircuts, legal expenses

Food and Beverages
breakfast cereal, milk, coffee, wine, chicken, snacks

FIGURE 3.6 Contents of the CPI Market Basket

SOURCE: Bureau of Labor Statistics, "Consumer Price Indexes: Frequently Asked Questions," http://www.bls.gov/cpi, accessed January 31, 2013.

44

looking for other employment, and former workers who have decided to return to the labor force. Service personnel who have recently left the armed forces fall into this category as well. However. for some of them, finding employment may have gotten a bit easier, as Walmart recently announced that they would hire 100,000 veterans.[6]

Cyclical unemployment includes people who are out of work because of a cyclical contraction in the economy. During periods of economic expansion, overall employment is likely to rise, but as growth

cyclical unemployment
people who are out of work due to contraction in the economy.

∨ Job fairs are popular for employers and job seekers alike.

structural unemployment people who remain unemployed for long periods of time, often with little hope of finding a new job like their old one.

slows and a recession begins, unemployment levels commonly rise. At such times, even workers with good job skills may face temporary unemployment.

Structural unemployment applies to people who remain unemployed for long periods of time, often with little hope of finding new jobs like their old ones. This situation may arise because these workers lack the necessary skills for available jobs or because the skills they have are no longer in demand, such as some types of factory workers.

>>> Quick Review

1 What two benefits should an economic system provide for its citizens?

2 What is productivity, and how do rises and declines in productivity affect the economy?

3 What is the Consumer Price Index and why is it important?

4 Managing the Economy's Performance

Government can use both monetary policy and fiscal policy in its efforts to fight unemployment, increase business and consumer spending, and reduce the length and severity of economic recessions. For instance, the Federal Reserve System can increase or reduce interest rates, and the federal government can enact tax cuts and rebates or propose other reforms.

monetary policy government actions to increase or decrease the money supply and change banking requirements and interest rates to influence bankers' willingness to make loans.

expansionary monetary policy government actions to increase the money supply in an effort to cut the cost of borrowing, which encourages business decision makers to make new investments, in turn stimulating employment and economic growth.

MONETARY POLICY

A common method of influencing economic activity is **monetary policy**, government actions to increase or decrease the money supply and change banking requirements and interest rates to influence spending by altering bankers' willingness to make loans. An **expansionary monetary policy** increases the money supply in an effort to cut the cost of borrowing, which encourages business decision makers to make new investments, in turn stimulating employment and economic growth. By contrast, a **restrictive monetary policy** reduces the money supply to curb rising prices, overexpansion, and concerns about overly rapid economic growth.

In the United States, the Federal Reserve System ("the Fed") is responsible for formulating and implementing the nation's monetary policy. It is headed by a chairman and board of governors, all of whom are nominated by the president. The current chairman is Ben Bernanke, who also serves as chairman of the Federal Open Market Committee, the Fed's main agency for monetary policymaking. All national banks must be members of this system and keep some percentage of their checking and savings funds on deposit at the Fed.

The Fed's board of governors uses a number of tools to regulate the economy. By changing the required percentage of checking and savings accounts that banks must deposit with the Fed, the governors can expand or shrink funds available to lend. The Fed also lends money to member banks, which in turn make loans at higher interest rates to business and individual borrowers. By changing the interest rates charged to commercial banks, the Fed affects the interest rates charged to borrowers and, consequently, their willingness to borrow.

FISCAL POLICY

Governments also influence economic activities by making decisions about taxes and spending. Through revenues and expenses, the government implements **fiscal policy**, a set of decisions designed to control inflation, reduce unemployment, improve the general standard of living, and encourage economic growth.

THE FEDERAL BUDGET

Each year, the president proposes a **budget** for the federal government, a plan for how it will raise and spend money during the coming year, and presents it to Congress for approval. A typical federal budget proposal undergoes months of deliberation and many modifications before receiving approval. The federal budget includes a number of different spending categories, ranging from defense and Social Security to interest payments on the national debt (**FIGURE 3.7**). The decisions about what to include in the budget have a direct effect on various sectors of the economy. For example, during a recession, the federal government may approve increased spending on interstate highway repairs to improve transportation and increase employment in the construction

restrictive monetary policy government actions to reduce the money supply to curb rising prices, overexpansion, and concerns about overly rapid economic growth.

fiscal policy government spending and taxation decisions designed to control inflation, reduce unemployment, improve the general standard of living, and encourage economic growth.

budget organization's plan for how it will raise and spend money during a given period of time.

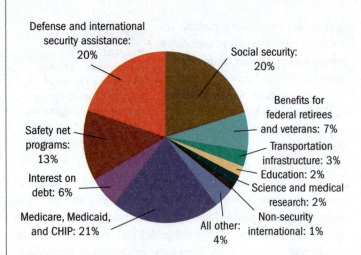

FIGURE 3.7 United States Federal Budget

SOURCE: Adapted from "Where Do Your Taxes Go?" CNN, http://yourmoney.blogs.cnn.com, April 20, 2012.

industry. During prosperity, the government may allocate more money for scientific research.

The primary sources of government funds to cover the costs of the annual budget are taxes, fees, and borrowing. Both the overall amount of these funds and their specific combination have major effects on the economic well-being of the nation. One way governments raise money is to impose taxes on sales, income, and other sources. But increasing taxes leaves people and businesses with less money to spend. This might reduce inflation, but overly high taxes can also slow economic growth. Governments then try to balance taxes to give people necessary services without slowing economic growth.

Taxes don't always generate enough funds to cover every spending project the government hopes to undertake. When the government spends more than the amount of money it raises through taxes, it creates a **budget deficit**. To cover the deficit, the U.S. government borrows money by selling Treasury bills, Treasury notes, and Treasury bonds to investors.

budget deficit situation in which the government spends more than the amount of money it raises through taxes.

All of this borrowing makes up the **national debt**. If the government takes in more money than it spends, it is said to have a **budget surplus**. A **balanced budget** means total revenues raised by taxes equal the total proposed spending for the year.

Achieving a balanced budget—or even a budget surplus—does not erase the national debt. U.S. legislators continually debate how to use revenues to reduce its debt. Most families want to wipe out debt—from credit cards, automobile purchases, and college, to name a few sources. To put the national debt into personal perspective, with roughly 314 million U.S. citizens, each one owes about $53,300 as his or her share.[7]

But for the federal government, the decision is more complex. When the government raises money by selling Treasury bills, it makes safe investments available to investors worldwide. If foreign investors cannot buy Treasury notes, they might turn to other countries, reducing the amount of money flowing into the United States. U.S. government debt has also been used as a basis for pricing riskier investments. If the government issues less debt, the interest rates it commands are higher, raising the overall cost of debt to private borrowers. In addition, the government uses the funds from borrowing, at least in part, to pay for such public services as education and scientific research.

national debt money owed by government to individuals, businesses, and government agencies who purchase Treasury bills, Treasury notes, and Treasury bonds sold to cover expenditures.

budget surplus excess funding that occurs when government spends less than the amount of funds raised through taxes and fees.

balanced budget situation in which total revenues raised by taxes equal the total proposed spending for the year.

> > > **Quick Review**

1. What two types of policy does the U.S. government use to influence economic activity?

2. Name the three primary sources of funds for the U.S. government.

What's Ahead? > > >

Global competition is a key factor in today's economy. In Chapter 4, we focus on the global dimensions of business. We cover basic concepts of doing business internationally and examine how nations can position themselves to benefit from the global economy. Then we describe the specific methods used by individual businesses to expand beyond their national borders and compete successfully in the global marketplace.

Don't miss the Weekly Updates located at http://contemporarybusinessupdates.com to help you take the first step toward success.

NOTES

1. Claudia Buck, "Lackluster Job Market Drives Thousands of Young Adults Back Home to Live with Parents," *The Sacramento Bee,* April 4, 2013, www.sacbee.com; Rebecca Trounson, "Boomerang Babies Don't Mind Return," *Chicago Tribune*, March 20, 2012.

2. Amy Chozick, "F.C.C Shift May Thwart a Murdoch Media Deal," *New York Times*, March 24, 2013, http://www.nytimes.com.

3. Company Web site, http://www.aircanada .com, accessed April 9, 2013.

4. *World Factbook*, Central Intelligence Agency, http://www.cia.gov, accessed April 9, 2013.

5. *Occupational Outlook Handbook 2012–2013 Edition*, U.S. Bureau of Labor Statistics, http://www.bls.gov, accessed April 9, 2013.

6. Emily Jane Fox, "Wal-Mart to Hire 100,000 Veterans," CNN Money, http://money.cnn.com, January 15, 2013.

7. U.S. National Debt Clock, http://www.brillig .com, accessed April 24, 2013.

Summary of Learning Objectives

1 Discuss microeconomics and explain the forces of demand and supply.

Microeconomics is the study of economic behavior among individual consumers, families, and businesses whose collective behavior in the marketplace determines the quantity of goods and services demanded and supplied at different prices. Macroeconomics is the study of the broader economic picture and how an economic system maintains and allocates its resources; it focuses on how a government's monetary and fiscal policies affect the overall operation of an economic system.

Demand is the willingness and ability of buyers to purchase goods and services at different prices. Factors that drive demand for a good or service include customer preferences, the number of buyers and their incomes, the prices of substitute goods, the prices of complementary goods, and consumer expectations about the future. Supply is the willingness and ability of businesses to offer products for sale at different prices. Supply is determined by the cost of inputs and technology resources, taxes, and the number of suppliers operating in the market.

economics social science that analyzes the choices people and governments make in allocating scarce resources.

microeconomics study of small economic units, such as individual consumers, families, and businesses.

macroeconomics study of a nation's overall economic issues, such as how an economy uses its resources and how national governmental policies affect people's standard of living.

demand willingness and ability of buyers to purchase goods and services at different prices.

supply amount of goods and services for sale at different prices.

demand curve graph of the amount of a product that buyers will purchase at different prices.

supply curve graph that shows the relationship between different prices and the quantities that sellers will offer for sale, regardless of demand.

equilibrium price prevailing market price at which you can buy an item.

2 Describe macroeconomics and the issues for the entire economy.

Four basic models characterize competition in a private enterprise system: pure competition, monopolistic competition, oligopoly, and monopoly. Pure competition is a market structure, like that in small-scale agriculture, in which large numbers of buyers and sellers exchange homogeneous products and no single participant has a significant influence on price. Monopolistic competition is a market structure, like that of retailing, in which large numbers of buyers and sellers exchange differentiated products, so each participant has some control over price. Oligopolies are market situations, like those in the steel and airline industries, in which relatively few sellers compete and high start-up costs form barriers to keep out new competitors. In a monopoly, one seller dominates trade in a good or service, for which buyers can find no close substitutes.

The major economic systems are private enterprise economy, planned economy (such as communism or socialism), and mixed market economy. In a private enterprise system, individuals and private businesses pursue their own interests—including investment decisions and profits—without undue governmental restriction. In a planned economy, the government exerts stronger control over business ownership, profits, and resources to accomplish governmental and societal—rather than individual—goals. Socialism, one type of planned economic system, is characterized by government ownership and operation of all major industries. Communism is an economic system with limited private property; goods are owned in common, and factors of production and production decisions are controlled by the state. A mixed market economy blends government ownership and private enterprise, combining characteristics of both planned and private enterprise economies.

pure competition market structure in which large numbers of buyers and sellers exchange homogeneous products and no single participant can significantly influence price.

monopolistic competition market structure in which large numbers of buyers and sellers exchange heterogeneous products so each participant has some control over price.

oligopoly market situation in which relatively few sellers compete and high start-up costs serve as barriers to new competitors.

monopoly market situation in which a single seller dominates trade in a good or service for which buyers can find no close substitutes.

regulated monopoly market situation in which a local, state, or federal government grants exclusive rights in a certain market to a single firm.

planned economy economic system in which government controls determine business ownership, profits, and resource allocation to accomplish government goals rather than those set by individual firms.

socialism economic system characterized by government ownership and operation of major industries such as communications.

communism economic system in which all property would be shared equally by the people of a community under the direction of a strong central government.

mixed market economy economic system that mixes both private enterprise systems and planned economies.

privatization conversion of government-owned and -operated companies into privately held businesses.

 Identify how to evaluate economic performance.

The four stages are prosperity, recession, depression, and recovery. Prosperity is characterized by low unemployment and strong consumer confidence. In a recession, consumers often postpone major purchases, layoffs occur, and household savings may be depleted. A depression occurs when an economic slowdown continues in a downward spiral over a long period of time. During recovery, consumer spending begins to increase and business activity accelerates, leading to an increased number of jobs.

As productivity rises, so do an economy's growth and the wealth of its citizens. In a recession, productivity stalls or possibly declines. Changes in general price levels—inflation or deflation—are important indicators of an economy's general stability. The U.S. government measures price-level changes by the Consumer Price Index. A nation's unemployment rate is an indicator of both overall stability and growth. The unemployment rate shows, as a percentage of the total labor force, the number of people actively seeking employment who are unable to find jobs.

recession cyclical economic contraction that lasts for six months or longer.

depression prolonged recession or one that causes a significant drop in GDP.

productivity relationship between the goods and services produced in a nation each year and the inputs needed to produce them.

Gross Domestic Product (GDP) sum of all goods and services produced within a country's boundaries.

inflation economic situation characterized by rising prices caused by a combination of excess consumer demand and increases in the costs of raw materials, component parts, human resources, and other factors of production.

core inflation rate inflation rate of an economy after energy and food prices are removed.

hyperinflation economic situation characterized by soaring prices.

deflation opposite of inflation, occurs when prices continue to fall.

Consumer Price Index (CPI) measurement of the monthly average change in prices of goods and services.

unemployment rate percentage of the total workforce actively seeking work but who are currently unemployed.

frictional unemployment joblessness of individuals who are temporarily not working but are looking for jobs.

cyclical unemployment people who are out of work due to contraction in the economy.

structural unemployment people who remain unemployed for long periods of time, often with little hope of finding a new job like their old one.

4 Discuss government's attempts to manage economic performance.

Monetary policy encompasses a government's efforts to control the size of the nation's money supply. Various methods of increasing or decreasing the overall money supply affect interest rates and therefore affect borrowing and investment decisions. By changing the size of the money supply, government can encourage growth or control inflation. Fiscal policy involves decisions regarding government revenues and expenditures. Changes in government spending affect economic growth and employment levels in the private sector. However, a government must also raise money, through taxes or borrowing, to finance its expenditures. Because tax payments are funds that might otherwise have been spent by individuals and businesses, any taxation changes also affect the overall economy.

monetary policy government actions to increase or decrease the money supply and change banking requirements and interest rates to influence bankers' willingness to make loans.

expansionary monetary policy government actions to increase the money supply in an effort to cut the cost of borrowing, which encourages business decision makers to make new investments, in turn stimulating employment and economic growth.

restrictive monetary policy government actions to reduce the money supply to curb rising prices, overexpansion, and concerns about overly rapid economic growth.

fiscal policy government spending and taxation decisions designed to control inflation, reduce unemployment, improve the general standard of living, and encourage economic growth.

budget organization's plan for how it will raise and spend money during a given period of time.

budget deficit situation in which the government spends more than the amount of money it raises through taxes.

national debt money owed by government to individuals, businesses, and government agencies who purchase Treasury bills, Treasury notes, and Treasury bonds sold to cover expenditures.

budget surplus excess funding that occurs when government spends less than the amount of funds raised through taxes and fees.

balanced budget situation in which total revenues raised by taxes equal the total proposed spending for the year.

>>> **Quick Review** >>>

LO1

1 Define macroeconomics and microeconomics.

2 Explain how demand and supply curves work.

LO2

1 What is the difference between pure competition and monopolistic competition? On which system is the U.S. economy based?

2 What is a mixed market economy? Give an example of this economy in practice today.

LO3

1 What two benefits should an economic system provide for its citizens?

2 What is productivity, and how do rises and declines in productivity affect the economy?

3 What is the Consumer Price Index, and why is it important?

LO4

1 What two types of policy does the U.S. government use to influence economic activity?

2 Name the three primary sources of funds for the U.S. government.

ANGELA MERKEL

© EdStock/iStockphoto

Competing in World Markets

Learning Objectives

1. **Explain** why nations trade.

2. **Describe** how trade is measured between nations.

3. **Identify** the barriers to international trade.

4. **Discuss** reducing barriers to international trade.

5. **Explain** the decisions to go global.

Toyota Reclaims Global Auto Sales Crown

It is good to be king and Toyota is—at least when it comes to recent auto sales. In 2012, Toyota Motor reported global sales of 9.75 million vehicles, topping its forecast of 9.7 million vehicles, while General Motors announced global sales of 9.29 million units and the Volkswagen Group finished third in the ranking with sales of 9.09 million.

While the worldwide sales numbers look good for Toyota, the crown might not be as shiny as Toyota would like. GM is the leading automaker in the world's two largest markets, China and the United States. Toyota is a clear leader in its home market of Japan, where non-Japanese automakers have had trouble competing due to limited dealerships. Also, Toyota enjoyed a bounce-back year in Japan, with sales rebounding 35 percent from the previous year when they were hurt by the earthquake and tsunami.

Toyota's sales totals were also helped by the fact that it made more than 600,000 heavy-duty trucks and buses during the year, a segment GM essentially pulled out of a few years ago.[1]

Will Toyota be able to keep their number 1 status and the bragging rights that go with that ranking? For now it appears so. However, in the hyper-competitive world of vehicle manufacturers, Toyota would do well to keep an eye on their competitors, as both GM and Volkswagen want to make Toyota's reign a short one.

Overview > > >

Consider for a moment how many products you used today that came from outside the United States. Maybe you drank Brazilian coffee with your breakfast, wore clothes manufactured in Honduras or Malaysia, drove to class in a German or Japanese car fueled by gasoline refined from Canadian crude oil, and watched a movie on a television set assembled in Mexico for a Japanese company such as Sony. A fellow student in Germany may be wearing Zara jeans, using a Samsung cell phone, and drinking Pepsi.

These and thousands of other products cross national borders every day. The computers that U.S. manufacturers produce in the United States and sell in Canada represent an example of an **export**, while an **import** is a product produced in another country and shipped to the United States for purchase by domestic consumers. Together, U.S. exports and imports make up about a quarter of the U.S. gross domestic product (GDP). The United States is fourth in the world among exporting nations, with exports exceeding $1.5 trillion and annual imports of more than $2.3 trillion. That total amount is more than double the nation's imports and exports of just a decade ago.[2]

export domestically produced good or service sold in markets in other countries.

import foreign-made product purchased by domestic consumers.

This chapter travels through the world of international business to see how both large and small companies approach globalization. First, we consider the reasons nations trade, the importance and characteristics of the global marketplace, and the ways nations measure international trade. Then we examine barriers to international trade that arise from cultural and environmental differences. To reduce these barriers, countries turn to organizations that promote global business. Finally, we look at the strategies firms implement for entering foreign markets and the way they develop international business strategies.

ʌ Where were the clothes manufactured that you're wearing today?

© DPD ImageStock/Alamy

① Why Nations Trade

As domestic markets mature and sales growth slows, companies in every industry recognize the increasing importance of efforts to develop business in other countries. Walmart operates stores in Mexico, Boeing sells jetliners in Asia, and Apple sells iPads in Germany. These are only a few of the thousands of U.S. companies taking advantage of large populations, substantial resources, and rising standards of living abroad to boost sales of their goods and services. Likewise, the U.S. market, with the world's greatest purchasing power, attracts thousands of foreign companies looking to increase their sales.

INTERNATIONAL SOURCES OF FACTORS OF PRODUCTION

Business decisions to operate abroad depend on the availability, price, and quality of labor, natural resources, capital, and entrepreneurship—the basic factors of production—in the foreign country. For example, Indian colleges and universities produce thousands of highly qualified computer scientists and engineers each year. To take advantage of this talent, many U.S. computer software and hardware firms have set up operations in India, and many others are outsourcing information technology and customer service jobs there.

Trading with other countries also allows a company to spread risk because different nations may be at different stages of the business cycle or in different phases of development. If demand falls off in one country, the company may still enjoy strong demand in other nations. Companies such as Kellogg's and IKEA have long used international sales to offset lower domestic demand.

SIZE OF THE INTERNATIONAL MARKETPLACE

As developing nations expand their involvement in global business, the potential for reaching new groups of customers dramatically increases. Firms looking for new revenue are inevitably attracted to giant markets such as China and India, with respective populations of about 1.3 billion and 1.2 billion. However, people alone are not enough to create a market. Consumer demand also requires purchasing power. As TABLE 4.1 shows, population size is no guarantee of economic prosperity. Of the ten most populous countries, only the United States appears on the list of those with the highest per-capita GDPs.

Although people in developing nations have lower per-capita incomes than those in the highly developed economies of North America and Western Europe, their huge populations do represent lucrative markets. Even when the higher-income segments are only a small percentage of the entire country's population, their sheer numbers may still represent significant and growing markets.

TABLE 4.1 Which countries make the top ten list based on populations and wealth?

Population		Wealth	
Country	Population (in millions)	Country	Pre-Capita GDP (in U.S. dollars)
China	1,343	Qatar	$98,900
India	1,205	Liechtenstein	$89,400
United States	315	Luxembourg	$80,600
Indonesia	248	Singapore	$59,700
Brazil	199	Norway	$53,400
Pakistan	190	Brunei	$49,500
Nigeria	170	Hong Kong	$49,400
Bangladesh	161	United States	$48,300
Russia	142	United Arab Emirates	$47,700
Japan	127	Switzerland	$44,500

SOURCE: *World Factbook*, https://www.cia.gov, accessed January 22, 2013.

In addition to large populations, many developing countries have posted high rates of annual GDP growth. In the United States, GDP generally averages between 2 and 4 percent growth per year. By contrast, GDP growth in less developed countries is much greater—China's GDP growth rate averaged nearly 10 percent over a recent three-year period, and India's averaged 8.2 percent.[3] These markets represent opportunities for global businesses, even though their per-capita incomes lag behind those in more developed countries. Many firms are establishing operations in these and other developing countries to position themselves to benefit from local sales driven by expanding economies and rising standards of living. Walmart is one of those companies. As the world's largest retailer, Walmart employs 2.2 million workers worldwide. Walmart International is growing fast, with more than 5,300 stores and 740,000 employees in 27 countries as far-ranging as Lesotho and Swaziland in Africa.[4]

The United States trades with many other nations. As FIGURE 4.1 shows, the top five U.S. trading partners are Canada, China, Mexico, Japan, and Germany. With the United Kingdom, South Korea, France, Brazil, and Saudi Arabia, they represent nearly two-thirds of U.S. imports and exports every year.[5] Within the United States, foreign trade makes up a large portion of the business activity in many individual states. Texas exports more than $206 billion of goods annually, and California exports more than $143 billion. Other big exporting states include Florida, Illinois, New York, and Washington.[6]

ABSOLUTE AND COMPARATIVE ADVANTAGE

Few countries can produce all the goods and services their people need. For centuries, trading has been the way that countries can meet consumer demands. If a country focuses on producing what it does best, it can export surplus domestic output and buy

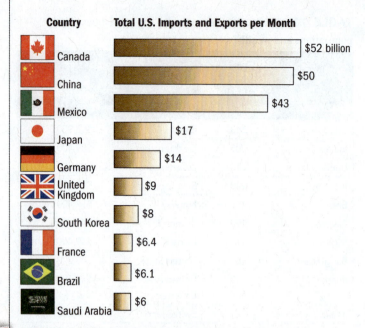

Country	Total U.S. Imports and Exports per Month
Canada	$52 billion
China	$50
Mexico	$43
Japan	$17
Germany	$14
United Kingdom	$9
South Korea	$8
France	$6.4
Brazil	$6.1
Saudi Arabia	$6

FIGURE 4.1 Top Ten Trading Partners with the United States

SOURCE: Data from U.S. Census Bureau, "Top Ten Countries with which the U.S. Trades," http://www.census.gov/foreign-trade/top/dst/current/balance.html, accessed January 24, 2013.

54

foreign products that it lacks or cannot efficiently produce. The potential for foreign sales of a particular item depends largely on whether the country has an absolute advantage or a comparative advantage.

absolute advantage The ability to produce more goods using fewer resources than other providers.

A country has an **absolute advantage** in making a product if it can maintain a monopoly in the production of that product or if it can consistently produce the product at a lower cost than any competitor. For example, China enjoyed an absolute advantage in silk production. The fabric was woven from fibers recovered from silkworm

V The Silk Road was a 5,000-mile route early traders used to move goods from ancient China to Europe.

cocoons, making it a prized raw material in high-quality clothing. Demand among Europeans for silk led to establishment of the famous Silk Road, a 5,000-mile link between Rome and the ancient Chinese capital city of Xian.

A nation can develop a **comparative advantage** if it can supply its products more efficiently—at a lower price—than it can supply other goods. Today China is profiting from its comparative advantage in producing textiles for the export market. China can produce them more efficiently than other products it could manufacture, thereby giving it a comparative advantage in textiles to other types of products it could manufacture—say, automobiles. Beyond the production of goods, ensuring that its people are well educated is another way a nation can develop a comparative advantage. For example, India offers the services of its educated tech workers at a lower wage.

comparative advantage the ability to produce one good at a relatively lower opportunity cost than other goods.

To see the differences between a comparative and absolute advantage, consider the following example. An accountant operates a CPA firm where she bills $200 per hour doing accounting work. In addition to being an excellent accountant, she is also a pretty good typist able to type 80 words per minute. As her business grows, she decides to hire an administrative assistant specifically to help with the typing. To find suitable candidates she posts an ad on Craigslist: "Wanted: administrative assistant for growing CPA firm. Pay $20 per hour." After interviewing several candidates, she finds that the best candidate can type only 40 words per minute. Should she hire this person?

It is clear that the accountant has an absolute advantage in typing compared to her administrative assistant candidate. However, the administrative assistant has a comparative advantage when it comes to typing. This is true because of the accountant's **opportunity cost** (the difference between what she could earn doing accounting work versus what she saves by doing her own typing). Even though she can type twice as fast as the assistant, she is much better off focusing on accounting work and letting her assistant handle the typing. And so it goes with international trade, where comparative advantages and opportunity costs form the basis for most trade between nations.

opportunity cost the highest valued alternative forgone in the pursuit of an activity.

>>> Quick Review

1. Why do nations trade?

2. Explain how population and per-capita GDP are important aspects of the global market.

3. What are absolute advantage and comparative advantage, and why are they important?

2 Measuring Trade between Nations

Clearly, engaging in international trade provides tremendous competitive advantages to both the countries and individual companies involved. But how do we measure global business activity? To understand what the trade inflows and outflows mean for a country, we need to examine the concepts of balance of trade and balance of payments. Another important factor is currency exchange rates for each country.

balance of trade difference between a nation's exports and imports.

trade surplus the positive difference between what a country exports compared to what it imports.

trade deficit the negative difference between what a country exports compared to what it imports.

balance of payments overall flow of money into or out of a country.

A nation's **balance of trade** is the difference between its exports and imports. If a country exports more than it imports, it achieves a positive balance of trade, called a **trade surplus**. If it imports more than it exports, it produces a negative balance of trade, called a **trade deficit**. The United States has run a trade deficit for years. Despite being one of the world's top exporters, the United States has an even greater appetite for foreign-made goods, which creates a trade deficit.

A nation's balance of trade plays a central role in determining its **balance of payments**—the overall flow of money into or out of a country. Other factors also affect the balance of payments, including overseas loans and borrowing, international investments, profits from such investments, and foreign aid payments. To calculate a nation's balance of payments, subtract the monetary outflows from the monetary inflows. A positive balance of payments, or a *balance-of-payments surplus*, means more money has moved into a country than out of it. A negative balance of payments, or *balance-of-payments deficit*, means more money has gone out of the country than entered it.

MAJOR U.S. EXPORTS AND IMPORTS

The United States, with combined exports and imports of about $3.8 trillion, leads the world in the international trade of goods and services. As listed in TABLE 4.2, the leading categories of goods exchanged by U.S. exporters and importers range from machinery and vehicles to crude oil and chemicals. Strong U.S. demand for imported goods is partly a reflection of the nation's prosperity and diversity.

With annual imports of over $2.3 trillion, the United States is by far the world's leading importer. American tastes for foreign-made goods for everything from clothing to consumer electronics show up as huge trade deficits with the consumer goods–exporting nations of China and Japan.

Although the United States imports more goods than it exports, the opposite is true for services. U.S. exporters sell more than $600 billion in services annually. Much of that money comes from travel and tourism—money spent by foreign nationals visiting the United States.[7] U.S. service exports also include business and technical services such as engineering, financial services, computing, legal services, and entertainment, as well as royalties and licensing fees. Major service exporters include Citibank, Walt Disney, Allstate Insurance, and Federal Express, as well as retailers such as McDonald's and Starbucks.

Businesses in many foreign countries want the expertise of U.S. financial and business professionals. Accountants are in high demand in Russia, China, the Netherlands, and Australia—Sydney has become one of Asia's biggest financial centers. Entertainment is another major growth area for U.S. service exports. The Walt Disney Company already has theme parks in Europe and Asia and is building Shanghai Disney Resort, a multi-billion-dollar park in China.[8]

EXCHANGE RATES

The value of a nation's currency is an important "thermometer" reflecting the state of a nation's economic health. A country with

TABLE 4.2 What exports and imports make the top ten list for U.S. merchandise?

Exports	Amount (in billions)	Imports	Amount (in billions)
Agricultural commodities	$115.82	Crude oil	$260.1
Vehicles	88.1	Vehicles	178.9
Mineral fuel	80.5	Television, VCR	137.3
Electrical machinery	77.0	Electrical machinery	119.6
Petroleum preparations	53.5	Automated data processing equipment	113.5
General industrial machinery	51.8	Agricultural commodities	82.0
Specialized industrial machinery	46.8	Clothing	78.5
Scientific instruments	44.3	Petroleum preparations	67.4
Chemicals—plastics	42.0	Chemicals—medicinal	65.2
Chemicals—medicinal	41.9	General industrial machinery	60.4

SOURCE: U.S. Census Bureau, "U.S. Exports and General Imports by Selected SITC Commodity Groups," *Statistical Abstract of the United States: 2012,* http://www.census.gov, accessed January 29, 2013.

a strong currency can generally purchase more goods and services in the international market than ones with a weaker currency. An **exchange rate** is a measure of the strength of the local currency as a nation's money is exchanged for the currencies of other nations. For example, roughly 13 Mexican pesos are needed to exchange for one U.S. dollar. A Canadian dollar can be exchanged for approximately $1 in the United States. The euro, the currency used in most of the European Union (EU) member countries, has made considerable moves in exchange value during its few years in circulation. European consumers and businesses now use the euro to pay bills by check, credit card, or bank transfer. Euro coins and notes are also used in many EU member-countries.

Foreign exchange rates are influenced by a number of factors, including domestic economic and political conditions, central bank intervention, balance-of-payments position, and speculation over future currency values. Currency values fluctuate, or "float," depending on the supply and demand for each currency in the international market. In this system of *floating exchange rates,* currency traders create a market for the world's currencies based on each country's relative trade and investment prospects. In theory, this market permits exchange rates to vary freely according to supply and demand. In practice however, exchange rates do not float in total freedom: national governments often intervene in currency markets to adjust their exchange rates.

Exchange rate changes can quickly create—or wipe out—a competitive advantage, so they are important factors in decisions about whether to invest abroad. In Europe, a declining dollar means that a price of ten euros is worth more, so companies are pressured to lower prices. **Devaluation** describes a drop in a currency's value relative to other currencies or to a fixed standard. At the same time, if the dollar falls it makes European vacations less affordable for U.S. tourists because their dollars are worth less relative to the euro.

< For a variety of reasons, exchange are constantly changing.

Jack Kurtz/ZUMA Press/NewsCom

Currencies that owners can easily convert into other currencies are called *hard currencies.* Examples include the euro, the U.S. dollar, and the Japanese yen. The Russian ruble and many central European currencies are considered soft currencies because they cannot be readily converted to other currencies. Exporters trading with these countries sometimes prefer to barter, accepting payment in oil, timber, or other commodities that they can resell for hard currency.

The foreign currency market is the largest financial market in the world, with a daily volume of about $4 trillion in U.S. dollars.[9] This is about ten times the size of all the world's stock markets combined, so the foreign exchange market is one of the largest most efficient financial markets in the world.

3 Barriers to International Trade

Whether they sell only to local customers or trade in international markets, all business encounter challenges—barriers—to their operations. For example, countries such as Australia and New Zealand regulate the hours and days retailers may be open. International companies may have to reformulate their products to accommodate different tastes in new locations. Some of the challenges shown in **FIGURE 4.2** are easily overcome, but others require major changes in a company's business strategy. To successfully compete in global markets, companies and their managers must understand not only how these barriers affect international trade but also how to overcome them.

SOCIAL, CULTURAL, AND ECONOMIC DIFFERENCES

The social and cultural differences among nations range from language and customs to educational background and religious holidays. Understanding and respecting these differences are critical to international business success. Businesspeople with knowledge of host countries' cultures, languages, social values, and religious attitudes and practices are well equipped for the marketplace and the negotiating table. Sensitivity to such elements as local attitudes, forms of address, and expectations regarding dress, body language, and timeliness also helps them win customers and achieve their business objectives.

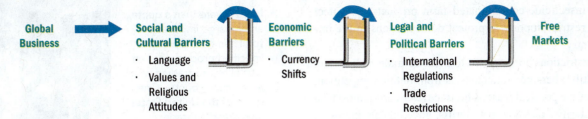

FIGURE 4.2 Barriers to International Trade

LANGUAGE

Understanding a business colleague's primary language may prove to be the difference between closing an international business transaction and losing the sale to someone else. Company representatives operating in foreign markets must not only choose correct and appropriate words but also translate words correctly to convey the intended meanings. Firms may also need to rename products or rewrite slogans for foreign markets.

VALUES

U.S. society places a higher value on business efficiency and low unemployment than does European society, where employee benefits are more valued. The U.S. government does not regulate vacation time, and in the U.S. employees typically have limited or no paid vacation during their first year of employment, then two weeks vacation, and eventually up to three or four weeks if they stay with the same employer for many years. In contrast, the EU mandates a minimum paid vacation of four weeks per year, and most Europeans get five or six weeks. In these countries, a U.S. company that opens a manufacturing plant would not be able to hire any local employees without offering vacations in line with a nation's business practices.

ECONOMICS

Business opportunities are flourishing in densely populated countries such as China and India, as local consumers eagerly buy Western products. Although such prospects might tempt American firms, managers must first consider the economic factors involved in doing business in these markets. A country's size, per-capita income, and stage of economic development are among the economic factors to consider when evaluating it as a candidate for an international business venture. Tata Motors, for instance, has an eye on Western auto buyers, even as it markets its low-priced Nano car for the home market in India.

POLITICAL AND LEGAL DIFFERENCES

Like social, cultural, and economic differences, legal and political differences in host countries can pose barriers to international trade. To compete in today's world marketplace, managers involved in international business must be well versed in legislation that affects their industries. Some countries impose general trade restrictions. Others have established detailed rules that regulate how foreign companies can operate. An important factor in any international business investment is the stability of the political climate. The political structures of many nations promote stability similar to that in the United States. Other nations, such as Indonesia, Congo, and Bosnia, feature quite different—and frequently changing—structures. Host nations often pass laws designed to protect their own interests, sometimes at the expense of foreign businesses.

LEGAL ENVIRONMENT

When conducting business internationally, managers must be familiar with three dimensions of the legal environment: U.S. law, international regulations, and the laws of the countries in which they plan to trade. Some laws protect the rights of foreign companies to compete in the United States. Others dictate actions allowed for U.S. companies doing business in foreign countries.

The Foreign Corrupt Practices Act forbids U.S. companies from bribing foreign officials, political candidates, or government representatives. Although the law has been in effect since 1977, in the past few years the U.S. government has increased its enforcement, including major proceedings in the pharmaceutical, medical device, and financial industries. The United States, United Kingdom, France, Germany, and 36 other countries have signed the Organization for Economic Cooperation and Development Anti-Bribery Convention. Still, corruption continues to be an international problem. Its pervasiveness, combined with U.S. prohibitions, creates a difficult obstacle for U.S. businesspeople who want to do business in many foreign countries. Chinese pay *huilu*, and Russians rely on *vzyatka*. In the Middle East, palms are greased with *baksheesh*.

TYPES OF TRADE RESTRICTIONS

Trade restrictions such as taxes on imports and complicated administrative procedures create additional barriers to international business. They may limit consumer choices while increasing the costs of foreign-made products. Trade restrictions are also imposed to protect citizens' security, health, and jobs. A government may limit exports of strategic and defense-related goods to unfriendly countries to protect its security, ban imports of insecticide-contaminated farm products to protect health, and restrict imports to protect domestic jobs in the importing country.

Other restrictions are imposed to promote trade with certain countries. Still others protect countries from unfair competition. Regardless of the political reasons for trade restrictions, most take the form of tariffs. In addition to tariffs, governments impose a number of nontariff—or administrative—barriers. These include quotas and embargoes.

TARIFFS

A tax, surcharge, or duty on foreign products is referred to as a **tariff**. Governments may assess two types of tariffs—revenue and protective tariffs—both of which make imports more expensive for domestic buyers. Revenue tariffs generate income for the government.

> **tariff** tax, surcharge, or duty on foreign products.

Upon returning home, U.S. leisure travelers who are out of the country more than 48 hours and who bring back goods purchased abroad may pay import taxes on the goods' value depending on the country of origin. This duty goes directly to the U.S. Treasury. The sole purpose of a protective tariff is to raise the retail price of imported products to match or exceed the prices of similar products manufactured in the home country. In other words, protective tariffs seek to limit imports and provide advantages for domestic competitors.

NONTARIFF BARRIERS

Nontariff, or administrative, trade barriers restrict imports in more subtle ways than tariffs. These measures may take such forms as quotas on imports, restrictive standards for imports, and export subsidies. Because many countries have recently substantially reduced tariffs or eliminated them entirely, they increasingly use nontariff barriers to control flows of imported products.

> **quota** limit set on the amounts of particular products that countries can import during specified time periods.

A **quota** limits the amount of a particular product that countries can import during specified time periods. Limits may be set as quantities, such as number of cars or bushels of wheat, or as values, such as dollars' worth of cigarettes. Governments regularly set quotas for agricultural products and sometimes for imported automobiles. The United States, for example, sets a quota on imports of sugar. Imports under the quota amount are subject to a lower tariff than shipments above the quota. However, sugar and related products imported at the higher rate may enter the country in unlimited quantities.[10]

> **dumping** selling products abroad at prices below production costs or below typical prices in the home market to capture market share from domestic competitors.

Quotas help prevent **dumping**. In one form of dumping, a company sells products abroad at prices below its cost of production. In another, a company exports a large quantity of a product at a lower price than the same product in the home market and drives down the price of the domestic product. Dumping benefits domestic consumers in the importing market, but it hurts domestic producers. It also allows companies to gain quick entry to foreign markets.

More severe than a quota, an **embargo** imposes a total ban on importing a specified product or even a total halt to trading with a particular country. The United States has a long-standing trade embargo with Cuba.

> **embargo** total ban on importing specific products or a total halt to trading with a particular country.

> More severe than a quota, an embargo imposes a total ban on importing a specified product or even a total halt to trading with a particular country. One result of the United States' long-standing trade embargo with Cuba is the lack of new cars in the country—as you can see in this Cuban neighborhood.

Michael Setboun/Getty Images, Inc.

> ### >>> Quick Review
>
> **1** How might cultural values create a barrier to trade, and how can such barriers be overcome?
>
> **2** What is a tariff, and how do tariffs work?
>
> **3** Why is dumping a problem for companies marketing goods internationally?

4 Reducing Barriers to International Trade

Although tariffs and administrative barriers still restrict trade, overall the world is moving toward free trade. Several types of organizations ease barriers to international trade, including groups that monitor trade policies and practices and institutions that offer monetary assistance. Another type of federation designed to ease trade barriers is the multinational economic community, such as the European Union. This section looks at the roles these organizations play.

ORGANIZATIONS PROMOTING INTERNATIONAL TRADE

For the 60-plus years of its existence, the **General Agreement on Tariffs and Trade (GATT)**, an international trade accord, sponsored a series of negotiations, called rounds, which substantially reduced worldwide tariffs and other barriers. Major industrialized nations founded the multinational organization in 1947 to work toward reducing tariffs and relaxing import quotas. The last set of completed negotiations—the Uruguay Round—cut average tariffs by one-third, in excess of $700 billion; reduced farm subsidies; and improved protection for copyright and patent holders. In addition, international trading rules now apply to various service industries. Finally, the new agreement established the **World Trade Organization (WTO)** to succeed GATT. This organization includes representatives from 153 countries.

> **General Agreement on Tariffs and Trade (GATT)** international trade accord that substantially reduced worldwide tariffs and other trade barriers.
>
> **World Trade Organization (WTO)** 153-member international institution that monitors GATT agreements and mediates international trade disputes.

WORLD TRADE ORGANIZATION

Since 1995, the WTO has monitored GATT agreements among the member-nations, mediated disputes, and continued the effort to reduce trade barriers throughout the world. Unlike provisions in GATT, the WTO's decisions are binding on parties involved in disputes.

The WTO has grown more controversial in recent years as it issues decisions that have implications for working conditions and the environment in member nations. Concerns have been expressed that the WTO's focus on lowering trade barriers encourages businesses to keep costs down through practices that may increase pollution and human rights abuses. Particularly worrisome is the fact that the organization's member-countries must agree on policies, and developing countries tend not to be eager to lose their low-cost advantage by enacting stricter labor and environmental laws. Other critics claim that if well-funded U.S. firms such as fast food chains, entertainment companies, and Internet retailers can freely enter foreign markets, they will wipe out smaller foreign businesses serving the distinct tastes and practices of other country's cultures.

WORLD BANK

> **World Bank** organization established by industrialized nations to lend money to less developed countries.

Shortly after the end of World War II, industrialized nations formed an organization to lend money to less developed and developing countries. The **World Bank** primarily

∧ The Gibe III dam in Ethiopia is a controversial World Bank–funded project. While it will provide water and electricity for the nation, it also displaces hundreds of thousands of native peoples and floods animal habitat and valuable farmland.

© National Geographic Image Collection/Alamy

funds projects that build or expand nations' infrastructure such as transportation, education, and medical systems and facilities. The World Bank and other development banks also provide advice and assistance to developing nations. Often, in exchange for granting loans, the World Bank imposes requirements intended to build the economies of borrower nations.

Although the World Bank provides many benefits to developing countries, it is not without its critics. For example, it has been criticized for making loans with conditions that ultimately hurt the borrower nations. When developing nations are required to balance government budgets, they are sometimes forced to cut vital social programs. Critics also say that the World Bank should consider the impact of its loans on the environment and working conditions. One controversial project funded by the World Bank is the Gibe III dam in Ethiopia. Once it is complete, this dam will provide water for irrigation and hydroelectric power for Ethiopia but will cause the removal of hundreds of thousands of residents from the Lower Omo Valley river basin.[11]

INTERNATIONAL MONETARY FUND

Established a year after the World Bank, the **International Monetary Fund (IMF)** was created to promote trade through financial cooperation and, in the process, eliminate barriers. The IMF makes short-term loans to member nations that are unable to meet their expenses. It operates as a lender of last resort for troubled nations. In exchange for these emergency loans, IMF lenders frequently require significant commitments from borrowing nations to address the problems that led to the crises. These steps may include curtailing imports or even devaluing currencies. Throughout its existence, the

> **International Monetary Fund (IMF)** organization created to promote trade, eliminate barriers, and make short-term loans to member nations that are unable to meet their budgets.

IMF has worked to prevent financial crises by warning the international business community when countries encounter problems meeting their financial obligations. Often, the IMF lends to countries to keep them from defaulting on prior debts and to prevent economic crises in particular countries from spreading to other nations.

INTERNATIONAL ECONOMIC COMMUNITIES

International economic communities reduce trade barriers and promote regional economic integration. In the simplest approach, countries may establish a *free-trade area* in which they trade freely among themselves without tariffs or trade restrictions. Each maintains its own tariffs for trade outside this area. A *customs union* sets up a free-trade area and specifies a uniform tariff structure for members' trade with nonmember nations.

> **North American Free Trade Agreement (NAFTA)** agreement among the United States, Canada, and Mexico to break down tariffs and trade restrictions.

In a *common market,* or economic union, members go beyond a customs union and try to bring all of their trade rules into agreement.

One example of a free-trade area is the **North American Free Trade Agreement (NAFTA)** enacted by the United States, Canada, and Mexico. Other examples of regional trading blocs include the MERCOSUR customs union (joining Brazil, Argentina, Paraguay, Uruguay, Chile, and Bolivia) and the ten-country Association of South East Asian Nations (ASEAN).

NAFTA

NAFTA became effective in 1994, creating the world's largest free-trade zone with the United States, Canada, and Mexico. With a combined population of more than 463 million and a total GDP of more than $18 trillion, North America represents one of the world's most attractive markets. By eliminating all trade barriers and investment restrictions among the United States, Canada, and Mexico over a 15-year period, NAFTA opened more doors for free trade. The agreement also eased regulations governing services, such as banking, and established uniform legal requirements for protection of intellectual property. The three nations can now trade with one another without tariffs or other trade barriers, simplifying shipments of goods across the partners' borders. Standardized customs and uniform labeling regulations create economic efficiencies and smooth import and export procedures. Trade among the partners has increased steadily, more than doubling since NAFTA took effect.

CAFTA-DR

The **Central America–Dominican Republic Free Trade Agreement (CAFTA-DR)** created a free-trade area among the United States, Costa Rica, the Dominican Republic (the DR of the title), El Salvador, Guatemala, Honduras, and Nicaragua. The agreement—the first of its kind between the United States and these smaller developing economies—ends tariffs on the nearly $40 billion in products traded between the United States and its Latin American neighbors. Agricultural producers such as corn, soybean, and dairy farmers stand to gain under the relaxed trade rules. Overall, CAFTA-DR's effects have increased both exports and imports substantially, much as NAFTA did.[12]

> **Central America–Dominican Republic Free Trade Agreement (CAFTA-DR)** agreement among the United States, Costa Rica, the Dominican Republic, El Salvador, Guatemala, Honduras, and Nicaragua to reduce tariffs and trade restrictions.

EUROPEAN UNION

Perhaps the best-known example of a common market is the **European Union (EU)**. The EU combines 28 countries, over 503 million people, and a total GDP of roughly $15.39 trillion to form a huge common market. **FIGURE 4.3** shows the member countries. Current candidates for membership are Iceland, Montenegro, Serbia, Turkey, and the former Yugoslav Republic of Macedonia.[13]

> **European Union (EU)** 28-nation European economic alliance.

The EU's goals include promoting economic and social progress, introducing European citizenship as a complement to national citizenship, and giving the EU a significant role in international affairs. To achieve its goal of a borderless Europe, the EU is removing barriers to free trade among its members. This highly complex process involves standardizing business regulations and requirements, standardizing import duties and taxes, and eliminating customs checks so that companies can

▼ With NAFTA allowing free trade for the United States, Canada, and Mexico, the amount of goods and services traded is healthy for Canada's economy as well as the United States.

Roger Lecuyer/iStockphoto

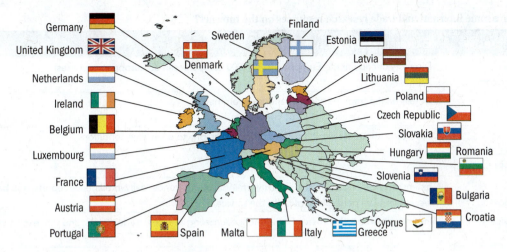

FIGURE 4.3 The 28 Nations of the European Union

transport goods from England to Italy or Poland as easily as from New York to Boston.

Unifying standards and laws can contribute to economic growth. But just as NAFTA sparked fears in the United States about free trade with Mexico, some people in Western Europe worried that opening trade with such countries as Poland, Hungary, and the Czech Republic would cause jobs to flow eastward to lower-wage economies.

The EU also introduced the euro to replace currencies such as the French franc and Italian lira. For the 17 member-states that have adopted the euro, potential benefits include eliminating the economic costs of currency exchange and simplifying price comparisons.

>>> **Quick Review**

1. What international trade organization succeeded GATT, and what is its goal?

2. Compare and contrast the goals of the World Bank and the International Monetary Fund.

3. What are the goals of the European Union, and how do they promote international trade?

5 Going Global

While expanding into overseas markets can increase profits and marketing opportunities, it also introduces new complexities to a firm's business operations. Before deciding to go global, a company faces a number of key decisions, beginning with the following:

- determining which foreign market(s) to enter
- analyzing the investment required to enter a new market
- deciding the best way to organize the overseas operations

These issues vary in importance depending on the level of involvement a company chooses. Education and employee training in the host country would be much more important for an electronics manufacturer building an Asian factory than for a firm that is simply planning to export American-made products.

The choice of which markets to enter usually follows extensive research focusing on local demand for the firm's products, availability of needed resources, and ability of the local workforce to produce world-class quality. Other factors include existing and potential competition, tariff rates, currency stability, and investment barriers. A variety of government and other sources are available to facilitate this research process. A good starting place is the CIA's *World Factbook,* which contains country-by-country information on geography, population, government, economy, and infrastructure.

U.S. Department of Commerce counselors working at district offices offer a full range of international business advice, including computerized market data and names of business and government contacts in dozens of countries. As TABLE 4.3 shows, the Internet provides access to many resources for international trade information.

LEVELS OF INTERNATIONAL INVOLVEMENT

After a firm has completed its research and decided to do business overseas, it can choose one or more strategies:

- exporting or importing
- entering into contractual agreements such as franchising, licensing, and subcontracting deals
- direct investment in the foreign market through acquisitions, joint ventures, or establishment of an overseas division

Although the company's risk increases with the level of its involvement, so does its overall control of all aspects of producing and selling its goods or services.

TABLE 4.3 **What are some international trade research resources on the Internet?**

Web Site and Address	General Description
Europages http://www.europages.com	Directory of and links to Europe's top 500,000 companies in 33 European countries
World Trade Organization http://www.wto.org	Details on the trade policies of various governments
CIA *World Factbook* https://www.cia.gov/cia/library /publications/the-world-factbook	Basic facts about the world's nations, from geography to economic conditions
STAT-USA http://www.stat-usa.gov	Extensive trade and economic data, information about trends, daily intelligence reports, and background data (access requires paid subscription to the service)
U.S. Commercial Service http://trade.gov/cs	Information about Commerce Department counseling services, trade events, and U.S. export regulations
U.S. Business Advisor http://www.SBA.gov	One-stop access to a range of federal government information, services, and transactions
U.S. State Department http://www.travel.state.gov /travel/cis_pa_tw/tw/tw_1764.html	Listing of the State Department's latest travel warnings about conditions that may affect safety abroad, supplemented by the list of consulate addresses and country information

IMPORTERS AND EXPORTERS

When a firm brings in goods produced abroad to sell domestically, it is an importer. Conversely, companies are exporters when they produce—or purchase—goods at home and sell them in overseas markets. An importing or exporting strategy provides the most basic level of international involvement, with the least risk and control.

Firms engage in exporting of two types: indirect and direct. A company engages in indirect exporting when it produces a product, such as an electronic component, that becomes part of another product that is ultimately sold in foreign markets. The second method, direct exporting, occurs as the name implies when a company directly sells its products in markets outside its own country. Often the first step for companies entering foreign

∨ Approximately 90 percent of non-bulk cargo worldwide is transported in containers, and modern container ships can carry up to 8,000 of these 40-foot-long containers.

markets, direct exporting is the most common form of international business. Firms that succeed at this may then move to other strategies.

CONTRACTUAL AGREEMENTS

One type of contractual agreement, **subcontracting**, involves hiring local companies to produce, distribute, or sell goods or

subcontracting international agreement that involves hiring local companies to produce, distribute, or sell goods or services in a specific country or geographical region.

services. This move allows a foreign firm to take advantage of the subcontractor's expertise in local culture, contacts, and regulations. Many companies simply modify their domestic business strategies by translating promotional brochures and product-use instructions into the languages of the host nations.

Subcontracting works equally well for mail-order companies, which can farm out order fulfillment and customer service functions to local businesses. Manufacturers practice subcontracting to save money on import duties and labor costs, and businesses go this route to market products best sold by locals in a given country. Some firms, such as Maryland-based Pacific Bridge Medical, help medical manufacturers find reliable subcontractors and parts suppliers in Asia.

A key disadvantage of subcontracting is that companies cannot always control their subcontractors' business practices. Several major U.S. companies have been embarrassed by reports that their subcontractors used child labor to manufacture clothing. Additionally, when a U.S. firm provides the subcontractor with the know-how to produce a product for them, there is the chance that they will use this intellectual property to aid a competitor.

INTERNATIONAL DIRECT INVESTMENT

Investing directly in production and marketing operations in a foreign country is the ultimate level of global involvement. Over time, a firm may become successful at conducting business in other countries through exporting and contractual agreements. Its managers may then decide to establish manufacturing facilities in those countries, open branch offices, or buy ownership interests in local companies. Making the decision to directly invest in another country can carry significant risks for the investing company. Political instability, currency devaluation, and changes in the competitive environment are but a few of the issues that a firm must consider before making a direct investment.

One type of direct investment is the **joint venture**, which allows companies to share risks, costs, profits, and management responsibilities with one or more host country nationals. By setting

joint venture partnership between companies formed for a specific undertaking.

up such an arrangement, a company can conduct a significant amount of its business overseas while reducing the risk of "going it alone" in a foreign country.

TABLE 4.4 World's largest multinational companies

Rank	Company	Industry	Country of Origin
1	ICBC	Major banks	China
2	China Construction Bank	Regional banks	China
3	JPMorgan Chase	Major banks	United States
4	General Electric	Conglomerates	United States
5	Exxon Mobil	Oil & gas operations	United States
6	HSBC Holdings	Major banks	United Kingdom
7	Royal Dutch Shell	Oil & gas operations	Netherlands
8	Agricultural Bank of China	Regional banks	China
9	Berkshire Hathaway	Investment services	United States
9	PetroChina	Oil & gas operations	China

SOURCE: "The Global 2000," *Forbes*, April 17, 2013, http://www.forbes.com.

FROM MULTINATIONAL CORPORATION TO GLOBAL BUSINESS

A **multinational corporation (MNC)** is an organization with significant foreign operations. As TABLE 4.4 shows, firms headquartered in the United States make up half the list of the world's largest multinationals. Brazil, China, the

multinational corporation firm with significant operations and marketing activities outside its home country.

Netherlands, and the United Kingdom make up the other half. Note that the two top industries are banking and oil and gas.

Many U.S. multinationals, including Nike and Walmart, have expanded their overseas operations because they believe that domestic markets are peaking and foreign markets offer greater sales and profit potential. Other MNCs are making substantial investments in developing countries in part because these countries provide low-cost labor compared with the United States and Western Europe. In addition, many MNCs are locating high-tech facilities in countries with large numbers of technical school graduates.

> > > **Quick Review**

1. What are some key decisions an organization must make before doing business overseas?

2. Name the various levels of involvement an organization could select in doing business overseas.

3. How does subcontracting work in global business?

What's Ahead? > > >

Examples in this chapter indicate that businesses of all sizes are relying on world trade. Chapter 5 examines the special advantages and challenges that small-business owners encounter. In addition, a critical decision facing any new business is the choice of the most appropriate form of business ownership. Chapter 5 also examines the major ownership structures—sole proprietorship, partnership, and corporation—and assesses the pros and cons of each. The chapter closes with a discussion of trends affecting business ownership such as business consolidations through mergers and acquisitions.

Don't miss the Weekly Updates located at http://contemporarybusinessupdates.com to help you take the first step toward success.

NOTES

1. Chester Dawson, "Toyota Again World's Largest Autor Maker," *The Wall Street Journal*, January 28, 2013, http://online.wsj.com; Chris Isidore, "Toyota Motor Set to Reclaim 'Top Car Maker' Spot from GM," CNN Money, December 26, 2012, http://money.cnn.com.

2. *World Factbook*, "United States," https://www.cia.gov, accessed April 9, 2013.

3. Organization Web site, http://data.worldbank.org, accessed April 9, 2013.

4. Company Web site, http://walmartstores.com, "International," accessed April 9, 2013.

5. U.S. Census, "Top Ten Countries with Which the U.S. Trades, for the Month of December 2011," http://www.census.gov, accessed April 9, 2013.

6. U.S. Census, "Origin of Movement of U.S. Exports of Goods by State by NAICS-Based Product Code Groupings, Not Seasonally Adjusted, 2010," http://www.census.gov, accessed April 9, 2013.

7. U.S. Bureau of Economic Analysis, "U.S. International Trade in Goods and Services," press release, February 10, 2012, http://www.bea.gov.

8. Company Web site, http://en.shanghaidisneyresort.com.cn/en, accessed April 9, 2013; Shanghai Disney Resort, "First Steel Column of the Shanghai Disney Resort Project Administration Building Installed," press release, November 22, 2012, http://en.shanghaidisneyresort.com.cn.

9. Bank for International Settlements, http://www.bis.org, accessed April 9, 2013.

10. U.S. Department of Agriculture, Foreign Agriculture Service, "U.S. Sugar Import Program," http://www.fas.usda.gov, accessed April 9, 2013.

11. John Vidal, "Ethiopia Dam Project Is Devastating the Lives of Remote Indigenous Groups," *The Guardian*, February 6, 2013, http://www.guardian.co.uk; John Vidal, "Ethiopia Dam Project Rides Roughshod over Heritage of Local Tribespeople," *The Guardian*, February 23, 2012, http://www.guardian.co.uk.

12. Office of the United States Trade Representative, "CAFTA-DR," http://www.ustr.gov, accessed April 9, 2013.

13. European Union Web site, "Countries," http://europa.eu, accessed April 9, 2013; *World Factbook,* www.cia.gov, accessed April 9, 2013.

Summary of Learning Objectives

 Explain why nations trade.

The United States is both the world's largest importer and the largest exporter, although less than 5 percent of the world's population lives within its borders. With the increasing globalization of the world's economies, the international marketplace offers tremendous opportunities for U.S. and foreign businesses to expand into new markets for their goods and services. Doing business globally provides new sources of materials and labor. Trading with other countries also reduces a company's dependence on economic conditions in its home market. Countries that encourage international trade enjoy higher levels of economic activity, employment, and wages than those that restrict it.

Nations usually benefit if they specialize in producing certain goods or services. A country has an absolute advantage if it holds a monopoly or produces a good or service at a lower cost than other nations. It has a comparative advantage if it can supply a particular product more efficiently or at a lower cost than it can produce other items.

export   domestically produced good or service sold in markets in other countries.

import   foreign-made product purchased by domestic consumers.

absolute advantage   the ability to produce more goods using fewer resources than other providers.

comparative advantage   the ability to produce one good at a relatively lower opportunity cost than other goods.

opportunity cost   the highest valued alternative forgone in the pursuit of an activity.

 Describe how trade is measured between nations.

Countries measure the level of international trade by comparing exports and imports and then calculating whether a trade surplus or a deficit exists. This is the balance of trade, which represents the difference between exports and imports. The term *balance of payments* refers to the overall flow of money into or out of a country, including overseas loans and borrowing, international investments, and profits from such investments. An exchange rate is the value of a nation's currency relative to the currency of another nation. Currency values typically fluctuate, or "float," relative to the supply and demand for specific currencies in the world market. When the value of the dollar falls compared with other currencies, the cost paid by foreign businesses and households for U.S. products declines, and demand for exports may rise. An increase in the value

of the dollar raises the prices of U.S. products sold abroad, but it reduces the prices of foreign products sold in the United States.

balance of trade   difference between a nation's exports and imports.

trade surplus   the positive difference between what a country exports compared to what it imports.

trade deficit   the negative difference between what a country exports compared to what it imports.

balance of payments   overall flow of money into or out of a country.

exchange rate   the rate at which a nation's currency can be exchanged for the currencies of other nations.

devaluation   drop in a currency's value relative to other currencies or to a fixed standard.

 Identify the barriers to international trade.

Businesses face several obstacles in the global marketplace. Companies must be sensitive to social and cultural differences, such as languages, values, and religions, when operating in other countries. Economic differences include standard-of-living variations and levels of infrastructure development. Legal and political barriers are among the most difficult to judge. Each country sets its own laws regulating business practices. Trade restrictions such as tariffs and administrative barriers also present obstacles to international business.

tariff   tax, surcharge, or duty on foreign products.

quota   limit set on the amounts of particular products that countries can import during specified time periods.

dumping   selling products abroad at prices below production costs or below typical prices in the home market to capture market share from domestic competitors.

embargo   total ban on importing specific products or a total halt to trading with a particular country.

4 **Discuss reducing barriers to international trade.**

Many international organizations seek to promote international trade by reducing barriers among nations. Examples include the World Trade Organization, the World Bank, and the International Monetary Fund. Multinational economic communities create partnerships to remove barriers to the flow of goods, capital, and people across the borders of members. Three such economic agreements are the North American Free Trade Agreement, CAFTA-DR, and the European Union.

General Agreement on Tariffs and Trade (GATT) international trade accord that substantially reduced worldwide tariffs and other trade barriers.

World Trade Organization (WTO) 153-member international institution that monitors GATT agreements and mediates international trade disputes.

World Bank organization established by industrialized nations to lend money to less developed countries.

International Monetary Fund (IMF) organization created to promote trade, eliminate barriers, and make short-term loans to member nations that are unable to meet their budgets.

North American Free Trade Agreement (NAFTA) agreement among the United States, Canada, and Mexico to break down tariffs and trade restrictions.

Central America–Dominican Republic Free Trade Agreement (CAFTA-DR) agreement among the United States, Costa Rica, the Dominican Republic, El Salvador, Guatemala, Honduras, and Nicaragua to reduce tariffs and trade restrictions.

European Union (EU) 28-nation European economic alliance.

5 Explain the decisions to go global.

Exporting and importing, the first level of involvement in international business, has the lowest degree of both risk and control. Companies may rely on export trading or management companies to help distribute their products. Contractual agreements such as franchising, foreign licensing, and subcontracting offer additional options. Franchising and licensing are especially appropriate for services. Companies may also choose local subcontractors to produce goods for local sales. International direct investment in production and marketing facilities provides the highest degree of control but also the greatest risk. Firms make direct investments by acquiring foreign companies or facilities, forming joint ventures with local firms and setting up their own overseas divisions.

subcontracting international agreement that involves hiring local companies to produce, distribute, or sell goods or services in a specific country or geographical region.

joint venture partnership between companies formed for a specific undertaking.

multinational corporation firm with significant operations and marketing activities outside its home country.

>>> Quick Review >>>

LO1

1. Why do nations trade?

2. Explain how population and per-capita GDP are important aspects of the global market.

3. What are absolute advantage and comparative advantage, and why are they important?

LO2

1. What are balance of trade and balance of payments, and how do they affect each other?

2. Explain the purpose of an exchange rate.

3. What happens when a country's currency is devalued?

LO3

1. How might cultural values create a barrier to trade, and how can such barriers be overcome?

2. What is a tariff, and how do tariffs work?

3. Why is dumping a problem for companies marketing goods internationally?

LO4

1. What international trade organization succeeded GATT, and what is its goal?

2. Compare and contrast the goals of the World Bank and the International Monetary Fund.

3. What are the goals of the European Union, and how do they promote international trade?

LO5

1. What are some key decisions an organization must make before doing business overseas?

2. Name the various levels of involvement an organization could select in doing business overseas.

3. How does subcontracting work in global business?

Joe Mahoney/Richmond Times Dispatch

SHAWN BOYER

Small Business and Forms of Business Ownership

Learning Objectives

1 **Discuss** why most businesses are small businesses.

2 **Determine** the contributions of small businesses to the economy.

3 **Discuss** why small businesses fail.

4 **Identify** the available assistance for small businesses.

5 **Outline** the forms of private business ownership.

6 **Describe** public and collective ownership of business.

7 **Discuss** organizing a corporation.

8 **Explain** what happens when businesses join forces.

Snagajob's Success Hooks Investors

When Shawn Boyer tried to help a friend find an internship online several years ago, he didn't know he would soon be the founder of a fast-growing company or the winner of a couple of prestigious business awards. Finding no Web sites for part-time or hourly jobseekers at that time, Boyer set up a job board to serve them and called it Snagajob.com.

A few years later the board had become a full-service, online job-search company, offering job opportunities, networking, and advice to a loyal community of over 30 million hourly workers, most between 18 and 32. Snagajob provides workforce solutions to employers as well.

The U.S. Small Business Administration named Boyer its National Small Business Owner of the Year, and his company continued to grow, relocating, adding employees, and developing a casual culture with employee benefits like backup child care, on-site fitness center, and paid resort vacations to celebrate five- and ten-year employment anniversaries. Recently, Snagajob was named the Outstanding Company of the Year for the wellness and fitness programs they provide to their employees.

Snagajob attracted $14 million in private equity funding on top of $27 million in investment money from a venture capital firm to help it keep expanding. It's a good thing the company was recently named the Best Small Company to Work For in the U.S., too. With the firm's continued expansion, it is rapidly on its way to becoming a mid-sized firm.[1]

Overview > > >

Do you hope to work for a big company or a small one? Do you plan to start your own business? But before you enter the business world—as an employee or an owner—you need to understand the industry in which a company operates, as well as the size and framework of the firm's organization. For example, Snagajob.com is a small but fast-growing business that could spawn a whole new industry. It's important to remember that larger businesses—like Ford and Apple—began as small businesses.

This chapter begins by focusing on small business and then moves on to an overview of the forms of private business ownership. Public and collective ownership are examined as well as not-for-profit organizations. The chapter concludes with an explanation of structures and operations typical of larger companies and a review of the major types of business alliances.

1 Most Businesses Are Small Businesses

Although many people associate the term *business* with corporate giants such as Walmart, 3M, and ExxonMobil, most people do not know that 99.7 percent of all U.S. companies are considered small businesses. These firms have generated 65 percent of new jobs over the past two decades and employ half of all private-sector (nongovernment) workers.[2] Small business is also the launching pad for new ideas and products. Small businesses hire 43 percent of high-tech workers such as scientists, engineers, and computer programmers, who devote their time to developing new goods and services.[3]

WHAT IS A SMALL BUSINESS?

How can you tell a small business from a large one? The Small Business Administration (SBA), the federal agency most directly involved with this sector of the economy, defines a **small business** as an independent business having fewer than 500 employees. However, those bidding for government contracts or applying for government assistance may vary in size according to industry. For example, small manufacturers fall in the 500-worker range, whereas wholesalers must employ fewer than 100. Retailers may generate up to $7 million in annual sales and still be considered small businesses, whereas farms or other agricultural businesses must generate less than $750,000 annually to be designated as small.[4]

small business an independent entity with fewer than 500 employees that is not dominant in its market.

TYPICAL SMALL-BUSINESS VENTURES

Small businesses have experienced steady erosion in some industries as larger firms have bought them out and replaced

∧ Food trucks are growing in popularity as a small business idea. Have you visited a food truck for lunch recently?

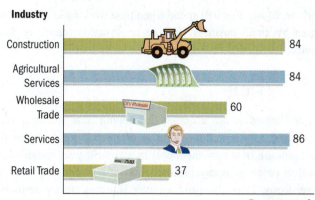

Percentage of firms with fewer than 500 employees

FIGURE 5.1 Major Industries Dominated by Small Businesses

SOURCE: U.S. Small Business Administration, Office of Advocacy, "Small Business Profile: United States," http://www.sba.gov, accessed April 18, 2013.

them with larger operations. The number of independent home improvement stores, for example, has fallen dramatically as Lowe's, Home Depot, Menard's, and other large brands have increased the size and number of their stores. But as TABLE 5.1 reveals, the businesses least likely to be gobbled up are those that sell personalized services, rely on certain locations, and keep their overhead costs low.

As **FIGURE 5.1** shows, small businesses provide most jobs in the construction, agricultural services, wholesale trade, services, and retail trade industries. Retailing to the consumer is another important industry for small firms. Retailing giants such as Amazon and Macy's may be the best-known firms, but smaller stores and Web sites outnumber them. And these small firms can be very successful, often because they can keep their overhead expenses low.

> > > **Quick Review**

1 How does the Small Business Administration define a small business?

2 In what industries do small businesses play a significant role?

② Contributions of Small Business to the Economy

Small businesses form the core of the U.S. economy. Businesses with fewer than 500 employees generate more than half the nation's gross domestic products (GDP). These businesses contribute in many ways, including creating jobs, new products, and even whole new industries. Small firms are credited with U.S. competitiveness in a number of global markets.[5]

CREATING NEW JOBS

One impressive contribution that small business makes to the U.S. economy is the number of new jobs created each year. On average, companies with fewer than 500 employees are responsible for creating two of every three new jobs in a year.[6] The smallest companies—those with four or fewer employees—are responsible for a significant share of those jobs. Several provisions of the recent Small Business Jobs Act may help give a further boost to these job numbers by raising the dollar amount of small business loans available to companies.[7]

Even if you never plan to start your own company, you will probably work for a small business at some point in your career, particularly at the beginning. Small firms often hire the youngest

TABLE 5.1 Which business sectors are most dominated and least dominated by small firms?

Most Likely to Be a Small Firm	Fewer Than 20 Workers
Home builders	97%
Florists	97%
Hair salons	96%
Auto repair	96%
Funeral homes	94%
Least Likely to Be a Small Firm	**Fewer Than 20 Workers**
Hospitals	14%
Nursing homes	23%
Paper mills	33%
Electric utilities	38%
Oil pipelines	38%

SOURCE: U.S. Census Bureau, "Number of Firms, Number of Establishments, Employment, and Annual Payroll by Employment Size of the Enterprise for the United States, All Industries," http://www.census.gov, accessed April 18, 2013.

workers. Most of us will spend some time working in areas dominated by small business such as construction, retail, or food service.

INNOVATION

Small businesses are adept at developing new and improved goods and services. Innovation is often the entire reason for the founding of a new business. In a typical year, small firms develop twice as many product innovations per employee as larger firms. They also produce over 16 times more patents per employee than larger firms.[8] Key 20th century innovations developed by small businesses include the airplane, the personal computer, soft contact lenses, and the zipper. Innovations that already drive small businesses in the 21st century include those that fall into the social networking, security, and green energy industries.

CREATING NEW INDUSTRIES

Small firms give businesspeople the opportunity and outlet for developing their new ideas. Sometimes these innovations become entirely new industries. TABLE 5.2 illustrates some of the newest jobs within both traditional and new industries, many of which can be found in small businesses. Many of today's largest and most successful firms, such as Whole Foods, Google, and Mattel, began as small businesses. Facebook co-founders Mark Zuckerberg, Dustin Moskovitz, Chris Hughes, and Eduardo Saverin launched their new business from their college dorm room. Within a few years, Facebook had logged more than 500 million active users, positioned itself as a leader in the new industry of social networking, and prompted others to start their own businesses.[9]

∧ New industries can be created when small businesses adapt to shifts in consumer interests and preferences. ThinkEco created a device that regulates outlet power, allowing its customers to save as much as 20 percent on their energy bills.

> >> **Quick Review**

1 In what three key ways do small businesses contribute to the economy?

2 How are new industries formed?

3 Why Small Businesses Fail

As we have seen, small businesses play a huge role in the U.S. economy. However, owning or even working in a small business is often more challenging than in a large firm. Some of the advantages of small business, such as lower costs, can also

TABLE 5.2 Can you list some of the new job opportunities within traditional and new industries?

Industry	Jobs and Recent Statistics
Green energy and construction	Wind-farm engineers; solar installers and technicians; green-collar specialists and consultants; green construction specialists; water conservation specialists (blue economy jobs); industry expected to reach $573.1 billion by 2017
Environmental consulting	Consultants; industry is expected to add 52,000 jobs over the next 5 years
Restaurants	Wait staff, host/hostess, chefs, food truck operators, management; industry currently employs 10% of the U.S. workforce
Internet publishing & broadcasting	Editors, writers, developers, includes services like Hulu; industry is expected to grow 16.2% over the next few years and reach $72 billion in revenue
Information technology	IT specialists, consultants, project managers, security consultants, digital forensic experts; industry added nearly 200,000 consulting jobs over recent 5-year span
E-commerce	Customer service, business owners; industry is slated to grow 8.8% annually through 2017
Mobile & social gaming	Developers, graphic artists; industry has $4.5 billion in sales and currently employs 28,000 people at 1,500 firms
Big data	Entrepreneurs to organize, analyze, and strategize, virtual data rooms to share secure information across virtual teams; industry is expected to soon increase to $17 billion
Pet care	Pet groomers, massage therapists, retail workers; industry boasts $52.87 billion in sales in a recent year

SOURCES: "Best Industries for Starting a Business in 2012," Inc.com, http://www.inc.com, accessed April 18, 2013; Carol Tice, "What Business Should You Start? Fast-Growing Sectors for 2013," *Forbes*, February 7, 2013, http://www.forbes.com.

be disadvantages. For example, suppose a firm has lower costs because it doesn't have a human resources department. In this case, the owner must deal with all human resource issues as well as all other duties. This same concept applies to other areas within a small business as well, from accounting to production to marketing and sales. The owner and the staff have to perform many duties, often without the resources of larger firms. To succeed, a small business owner must have a clear focus, stick to a plan, and hope for a bit of luck. However, even in the best case, owning small business can be difficult. Some of the more common issues that plague small firms include management inexperience, inadequate financing, and the challenge of meeting government regulations.

As **FIGURE 5.2** shows, seven out of ten new businesses survive at least two years and about half make it to the five-year mark. But by the tenth year, just 34 percent survive.[10] Let's look a little more closely at why this happens.

MANAGEMENT SHORTCOMINGS

Management shortcoming may include lack of people skills, inadequate knowledge of finance, inability to track inventory or sales, poor assessment of the competition, or simply the lack of time to do everything required. As we have seen, large firms

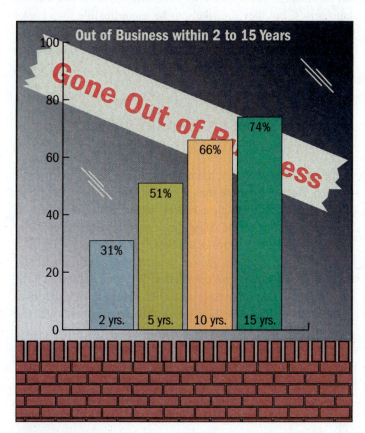

FIGURE 5.2 Rate of Business Failures

SOURCE: Office of Advocacy, U.S. Small Business Administration, "Frequently Asked Questions: Advocacy Small Business Statistics and Research," http://www.sba.gov, accessed April 18, 2013.

often have the resources to recruit specialists in areas such as marketing and finance, whereas the owner of a small business often must wear many hats.

Also, the challenge of scaling is especially difficult for small business. For example, imagine a highly profitable restaurant owned by a celebrity chef who enjoys creating exciting, new dishes. As the business grows, she may want to expand her restaurant to multiple locations. However, with multiple locations, the chef must divide her time among several restaurants, deal with an expanded staff, and handle all the other problems that come from running a larger operation. She must hire chefs for the other locations who may not be as talented or motivated as she. What was a once a great single restaurant has become a collection of average restaurants that are not as stellar as the original one. The chef, now more of a manager than a cook, is likely to wonder where she went wrong. Where indeed?

INADEQUATE FINANCING

Many of the challenges that small businesses face can be traced to inadequate financing. Money is the foundation of any business. Every business, large or small, needs a certain amount of financing in order to operate, grow, and thrive. First-time business owners often assume their firms will generate enough funds from initial sales to finance continuing operations. But building a business takes time. Products need to be developed, employees have to be hired, a Web site must be constructed, a distribution strategy has to be determined, office or retail space might have to be secured, and so forth. Most small businesses—even those with minimal start-up costs—sometimes don't turn a profit for months or even years.[11]

GOVERNMENT REGULATION

Small-business owners cite their struggle to comply with government regulations as one of the biggest challenges they face. Some firms falter because of this burden alone. Paperwork costs account for billions of small-business dollars each year. A large company can better cope with requirements for forms and reports. Larger firms often find it makes economic sense to hire or contract with specialists in specific types of regulation, such as employment law and workplace safety regulations. By contrast, small businesses often struggle to absorb the costs of government paperwork because of their smaller staff and budgets. The smallest firms—those with fewer than 20 employees—spend 45 percent more per employee than larger firms just to comply with federal regulations.[12]

>>> Quick Review

1 What percentage of small businesses remain in operation after five years? Ten years?

2 Name the three main causes of small-business failure.

4 Available Assistance for Small Businesses

An important part of organizing a small business is financing its activities. Once a business plan has been created, various sources can be tapped for loans and other types of financing. These include government agencies as well as private investors.

SMALL BUSINESS ADMINISTRATION

Not all government involvement in small business is burdensome. Small businesses can benefit from using the resources provided by the U.S. government's **Small Business Administration (SBA)**. The SBA is the principal agency concerned with helping small U.S. firms, and it is the advocate for small businesses within the federal government. Several thousand employees staff the SBA's Washington headquarters and its 1,800 regional and field offices.[13] The SBA's mission statement declares that "Small business is critical to our economic recovery and strength, to building America's future, and to helping the United States compete in today's global marketplace."[14]

Small Business Administration (SBA) principal government agency concerned with helping small U.S. firms.

Contrary to popular belief, the SBA seldom provides direct business loans or outright grants to start or expand small businesses. Rather, the SBA guarantees small-business loans made by private lenders, including banks and other institutions. To qualify for an SBA-backed loan, borrowers must be unable to secure conventional commercial financing on reasonable terms and be a "small business" as defined by SBA size standards.[15] Direct SBA loans are available in only a few special situations, such as natural disaster recovery, energy conservation, or development programs. Under the 2009 Recovery Act, the SBA temporarily eliminated specific loan fees and raised the guarantee level on some of its loans.[16] The previously mentioned Small Business Jobs Act was also intended to make more capital available to entrepreneurs and small business owners.[17]

Start-ups and other small firms can obtain an SBA-guaranteed **microloan** of up to $35,000, with the average being $13,000 with a maximum term of six years.[18] Microloans may be used to buy equipment or operate a business but not to buy real estate or pay off other loans. These loans are available from nonprofit organizations located in most states. Other sources of microloans include the federal Economic Development Administration; some state governments; and certain private lenders, such as credit unions and community development groups. The most frequent suppliers of credit to small firms are banks.

microloan small-business loan often used to buy equipment or operate a business.

RiverNorthPhotography/iStockphoto

∧ Small Business Investment Companies (SBICs) are for-profit businesses licensed by the Small Business Administration. Using their own capital, SBICs provide loans to small businesses. FedEx used SBIC financing when it was a small start-up company.

Small-business loans are also available through a Small Business Investment Company (SBIC), an SBA-licensed organization operated by experienced venture capitalists. SBICs use their own capital, supplemented with government loans, to invest in small businesses. Like banks, SBICs are profit-making enterprises, but they are likely to be more flexible than banks in their lending decisions. Large companies that used SBIC financing when they were small start-ups include Callaway Golf, FedEx, and Costco.[19]

SMALL-BUSINESS OPPORTUNITIES FOR WOMEN AND MINORITIES

In the United States today, more than 8 million firms are owned by women, employing more than 7 million workers and generating nearly $1.3 trillion in sales. In fact, women own 40 percent of companies in the United States, and those firms are growing at twice the rate of U.S. firms as a whole.[20]

Like male business owners, women have a variety of reasons for owning their own companies. Some have a unique business idea that they want to bring to life. Others decide to form a business when they lose their jobs or become frustrated with the bureaucracies in large companies. In some cases, women leave large corporations when they feel blocked from opportunities for advancement—when they hit the so-called "glass ceiling." Because women are more likely than men to be their family's primary caregiver, many seek self-employment as a way to achieve flexible working hours so they can spend more time with their families.

Business ownership is also an important opportunity for America's racial and ethnic minorities. In recent years, the growth in the number of businesses owned by African Americans,

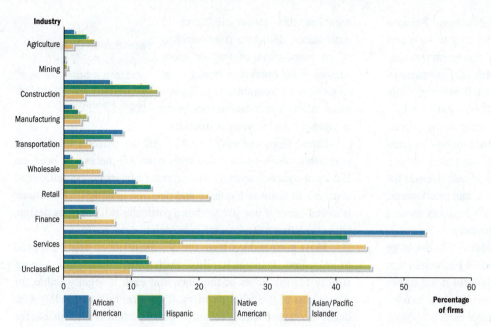

Industry

Agriculture

Mining

Construction

Manufacturing

Transportation

Wholesale

Retail

Finance

Services

Unclassified

0   10   20   30   40   50   60

Percentage of firms

- African American
- Hispanic
- Native American
- Asian/Pacific Islander

FIGURE 5.3 Types of Businesses Owned by Racial and Ethnic Minorities

SOURCE: Data from Office of Advocacy, U.S. Small Business Administration, "Minorities in Business," http://www.sba.gov/advocacy, accessed April 18, 2013.

Hispanics, and Asian Americans has far outpaced the overall growth of U.S. businesses. **FIGURE 5.3** shows the percentages of minority ownership in major industries. The relatively strong presence of minorities in the services and retail industries is especially significant because these industries contain the greatest number of businesses.

>>> Quick Review

1 In what ways does the SBA help small businesses?

2 Why do small businesses represent a good opportunity for women and minorities?

SOLE PROPRIETORSHIPS

The most common form of business ownership, the **sole proprietorship** is also the oldest and the simplest. In a sole proprietorship, no legal distinction separates the sole proprietor's status as an individual from his or her status as a business owner. Although sole proprietorships are common in a variety of industries, they are concentrated primarily among small businesses such as repair shops, small retail stores, and service providers such as plumbers, hair stylists, and photographers.

> **sole proprietorship** business ownership in which there is no legal distinction between the sole proprietor's status as an individual and his or her status as a business owner.

5 Forms of Private Business Ownership

Regardless of its size, every business is organized according to one of three categories of legal structure: sole proprietorship, partnership, or corporation. Each legal structure offers unique advantages and disadvantages. But because there is no universal formula for every situation, U.S. state governments have created or adopted a variety of organizational structures. Business owners can then choose the structure that best meets their needs. For example, within the corporate organizational form there are C corporations, S corporations, and, depending on size and other factors, limited liability companies (LLC). Within partnerships, there are general partnerships, limited partnerships, and limited liability partnerships. And there are even variations on sole proprietors, such as a single person LLC. **FIGURE 5.4** shows the breakdown of organizational forms, with sole proprietorships being the most common form of business ownership, accounting for more than 70 percent of all firms in the United States.

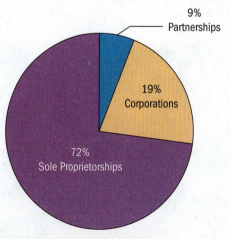

9% Partnerships

19% Corporations

72% Sole Proprietorships

FIGURE 5.4 Forms of Business Ownership

SOURCE: Data from U.S. Census Bureau, "Business Enterprise: Sole Proprietorships, Partnerships, Corporations, Table 744," *2012 Statistical Abstract*, http://www.uscensus.gov, accessed April 18, 2013.

A sole proprietorship offers some unique advantages. Because such businesses involve a single owner, they are easy to form and dissolve. A sole proprietorship gives the owner maximum management flexibility, along with the right to all profits after payment of business-related bills and taxes. A highly motivated owner of a sole proprietorship directly reaps the benefits of his or her hard work.

Minimal legal requirements simplify creating a sole proprietorship. The owner registers the business or trade name—to guarantee that two firms do not use the same name—and takes out any necessary licenses. Local governments require certain licenses for businesses such as restaurants, motels or hotels, and retail stores. In addition, some occupational licenses require business owners to obtain specific insurance such as liability coverage.

Sole proprietorships are also easy to dissolve. This advantage is particularly important to temporary or seasonal businesses that set up for a limited period of time. It's also helpful if the owner wants or needs to close the business for any reason—say, to relocate or to accept a full-time position with a larger firm.

Management flexibility is another advantage of a sole proprietorship. The owner can make decisions without reporting to a manager, take quick action, and keep trade secrets. A sole proprietorship always bears the individual stamp or flair of its owner, whether it's a discount loyalty program or longer warranty.

The greatest disadvantage of the sole proprietorship is the owner's personal financial liability for all debts of the business. Also, the business must operate with financial resources limited to the owner's personal funds and money that he or she can borrow. Such financing limitations can keep the business from expanding.

PARTNERSHIPS

Another option for organizing a business is to form a partnership. The Uniform Partnership Act, which regulates this ownership form in most states, defines a **partnership** as an association of two or more persons who operate a business as co-owners by voluntary legal agreement. Many small businesses begin as partnerships between co-founders.

Partnerships are easy to form. All the partners need to do is register the business name and obtain any necessary licenses. Having a partner generally means greater financial capability and someone to share in the tasks and decision making of a business. It's even better if one partner has a particular skill, such as design, while the other has a knack for financials.

Most partnerships have the disadvantage of being exposed to unlimited financial liability. Each partner bears full responsibility for the debts of the firm, and each is legally liable for the actions of the other partners. If the firm fails and is left with debt—no matter who is at fault—every partner is responsible for those debts. If one partner defaults, the others are responsible for the firm's debts, even if it means dipping into personal funds. To avoid these problems, many firms establish a limited partnership or a limited-liability partnership, which limits the liability of partners to the value of their interests in the company. In the case of a limited partnership, the general partners have complete liability, while the liability of limited partners is limited to the amount of their investment. Limited-liability partnerships go a step further in limiting the liability for all partners to the assets of the partnership.

Breaking up a partnership is more complicated than dissolving a sole proprietorship. Rather than simply withdrawing funds from the bank, the partner who wants out may need to find someone to buy his or her interest in the firm. The death of a partner also threatens the survival of a partnership. A new partnership must be formed, and the estate of the deceased is entitled to a share of the firm's value. To ease the financial strains of

> A highly motivated owner of a sole proprietorship directly reaps the benefits of his or her hard work.

74

such events, business planners often recommend life insurance coverage for each partner, combined with a buy–sell agreement. The insurance proceeds can be used to repay the deceased partner's heirs and allow the surviving partner to retain control of the business. Because partnerships are vulnerable to personal conflicts that can quickly escalate, it's important for partners to choose each other carefully—not just because they are friends—and try to plan for the future.

CORPORATIONS

A **C corporation** is a legal organization with assets and liabilities separate from those of its owner(s). A corporation can be a large or small business. It can be Ford Motor Corp. or a local auto repair shop.

> **C corporation** a form of legal organization with assets and liabilities separate from those of its owner(s).

Corporate ownership offers considerable advantages. Because a corporation is a separate legal entity, its stockholders have only limited financial risk. If the firm fails, stockholders lose only the money they invested. This applies to the firm's managers and executives as well. Because they are not the sole proprietors or partners in the business, their personal savings are not at risk if the company folds or goes bankrupt. This protection also extends to legal risk. Class-action suits involving automakers, drug manufacturers, and food producers are filed against the companies, not the owners of those companies. Although companies such as BP recently experienced class-action suits, their employees and stockholders were not required to pay the settlements from their own bank accounts.[21]

Corporations offer other advantages. They gain access to expanded financial capabilities based on the opportunity to offer direct outside investments such as stock sales. A large corporation can legally generate internal financing for many projects by transferring money from one part of the corporation to another.

v Corporations, as shown here with the different logos, are a form of legal organization with assets and liabilities separate from those of its owners.

© Linda Steward/iStockphoto

One major disadvantage for a corporation is the double taxation of corporate earnings. After a corporation pays federal, state, and local income taxes on its profits, its owners (stockholders) also pay personal taxes on any distributions of those profits they receive from the corporation in the form of dividends.

S CORPORATIONS AND LIMITED LIABILITY CORPORATIONS

To avoid double taxation of business income while minimizing financial liability for their owners, many smaller firms (those with fewer than 100 stockholders) organize as an **S corporation**. An S corporation can elect to pay federal income taxes as a partnership while retaining the liability limitations typical of corporations. S corporations are only taxed once. Unlike regular corporations, S corporations do not pay corporate taxes on their profits. Instead, the untaxed profits of S corporations are paid directly as dividends to shareholders, who then pay the individual tax rate. This tax advantage has resulted in a tremendous increase in the number of S corporations. Consequently, the IRS closely monitors S corporations because some businesses don't meet the legal requirements to form S corporations.[22]

> **S corporation** a form of business organization in which the entity does not pay corporate taxes on profits; instead, profits are distributed to shareholders, who pay individual income taxes.

Business owners may also form a **limited-liability company (LLC)** to secure the corporate advantage of limited liability while avoiding the double taxation characteristic of corporations. An LLC combines the pass-through taxation of a partnership or sole proprietorship with the limited liability of a corporation.

> **limited-liability company (LLC)** a business entity that secures the corporate advantage of limited liability while avoiding the double taxation characteristic of a traditional corporation.

EMPLOYEE-OWNED CORPORATIONS

Another alternative for creating a corporation is **employee ownership**, in which workers buy shares of stock in the company that employs them. The corporate organization stays the same, but most stockholders are also employees. The popularity of this form of corporation is growing, with the number of employee ownership plans increasing dramatically. Today about 20 percent of all employees of for-profit companies report owning stock in their companies; approximately 25 million Americans own employer stock through employee stock ownership plans (ESOPs), options, stock purchase plans, 401(k) plans, and other programs.

> **employee ownership** business arrangement in which workers buy shares of stock in the company that employs them.

∧ City Year Inc. is a not-fot-profit organization supporting community service efforts of people in their late teens and early twenties.

76

NOT-FOR-PROFIT CORPORATIONS

The same business concepts that apply to commercial companies also apply to the **not-for-profit corporation**—an organization whose goals do not include pursuing a profit. About 1.5 million not-for-profits operate in the United States, including charitable groups, social-welfare organizations, government agencies, and religious congregations. This sector also includes museums, libraries, hospitals, conservation groups, private schools, and the like.

not-for-profit corporation

organization whose goals do not include pursuing a profit.

City Year Inc., a not-for-profit organization, supports the community service efforts of people in their late teens and early twenties. The organization offers a number of programs in which volunteers can participate. Its signature program, the City Year Youth Corps, invites 1,750 volunteers between the ages of 17 and 24 to commit to a year of full-time community service in activities such as mentoring and tutoring inner-city school children, helping to restore and re-claim public spaces, and staffing youth summer camps. The organization also partners with for-profit corporations such as Timberland, Comcast, and Pepsi to fund and implement its efforts.[23]

>>> Quick Review

1 What are some key differences between sole proprietorships and partnerships?

2 What is a corporation?

3 What is the main distinction of a not-for-profit organization?

6 Public and Collective Ownership of Business

One alternative to private ownership is some form of public ownership owned and operated by a government unit or agency. In the United States, local governments often own parking structures and water systems. The Pennsylvania Turnpike Authority operates a vital highway link across the Keystone State. The federal government operates Hoover Dam in Nevada to provide electricity over a large region.

Collective ownership establishes an organization referred to as a cooperative (or co-op), whose owners join forces to operate all or part of the activities in their firm or industry. Currently, about 100 million people worldwide are employed by cooperatives.[24] Cooperatives allow small businesses to pool their resources on purchases, marketing, equipment, distribution, and the like. Discount savings can be split among members. Cooperatives can share equipment and expertise. During difficult economic times, members find a variety of ways to support each other. Ocean Spray is an example of an agricultural cooperative.

>>> Quick Review

1 What is public ownership?

2 What is collective ownership? Where are collectives typically found, and what benefits do they provide small businesses?

7 Organizing a Corporation

A corporation is a legal structure, but it also requires a certain organizational structure that is more complex than the structure of a sole proprietorship or a partnership. This is why people often think of a corporation as a large entity, even though it does not have to be a specific size.

TYPES OF CORPORATIONS

Corporations fall into three categories: domestic, foreign, and alien. A firm is considered a domestic corporation in the state where it is incorporated. When a company does business in states other than the one where it has filed incorporation papers, it is registered as a foreign corporation in each of those states. A firm incorporated in one nation that operates in another is known as an alien corporation where it operates. Many firms—particularly large corporations with operations scattered around the world—may operate under all three of these designations.

THE CORPORATE CHARTER

Each state has a specific procedure for incorporating a business. Most states require at least three incorporators—the individuals

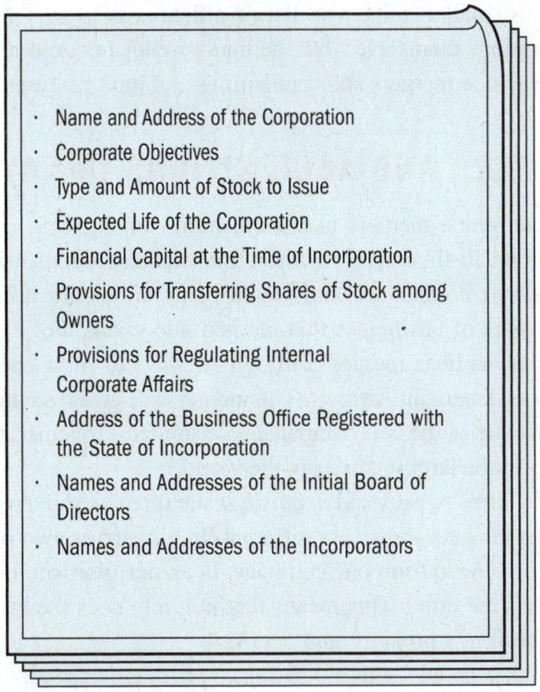

- Name and Address of the Corporation
- Corporate Objectives
- Type and Amount of Stock to Issue
- Expected Life of the Corporation
- Financial Capital at the Time of Incorporation
- Provisions for Transferring Shares of Stock among Owners
- Provisions for Regulating Internal Corporate Affairs
- Address of the Business Office Registered with the State of Incorporation
- Names and Addresses of the Initial Board of Directors
- Names and Addresses of the Incorporators

FIGURE 5.5 Traditional Articles of Incorporation

who create the corporation. In addition, the new corporation must select a name that is different from names used by other businesses. **FIGURE 5.5** lists the ten elements that most states require for chartering a corporation.

The information provided in the articles of incorporation forms the basis on which a state grants a corporate charter, which is the legal document that formally establishes a corporation. After securing the charter, the owners prepare the company's by-laws, which describe the rules and procedures for its operation.

CORPORATE MANAGEMENT

Regardless of its size, every corporation has levels of management and ownership. **FIGURE 5.6** illustrates those that are typical—although a smaller firm might not contain all five of these. These levels range from stockholders down to supervisory management.

STOCK OWNERSHIP AND STOCKHOLDER RIGHTS

At the top of Figure 5.6 are **stockholders**. They buy shares of stock in the corporation, becoming part owners. Some companies, such as family businesses, are owned by relatively few stockholders, and the stock is generally unavailable to outsiders. In such a firm, known as a private, closed, or closely held corporation, the stockholders also control and manage all of the company's activities. S. C. Johnson & Son, Bose Corporation, and W. L. Gore & Associates are examples of closely held corporations.

stockholder an owner of a corporation due to his or her purchase of stock in the corporation.

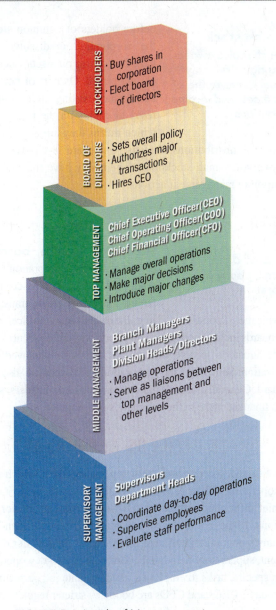

FIGURE 5.6 Levels of Management in a Corporation

In contrast, an open corporation, also called a publicly held corporation, sells stock to the general public, establishing diversified ownership and often leading to a broader scope of operations than those of a closed corporation. Publicly held corporations usually hold annual stockholders' meetings. During these meetings, managers report on corporate activities, and stockholders vote on any decisions that require their approval, including elections of officers. Walmart holds the nation's largest stockholder meeting at the University of Arkansas Bud Walton Arena; approximately 16,000 people attend.

Stockholders' role in the corporation depends on the class of stock they own. Shares are usually classified as common or preferred stock. Although owners of **preferred stock** have limited voting rights, they are entitled to receive dividends

preferred stock shares that give owners limited voting rights, and the right to receive dividends or assets before owners of common stock.

before holders of common stock. If the corporation is dissolved, they have first claims on assets, once debtors are repaid. Owners of **common stock** have voting rights but only residual claims on the firm's assets, which means they are last to receive any income distributions. Because one share is typically worth only one vote, small stockholders generally have little influence on corporate management actions.

BOARD OF DIRECTORS

Stockholders elect a **board of directors**—the corporation's governing body. The board sets overall policy, authorizes major transactions involving the corporation, and hires the chief executive officer (CEO). Most boards include both inside directors (corporate executives) and outside directors—people who are not otherwise employed by the organization. Sometimes the corporation's top executive also chairs the board. Generally, outside directors are also stockholders, so they have a financial stake in the company's performance.

CORPORATE OFFICERS AND MANAGERS

The CEO and other members of top management—such as the chief operating officer (COO), chief financial officer (CFO), and the chief information officer (CIO)—make most major corporate decisions. Managers at the middle management level handle the company's ongoing operational functions. At the first tier of management, supervisory personnel coordinate day-to-day operations, assign specific tasks to employees, and evaluate job performance.

Today's CEOs and CFOs are bound by stricter regulations than in the past. They must verify in writing the accuracy of their firm's financial statements, and the process for nominating candidates for the board has become more complex. In short, more checks and balances are in place for the governance of corporations.

> **>>> Quick Review**
>
> 1 Name the three types of corporations.
>
> 2 Describe the five main levels of corporate management and ownership.

8 When Businesses Join Forces

Today's business environment contains many complex relationships among businesses as well as not-for-profit organizations. Two firms may team up to develop a product or co-market products. One company may buy out another. Large corporations may split into smaller units. The list of alliances is as varied as the organizations themselves, but the major trends in corporate ownership include mergers and acquisitions and joint ventures.

MERGERS AND ACQUISITIONS (M&A)

In recent years, mergers and acquisitions among U.S. corporations hit an all-time high. Airlines, financial institutions, telecommunications companies, and media corporations are just a few of the types of businesses that merged into giants. For example, American Airlines merged with US Airways to form one entity known as American Airlines. The merger will create savings and new revenue as the two companies consolidate. Together, the airlines form the largest carrier in the world.[25]

The terms *merger* and *acquisition* are often used interchangeably, but their meanings are different. In a **merger**, two or more firms combine to form one company. In an **acquisition**, one firm purchases the other. This means that not only does the buyer acquire the firm's property and assets; it also takes on any debt obligations. The recent acquisition of Lucas Films by the Disney Corporation is an example. Acquisitions also occur when one firm buys a division or subsidiary from another firm. For example, a private equity firm recently purchased the subsidiary GE Healthcare Strategic Sourcing from GE Healthcare.[26]

Mergers can be classified as vertical, horizontal, or conglomerate. A **vertical merger** combines

▼ Lucas Films was recently acquired by the Disney Corporation.

Disney, Todd Anderson/AP Photo

firms operating at different levels in the production and marketing process—the combination of a manufacturer and a large retailer, for instance. A vertical merger pursues one of two primary goals: (1) to ensure adequate flows of raw materials and supplies needed for a firm's products or (2) to increase distribution. Software giant Microsoft is well known for acquiring small firms that have developed products with strong market potential, such as Teleo, a provider of voice over Internet protocol (VoIP) software and services that can be used to make phone calls via the Internet.

horizontal merger agreement that joins firms in the same industry for the purpose of diversification, increasing customer bases, cutting costs, or expanding product lines.

A **horizontal merger** joins firms in the same industry. This is done for the purpose of diversification, increasing customer bases, cutting costs, or expanding product lines. This type of merger is particularly popular in the auto and health care industries. Volkswagen now owns the Porsche brand, while CVS Caremark purchased another firm's Medicaid prescription business.

conglomerate merger agreement that combines unrelated firms, usually with the goal of diversification, spurring sales growth, or spending a cash surplus in order to avoid a takeover attempt.

A **conglomerate merger** combines unrelated firms. The most common reasons for a conglomerate merger are to diversify, spur sales growth, or spend a cash surplus that might otherwise make the firm a tempting target for a takeover effort. Conglomerate mergers may join firms in totally unrelated industries. General Electric is, in fact, well known for its conglomerate mergers, including its ownership of health care services and household appliances. Experts debate whether conglomerate mergers are beneficial. The usual argument in favor of such mergers is that a company can use its management expertise to succeed in a variety of industries. But the obvious drawback is that a huge conglomerate can spread its resources too thin to be dominant in any one market.

JOINT VENTURES: SPECIALIZED PARTNERSHIPS

joint venture partnership between companies formed for a specific undertaking.

A **joint venture** is a partnership between companies formed for a specific undertaking. Sometimes a company enters into a joint venture with a local firm, sharing the operation's costs, risks, management, and profits with its local partner. This is particularly common when a firm wants to enter into business in a foreign market. DreamWorks Animation recently entered a joint venture with three Chinese firms. The four companies will invest $330 million in a new company, Oriental DreamWorks. Based in Shanghai, the new venture will specialize in family films.[27]

Joint ventures between for-profit firms and not-for-profit organizations are becoming more and more common. These partnerships provide great benefits for both parties. Not-for-profit organizations receive the funding, marketing exposure, and sometimes manpower they might not otherwise generate.

> > > **Quick Review**

1 Distinguish between a merger and an acquisition.

2 What are the different kinds of mergers?

3 What is a joint venture?

What's Ahead? > > >

The next chapter focuses on the driving force behind the formation of new businesses: entrepreneurs. It examines the differences between a small-business owner and an entrepreneur and identifies certain personality traits typical of entrepreneurs. The chapter also details the process of launching a new venture, including identifying opportunities, locating needed financing, and turning good ideas into successful businesses. The chapter also details the advantages and disadvantages of owning and operating a business franchise. Finally, Chapter 6 explores a method for infusing the entrepreneurial spirit into established businesses—intrapreneurship.

Don't miss the Weekly Updates located at http://www.contemporarybusinessupdates.com to help you take the first step toward success.

NOTES

1. Company Web site, www.snagajob.com, accessed April 18, 2013; John Reid Blackwell, "Snagajob Hires New CEO; Founder to Become Chairman," *Richmond Times-Dispatch*, March 7, 2013, http://www.timesdispatch.com; Pete Woody, "Corporate Wellness on the Menu at Active RVA Awards Luncheon," Sports Backers, February 14, 2013, http://www.sportsbackers.org.

2. U.S. Small Business Administration, "Advocacy Small Business Statistics and Research," http://web.sba.gov/faqs, accessed April 18, 2013.

3. Ibid.

4. U.S. Small Business Administration, "Guide to SBA's Definitions of Small Business," http://archive.sba.gov, "Table of Small Business Size Standards Matched to North American Industry Classification System Codes," http://www.sba.gov, accessed April 18, 2013.

5. Gwen Moran, "10 Hot Export Markets for Small Businesses," *Entrepreneur*, accessed September 17, 2013, http://www.entrepreneur.com.

6. U.S. Small Business Administration, "Frequently Asked Questions," http://archive.sba.gov/advo/stats/sbfaq.pdf, April 18, 2013.

7. U.S. Small Business Administration, "Small Business Jobs Act of 2010," http://www.sba.gov, accessed April 18, 2013; David Ferris, "Law Can Have Big Impact on Small Businesses," February 1, 2012, http://www.workforce.com.

8. U.S. Small Business Administration, Office for Advocacy "Frequently Asked Questions," http://www.sba.gov, accessed April 18, 2013.

9. Company Web site, http://www.newsroom.fb.com, accessed April 18, 2013.

10. U.S. Small Business Administration, Office of Advocacy, "Frequently Asked Questions: Advocacy Small Business Statistics and Research," http://www.sba.gov, accessed April 18, 2013.

11. Nick Reese, "10 Common Pitfalls of New Entrepreneurs—and How to Avoid Them," *Forbes,* July 13, 2012, http://www.forbes.com.

12. W. Mark Crain, "The Impact of Regulatory Costs on Small Firms," Office of Advocacy, U.S. Small Business Administration, http://www.sba.gov, accessed April 18, 2013.

13. U.S. Small Business Administration, "What We Do," http://www.sba.gov, accessed April 18, 2013.

14. U.S. Small Business Administration, "Mission Statement," http://www.sba.gov, accessed April 18, 2013.

15. U.S. Small Business Administration, "Loans and Grants," http://www.sba.gov, accessed April 18, 2013.

16. U.S. Small Business Administration, "Disaster Assistance," http://www.sba.gov, accessed April 18, 2013.

17. U.S. Small Business Administration, "Small Business Jobs Act of 2010," http://www.sba.gov, accessed April 18, 2013.

18. U.S. Small Business Administration, "Microloan Program," http://www.sba.gov, accessed April 18, 2013.

19. Small Business Investor Alliance, "SBIC Program History," http://www.sbia.org, accessed April 18, 2013.

20. Women Moving Millions, "Facts: Entrepreneurship & Small Business," http://www.womenmovingmillions.org, accessed April 18, 2013.

21. Associated Press, "BP Seeks to Block Payment of Business Claims under Gulf Spill Settlement," Fox News, March 15, 2013, http://www.foxnews.com.

22. Lewis Taub, "Maximizing the Benefits of the S Corporation in Turbulent Times," McGladrey, http://www.mcgladrey.com, accessed May 2, 2013.

23. Organization Web site, "About City Year," http://www.cityyear.org, accessed April 18, 2013.

24. Organization Web site, National Cooperative Business Association, http://usa2012.coop, accessed April 18, 2013.

25. Mary Schlangenstein, "US Airways Leads AMR Merger to Create Largest Airline," *Bloomberg*, February 14, 2013, http://www.bloomberg.com.

26. Rachel Landen, "Private-Equity Firm Buys EHR Subsidiary from GE," ModernHealthcare.com, March 7, 2013, http://www.modernhealthcare.com.

27. Richard Verrier, "Oriental DreamWorks and Chinese Partners Announce Tibet Movie," *Los Angeles Times*, April 20, 2013, http://www.latimes.com; Brookes Barnes, "DreamWorks Animation Forms Studio with Chinese Partners," *The New York Times*, February 17, 2012, http://mediacoder.blogs.nytimes.com; Brent Lang, "DreamWorks Animation Announces China Joint Venture," *The Wrap*, February 17, 2012, http://www.thewrap.com.

Summary of Learning Objectives

 Discuss why most businesses are small businesses.

A small business is an independently owned business having fewer than 500 employees. Generally it is not dominant in its field and meets industry-specific size standards for income or number of employees. A business is classified as large when it exceeds these specifications.

small business an independent entity with fewer than 500 employees that is not dominant in its market.

 Determine the contributions of small businesses to the economy.

Small businesses create new jobs and new industries. They often hire workers who traditionally have had difficulty finding employment at larger firms. Small firms give people the opportunity and outlet for developing new ideas, which can turn into entirely new industries. Small businesses also develop new and improved goods and services.

 Discuss why small businesses fail.

About seven of every ten new (small) businesses survive at least two years. But by the tenth year, 82 percent have closed. Failure is often attributed to management shortcomings, inadequate financing, and difficulty meeting government regulations.

 Identify the available assistance for small businesses.

The SBA guarantees loans made by private lenders, including microloans and those funded by Small Business Investment Companies. It offers training and information resources so business owners can improve their odds of success. The SBA also provides specific support for businesses owned by women and minorities. State and local governments also have programs designed to help small businesses get established and grow. Venture capitalists are firms that invest in small businesses in return for an ownership stake.

Small Business Administration (SBA) principal government agency concerned with helping small U.S. firms.

microloan small-business loan often used to buy equipment or operate a business.

5 **Outline** the forms of private business ownership.

A sole proprietorship is owned and operated by one person. Although sole proprietorships are easy to set up and offer great operating flexibility, the owner remains personally liable for all of the firm's debts and legal settlements. In a partnership, two or more individuals share responsibility for owning and running the business. Partnerships are relatively easy to set up, but they do not offer protection from liability. When a business is set up as a corporation, it becomes a separate legal entity. Investors receive shares of stock in the firm. Owners have no legal and financial liability beyond their individual investments. In an employee-owned business, most stockholders are also employees. Family-owned businesses may be structured legally in any of these three ways but face unique challenges, including succession and complex relationships. The legal structure of a not-for-profit corporation stipulates that its goals do not include earning a profit.

sole proprietorship business ownership in which there is no legal distinction between the sole proprietor's status as an individual and his or her status as a business owner.

partnership association of two or more persons who operate a business as co-owners by voluntary legal agreement.

C corporation a form of legal organization with assets and liabilities separate from those of its owner(s).

S corporation a form of business organization in which the entity does not pay corporate taxes on profits; instead, profits are distributed to shareholders, who pay individual income taxes.

limited-liability company (LLC) a business entity that secures the corporate advantage of limited liability while avoiding the double taxation characteristic of a traditional corporation.

employee ownership business arrangement in which workers buy shares of stock in the company that employs them.

not-for-profit corporation organization whose goals do not include pursuing a profit.

 Describe public and collective ownership of business.

Public ownership occurs when a unit or agency of government owns and operates an organization. Collective ownership establishes an organization referred to as a cooperative, whose owners join forces to operate all or part of the functions in their firm or industry.

7 **Discuss organizing a corporation.**

There are three types of corporations: domestic, foreign, and alien. Stockholders, or shareholders, own a corporation. In return for their financial investments, they receive shares of stock in the company. Stockholders elect a board of directors, which sets overall policy. The board hires the chief executive officer (CEO), who then hires managers.

stockholder an owner of a corporation due to his or her purchase of stock in the corporation.

preferred stock shares that give owners limited voting rights, and the right to receive dividends or assets before owners of common stock.

common stock shares that give owners voting rights but only residual claims to the firm's assets and income distributions.

board of directors governing body of a corporation.

8 **Explain what happens when businesses join forces.**

In a merger, two or more firms combine to form one company. A vertical merger combines firms operating at different levels in the production and marketing process. A horizontal merger joins firms in the same industry. A conglomerate merger combines unrelated firms. An acquisition occurs when one firm purchases another. A joint venture is a partnership between companies formed for a specific undertaking.

merger agreement in which two or more firms combine to form one company.

acquisition agreement in which one firm purchases another.

vertical merger agreement that combines firms operating at different levels in the production and marketing process.

horizontal merger agreement that joins firms in the same industry for the purpose of diversification, increasing customer bases, cutting costs, or expanding product lines.

conglomerate merger agreement that combines unrelated firms, usually with the goal of diversification, spurring sales growth, or spending a cash surplus in order to avoid a takeover attempt.

joint venture partnership between companies formed for a specific undertaking.

>>> Quick Review >>

LO1

1 How does the Small Business Administration define a small business?

2 In what industries do small businesses play a significant role?

LO2

1 In what three key ways do small businesses contribute to the economy?

2 How are new industries formed?

LO3

1 What percentage of small businesses remain in operation after five years? Ten years?

2 Name the three main causes of small-business failure.

LO4

1 In what ways does the SBA help small businesses?

2 Why do small businesses represent a good opportunity for women and minorities?

LO5

1 What are some key differences between sole proprietorships and partnerships?

2 What is a corporation?

3 What is the main distinction of a not-for-profit organization?

LO6

1 What is public ownership?

2 What is collective ownership? Where are collectives typically found, and what benefits do they provide small businesses?

LO7

1 Name the three types of corporations.

2 Describe the five main levels of corporate management and ownership.

LO8

1 Distinguish between a merger and an acquisition.

2 What are the different kinds of mergers?

3 What is a joint venture?

chapter six

Starting Your Own Business

Learning Objectives

1 **Define** what is an *entrepreneur*.

2 **Describe** the environment for entrepreneurs.

3 **Outline** the process of starting a new venture.

4 **Summarize** different ways to finance new ventures.

5 **Explain** why people choose entrepreneurship.

6 **Identify** the different categories of entrepreneurs.

7 **Describe** the franchising alternative.

8 **Explain** how organizations promote intrapreneurship.

The Marketing Zen Group: From $1,500 to Millions in Five Years

"Young entrepreneurs have to create their own opportunities. This economy needs fresh blood and bold new ideas." That forthright attitude is what took The Marketing Zen Group, Shama Kabani's entrepreneurial Web marketing firm, from a one-person startup to a 30-person global firm in two short years.

Kabani, who founded the firm at age 24 with $1,500 of her own money, saw an opportunity while still in college to help firms struggling to get up to speed with online marketing and social media. Their needs and Kabani's interests were a match, so she quickly adapted her original idea, which was to start a general consulting firm, and shifted to building a company that takes over Web marketing services for clients.

For clients like Arthur Murray Dance Studios and k9cuisine.com, The Marketing Zen Group handles everything from setting up a Facebook and Twitter presence to creating interactive Web sites, developing e-mail marketing campaigns, optimizing search engine results, and launching blogs aimed at clients' target markets. Clients have already seen record results from the firm's efforts, in terms of both Web traffic and sales dollars.

Kabani, who has also written a best-selling book about social media marketing, expects her firm to soon reach multimillion-dollar status. She keeps overhead low by using virtual hiring and lets most employees work off-site, for example. Kabani says hiring is different in an entrepreneurial firm. A large corporation can accommodate many different types of employees, but "in a smaller business, passion is a must in every position. Hire people who are driven to do well and see your business succeed." Kabani herself brings the same degree of passion to her work.[1]

Overview > > >

This chapter focuses on pathways for entering the world of entrepreneurship, describing the activities, the different kinds of enterprises, and the reason a growing number of people choose to be entrepreneurs. It discusses the business environment in which business owners work, characteristics that help them succeed, and the ways they start and fund new ventures. The chapter includes a discussion on franchising as a way to start a business using established methods and ends by identifying methods by which large companies try to incorporate the entrepreneurial spirit in their operations.

84

1 What Is an Entrepreneur?

An **entrepreneur** is a person who seeks a profitable opportunity and takes the necessary risks to set up and operate a business. The history of business is full of examples of entrepreneurs who through their innovation and hard work created very successful companies. From John Deere (Deere and Company) to Thomas Edison (General Electric), Henry Ford (Ford Motor Company), Sam Walton (Walmart), and Steve Jobs (Apple), these entrepreneurs' visions for the future were the driving force behind revolutions in farming, manufacturing, retailing, and computer technology. For example, Sam Walton wasn't satisfied owning just one successful Ben Franklin franchise, so he purchased others. And when that wasn't enough, he started his own stores and grew them. Entrepreneurs like Walton combine

entrepreneur a person who seeks a profitable opportunity and takes the necessary risks to set up and operate a business.

their ideas and drive with money, employees, and other resources to create a business that fills a market need. That entrepreneurial role can make something significant out of a small beginning. Walmart, the company that Sam Walton started, recently reported net sales in excess of $411 billion.[2]

∨ Logos of familiar companies started by entrepreneurs.

John Deere: ©Clare Gainey/Alamy; GE: ©imagebroker/Alamy; Walmart: ©Newsies Media/Alamy; Ford: Philip Lange/Shutterstock; Apple: ©TP/Alamy

Entrepreneurs differ from many small-business owners. Although many small-business owners possess the same drive, creative energy, and desire to succeed, what makes entrepreneurs different is that one of their major goals is expansion and growth. By contrast, small-business owners without a strong entrepreneurial spirit may prefer to keep their businesses small. For them, maintaining a small, profitable enterprise may be more important than growth.

Entrepreneurs also differ from managers. Managers are employees of a firm who direct the efforts of others to achieve the organization's goals. Entrepreneurs may also perform a managerial role, but their overriding responsibility is to use the resources of their organizations to accomplish their goals. Those resources may include:

- employees
- money
- equipment
- facilities

Studies have identified certain personality traits and behaviors common to entrepreneurs that differ from those required for managerial success. One of these traits is the willingness to assume the risks involved in starting a new venture. Others want a challenge or a different quality of life. And still others want to pursue their vision. Regardless of their motivation, entrepreneurs are a breed apart from traditional business managers, for they are the ones whose drive, energy, and creativity create new jobs, new businesses, and even whole new industries. The characteristics of successful entrepreneurs are examined in detail later in this chapter.

> >> **Quick Review**

1 What is an entrepreneur?

2 How are entrepreneurs different from some small-business owners?

> Terry Gou combined technical excellence with low-cost labor to create one of the world's largest electronics manufacturers, Foxconn Technology.

©PHOTO-DEF/Alamy

② The Environment for Entrepreneurs

When considering a new venture, entrepreneurs are wise to consider broader socioeconomic trends as well as those connected with their particular business. Several ongoing trends that support and expand the opportunities for entrepreneurs are globalization, education, and information technology. Each of these factors is discussed in the following sections.

GLOBALIZATION

The next time you look into your closet, reach for your smart phone, or bend down to tie your shoes, you are likely experiencing one of the results of globalization: low-cost, high-quality products produced in developing nations. These products and a host of others are often created by companies founded by entrepreneurs. "With $7,500 and guided by a belief that electronics products would be an integral part of everyday life in every office and in every home, Terry Gou founded Hon Hai Precision Industry Company Ltd, the anchor company of Foxconn Technology Group, in 1974."[3] Foxconn is just one example of the increasing globalization of manufacturing. Gou was able to take advantage of this trend, combining technical excellence with low-cost labor to create one of the world's largest electronics manufacturers. Foxconn's customer list includes many well-known consumer brands, including Apple.[4]

EDUCATION

You don't have to major in business to become an entrepreneur, but students who do major in entrepreneurship or take entrepreneurship courses are three times more likely to start their own business or help someone else start one.[5] The past two decades have brought tremendous growth in the number of educational opportunities for would-be entrepreneurs. Today, more than 100 U.S. universities offer full-fledged majors in entrepreneurship, dozens of

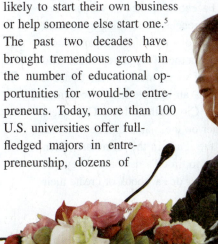

others offer an emphasis in entrepreneurship, and hundreds more offer one or two courses in how to start a business. In fact, you don't have to wait for graduation to develop your first start-up. FedEx, Facebook, Napster, and Google were all conceived by college students. And who would have thought that student housing was the best place to start a company? Michael Dell did exactly that, turning his University of Texas dorm room into the first company headquarters for Dell Computer.[6] Learning about business is important for entrepreneurs, but the opportunity to put your ideas into practice is—as they say in the MasterCard commercials—"priceless."

INFORMATION TECHNOLOGY

The explosion in information technology (IT) has provided one of the biggest boosts for entrepreneurs. As computer and communications technologies have merged and dropped dramatically in cost, entrepreneurs have gained tools that help them compete with large companies. IT helps entrepreneurs

FedEx, Facebook, Napster, and Google were all conceived by college students.

- work quickly and efficiently
- provide immediate and attentive customer service
- increase sales
- project professional images

In fact, technology has leveled the playing field to the point that, with the use of smart phones and other wireless devices, a dorm room innovator can compete with a much larger firm.

Social networking has further transformed the business environment for entrepreneurs. Mark Zuckerberg's entrepreneurial venture Facebook opened up vast new opportunities for other entrepreneurs. According to a recent study, more than 90 percent of successful companies now use at least one social media tool. One entrepreneur who embraces the full impact of social media on his business is Adam Kidron, who runs an upscale health-conscious burger joint in New York City, called 4food. Customers "design" their own burger on their smart phone or home computer or on one of the iPads in the restaurant. Then they save the information to 4food's database. They can post their creation on Twitter or Facebook or create their own YouTube commercial.[7]

3 The Process of Starting a New Venture

The examples of entrepreneurs presented so far have introduced many different types of businesses. This section discusses the process of choosing an idea for a new venture and transforming the idea into a working business.

SELECTING A BUSINESS IDEA

In choosing an idea for your business, the two most important considerations are (1) finding something you are passionate about and (2) determining whether your idea can satisfy a need in the marketplace. People willingly work hard doing something they love, and the experience will bring personal fulfillment. Success also depends on customers, so would-be entrepreneurs must also be sure that the idea they choose has interest in the marketplace. The most successful entrepreneurs tend to operate in industries in which a great deal of change is taking place and in which customers have difficulty pinpointing their precise needs. These industries allow entrepreneurs to capitalize on their strengths (such as creativity, hard work, and vision) despite market uncertainty.

Nevertheless, examples of outstanding entrepreneurial success occur in every industry. Whether you want to build a business

▾ Entrepreneurs are more likely to succeed by asking the right questions from the beginning.

alphaspirit/Shutterstock

based on your grandmother's cookie recipes or know that you have a better idea for tax-preparation software, you are more likely to succeed if you ask yourself the right questions from the beginning.

Consider the following guidelines as you think about your business ideas:

- List your interests and abilities. Include your values and beliefs, your goals and dreams, things you like and dislike doing, and your job experiences.

- Make another list of the types of businesses that match your interests and abilities.

- Read newspapers and business and consumer magazines to learn about demographic and economic trends that identify future needs for products that no one yet offers.

- Carefully evaluate existing goods and services, looking for ways you can improve them.

- Decide on a business that matches what you want and offers profit potential.

- Conduct marketing research to determine whether your business idea will attract enough customers to earn a profit.

- Learn as much as you can about your industry, your goods or service, and your competitors.

- Read surveys that project growth in various industries.

Turning a good idea into a good business, Turning Technologies developed the audience-response wireless keypad systems used on TV game shows to register opinions or answer questions. Beyond TV game shows, teachers from kindergarten through college also use Turning's audience-response technology. Instructors can ask questions in class using other programs; have students key in answers—anonymously or not—using their remotes; and instantly collate the responses to see how many students answered correctly. Says a school official about applications of the Turning program, "You're really only limited by your creativity."[8]

Planning is an integral part of managing in contemporary business.

> Ever wondered who developed the audience-response wireless keypad systems used on TV game shows?

Courtesy of Turning Technologies

Government agencies and nonprofit organizations use Turning Technologies' systems for their training programs. Turning has already been called the fastest-growing privately held software company in the United States. The firm boasts more than 6,500 clients, and more than a million people use its audience-response products.

CREATING A BUSINESS PLAN

Large or small, every business needs a plan in order to succeed. While there are tales of firms launched from an idea scribbled on a napkin at a restaurant or sketched out on graph paper on a college campus, the idea must be backed by a solid plan in order to become reality. A **business plan** is a written document that provides an orderly statement of a company's goals, the methods by which it intends to achieve these goals, and the standards by which it will measure its achievements. The business plan is often the document that secures financing for a firm and creates a framework for the organization.

In the past, many entrepreneurs launched their ventures without creating formal business plans. Although planning is an integral part of managing in contemporary business, what often defines entrepreneurs is the ability to seize opportunities as they arise and change course as necessary. Flexibility seems to be the key to business start-ups, especially in rapidly changing markets. However, due to the inherent risks of starting a business, it has become apparent that at least some planning is not only advisable but necessary, particularly if an entrepreneur is seeking funds from outside sources. Business plans give the organization a sense of purpose. They identify the firm's mission and goals. They create measurable standards and outline a strategy for reaching company objectives.

> **business plan** a written document that provides an orderly statement of a company's objectives, methods, and standards.

THE BUSINESS PLAN

A typical business plan includes the following sections:

- An *executive summary* that briefly answers the who, what, where, when, why, and how questions for the firm.

- *The company's mission and the vision.* For an example of a firm's mission statement, visit a business's Web site.

- *An outline of what makes the company unique.* Why start a business that's just like hundreds of others? An effective business plan describes what distinguishes the firm and its products from the rest of the pack. TOMS Shoes illustrates a unique business model with its "one-for-one" donation program.

- *Customers.* A business plan identifies the company's prospective customers and how it will serve their needs.

- *Competition.* A business plan addresses the firm's existing and potential competitors as legitimate entities, with a strategy for creating superior or unique offerings. Studying the competition can provide valuable information about what works and what doesn't in the marketplace.
- *Financial evaluation of the industry and market conditions.* This knowledge helps develop a credible financial forecast and budget.
- *Assessment of the risks.* Every business undertaking involves risks. A solid business plan acknowledges these and outlines a strategy for dealing with them.
- *Résumés of principals*—especially in plans written to obtain financing.

Whether a firm's intention is to revolutionize an entire industry on a global scale or improve the lives of children by providing them with shoes, the business plan is a major factor in its success.

>>> Quick Review

1. What are the two most important considerations in choosing an idea for a new business?

2. What information should a business plan include?

4 Financing Your Venture

A key issue in any business plan is financing. Requirements for seed capital, the funds used to launch a company, depend on the nature of the business. Seed capital can range as high as several million—say, for the purchase of a McDonald's franchise in a lucrative area—or as low as $1,000 for Web site design. Many entrepreneurs rely on personal savings or loans from business associates, family members, or even friends for start-up funds. TABLE 6.1 lists the common sources of start-up capital.

> **seed capital** initial funding used to launch a company.

SELF-FINANCING

Financing a venture using your own funds has many advantages over other methods. Since the funds belong to you as the entrepreneur, they can be used without restrictions or conditions. There also is no need to repay the funds, nor must you give up ownership of the venture in exchange for funding. At the very earliest stages of a new venture, entrepreneurs should use their own funds to advance their ideas and business processes. Not only does it help validate the entrepreneur's ideas, but it demonstrates commitment to the project and shows prospective investors that the entrepreneur has "skin in the game." Spending their own money also forces entrepreneurs to be more creative in the use of the funds.

TABLE 6.1 Where does funding come from for entrepreneurial start-ups?

Source	Percentage of Entrepreneurs*
Self-financing	82%
Loans from family, friends, or business associates	22%
Bank loans	18%
Lines of credit	18%
Venture capital	8%
SBA or other government funds	4%

*Percentages exceed 100 because entrepreneurs often use multiple sources to finance start-ups.

SOURCE: "Entrepreneurial America: A Comprehensive Look at Today's Fastest-Growing Private Companies," *Inc.*, *The Handbook of the American Entrepreneur*, http://www.inc.com, February 8, 2012.

However, at some point the cash demands of a growing business may exceed an entrepreneur's resources, and he or she will have to seek out additional sources of funds. **Other People's Money (OPM)** is the general term for the funds business people raise from others. By using OPM, entrepreneurs can leverage their own investment, allowing their businesses to grow faster while sharing financial risks with others. Outside funds can be raised in a number of ways including traditional debt financing, equity financing, and more recently crowd funding. The following sections detail each of these methods.

> **OPM** money an entrepreneur raises from others to help start or expand a business.

DEBT FINANCING

When entrepreneurs use **debt financing**, they borrow money that they must repay. Loans from banks, finance companies, credit-card companies, and family or friends are all sources of debt financing. Although some entrepreneurs charge business expenses to personal credit cards because they are relatively easy to obtain, high interest rates make this source of funding expensive.

> **debt financing** borrowed funds that entrepreneurs must repay.

Many banks turn down requests for loans to fund start-ups, fearful of the high risk such ventures entail. This has been particularly true over the last several years. Only a small percentage of startups raise seed capital through bank loans, although some new firms can get Small Business Administration (SBA)–backed loans, as discussed in Chapter 5. Applying for a bank loan requires careful preparation. Bank loan officers want to see a business plan and will evaluate the entrepreneur's credit history. Because a start-up has not yet established a business credit history, banks often base lending decisions on evaluations of entrepreneurs' personal credit histories. Banks are more willing to make loans to entrepreneurs who have been in business for a while, show a profit on rising revenues, and need funds to finance expansion. Some entrepreneurs find that local community banks are more interested in business than are major national banks.

EQUITY FINANCING

To secure equity financing, entrepreneurs exchange a share of ownership in their company for money supplied by one or more investors. Entrepreneurs invest their own money along with funds supplied by other people and firms that become co-owners of the start-ups. An entrepreneur does not have to repay equity funds. Instead, investors share in the success of the business. Sources of equity financing include family and friends, business partners, venture capital firms, and private investors.

A venture capitalist is a business organization or a group of private individuals that invests in early-stage, high-potential, and growth companies. Venture capitalists often back companies in high-technology industries such as biotechnology. FIGURE 6.1 details venture capital investment by sector during a recent period. In exchange for taking a risk with their own funds, these investors expect high rates of return, along with a stake in the company. Typical terms for accepting venture capital include agreement on how much the company is worth, how much stock both the investors and the founders will retain, control of the company's board, payment of dividends, and the period of time during which the founders are prohibited from seeking further investors. When investing, venture capitalists look for a combination of extremely rare qualities, such as innovative technology, potential for rapid growth, a well-developed business model, and an impressive management team.

equity financing funds invested in new ventures in exchange for part ownership.

venture capitalist a business organization or group of individuals that invests in early-stage, high-potential, and growth companies.

An angel investor, a wealthy individual who invests money directly in new ventures in exchange for equity, represents another source of investment capital for start-up firms. In contrast to venture capitalists, angels focus primarily on new ventures and, because most entrepreneurs have trouble finding wealthy private investors, angel networks are formed to match business angels with start-ups in need of capital. One such network of angel investors is Keiretsu Forum, an association with worldwide affiliates.[9]

NEW FINANCING METHODS

In addition to more traditional funding sources, a number of interesting new ways exist to raise funds for entrepreneurial ventures. The Internet has made these methods possible by crowd funding, effectively linking entrepreneurs directly with their supporters.

A growing list of Web-based businesses has been established specifically to facilitate these exchanges, which include direct donations, patronage, and advanced orders.[10] For many years, philanthropic groups have raised money for their causes by soliciting online donations. Social entrepreneurs may use this approach to help raise money for victims of natural disasters. Alternatively, a musical group or other artist may use a Web-based appeal to raise money to pursue their careers. This approach is a replay of the patronage model from centuries ago, when wealthy individuals would pay an artist to create

angel investor a wealthy individual who invests money directly in new ventures in exchange for equity.

crowd funding a source of financial support involving groups of individuals, often connected through the Internet, that pool small sums of money to support new businesses as well as philanthropic causes and artistic endeavors.

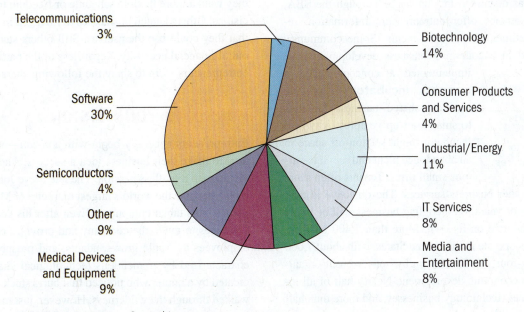

FIGURE 6.1 Venture Capital Investments

SOURCE: Data adapted from PricewaterhouseCoopers/National Venture Capital Association Money Tree™ Report, Data: Thomson Reuters, http://www.nvca.org, accessed March 5, 2013.

< Britta Riley expanded her company, Windowfarms, using Kickstarter.

Anthony Collins Photography

art for them. Much of the great art and music of the Renaissance was produced this way. Entrepreneurs can also use crowd-funding sites to obtain pre-orders for their products. In this approach, an individual or group will make an appeal for funds to start or expand their business in exchange for their product. For example, entrepreneur Britta Riley used Kickstarter to raise $257,307 from 1,577 backers to expand her hydroponic systems business, called Windowfarms.[11]

GOVERNMENT SUPPORT FOR NEW VENTURES

Federal, state, and local governments support new ventures in a number of ways, as discussed in Chapter 5. Through the SBA, state and local agencies offer entrepreneurs information, resources, and sometimes access to financing. Some community agencies interested in encouraging business development have implemented a concept called a **business incubator** to provide low-cost shared business facilities to small start-up ventures. A typical incubator might section-off space in an abandoned plant and rent it to various small firms. Tenants often share clerical staff and other business services. The objective is that, after a few months or years, the fledgling business will be ready to move out and operate on its own. More than 1,400 business incubator programs operate in the United States, with about 7,000 worldwide. Ninety-four percent are run by not-for-profit organizations focused on economic development. Nearly half of all incubators focus on new technology businesses, and more than half operate in urban areas.[12]

Another way to encourage entrepreneurship is through *enterprise zones,* specific geographic areas designated for

business incubator
a local program designed to provide low-cost shared business facilities to small start-up ventures.

economic revitalization. Enterprise zones encourage investment, often in distressed areas, by offering tax advantages and incentives to businesses locating within the boundaries of the zone. The state of Florida, for example, has 56 enterprise zones and allows a business located within urban zones to take tax credits for 20 or 30 percent of wages paid to new employees who reside within the urban enterprise zone. Colorado has 16 zones, and Ohio has over 360 active zones.

The government may also support new ventures through direct procurement of goods and services. The Commerce Business Daily is a U.S. government publication that lists opportunities for entrepreneurs to obtain government contracts. Many government agencies such as NASA, the Department of Defense (DOD), and the Department of Energy (DOE) have active research programs and support entrepreneurs and business organizations working in their areas of responsibility.[13]

>>> Quick Review

1 List the ways of financing an entrepreneurial venture.

2 What is the difference between debt financing and equity financing?

3 How could an entrepreneur use the Internet to raise funds for a new venture?

5 Reasons to Choose Entrepreneurship

People choose to become entrepreneurs for many reasons. Some are motivated by dissatisfaction with the traditional work world—they want a more flexible schedule or freedom to make all the decisions. Others launch businesses to fill a gap in goods or services that they could use themselves. Still others start their own firms out of financial necessity. Regardless of the particular motivation, entrepreneurs seem to share the following characteristics.

PURSUING YOUR VISION

Entrepreneurs generally begin with a *vision*—an overall idea for how to make their business idea a success. And they pursue this vision with relentless passion. The late Steve Jobs's vision helped Apple become the world's largest marketer of MP3 players, smart phones, and tablet computers. Even after his death, Jobs's vision continues to guide the company and provides clear direction for employees as Apple grows, adapts, and prospers in an industry characterized by tremendous technological change. Velcro was created by a hunter who noticed that burrs stuck to his socks as he walked through the wilderness. However, just making a discovery is not enough; entrepreneurs must know how to turn their vision into a profitable business. Although Sir Alexander Fleming discovered penicillin, he was unable to turn his discovery into a cure for bacterial infections. It took others to develop the process to produce usable quantities of the drug.[14]

BEING YOUR OWN BOSS

The freedom to make all the decisions—being your own boss—is one of the biggest lures of entrepreneurship. After 20 years of working in the fitness industry, Peter Taunton wanted out of the big-box health club scene, but he wasn't finished with fitness. He decided to create a different kind of gym, one for average people who prefer to work out without wearing Spandex shorts or being bombarded by loud music and big-screen TVs. Taunton founded Taunton's Snap Fitness—small, neighborhood-oriented fitness clubs based on affordability, convenience, and cleanliness. Now, the nearly 2,000 franchised Snap Fitness clubs are smaller than the average gym but are open 24 hours a day. They feature up-to-date cardio and training equipment, but that's about all. There are no child-care facilities or smoothie bars, no pools or racquetball courts. What there is, however, is state-of-the-art equipment and employees who are willing to help each Snap Fitness member achieve their fitness goals.[15]

ACHIEVING FINANCIAL SUCCESS

Entrepreneurs are wealth creators. Many start their ventures with the specific goal of becoming rich—or at least financially successful. Often they believe they have an idea for a superior product and they want to be the first to bring it to market, reaping the financial rewards as a result. Entrepreneurs believe they won't achieve their greatest success by working for someone else, and they're generally right. Of course, the downside is that, when they fail, they don't have the cushion of employment.

John Vechey, with Jason Kapalka and Brian Fiete, founded PopCap and developed such popular games as Bejeweled and Plants vs. Zombies on the premise that online games should be simple and fun for everyone. As Vechey says, "PopCap Games began with just a couple of college guys who didn't know how to run a business." However, it turns out that they did know how to run a business after all. In 2011, Electronic Arts bought PopCap in a deal worth $750 million.[16]

> Velcro was created by a hunter who noticed that burrs stuck to his socks as he walked through the wilderness.

6 Categories of Entrepreneurs

Entrepreneurs apply their talents in different situations. These differences can be classified into distinct categories:

- classic entrepreneurs
- serial entrepreneurs
- social entrepreneurs

A **classic entrepreneur** identifies business opportunities and allocates available resources to tap those markets. Dana Hood is a classic entrepreneur. She recognized that dog owners want special attention for their pets when they leave those animals in the care of others. She also knew that pet owners spent $3.4 billion for boarding and daycare centers during a recent year. So, when she founded For the Love of Dogs, a canine daycare center, she made certain that her services stood out from the average kennel. Hood's firm offers customized services such as grooming and anesthesia-free teeth-cleaning, a treadmill, swimming pools, and water misters to

classic entrepreneur
a person who identifies a business opportunity and allocates available resources to tap that market.

< Have you ever played Bejeweled or Plants vs. Zombies? John Vechey developed those games at PopCap.

John Keatley/Redux

>>> Quick Review

1 Why do people choose to become entrepreneurs?

2 What is meant by an entrepreneur's vision?

cool off customers' pets during hot weather. In addition, pet owners can purchase high-end organic foods and treats, beds, toys, and other retail goods.[17]

While a classic entrepreneur starts a new company by identifying a business opportunity and allocating resources to tap a new market, a **serial entrepreneur** starts one business, runs it, and then starts and runs additional businesses in succession. Elon Musk cofounded the electronic payment firm PayPal and the spacecraft and launch vehicle company SpaceX. He was also chairman and chief executive officer and primary investor in the electric car manufacturer Tesla Motors.[18] Successful serial entrepreneurs achieve rock star status. For the movie *Iron Man,* actor Robert Downey Jr. patterned his portrayal of the fictional character Tony Stark after the real-life accomplishments of Elon Musk.[19]

serial entrepreneur person who starts one business, runs it, and then starts and runs additional businesses in succession.

Some entrepreneurs focus on solving society's challenges through their businesses. A **social entrepreneur** recognizes a societal problem and uses business principles to develop innovative solutions. Social entrepreneurs are pioneers of innovations that benefit humanity. Samuel Kaymen's Stonyfield Farm is a hugely successful company and a model for social entrepreneurs. In addition to producing a healthy organic yogurt, the company established a "Profits for the Planet" program that commits 10 percent of its annual profits to people and organizations working to restore and protect the environment. Stonyfield is also known for using its yogurt lids—millions of them each week—to promote causes, organizations, and environmental initiatives.[20]

social entrepreneur a person who recognizes societal problems and uses business principles to develop innovative solutions.

CHARACTERISTICS OF SUCCESSFUL ENTREPRENEURS

People who start businesses are pioneers in their own right. They aren't satisfied with the status quo and want to achieve certain goals on their own terms. They also tend to possess specific personality traits. Researchers who study successful entrepreneurs report that they are more likely to be curious, passionate, self-motivated, honest, courageous, and flexible. The eight traits summarized in **FIGURE 6.2** are especially important for people who want to succeed as entrepreneurs.

< Have you heard of PayPal, SpaceX, and Tesla Motors? Elon Musk had a major role in each of those companies.

©Kristoffer Tripplaar /Alamy

Entrepreneurial Personality

Vision

High Energy Level

Need to Achieve

Self-Confidence and Optimism

Tolerance for Failure

Creativity

Tolerance for Ambiguity

Internal Locus of Control

FIGURE 6.2 Characteristics of Entrepreneurs

Entrepreneurs work hard because they want to excel. Their strong competitive drive helps them enjoy the challenge of reaching difficult goals and promotes dedication to personal success. A poll conducted by About.com showed Oprah Winfrey as the most admired entrepreneur among adults. The first African American woman billionaire, Winfrey built an empire stretching from television to magazines to radio. Her own words best illustrate her strong drive: "I don't think of myself as a poor, deprived ghetto girl who made good. I think of myself as somebody who from an early age knew I was responsible for myself, and had to make good."[21]

Entrepreneurs believe in their ability to succeed, and they instill their optimism in others. Often their optimism resembles fearlessness in the face of difficult odds. They see opportunities where others see danger lurking. Entrepreneurs often succeed by sheer will and the ability to try and try again when others would give up. They also view setbacks and failures as learning experiences and are not easily discouraged or disappointed when things don't go as planned. When things go well, it's easy to take personal credit. But when poor business decisions result in failure, it's a bit more difficult. Truly successful entrepreneurs are willing to take responsibility for their mistakes.

Entrepreneurs work long and hard to realize their visions. Many entrepreneurs work full-time at their regular day jobs and spend weeknights and weekends launching their start-ups. Entrepreneurs often work alone or with a very small staff, which means that they often wear most—if not all—of the hats required to get the business going. Most entrepreneurs spend at least 70 hours a week on their new business.[22] Thus they need a high level of energy in order to succeed.

If this sounds like you, then you may have what it takes to be an entrepreneur.

>>> **Quick Review**

1 Identify the different types of entrepreneurs.

2 What are some characteristics of successful entrepreneurs?

7 The Franchising Alternative

While we might all like to think we can come up with the next "new big thing," the reality is that many entrepreneurs are not able to transform their business ideas into successful enterprises.[23] As we will see in Chapter 12, business people face significant challenges in turning new ideas into successful products. And not only must entrepreneurs worry about developing their products; they also have to work diligently to

- establish their business operations
- hire employees
- obtain financing
- contract with suppliers
- set up product distribution, marketing, and promotion

Failure in any one of these areas can lead to failure of the entire venture.

To reduce these risks, some entrepreneurs may choose to follow business models that have been developed and successfully implemented by others. Franchising is just such an approach, where an entrepreneur acquires a license to use a company's name, suppliers, know-how, and advertising in their own business. For entrepreneurs, franchises often combine the best of both worlds, offering them the ability to develop their own business while at the same time enjoying the advantages of being part of a larger organization. **Franchising**

franchising contractual business arrangement between a manufacturer or other supplier and a dealer, such as a restaurant operator or retailer.

is a contractual business arrangement between a manufacturer or another supplier and a dealer such as a restaurant operator or a retailer. The contract specifies the methods by which the dealer markets the product of the supplier. Franchises can involve both goods and services, such as food staff and servers. The top ten franchises from *Entrepreneur*'s Franchise 500 are shown in TABLE 6.2. The ranking is based on a set of criteria developed by *Entrepreneur,* and the annual list is in its 34th year.

THE FRANCHISING SECTOR

Franchised businesses are a huge part of the U.S. economy, accounting for over 9 million jobs in the U.S. workforce. The International Franchise Association reported that franchising is responsible for over 800,000 businesses at a gross value of over $8 billion. Business sectors currently experiencing the most growth are quick-service restaurants, retail food, and personal and business services.[24]

Franchising overseas is also a growing trend for businesses whose goal is to expand into foreign markets. It seems that, anywhere you go in the world, you can get a McDonald's burger. But other international franchises are also common. Baskin-Robbins—owned by Dunkin' Brands—has more than 6,700 stores worldwide in such countries as Australia, Canada, China, Japan, Malaysia, and Russia.[25]

TABLE 6.2 Can you name the Top Ten Franchises?

1	Hampton Hotels (hotel chain)
2	SUBWAY (submarine sandwiches & salads)
3	Jiffy Lube Int'l. Inc. (oil change service)
4	7-Eleven Inc. (convenience store)
5	Supercuts (hair salon)
6	Anytime Fitness (fitness center)
7	Servpro (insurance/disaster cleaning & restoration)
8	Denny's Inc. (full-service family restaurant)
9	McDonald's (fast food restaurant)
10	Pizza Hut Inc. (fast food restaurant)

SOURCE: "Franchises: America's Top Franchises from *Entrepreneur*'s Franchise 500," *Entrepreneur,* http://www.entrepreneur.com, accessed March 19, 2013.

FRANCHISING AGREEMENTS

The two principals in a franchising agreement are the franchisee and the franchisor. The individual or business firm purchasing the franchise is called the **franchisee**. This business owner agrees to sell the goods or services of the franchisor under certain terms. The **franchisor** is the firm whose products are sold by the franchisee. For example, McDonald's Corp. is a franchisor. Your local McDonald's restaurant owner is most likely a franchisee.

franchisee individual or business firm purchasing a franchise.

franchisor firm whose products are sold to customers by the franchisee.

Franchise agreements can be complex. They involve an initial purchase fee plus agreed-on start-up costs. Because the franchisee is representing the franchisor's brand, the franchisor usually stipulates the purchase of certain ingredients or equipment, pricing, and marketing efforts. The total start-up cost for a SUBWAY franchise may be as low as $78,600.[26] In contrast, McDonald's is one of the more expensive franchises—total start-up costs can run more than $1 million. For this reason, business people interested in purchasing a more expensive franchise often group together.

BENEFITS AND PROBLEMS OF FRANCHISING

Like any other type of business arrangement, franchising has its benefits and drawbacks. Benefits for the franchisor include opportunities for expansion that might not otherwise be available. A franchised business can move into new geographic locations, including overseas, employing workers with knowledge of local preferences. A good franchisor can manage a much larger and more complex business—with fewer direct employees—than could be handled without the franchise option.

⌄ SUBWAY is one franchise opportunity in the restaurant industry.

Newscast/Associate Press

Franchising can also have its downside—for both franchisors and franchisees. For the franchisor, if its franchisees fail in any way, that failure reflects on the brand as well as the bottom line. The same holds true for the franchisee: A firm that is mismanaged at the top level can spell doom for the people who are actually running the individual units. Of course, in offering franchise opportunities, the franchisor—often the founder of what was once a small business—loses absolute control over every aspect of the business. This uncertainty can make the process of selecting the right franchisees to carry out the company's mission a difficult one.[27]

Because franchises are so closely linked to their brand, franchisors and franchisees must work well together to maintain standards of quality in their goods and services. If customers are unhappy with their experience at one franchise location, they might avoid stopping at another one several miles away, even if the second one is owned and operated by someone else. This is especially true where food is involved. The discovery of tainted meat or produce at one franchise restaurant can negatively affect the entire chain. A potential franchisee would be wise to thoroughly research the financial performance and reputation of the franchisor, using resources such as other franchisees and the Federal Trade Commission.

> > > **Quick Review**

1 What is franchising and how does it work?

2 What are some of the advantages and disadvantages of franchising?

8 Promoting Intrapreneurship

Franchising illustrates one way to integrate entrepreneurs into established businesses. Companies can also try to foster an entrepreneurial spirit in their employees by encouraging **intrapreneurship**, the process of promoting innovation within their organizational structures. Today's fast-changing business climate compels established firms to innovate continually to maintain their competitive advantages. Another form of intrapreneurship is

intrapreneurship
process of promoting innovation within the structure of an existing organization.

> At the 3M Innovation Center, intrapreneurship is encouraged, and researchers can devote a portion of their time at work to pursue their own ideas.

© ZUMA Press, Inc./Alamy

skunkworks
project initiated by an employee who conceives an idea, convinces top management of its potential, and then recruits human and other resources from within the company to the idea into a commercial project.

a **skunkworks**, a project initiated by an employee who conceives an idea, convinces top management of its potential, and then recruits human and other resources from within the company to turn that idea into a commercial project.

Many companies encourage intrapreneurship—some organizations, including Google, have formalized the role of the intrapreneur through official positions such as the "Entrepreneur In Residence" (EIR) or "Chief Innovation Officer."[28] 3M is a firm that has long been known for its innovative products. Ranging from Post-It Notes and Scotch Tape to Nutri Dog Chews and Thinsulate insulation, there are more than 55,000 3M products either on store shelves or embedded in other firms' goods.[29]

Coming up with the ideas for these products, developing them, and testing them before bringing them to market takes time and resources. Former 3M CEO George Buckley believes that the only way to do this is to allocate both time and money in support of intrapraneurship. Despite the recent recession, Buckley maintained $1 billion for research and development. 3M allows its researchers to devote 15 percent of their time to pursue their own ideas. One recent successful product that resulted from this is the first electronic stethoscope with Bluetooth technology. The company also awards annual Genesis Grants, worth up to $100,000, to 3M scientists for research.[30]

> > > **Quick Review**

1 Why would a company support intrapreneurship?

2 What is a skunkworks?

What's Ahead? > > >

In upcoming chapters, we look at other trends that are reshaping the business world of the 21st century. For example, in the next chapters of *Contemporary Business Essentials,* we explore the critical issues of how companies organize, lead, and manage their work processes; manage and motivate their employees; empower their employees through teamwork and enhanced communication; handle labor and workplace disputes; and create and produce world-class goods and services.

Weekly Updates spark classroom debate around current events that apply to your business course topics. http://contemporarybusinessupdates.com

NOTES

1. Company Web site, www.marketingzen.com, accessed March 13, 2013; Claudia Chan, "Meet Shama Kabani," www.claudiachan .com, February 15, 2012; Matt Vilano, "From Grad Student to Social Media Millionaire," Entrepreneur.com, September 5, 2011, www .entrepreneur.com; Shama Kabani, "26 Lessons from a 26 Year Old CEO," Forbes.com, July 25, 2011, www.forbes.com.

2. Company Web site, http://investors .walmartstores.com, accessed March 13, 2013.

3. Company Web site, http://www.foxconn .com/companyintro.html, accessed March 13, 2013.

4. "Terry Gou," Forbes Profile, www.forbes .com, accessed September 9, 2013; Foxconn Technology, "Business Day," *New York Times*, September 24, 2012, http://topics.nytimes.com.

5. Mark Henricks, "Honor Roll," *Entrepreneur*, http://www.entrepreneur.com, accessed March 13, 2013.

6. Company Web site, http://www.dell.com, accessed March 10, 2013.

7. Company Web site, http://www.4food.com, accessed September 9, 2013; Amelia Levin, "4FOOD," Restaurant Development and Design, September 28, 2012, http://www .rddmag.com.

8. Company Web site, http://www .turningtechnologies.com, accessed March 13, 2013.

9. Organization Web site, http://www .keiretsuforum.com, accessed March 13, 2013.

10. Devin Thorpe, "Eight Crowdfunding Sites for Social Entrepreneurs," *Forbes*, September 10, 2012, http://www.forbes.com.

11. Organization Web site, "View Profile: Britta Riley, Windowfarms," http:// socialcapitalmarkets.net, accessed March 13, 2013; company Web site, http://www .windowfarms.com, accessed March 13, 2013.

12. Association Web site, http://www.nbia.org, accessed March 13, 2013.

13. Organization Web site, http://www.nasa.gov, accessed March 13, 2013.

14. Science Daily Web site, "Ernest H. Volwiler Information," http://inventors.sciencedaily.com, accessed March 12, 2013.

15. Company Web site, "Peter Taunton video," http://www.snapfitness.com, accessed March 10, 2013.

16. Liz Welch, "John Vechey: Don't Waste Time with Mission Statements," *Inc.* magazine, http://www.inc.com, March 6, 2013.

17. Company website, http://www.fortheloveofdog .com, accessed April 9, 2013.

18. Personal Web site, http://elonmusk.com, accessed March 10, 2013.

19. Personal Web site, http://elonmusk.com, accessed March 10, 2013; Damon Poeter, "Is Elon Musk the Real-Life Tony Stark? Not So Fast," *PC Magazine*, May 23, 2012, http://www .pcmag.com.

20. Meg Cadoux Hirshberg, "The Full Story," http://www.stonyfield.com, accessed March 13, 2013.

21. Jone Johnson Lewis, "Oprah Winfrey Quotes," About Women's History, http:// womenshistory.about.com, accessed April 10, 2013.

22. Hannah Seligson, "When the Work-Life Scales Are Unequal," *New York Times*, September 1, 2012, http://www.nytimes.com.

23. Deborah Gage, "The Venture Capital Secret: 3 Out of 4 Start-Ups Fail," *The Wall Street Journal Online*, September 19, 2012, http://online.wsj.com.

24. Association Web site, http://www.franchise .org, accessed March 13, 2013.

25. Company Web site, http://www. baskinrobbins.com, accessed March 13, 2013.

26. Company Web site, http://www.subway .com, accessed March 13, 2013.

27. Edward N. Levitt, "What's So Great about Franchising?" *FranchiseKnowHow*, http:// www.franchiseknowhow.com, accessed March 13, 2013.

28. John Webb, "How Dreamworks, LinkedIn and Google Build Intrapreneurial Cultures," January 23, 2013, http://www .innovationexcellence.com.

29. Company Web site, http://www.3m.com, accessed March 13, 2013.

30. Company Web site, http://www.3m.com, accessed March 13, 2013.

Summary of Learning Objectives

 Define what is an *entrepreneur*.

Unlike many small-business owners, entrepreneurs typically own and run their businesses with the goal of building significant firms that create wealth and add jobs. Entrepreneurs are visionaries. They identify opportunities and take the initiative to gather the resources they need to start their businesses quickly. Both managers and entrepreneurs use the resources of their companies to achieve the goals of those organizations.

entrepreneur   a person who seeks a profitable opportunity and takes the necessary risks to set up and operate a business.

 Describe the environment for entrepreneurs.

A favorable public perception, availability of financing, the falling cost and widespread availability of information technology, globalization, entrepreneurship education, and changing demographic and economic trends all contribute to a fertile environment for people to start new ventures.

 Outline the process of starting a new venture.

Entrepreneurs must select an idea for their business, develop a business plan, obtain financing, and organize the resources they need to operate their start-ups.

business plan   a written document that provides an orderly statement of a company's objectives, methods, and standards.

 Summarize different ways to finance new ventures.

Entrepreneurs need seed capital to launch a business venture. Sometimes they use their own money to fund a project. They may ask friends or family to pitch in (OPM: "other people's money"). They may obtain a loan from a bank or apply for Small Business Administration (SBA) or other government funding. Most commonly, however, entrepreneurs raise money from venture capitalists.

seed capital   initial funding used to launch a company.

OPM   "other people's money"; money an entrepreneur raises from others to help start or expand a business.

debt financing   borrowed funds that entrepreneurs must repay.

equity financing   funds invested in new ventures in exchange for part ownership.

venture capitalist   a business organization or group of individuals that invests in early-stage, high-potential, and growth companies.

angel investor   a wealthy individual who invests money directly in new ventures in exchange for equity.

crowd funding   a source of financial support involving groups of individuals, often connected through the Internet, that pool small sums of money to support new businesses and philanthropic causes, as well as artistic endeavors.

business incubator   a local program designed to provide low-cost shared business facilities to small start-up ventures.

 Explain why people choose entrepreneurship.

There are many reasons people choose to become entrepreneurs: the desire to be one's own boss, the desire to achieve financial success, the desire for job security, and the desire to improve one's quality of life.

 Identify the different categories of entrepreneurs.

A classic entrepreneur identifies a business opportunity and allocates available resources to tap that market. A serial entrepreneur starts one business, runs it, and then starts and runs additional businesses in succession. A social entrepreneur uses business principles to solve social problems.

classic entrepreneur   a person who identifies a business opportunity and allocates available resources to tap that market.

serial entrepreneur   a person who starts one business, runs it, and then starts and runs additional businesses in succession.

social entrepreneur   a person who recognizes societal problems and uses business principles to develop innovative solutions.

 Describe the franchising alternative.

A franchisor is a large firm that permits a small-business owner (franchisee) to sell its products under its brand name in return for a fee. Benefits to the franchisor include opportunities for expansion and greater profits. Benefits to the franchisee include name recognition, quick start-up, support from the franchisor, and the freedom of small-business ownership.

franchising   contractual business arrangement between a manufacturer or other supplier and a dealer, such as a restaurant operator or retailer.

franchisee   individual or business firm purchasing a franchise.

franchisor   firm whose products are sold to customers by the franchisee.

8 Explain how organizations promote intrapreneurship.

Organizations encourage intrapreneurial activity within the company in a variety of ways, including hiring practices, dedicated programs such as skunkworks, access to resources, and wide latitude to innovate within established firms.

intrapreneurship   process of promoting innovation within the structure of an existing organization.

skunkworks   project initiated by an employee who conceives an idea, convinces top management of its potential, and then recruits human and other resources from within the company to put the idea into a commercial project.

>>> Quick Review >>

LO1

1 What is an entrepreneur?

2 How are entrepreneurs different from most small-business owners?

LO2

1 What socioeconomic trends provide opportunities for entrepreneurs?

2 How has social networking affected the environment for entrepreneurs?

LO3

1 What are the two most important considerations in choosing an idea for a new business?

2 What information should a business plan include?

LO4

1 List the ways of financing an entrepreneurial venture.

2 What is the difference between debt financing and equity financing?

3 How could an entrepreneur use the Internet to raise funds for a new venture?

LO5

1 Why do people choose to become entrepreneurs?

2 What is meant by an entrepreneur's vision?

LO6

1 Identify the different types of entrepreneurs.

2 What are some characteristics of successful entrepreneurs?

LO7

1 What is franchising, and how does it work?

2 What are some of the advantages and disadvantages of franchising?

LO8

1 Why would a company support intrapreneurship?

2 What is a skunkworks?

chapter seven

7

Management, Leadership, and the Internal Organization

Learning Objectives

1 Define *management*.

2 Evaluate managers as leaders.

3 Discuss leading by setting a vision.

4 Describe managers as decision makers.

5 Summarize the importance of planning.

6 Describe the strategic planning process.

7 Discuss organizational structures.

Wegmans Food Markets: Still a Great Place to Work

If a company has spent 15 consecutive years on *Fortune's* list of "100 Best Companies to Work For" and consistently ranks in the top five, credit must go to its top management team for creating a culture and policies that foster a great work environment. If that company is Wegmans Food Markets, a 79-store, family-owned grocery chain based in Gates, NY, CEO Danny Wegman explains it best: "Our employees are the No. 1 reason our customers shop at Wegmans," CEO Danny Wegman said in a release. "I'm convinced there is only one path to great customer service, and that is through employees who feel they are cared about and empowered."

Wegman and his management team can feel pretty good about what they've accomplished. While turnover among the 42,000 employees is already low, the $6.2 billion company constantly adds new employee benefits, like a recently introduced 24-hour health hotline. Employees already enjoy job sharing, compressed workweeks, subsidized gym membership, and free programs to quit smoking. In fact, more than 2,000 workers have enrolled in the smoking-cessation program over the last few years.

Giving back to its employees and surrounding communities is also high on the company's list. Since its founding in 1984, Wegmans' scholarship program has awarded more than $80 million in scholarships to over 25,000 employees. And recently the company gave more than 16 million pounds of food to local food banks. Wegmans is truly a great place to work and one that attracts more than 200,000 people for about 900 job openings a year.[1]

Overview > > >

When asked about their professional objectives, many students say, "I want to be a manager." You may think the role of a manager is basically being the boss. But in today's business world, companies are looking for much more than bosses. They want managers who understand technology, can adapt quickly to change, motivate employees, and realize the importance of satisfying customers. Managers who can master those skills will continue to be in great demand because their commitment strongly affects their firms' performance. And Danny Wegman's management of his family's grocery chain has ensured the prosperity of the firm, still going strong after almost 80 years.

This chapter begins by examining levels of management, the skills that managers need, and the functions that managers perform. The chapter explains the importance of managers being effective leaders. Other sections of the chapter explore the importance of decisions that managers make. The chapter concludes by examining the additional functions of management—organizing, directing, and controlling.

1 What Is Management?

Management is the process of achieving organizational objectives through people and other resources. The manager's job is to combine human and technical resources in the best way possible to achieve the company's goals. Management principles and concepts apply to not-for-profit organizations as well as profit-seeking firms. A city mayor, the president of the Appalachian Mountain Club, and a superintendent of schools all perform the managerial functions described later in this chapter. Management happens at many levels, from that of the manager of a family-owned restaurant to a national sales vice president for a major manufacturer.

management process of achieving organizational objectives through people and other resources.

THE MANAGEMENT HIERARCHY

A firm's management usually has three levels: top, middle, and supervisory. These levels of management form a management hierarchy, as shown in **FIGURE 7.1**. The hierarchy is the traditional structure found in most organizations. Managers at each level perform different activities. This hierarchy is often shown as a

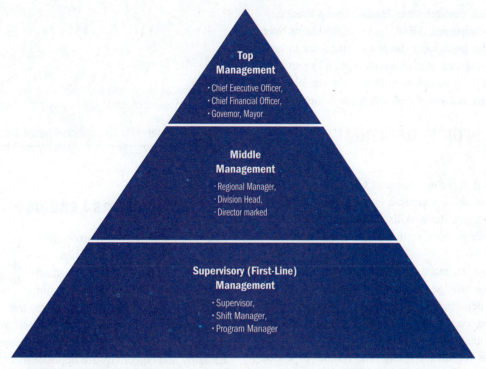

FIGURE 7.1 The Management Pyramid

pyramid to illustrate that, at the top of the pyramid, the company president is supported by many other managers, with the numbers increasing as the job titles go from top to middle to supervisor.

The highest level of management is *top management*. Top managers include such positions as chief executive officer (CEO), chief financial officer (CFO), and executive vice president. Top managers devote most of their time to developing long-range plans for their organizations. They make decisions such as whether to introduce new products, purchase other companies, or enter new geographical markets. Top managers set a direction for their organization and inspire the company's executives and employees to achieve their vision for the company's future.

Middle management, the second tier in the executive hierarchy, includes positions such as general managers, plant managers, division managers, and unit managers. A middle manager's attention focuses on specific operations, products, or customer groups within an organization. They are responsible for developing detailed plans and procedures to implement the firm's strategic plans. If top management decided to broaden the distribution of a product, a sales manager would be responsible for determining the number of sales personnel required. Middle managers are responsible for targeting the products and customers who are the source of the sales and profit growth expected by their CEOs. To achieve these goals, middle managers might budget money for product development, identify new uses for existing products, and improve the ways they train and motivate

salespeople. Because they are more familiar with day-to-day operations than CEOs, middle managers often come up with new ways to increase sales or solve company problems.

Supervisory management, or first-line management, includes positions such as supervisor, section chief, and team leader. These managers are directly responsible for assigning nonmanagerial employees to specific jobs and evaluating their performance. Managers at this first level of the hierarchy work directly with the employees who produce and sell the firm's goods and services. They are responsible for implementing middle managers' plans by motivating workers to accomplish daily, weekly, and monthly goals. A recent

> Kohl's Department Stores ranks in the top tier of the Temkin Group's annual list of top providers of customer service. First-line managers make sure that customer service is a priority for all employees.

kali9/iStockphoto

survey by the marketing research firm Temkin Group rated customer service at U.S. companies. All of the top-ranked firms have first-line managers who implement the firms' strategies to provide superior customer service. Amazon.com, Kohl's Department Stores, and Costco all have in common first-line managers who see that customer service is a top priority among their employees.[2]

SKILLS NEEDED FOR MANAGERIAL SUCCESS

Managers at every level in the management hierarchy must exercise three basic types of skills: technical, human, and conceptual. All managers must acquire these skills in varying proportions, although the importance of each skill changes at different management levels.

Technical skills are the manager's ability to understand and use the techniques, knowledge, and tools and equipment of a specific discipline or department. Technical skills are especially important for first-line managers and become less important at higher levels of the management hierarchy. But most top executives started out as technical experts. The résumé of a vice president for information systems probably lists experience as a computer analyst, and that of a vice president for marketing usually shows a background in sales. Many firms, including Home Depot and Dell, have increased training programs for first-line managers to boost technical skills and worker productivity.

Human skills are interpersonal skills that enable managers to work effectively with and through people. Human skills include the ability to communicate with, motivate, and lead employees to complete assigned activities. Managers need human skills to interact with people both inside and outside the organization. It would be tough for a manager to succeed without such skills, even though they must be adapted to different forms—for instance, mastering and communicating effectively with staff through e-mail, cell phones, videoconferencing, and text messaging, all of which are widely used in today's offices.

Conceptual skills determine a manager's ability to see the organization as a unified whole and to understand how each part of the overall organization interacts with other parts. These skills involve an ability to see the big picture by acquiring, analyzing, and interpreting information. Conceptual skills are especially important for top-level managers, who must develop long-range plans for the future direction of their organization.

> Don Thompson looks to follow Jim Skinner's results during his tenure as CEO at McDonald's.

Yves Logghe/AP images

> > > **Quick Review**

1 What is management?

2 How do the responsibilities of top management, middle management, and supervisory management differ?

3 Name the skills an individual needs for managerial success.

2 Managers as Leaders

Above all else, business executives must demonstrate **leadership**, directing or inspiring people to attain certain goals. Great leaders do not

leadership ability to direct or inspire people to attain certain goals.

all share the same qualities, but three traits are often mentioned: empathy (the ability to imagine yourself in someone else's position), self-awareness, and objectivity. Although it might seem as if empathy and objectivity are opposite traits, they do balance each other. Many leaders share other traits—courage, passion, commitment, innovation, and flexibility, to name a few.

Leadership involves the use of influence or power. This influence may come from one or more sources. One source of power is the leader's position in the company. A national sales manager has the authority to direct the activities of the sales force. Another source of power is a leader's expertise and experience. A first-line supervisor with expert machinist skills will most likely be respected by employees in the machining department.

Some leaders derive power from their personalities. Employees may admire a leader because they recognize an exceptionally kind, fair, humorous, energetic, or enthusiastic person. Admiration, inspiration, and motivation are especially important during difficult economic times or when a leader has to make tough decisions for the company.

When Jim Skinner took over as CEO of McDonald's, the company had just lost two previous CEOs in a very short time, and same-store sales were stagnant. Replacing CEOs who died unexpectedly was a delicate situation, and the company's board looked to Skinner to provide stability. His

102

ability to lead the company to record revenues and sales can be attributed to his confident, no-nonsense approach to management. Known as an operations whiz, he focused on the performance of the 33,000 restaurants worldwide and the company infrastructure that supports them. Skinner's approach to leadership recently led the company to an annual 5 percent growth with revenues of more than $24 billion. Same-store sales have increased every year since he took over the top job. Skinner requires McDonald's executives to train at least two potential successors—one for now and one for the future. This policy came in handy in 2012, when longtime McDonald's USA president Don Thompson took over Skinner's CEO duties.[3]

LEADERSHIP STYLES

The way a person uses power to lead others determines his or her leadership style. Leadership styles range along a continuum with autocratic leadership at one end and free-rein leadership at the other. *Autocratic leadership* is centered on the boss. Autocratic leaders make decisions on their own without consulting employees. They reach decisions, communicate them to subordinates, and expect automatic implementation.

empowerment in an organization, employees' shared authority, responsibility, and decision making with their managers.

Democratic leadership includes subordinates in the decision-making process. This leadership style centers on employees' contributions. Democratic leaders delegate assignments, ask employees for suggestions, and encourage participation. An important outgrowth of democratic leadership in business is **empowerment**, employees' sharing of authority, responsibility, and decision making with their managers.

At the other end of the continuum is *free-rein leadership*. Free-rein leaders believe in minimal supervision and allow subordinates to make most of their own decisions. Free-rein leaders communicate with employees frequently, as the situation warrants. For the first decade of its existence, Google was proud of its free-rein leadership style. Engineers were encouraged to pursue any and all ideas; teams formed or disbanded on their own; employees spent as much or as little time as they wanted to on any given project. But as the firm entered its second decade, it became apparent that not every innovation was worth pursuing—and some valuable ideas were not getting the attention they deserved. Chief Executive Larry Page has spent time trying to bring a renewed sense of urgency and focus to the search company, in what he calls putting, "more wood behind fewer arrows."[4]

WHICH LEADERSHIP STYLE IS BEST?

No single leadership style is best for every firm in every situation. Sometimes leadership styles require change in order for a company to grow, as has been the case for Google. In a crisis, an autocratic leadership style might save the company—and sometimes the lives of customers and employees. This was the case when

US Airways flight 1549 was forced to ditch into the Hudson River after hitting a wayward flock of Canadian geese. Quick, autocratic decisions made by the pilot, Captain Chesley Sullenberger, resulted in the survival of everyone on board the flight. Yet, on the ground US Airways practiced a democratic style of leadership in which managers at many levels were empowered to take actions to help passengers and their families. For example, one executive arrived on the scene with a bag of emergency cash for passengers and credit cards for employees so they could purchase medicines, food, or anything else survivors needed.[5] A company that recognizes which leadership style works best for its employees, customers, and business conditions is most likely to choose the best leaders for its particular needs.

>>> Quick Review

1 Identify and describe leadership styles as they appear along a continuum of employee participation.

2 Explain why no single leadership style is best for every organization.

3 Leading by Setting a Vision for the Firm

All businesses begin with a **vision**, its founder's perception of what the organization wants to be or how it wants the world to be in an idealized way. Typically, a vision is a long-term view of the future. A vision statement is often emotive and inspirational.[6] The best vision statements serve as the target for a firm's actions, helping direct the company toward opportunities and differentiating it from its competitors. In articulating his vision for Apple Computer, founder Steve Jobs is reported to have said "An Apple on every desk."

vision perception of marketplace needs and the ways a firm can satisfy them.

Whether they are the president of a Fortune 500 company or a small business, a key part of a leader's vision for their firm is the **corporate culture**, an organization's system of principles, beliefs, and values. A corporate culture is typically shaped by the leaders who founded and developed the company

corporate culture an organization's system of principles, beliefs, and values.

and by those who succeed them. Although Google grew by leaps and bounds after its launch, the firm still tries to maintain the culture of innovation, creativity, and flexibility that co-founders Larry Page and Sergey Brin promoted from the beginning. Google now has offices around the world, staffed by thousands of workers who speak a multitude of languages. "We are aggressively inclusive in our hiring, and we favor ability over experience," states the Web site. "The result is a team that reflects the global audience Google serves. When not at work, Googlers pursue interests from cross-country cycling to wine tasting, from flying to Frisbee."[7]

 Although Google is no longer a start-up venture, the company still tries to maintain a culture of innovation, creativity, and flexibility that the founders promoted from the beginning.

Managers use symbols, rituals, ceremonies, and stories to reinforce corporate culture. The corporate culture at the Walt Disney Company is almost as famous as the original Disney characters themselves. In fact, Disney employees are known as cast members. All new employees attend training seminars in which they learn the language, customs, traditions, stories, product lines—everything there is to know about the Disney culture and its original founder, Walt Disney.[8]

Corporate culture can be strong and enduring, but sometimes it is forced to change to meet new demands in the business environment. A firm steeped in tradition and bureaucracy might have to shift to a leaner, more flexible culture in order to respond to shifts in technology or customer preferences. A firm that grows quickly—like Google—generally has to make some adjustments in its culture to accommodate more customers and employees.

> > > **Quick Review**

1 What is meant by a firm's vision?

2 Describe the relationship between leadership style and corporate culture.

3 How would you characterize a strong corporate culture?

4 Managers as Decision Makers

decision making
process of recognizing a problem or opportunity, evaluating alternative solutions, selecting and implementing an alternative, and assessing the results.

Managers make decisions every day, whether they involve shutting down a manufacturing plant or adding grilled cheese sandwiches to a lunch menu. **Decision making** is the process of recognizing a problem or opportunity, evaluating alternative solutions, selecting and implementing an alternative, and assessing the results.

DELEGATING WORK ASSIGNMENTS

One decision managers make involves assigning work to employees, a process called **delegation**. Employees might be responsible for answering customer calls, scooping ice cream, processing returns, making deliveries, opening or closing a store, cooking or serving food, contributing to new-product design, calculating a return on investment, or any of thousands of other tasks. Just as important, employees are given a certain amount of authority to make decisions.

delegation
managerial process of assigning work to employees.

Companies like Zappos, the online shoe retailer, empower their workers to make decisions that could better serve their customers. As a result, such firms generally have happier employees and more satisfied customers.[9] As employees receive greater authority, they also must be accountable for their actions and decisions—they receive credit when things go well and must accept responsibility when they don't. Managers also must figure out the best way to delegate responsibilities to employees from different age groups, who may have very different interests and motivation.

SPAN OF MANAGEMENT

The *span of management,* or span of control, is the number of employees a manager supervises. These employees are often referred to as direct reports. First-line managers have a wider span of management, monitoring the work of many employees. The span of management depends on many factors, including employees' training and the type of work performed. In recent years, a growing trend has brought wider spans of control as companies have reduced their layers of management to flatten their organizational structures, in the process increasing the decision-making responsibility they give employees.

CENTRALIZATION AND DECENTRALIZATION

How widely should managers disperse decision-making authority throughout an organization? A company that emphasizes *centralization* retains decision making at the top of the management hierarchy. A company that emphasizes *decentralization* locates decision making at lower levels. A trend toward decentralization has pushed decision making down to operating employees in many cases. Firms that have decentralized believe that the change can improve their ability to serve customers. For example, the front-desk clerk at a hotel is much better equipped to fulfill a guest's request for a crib or a wake-up call than the hotel's general manager.

MANAGERS AS PLANNERS

Planning is the process of anticipating future events and conditions and determining courses of actions for achieving organizational objectives.

planning process of anticipating future events and conditions and determining courses of action for achieving organizational objectives.

Effective planning helps a business focus its vision, avoid costly mistakes, and seize opportunities. Planning should be flexible and responsive to changes in the business environment and should involve managers from all levels of the organization. As global competition intensifies, technology expands, and the speed at which firms bring new innovations to market increases, planning for the future becomes even more critical. For example, a CEO and other top-level managers need to plan for succession—those who will follow in their footsteps.

Matt Born/AP images

∧ Helping consumers make more environmentally conscious purchases is a key part of Whole Foods sustainability strategy.

> > > ## Quick Review

1 What is delegation? Why do managers delegate?

2 How does decision-making authority vary between organizations that emphasis centralization and those that emphasize decentralization?

5 Importance of Planning

Although some firms manage to launch without a clear strategic plan, they won't last long if they don't map out a future. Facebook founder Mark Zuckerberg claims he didn't have a major plan for the site at the beginning. But Facebook's nearly global reach—and membership of more than 800 million—means that Zuckerberg must plan the firm's next moves in order to outrun competitors and avoid major stumbles.

TYPES OF PLANNING

Planning can be categorized by scope and breadth. Some plans are very broad and long range, whereas others are short range and very narrow, affecting selected parts of the organization rather than the company as a whole. Planning can be divided into the following categories: strategic, tactical, operational, and contingency, with each step including more specific information than the last. From the mission statement (described in the next section) to objectives to specific plans, each phase must fit into a comprehensive planning framework. The framework also must include narrow, functional plans aimed at individual employees and work areas relevant to individual tasks. These plans must fit within the firm's overall planning framework and help it reach objectives and achieve its mission.

● *Strategic planning* is the most far-reaching level of planning—the process of determining the primary objectives of an organization and then acting and allocating resources to achieve those objectives. Generally, a company's top executives have responsibility for strategic planning. As part of its strategy to use company resources to help lessen their impact on the environment, Whole Foods has created sustainability programs

in many areas of their business. From their Reduce, Recycle and Reuse programs, to special labeling for wild-caught seafood, the company is fulfilling its environment objectives while accomplishing its mission of bringing the highest quality natural and organic food to market. The company recently documented the results of these and other strategic initiatives at its first ever "Green Mission Report" report.[10]

● *Tactical planning* involves implementing the activities specified by strategic plans. Tactical plans guide the current and near-term activities required to implement overall strategies. As part of a strategy to increase profitability, a firm may develop tactical plans around building sales revenue, reducing expense, or developing new products. Business executives often look at tactical plans as blueprints for the organization they want to create and the performance they want to achieve.

● *Operational planning* creates the detailed standards that guide implementation of tactical plans. This activity involves choosing specific work targets and assigning employees and teams to carry out plans. Unlike strategic planning, which focuses on the organization as a whole, operational planning deals with developing and implementing tactics in specific functional areas. The operation plan for Whole Foods new seafood-labeling program included partnering with the Blue Ocean Institute and Monterey Bay Aquarium and developing a color-coded rating system with sustainability status information for all wild-caught seafood not certified by the Marine Stewardship Council.[11]

● *Contingency planning* takes into account all the possibilities that actual planning cannot foresee. Major accidents, natural disasters, and rapid economic downturns can throw even the best-laid plans into chaos. Many firms use *contingency planning* to address the possibility of business disruption from such events, allowing them to resume operations as quickly and as smoothly as possible while communicating with the public about what happened.

6 The Strategic Planning Process

Strategic planning often makes the difference between an organization's success and failure. Strategic planning has formed the basis of many fundamental management decisions. Successful strategic planners typically follow the six steps shown in **FIGURE 7.2**: defining a mission, assessing the organization's competitive position, setting organizational objectives, creating strategies for competitive differentiation, implementing the strategy, and evaluating the results and refining the plan.

DEFINING THE ORGANIZATION'S MISSION

The first step in strategic planning is to translate the firm's vision into a **mission statement**—a written description of an organization's business intentions and aims. It is an enduring statement of a firm's purpose, possibly highlighting the scope of operations, the market it seeks to serve, and the ways it will attempt to set itself apart from competitors. A mission statement guides the actions of employees and publicizes the company's reasons for existence.

mission statement written explanation of an organization's business intentions and aims.

ASSESSING YOUR COMPETITIVE POSITION

Once a mission statement has been created, the next step in the planning process is to determine the firm's current—or potential—position in the marketplace. The company's founder or top managers evaluate the factors that could help it grow or cause it to fail. A frequently used tool in this phase of strategic planning is the **SWOT analysis**. SWOT is an acronym for *strengths, weaknesses, opportunities*, and *threats*. By systematically evaluating all four of these factors, a firm can then develop the best strategies for gaining a competitive advantage. The framework for a SWOT analysis appears in **FIGURE 7.3**.

To evaluate their firm's strengths and weaknesses, managers may examine the functional areas—such as finance, marketing, information technology, and human resources—or each office, plant, or store. Entrepreneurs may focus on the individual skills and experience they bring to a new business.

For Starbucks, a key strength is consumers' positive image of the company's brand, which gets them to stand in line to pay premium prices for coffee. That positive image comes from Starbucks' socially responsible corporate policies and its stature on the *Fortune* list of the 100 best companies to work for in the United States. The company's strategic plans have included various ways to build on Starbucks' strong brand loyalty by attaching it to new products and expanding into new markets. The expansion efforts have included creating a Music WiFi Community on its Web site; offering bottled Frappuccino drinks in grocery stores; and opening thousands of Starbucks outlets in Europe, Asia, and the Middle East. Weaknesses include saturating some markets with too many stores and not paying attention to store design. Starbucks eventually addressed these weaknesses by closing some stores and redesigning others.[12]

SWOT analysis defines a firm's opportunities and threats. Threats might include an economic recession—during which consumers are not willing to pay a premium for products—or a change in federal regulations. Starbucks addressed the threat of an economic downturn by beginning to offer less-expensive instant coffee in stores like Costco and Target. Opportunities like the growth of social media encouraged Starbucks to add Facebook and Twitter links to its Web site.[13]

A SWOT analysis isn't carved in stone. Strengths, weaknesses, opportunities, and threats may shift over time. A strength

SWOT analysis SWOT is an acronym for *strengths, weaknesses, opportunities,* and *threats.* By systematically evaluating all four of these factors, a firm can then develop the best strategies for gaining a competitive advantage.

FIGURE 7.2 Steps in the Strategic Planning Process

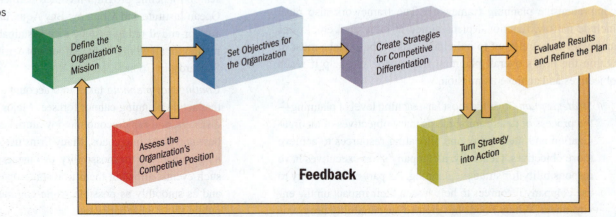

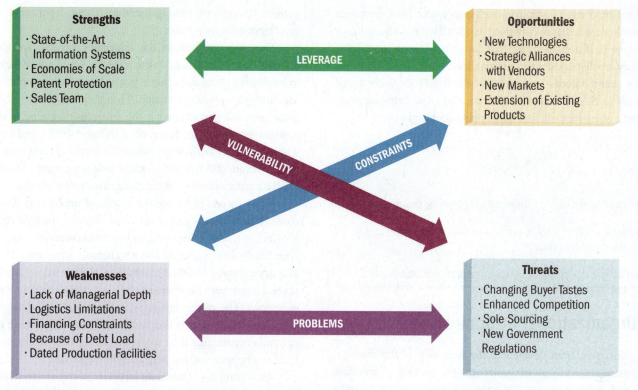

FIGURE 7.3 Elements of SWOT Analysis

may eventually become a weakness, and a threat may turn into an opportunity. But the analysis gives managers a place to start.

SETTING OBJECTIVES FOR THE ORGANIZATION

objective quantitative (measurable) outcome by which managers define the organization's desired performance in such areas as new-product development, sales, customer service, growth, environmental and social responsibility, and employee satisfaction.

In the next step in planning, a firm's leadership develops objectives. Objectives set guideposts by which managers define the organization's desired performance in such areas as new-product development, sales, customer service, growth, environmental and social responsibility, and employee satisfaction. Though the mission statement identifies a company's overall goals, objectives are more concrete and usually involve measurable (quantitative) outcomes.

CREATING STRATEGIES FOR COMPETITIVE DIFFERENTIATION

Developing a mission statement and setting objectives point a business in a specific direction. But the firm needs to identify the strategies it will use to reach its destination ahead of the competition. The underlying goal of strategy development is *competitive differentiation*—the unique combination of a company's abilities and resources that set it apart from its competitors. A firm might differentiate itself by being the first to introduce a product such

as the iPad to a widespread market; or by offering exceptional customer service, as Nordstrom does; or by offering bargains, as Costco does. After using mobile text messaging to tutor his sister in organic chemistry, Breanden Beneschott founded smsPREP while he was still a college student. The company sends its subscribers text messages with practice test questions for the SAT and ACT.[14]

IMPLEMENTING THE STRATEGY

Once the first four phases of the strategic planning process are complete, managers are ready to put those plans into action. Often, it's the middle managers or supervisors who actually implement a strategy. However, top company officials in some companies may still be reluctant to empower managers and employees with the authority to make decisions that could benefit the company. Companies that are willing to empower all employees generally reap the benefits. "The greatest power on earth is human potential," said Mark Lamoncha, CEO of Humtown Products, "It has been enslaved and exploited, but never truly empowered."[15]

MONITORING AND ADAPTING STRATEGIC PLANS

The final step in the strategic planning process is to monitor and adapt plans when the actual performance fails to meet goals. Monitoring involves securing feedback about performance. Managers might compare actual sales against forecasts; compile information from surveys; listen to complaints from the customer hotline; interview employees who are involved; and review reports prepared by production, finance, marketing, or other company units. If Internet advertisement doesn't result in enough response or sales, managers might evaluate whether to continue the advertisement, change it, or discontinue it. If a retailer observes customers buying more jeans when they are displayed near the front door, likely the display area will stay near the door—and perhaps be enlarged. Ongoing use of such tools as SWOT analysis and forecasting can help managers adapt their objectives and functional plans as changes occur.

>>> **Quick Review**

1. Name the six steps in the strategic planning process.

2. What is a SWOT analysis and how does it help organizations in the planning process?

3. What is the purpose of setting organizational objectives?

7 Organizational Structures

Once plans have been developed, the next step in the management process typically is **organizing**—the process of blending human and material resources through a formal structure of tasks and authority: arranging work, dividing tasks among employees, and coordinating them to ensure implementation of plans and accomplishment of objectives. Organizing involves classifying and dividing work into manageable units with a logical structure. Managers staff the organization with the best possible employees for each job. Sometimes the organizing function requires studying a company's existing structure and determining whether to restructure it in order to operate more efficiently, cost effectively, or sustainably.

An **organization** is a structured group of people working together to achieve common goals. An organization features three key elements: human interaction, goal-directed activities, and structure. The organizing process, much of which is led by managers, should result in an overall structure that permits interactions among individuals and departments needed to achieve company goals.

The steps involved in the organizing process are shown in **FIGURE 7.4**. Managers first determine the specific activities needed to implement plans and achieve goals. Next, they group these work activities into a logical structure. Then they assign work to specific employees and give the people the resources they need to complete it. Managers coordinate the work of different groups and employees within the firm. Finally, they evaluate the results of the organizing process to ensure effective and efficient progress toward planned goals. Evaluation sometimes results in changes to the way work is organized.

Many factors influence the results of organizing. The list includes a firm's goals and competitive strategy, the type of product it offers, the way it uses technology to accomplish work, and its size. Small firms typically use very simple structures. The owner of a dry-cleaning business generally is the top manager who hires several employees to process orders, clean the clothing, and make deliveries. The owner handles the functions of purchasing supplies such as detergents and hangers, hiring and training employees and coordinating their work, preparing advertisements for the local newspaper, and keeping accounting records.

As a company grows, its structure increases in complexity. With increased size comes specialization and growing numbers of employees. A larger firm may employ many salespeople, along with a sales manager to direct and coordinate their work or organize an accounting department.

An effective structure is one that is clear and easy to understand: employees know what is expected of them and to whom they report. They also know how their jobs contribute to the company's mission and overall strategic plan. An *organization chart* can help clarify the structure of a firm. **FIGURE 7.5** illustrates a sample organization chart.

Not-for-profit organizations also organize through formal structures so they can function efficiently and carry out their goals. These organizations, such as the Salvation Army and the American Society for Prevention of Cruelty to Animals (ASPCA), sometimes have a blend of paid staff and volunteers in their organizational structure.

DEPARTMENTALIZATION

Departmentalization is the process of dividing work activities into units within the organization. In this arrangement, employees specialize

organizing process of blending human and material resources through a formal structure of tasks and authority: arranging work, dividing tasks among employees, and coordinating them to ensure implementation of plans and accomplishment of objectives.

organization structured group of people working together to achieve common goals.

departmentalization process of dividing work activities into units within the organization.

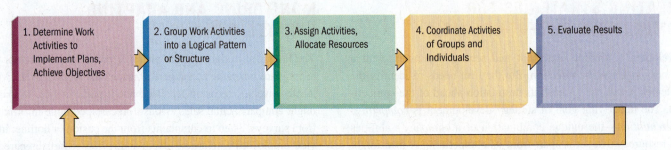

1. Determine Work Activities to Implement Plans, Achieve Objectives

2. Group Work Activities into a Logical Pattern or Structure

3. Assign Activities, Allocate Resources

4. Coordinate Activities of Groups and Individuals

5. Evaluate Results

FIGURE 7.4 Steps in the Organizing Process

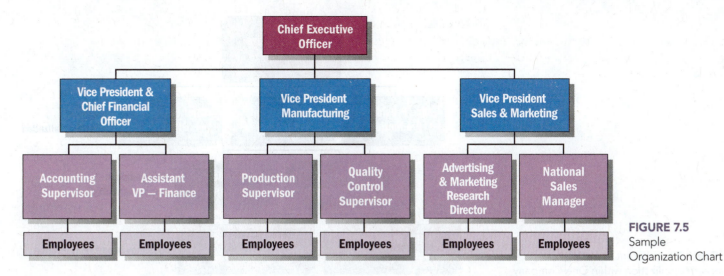

FIGURE 7.5
Sample Organization Chart

in certain jobs—such as marketing, finance, or design. Depending on the size of the firm, usually an executive runs the department, followed by middle-level managers and supervisors. The five major forms of departmentalization subdivide work by product, geographical area, customer, function, and process.

● *Product departmentalization* organizes work units based on the goods and services a company offers. Video game publisher Activision Blizzard has three operating segments: Activision Publishing, Inc., developer of interactive entertainment software products such as Call of Duty; Blizzard Entertainment, Inc., maker of the online game World of Warcraft; and Activision Blizzard Distribution, a subsidiary set up to manage Activision European businesses.[16]

● *Geographical departmentalization* organizes units by geographical regions within a country or, for a multinational firm, by region throughout the world. The Web site Petswelcome.com makes it easy for traveling pet owners to locate hotel chains, rentals, amusement parks, and other recreational locations around the country that welcome pets. Users can search by type of lodging, route planned, and destination.[17]

∨ These familiar office products represent only one of 3M Corporation's many product lines. Because 3M serves such a broad spectrum of customers, it is organized on the basis of customer departmentalization.

© R. Alcorn, Photographed for John Wiley & Sons

● *Customer departmentalization targets its* goods and services at different types of customers. Procter & Gamble divides its management across two major business units: Beauty and Grooming and Household Care.[18]

● *Functional departmentalization* organizes work units according to business functions such as finance, marketing, human resources, and production. An advertising agency may create departments for creative personnel (say, copywriters), media buyers, and account executives.

● *Process departmentalization* organizes a firm by steps in a production process. For example, a manufacturer may set up separate departments for cutting material, heat-treating it, forming it into its final shape, and painting it.

As **FIGURE 7.6** illustrates, a single company may implement several different departmentalization schemes. In deciding on a form of departmentalization, managers take into account the type of product they produce, the size of their company, their customer base, and the locations of their customers.

TYPES OF ORGANIZATION STRUCTURES

The four basic types of organization structures are line, line-and-staff, committee, and matrix. While some companies do follow one type of structure, most use a combination.

● *Line organization*, the oldest and simplest organization structure, establishes a direct flow of authority from the chief executive to employees. The line organization defines a simple, clear chain of command, or hierarchy of managers and workers. With a clear chain of command, everyone knows who is in charge and decisions can be made quickly. While line organization is particularly effective in a crisis, it has its drawbacks. Each manager has complete responsibility for a range of activities; in a midsize or large organization, however, this person can't possibly be expert in all of them. In a small organization such as a local hair salon or dentist's office, a line organization is probably the most efficient way to run the business.

FIGURE 7.6 Different Forms of Departmentalization within One Company

- *Line-and-staff organization* combines the direct flow of authority of a line organization with staff departments that support the line departments. Line departments participate directly in decisions that affect the core operations of the organization. Staff departments lend specialized technical support. **FIGURE 7.7** illustrates a line-and-staff organization. Accounting, legal, engineering, and human resources are typical staff departments that support the line authority extending from the plant manager to the production manager and supervisors.

A line manager and a staff manager differ significantly in their authority relationships. A line manager forms part of the primary line of authority that flows throughout the organization. Line managers interact directly with the functions of production, financing, or marketing—the functions needed to produce and sell goods and services. A staff manager provides information, advice, or technical assistance to aid line managers. Staff managers do not

have authority to give orders outside their own departments or to compel line managers to take action.

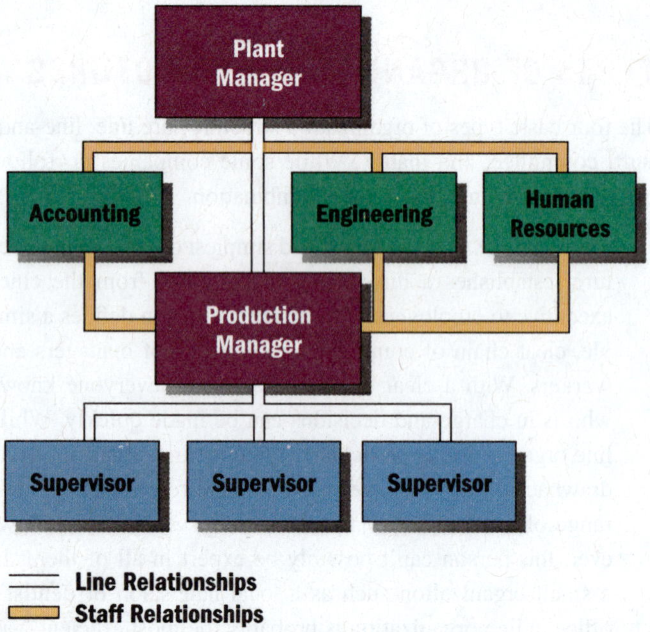

The line-and-staff organization is common in midsize and large organizations. It is an effective structure because it combines the line organization's capabilities for rapid decision making and direct communication with the expert knowledge of staff specialists.

- *Committee organization* places authority and responsibility jointly in the hands of a group of individuals rather than a single manager. This model typically appears as part of a regular line-and-staff structure.

Committees also work in areas such as new-product development. A new-product committee may include managers from such areas as accounting, engineering, finance, manufacturing, marketing, and technical research. By including representatives from all areas involved in creating and marketing products, such a committee generally improves planning and employee morale because decisions reflect diverse perspectives.

Committees tend to act slowly and conservatively, however, and may make decisions by compromising conflicting interests rather than by choosing the best alternative. The definition of a camel as "a racehorse designed by committee" provides an apt description of some limitations of committee decisions.

- *Matrix organization* links employees from different parts of the firm to work together on specific projects. In a matrix structure, each employee reports to two managers: one line manager and one project manager. Employees chosen to work on a special project receive instructions from the project manager (horizontal authority), but they continue as employees in their permanent functional departments (vertical authority). The term *matrix* comes from the intersecting grid of horizontal and vertical lines of authority.

FIGURE 7.8 depicts a matrix structure in which a project manager assembles a group of employees from different functional areas. The employees keep their ties to the line-and-staff structure, as shown in the vertical white lines. As the horizontal gold lines show, employees are also members

FIGURE 7.7 Line-and-Staff Organization

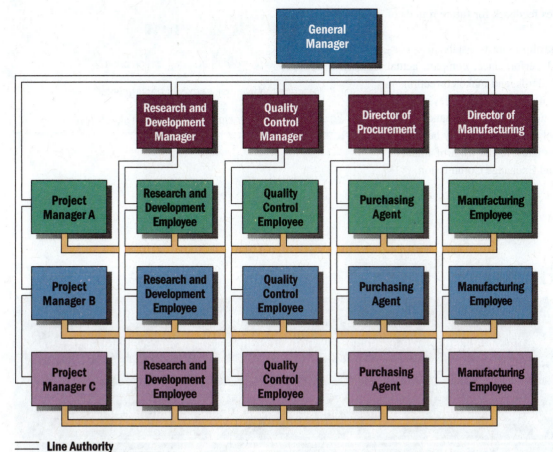

───	**Line Authority**
▬▬▬	**Project Authority**

FIGURE 7.8 Matrix Organization

of project teams. When the project is completed, employees return to their regular jobs.

The matrix structure is popular at high-technology and multinational corporations, as well as hospitals and consulting firms. Both Dow Chemical and Procter & Gamble have used matrix structures. The major benefits of the matrix structure come from its flexibility in adapting quickly to rapid changes in the environment and its capability of focusing resources on major problems or products. It also provides an outlet for employees' creativity and initiative. However, it challenges project managers to integrate the skills of specialists from many departments into a coordinated team. It also means that team members' permanent functional managers must adjust their employees' regular workloads.

The matrix structure is most effective when company leaders empower project managers to use whatever resources are available to achieve the project's objectives. Good project managers know how to make the project goals clear and keep team members focused. A firm that truly embraces the matrix structure also nurtures a project culture by making sure staffing is adequate, the workload is reasonable, and other company resources are available to project managers.

MANAGERIAL FUNCTIONS

In addition to planning and organizing, managers need to be able to perform a multitude of other functions. These include hard skills such as technical analysis, operating computer software, and reading financial statements. Managers must also perfect soft skills such as public speaking, networking, and writing. Of the additional skills a manager requires, two stand out as critical to a managers success: directing and controlling.

Directing: Once an organization has been established, managers focus on **directing**, or guiding and motivating employees to accomplish organizational objectives. Directing might include training (or retraining), setting up schedules, delegating certain tasks, and monitoring progress. To fulfill the objective of reducing the office electricity bill, an office manager might have incandescent light bulbs replaced by compact fluorescents, ask employees to turn off the lights when they leave a room or use occupancy sensors, and direct the IT staff to program all the office computer screens to turn off after 10 or 15 minutes of inactivity.

Often when managers take time to listen to their employees, the manager gains insight and the employee gets a motivational boost. Fashion designer Eileen Fisher says, "Share information and your own ideas. Be present. Be accessible. Listen."[19]

Controlling: The **controlling** function evaluates an organization's performance against its objectives. Controlling assesses the success of

directing guiding and motivating employees to accomplish organizational objectives.

controlling function of evaluating an organization's performance against its objectives.

the planning function and provides feedback for future rounds of planning.

The four basic steps in controlling are to establish performance standards, monitor actual performance, compare actual performance with established standards, and make corrections if necessary. Under the provisions of the Sarbanes-Oxley Act, for example, CEOs and CFOs must monitor the performance of the firm's accounting staff more closely than has typically been done in the past. They must personally attest to the truth of financial reports filed with the Securities and Exchange Commission.

>>> **Quick Review**

1. What is the purpose of an organization chart?
2. Describe the five major types of departmentalization.
3. What are the four types of organization structures?

What's Ahead? > > >

In the next chapter, we sharpen our focus on the importance of people—the human resource—in shaping the growth and profitability of the organization. We examine how firms recruit, select, train, evaluate, and compensate employees in their attempts to attract, retain, and motivate a high-quality workforce. The concept of motivation is examined, and we will discuss how managers apply theories of motivation in the modern workplace. The next chapter also looks at the important topic of labor–management relations.

Weekly Updates spark classroom debate around current events that apply to your business course topics. http://wileybusinessupdates.com

NOTES

1. Fortune's "100 Best Companies to Work For" 2013, *CNNMoney,* http://money.cnn.com, accessed April 16, 2013; Emma Sapong "Wegmans Ranked among Best Places to Work for 16th Straight Year," *The Buffalo News,* January 16, 2013, http://www.buffalonews.com; "FMI Presents Robert B. Wegman Award to Danny Wegman," *Progressive Grocer,* January 30, 2012, http://www.progressivegrocer.com.

2. Brad Tuttle, "Apple, L.L. Bean—and Especially, Amazon—Score Big in Online Shopping Satisfaction," *Time,* May 14, 2012, http://business.time.com.

3. Company Web site, "Leadership," http://www.aboutmcdonalds.com, accessed May 3, 2013; Shaila Dewan, "McDonald's Says Its Chief Will Retire This Summer," *New York Times,* March 21, 2012, http://www.nytimes.com.

4. Company Web site, http://www.google.com, accessed May 3, 2013; Joseph Walker, "School's in Session at Google," *The Wall Street Journal,* July 5, 2012, http://onlinw.wsj.com.

5. Katie Couric, "The Man behind the Miracle on the Hudson: Captain Sully Sullenberger," *The Katie Show,* aired January 15, 2013, http://www.katiecouric.com.

6. Craig Chappelow, "5 Rules for Making Your Vision Stick," *Fast Company,* September 5, 2012, http://www.fastcompany.com/3000998/5-rules-making-your-vision-stick.

7. Company Web site, "Corporate Information," http://www.google.com, accessed March 13, 2013.

8. Bruce I. Jones, "People Management Lessons from Disney," http://www.trainingindustry.com, accessed April 16, 2013.

9. Gwen Moran, "Zappos' Secrets to Building an Empowering Company Culture," *Entrepreneur,* March 6, 2013, http://www.entrepreneur.com.

10. Company Web site, "Whole Foods Market's: Green Mission Report" http://www.wholefoodsmarket.com, accessed April 30, 2013.

11. Ibid.

12. Company Web site, http://www.starbucks.com, accessed April 16, 2013.

13. Ibid.

14. "Coolest College Startups 2013," *Inc.,* http://www.inc.com, accessed April 30, 2013.

15. Brandon Lamoncha, "Company Thrives on Empowering Employees," Interise, February 4, 2013, http://interise.org.

16. Company Web site, http://investor.activision.com, accessed April 16, 2013.

17. Company Web site, http://www.petswelcome.com, accessed April 16, 2013.

18. Company Web site, http://www.pg.com, accessed April 16, 2013.

19. Susan Schor, "10 Leadership Tips from Eileen Fisher," *Inc.,* http://www.inc.com, accessed April 16, 2013.

Summary of Learning Objectives

 Define *management.*

Management is the process of achieving organizational objectives through people and other resources. Generally in the management hierarchy, top managers provide overall direction for company activities; middle managers implement the strategies of top managers and direct the activities of supervisors; and supervisors interact directly with workers. The three basic managerial skills are technical, human or interpersonal, and conceptual.

management process of achieving organizational objectives through people and other resources.

 Evaluate **managers as leaders.**

Leadership is the act of motivating others to achieve certain goals. The basic leadership styles are autocratic, democratic, and free-rein leadership. The best leadership style depends on three elements: the leader, the followers, and the situation.

leadership ability to direct or inspire people to attain certain goals.

empowerment in an organization, employees' shared authority, responsibility, and decision making with their managers.

 Discuss **leading by setting a vision.**

Vision is the founder's perception of the needs of the marketplace and the firm's methods for meeting them. Vision helps clarify a firm's purpose and the actions it can take to make the most of opportunities.

vision perception of marketplace needs and the ways a firm can satisfy them.

corporate culture an organization's system of principles, beliefs, and values.

 Describe **managers as decision makers.**

Managers make decisions every day. Decision making is a five-step process that involves recognizing a problem or opportunity, evaluating alternative solutions, selecting and implementing an alternative, and assessing the results.

decision making process of recognizing a problem or opportunity, evaluating alternative solutions, selecting and implementing an alternative, and assessing the results.

delegation managerial process of assigning work to employees.

planning process of anticipating future events and conditions and determining courses of action for achieving organizational objectives.

 Summarize **the importance of planning.**

The planning process identifies organizational goals and develops the actions necessary to reach them. Planning helps a company turn vision into action, take advantage of opportunities, and avoid costly mistakes. Strategic planning is a far-reaching process. It views the world through a wide-angle lens to determine the long-range focus and activities of the organization. Tactical planning focuses on the current and short-range activities required to implement an organization's strategies. Operational planning sets standards and work targets for functional areas such as production, human resources, and marketing.

 Describe **the strategic planning process.**

The first step of strategic planning is to translate the firm's vision into a mission statement that explains its overall intentions and aims. Next, planners must assess the firm's current competitive position using tools such as SWOT analysis. Managers then set specific objectives. The next step is to develop strategies for reaching objectives that will differentiate the firm from its competitors. Managers then develop an action plan that outlines the specific methods for implementing the strategy. Finally, the results achieved by the plan are evaluated, and the plan is adjusted as needed.

mission statement written explanation of an organization's business intentions and aims.

SWOT analysis an acronym for *strengths, weaknesses, opportunities,* and *threats*; the systematic evaluation of these factors enables a firm to develop the best strategies for gaining a competitive advantage.

objective quantitative (measurable) outcome by which managers define the organization's desired performance in such areas as new-product development, sales, customer service, growth, environmental and social responsibility, and employee satisfaction.

7 Discuss organizational structures.

The subdivision of work activities into units within an organization is called *departmentalization*. It may be based on products, geographical locations, customers, functions, or processes. Most firms implement one or more of four structures: line, line-and-staff, committee, and matrix structures.

organizing process of blending human and material resources through a formal structure of tasks and authority: arranging work, dividing tasks among employees, and coordinating them to ensure implementation of plans and accomplishment of objectives.

organization structured group of people working together to achieve common goals.

departmentalization process of dividing work activities into units within the organization.

directing guiding and motivating employees to accomplish organizational objectives.

controlling function of evaluating an organization's performance against its objectives.

>>> Quick Review >>

LO1

1. What is management?

2. How do the responsibilities of top management, middle management, and supervisory management differ?

3. Name the skills an individual needs for managerial success.

LO2

1. Identify and describe leadership styles as they appear along a continuum of employee participation.

2. Explain why no single leadership style is best for every organization.

LO3

1. What is meant by a firm's vision?

2. Describe the relationship between leadership style and corporate culture.

3. How would you characterize a strong corporate culture?

LO4

1. What is delegation? Why do managers delegate?

2. How does decision-making authority vary between organizations that emphasize centralization and those that emphasize decentralization?

LO5

1. Outline the planning process.

2. Explain the purpose of tactical planning.

3. Compare the kinds of plans made by top managers and middle managers. How does their focus differ?

LO6

1. Name the six steps in the strategic planning process.

2. What is a SWOT analysis and how does it help organizations in the planning process?

3. What is the purpose of setting organizational objectives?

LO7

1. What is the purpose of an organization chart?

2. Describe the five major types of departmentalization.

3. What are the four types of organization structures?

Reed Saxon/Associated Press

ROBERT IGER

chapter eight

Human Resource Management: From Recruitment to Labor Relations

Learning Objectives

1 **Explain** the role of human resources: the people behind the people.

2 **Describe** recruitment and selection.

3 **Discuss** orientation, training, and evaluation.

4 **Describe** compensation.

5 **Discuss** employee separation.

6 **Explain** the different methods for motivating employees.

7 **Discuss** labor–management relations.

Hiring Heroes Is Good Business

U.S. military veterans returning from wars in Afghanistan and Iraq have had a tough time finding employment, making the transition from military to civilian life even more difficult. A recent government study reports that the unemployment rate among military vets is 4 percent above the national unemployment rate. And an estimated 30 percent of veterans under the age of 25 are jobless. But with help from several well-known companies, veterans may see those unemployment numbers change dramatically for the better.

The Walt Disney Company recently announced a new initiative to hire

1,000 military veterans over the next several years. Dubbed "Heroes Work Here," the program will span across all segments of the company and will be implemented through career fairs designed to showcase opportunities for returning military personnel. In addition, the company will assist military families and veterans during their transition to civilian life and launch a national public awareness campaign to encourage other employers across the country to hire veterans. Announcing the new program, Disney CEO Robert Iger said, "It's a measure of our respect for how much they have sacrificed on our behalf, and our sincere gratitude for their extraordinary contributions to this country."

Over the years, returning military veterans have played an important role in helping the U.S. economy get back on track by bringing their talents to the civilian workforce.[1]

Overview > > >

This chapter explores the important issues of human resource management and motivation. It begins with a discussion of how organizations attract, develop, and retain employees. Next it describes the concepts behind motivation and how human resource (HR) managers apply them to increase employee satisfaction and organizational effectiveness. The chapter also discusses why labor unions exist and focuses on legislation that affects labor–management relations. The process of collective bargaining is then discussed, along with tools used by unions and management in seeking their objectives.

1 Human Resources: The People Behind the People

Like a professional sports team, a company is only as good as its workers. If people come to work each day to do their very best, serve their customers, and help their firm compete, it's very likely that company will be a success. The best companies value their employees as much as they value customers—without workers, there would be no goods or services to offer customers. Management at such companies know that hiring good workers—including military veterans—is vital to their overall success. Achieving the highest level of job satisfaction and dedication among employees is the goal of **human resource management**, which attracts, develops, and retains the employees who can perform the activities necessary to accomplish organizational objectives.

human resource management the function of attracting, developing, and retaining employees who can perform the activities necessary to accomplish organizational objectives.

>>> **Quick Review**

1 What is human resource management?

2 Why is it sometimes said that an organization is only as good as its employees?

2 Recruitment and Selection

Nowhere is the role of HR more important than in recruiting and selecting workers for a company. To ensure that candidates bring the necessary skills to the job or have the desire and ability to learn them, most firms implement the recruitment and selection process shown in **FIGURE 8.1**.

Before seeking candidates for a position, a manager must first determine what tasks are to be done and the best way to accomplish those tasks. This step often leads to a discussion within top management on how staff is currently deployed. For example, do any

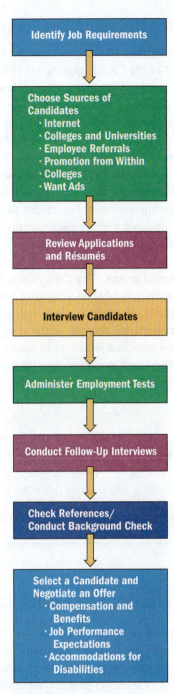

Identify Job Requirements

Choose Sources of Candidates
· Internet
· Colleges and Universities
· Employee Referrals
· Promotion from Within
· Colleges
· Want Ads

Review Applications and Résumés

Interview Candidates

Administer Employment Tests

Conduct Follow-Up Interviews

Check References/ Conduct Background Check

Select a Candidate and Negotiate an Offer
· Compensation and Benefits
· Job Performance Expectations
· Accommodations for Disabilities

FIGURE 8.1 Steps in the Recruitment and Selection Process

projects or businesses in the organization have a surplus of workers? Or does the firm have employees on furlough or not working full-time? Senior management is responsible for making sure current employees are working at capacity and at maximum productivity. Even then, a hiring manager must determine whether the company should hire additional employees. Outsourcing the work to an outside firm, using temporary staff, or engaging independent contractors to do the work may be better solutions. Clearly, managers have many choices when it comes to staffing their operations.

FINDING QUALIFIED CANDIDATES

After analyzing the situation, if a manager wants to hire a new employee, he or she needs to think about the type of person to target. This process often begins with the hiring manager generating a document listing the **job requirements**—the minimum skills, education, and experience a candidate needs for the position. Additionally, the hiring manager must think about the salary or wages and benefits required to attract the appropriate candidate. Hiring managers also guide HR to the likely sources of such individuals. Whether the position calls for a highly technical individual (such as a Web programmer) or an entry-level college graduate, the hiring manager plays an important role in identifying, interviewing, and selecting new employees. In all likelihood, the hiring manager will be working with the new employee, so making the right hiring decision is critical not only to their own success but also to that of their organization.

Besides the traditional methods of recruiting—such as college job fairs, personal referrals, and want ads—most companies now rely on their Web sites for job applicants. A firm's Web site might contain a career section with general employment information and a listing of open positions. Applicants are often able to submit a résumé and apply for an open position online. Internet recruiting is such a quick, efficient, and inexpensive way to reach a large pool of job seekers that the vast majority of companies currently use the Internet, including social networking sites, to fill job openings. This is also the best way for firms to reach new graduates and current workers. Using such social media sites such as LinkedIn or Facebook allows firms to communicate directly with candidates and streamline the selection process.

job requirements the minimum skills, education, and experience that a candidate must have to be considered for the position.

< Posting job openings online (including social networking sites) is a quick, efficient, and inexpensive way for companies to reach a large pool of job seekers.

Elena Elisseeva/Shutterstock

INTERVIEWING

Probably no conversation is more important or more stressful than a job interview. The interview is a chance for a manager to get to know a candidate, to see how he or she responds to questions, and to assess the candidate's "fit" within the organization. For job seekers, the interview is an opportunity to see an organization up close, perhaps meet their prospective manager, and better understand the job requirements. Finding the right fit is important for both the organization and the candidate

Interviews often start with a manager asking a candidate to "Tell me about yourself" or asking "How did you happen to learn about this opening?" Questions like these help break the ice, put candidates at ease, and allow them to speak with confidence about something they know. As the interview progresses, the interviewer will ask more detailed questions, often based on a candidate's résumé or experience. These types of questions help the interviewer assess whether the candidate has the right skill set, work experience, or on-the-job behaviors that the organization has determined the position needs. For example, suppose the firm wanted an information technology professional whose experience included a major software launch. The interviewer might say to the candidate, "Tell me about a time when you had to implement a companywide software changeover." Interviews often conclude with questions like, "What contribution would you envision making to ABC Company?" "What would you regard as your greatest accomplishment?" or "What questions do you have for me?" Good candidates will have anticipated a broad range of interview questions and practiced answers to them, demonstrating that they are the right fit for the position and the organization.

After the interviews, a hiring manager will often meet with the HR manager to discuss the candidates. Some will be immediately eliminated as they lacked some of the requirements, they appeared unprepared for the interview, or were not a good fit for the organization. The remaining candidates are typically ranked, and the top three or four selected for a next round of interviewing, possibly with other members of the management team, prospective colleagues, or senior employees. The HR manager will then begin checking references, verifying past employment, and confirming that the candidate has the degrees and certificates that they are claiming on their application. Managers might also Google the candidate to see what else they might learn about the individual. For certain positions, some organizations perform a background check of the top candidates. Once this process is completed, the HR manager and the hiring manager will meet and review the information. As this point, the top candidate is selected and the HR manager will contact the individual to offer them a position. Pay, benefits, and work responsibilities are discussed and placed in an offer letter. If the terms are acceptable, the candidate typically signs and returns a copy of the offer letter, and the start date is determined.

LEGAL ASPECTS OF HIRING EMPLOYEES

When hiring employees, every firm must follow state and federal employment laws. Title VII of the Civil Rights Act of 1964 prohibits employers from discriminating against applicants based on their race, religion, color, gender, or national origin. The Americans with Disabilities Act of 1990 prohibits employers from discriminating against disabled applicants. The Civil Rights Act created the *Equal Employment Opportunity Commission (EEOC)* to investigate discrimination complaints. The Uniform Employee Selection Guidelines were adopted by the EEOC in 1978 to further clarify ways in which employers must ensure that their employees will be hired and managed without discrimination.[2] The EEOC also helps employers set up *affirmative action programs* to increase job opportunities for women, minorities, people with disabilities, and other protected groups. The Civil Rights Act of 1991 expanded the alternatives available to victims of employment discrimination by including the right to a jury trial, punitive damages, and damages for emotional distress. At the same time, opponents to such laws have launched initiatives to restrict affirmative action standards and protect employers against unnecessary litigation.

> >>> **Quick Review**
>
> **1** List the steps in the recruiting and selection process.
>
> **2** What is the function of the Equal Employment Opportunity Commission (EEOC)?

3 Orientation, Training, and Evaluation

Once hired, employees need to know what is expected of them and how well they are performing. Companies provide this information through orientation, training, and evaluation. New hires may complete an orientation program administered jointly by HR and the department in which they will work. During orientation, employees learn about company policies regarding their rights and benefits. They might receive an employee manual that includes the company's code of ethics and code of conduct. And they'll usually receive some form of training.

TRAINING PROGRAMS

Training is a good investment for both employers and employees. Training helps workers build their skills and knowledge, preparing them for new job opportunities within the company. It also gives employers a better chance of retaining long-term, loyal, high-performing workers. Companies of all sizes take creative approaches to training. Nugget Market, a supermarket chain on *Fortune*'s list of "The 100 Best Companies to Work For," rolls out continuous information about products, the company, and updates from executives on a large, flat-screen monitor in each store. Employees who watch—and absorb—the information are eligible for bonus rewards that range from $20 to $1,000.[3]

● *On-the-job training,* a popular teaching method, prepares employees for job duties by allowing them to perform tasks under the guidance of experienced employees. A variation of on-the-job training is apprenticeship training, in which an employee learns a job by serving for a time as an assistant to a trained worker. American apprenticeships usually focus on blue-collar trades—such as plumbing and heating services—whereas in Europe, many new entrants to white-collar professions complete apprenticeships. McDonald's sponsors apprenticeship-training programs in its UK restaurants as part of an economic stimulus plan launched by the British government. Offering 10,000 apprenticeships per year, the company says, "We're as serious about education as we are about burgers and fries."[4]

● *Classroom and computer-based training* offer another option. Many firms are replacing classroom training with computer-based training programs, which can significantly reduce costs. Computer-based training offers consistent presentations along with videos that can simulate the work environment. Employees can learn at their own pace without having to sign up for a class. Through online training programs, employees can engage in interactive learning—they might conference with a mentor or instructor located elsewhere or they might participate in a simulation requiring them to make decisions related to their work.

∨ On-the-job training is a widely used training method offering employees the opportunity for a hands-on education.

∧ Employees value face-to-face feedback on their performance. Evaluations that are fair and consistent can improve an organization's productivity and profitability.

PERFORMANCE APPRAISALS

Feedback about performance is the best way for a company—and its employees—to improve. Most firms use an annual **performance appraisal** to evaluate an employee's job performance and provide feedback about it. A performance appraisal can include assessments of everything from attendance to goals met. Based on this evaluation, a manager will make decisions about compensation, promotion, additional training needs, transfers, or even termination. Performance appraisals are common, but not everyone agrees about their usefulness.

> **performance appraisal** evaluation of and feedback on an employee's job performance.

Some management experts argue that a performance review is skewed in favor of a single manager's subjective opinion—whether it's positive or negative—and that most employees are afraid to speak honestly to their managers during a performance review. If a performance review is to be at all effective, it should meet the following criteria:

● Establish clear, measurable, agreed-upon objectives

● Have thorough documentation

● Be a formal midyear evaluation

● Consist of frequent meetings with meaningful feedback (no conflict avoidance!)[5]

>>> **Quick Review**

1. What are the benefits of computer-based training programs?

2. Name the four important criteria of an effective performance appraisal.

4 Compensation

compensation amount employees are paid in money and benefits.

Compensation—how much employees are paid in money and benefits—is one of the most highly charged issues that HR managers face. The amount employees are paid, along with whatever benefits they receive, has a tremendous influence on where they live, their lifestyle, and how they spend their leisure time. Compensation also affects job satisfaction. Balancing compensation for employees at all job levels can be a challenge for human resource managers.

The terms *wages* and *salary* are often used interchangeably, but they actually are different. A **wage** is based on an hourly pay rate or the amount of work accomplished.

wage pay based on an hourly rate or the amount of work accomplished.

salary pay calculated on a periodic basis, such as weekly or monthly.

Typical wage earners are factory workers, construction workers, auto mechanics, retail salespeople, and restaurant servers. A **salary** is calculated periodically, such as weekly or monthly. Salaried employees receive a set amount of pay that does not fluctuate with the number of hours they work: wage earners may receive overtime pay, and salaried workers do not. Office personnel, executives, and professional employees usually receive salaries.

Most firms base their compensation policies on the following factors:

- What competing companies are paying
- Government regulation
- Cost of living
- Company profits
- An employee's productivity

Many firms try to balance rewarding workers with maintaining profits by linking more of an employee's pay to superior performance. Firms try to motivate employees to excel by offering some type of incentive compensation in addition to salaries or wages. **FIGURE 8.2** lists four common types of incentive compensation programs.

- Profit sharing, which awards bonuses based on company profits

- Gainsharing, a company's sharing of the financial value of productivity gains, cost savings, or quality improvements with its workers
- Lump-sum bonuses and stock options, which provide one-time cash payments and the right to purchase company stock based on performance
- Pay for knowledge, which distributes wage or salary increases as employees learn new job tasks

EMPLOYEE BENEFITS

employee benefits additional compensation such as vacation, retirement plans, profit-sharing, health insurance, gym memberships, child and elder care, and tuition reimbursement, offered by the employer.

In addition to wages and salaries, firms provide benefits to employees and their families as part of their compensation. **Employee benefits**—such as vacation, retirement plans, profit-sharing, health insurance, gym memberships, child and elder care, and tuition reimbursement—are sometimes offered by the employer. Benefits represent a large component of an employee's total compensation. Although wages and salaries account for around 70 percent of the typical employee's compensation, the other 30 percent takes the form of employee benefits.[6] TABLE 8.1 shows the breakdown of an average worker's benefits as compared to wages or salary.

Some benefits are required by law. U.S. firms are required to make Social Security and Medicare contributions, as well as payments to state unemployment insurance and workers' compensation programs, which protect workers in case of job-related injuries or illnesses. The Family and Medical Leave Act of 1993 requires covered employers to offer up to 12 weeks of unpaid, job-protected leave to eligible employees. Firms voluntarily provide other employee benefits, such as child care and health insurance, to help them attract and retain employees. Some states, such as California, New Jersey, and Washington, have laws mandating paid family leave.

Profit Sharing Bonus based on company profits	Gainsharing Bonus based on productivity gains, cost savings, or quality improvements
Bonus One-time cash payment or option to buy shares of company stock based on performance	Pay for Knowledge Salary increase based on learning new job tasks

FIGURE 8.2 Four Forms of Incentive Compensation

TABLE 8.1 What are average costs for employee compensation?

Type of Compensation	Percentage of Total Compensation
Wages and salaries	70.3%
Benefits	29.7
Paid leave	6.9
Supplemental pay	2.8
Insurance	8.2
Health benefits	7.7
Retirement and savings	3.6
Legally required benefits	8.2

SOURCE: Bureau of Labor Statistics, "Private Sector Employer Costs for Employee Compensation," released March 12, 2013, http://www.bls.gov.

∧ Benefits like on-site fitness facilities improve both a company's health and that of its employees.

In the past, companies have paid the greater share of the cost of health care benefits, with employees paying a much smaller share. However, as health care costs rise, employers are passing along premium increases to employees. Many companies now offer incentives for workers to live healthier lives. Gym memberships, nutrition programs, wellness visits to the doctor, and smoking-cessation classes are all examples of these incentives. At Qualcomm, a global mobile technologies firm, employee benefits include unlimited sick days, on-site gyms, tuition assistance, and work-life balance programs like job sharing, compressed workweeks, and telecommuting. In addition, Qualcomm provides a generous company match on its retirement savings plan and pays 100 percent of the monthly health insurance premium.[7]

Retirement plans make up a chunk of employee benefits. Some companies have reduced the contributions they make to workers' *401(k) plans*—retirement savings plans to which employees can make pretax contributions. Some firms have cut back on cash contributions to the plans and contribute company stock instead. However, others provide a high level of funding. Raytheon Solipsys offers a 401(k) with company match of up to 200 percent on employee contributions.[8]

FLEXIBLE BENEFITS

In response to increasing diversity in the workplace, firms look for creative ways to structure their benefit plans to the needs of employees. One approach offers *flexible benefits,* also called a cafeteria plan. Under this system, employees have a choice of benefits, including different types of medical insurance, dental and vision plans, and life and disability insurance. Typically, each employee receives a set allowance (called flex dollars or credits) to pay for benefits, depending on his or her needs. One working spouse, for example, might choose medical coverage for the entire family while the other spouse uses benefit dollars to elect other types of coverage. Contributions to cafeteria accounts can be made by both the employee and employer. Cafeteria plans also offer tax benefits to both employees and employers.

Another way of increasing the flexibility of employee benefits involves time off from work. Instead of establishing set numbers of holidays, vacation days, and sick days, some employers give each employee a bank of *paid time off (PTO)*. Employees use days from their PTO account without having to explain why they need the time. The greatest advantage of PTO is the freedom it gives workers to make their own choices; the greatest disadvantage is that it is an expensive benefit for employers.

FLEXIBLE WORK

Some firms are moving toward the option of *flexible work plans,* which are benefits that allow employees to adjust their working hours or places of work according to their needs. Flexible work plan options include flextime, compressed workweeks, job sharing, and home-based work (telecommuting). These benefit programs have reduced employee turnover and absenteeism and boosted productivity and job satisfaction. Flexible work has become critical in attracting and keeping talented human resources.

● *Flextime* allows employees to set their own work hours within certain parameters. Rather than mandating that all

∨ Many employees use flextime to mesh their work schedules with opening and closing times at schools and daycare programs.

employees work, say, from 8:00 a.m. to 5:00 p.m., a manager might stipulate that everyone works between the core hours of 10:00 a.m. and 3:00 p.m. Outside the core hours, employees could choose to start and end early or start and end late.

- Some companies offer a *compressed workweek*, which allows employees to work longer hours on fewer days. Employees might work four 10-hour days and then have three days off each week.

- A *job sharing program* allows two or more employees to divide the tasks of one job. This plan appeals to a growing number of people—such as students, working parents, and people of all ages who want to devote time to personal interests—who prefer to work part-time rather than full-time. Job sharing requires a lot of cooperation and communication between the partners, but an employer can benefit from the talents of both people.

- Home-based work programs allow employees to become *telecommuters*, performing their jobs from home via the Internet, voice and video conferencing, and mobile devices.

122

>>> Quick Review

1. Explain the difference between a *wage* and a *salary*.

2. On what factors do employers typically base their compensation decisions?

3. Name some flexible benefits in the workplace. Why do some employers offer flexible benefits?

5 Employee Separation

employee separation broad term covering the loss of an employee for any reason, voluntary or involuntary.

Employee separation is a broad term covering the loss of an employee for any reason, voluntary or involuntary. Voluntary separation includes workers who resign to take a job at another firm or start a business. Involuntary separation includes downsizing, outsourcing, and dismissal.

VOLUNTARY AND INVOLUNTARY TURNOVER

Turnover occurs when an employee leaves a job. Voluntary turnover occurs when the employee resigns—perhaps to take another job that pays better, start a new business, or retire. The human resource manager might conduct an exit interview with the employee to learn why he or she is leaving; this conversation can provide valuable information to a firm. An employee might decide to leave because of lack of career opportunities. Learning this, the human resource manager might offer ongoing training. Sometimes employees accept jobs at other firms because they fear upcoming layoffs. In this case, the human resource manager might be able to allay fears about job security.

Involuntary turnover occurs when employees are terminated because of poor job performance or unethical behavior. No matter how necessary a termination may be, it is never easy for the manager or the employee. The employee may react with anger or tears; co-workers may take sides. Managers should remain calm and professional and must be educated in employment laws. Protests against wrongful dismissal are often involved in complaints filed by the EEOC or by lawsuits brought by fired employees. Involuntary turnover also occurs when firms are forced to eliminate jobs as a cost-cutting measure, as in the case of downsizing or outsourcing.

DOWNSIZING

As the economy tightens, companies are often faced with the hard choice of terminating employees in order to cut costs or streamline the organization. **Downsizing** is the process of reducing the number of employees within a firm by eliminating jobs. Downsizing can be accomplished through early retirement plans or voluntary severance programs.

downsizing process of reducing the number of employees within a firm by eliminating jobs.

OUTSOURCING

Firms also shrink themselves into leaner organizations by **outsourcing**. Outsourcing involves transferring jobs from inside a firm to outside the firm. Jobs that are typically outsourced include office maintenance, deliveries, food service, and security. However, other job functions can be outsourced as well, including manufacturing, design, information technology, and accounting. In general, in order to save expenses and remain flexible, many companies try to outsource functions that are not part of their core business.

outsourcing transferring jobs from inside a firm to outside the firm.

>>> Quick Review

1. What is the difference between voluntary and involuntary turnover?

2. What is downsizing? How is it different from outsourcing?

TABLE 8.2 Can you name the top ten companies on *Fortune*'s work list?

1	Google	6	NetApp
2	SAS	7	Hilcorp Energy Company
3	CHG Healthcare Services	8	Edward Jones
4	Boston Consulting Group	9	Ultimate Software
5	Wegmans Food Markets	10	Camden Property Trust

SOURCE: "100 Best Companies to Work For 2013," *Fortune*, January 17, 2013, http://money.cnn.com.

6 Motivating Employees

Everyone wants to enjoy going to work. Smart employers know that and look for ways to motivate workers to commit to their company's goals and perform their best. Motivation starts with high employee morale—a positive attitude toward the job. Each year, *Fortune* announces its list of the "100 Best Companies to Work For." The most recent top ten are listed in TABLE 8.2. Based on these rankings, it's reasonable to believe that employees at these firms tend to have higher morale because they feel valued and empowered.

High morale generally results from good management, including an understanding of human needs and an effort to satisfy those needs in ways that move the company forward. Low employee morale, on the other hand, usually signals a poor relationship between managers and employees and often results in absenteeism, voluntary turnover, and a lack of motivation.

Generally speaking, managers use rewards and punishments to motivate employees. Extrinsic rewards are external to the work itself, such as pay, fringe benefits, and praise. Intrinsic rewards are feelings related to performing the job, such as feeling proud about meeting a deadline or achieving a sales goal. Punishment involves a negative consequence for such behavior as being late, skipping staff meetings, or treating a customer poorly.

There are several theories of motivation, all of which relate back to the basic process of motivation itself, which involves the recognition of a need, the move toward meeting that need, and the satisfaction of that need. For instance, if you are hungry you might be motivated to make yourself a peanut butter sandwich. Once you have eaten the sandwich, the need is satisfied and you are no longer hungry. **FIGURE 8.3** illustrates the process of motivation.

MASLOW'S HIERARCHY OF NEEDS THEORY

The studies of psychologist Abraham H. Maslow suggest how managers can motivate employees. **Maslow's hierarchy of needs** has become a widely accepted list of human needs based on these important assumptions:

> **Maslow's hierarchy of needs** theory of motivation proposed by Abraham Maslow.

- People's needs depend on what they already possess.

- A satisfied need is not a motivator; only needs that remain unsatisfied can influence behavior.

- People's needs are arranged in a hierarchy of importance; once they satisfy one need, at least partially, another emerges and demands satisfaction.

According to the theory, people have five levels of needs that they seek to satisfy: physiological, safety, social, esteem, and self-actualization.

In his theory, Maslow proposed that all people have basic needs such as hunger and protection that they must satisfy before they can consider higher-order needs such as social relationships or self-worth. He identified five types of needs:

1. *Physiological needs* include food, shelter, and clothing. On the job, employers satisfy these needs by paying salaries and wages and providing a temperature-controlled workspace.

2. *Safety needs* refer to desires for physical and economic protection. Companies satisfy these needs with benefits like health insurance and meeting safety standards in the workplace.

3. *Social (belongingness) needs* refer to people's desire to be accepted by family, friends, and co-workers. Managers might satisfy these needs through teamwork and group lunches.

4. *Esteem needs* have to do with people's desire to feel valued and recognized by others. Managers can meet these needs through special awards or privileges.

5. *Self-actualization needs* drive people to seek fulfillment of their dreams and capabilities. Employers can satisfy these needs by offering challenging or creative projects, along with opportunities for education and advancement.[9]

According to Maslow, people must satisfy the lower-order needs in the hierarchy, specifically their physiological and safety needs, before they are motivated to satisfy higher-order needs such as social, esteem, and self-actualization.

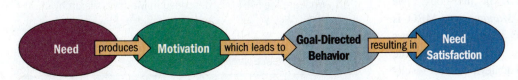

Need produces **Motivation** which leads to **Goal-Directed Behavior** resulting in **Need Satisfaction**

FIGURE 8.3 The Process of Motivation

ᵥ During difficult economic times when annual raises are not given to employees, companies need to find alternate ways to keep them motivated.

"No raise … he said he wants to test my self motivation skills."

Ron Morgan/www.cartoonstock.com

OTHER MOTIVATIONAL THEORIES

Equity theory is concerned with an individual's perception of fair and equitable treatment. In their work, employees first consider their effort and then their rewards. Next, employees compare their results against those of their co-workers. As shown in Figure 8.3, if employees feel they are under-rewarded for their effort in comparison with others doing similar work, equity theory suggests they will be motivated to decrease their effort. Conversely, if employees feel they are over-rewarded, they will feel guilty and put more effort into their job to restore equity and reduce guilt.

equity theory an individual's perception of fair and equitable treatment.

goal-setting theory says that people will be motivated to the extent to which they accept specific, challenging goals and receive feedback that indicates their progress toward goal achievement.

management by objectives systematic approach that allows managers to focus on attainable goals and to achieve the best results based on the organization's resources.

Goal-setting theory says that people will be motivated to the extent to which they accept specific, challenging goals and receive feedback that indicates their progress toward goal achievement. The basic components of goal-setting theory are goal specificity, goal difficulty, goal acceptance, and performance feedback.

Fifty years ago, Peter Drucker introduced a goal-setting technique called **management by objectives (MBO)** in his book, *The Practice of Management*. MBO is a systematic approach that allows managers to focus on attainable goals and to achieve the best results based on the organization's resources. MBO helps motivate individuals by aligning their objectives with the goals of the organization, increasing overall organizational performance. MBO clearly outlines people's tasks, goals, and contributions to the company.

MANAGERS' ATTITUDES AND MOTIVATION

A manager's attitude toward his or her employees greatly influences their motivation. Maslow's theory, described earlier, has helped managers understand that employees have a range of needs beyond their paychecks. Psychologist Douglas McGregor, a student of Maslow, studied motivation from the perspective of how managers view employees. After observing managers' interactions with employees, McGregor created two basic labels for the assumptions that different managers make about their workers' behavior and how these assumptions affect management styles:

● *Theory X* assumes that employees dislike work and try to avoid it whenever possible, so management must coerce them to do their jobs. Theory X managers believe that the average worker prefers to receive instructions, avoids responsibility, takes little initiative, and views money and job security as the only valid motivators—Maslow's lower order of needs.

● *Theory Y* assumes that the typical person actually likes work and will seek and accept greater responsibility. Theory Y managers assume that most people can think of creative ways to solve work-related problems and should be given the opportunity to participate in decision making. Unlike the traditional management philosophy that relies on external control and constant supervision, Theory Y emphasizes self-control and self-direction—Maslow's higher order of needs.

Another perspective on management, proposed by management professor William Ouchi, has been labeled *Theory Z*. Organizations structured on Theory Z concepts attempt to blend the best of American and Japanese management practices. This approach views worker involvement as the key to increased productivity for the company and improved quality of work life for employees. Many U.S. firms have adopted the participative management style used in Japanese firms by asking workers for suggestions to improve their jobs and then giving them the authority to implement proposed changes.

> >>> **Quick Review**

1 Name the four steps in the process of motivation.

2 What are the five levels described in Maslow's hierarchy of needs theory?

3 Compare and contrast the Theory X, Theory Y, and Theory Z management approaches.

7 Labor–Management Relations

The U.S. workplace is far different from what it was a century ago, when child labor, unsafe working conditions, and a 72-hour workweek were common. The development of labor unions, labor legislation, and the collective bargaining process have contributed to the changed environment. Today's HR managers must be educated in labor–management relations, the settling of disputes, and the competitive tactics of unions and management.

DEVELOPMENT OF LABOR UNIONS

A **labor union** is a group of workers who have banded together to achieve common goals in the areas of wages, hours, and working conditions. The organized efforts of Philadelphia printers in 1786 resulted in the first U.S. minimum wage—$1 a day. One hundred years later, New York City streetcar conductors were able to negotiate a reduction in their workday from 17 to 12 hours.

> **labor union** group of workers who have banded together to achieve common goals in the areas of wages, hours, and working conditions.

Labor unions can be found at the local, national, and international levels. A *local union* represents union members in a specific area, such as a single community, while a *national union* is a labor organization consisting of numerous local chapters. An *international union* is a national union with membership outside the United States, usually in Canada. About 14.8 million U.S. workers—just under 12 percent of the nation's full-time workforce—belong to labor unions.[10] Although only about 8 percent of workers in the private sector are unionized, more than one-third of government workers belong to unions. The largest union in the United States is the 3.2 million-member National Education Association (NEA), representing public school teachers and other support personnel. Other large unions include the 2.1 million members of the Service Employees International Union (SEIU), the 1.6 million members of the American Federation of State, County & Municipal Employees, the 1.4 million members of the International Brotherhood of Teamsters, the 1.3 million members of the United Food and Commercial Workers, and the 538,000 members of the United Automobile, Aerospace and Agricultural Implement Workers of America.[11]

LABOR LEGISLATION

Over the past century, some major pieces of labor legislation have been enacted, including the following:

- The *National Labor Relations Act of 1935 (Wagner Act)* legalized collective bargaining and required employers to negotiate with elected representatives of their employees. It established the National Labor Relations Board (NLRB) to supervise union elections and prohibit unfair labor practices such as firing workers for joining unions, refusing to hire union sympathizers, threatening to close if workers unionize, interfering with or dominating the administration of a union, and refusing to bargain with a union.

- The *Fair Labor Standards Act of 1938* set the first federal minimum wage (25 cents an hour) and a maximum basic workweek for certain industries. It also outlawed child labor.

- The *Taft-Hartley Act of 1947 (Labor–Management Relations Act)* limited unions' power by banning such practices as coercing employees to join unions; coercing employers to discriminate against employees who are not union members; discriminating against nonunion employees; picketing or conducting secondary boycotts or strikes for illegal purposes; and excessive initiation fees.

- The *Landrum-Griffin Act of 1959 (Labor–Management Reporting and Disclosure Act)* amended the Taft-Hartley Act to promote honesty and democracy in running unions' internal affairs. The law requires unions to set up a constitution and bylaws and to hold regularly scheduled elections of union officers by secret ballot. It set forth a bill of rights for union members and required unions to submit certain financial reports to the U.S. Secretary of Labor.

THE COLLECTIVE BARGAINING PROCESS

Labor unions work to increase job security for their members and to improve wages, hours, and working conditions. These goals are achieved primarily through **collective bargaining**, the process of negotiation between management and union representatives.

> **collective bargaining** process of negotiation between management and union representatives.

Union contracts, which typically cover a two- or three-year period, are often the result of weeks or months of discussion, disagreement, compromise, and eventual agreement. Once agreement is reached, union members must vote to accept or reject the contract. If the contract is rejected, union representatives may resume the bargaining process with management representatives, or union members may strike to obtain their demands.

SETTLING LABOR–MANAGEMENT DISPUTES

Strikes make the headlines, but most labor–management negotiations result in a signed contract without a strike. If a dispute arises, it is usually settled through a mechanism such as a grievance procedure, mediation, or arbitration. Any of these alternatives is quicker and less expensive than a strike.

The union contract serves as a guide to relations between the firm's management and its employees. The rights of each party are stated in the agreement. But no contract, regardless of how detailed, will eliminate the possibility of disagreement. Such differences can be the beginning of a *grievance,* a complaint by a single employee or by the entire union that management is violating some portion of the contract. Almost all union contracts

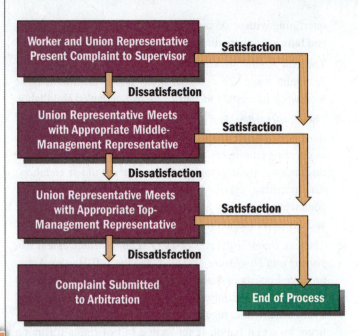

FIGURE 8.4 Steps in the Grievance Procedure

require these complaints to be submitted through a formal grievance procedure similar to the one shown in **FIGURE 8.4**. A grievance might involve a dispute about pay, working hours, or the workplace itself. The grievance procedure usually begins with an employee's supervisor and then moves up the company's hierarchy. If the highest level of management can't settle the grievance, it is submitted to an outside party for mediation or arbitration.

Mediation is the process of settling labor–management disputes through an impartial third party. Although the mediator does not make the final decision, he or she hears the whole story and makes objective recommendations. If the dispute remains unresolved, the two parties can turn to *arbitration*—bringing in an outside arbitrator who renders a legally binding decision. The arbitrator must be acceptable both to the union and to management, and his or her decision is final. Most union negotiations go to arbitration if union and management representatives fail to reach a contract agreement.

Both unions and management use tactics to make their views known and to win support. Generally, unions are concerned with issues such as pay, job security, and benefits. Unions generally want to improve compensation and security for their members. They are also concerned about the overall health of the business and will make concessions if they feel that they

> When the company and the union failed to reach an agreement, it appeared that Twinkies and other Hostess brands would be riding off into the sunset. However, an investment firm bought the brands and will restart the bakeries without union labor.

need to in order for the company to continue to operate. Managers think about many of the same issues but are primarily concerned with the competitiveness of their business. Financial performance is the most important element because if the business cannot thrive, there will be no money to pay anyone. Usually, labor and management can come to some understanding and through a process of negotiation arrive at a contract acceptable to both parties. However, if there is an impasse in negotiations the union and management may need to resort to other means to get their needs met.

THE COMPETITIVE TACTICS OF UNIONS

Unions chiefly use three tactics—strikes, picketing, and boycotts—to press for what they want:

● The *strike,* or walkout, is one of a union's most effective tools. It involves a temporary work stoppage by workers until a dispute has been settled or a contract signed. A strike generally seeks to disrupt business as usual, calling attention to workers' needs and union demands. Strikes can last for days or weeks and can be costly to both sides. In addition, strikes are often damaging to the very people the union is trying to help—for example, students lose valuable class time when teachers go on strike. Surrounding businesses may suffer, too. If striking workers aren't eating at their usual lunch haunts, those businesses will lose profits. Strikes seem to be on the decline, however. During the last decade, there were an average of 16 major work stoppages per year, half the number that took place in the 1990s.[12]

● *Picketing* consists of workers marching in a public protest against their employer. As long as picketing does not involve violence or intimidation, it is protected under the U.S. Constitution as freedom of speech. Picketing may accompany a strike, or it may be a protest against alleged unfair labor

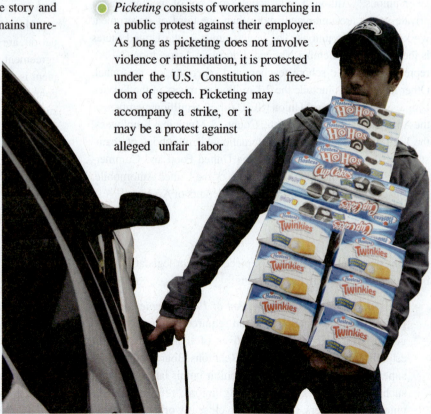

MCT/Getty Images

practices. During a recent labor dispute, Verizon union workers set up picket lines to show solidarity with other Verizon striking union members on the East Coast.[13]

- A *boycott* is an organized attempt to keep the public from purchasing a firm's goods or services. Some unions have been quite successful in organizing boycotts, and some unions even fine members who defy a boycott.

THE COMPETITIVE TACTICS OF MANAGEMENT

Management also has tactics for competing with organized labor when negotiations break down. In the past, it has used the lockout—a management "strike" to put pressure on union members by closing the firm. More commonly, however, organizations try to recruit strikebreakers (in highly visible fields such as professional sports) or transfer supervisors and other nonunion employees to continue operations during strikes. When union workers at British Airways went on strike, management leased aircraft from other airlines and used volunteer pilots and managers to take the place of the striking cabin crews.[14]

In extreme cases, management might go so far as to close the plant and outsource the work to another company or even shut down the operation entirely and file for bankruptcy, such as what happened with Hostess Brands, bakers of the iconic Twinkie and other snack cakes. After failing to reach an agreement with the union, Hostess filed for bankruptcy. Private equity groups Apollo Global Management and Metropolis & Co.—now doing business as Hostess Brands—paid $410 million to buy the Hostess and Dolly Madison snack cake lines as well as five plants as part of the company's liquidation process. And soon after, they relaunched the iconic products.[15]

THE FUTURE OF LABOR UNIONS

Union membership and influence grew through most of the 20th century by giving industrial workers a voice in decisions about their wages, benefits, and working conditions. However, as the United States, western Europe, and Japan have shifted from manufacturing economies to information and service economies, union membership and influence have declined. In a recent year, about 11.3 percent of wage and salary workers belonged to a union, down from 11.8 percent the year before. Subsets of that group have also seen a decline: 6.6 percent of private sector workers belonged to a union, down from 6.9 percent the previous year.[16]

How can labor unions change to maintain their relevance? They can be more flexible and adapt to a global economy and diverse workforce. They can respond to the growing need for environmentally responsible business and manufacturing processes. Unions can establish collaborative relationships with human resource managers and other managers. And they can recognize the potential for prosperity for all—management and union workers included.

> > > **Quick Review**

1. What is a labor union? What is collective bargaining?

2. Describe the three main tactics of a labor union.

3. Name the steps in a grievance procedure.

What's Ahead? > > >

Treating employees well by enriching the work environment will continue to gain importance as a way to recruit and retain a highly motivated workforce. In addition, managers can tap the full potential of their employees by empowering them to make decisions, leading them to work effectively as teams, and fostering clear, positive communication. The next chapter covers these three means of improving performance. By involving employees more fully through empowerment, teamwork, and communication, companies can benefit from their knowledge while employees enjoy a more meaningful role in the company.

Weekly Updates spark classroom debate around current events that apply to your business course topics. http://www.wileybusinessupdates.com

NOTES

1. Bureau of Labor Statistics, "Employment Situation of Veterans Summary," news release, March 20, 2013, http://www.bls.gov; "Disney to Hire 1,000 Vets, Launches PR Campaign," *West Orlando News,* March 13, 2012, http://westorlandonews.com; Halimah Abdullah, "Hiring Our Heroes: McChrystal on Hiring Veterans: We Need to Understand Where Soldiers Come From," *MSNBC,* March 26, 2012, http://hiringourheroes.today.com; company Web site, "Walmart U.S. CEO Bill Simon Calls on Veterans to Help Lead an 'American Renewal,'" press release, August 31, 2011, http://news.walmart.com.

2. Government Web site, "Fact Sheet on Employment Tests and Selection Procedures," http://eeoc.gov, accessed April 24, 2013.

3. "100 Best Companies to Work For (2013)," *CNN Money.com,* http://money.cnn.com, accessed April 24, 2013; "Nugget Market" in "100 Best Companies to Work For (2013)," *CNN Money.com,* http://money.cnn.com, accessed April 24, 2013; company Web site, "Nugget Markets Ranked in FORTUNE Magazine's '100 Best Companies to Work For' List for Seventh Consecutive Year," press release, January 20, 2012, http://www.nuggetmarket.com.

4. Tricia Phillips, "Job Focus: How to Get an Apprenticeship," *Mirror,* March 8, 2013, http://www.mirror.co.uk; company Web site, "McDonald's Puts Apprenticeships on the Menu," http://www.aboutmcdonalds.com, accessed April 24, 2013.

5. Victor Lipman, "4 Steps to Painless (and Effective) Performance Evaluations," *Forbes*, October 4, 2012, http://www.forbes.com.

6. Bureau of Labor Statistics, "Employer Costs for Employee Compensation," press release, March 12, 2013, http://www.bls.gov.

7. Company Web site, "Benefits Overview," http://www.qualcomm.com, accessed April 24, 2013; "100 Best Companies to Work For 2012: Best Benefits," *Fortune,* February 6, 2012, http://money.cnn.com.

8. Company Web site, "Careers," http://www.solipsys.com, accessed April 24, 2013.

9. "Abraham Maslow's Hierarchy of Needs," *Accel-Team.com,* http://www.accel-team.com, accessed April 24, 2013.

10. Bureau of Labor Statistics, "Union Membership News Release," January 23, 2013, http://www.bls.gov.

11. Organization Web site, http://www.afscme.org, accessed April 24, 2013; organization Web site, http://www.seiu.org, accessed April 24, 2013; organization Web site, http://www.teamster.org, accessed April 24, 2013; organization Web site, http://www.ufcw.org,

accessed April 24, 2013; John C. Henry, "Largest Unions Pay Leaders Well, Give Extensively to Democrats," *Milwaukee Journal Sentinel,* March 3, 2011, http://www.jsonline.com.

12. Bureau of Labor Statistics, "Work Stoppages Summary," news release, February 8, 2013, http://www.bls.gov.

13. Steve Greenhouse, "4-Year Deals for Unions at Verizon," *New York Times*, September 19, 2012, http://www.nytimes.com.

14. "BA: United We Stand Campaign," http://archive.unitetheunion.org, accessed April 24, 2013; "BA Strike: Airline and Union Agree to End Dispute," *BBC,* May 12, 2011, http://www.bbc.co.uk.

15. Associated Press, "Hostess Reopens Bakery for Twinkies, Ho Hos," *USA Today*, April 29, 2013, http://www.usatoday.com; Rachel Feintzeig, "New Twinkie Maker Shuns Union Labor," *Wall Street Journal*, April 23, 2013, http://online.wsj.com.

16. Organization Web site, "About the American Postal Workers Union," http://www.apwu.org, accessed April 24, 2013; Bureau of Labor Statistics, "Union Members—2012," news release, January 23, 2013, http://www.bls.gov.

Summary of Learning Objectives

 Explain the role of human resources: the people behind the people.

Human resource managers are responsible for attracting, developing, and retaining the employees who can perform the activities necessary to accomplish organizational objectives. They plan for staffing needs, recruit and hire workers, provide for training, evaluate performance, determine compensation and benefits, and oversee employee separation.

human resource management the function of attracting, developing, and retaining employees who can perform the activities necessary to accomplish organizational objectives.

 Describe recruitment and selection.

Human resource managers use internal and external methods to recruit qualified employees. They may use college job fairs, personal referrals, want ads, and other resources. Internet recruiting is now the fastest, most efficient, and inexpensive way to reach a large pool of job seekers. Firms must abide by employment laws during selection. Before hiring candidates, human resource managers may require employment tests that evaluate certain skills or aptitudes. When all of this is complete, there is a better chance that the right person will be hired for the job.

job requirements the minimum skills, education, and experience that a candidate must have to be considered for the position.

 Discuss orientation, training, and evaluation.

New employees often participate in an orientation where they learn about company policies and practices. Training programs provide opportunities for employees to build their skills and knowledge and prepare them for new job opportunities within the company. Such programs also give employers a better chance of retaining employees. Performance appraisals give employees feedback about their strengths and weaknesses and how they can improve.

performance appraisal evaluation of and feedback on an employee's job performance.

 Describe compensation.

Firms compensate employees with wages, salaries, incentive pay systems, and benefits. Benefit programs vary among firms, but most companies offer health insurance and other health-related

programs, retirement plans, paid time off, and sick leave. A growing number of companies are offering flexible benefit plans and flexible work plans, such as flextime, compressed workweeks, job sharing, and home-based work.

compensation amount employees are paid in money and benefits.

wage pay based on an hourly rate or the amount of work accomplished.

salary pay calculated on a periodic basis, such as weekly or monthly.

employee benefits additional compensation such as vacation, retirement plans, profit-sharing, health insurance, gym memberships, child and elder care, and tuition reimbursement, offered by the employer.

 Discuss employee separation.

Employee separation occurs when a worker leaves his or her job, voluntarily or involuntarily. Sometimes an employee is terminated because of poor job performance or unethical behavior. Downsizing is the process of reducing the number of employees within a firm in order to cut costs and achieve a leaner organization. However, some negative effects include anxiety and lost productivity among remaining workers; expensive severance packages; and a domino effect in the local economy. Outsourcing involves transferring jobs from inside a firm to outside the firm. While some expenses may be cut, a firm may experience a backlash in performance and public image.

employee separation broad term covering the loss of an employee for any reason, voluntary or involuntary.

downsizing process of reducing the number of employees within a firm by eliminating jobs.

outsourcing transferring jobs from inside a firm to outside the firm.

 Explain the different methods for motivating employees.

Employee motivation starts with high employee morale. According to Maslow's hierarchy of needs, people satisfy lower-order needs (such as food and safety) before moving to higher-order needs (such as esteem and fulfillment). Equity theory refers to a person's perception of fair and equitable treatment. Goal-setting theory says that people will be motivated to the extent to which they accept specific, challenging goals.

Maslow's hierarchy of needs theory of motivation proposed by Abraham Maslow. According to the theory, people have five levels of needs that they seek to satisfy: physiological, safety, social, esteem, and self-actualization.

equity theory an individual's perception of fair and equitable treatment.

goal-setting theory says that people will be motivated to the extent to which they accept specific, challenging goals and receive feedback that indicates their progress toward goal achievement.

management by objectives (MBO) systematic approach that allows managers to focus on attainable goals and to achieve the best results based on the organization's resources.

7 Discuss labor–management relations.

Labor unions have resulted in the improvement of wages and working conditions for many workers over the past century, along with the passage of significant labor laws. Unions achieve these improvements through the collective bargaining process, resulting in an agreement. Most labor–management disputes are settled through the grievance process, in which sometimes mediation or arbitration is necessary.

labor union group of workers who have banded together to achieve common goals in the areas of wages, hours, and working conditions.

collective bargaining process of negotiation between management and union representatives.

>>> Quick Review >>

LO1

1. What is human resource management?

2. Why is it sometimes said that an organization is only as good as its employees?

LO2

1. List the steps in the recruiting and selection process.

2. What is the function of the Equal Employment Opportunity Commission (EEOC)?

LO3

1. What are the benefits of computer-based training programs?

2. Name the four important criteria of an effective performance appraisal.

LO4

1. Explain the difference between a *wage* and a *salary*.

2. On what factors do employers typically base their compensation decisions?

LO5

1. What is the difference between voluntary and involuntary turnover?

2. What is downsizing? How is it different from outsourcing?

LO6

1. Name the four steps in the process of motivation.

2. What are the five levels described in Maslow's hierarchy of needs theory?

3. Compare and contrast the Theory X, Theory Y, and Theory Z management approaches.

LO7

1. What is a labor union? What is collective bargaining?

2. Describe the three main tactics of a labor union.

3. Name the steps in a grievance procedure.

chapter nine

© Szepy/iStockphoto

Top Performance through Empowerment, Teamwork, and Communication

Learning Objectives

1. **Discuss** empowering employees.

2. **Name** and describe the five types of teams.

3. **Identify** the stages of team development.

4. **Evaluate** team cohesiveness and norms.

5. **Describe** team conflict.

6. **Explain** the importance of effective communication.

7. **Compare** the basic forms of communication.

Enterprise Rent-a-Car Thrives on Empowerment, Teamwork

What harried customer wouldn't love to hear a customer service rep say, "You haven't described anything we can't solve"? That's exactly what happened to a couple of insurance executives racing to make the last plane home one evening. Frantic, they couldn't stop to fill the gas tank of their rental car, so the Enterprise Rent-a-Car employee who met them calmly drove them to their gate in a company van, filled out their paperwork, and e-mailed them copies so they could make their flight.

Enterprise Holdings is a 55-year-old family-run business with about $14 billion in revenue a year as the world's largest car rental firm, which now includes the Enterprise, Alamo, and National brands. The company was founded by Jack Taylor on a simple principle: "Take care of your customers and your employees first, and the profits will follow." Managed today by CEO Andy Taylor, son of the founder, the company honors employee empowerment and encourages teamwork. Andy started working for the company at age 16, washing cars during the holidays and summer vacations to learn the basics of the business.

Enterprise is a top recruiter at colleges, hiring thousands of graduates every year as management trainees, if they have the right stuff: a passion for helping others, sales skills, a flexible approach toward work assignments, and lots of motivation to get things done right. To raise customer satisfaction, Taylor instituted better hiring practices to ensure employees have good communication skills. He insisted they know their customers' names, offer help without being asked, and never use industry jargon. Growth and profits increased dramatically, and Enterprise ranks number one among car rental companies in the J.D. Power customer satisfaction survey.

The company's strong focus on customer service and employees' ability to make decisions on their own have been major reasons for Enterprise's success at building a loyal customer base. Its loyalty program, Enterprise Plus, was upgraded to provide members with rewards and free rental days as well as members-only check-in and special offers through its "Email Extras" e-newsletter. Enterprise believes upgrading its loyalty program is just one more way to demonstrate how much it appreciates its customers and their loyalty. Enterprise was recently recognized as the "Most Iconic Brand" in the car rental category.[1]

Overview > > >

Top managers at organizations like Enterprise Rent-a-Car recognize that teamwork and communication are essential for empowering employees to perform their best. This chapter focuses on how organizations involve employees by sharing information and empowering them to make critical decisions, allowing them to work in teams, and fostering communication. It discusses how managers empower their employees' decision-making authority and responsibility. Then it explains why and how a growing number of firms rely on teams of workers rather than individuals to make decisions and carry out assignments. Finally, the chapter analyzes how effective communication helps workers share information that improves the quality of decision making.

1 Empowering Employees

empowerment giving employees authority and responsibility to make decisions about their work.

An important component of effective management is the **empowerment** of employees. Managers empower employees by giving them authority and responsibility to make decisions about their work. Empowerment seeks to tap the brainpower of all workers to find improved ways of doing their jobs, better serving customers, and achieving organizational goals. It also motivates workers by adding challenges to their jobs and giving them a feeling of ownership. Managers empower employees by sharing company information and decision-making authority and by rewarding them for their performance—as well as the company's.

SHARING INFORMATION AND DECISION-MAKING AUTHORITY

One of the most effective methods of empowering employees is to keep them informed about the company's financial performance. Anderson & Associates (A&A), an engineering firm, gives its employees regular reports on key financial information, such as profit-and-loss statements. A&A designs roads, water and sewer lines, and water treatment plants for municipalities, along with private construction projects like retirement community Warm Hearth Village, whose residents were consulted during the planning process. The firm practices open-book management, giving every employee access to the same financial information about his or her employer. Like other companies that practice this strategy, A&A also trains employees to interpret financial statements so that they can understand how their work contributes to company profits. Using information technology to empower employees does carry some risks, however; for example, information may reach a firm's competitors. Although A&A considered this problem, management decided that sharing information was essential to the company's strategy.[2]

The second way in which companies empower employees is to give them broad authority to make workplace decisions that implement a firm's vision and its competitive strategy. Even among non-management staff, empowerment extends to decisions and activities traditionally handled by managers. Employees might be responsible for such tasks as purchasing supplies, making hiring decisions, scheduling production or work hours, overseeing the safety program, and granting pay increases.

This can be an especially powerful tool in many health care environments. At Lebanon Valley Brethren Home, a long-term care facility, workers at all levels are empowered to do whatever it takes to improve the quality of their elderly residents' lives. Each care worker attends to the same residents every day, so caregivers and residents form a strong personal bond. Caregivers are responsible for the overall management of their households, including meals and housekeeping. They make decisions for individual residents ranging from sleep schedules to room lighting. As a result, each Green House—or household within the larger community—feels like a home.[3]

LINKING REWARDS TO COMPANY PERFORMANCE

Whether they work in a small team or a large organization or are individual contributors, aligning employees' motivation and performance with that of the company is critical to success of both. Two widely used ways that companies provide workers with a sense of ownership are employee stock ownership plans and stock options. TABLE 9.1 compares these two methods of employee ownership.

EMPLOYEE STOCK OWNERSHIP PLANS

Over 10 million workers participate in 10,900 *employee stock ownership plans (ESOPs)* worth almost $870 billion.[4] These plans benefit employees by giving them ownership stakes in their companies, leading to potential profits as the value of their firm increases. Under ESOPs, the employer buys shares of company stock on behalf of its employees as a retirement benefit. The accounts continue to grow in value tax-free, and when employees leave the company they can cash in their shares. Employees are motivated to work harder and smarter than they would without ESOPs because, as part owners, they share in their firm's financial success. Of companies that offer ESOPs, over 92 percent of those surveyed report an increase in employee productivity.[5]

As a retirement plan, an ESOP must comply with government regulations designed to protect pension benefits. Because ESOPs

▼ Companies can empower employees by giving them broad authority to make workplace decisions that implement the firm's vision and advances its competitive strategy without seeking managerial input. At some long-term care facilities, workers are empowered to do whatever it takes to improve the quality of their residents' lives.

Jacob Wackerhausen/iStockphoto

TABLE 9.1 Can you compare two methods of employee ownership?

Employee Stock Options and Ownership (ESOP)	Stock Options
Company-sponsored trust fund holds shares of stock for employees	Company gives employees the option to buy shares of its stock
Usually covers all full-time employees	Can be granted to one, a few, or all employees
Employer pays for the shares of stock	Employees pay a set price to exercise the option
Employees receive stock shares (or value of stock) upon retiring or leaving the company	Employees receive shares of stock when (and if) they exercise the option, usually during a set period

SOURCE: "Employee Stock Options and Ownership (ESOP)," Reference for Business, http://www.referenceforbusiness.com, accessed May 15, 2013; "Employee Stock Options Fact Sheet," National Center for Employee Ownership, http://www.nceo.org, accessed May 15, 2013.

can be expensive to set up, they are more common in larger firms than in smaller ones. Public companies with ESOPs average around 14,000 employees, and private companies average about 1,500 employees.[6] One danger with ESOPs is that if the majority of an employee's retirement funds are in company stock and the value falls dramatically, the employee—like other investors—will be financially harmed.[7]

STOCK OPTIONS

Another popular way for companies to share ownership with their employees is through the use of *stock options*—the right to buy a specified amount of company stock at a given price within a given time period. In contrast to an ESOP, a stock option gives employees a chance to own the stock themselves if they exercise their options by completing the stock purchase. If an employee receives an option on 100 shares at $10 per share and the stock price goes up to $20, the employee can exercise the option to buy those 100 shares at $10 each, sell them at the market price of $20, and pocket the difference. If the stock price never goes above the option price, the employee isn't required to exercise the option.[8]

Although options were once limited to senior executives and members of the board of directors, some companies now grant stock options to employees at all levels. Federal labor laws allow stock options to be granted to both hourly and salaried employees. An estimated 9 million employees in thousands of companies hold stock options.[9] About one-third of all stock options issued by U.S. corporations go to the top five executives at each firm. Much of the remainder goes to other executives and managers, who make up only about 2 percent of the U.S. workforce. Yet there is solid evidence that stock options motivate regular employees to perform better. Some argue that to be most effective as motivators, stock options need to be granted to a broad base of employees.

Stock options have turned hundreds of employees at firms such as Home Depot, Microsoft, and Google into millionaires. But such success is no guarantee, especially when stock prices drop during an economic downturn. As with ESOPs, employees face risks when they rely on a single company's stock to provide for them.

> >> **Quick Review**

1. What is empowerment?

2. What kinds of information can employers share with their workforce to help enhance their decision-making responsibility?

3. How do employee stock ownership plans and stock options reward employees and encourage empowerment?

2 Five Types of Teams

According to a saying attributed to Aristotle, "The whole is greater than the sum of its parts." And so it is with employees—individually they may be "just" workers, but collectively they do amazing things: build new products, launch companies, and create whole new industries. To accomplish these tasks, a manager often creates a **team**—a group of people with certain skills who are committed to a common purpose, approach, and set of performance goals. All team members hold themselves mutually responsible and accountable for accomplishing their objectives.

team group of people with certain skills who are committed to a common purpose, approach, and set of performance goals.

Teams are widely used in business and in many not-for-profit organizations such as hospitals and government agencies. Teams are one of the most frequently discussed topics in employee training programs because teams require that people learn how to work effectively together. Many firms emphasize the importance of teams during their hiring processes, asking job applicants about their previous experiences as team members. Why? Because companies want to hire people who can work well with other people and pool their talents and ideas to achieve more together than they could achieve working alone. **FIGURE 9.1** outlines five basic types of teams: work teams, problem-solving teams, self-managed teams, cross-functional teams, and virtual teams.

work team relatively permanent group of employees with complementary skills who perform the day-to-day work of organizations.

About two-thirds of U.S. firms currently use **work teams**, which are relatively permanent groups of

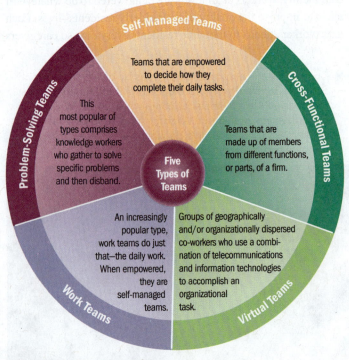

FIGURE 9.1 Five Types of Teams

employees. In this approach, people with complementary skills perform the day-to-day work of the organization. A **work team** might include all the workers involved in assembling and packaging a product—it could be anything from cupcakes to cars. Most of Walmart's major vendors maintain offices near Walmart headquarters. Typically, each vendor office operates as a work team, with the head of the vendor office often holding the title of "team leader."

In contrast to a work team, a **problem-solving team** is a temporary combination of workers who gather to solve a specific problem and then disband. This team differs from a work team in important ways, though. Work teams are permanent units designed to handle any business problem that arises, but problem-solving teams pursue specific missions. When Toyota faced serious quality problems—unintended acceleration, faulty brakes, questions about tires—and was forced to recall thousands of vehicles, the company formed Rapid Response SMART Teams to deal with the technical problems. The teams were made up of field technology specialists, engineers from manufacturing and design, and product engineers. Together, team members worked with dealers across the country to contact customers and arrange for on-site analyses of each problem vehicle to determine what went wrong and why. Teams were encouraged to "listen and react" to customers' descriptions of their experiences as part of their investigation.[10]

Typically, when a problem is solved, a problem-solving team disbands, but in some cases, it may develop a more permanent role within the firm.

problem-solving team temporary combination of workers who gather to solve a specific problem and then disband.

self-managed team work group with authority to decide how its members complete their daily tasks.

A work team empowered with the authority to decide how its members complete their daily tasks is called a **self-managed team**. A self-managed team works most effectively when it combines employees with a range of skills and functions. Members are cross-trained to perform each other's jobs as needed. Distributing decision-making authority in this way can free members to concentrate on satisfying customers.

Whole Foods Market has a structure based on self-managed work teams. Company managers decided that Whole Foods could be most innovative if employees made decisions themselves. Every employee is part of a team, and each store has about ten teams handling separate functions, such as groceries, bakery, and customer service. Each team handles responsibilities related to setting goals, hiring and training employees, scheduling team members, and purchasing merchandise. Teams meet at least monthly to review goals and performance, solve problems, and explore new ideas. Whole Foods awards bonuses based on the teams' performance relative to their goals.[11]

Λ Although members of a virtual team rarely meet in person, they stay in touch through technologies like videoconferencing. In today's global marketplace, the flexibility of virtual teams is a distinct advantage.

A team made up of members from different functions, such as production, marketing, and finance, is called a **cross-functional team**. Most often, cross-functional teams work on specific problems or projects, but they can also serve as permanent work team arrangements. The value of cross-functional teams comes from their ability to bring different perspectives—as well as different types of expertise—to a work effort. Communication is key to the success of cross-functional teams.

cross-functional team a working group of members from different functions, such as production, marketing, and finance.

A **virtual team** is a group of geographically or organizationally dispersed co-workers who use a combination of telecommunications and information technologies to accomplish an organizational task. Because of the availability of e-mail, videoconferencing, and group-communication software, members of virtual teams rarely meet face to face. Their principal advantage is their flexibility. Team members can work with each other regardless of physical location, time zone, or organizational affiliation. Virtual teams whose members are scattered across the globe can be difficult to manage, but firms that are committed to them believe the benefits outweigh the drawbacks.

virtual team a group of geographically or organizationally dispersed co-workers who use a combination of telecommunications and information technologies to accomplish an organizational task.

Image Source/Getty Images

> > > **Quick Review**

1 What is a team?

2 Name the five types of teams. How are they different?

3 Stages of Team Development

Teams typically progress through five stages of development: forming, storming, norming, performing, and adjourning. Although not every team passes through each of these stages, those that do usually perform better. These stages are summarized in **FIGURE 9.2**.

STAGE 1: FORMING

Forming is an orientation period during which team members get to know each other and find out what behaviors are acceptable to the group. Team members begin with curiosity about expectations of them and whether they will fit in with the group. An effective team leader provides time for members to become acquainted.

STAGE 2: STORMING

The personalities of team members begin to emerge during the storming stage, as members clarify their roles and expectations. Conflicts may arise as people disagree over the team's mission and jockey for position and control of the group. Subgroups may form based on common interests or concerns. At this stage, the team leader must encourage everyone to participate, allowing members to work through their uncertainties and conflicts. Teams must move beyond this stage to achieve real productivity.

STAGE 3: NORMING

During the norming stage, members resolve differences, accept each other, and reach broad agreement about the roles of the team

leader and other participants. This stage is usually brief, and the team leader should use it to emphasize the team's unity and the importance of its objectives.

STAGE 4: PERFORMING

While performing, members focus on solving problems and accomplishing tasks. They interact frequently and handle conflicts in constructive ways. The team leader encourages contributions from all members. He or she should attempt to get any nonparticipating team members involved.

STAGE 5: ADJOURNING

The team adjourns after members have completed the assigned task or solved the problem. During this phase, the focus is on wrapping up and summarizing the team's experiences and accomplishments. The team leader may recognize the team's accomplishments with a celebration, perhaps distributing plaques or awards.

>>> **Quick Review**

1 What are the five stages of team development?

2 Explain how a team progresses through each stage of development.

4 Team Cohesiveness and Norms

A team tends to maximize productivity when it becomes a highly cohesive unit. **Team cohesiveness** is the extent to which members feel attracted to the team and motivated to remain part of it. This cohesiveness typically increases when members interact frequently, share common attitudes and goals, and enjoy being together. Cohesive groups have a better chance of retaining their members than those that do not achieve cohesiveness. As a result, cohesive groups typically experience lower turnover. In addition, team cohesiveness promotes cooperative behavior, generosity, and a willingness on the part of team members to help each other. When team cohesiveness is high, team members are more motivated to contribute to the team because they want the approval of other team members. Not surprisingly, studies have clearly established that cohesive teams quickly achieve high levels of performance and consistently perform better.

Team-building retreats are one way to encourage cohesiveness and improve satisfaction and retention. Firms that specialize in conducting these retreats offer a wide range of options. CEO

> **team cohesiveness** extent to which team members feel attracted to the team and motivated to remain part of it.

FIGURE 9.2 Stages of Team Development

136

Chef offers to bring its team-building program to clients—an option typically less expensive than a traditional retreat. The culinary team from CEO Chef can travel to an off-site meeting location or to a company's own cafeteria for a team-building exercise in which participants work together to create a gourmet meal—then enjoy eating it.[12]

team norm standard of conduct shared by team members that guides their behavior.

A **team norm** is a standard of conduct shared by team members that guides their behavior. Norms are not formal written guidelines; they are informal standards that identify key values and clarify team members' expectations. In highly productive teams, norms contribute to constructive work and the accomplishment of team goals.

Team norms can be simple such as a group's expectations for working hours (staying late) or employee dress (casual Fridays). Or they can be involved and complex such as a member's willingness to accept a groups' decision after a decision has been made. In either case, members who follow the norms are more likely to be seen as a valuable part of the team, whereas members who do not embrace the team norms are often seen as less productive. As will be seen in the next section, when team conflicts arise, they often occur because one or more members of the team are not adhering to the team's norms.

>>> **Quick Review**

1. How does cohesiveness affect a team?

2. Explain how team norms positively and negatively affect a team.

5 Team Conflict

Conflict occurs when one person's or a group's needs do not match those of another, and attempts may be made to block the opposing side's intentions or goals. Conflict and disagreement are inevitable in most teams. But this shouldn't surprise anyone. People who work together sometimes disagree about what and how things are done. What causes conflict in teams? Although almost anything can lead to conflict—casual remarks that unintentionally offend a team member or fighting over scarce resources—the primary cause of team conflict is disagreement over goals and priorities. Other common causes of team conflict include disagreements over task-related issues, interpersonal incompatibilities, simple fatigue, and team diversity.

conflict situation in which the needs of a person or group do not match those of another and attempts may be made to block the opposing side's intentions or goals.

Strong teams are diverse in their members' experience, ability, and background. And though diversity brings stimulation, challenge, and energy, it can also lead to conflict. The manager must create an environment in which differences are appreciated and a team of diverse individuals can work productively together. Diversity awareness training programs can reduce conflict by bringing these differences out in the open and identifying the unique talents of diverse individuals.

Although most people think conflict should be avoided, management experts note that conflict can actually enhance team performance. The key to dealing with conflict is making sure the team experiences the right kind of conflict. **Cognitive conflict** focuses on problem-related differences of opinion; reconciling these differences strongly improves team performance. With cognitive conflict, team members disagree because their different experiences and expertise lead them to different views of the problem and its solutions. Cognitive conflict is also characterized by a willingness to examine, compare, and reconcile differences to produce the best-possible solution.

cognitive conflict disagreement that focuses on problem- and issue-related differences of opinion.

By contrast, **affective conflict** refers to the emotional reactions that can occur when disagreements become personal rather than professional, and these differences strongly decrease team performance. Because affective conflict often results in hostility, anger, resentment, distrust, cynicism, and apathy, it can make people uncomfortable, cause them to withdraw, decrease their commitment to a team, lower the satisfaction of team members, and decrease team cohesiveness. Unlike cognitive conflict, affective conflict undermines team performance by preventing teams from engaging in activities that are critical to team effectiveness.

affective conflict disagreement that focuses on individuals or personal issues.

What can managers do to manage team conflict—and even make it work for them? Perhaps the team leader's most important contribution to conflict resolution can be facilitating good communication so that teammates respect each other and are free to disagree with each other. Ongoing, effective communication ensures that team members perceive each other accurately, understand what is expected of them, and obtain the information they need. Taking this a step further, organizations should evaluate situations or conditions in the workplace that might be causing conflict. Solving a single conflict isn't helpful if there are problems systemic to the team or to the company. Team-building exercises, listening exercises, and role-playing can help employees learn to become better team members.[13]

>>> **Quick Review**

1. What is cognitive conflict? How does it affect a team?

2. Describe affective conflict and its effect on a team.

3. How can a team leader manage conflict—and even use it to work for the team?

6 The Importance of Effective Communication

No matter how well the rest of an organization operates, few businesses can succeed without effective **communication**, the meaningful exchange of information through messages. Toyota Motor Corp. became embroiled in miscommunication when it tried to establish a clear timeline for the reporting of the number of its vehicles that were affected by unintended acceleration worldwide. While the National Highway Traffic Safety Administration (NHTSA) investigated, Toyota continued the recalls over a period of several years, reaching a total of more than 8 million total vehicles. By the time the NHTSA closed its investigation, Toyota had been ordered to pay more than $66 million for not notifying the agency in a timely manner on the acceleration issues and was fined an additional $17 million for not telling the agency about a floormat issue in a separate recall of Lexus vehicles.[14]

> **communication** the meaningful exchange of information through messages.

Managers spend about 80 percent of their time—6 hours and 24 minutes of every 8-hour day—in direct communication with others, whether on the telephone, in meetings, via e-mail, or in individual conversations. Company recruiters consistently rate effective communication, such as listening, conversing, and giving feedback, as the most important skill they look for when hiring new employees.

THE PROCESS OF COMMUNICATION

Every communication follows a step-by-step process that involves interactions among six elements: sender, message, channel, audience, feedback, and context. This process is illustrated in **FIGURE 9.3**.

In the first step, the *sender* composes the *message* and sends it through a communication carrier, or *channel*. Encoding a message means that the sender crafts its meaning in understandable terms and in a form that allows transmission through a chosen channel. The sender can communicate a particular message through many different channels, including face-to-face conversations, phone calls, and e-mail or texting. A promotional message to the firm's customers may be communicated through such forms as radio and television ads, billboards, magazines and newspapers, sales presentations, and social media such as Facebook and Twitter. The *audience* consists of the person or persons who receive the message. In decoding, the receiver of the message interprets its meaning. *Feedback* from the audience—in response to the sender's communication—helps the sender determine whether the audience has correctly interpreted the intended meaning of the message.

Every communication takes place in some sort of situational or cultural context. The *context* can exert a powerful influence on how well the process works. A conversation between two people in a quiet office, for example, may be a very different experience from the same conversation held at a noisy party. And words have different meanings in different cultures. An American who orders chips in an English tavern will receive French fries.

Anthropologists classify cultures as *low context* or *high context*. Communication in low-context cultures such as Switzerland, Austria, Germany, and the United States tends to rely on explicit written and verbal messages. In contrast, communication in high-context cultures—such as those of Japan, Latin America, and India—depends not only on the message itself but also on the conditions that surround it, including nonverbal cues, past and present experiences, and personal relationships among the parties. Westerners must carefully temper their low-context style to the expectations of colleagues and clients from high-context countries. Although Americans tend to favor direct interactions and want to "get down to business" soon after shaking hands or sitting down to a business dinner, businesspeople in Mexico and Asian countries prefer to become acquainted before

> The noise shown in this photo is the result of communication overload.

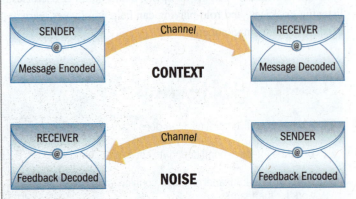

FIGURE 9.3 The Communication Process

Joe Potato Photo/iStockphoto

discussing details. When conducting business in these cultures, wise visitors allow time for relaxed meals during which business-related topics are avoided.

Senders must pay attention to audience feedback, even requesting it if none is forthcoming, because this response clarifies whether the communication has conveyed the intended message. Feedback can indicate whether the receiver heard the message and was able to decode it accurately. Even when the receiver tries to understand, the communication may fail if the message contained jargon or ambiguous words.

Noise during the communication process is any type of interference that affects the transmission of messages and feedback. Noise can result from simple physical factors, such as poor reception of a cell phone message or static that drowns out a radio commercial. It can also be caused by more complex differences in people's attitudes and perceptions. Consequently, even when people are exposed to the same communications, they can end up with very different perceptions and understandings because of communication noise.

7 Basic Forms of Communication

Managers and co-workers communicate in many different ways—by making a phone call, sending an e-mail, holding a staff meeting, or chatting in the hallway. They also communicate with facial expressions, gestures, and other body language. Subtle variations can significantly influence the reception of a message. As TABLE 9.2 points out, communication takes various forms: oral and written, formal and informal, and nonverbal.

ORAL COMMUNICATION

Managers spend much time engaged in oral communication, both in person and on the phone. Some people prefer to communicate this way, believing that oral channels convey messages more accurately. Face-to-face oral communication allows people to combine words with such cues as facial expressions and tone of voice. Oral communication over the telephone lacks visual cues, but it does allow people to hear the tone of voice and creates an opportunity to provide immediate feedback by asking questions or restating the message. Because of its immediacy, oral communication has drawbacks. If one person is agitated or nervous during a conversation, noise enters the communication process. A hurried manager might brush off an employee who has an important message to deliver. A frustrated employee might feel compelled to fire a harsh retort at an unsupportive supervisor instead of thinking before responding.

In any medium, a vital component of oral communication is **listening**—receiving a message and interpreting its genuine meaning by accurately grasping the facts and feelings conveyed. Although listening may be the most important communication skill, most of us don't use it enough—or as well as we should.

listening receiving a message and interpreting its intended meaning by grasping the facts and feelings it conveys.

Listening may seem easy because the listener appears to make no effort. But the average person talks at a rate of roughly 150 words per minute, while the brain can handle up to 400 words per minute. This gap can lead to listener boredom, inattention, and misinterpretation. In fact, immediately after listening to a message, the average person can recall only half of it. After several

TABLE 9.2 How would you describe the various forms of communication?

Form	Description	Examples
Oral communication	Communication transmitted through speech	Personal conversations, speeches, meetings, voice mail, telephone conversations, videoconferences
Written communication	Communication transmitted through writing	E-mails, letters, memos, formal reports, news releases, online discussion groups, Internet messaging, faxes
Formal communication	Communication transmitted through the chain of command within an organization to other members or to people outside the organization	Internal—memos, reports, meetings, written proposals, oral presentations, meeting minutes; external—letters, written proposals, oral presentations, speeches, news releases, press conferences
Informal communication	Communication transmitted outside formal channels without regard for the organization's hierarchy of authority	Rumors spread among employees via the grapevine
Nonverbal communication	Communication transmitted through actions and behaviors rather than through words	Gestures, facial expressions, posture, body language, dress

days, the proportion of a message that a listener can recall falls to 25 percent or less.

Certain types of listening behaviors are common in both business and personal interactions:

- *Cynical or defensive listening.* Occurs when the receiver of a message feels the sender is trying to gain some advantage from the communication.
- *Offensive listening.* Receiver tries to catch the speaker in a mistake or contradiction.
- *Polite listening.* Receiver listens to be polite rather than to contribute to communication. Polite listeners are usually inattentive and spend their time rehearsing what they want to say when the speaker finishes.
- *Active listening.* Receiver is involved with the information and shows empathy for the speaker's situation. In both business and personal life, active listening is the basis for effective communication.

Learning how to be an active listener is an especially important goal for business leaders because effective communication is essential to their role. Listening is hard work, but it pays off with increased learning, better interpersonal relationships, and greater influence.

WRITTEN COMMUNICATION

Channels for written communication include reports, letters, memos, online discussion boards and social media, e-mails, and text messages. Many of these channels permit only delayed feedback and create a record of the message. It is important for the sender of a written communication to prepare the message carefully and review it to avoid misunderstandings—particularly before pressing that "send" button.

Effective written communication reflects its audience, the channel carrying the message, and the appropriate degree of formality. When writing a formal business document such as a complex marketing research report, a manager must plan in advance and carefully construct the document. The process of writing a formal document involves planning, research, organization, composition and design, and revision. Written communication

> Listening may seem easy. However, because the brain can handle many more words per minute than the average person can speak, this gap makes attentive listening a real challenge.

GlobalStock/iStockphoto

via e-mail may call for a less-formal writing style, including short sentences, phrases, and lists.

E-mail is an effective communication channel for delivering straightforward messages and information. But e-mail's perceived effectiveness also leads to one of its biggest drawbacks: too much e-mail! Many workers find their valuable time being consumed with e-mail. To relieve this burden and leave more time for performing the most important aspects of the job, some companies are looking into ways to reduce the time employees spend sending and reading e-mail. To fulfill this need, some firms provide e-mail management services. DakotaPro.biz provides customized e-mail solutions for firms that struggle to keep up with the volume of e-mail they receive and the time it takes to operate an in-house server.[15]

Security and retention present other e-mail concerns. Because e-mail messages are often informal, senders occasionally forget they're creating a written record. Even if the recipient deletes an e-mail message, other copies exist on company e-mail servers. Such e-mails can be used as evidence in lawsuits or disciplinary actions.

FORMAL COMMUNICATION

A *formal communication channel* carries messages that flow within the chain-of-command structure defined by an organization. The most familiar channel, downward communication, carries messages from someone senior in the organization to subordinates. Managers may communicate downward by sending employees e-mail messages, presiding at department meetings, distributing policy manuals, posting notices on bulletin boards, and reporting news in company newsletters. The most important factor in formal communication is to be open and honest. "Spinning" bad news to make it look better almost always backfires. In a work environment characterized by open communication, employees feel free to express opinions, offer suggestions, and even voice complaints. Research has shown that open communication has the following seven characteristics:

1. *Employees are valued.* Employees are happier and more motivated when they feel they are valued and their opinions are heard.

2. *A high level of trust exists.* Telling the truth maintains a high level of trust, forming a foundation for open communication and employee motivation and retention.

3. *Conflict is invited and resolved positively.* Without conflict, innovation and creativity are stifled.

4. *Creative dissent is welcomed.* By expressing unique ideas, employees feel they have contributed to the organization and improved performance.

5. *Employee input is solicited.* The key to any organization's success is input from employees, which establishes a sense of involvement and improves working relations.

6. *Employees are well informed.* Employees are kept informed about what is happening within the organization.

7. *Feedback is ongoing.* Both positive and negative feedback are ongoing and are provided in a manner that builds relationships rather than assigns blame.[16]

Many firms also define formal channels for upward communications, encouraging communication from employees to supervisors and upward to leadership. Some examples of upward communication channels are employee surveys, suggestion boxes, and systems that allow employees to propose ideas for new products or voice complaints. Upward communication is also necessary for managers to evaluate the effectiveness of downward communication. **FIGURE 9.4** illustrates the forms of organizational communication, both formal and informal.

INFORMAL COMMUNICATION

Informal communication channels carry messages outside formally authorized channels within an organization's hierarchy. A familiar example of an informal channel is the **grapevine,** an internal channel that

> **grapevine** internal information channel that transmits information from unofficial sources.

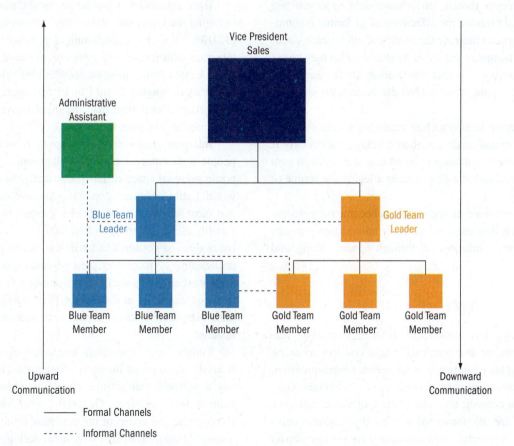

FIGURE 9.4 Formal and Informal Channels of Communication

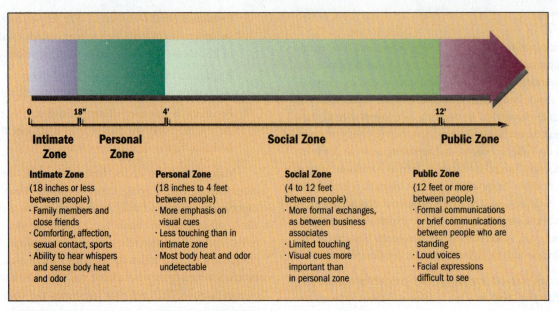

FIGURE 9.5 Influence of Personal Space in Nonverbal Communication

The figure shows a continuum arrow with measurements and four zones:

Intimate Zone

Personal Zone

Social Zone

Public Zone

Measurements along the arrow: 0, 18", 4', 12'

Intimate Zone
(18 inches or less between people)
· Family members and close friends
· Comforting, affection, sexual contact, sports
· Ability to hear whispers and sense body heat and odor

Personal Zone
(18 inches to 4 feet between people)
· More emphasis on visual cues
· Less touching than in intimate zone
· Most body heat and odor undetectable

Social Zone
(4 to 12 feet between people)
· More formal exchanges, as between business associates
· Limited touching
· Visual cues more important than in personal zone

Public Zone
(12 feet or more between people)
· Formal communications or brief communications between people who are standing
· Loud voices
· Facial expressions difficult to see

carries information from unofficial sources. All organizations, large or small, have grapevines. Grapevines disseminate information with speed and economy and are surprisingly reliable. But company communications must be managed effectively so that the grapevine is not the main source of information.

When properly nurtured, the grapevine can help managers get a feel for employee morale, understand what employees are thinking about, and evaluate the effectiveness of formal communications. Managers can improve the quality of information circulating through the company grapevine by sharing what they know, even if it is preliminary or partial information. By feeding information to selected people, smart leaders can harness the power of the grapevine.

But the grapevine is also a chief carrier of gossip. And because gossip can spread misinformation quickly—particularly if it reaches the Internet—a manager should deal directly with gossip to attempt to maintain the grapevine as a legitimate source of information.

More than ever before, as organizations become more decentralized and globally dispersed, informal communication provides an important source of information, through e-mail, texting, and social media.

NONVERBAL COMMUNICATION

So far, this section has considered different forms of verbal communication, or communication that conveys meaning through words. Equally important is *nonverbal communication,* which transmits messages through actions and behaviors. Gestures, posture, eye contact, tone and volume of voice, and even clothing choices are all nonverbal actions that become communication cues. Nonverbal cues can have a far greater impact

on communications than many people realize. In fact, an estimated 70 percent of interpersonal communication is conveyed through nonverbal cues. Top salespeople are particularly adept at reading and using these cues. For example, they practice "mirroring" a customer's gestures and body language in order to indicate agreement.[17]

Even personal space—the physical distance between people engaging in communication—can convey powerful messages. **FIGURE 9.5** shows a continuum of personal space and social interaction with four zones: intimate, personal, social, and public. In the United States, most business conversations occur within the social zone, roughly from 4 to 12 feet apart. If one person tries to approach closer than that, the other individual will likely feel uncomfortable or even threatened.

Interpreting nonverbal cues can be especially challenging for people with different cultural backgrounds. Concepts of appropriate personal space differ dramatically throughout most of the world. Latin Americans conduct business discussions in positions that most Americans and northern Europeans would find uncomfortably close. Americans often back away to preserve their personal space, a gesture that Latin Americans perceive as a sign of unfriendliness. To protect their personal space, some Americans separate themselves across desks or tables from their Latin American counterparts—at the risk of challenging their colleagues to maneuver around those obstacles to reduce the uncomfortable distance.

People send nonverbal messages even when they consciously try to avoid doing so. Sometimes nonverbal cues convey a person's true attitudes and thoughts, which may differ from spoken meanings. Generally, when verbal and nonverbal cues conflict, receivers of the communication tend to believe the nonverbal content. This is why firms seeking to hire people with good attitudes and a team orientation closely watch nonverbal behavior during job interviews in which job applicants participate in group sessions with other job candidates applying for the same job. If in those group interviews an applicant frowns or looks discouraged when a competing candidate gives a good answer, that nonverbal behavior suggests that this person may not be strongly team oriented.

EXTERNAL COMMUNICATION

external communication *meaningful exchange of information through messages transmitted between an organization and its major audiences.*

External communication is a meaningful exchange of information through messages transmitted between an organization and its major audiences, such as customers, suppliers, other firms, the general public, the media, and government officials. Businesses use external communication for many purposes:

- To keep their operations functioning
- To maintain their position in the marketplace
- To preserve their corporate reputation
- To build customer relationships

Using external communication, organizations provide information on such topics as product modifications and price changes. Every communication with customers—including sales presentations and advertisements—should create goodwill and contribute to customer satisfaction. For example, SC Johnson uses its annual report, its Web site, press releases, product packaging, and even the phone to communicate good news about the company.

Jacob Wackerhausen/iStockphoto

∧ Businesses use external communication to keep their operations functioning, preserve their reputation and their position in the marketplace, and to build customer relationships.

Letting the public know about the firm's new initiatives for environmentally friendly processes, community projects, and other socially responsible activities is an important function of external communication.

> > > **Quick Review**

1 Define the four common listening behaviors.

2 Explain the differences between formal and informal communication.

3 What is external communication?

What's Ahead? > > >

Today's consumers expect the products they buy to be of the highest value for the price. Firms ensure this value by developing efficient systems for producing goods and services and maintaining high quality. The next chapter examines how businesses produce world-class goods and services, efficiently organize their production facilities, purchase what they need to produce their goods and services, and manage large inventories to maximize efficiency and reduce costs.

Weekly Updates spark classroom debate around current events that apply to your business course topics. http://www.wileybusinessupdates.com

NOTES

1. Company Web site, "Culture of Customer Service," http://www.aboutus.enterprise.com, accessed April 30, 2013; "Enterprise Rent-a-Car Ranked One of the 'Most Iconic Brands' of 2012," *KMOX News,* March 30, 2012, http://stlouis.cbslocal.com; "New Enterprise Plus Program Rewards Loyal Enterprise Rent-a-Car Customers," press release, March 13, 2012, http://www.finance.yahoo.com; Scott S. Smith, "The Car-Rental Enterprise of CEO Andy Taylor," *Investor's Business Daily,* January 24, 2012, http://news.investors.com; Christine M. Riordan, "Give the Holiday Gift of a Remarkable Customer Experience," *Forbes,* December 21, 2011, www.forbes.com; "Campaign Highlights Customer Service, Employee Empowerment, Family Heritage," *MarketWire,* February 28, 2011, www.marketwire.com.

2. Company Web site, http://www.andassoc.com, accessed April 30, 2013; Su Clauson-Wicker, "Warm Hearth CEO Ferne Moschella: Seeing the Trees & the Forest," *Ampersand* 24, no. 1, http://www.andassoc.com, accessed April 30, 2013.

3. Retirement Community Web site, http://www.lvbh.org, accessed May 15, 2013; David Farrell, "Empowerment Is Foundational to Success: Herzberg and the Green House Model," The Green House Project Blog, March 11, 2013, http://blog.thegreenhouse-project.org.

4. Organization Web site, http://www.nceo.org, accessed April 30, 2013.

5. Association Web site, http://www.esopassociation.org, accessed April 30, 2013.

6. Organization Web site, http://www.nceo.org, accessed April 30, 2013.

7. Organization Web site, "Employee Ownership as a Retirement Plan," http://www.nceo.org, accessed April 30, 2013.

8. Organization Web site, "Employee Stock Options Fact Sheet," http://www.nceo.org, accessed April 30, 2013.

9. Ibid.

10. Company Web site, https://secure.toyota.com/safety/smart-team/videos/rapid-response-smart-team.html, accessed April 30, 2013.

11. Company Web site, "Whole Foods Market's Core Values," http://www.wholefoodsmarket.com, accessed April 30, 2013.

12. Company Web site, http://ceochef.com, accessed April 30, 2013.

13. Tara Duggan, "Leadership vs. Conflict Resolution," *Chron.com,* http://smallbusiness.chron.com, accessed April 30, 2013.

14. Mike Ramsey, "Toyota in $1.1 Billion Gas-Pedal Settlement," *The Wall Street Journal*, December 27, 2012, http://online.wsj.com; Christopher Jensen, "Toyota Recalls Nearly 700,000 Vehicles for Potential Brake Light and Air-Bag Failures," *New York Times,* March 9, 2012, http://www.nytimescom.

15. Company Web site, "Why Outsource Email?" http://www.dakotapro.biz, accessed April 30, 2013.

16. "Expand Trust in Your Organization," *Peter Stark.com,* http://www.peterstark.com, accessed April 30, 2013.

17. John Boe, "How to Read Your Prospect like a Book!" John Boe International, http://johnboe.com, accessed April 30, 2013.

Summary of Learning Objectives

 Discuss empowering employees.

Empowerment comes from giving employees authority and responsibility to make decisions about their work without traditional managerial approval and control.

empowerment giving employees authority and responsibility to make decisions about their work.

 Name and describe the five types of teams.

The five basic types of teams are work teams, problem-solving teams, self-managed teams, cross-functional teams, and virtual teams.

1. Work teams are permanent groups of coworkers who perform the day-to-day tasks necessary to operate the organization.
2. Problem-solving teams are temporary groups of employees who gather to solve specific problems and then disband.
3. Self-managed teams have the authority to make decisions about how their members complete their daily tasks.
4. Cross-functional teams are made up of members from different units, such as production, marketing, and finance.
5. Virtual teams are groups of geographically or organizationally dispersed coworkers who use a combination of information and telecommunications technologies to accomplish an organizational task.

team group of people with certain skills who are committed to a common purpose, approach, and set of performance goals.

work team relatively permanent group of employees with complementary skills who perform the day-to-day work of organizations.

problem-solving team temporary combination of workers who gather to solve a specific problem and then disband.

self-managed team work group with authority to decide how its members complete their daily tasks.

cross-functional team a working group of members from different functions, such as production, marketing, and finance.

virtual team a group of geographically or organizationally dispersed co-workers who use a combination of telecommunications and information technologies to accomplish an organizational task.

 Identify the stages of team development.

Teams pass through five stages of development:

1. Forming, an orientation period during which members get to know each other and find out what behaviors are acceptable to the group

2. Storming, the stage during which individual personalities emerge as members clarify their roles and expectations.
3. Norming, during which differences are resolved, members accept each other, and consensus emerges about the roles of the team leader and other participants
4. Performing, a stage characterized by problem solving and a focus on task accomplishment.
5. Adjourning, the final stage, focuses on wrapping up and summarizing the team's experiences and accomplishments.

 Evaluate team cohesiveness and norms.

Team cohesiveness is the extent to which team members feel attracted to the team and motivated to remain on it. Team norms are standards of conduct shared by team members that guide their behavior. Highly cohesive teams whose members share certain standards of conduct tend to be more productive and effective.

team cohesiveness extent to which team members feel attracted to the team and motivated to remain part of it.

team norm standard of conduct shared by team members that guides their behavior.

 Describe team conflict.

Conflict and disagreement are inevitable in most teams. Conflict can stem from many sources:

- Disagreements about goals and priorities
- Task-related issues
- Interpersonal incompatibilities
- Scarce resources
- Simple fatigue

The key to dealing with team conflict is not avoiding it, but making sure the team experiences the right kind of conflict.

- Cognitive conflict focuses on problem-related differences of opinion and, when reconciled, strongly improves team performance.
- Affective conflict refers to the emotional reactions that can occur when disagreements become personal rather than professional, and these differences strongly decrease team performance.

A team leader can manage team conflict by fostering good communication so team members perceive each other accurately, understand what is expected of them, and obtain the information they need.

conflict situation in which the needs of a person or group do not match those of another and attempts may be made to block the opposing side's intentions or goals.

cognitive conflict disagreement that focuses on problem- and issue-related differences of opinion.

affective conflict disagreement that focuses on individuals or personal issues.

6 Explain the importance of effective communication.

Managers spend about 80 percent of their time in direct communication with others. Company recruiters consistently rate effective communication—such as listening, conversing, and giving feedback—as the most important skill they look for when hiring new employees. The communication process follows a step-by-step process that involves interactions among six elements: sender, message, channel, audience, feedback, and context. The sender composes the message and sends it through the channel. The audience receives the message and interprets its meaning. The receiver gives feedback to the sender. The communication takes place in a situational or cultural context.

communication the meaningful exchange of information through messages.

7 Compare the basic forms of communication.

People exchange messages in many ways: oral and written, formal and informal, verbal and nonverbal communication. Effective written communication reflects its audience, its channel, and the appropriate degree of formality. Formal communication channels carry messages within the chain of command. Informal communication channels, such as the grapevine, carry messages outside the formal chain of command. Nonverbal communication plays a larger role than most people realize. Generally, when verbal and nonverbal cues conflict, the receiver of a message tends to believe the meaning conveyed by nonverbal cues.

External communication is a meaningful exchange of information through messages transmitted between an organization and its major audiences, such as customers, suppliers, other firms, the general public, and government officials. Every communication with customers should create goodwill and contribute to customer satisfaction. However, all of this is threatened when companies experience a public crisis that threatens their reputation or goodwill. To manage a public crisis, businesses should respond quickly and honestly, with a member of top management present.

listening receiving a message and interpreting its intended meaning by grasping the facts and feelings it conveys.

grapevine internal information channel that transmits information from unofficial sources.

external communication meaningful exchange of information through messages transmitted between an organization and its major audiences.

>>> Quick Review >>

LO1

1. What is empowerment?

2. What kinds of information can employers share with their workforce to help enhance their decision-making responsibility?

3. How do employee stock ownership plans and stock options reward employees and encourage empowerment?

LO2

1. What is a team?

2. Name the five types of teams. How are they different?

LO3

1. What are the five stages of team development?

2. Explain how a team progresses through each stage of development.

LO4

1. How does cohesiveness affect a team?

2. Explain how team norms positively and negatively affect a team.

LO5

1. What is cognitive conflict? How does it affect a team?

2. Describe affective conflict and its effect on a team.

3. How can a team leader manage conflict—and even use it to work for the team?

LO6

1. Describe the difference between communication in low-context cultures and high-context cultures.

2. In the context of the communication process, what is noise? Can a manager decrease this kind of noise in the workplace?

LO7

1. Define the four common listening behaviors.

2. Explain the differences between formal and informal communication.

3. What is external communication?

chapter ten

Production and Operations Management

Learning Objectives

1 **Identify** and describe the four main categories of production processes.

2 **Identify** and describe the three major production methods.

3 **Describe** the strategic decisions made by production and operations managers.

4 **Identify** the steps in the production control process.

5 **Discuss** the importance of quality control.

Intel's "Fab" New Manufacturing Facility

What's it like inside one of Intel's secure microprocessor chip fabricating facilities? If you're lucky enough to visit a "fab" plant— and few people are—you'll enter dressed in a white jumpsuit, double-layered gloves, and special shoes, hairnet, and goggles. All that gear is to protect the chips, by the way, not you.

Intel supplies chips for about 80 percent of all laptops, its core market, but with the rapid growth of smart phones and tablets, which require different, smaller microprocessors, the firm is investing $9 billion to increase its production capacity and stay ahead of demand for the new 22-nanometer technology. "By continuing to push our manufacturing leadership," says a company spokesperson, "Intel has a great opportunity to be a significant force in markets where it hasn't traditionally been a factor."

Intel's latest factory, the 1 million-square-foot Fab 42 now under construction in Arizona, will consume about $5 billion of the firm's production investment on its way to becoming the most advanced high-volume semiconductor manufacturing plant in the world. Fab 42 will require 11 million skilled-labor hours, the efforts of 2,000 to 3,000 construction workers, almost 600 miles of wiring, 86,000 cubic yards of concrete, more than 130 miles of mechanical piping, and 21,000 tons of structural steel. To lift 300-ton roof trusses into place, Intel also needed the largest land-based crane in the world, which was assembled on the site from pieces that filled 250 trucks.

Building the new facility (set to employ about 1,000 people when it opens) is "a very large, complex construction process," says the company's head of manufacturing. The rest of Intel's investment in production will help upgrade its existing facilities. At Fab 32, for instance, 30 quality-control specialists monitor the automated manufacturing processes 24/7, speedily shutting equipment down in the rare case of a defect. The facility can test for 1,500 different defects in silicon wafers the width of a human hair. Fab 42 will doubtless do likewise and more. "We think Fab 42 will lead us into the future," says Intel's head of manufacturing.[1]

148

Overview >>>

Businesses create what economists call **utility**, a measure of the value of a good or service to a consumer by producing and marketing products that people want. Businesses can create or enhance four basic kinds of utility: time, place, ownership, and form. A firm's marketing operation generates time, place, and ownership utility by offering products to customers at a time and place that is convenient for purchase. Production creates form utility by converting raw materials and other inputs into finished products, such as Boeing's 737 jets. **Production** uses resources, including workers and machinery, to convert materials into finished goods and services. This conversion process may make major changes in raw materials or simply combine already finished parts into new products. The task of **production and operations management** in a firm is to oversee the production process by managing people and machinery in converting materials and resources into finished goods and services (which is illustrated by **FIGURE 10.1**).

utility a measure of the value of a good or service to a consumer.

production use of resources, such as workers and machinery, to convert materials into finished goods and services.

production and operations management overseeing the production process by managing people and machinery in converting materials and resources into finished goods and services.

FIGURE 10.1 The Production Process: Converting Inputs to Outputs

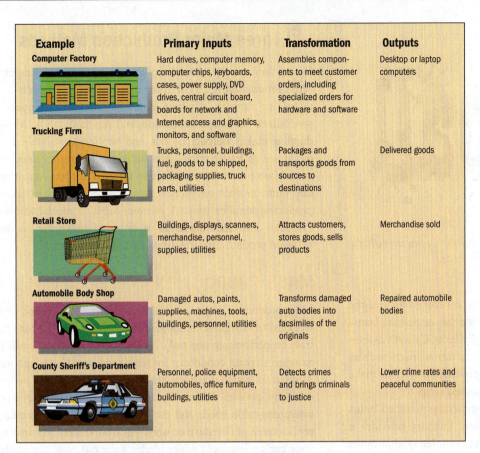

Example	Primary Inputs	Transformation	Outputs
Computer Factory	Hard drives, computer memory, computer chips, keyboards, cases, power supply, DVD drives, central circuit board, boards for network and Internet access and graphics, monitors, and software	Assembles components to meet customer orders, including specialized orders for hardware and software	Desktop or laptop computers
Trucking Firm	Trucks, personnel, buildings, fuel, goods to be shipped, packaging supplies, truck parts, utilities	Packages and transports goods from sources to destinations	Delivered goods
Retail Store	Buildings, displays, scanners, merchandise, personnel, supplies, utilities	Attracts customers, stores goods, sells products	Merchandise sold
Automobile Body Shop	Damaged autos, paints, supplies, machines, tools, buildings, personnel, utilities	Transforms damaged auto bodies into facsimiles of the originals	Repaired automobile bodies
County Sheriff's Department	Personnel, police equipment, automobiles, office furniture, buildings, utilities	Detects crimes and brings criminals to justice	Lower crime rates and peaceful communities

FIGURE 10.2 Typical Production Systems

People sometimes use the terms *production* and *manufacturing* interchangeably, but the two are actually different. Production spans both manufacturing and nonmanufacturing industries. For instance, companies that engage in fishing or mining engage in production, as do firms that provide package deliveries or lodging. Similarly, a hospital's services could be thought of as production—in this case, the number of patients seen versus the number of cars produced or the number of packages delivered. **FIGURE 10.2** lists five examples of production systems for a variety of goods and services.

But whether the production process results in a tangible good such as a car or an intangible service such as cable television, it always converts *inputs* into *outputs*. A cabinetmaker combines wood, tools, and skill to create finished kitchen cabinets for a new home. A transit system combines buses, trains, and employees to create its output: passenger transportation. Both of these production processes create utility.

This chapter describes the process of producing goods and services, the importance of production and operations management, and discusses the new technologies that are transforming the production function.

1 The Four Main Categories of Production Processes

Along with marketing and finance, production is a vital business activity. Without goods or services to sell, companies cannot generate money to pay their employees, lenders, and stockholders.

And without profits, firms quickly fail. The production process is just as crucial in not-for-profit organizations, such as St. Jude Children's Research Hospital, because without financially profitable operations they too will fail. Effective production and operations management can lower a firm's costs of production, allowing it to respond dependably to customer demands and create sufficient cash to renew itself, providing new products to its customers. Throughout their business operations, firms must continually strive to provide high-quality goods and services. Quality is an essential element of all modern business operations. By building quality into every one of its business processes, a firm will be able to consistently meet customers' expectations and compete in their industry. The most successful firms in any industry are those that are able to provide the greatest utility to their customers.

When thinking about production, it is not surprising that an Apple iPad and a computer mouse pad are produced with very different processes. Some products, like the iPad, require a wide range of processes. Others, like the mouse pad, may require only a few. However, whether it's one process or many thousand, almost all production processes can be separated into several unique groups.

An *analytic production process* reduces a raw material to its component parts in order to extract one or more marketable products. Petroleum refining breaks down crude oil into several marketable products, including gasoline, heating oil, and aviation fuel. When corn is processed, the resulting marketable food products include animal feed and corn sweetener.

Serdar Tibet/Shutterstock

∧ Paintballs—have you ever wondered how they are made? It's an interesting production process.

A *synthetic production process* is the reverse of an analytic process. It combines a number of raw materials or parts or transforms raw materials to produce finished products. Canon's assembly line produces a camera by assembling various parts such as a shutter or a lens cap. Other synthetic production systems make drugs, chemicals, computer chips, and canned soup.

A *continuous production process* generates finished items over a lengthy period of time. The steel industry provides a classic example. Its blast furnaces never completely shut down except for malfunctions. Petroleum refineries, chemical plants, and nuclear power facilities also practice continuous production. A shutdown can damage sensitive equipment, with extremely costly results.

An *intermittent production process* generates products in short production runs, shutting down machines frequently or changing their configurations to produce different products. Most services result from intermittent production systems. For instance, accountants, plumbers, and dentists traditionally have not attempted to standardize their services because each service provider confronts different problems that require individual approaches.

To view some interesting production processes, take a look at the Discovery Channel *How Its Made* series on the Internet. This series details the many processes used to create some everyday products, from stackable chips to turbine blades to paintballs. The manufacture of paintballs is a good example of a synthetic process using both intermittent (the production of the shell material) and continuous processes (the molding and filling of the shell).[2]

>>> Quick Review

1 Why is production an important activity for all organizations?

2 What are the four types of production processes?

2 Three Major Production Methods

Production activity can take place under various arrangements. *Mass production* is a system for manufacturing products in large quantities through effective combinations of employees with specialized skills, mechanization, and standardization. Mass production makes outputs (goods and services) available in large quantities at lower prices than individually crafted items would cost. Mass production is effective for creating large quantities of one item; *flexible production* is usually more cost-effective for producing smaller runs. A *customer-driven production* system evaluates customer demands in order to make the connection between products manufactured and products bought.

MASS PRODUCTION

Mass production begins with the *specialization of labor,* dividing work into its simplest components so that each worker can concentrate on performing one task. By separating jobs into small tasks, managers create conditions for high productivity through *mechanization*, in which machines perform much of the work previously done by people. *Standardization* involves producing uniform, interchangeable goods and parts. Standardized parts simplify the replacement of defective or worn-out components. For instance, if your car's windshield wiper blades wear out, you can easily buy replacements at a local auto parts store such as AutoZone.

A logical extension of these principles of specialization, mechanization, and standardization led to development of the *assembly line process,* a common process in today's industries. This manufacturing method moves the product along a conveyor belt past a number of workstations, where workers perform specialized tasks such as welding, painting, installing individual parts, and tightening bolts. Henry Ford's application of this concept revolutionized auto assembly. Before the assembly line, it took Ford's workers 12 hours to assemble a Model T car. But with an assembly line, it took just 1.5 hours to make the same car.

Although mass production has important advantages, it has limitations, too. Mass production is highly efficient for producing large numbers of similar products, but it is highly inefficient when producing small batches of different items. This trade-off might tempt some companies to focus on efficient production methods rather than on making what customers really want. In addition, the labor specialization associated with mass production can lead to boring jobs because workers keep repeating the same task. To improve their competitive capabilities, many firms adopt flexible production and customer-driven production systems. These methods won't replace mass production in every case, but in many instances might lead to improved product quality and greater job satisfaction. It might also enhance the use of mass production.

FLEXIBLE PRODUCTION

Flexible production can take many forms, but it generally involves using information technology to share the details of customer

^ This Honda auto plant uses flexible production techniques to turn out several different models. The auto industry, which developed mass production methods, now finds flexible production to be more efficient.

orders, programmable equipment to fulfill the orders, and skilled people to carry out whatever tasks are needed to fill a particular order. This system is even more beneficial when combined with lean production methods that use automation and information technology to reduce requirements for workers and inventory. Flexible production requires a lot of communication among everyone in the organization.

Flexible production is now widely used in the auto industry: Henry Ford revolutionized auto production in the early 20th century; current automakers such as Toyota and Honda are innovating with new methods of production. Changing from mass production to flexible production has enabled these companies to produce different kinds of cars at the same plant. Honda's flexible manufacturing plant in Marysville, Ohio, now builds more than 90 percent of all Honda sedans sold in the United States. The facility accomplishes this through team-based operations, relying on the expertise and knowledge of individual workers to innovate and improve manufacturing processes.[3]

CUSTOMER-DRIVEN PRODUCTION

A customer-driven production system evaluates customer demands in order to make the connection between products manufactured and products bought. Many firms use this approach with great success. One method is to establish computer links between factories and retailers' scanners, using data about sales as the basis for creating short-term forecasts and designing production schedules to meet those forecasts. Another approach to customer-driven production systems is simply not to make the product until a customer orders it—whether it's a taco or a computer.

Shibui Designs creates custom-made dresses in high-end fabrics for female executives and other women over 40. Each item of clothing is custom cut and fit to a single customer's measurements. Founder Elizabeth Nill started the business because she couldn't find clothing that fit well. "I don't have the body of a model, and the bulges are real. Truly made classic clothing that is custom made-to-measure helps camouflage these inevitable imperfections and makes me feel more elegant." Nill's customers agree.[4]

>>> **Quick Review**

1 What are the three major production methods?

2 How does Honda use a flexible production method?

3 The Strategic Decisions Made by Production and Operations Managers

Developing a production strategy often begins with a rereading of a firm's mission statement, identifying its core strengths, comparative advantages, and vision for the future. For example, an Internet retailer may decide that one of its core strengths is the management of a complex inventory system. Consequently, the organization may create an extensive warehousing system to offer customers quick, efficient product delivery (Amazon). Or a firm may decide the customer interface is its core strength, and it may then choose to rely on others to fulfill customer orders (eBay). Similarly, a firm may decide that they want to develop an extensive manufacturing capability (GE), or they may decide that they want to let others produce merchandise for them (Apple). These types of strategic choices often come down to what is known as a **make, buy, or lease decision**, choosing whether to produce a good or service in-house or purchase it from an outside supplier.

> **make, buy, or lease decision** choosing whether to manufacture a product or component in-house, purchase it from an outside supplier, or lease it.

Many factors affect the make, buy, or lease decision, including the costs of leasing or purchasing parts from vendors compared with the costs of producing them in-house. The decision sometimes hinges on the availability of outside suppliers that can dependably meet a firm's standards for quality and quantity. A firm might not yet have the technology to produce certain components or materials, the technology might be too costly, or the firm may be concerned about maintaining control over its intellectual property (patents and copyrights).

THE LOCATION DECISION

Once the basic strategy is established, one of the next decisions is where to locate an output facility. This decision often hinges on well-understood factors such as the cost of construction, availability of utilities, transportation, and availability of workers (as shown in TABLE 10.1). Transportation factors include proximity to markets and raw materials and the availability of alternative modes for transporting both inputs and outputs. Automobile assembly plants are located near major rail lines. Inputs—such as engines, plastics, and metal parts—arrive by rail, and the finished vehicles are shipped out by rail. Shopping malls are often located

TABLE 10.1 What are the factors in the location decision?

Location Factor	Examples of Affected Businesses
Transportation	
Proximity to markets	Baking companies and manufacturers of other perishable products, dry cleaners, hotels, other services
Proximity to raw materials	Paper mills
Availability of transportation alternatives	Brick manufacturers, retail stores
Physical Factors	
Water supply	Computer chip fabrication plants
Energy	Aluminum, chemical, and fertilizer manufacturers
Hazardous wastes	All businesses
Human Factors	
Labor supply	Auto manufacturers, software developers
Local zoning regulations	Manufacturing and distribution companies
Community living conditions	All businesses
Taxes	All businesses

next to major streets and freeways in suburban areas because most customers arrive by car.

Physical variables involve such issues as weather, water supplies, available energy, and options for disposing of hazardous waste. Theme parks, such as Walt Disney World, are often located in warm climates so they can be open and attract visitors year-round. A manufacturing business that wants to locate near a community must prepare an *environmental impact study* that analyzes how a proposed plant would affect the quality of life in the surrounding area. Regulatory agencies typically require these studies to cover topics such as the impact on transportation facilities; energy requirements; water and sewage treatment needs; natural plant life and wildlife; and water, air, and noise pollution.

Human factors in the location decision include an area's labor supply, local regulations, taxes, and living conditions. Management considers local labor costs as well as the availability of qualified workers. Software makers and other computer-related firms concentrate in areas with the technical talent they need, including Boston, California's Silicon Valley, and Austin, Texas. By contrast, some labor-intensive industries have located plants in rural areas with readily available labor pools and limited high-wage alternatives. And some firms with headquarters in the United States and other industrialized countries have moved production offshore in search of low wages.

A recent trend in location strategy is bringing production facilities closer to the markets where the goods will be sold. One reason for this is reduced time and cost for shipping. Another reason is a closer cultural affinity between the parent company and

supplier (in cases where production remains overseas). German automaker Volkswagen decided to build a $1 billion manufacturing plant in Chattanooga, Tennessee, for the construction of its new midsize sedan. The new Passat was engineered specifically for the U.S. market, featuring a clean diesel fuel option and a larger interior than competing models. Volkswagen plans to roll 150,000 vehicles out of the Chattanooga plant each year, with possibilities for a major expansion that would increase production capacity for even more.[5]

DETERMINING THE FACILITY LAYOUT

Once decisions are made as to the basic design of the production process and location, production management's task is determining the best layout for the facility. An efficient facility layout can reduce material handling, decrease costs, and improve product flow through the facility. This decision requires managers to consider all phases of production and the necessary inputs at each step. **FIGURE 10.3** shows three common layout designs: process, product, and fixed-position layouts.

A *process layout* groups machinery and equipment according to their functions. The work in process moves around the plant to reach different workstations. A process layout often facilitates production of a variety of nonstandard items in relatively small batches. Its purpose is to process goods and services that have a variety of functions. For instance, a typical machine shop generally has separate departments where machines are grouped by functions such as grinding, drilling, pressing, and lathing. Process layouts accommodate a variety of production functions and use general-purpose equipment that can be less costly to purchase and maintain than specialized equipment. Similarly, a service firm should arrange its facilities to enhance the interactions between customers and its services. If you think of patients as inputs, a hospital implements a form of the process layout. Banks, libraries, dental offices, and hair salons also use process layouts.

A *product layout*, also referred to as an assembly line, sets up production equipment along a product-flow line, and the work in process moves along this line past workstations. This type of layout efficiently produces large numbers of similar items, but it may prove inflexible and able to accommodate only a few product variations. Although product layouts date back at least to the Model T assembly line, companies are refining this approach with modern touches. Many auto manufacturers continue to use a product layout, but robots perform many of the activities that humans once performed. Automation overcomes one of the major drawbacks of this system—unlike humans, robots don't get bored doing a dull, repetitive job.

A *fixed-position layout* places the product in one spot, and workers, materials, and equipment come to it. This approach suits production of very large, bulky, heavy, or fragile products. For example, a bridge cannot be built on an assembly line. Fixed-position layouts dominate several industries including

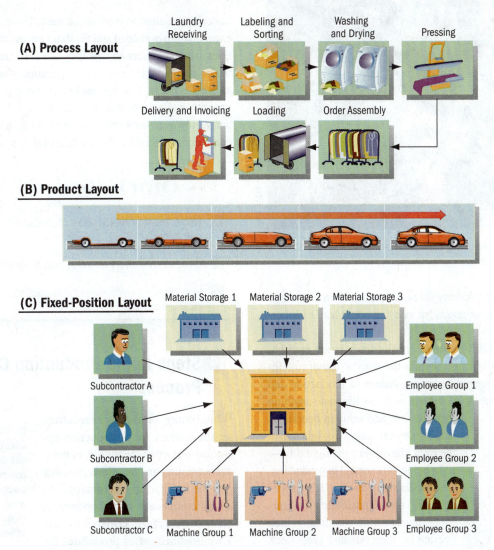

(A) Process Layout

Laundry Receiving → Labeling and Sorting → Washing and Drying → Pressing

Delivery and Invoicing ← Loading ← Order Assembly

(B) Product Layout

(C) Fixed-Position Layout

Subcontractor A
Subcontractor B
Subcontractor C

Material Storage 1
Material Storage 2
Material Storage 3

Employee Group 1
Employee Group 2
Employee Group 3

Machine Group 1
Machine Group 2
Machine Group 3

FIGURE 10.3 Basic Facility Layouts

construction, shipbuilding, aircraft and aerospace, and oil drilling, to name a few. In all of these industries, the nature of the product generally dictates a fixed-position layout.

SELECTION OF SUPPLIERS

Once a company decides what inputs to purchase, it must choose the best vendors for its needs. To make this choice, production managers compare the quality, prices, dependability of delivery, and services offered by competing companies. Different suppliers may offer virtually identical quality levels and prices, so the final decision often rests on factors such as the firm's experience with each supplier, speed of delivery, warranties on purchases, and other services.

For a major purchase, negotiations between the purchaser and potential vendors may stretch over several weeks or even months, and the buying decision may rest with a number of colleagues who must say yes before the final decision is made. The choice of a supplier for an industrial drill press, for example, may require a joint decision by the production, engineering, purchasing, and

quality-control departments. These departments often must reconcile their different views to settle on a purchasing decision.

The Internet has given buyers powerful tools for finding and comparing suppliers. Buyers can log on to business exchanges to compare specifications, prices, and availability. Ariba, with headquarters in California, offers organizations online software and other tools that allow them to source $120 billion worth of goods and services from suppliers around the world.[6]

APPROACH TO INVENTORY CONTROL

Production and operations managers' responsibility for **inventory control** requires them to balance the need to keep stock on hand to meet demand against the costs of carrying inventory. Among the expenses involved in storing inventory are warehousing costs, taxes, insurance, and maintenance. Firms waste money if they hold more inventory than they need. On the other

inventory control
the act of balancing the need to keep stock on hand to meet demand against the costs of carrying inventory.

Marc F. Henning/Alamy

∧ Associate at Walmart using a Telxon handheld scanner to read labels on clothing.

hand, having too little inventory on hand may result in a shortage of raw materials, parts, or goods for sale that could lead to delays and unhappy customers.

154

A **just-in-time (JIT) system** implements a broad management philosophy that reaches beyond the narrow activity of inventory control to influence the entire system of production and operations management. A JIT system seeks to eliminate anything that does not add value in operations activities by providing the right part at the right place at just the right time—right before it is needed in production.

Production using JIT shifts much of the responsibility for carrying inventory to vendors, which operate on forecasts and keep stock on hand to respond to manufacturers' needs. This concept is known as *vendor-managed inventory*. Suppliers that cannot keep enough high-quality parts on hand may be assessed steep penalties by purchasers. Another risk of using JIT systems is what happens if manufacturers underestimate demand for a product. Strong demand will begin to overtax JIT systems, as suppliers and their customers struggle to keep up with orders with no inventory cushion to tide them over.

Besides efficiency, effective inventory control requires careful planning to ensure the firm has all the inputs it needs to make its products. How do production and operations managers coordinate all of this information? They rely on **materials requirement planning (MRP)**, a computer-based production planning system that ensures a firm has all the parts and materials it needs to produce its output at the right time and place and in the right amounts.

Production managers use MRP programs to create schedules that identify the specific parts and

just-in-time (JIT) system
broad management philosophy that reaches beyond the narrow activity of inventory control to influence the entire system of production and operations management.

materials requirement planning (MRP)
a computer-based production planning system that ensures a firm has all the parts and materials it needs to produce its output at the right time and place and in the right amounts.

materials required to produce an item. These schedules specify the exact quantities needed and the dates on which to order those quantities from suppliers so that they are delivered at the correct time in the production cycle. A small company might get by without an MRP system. If a firm makes a simple product with few components, a telephone call may ensure overnight delivery of crucial parts. However, for a complex product like a high-definition TV or commercial aircraft, a more sophisticated system is required.

>>> **Quick Review**

1 Name the four major tasks of production and operations managers.

2 What factors affect a make, buy, or lease decision?

3 How does an environmental impact study influence the location decision?

4 Steps in the Production Control Process

While senior production executives set the strategy for a production operation, it is often the mid-level managers creating an operations plan that gets the facility "up and running." As a key component of an operations plan, **production control** creates a well-defined set of procedures for coordinating people, materials, and machinery to provide maximum production efficiency.

production control
creates a well-defined set of procedures for coordinating people, materials, and machinery to provide maximum production efficiency.

Suppose a watch factory must produce 80,000 watches during October. Production control managers break down this total into a daily production assignment of 4,000 watches for each of the month's 20 working days. Next, they determine the number of workers, raw materials, parts, and machines the plant needs to

∨ At a watch factory, monthly production quotas are broken into daily assignments, which determine the necessary quantities of workers and raw materials.

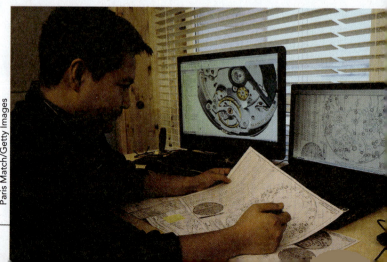

Paris Match/Getty Images

meet the production schedule. Similarly, a manager in a service business such as a restaurant must estimate how many dinners the kitchen will serve each day and then determine how many people are needed to prepare and serve the food, as well as what food to purchase. Production managers are responsible for all aspects of the production process, and careful planning, scheduling, routing, and monitoring are critical to their success.

PLANNING DETAILS

In manufacturing, a production manager often starts with a *Bill of Materials (BOM),* a document that lists all the parts and materials needed to create the product. By comparing information about needed parts and materials with the firm's inventory data, purchasing staff can identify necessary purchases. Production managers will also identify the equipment, supplies, and labor required to build the product. Building more of a product, where the product design, manufacturing process, and production equipment exist, may be relatively straightforward. However, when a company is considering a new product (as Apple did with the iPad), it will spend considerable time and effort understanding the costs and the *lead times* of the new production processes, equipment, materials, and worker skills. Establishing the costs and times for production is an important part of a production manager's work, and often a company's success or failure is built on getting these details right.

SCHEDULING

In the *scheduling* phase of production control, managers develop timetables that specify how long each operation in the production process takes and when workers should perform it. Efficient scheduling ensures that production will meet delivery schedules and make efficient use of resources.

Whether the product is complex or simple to produce and whether it is a tangible good or a service, scheduling is important. A pencil is simpler to produce than a computer, but each production process has scheduling requirements. A stylist may take 25 minutes to complete each haircut with just one or two tools, whereas every day a hospital has to schedule procedures and treatments ranging from Xrays to surgery to follow-up appointments.

Production managers use a number of analytical methods for scheduling. One of the oldest methods, the *Gantt chart,* tracks projected and actual work progress over time. Gantt charts like the one in **FIGURE 10.4** remain popular because they show at a glance the status of a particular project. However, they are most effective for scheduling relatively simple projects.

A complex project might require a *PERT (program evaluation and review technique)* chart, which seeks to minimize delays by coordinating all aspects of the production process. First developed for the military, PERT has been modified for industry. The simplified PERT diagram in **FIGURE 10.5** summarizes the

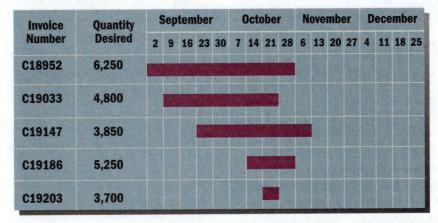

Invoice Number	Quantity Desired	September					October				November				December			
		2	9	16	23	30	7	14	21	28	6	13	20	27	4	11	18	25
C18952	6,250																	
C19033	4,800																	
C19147	3,850																	
C19186	5,250																	
C19203	3,700																	

FIGURE 10.4 Sample Gantt Chart

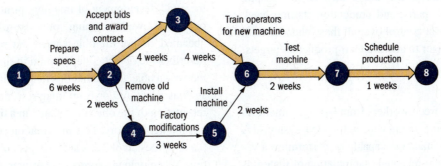

1. Project started
2. Specs completed
3. Contract awarded
4. Old machine removed
5. Plant modifications completed
6. Training and installation completed
7. Testing completed
8. Project completed

Critical path

FIGURE 10.5 PERT Diagram for the Purchase and Installation of a New Robot

schedule for purchasing and installing a new robot in a factory. The heavy, gold line indicates the *critical path*—the sequence of operations that requires the longest time for completion. In this case, the project cannot be completed in fewer than 17 weeks.

In practice, a PERT network may consist of thousands of events and may cover months of time. Complex computer programs help production managers develop such a network and find the critical path among the maze of events and activities. The construction of a huge office building requires complex production planning of this nature.

ROUTING AND DISPATCHING

Moving an item through the production process is called *routing*. In general, routing determines the path or sequence of work throughout the facility, specifying who will perform the work at what location. Routing choices depend on two factors: the nature of the good or service and the facility layouts (discussed earlier in the chapter)—product, process, fixed position, or customer oriented. *Dispatching* is the phase of production control in which management instructs operators when to do the work. The dispatcher (often an automated system) authorizes performance, provides instructions, and sets priorities. For example, FedEx trucks are routed and then dispatched based on a complicated formula of package pick-up time, location, and type of shipment. Minimizing cost, maximizing employee productivity, and creating a high level of customer satisfaction are key goals of the FedEx operations.

METRICS AND MEASURES

Measuring output is an important part of a production manager's responsibilities. The first step in implementing financial controls is to create a *budget* for the expected cost of the good or service. Budget elements include labor, materials, and overhead as well as test and inspection costs. Once the budget is established, the production manager can use the budget to determine whether the process is in financial control. Cost *variances* are the differences between the actual cost and the budgeted costs, with positive cost variances indicating that a process has higher costs than budgeted and negative cost variances showing a process costing less than budgeted. Operational controls are items such as throughput, yield, number of reworked parts, and production staffing level. Obviously, maintaining strict control over all these elements will allow the production manager to achieve their production targets.

AUTOMATION

Many manufacturers have freed workers from boring, sometimes dangerous jobs by replacing them with automated systems. A *robot* is a reprogrammable machine capable of performing a variety of tasks that require the repeated manipulation of materials and tools. Robots can repeat the same tasks many times without varying their movements. Many factories use robots today to stack their output on pallets and shrink-wrap them for shipping. Other types of automated systems include those that inspect, transport,

^ Many companies use robots today to automate their systems, resulting in lower costs, high yields, faster throughput, and better quality in production processes.

and measure products. Inspection technology, for example, allows production managers to continuously track a process, including those that measure a product's length, width, weight, fill level, and the like. Automated systems extend well beyond individual robots and measurement stations. The whole assembly line can be automated with many robotic systems linked together. The end results of these efforts are production processes with lower costs, high yields, faster throughput, and better quality.

COMPUTER-AIDED DESIGN AND MANUFACTURING

Of all the technologies used in the *Star Trek* series, probably none is as interesting as the transporter. "Beam me up, Scotty" became one of the more memorable lines from the television show and movies. Being able to decompose a solid, transport it through space, and reconstruct it perfectly would be an extraordinary technical accomplishment. For now, "beaming" Captain Kirk or anyone "up" is clearly in the realm of science fiction. However, the rapid development of imaging, printing, and material technology has allowed "beaming" of a sort to take place. Today what is "beamed" is not the object itself but rather the information that describes the object. Teleportation in this way starts with a digital map of an object. Whether this map is made in a computer program such as AutoCAD or from images of the object, a geometric representation of the object is created in a digital format and stored in a computer memory. This information composed solely of 1's and 0's describes an object's size, shape, color, and material composition. When uploaded onto a 3D printer, the image becomes real.

Chuck Hull developed many of the key technologies for this process, which he went on to name photo stereo lithography. His process used a liquid compound called photo resist (a material that hardens when exposed to light). By illuminating the photo resist with

156

carefully directed beams of light, he was able to produce solid objects from the liquid photo resist. The company Hull founded, 3D Systems Inc., brought this technology to market.[7]

In addition to photoresist, today's 3D printers use a wide variety of processes and materials to create solid objects. And instead of costing many tens of thousands of dollars, desktop versions can be purchased for a few thousand dollars. While the object itself is not transported, the information used to describe the object can be "beamed" around the world and even into space.

computer-aided design (CAD) process that allows engineers to design components as well as entire products on computer screens faster and with fewer mistakes than they could achieve by working with traditional drafting systems.

computer-aided manufacturing (CAM) computer tools to analyze CAD output and enable a manufacturer to analyze the steps that a machine must take to produce a needed product or part.

What makes this technology possible is the combination of **computer-aided design (CAD)** software and **computer-aided manufacturing (CAM)** processes. Using these technologies, engineers can design components as well as entire products faster and with fewer mistakes that they could achieve using traditional systems. Software such as AutoCAD or TurboCAD allows designers to create entire products in the computer, specifying the physical dimensions, materials finishes, and mechanical properties. In the realm of architecture, AutoCAD is often the first and only drafting program used to render a building, creating wall, window, door, and structural elements as well as the mechanical and electrical fixtures. The customer gets a chance to see the building, including the ability to "fly" through the rooms long before it is built. When created in this fashion, engineers can make any changes required in the computer, saving both cost and time.

The process of CAM picks up where CAD systems leave off. When using CAM, engineers first develop a plan for creating the product. For example, if a metal part is required, the engineer would specify the size and shape of the block of metal from which the part will be fabricated. Then, the engineer would determine which parts of a block are to be cut away and which are to remain.

Programmable tools such as milling machines, lathes, laser cutters, and water jets are then chosen to perform these steps based on the amount of material to be removed and the configuration of the final product. Electronic files with this information are created and transmitted to the processing equipment. Automated systems take over from there with operators standing by to load and unload finished product. In the production of integrated circuits, no humans are involved, and the entire CAM process is handled by automated equipment. CAD and CAM technologies are used together in most modern production facilities, saving time and money and creating more precise products.

>>> **Quick Review**

1 What steps are involved in controlling the production process?

2 Why do some companies invest in robots?

3 How do CAD and CAM work together to enhance production?

▼ AutoCAD can be used by architects to render the complete building, including the structural elements and mechanical and electrical fixtures.

Business/Alamy

5 The Importance of Quality Control

As it relates to the production of goods and services, **quality** is defined as being free of deficiencies. Quality matters because fixing, replacing, or redesigning deficient products or services is costly. If Seagate makes a defective computer hard drive, it has to either fix the drive or replace it to keep a customer happy. If American Airlines books too many passengers for a flight, it has to offer vouchers worth several hundred dollars to encourage passengers to give up their seats and take a later flight. As such, quality defines virtually all of a firm's processes from the way it designs products, delivers services, and handles customer complaints.

quality good or service that is free of deficiencies.

For most companies, the costs of poor quality can amount to 20 percent of sales revenue, if not more. Some typical costs of poor quality include downtime, repair costs, rework, and employee turnover. Poor quality can also result in lost sales and a tarnished image, something companies want to avoid. Bumble Bee Foods recently voluntarily recalled cans of tuna because the seal on the cans didn't meet company standards. The company was concerned with maintaining their high-quality standards and didn't want anyone to get sick from bacteria entering the cans because of a loose seal.[9]

STATISTICAL PROCESS CONTROL

Quality control involves measuring output against established quality standards. Firms need such checks to spot defective products and to avoid delivering inferior shipments to customers. Standards should be set high enough to meet customer expectations. A 90 or 95 percent success rate might seem to be a good number, but consider what your phone service or ATM network would be like if it worked only 90 percent of the time. You would feel frustrated and inconvenienced and would probably switch your account to another phone service or ATM network provider.

quality control involves measuring output against established quality standards.

Because the typical factory can spend up to half its operating budget identifying and fixing mistakes, a company cannot rely solely on inspections to achieve its quality goals. Instead, quality-driven production managers identify all processes involved in producing goods and services and work to maximize their efficiency. The causes of problems in the processes must be found and eliminated. If a company concentrates its efforts on better designs of products and processes with clear quality targets, it can ensure virtually defect-free production.

Statistical Process Control (SPC) is one method that companies use to evaluate a product or process quality. This method requires knowledge of the capabilities of the process and the requirement for the output. The process is then designed to achieve the desired result with data collected on the process measurements. With these data, production managers can create charts

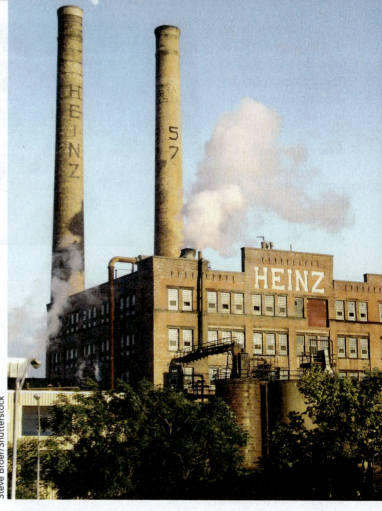

∧ Heinz, along with other companies, uses Six Sigma to achieve quality goals in making error-free products.

Steve Broer/Shutterstock

showing the process performance over time and allow corrections in the process before it creates out-of-tolerance parts.

General Electric, Heinz, 3M, Sears, and the U.S. military are just a few of the major organizations using the Six Sigma concept to achieve quality goals. *Six Sigma* means a company tries to make error-free products 99.9997 percent of the time—a tiny 3.4 errors per million opportunities. The goal of Six Sigma programs is for companies to eliminate virtually all defects in output, processes, and transactions. Motorola—a Six Sigma firm—recently completed an initiative to redesign and simplify much of its software architecture in order to improve operational efficiencies and cut costs by reducing redundant IT applications.[10]

BENCHMARKING

One process that companies use to ensure that they produce high-quality products from the start is **benchmarking**—determining how well other companies perform

benchmarking determining how well other companies perform business functions or tasks.

business functions or tasks. In other words, benchmarking is the process of determining other firms' standards and best practices. Automobile companies routinely purchase each other's cars and then take them apart to examine and compare the design, components, and materials used to make even the smallest part. They then make improvements to match or exceed the quality found in their competitors' cars.

Companies may use many different benchmarks, depending on their objectives. For instance, some organizations that want to make more money may compare their operating profits or expenses to those of other firms. Retailers concerned with productivity may want to benchmark sales per square foot. It's important when benchmarking for a firm to establish what it wants to accomplish, what it wants to measure, and which company can provide the most useful benchmarking information. A firm might choose a direct competitor for benchmarking, or it might select a company in an entirely different industry—but one that has processes the firm wants to study and emulate.

ISO STANDARDS

The International Organization for Standardization (ISO, as it is often called) is an organization whose mission is to develop and promote international standards for business, government, and society to facilitate global trade and cooperation.

Operating since 1947, ISO is a network of national standards bodies from 163 countries. Its mission is to develop and promote international standards to facilitate global trade and cooperation. ISO has developed voluntary standards for everything from the format of banking and telephone cards to freight containers to paper sizes to metric screw threads. The U.S. member body of ISO is the American National Standards Institute.

The ISO 9000 family of standards gave requirements and guidance for quality management to help organizations ensure that their goods and services achieve customer satisfaction and also provide a framework for continual improvement. The ISO 14000 family of standards for environmental management helps organizations ensure that their operations cause minimal harm to the environment and achieve continual improvement of their environmental performance.

Both ISO 9001:2008 and ISO 14001:2004 can be used for certification, which means that the organization's management system (the way it manages its processes) is independently audited by a certification body (also known in North American as a registration body, or registrar) and confirmed as conforming to the requirements of the standard. The organization is then issued an ISO 9001:2008 or an ISO 14001:2004 certificate.

It should be noted that certification is not a requirement of either standard, which can be implemented solely for the benefits it provides the organization and its customers. However, many organizations opt to seek certification because of the perception that an independent audit adds confidence in its abilities. Business partners, customers, suppliers, and consumers may prefer to deal with or buy products from a certified organization. Certifications have to be periodically renewed through accompanying audits.

Though ISO develops standards, it does not itself carry out auditing and certification activities. This is done independently by hundreds of certification bodies around the world. The certificates they issue carry their own logo but not ISO's because the latter does not approve or control their activities.[11]

> > > **Quick Review**

1 Why is quality important to an organization?

2 What are some benefits to obtaining ISO certification?

What's Ahead? > > >

Maintaining high quality is an important part of satisfying customers. Product quality and customer satisfaction are also objectives of the business function of marketing. The next part consists of three chapters that explore the many activities involved in customer-driven marketing. These activities include product development, distribution, promotion, and pricing.

Don't miss the Weekly Updates located at http://contemporarybusinessupdates.com to help you take the first step toward success.

NOTES

1. Company Web site, http://www.intel.com, accessed April 9, 2013; Esther Andrews, "What's behind the Products You Love?" Technology@Intel, January 22, 2012, http://blogs.intel.com; Chris Nuttall, "Intel's Chip Plans Bloom in Arizona Desert," *Financial Times*, January 22, 2012, http://www.ft.com; Jon Swartz, "Intel Bets Big on Manufacturing," *USA Today*, March 29, 2011, pp. 1B, 2B.

2. "How It's Made: Paintballs," Discovery Channel, http://www.youtube.com, accessed March 22, 2013.

3. Company Web site, "Operations Facilities," http://corporate.honda.com, accessed March 22, 2013.

4. Company Web site, http://www.shibuidesignsltd.com, accessed March 22, 2013.

5. Company Web site, "Chattanooga Plant," http://www.volkswagengroupamerica.com, accessed April 9, 2013; Dave Flessner, "VW Contractor Hiring More Workers in Chattanooga," *Chattanooga Times Free Press*, April 4, 2012, http://www.timesfreepress.com; "Volkswagen Chattanooga Earns LEED Platinum," press release, December 1, 2011, http://www.volkswagengroupamerica.com; Mike Ramsey, "VW Chops Labor Costs in U.S.," *Wall Street Journal*, May 23, 2011, http://online.wsj.com.

6. Company Web site, http://www.ariba.com, accessed March 22, 2013.

7. Company Web site, http://www.3dsystems.com/about-us, accessed March 21, 2013.

8. Katie Moisse, "Bumble Bee, Chicken of the Sea, Expand Tuna Recall," *ABC News*, March 8, 2013, http://www.abcnews.go.com.

9. Organization Web site, "What Is Six Sigma?" http://www.isixsigma.com, accessed March 22, 2013.

10. Organization Web site, http://www.iso.org, accessed March 22, 2013.

Summary of Learning Objectives

 Identify and describe the four main categories of production processes.

Production and operations management is a vital business function. Without a quality good or service, a company cannot create profits, and it soon fails. The production process is also crucial in a not-for-profit organization because the good or service it produces justifies the organization's existence. Production and operations management plays an important strategic role by lowering the costs of production, boosting output quality, and allowing the firm to respond flexibly and dependably to customers' demands.

The four main categories of production processes are

- the analytic production system, which reduces a raw material to its component parts in order to extract one or more marketable products

- the synthetic production system, which combines a number of raw materials or parts to produce finished products

- the continuous production process, which generates finished items over a lengthy period of time

- the intermittent production process, which generates products in short production runs

utility a measure of the value of a good or service to a consumer.

production use of resources, such as workers and machinery, to convert materials into finished goods and services.

production and operations management overseeing the production process by managing people and machinery in converting materials and resources into finished goods and services.

 Identify and describe the three major production methods.

The three major production methods are

- mass production, a system for manufacturing products in large quantities through effective combinations of employees with specialized skills, mechanization, and standardization

- flexible production, usually more cost-effective for smaller runs

- customer-driven production, a system that evaluates customer demands in order to make the connection between products manufactured and products bought

Describe the strategic decisions made by production and operations managers.

Production and operations managers use people and machinery to convert inputs (materials and resources) into finished goods and services. Four major tasks are involved. First, the managers must plan the overall production process. Next, they must pick the best layout for their facilities. Then they implement their production plans. Finally, they control the production process and evaluate results to maintain the highest possible quality.

Criteria for choosing the best site for a production facility fall into three categories: transportation, human, and physical factors.

- Transportation factors include proximity to markets and raw materials, along with availability of transportation alternatives.

- Physical variables involve such issues as water supply, available energy, and options for disposing of hazardous wastes.

- Human factors include the area's labor supply, local regulations, taxes, and living conditions.

Implementation involves deciding whether to make, buy, or lease components; selecting the best suppliers for materials; and controlling inventory to keep enough, but not too much, on hand.

make, buy, or lease decision choosing whether to manufacture a product or component in-house, purchase it from an outside supplier, or lease it.

inventory control the act of balancing the need to keep stock on hand to meet demand against the costs of carrying inventory.

just-in-time (JIT) system broad management philosophy that reaches beyond the narrow activity of inventory control to influence the entire system of production and operations management.

materials requirement planning (MRP) computer-based production planning system that ensures a firm has all the parts and materials it needs to produce its output at the right time and place and in the right amounts.

 Identify the steps in the production control process.

The production control process consists of five steps: planning, routing, scheduling, dispatching, and follow-up. Quality control is an important consideration throughout this process. Coordination of each of these phases should result in high production efficiency and low production costs.

Computer-driven automation allows companies to design, create, and modify products rapidly and produce them in ways that effectively meet customers' changing needs. Important design and production technologies include robots, computer-aided design (CAD), and computer-aided manufacturing (CAM).

production control   creating a well-defined set of procedures for coordinating people, materials, and machinery to provide maximum production efficiency.

computer-aided design (CAD)   process that allows engineers to design components as well as entire products on computer screens faster and with fewer mistakes than they could achieve working with traditional drafting systems.

computer-aided manufacturing (CAM)   computer tools to analyze CAD output and enable a manufacturer to analyze the steps that a machine must take to produce a needed product or part.

5 Discuss the importance of quality control.

Quality control involves evaluating goods and services against established quality standards. Such checks are necessary to spot defective products and to see that they are not shipped to customers. Devices for monitoring quality levels of the firm's output include visual inspection, electronic sensors, robots, and Xrays. Companies are increasing the quality of their goods and services by using Six Sigma techniques, benchmarking their practices against those of their competitors, and by becoming ISO-9000 and -14000 certified.

quality   good or service that is free of deficiencies.

benchmarking   determining how well other companies perform business functions or tasks.

>>> Quick Review >>>

LO1

1 Why is production an important activity for all organizations?

2 What are the four types of production processes?

LO2

1 What are the three major production methods?

2 How does Honda use a flexible production method?

LO3

1 Name the four major tasks of production and operations managers.

2 What factors affect a make, buy, or lease decision?

LO3

3 How does an environmental impact study influence the location decision?

LO4

1 What steps are involved in controlling the production process?

2 Why do some companies invest in robots?

3 How do CAD and CAM work together to enhance production?

LO5

1 Why is quality important to an organization?

2 What are some benefits to obtaining ISO certification?

chapter eleven

Customer-Driven Marketing

Learning Objectives

1. **Define** marketing.

2. **Discuss** the evolution of the marketing concept.

3. **Summarize** consumer behavior.

4. **Describe** marketing research.

5. **Explain** market segmentation.

6. **List** the steps in building a marketing strategy.

7. **Discuss** relationship marketing.

Walmart Introduces "Great for You"

Walmart, already the undisputed leader in low-price retail, is identifying healthier, low-cost food choices for consumers by adding a bright green-and-white "Great for You" label to foods that meet the store's new set of nutritional quality standards.

Fresh fruits and vegetables make the cut; sugary cereals don't. "There are no candy bars," said the company's senior vice president of sustainability. Brown rice, skim milk, and lean cuts of meat also qualify and, after a long debate about their protein value versus their cholesterol content, so do eggs. About 20 percent of packaged food products sold in Walmart's nearly 3,600 stores—both its own brands and those of its suppliers—will eventually carry the "Great for You" label. The U.S. Food and Drug Administration (FDA) has yet to unveil an official food quality designation of its own. When it does, says Walmart's sustainability officer, "We'll be happy to make a switch. At this point we feel like our customers need help right now."

Walmart is also lowering the prices of about 350 healthier foods, such as low-fat peanut butter and fat-free salad dressings, making them as affordable as regular products to encourage customers to purchase them. The company has worked with suppliers to reduce the sugar, trans fats, and sodium in many of the prepared products it carries. And it reduced prices on fresh fruits and vegetables enough to save consumers more than $1 billion a year over the prices charged at competing stores.

Many observers give the company credit for establishing pretty strict criteria for its "Great for You" label. "Customers asked us to make healthier food choices easy while keeping prices low," said an executive vice president of grocery for Walmart. Experts in nutrition advised the company to make the criteria tough and significant. Walmart executives have confidence that the "Great for You" icon meets those objectives and will encourage Walmart shoppers to fill up on healthier food choices at the lower prices they expect from the brand.[1]

Overview > > >

Business success in the 21st century is directly tied to a company's ability to identify and serve its target markets. In fact, all organizations—profit-oriented and not-for-profit, manufacturing and retailing—*must* serve customer needs to succeed, just as Walmart does by offering multiple choices to its shoppers. Marketing is the link between the organization and the people who buy and use its goods and services. It is the way organizations determine buyer needs and inform potential customers that their firms can meet those needs by supplying a quality product at a reasonable price. And it is the path to developing loyal, long-term customers.

Consumers who purchase goods for their own use and business purchasers seeking products to use in their firm's operation may seem to fall in the same category, but marketers see distinct wants and needs for each group. To understand buyers—from manufacturers to Web surfers to shoppers in the grocery aisles—companies gather mountains of data on every aspect of consumer lifestyles and buying behaviors. Marketers use the data to understand the needs and wants of both final customers and business buyers. Satisfying customers goes a long way toward building relationships with them. It's not always easy.

This chapter begins with an examination of the marketing concept and the way businesspeople develop a marketing strategy. It then turns to marketing research techniques and how businesses apply data to market segmentation and understanding customer behavior. The chapter closes with a detailed look at the important role customer relationships play in today's highly competitive business world.

1 What Is Marketing?

Every organization—from profit-seeking firms such as Jimmy John's and Kellogg's to not-for-profits such as the Make-a-Wish Foundation and the American Cancer Society—must serve customer needs to succeed. Perhaps the retail pioneer J. C. Penney best expressed this priority when he told his store managers, "Either you or your replacement will greet the customer within the first 60 seconds."

marketing
organizational function and set of processes for creating, communicating, and delivering value to customers and for managing customer relationships in ways that benefit the organization and its stakeholders.

According to the American Marketing Association Board of Directors, **marketing** is "the activity, set of institutions, and processes for creating, communicating, delivering, and exchanging offerings that have value for customers, clients, partners, and society at large."[2] In addition to selling goods and services, marketing techniques help people advocate ideas or viewpoints and educate others. The American Heart Association mails out questionnaires that ask, "Are you at risk for a heart attack?" The documents help educate the general public about this widespread condition by listing its risk factors and common symptoms and describing the work of the association.

To be a marketing professional means to understand a consumer's hopes, dreams, desires, and fears better than they do themselves and to create goods and services that will satisfy those needs. Marketers know that, while consumers are almost always open to a better way to address their needs, they are rarely able to anticipate or articulate their needs.[3] Apple founder Steve Jobs famously said, "Some people say, 'Give customers what they want.' But that's not my approach. Our job is to figure out what they're going to want before they do."[4] Jobs and visionaries like him create amazing new products that revolutionize the marketplace. Even if companies are not changing the world with their products, marketers are always looking to understand a consumers' needs before those needs surface. Anticipating consumer needs allows a firm to get a jump on the competition, creating a link in consumers' minds between the new need and the fulfillment of that need by the marketers' products. Examples of this approach include:

- Principal Financial Group markets employee retirement plans to organizations that then custom-tailor those plans to retain key employees.

> The best marketers give consumers what they want and anticipate their needs. Samsung's Smart TVs allow consumers to interact, connect, and multitask without leaving their homes.

STANCA SANDA/Alamy

- NetJets offers fractional jet ownership to executives who want the luxury and flexibility of private ownership without the cost of owning their own plane.

- Samsung offers its next generation of high-definition TV with its Smart TVs. Owners can connect their television to their home Internet connection, then add widgets to track the weather, use Skype, stream video content, and check for Twitter updates—all in real time. In addition, they can get video-on-demand service and other apps through the company's Web site. "Get the best of the Web right on your TV," one of Samsung's promotions says.

As these examples also illustrate, marketing is more than just developing exciting new products. It is a systematic process that begins with discovering unmet customer needs, researching the potential market; producing a good or service capable of satisfying the targeted customers; and promoting, pricing, and distributing that good or service. Throughout the entire marketing process, a successful organization focuses on building customer relationships.

Consider the simple act of purchasing a cup of coffee. Your purchase decision begins with the thought that a cup of coffee will satisfy a need you have, whether it be something warm to drink, to see your favorite barista, or to fulfill a morning ritual. Meeting this need (or any need, for that matter) requires that you identify a willing partner to the transaction. In the case of a cup of coffee, the other party may be a convenience store clerk, a vending machine, or a Seattle's Best server. When two or more parties benefit from trading things of value, they have entered into an **exchange process**.

exchange process
activity in which two or more parties give something of value to each other to satisfy perceived needs.

On the surface, the exchange seems simple—some money changes hands, and you receive your cup of coffee. But the exchange process is more complex than that. It could not

occur if you didn't feel the need for a cup of coffee or if the convenience store or vending machine were not available. You wouldn't choose Seattle's Best Coffee unless you were aware of the brand. Marketing plays a role in all aspects of this transaction.

HOW MARKETING CREATES UTILITY

The ability of a good or service to satisfy the wants and needs of customers is called **utility**. A company's production function creates *form utility* by converting raw materials, components, and other inputs from less valuable forms to more valuable finished goods and services. In the case of a cup of coffee, the beans, water, sugar, and cream (which together are worth only a few cents) are transformed into hot coffee (worth many times as much). In addition to form utility, the marketing function also creates time, place, and ownership utility.

> **utility** power of a good or service to satisfy a want or need.

- *Time utility* is created by making a good or service available when customers want to purchase it.
- *Place utility* is created by making a product available in a location convenient for customers.
- *Ownership utility* refers to an orderly transfer of goods and services from the seller to the buyer.

166

>>> **Quick Review**

1 What is utility?

2 Identify some ways in which marketing creates utility.

2 Evolution of the Marketing Concept

Marketing has always been a part of business, from the earliest village traders to large 21st century organizations producing and selling complex goods and services. Over time, however, marketing activities evolved through the five eras shown in **FIGURE 11.1**: the production, sales, marketing, and relationship eras, and now the social era. Note that these eras parallel some of the time periods discussed in Chapter 1.

For centuries, organizations operating in the *production era* stressed efficiency in producing quality products. Their philosophy could be summed up by the remark, "A good product will sell itself." Although this production orientation continued into the 20th century, it gradually gave way to the *sales era*, in which businesses assumed that consumers would buy as a result of their energetic sales efforts. Organizations didn't fully recognize the importance of their customers until the *marketing era* of the 1950s, when they began to adopt a consumer orientation.

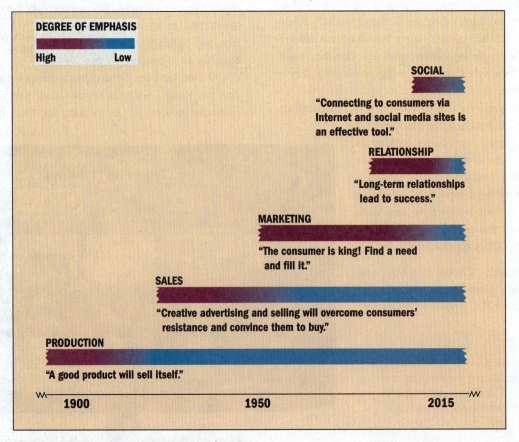

FIGURE 11.1 Five Eras in the History of Marketing

The emergence of the marketing era can be explained best by the shift from a *seller's market,* one with a shortage of goods and services, to a *buyer's market,* one with an abundance of goods and services. During the 1950s, the United States became a strong buyer's market, forcing companies to satisfy customers rather than just producing and selling goods and services. The marketing era continues today with companies focused on understanding their customers' needs and creating goods and services to meet these needs.

Recently, this focus has intensified, leading to the emergence of the *relationship era* in the 1990s and the *social era* of today. In the relationship era, companies emphasized customer satisfaction and building long-term business relationships. As the second decade of the new century gets under way, the social era of marketing is in full swing, thanks to the Internet and the creation of social media sites such as Twitter and Facebook. Companies now routinely use the Web and social media sites to connect to consumers as a way of marketing their goods and services.

EMERGENCE OF THE MARKETING CONCEPT

marketing concept companywide consumer orientation to promote long-run success.

The marketing era can also be identified with the term **marketing concept**, which refers to a companywide customer orientation with the objective of achieving long-run success. The basic idea of the marketing concept is that marketplace success begins with the customer. Successful firms analyze their customers' needs and then work backward to offer products that fulfill them. Exceptional firms are those that do a better job of understanding and meeting their customers' needs than their competitors. Apple, Nike, Budweiser, and GEICO are examples of firms that do an outstanding job marketing their products.

> The reptilian mascot of GEICO uses humor and satire to introduce and remind customers of GEICO's insurance products.

Walter G Arce/Cal Sport Media/NewsCom

>>> **Quick Review**

1. Name the five eras in the history of marketing.

2. What is the marketing concept?

3. How is the marketing concept tied to the relationship and social eras of marketing?

3 Consumer Behavior

In the marketing era, all businesses, large or small, work diligently to provide the goods and services that satisfy their customers' needs. But who exactly are these customers? What are their needs? Where do they purchase and how do they use these products? The answers to these and many other questions are critical to a firm's understanding of their customers and the larger market for their products.

Both personal and interpersonal factors influence the way buyers behave. Personal influences on **consumer behavior** include individual needs and motives, perceptions, attitudes, learned experiences, and self-concept. For instance, today people are constantly looking for ways to save time, so firms do everything they can to provide goods and services designed for convenience. However, when it comes to products such as dinner foods, consumers want convenience, but they also want to enjoy the flavor of a home-cooked meal and spend quality time with their families. So companies such as Stouffer's offer frozen lasagna or manicotti in family sizes, and supermarkets have entire sections devoted to freshly prepared take-out meals that range from roast turkey to filet mignon. Sometimes external events influence consumer behavior. After the recent recession, consumers are less likely to go into debt to make purchases. The Federal Reserve data show that in a previous year, consumers spent about 14 percent of their income to pay off their debts. In a more recent year, that number was down to 10 percent, indicating that consumers are unwilling to take on new debt to make purchases. Since about 70 percent of the U.S. GDP is the result of consumer spending, manufacturers and retailers—and especially small businesses—will need to rethink their consumers' profiles to respond to these challenges.[5]

consumer behavior actions of ultimate consumers directly involved in obtaining, consuming, and disposing of products and the decision processes that precede and follow these actions.

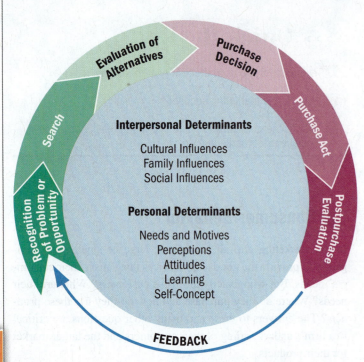

Interpersonal Determinants

Cultural Influences
Family Influences
Social Influences

Personal Determinants

Needs and Motives
Perceptions
Attitudes
Learning
Self-Concept

FEEDBACK

FIGURE 11.2 Steps in the Consumer Behavior Process

STEPS IN THE CONSUMER BEHAVIOR PROCESS

In general, consumer decision making follows the sequential process outlined in **FIGURE 11.2**, with interpersonal and personal influences affecting every step. The process begins when the consumer recognizes a problem or opportunity. If someone needs a new pair of shoes, that need becomes a problem to solve. If you receive a promotion at work and a 20 percent salary increase, that change may also become a purchase opportunity.

To solve the problem or take advantage of the opportunity, consumers seek information about their intended purchase and evaluate alternatives, such as available brands. The goal is to find the best response to the problem or opportunity. Eventually, consumers reach a decision and complete the transaction. Later, they evaluate the experience by making a post-purchase evaluation. Feelings about the experience serve as feedback that will influence future purchase decisions. The various steps in the sequence are affected by both interpersonal and personal factors.

> **>>> Quick Review**
>
> **1** What is consumer behavior?
>
> **2** What are some influences on consumer behavior?
>
> **3** Name the steps in the consumer behavior process.

4 Marketing Research

In addition to studying individual consumers, a firm can also investigate the larger market for their products. Whether it is conducted by the owner of a small business or by the marketing department of a Fortune 500 company, marketing research is more than just collecting data.

Marketing research is the process of collecting and evaluating information to help marketers make effective decisions. Researchers must decide how to collect data, interpret the results, convert the data into decision-oriented information, and communicate those results to managers for use in decision making. This research links business decision makers to the marketplace by providing data about potential target markets that help them design—as in the case of GEICO Insurance—effective marketing approaches.

> **marketing research**
> collecting and evaluating information to help marketers make effective decisions.

OBTAINING MARKET DATA

To get a complete picture of their markets, researchers need both internal and external data. Firms generate *internal data* within their organizations. Financial records provide a tremendous amount of useful information, such as changes in unpaid bills; inventory levels; sales generated by different categories of customers or product lines; profitability of particular divisions; or comparisons of sales by territories, salespeople, customers, or product lines.

Researchers gather *external data* from outside sources, including previously published data. Trade associations publish reports on activities in particular industries. Advertising agencies collect information on the audiences reached by various media. National marketing research firms offer information through subscription services. Some of these professional research firms specialize in specific markets, such as teens or ethnic groups. This information helps companies make decisions about developing or modifying products.

The world's largest consumer-goods manufacturer, Procter & Gamble, has excelled in marketing research for a long time. It created its own marketing research department in 1923 and began conducting its research online in 2001. P&G CEO Bob McDonald has set the goal of reaching 1 billion new customers worldwide over the next few years. This expansion involves reaching customers in developing regions. As part of this strategy, he traveled undercover to 30 countries, posing as a marketing researcher.[6]

Secondary data, or previously published data, are low cost and easy to obtain. Federal, state, and local government publications are excellent data sources, and most are available online. The most frequently used government statistics include census data, which contain the population's age, gender, education level, household size and composition, occupation, employment status, and income. Even private research firms such as TRU (formerly Teenage Research Unlimited), which studies the purchasing habits of teens, provide some free information on their Web sites. This information helps firms evaluate consumers' buying behavior, anticipate possible changes in the marketplace, and identify new markets.

Even though secondary data are a quick and inexpensive resource, marketing researchers sometimes discover that this information isn't specific or current enough for their needs. If so, researchers may conclude that they must collect *primary data*—data collected firsthand through such methods as observation and surveys.

Simply observing customers cannot provide some types of information. A researcher might observe a customer buying a red sweater but have no idea why the purchase was made—or for whom. When researchers need information about consumers' attitudes, opinions, and motives, they need to ask the consumers themselves. They may conduct surveys by telephone, in person, online, or in focus groups.

One method that companies might use to obtain primary research is a *focus group*. A focus group gathers 8 to 12 people in a room or over the Internet to discuss a particular topic. A focus group can generate new ideas, address consumers' needs, and even point out flaws in existing products. For example, when Frito-Lay develops a new potato chip flavor, they use the new Lay's Facebook app to suggest new flavors and ask their focus group members to click an "I'd Eat That" button to register their preferences. So far, the results show that a beer-battered onion-ring flavor is popular in California and Ohio, while a churros flavor is a hit in New York. "It's a new way of getting consumer research," said the chief marketing officer of Frito-Lay North America. "We're going to get a ton of new ideas."[7]

ADVANCED RESEARCH TECHNIQUES

Once a company has built a database, marketers must be able to analyze the data and use the information it provides. **Data mining**, part of the broader field of **business intelligence**, is the task of using computer-based technology to evaluate data in a database and identify useful trends. These trends or patterns may suggest predictive models of real-world business activities. Accurate data mining can help researchers forecast sales levels and pinpoint sales prospects.

data mining the task of using computer-based technology to evaluate data in a database and identify useful trends.

business intelligence activities and technologies for gathering, storing, and analyzing data to make better competitive decisions.

Companies such as Rapleaf Inc. collect publicly available personal information from social-networking sites like Facebook, Twitter, and other forums. They then sell this information to entities such as airlines and credit card companies that regard those individuals as potential customers. Such information can include everything from your blogging or posting habits to your credit rating. Among the issues arising from data mining are ownership of Web user data, the targeting capabilities of the Web, government supervision—and, of course, privacy.

>>> **Quick Review**

1. Give examples of internal data and external data. How are they gathered?

2. Differentiate between primary and secondary data.

3. What is data mining and how is it useful to marketers?

5 Market Segmentation

As a firm begins to develop a picture of its customers' needs, companies will often attempt to form their customers into groups called market segments. This is an important process, as companies can be much more efficient with their product design, production process, and promotional activities if they are targeting similar customers. Simply put, **market segmentation** is the process of dividing a market into homogeneous groups by isolating the traits that distinguish a certain group of customers from the overall market.

market segmentation process of dividing a total market into several relatively homogeneous groups.

Firms have been segmenting markets since people first began selling products. Tailors made some clothing items for men and others for women. Tea was imported from India for tea drinkers in England and in other European countries. In addition to the segments based on demographic (gender, for example) and geographical (location) segmentation, today's marketers also define customer groups based on psychographic criteria—lifestyle and values—as well as product-related distinctions. **FIGURE 11.3** illustrates the segmentation methods for consumer markets.

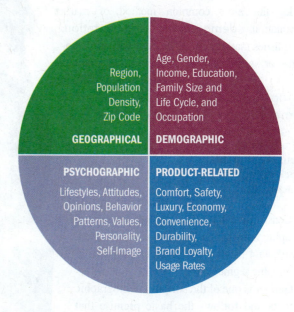

Consumer (B2C) Markets

FIGURE 11.3 Methods of Segmenting Consumer Markets

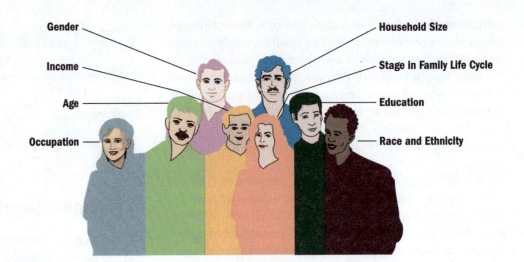

FIGURE 11.4 Common Demographic Measures

GEOGRAPHIC SEGMENTATION

The oldest segmentation method is **geographic segmentation**— dividing a market into homogeneous groups on the basis of their locations. Geographic location does not guarantee that consumers in a certain region will all buy the same kinds of products, but it does provide some indication of needs. For instance, suburbanites buy more lawn care products than do central-city dwellers. Consumers who live in northern states, where winter is more severe, are more likely to buy ice scrapers, snow shovels, and snow blowers than those who live in warmer climates. Marketers also look at the size of the population of an area, as well as who lives there.

geographic segmentation
dividing a market into homogeneous groups on the basis of their location.

DEMOGRAPHIC SEGMENTATION

By far the most common method of market segmentation, **demographic segmentation**, distinguishes markets on the basis of various demographic or socioeconomic characteristics. Common demographic measures include gender, income, age, occupation, household size, stage in the family life cycle, education, and racial or ethnic group. The U.S. Census Bureau is one of the best sources of demographic information for the domestic market. **FIGURE 11.4** lists some of the measures used in demographic segmentation.

demographic segmentation
distinguishes markets on the basis of various demographic or socioeconomic characteristics.

Gender is one of the simplest demographic segments and follows the basic premise that shopping and buying patterns are different between men and women. A traditional view is that some types of products are more appealing to women, such as jewelry and skin care, and therefore should be more heavily marketed toward women than men. The same could be said about traditional male products, such as sporting equipment and tools. What may have been true for the old "brick and mortar" retailers still seems to be true today, with 29 percent of women shopping online for shoes, clothing, and accessories, compared with 17 percent for men. Gender differences also are seen in the total volume of Internet purchases. While men and women are online about the same amount of time, 58 percent of e-commerce sales revenue comes from women. Shopping habits also differ, as men generally complete more transactions online while women have a higher average order value.[8]

With a rapidly aging population, age is perhaps the most volatile factor in demographic segmentation in the United States. Of the 325-plus million people projected to live in the United States by 2015, almost 87 million will be age 55 or older.[9] Working from these statistics, marketers in the travel and leisure, retirement, and investments industries work hard to attract the attention of these Baby Boomers—people born between 1946 and 1964. Active-adult housing communities are one result of these efforts.

Young adults are another rapidly growing market. The entire scope of Generation Y—those born

< Tech-savvy Millennials influence the purchases of their families and friends.

Thomas Northcut/ Photodisc/Getty Images

between 1976 and 1997—encompasses about 113 million Americans, a little more than one-third of the total U.S. population. Often called Millennials, these consumers are tech-savvy shoppers who are more likely than their Baby Boomer parents to use digital and mobile technologies to guide their purchase decisions.[10]

PSYCHOGRAPHIC SEGMENTATION

Although demographic classifications such as age, gender, and income are relatively easy to identify and measure, researchers also need to define **psychographic segmentation** categories. Often marketing research firms conduct extensive studies of consumers and then share their psychographic data with clients. In addition, businesses look to studies done by sociologists and psychologists to help them understand their customers.

psychographic segmentation dividing consumer markets into groups with similar psychological characteristics, values, and lifestyles.

For instance, while children may fall into one age group and their parents in another, they also live certain lifestyles together. Recent marketing research reveals that today's parents are willing and able to spend more on goods and services for their children than parents were a generation or two ago. Current estimates are that middle income parents who had a baby last year will spend nearly $300,000 over the next 17 years, while higher income families will spend about $500,000 per child.[11] Psychographic information of this sort may give a company's management confidence that their proposed exclusive preschool or high-priced children's shoes might now be successful.

PRODUCT-RELATED SEGMENTATION

Using **product-related segmentation**, sellers can divide a consumer market into groups based on buyers' relationships to the good or service. The three most popular approaches to product-related segmentation are based on benefits sought, usage rates, and brand loyalty levels.

product-related segmentation dividing consumer markets into groups based on buyers' relationships to the good or service.

Segmenting by *benefits sought* focuses on the attributes that people seek in a good or service and the benefits they expect to receive from it. As more firms respond to consumer demand for eco-friendly products, marketers find ways to emphasize the benefits of these products. Home-goods retailer IKEA follows strict guidelines for sourcing its solid-wood furniture products. For example, the worldwide company does not accept any illegally felled wood. IKEA's own forest specialists trace batches of timber to their origins to ensure that the lumber is properly documented and certified by the Forest Stewardship Council. In addition, these specialists work with suppliers to promote more sustainably managed forests worldwide. IKEA uses its Web site and signage in its stores to educate consumers about its wood-source policies.[12]

Consumer markets can also be segmented according to the amounts of a product that people buy and use. Segmentation by *product usage rate* usually defines such categories as light, medium, and heavy users. According to what is commonly referred to as the "80/20 principle," roughly 80 percent of a product's revenues come from only 20 percent of its buyers. Companies can now pinpoint which of their customers are the heaviest users—and even the most profitable customers—and direct their greatest marketing efforts toward those customers.

Marketers also segment users by *brand loyalty*—the degree to which consumers recognize, prefer, and insist on a particular brand. They then attempt to tie loyal customers to a good or service by giving away premiums, which can be anything from a logo-emblazoned T-shirt to a pair of free tickets to a concert or sports event.

> **>>> Quick Review**
>
> **1** Name the most common forms of market segmentation.
>
> **2** What are the three most popular approaches to product-related segmentation?

6 Steps in Building a Marketing Strategy

Once a firm has a good understanding about likely customer behavior, the market in which it will operate, and how customers might group together, it transforms this information into a *marketing strategy*. Decision makers in any successful organization, for-profit or not-for-profit, follow a two-step process to develop their strategy. First, they study and analyze potential target markets, choosing those likely to yield the greatest profit, give them long-term growth potential, and provide defensible positions relative to their competitors. Second, they create a series of goods or services that will satisfy the chosen market.

A marketing plan is a key component of a firm's overall business plan. The marketing plan outlines its marketing strategy and includes information about the target market, sales and revenue goals, the marketing budget, and the timing for implementing the elements of the marketing mix.

SELECTING TARGET MARKETS

Markets can be classified by type of product. **Consumer products (B2C)**—often known as business-to-consumer products—are goods and services, such as an SUV, tomato sauce, or a haircut, that are purchased by end users. **Business products (B2B)**—or business-to-business products—are goods and services

consumer (B2C) product good or service that is purchased by end users.

business (B2B) product good or service purchased to be used, either directly or indirectly, in the production of other goods for resale.

target market group of people toward whom an organization markets its goods, services, or ideas with a strategy designed to satisfy their specific needs and preferences.

marketing mix blending of the four elements of marketing strategy—product, distribution, promotion, and pricing—to fit the needs and preferences of a specific target market.

purchased to be used, either directly or indirectly, in the production of other goods for resale. Some products can fit either classification, depending on who buys them and why. For example, your neighbors may buy a global positioning system (GPS) for their next road trip, or General Motors buys GPS systems by the thousands for installation on its assembly lines.

An organization's **target market** is the group of potential customers toward whom it directs its marketing efforts. Customer needs and wants vary considerably, and no single organization has the resources to satisfy everyone. *Popular Science* is geared toward readers who are interested in science and technology, whereas *Bon Appétit* is aimed at readers who are interested in fine food and cooking.

Decisions about marketing involve strategies for four areas of marketing activity: product, distribution, promotion, and pricing. A firm's **marketing mix** blends the four strategies to fit the needs and preferences of a specific target market. Marketing success depends not on the four individual strategies but on their unique combination.

- *Product strategy* involves more than just designing a good or service with needed attributes. It also includes decisions

about package design, brand names, trademarks, warranties, product image, new product development, and customer service. Think about your favorite pair of jeans. Do you like them because they fit the best, or do other attributes—such as styling and overall image—also contribute to your brand preference?

- *Distribution strategy* ensures that customers receive their purchases in the proper quantities at the right times and locations.

- *Promotional strategy* effectively blends advertising, personal selling, sales promotion, and public relations to achieve its goals of informing, persuading, and influencing purchase decisions.

- *Pricing strategy* involves one of the most difficult areas of marketing decision making: setting prices for a good or service. Pricing is sometimes subject to government regulation and considerable public scrutiny. It also represents a powerful competitive weapon and frequently produces responses by industry competitors who match price changes to avoid losing customers. Think about your jeans again. Would you continue to purchase them if they were priced either much higher or much lower?

FIGURE 11.5 shows the relationships among the target market, the marketing mix variables, and the marketing environment.

To see how the marketing mix affects a particular product offering, consider a walk-in medical clinic like the ones found

FIGURE 11.5 Target Market and Marketing Mix within the Marketing Environment

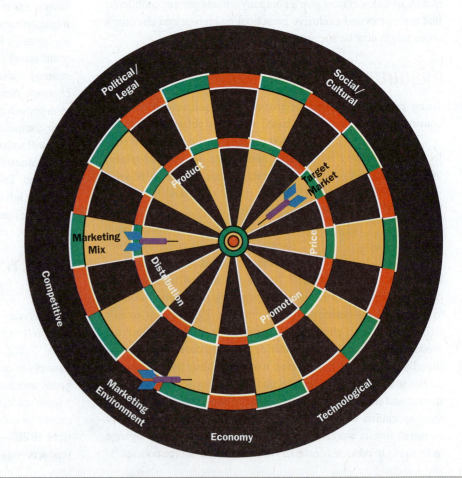

in supermarkets, chain drugstores, or big-box stores. Patients typically see nurse practitioners or physician assistants who can diagnose and treat minor medical conditions and prescribe some medications. The product strategy is, of course, medical services, but these clinics represent more than just medical care. They are open evenings and on weekends, and they are located where the consumers are. No need for a separate trip to a doctor's office: the physical location of a walk-in clinic is an important part of the distribution strategy. Letting consumers know that these clinics are available to provide seasonal flu shots and summer camp physicals helps establish the value of these centers to the public.

As part of its promotional strategy, drugstore chain Walgreens markets its Take Care Clinics with some nationwide health care organizations. Pricing strategy, the last element of the marketing mix, is addressed by setting pricing that represents a relatively low cost to the consumer: usually about $80 per visit. Marketers use product, distribution, promotion, and pricing strategies to create clinics that meet consumer needs.[13]

>>> **Quick Review**

1 Identify the two steps in building a marketing strategy and describe what is involved.

2 Distinguish between a consumer product and a business product.

3 What are the elements of a marketing mix?

7 Relationship Marketing

The past decade has brought rapid change to most industries, as consumers have become better informed and more demanding purchasers by comparing competing goods and services. They expect, even demand, new benefits from product offerings, making it harder for firms to gain a competitive advantage based on product features alone.

In these competitive times, businesses need to find new ways of relating to customers if they hope to maintain long-term success. Businesses are developing strategies and tactics that draw them into tighter connections with their customers, suppliers, and even employees. As a result, many firms are turning their attention to the issues of relationship marketing. **Relationship marketing** goes beyond making the sale. It develops and maintains long-term,

relationship marketing developing and maintaining long-term, cost-effective exchange relationships with partners.

cost-effective exchange relationships with such partners as individual customers, suppliers, and employees. Its ultimate goal: customer satisfaction.

Managing relationships instead of simply completing transactions often leads to creative partnerships. However, customers enter into relationships with firms only if they are assured that the relationship will somehow benefit them. As the intensity of commitment increases, so does the likelihood of a business continuing a long-term relationship with its customers.

Businesses are building relationships by partnering with customers, suppliers, and other businesses. Timberland, maker of footwear and clothing, creates many partnerships that foster long-term relationships. The firm partners with not-for-profit organizations such as City Year and the Planet Water Foundation to complete service projects for communities and the environment. Through its Serv-a-Palooza, hundreds of Timberland employees engage in volunteer tasks in their communities. Those opportunities even extend to customers who have expressed an interest in participating in programs in their own regions. To volunteer for a food drive or help restore a marsh, log on to the Timberland Web site to see what's available. Marketers find these activities help build relationships with customers, communities, and other organizations.[14]

BENEFITS OF RELATIONSHIP MARKETING

Relationship marketing helps all parties involved. In addition to providing mutual protection against competitors, businesses that forge solid links with vendors and customers are often rewarded with lower costs and higher profits than they would generate on their own. Long-term agreements with a few high-quality suppliers frequently reduce a firm's production costs. Unlike one-time sales, these ongoing relationships encourage suppliers to offer customers preferential treatment, quickly adjusting shipments to accommodate changes in orders and correcting any quality problems that might arise.

Good relationships with customers can be vital strategic weapons for a firm. By identifying current purchasers and maintaining positive relationships with them, organizations can efficiently target their best customers. Studying current customers' buying habits and preferences can help marketers identify potential new customers and establish ongoing contact with them. Attracting a new customer can cost five times as much as keeping an existing one. Not only are marketing costs lower with existing customers, they usually buy more, require less service, refer other customers, and provide valuable feedback. Together, these elements contribute to a higher **lifetime value of a customer**—the revenues and intangible benefits (referrals and customer feedback)

lifetime value of a customer revenues and intangible benefits (referrals and customer feedback) from a customer over the life of the relationship, minus the amount the company must spend to acquire and serve that customer.

from the customer over the life of the relationship, minus the amount the company must spend to acquire and serve that customer. Keeping that customer may occasionally require some extra effort, especially if the customer has become upset or dissatisfied with a good or service.

Businesses also benefit from strong relationships with other companies. Purchasers who repeatedly buy from one business may find they save time and gain service quality as the business learns their specific needs. Some relationship-oriented companies also customize items based on customer preferences. Because many businesses reward loyal customers with discounts or bonuses, some buyers may even find they save money by developing long-term relationships.

Alliances with other firms to serve the same customers also can be rewarding. The partners combine their capabilities and resources to accomplish goals that they could not reach on their own. In addition, alliances with other firms may help businesses develop the skills and experiences they need to successfully enter new markets or improve service to current customers.

TOOLS FOR NURTURING CUSTOMER RELATIONSHIPS

Although relationship marketing has important benefits for both customers and businesses, most relationship-oriented businesses quickly discover that some customers generate more profitable business than others. Assume 20 percent of a firm's customers account for roughly 80 percent of its sales and profits—the 80/20 principle mentioned earlier in the chapter—a customer in that category undoubtedly has a higher lifetime value than one who buys only once or twice or who makes small purchases.

While businesses shouldn't ignore any customer, they need to allocate their marketing resources wisely. A firm may choose to customize goods or services for high-value customers while working to increase repeat sales of stock products to less valuable customers. Differentiating between these two groups also helps marketers focus on each in an effort to increase their commitment.

FREQUENCY MARKETING AND AFFINITY MARKETING PROGRAMS

Marketers try to build and protect customer relationships with **frequency marketing** programs. Such programs reward frequent customers with cash, rebates, merchandise, or other premiums. Frequency programs have grown more sophisticated over the years, offering more personalization and customization than in the past. Airlines, hotel groups, restaurants, and many retailers, including supermarkets, offer frequency programs. For example, vacationers who book

frequency marketing marketing initiative that rewards frequent purchases with cash, rebates, merchandise, or other premiums.

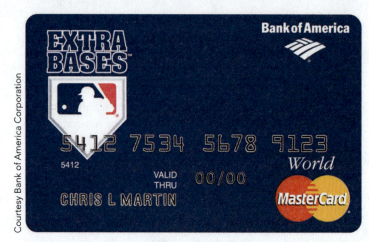

Courtesy Bank of America Corporation

∧ Affinity programs build emotional links with customers and are common in the credit card industry. Bank of America offers credit cards featuring the logos of all 30 Major League Baseball clubs.

a certain number of nights at the Atlantis resort in the Bahamas may earn airfare credit for their trip.[15]

Affinity programs build emotional links with customers. In an **affinity program**, an organization solicits involvement by individuals who share common interests and activities. Affinity programs are common in the credit card industry. For instance, a person can sign up for a credit card emblazoned with the logo of his or her college, favorite charity, or a sports team. Bank of America offers credit cards featuring the logos of all 30 Major League Baseball clubs.

affinity program marketing effort sponsored by an organization that solicits involvement by individuals who share common interests and activities.

ONE-ON-ONE MARKETING

The ability to customize products and rapidly deliver goods and services has become increasingly dependent on technology such as computer-aided design and manufacturing (CAD/CAM). The Internet offers a way for businesses to connect with customers in a direct and intimate manner. Companies can take orders for customized products, gather data about buyers, and predict what items a customer might want in the future. Computer databases provide strong support for effective relationship marketing. Marketers can maintain databases on customer tastes, price range preferences, and lifestyles, and they can quickly obtain names and other information about promising prospects.

Amazon.com greets each online customer with a list of suggested books he or she might like to purchase. Many online retailers send their customers e-mails about upcoming sales, new products, and special events.

Small and large companies often rely on *customer relationship management* software technology that helps them gather, sort, and interpret data about customers. Software firms develop this software to help businesses build and manage their relationships with customers. QueueBuster is one such product. The software offers a caller the choice of receiving an automated return call at a convenient time instead of waiting on hold for the next available representative. After implementing the software to support its central reservations team, the Apex Hotel chain minimized the number of dropped customer calls and increased customer-service levels. This simple solution to customers' frustration not only helped build customer loyalty and improve employee morale but also helped save Apex Hotels from losing business.[16]

>>> **Quick Review**

1 What is the lifetime value of a customer, and why is this concept important to marketers?

2 Identify some tools for nurturing customer relationships.

What's Ahead? > > >

The next two chapters examine each of the four elements of the marketing mix that marketers use to satisfy their selected target markets. Chapter 12 focuses on products and their distribution through various channels to different outlets. Chapter 13 covers promotion and the various methods marketers use to communicate with their target customers, along with strategies for setting prices for different products.

Weekly Updates spark classroom debate around current events that apply to your business course topics. http://www.wileybusinessupdates.com

NOTES

1. Company Web site, "Here's What's Great for You," http://instoresnow.walmart.com, accessed May 13, 2013; Stephanie Strom, "Walmart to Label Healthy Foods," *New York Times*, February 7, 2012, http://www.nytimes.com; Jessica Wohl, "Walmart to Label Healthier Food as 'Great for You,'" *Reuters*, February 7, 2012, http://www.reuters.com.

2. Association Web site, "Definition of Marketing," http://www.marketingpower.com, accessed May 2, 2013.

3. Steve Carlotti and Jason Green, "Give the People What They Don't Know They Want," *The Washington Post*, May 14, 2012, http://articles.washingtonpost.com.

4. Reineke Reitsma, "Market Research That Goes beyond 'a Faster Horse,'" *RW Connect*, Septermber 27, 2012, http://rwconnect.esomar.org.

5. Kevin G. Hall, "Consumers Coming Back, but They May Not Run Up Credit Cards," *McClatchy Newspapers*, February 14, 2013, http://www.mcclatchydc.com.

6. Company Web site, http://www.pg.com, accessed May 13, 2013.

7. Stephanie Clifford, "Social Media Are Giving a Voice to Taste Buds," *New York Times*, July 30, 2012, http://www.nytimes.com.

8. Matthew Brown, "Understanding Gender and eCommerce," PFSweb blog, August 10, 2012, http://www.pfsweb.com.

9. U.S. Census Bureau, *2012 Statistical Abstract*, "Resident Population Projections by Sex and Age: 2010 to 2050," http://www.census.gov, accessed May 2, 2013.

10. Patricia Orsini, "Millennials in Aisle 2.0: Keeping Young Supermarket Shoppers Engaged with Brands," *eMarketer*, November 20, 2012, http://bx.businessweek.com.

11. Amy Morin, "How Much Money Do Parents Spend on Their Kids?," Mom.me, May 2013, http://mom.me.

12. Company Web site, "Forestry and Wood," http://www.ikea.com, accessed May 2, 2013.

13. Company Web site, http://www.takecarehealth.com, accessed May 2, 2013; "Take Care Clinics at Select Walgreens Offer Families Convenient and Affordable Option for Camp and Sports Physicals," press release, March 7, 2012, http://www.businesswire.com.

14. Company Web site, http://www.timberland.com, accessed May 2, 2013.

15. Company Web site, http://www.atlantis.com, accessed May 2, 2013.

16. Company Web site, http://www.netcall.com, accessed May 2, 2013.

Summary of Learning Objectives

 Define *marketing.*

Utility is the ability of a good or service to satisfy the wants and needs of customers. Marketing creates time, place, and ownership utility by making a product or service available when and where consumers want to buy and by arranging for orderly transfers of ownership.

marketing organizational function and set of processes for creating, communicating, and delivering value to customers and for managing customer relationships in ways that benefit the organization and its stakeholders.

exchange process activity in which two or more parties give something of value to each other to satisfy perceived needs.

utility power of a good or service to satisfy a want or need.

2 Discuss **the evolution of the marketing concept.**

The marketing concept is a companywide customer orientation with the objective of achieving long-run success. This concept is essential in today's marketplace, which is primarily a buyer's market, meaning buyers can choose from an abundance of goods and services. Marketing focuses on creating customer satisfaction and building long-term relationships with customers.

marketing concept companywide consumer orientation to promote long-run success.

 Summarize **consumer behavior.**

Consumer behavior refers to the actions of ultimate consumers with direct effects on obtaining, consuming, and disposing of products, as well as the decision processes that precede and follow these actions. Personal influences on consumer behavior include an individual's needs and motives, perceptions, attitudes, learned experiences, and self-concept. The interpersonal determinants include cultural influences, social influences, and family influences. A number of people within a firm may participate in business purchase decisions, so business buyers must consider a variety of organizational influences in addition to their own preferences.

consumer behavior actions of ultimate consumers directly involved in obtaining, consuming, and disposing of products and the decision processes that precede and follow these actions.

 Describe **marketing research.**

Marketing research is the information-gathering function that links marketers to the marketplace. It provides valuable information about potential target markets. Firms may generate internal data or gather external data. They may use secondary data or conduct research to obtain primary data. Data mining, which involves computer searches through customer data to detect patterns or relationships, is one helpful tool in forecasting various trends such as sales revenues and consumer behavior.

marketing research collecting and evaluating information to help marketers make effective decisions.

data mining the task of using computer-based technology to evaluate data in a database and identify useful trends.

business intelligence activities and technologies for gathering, storing, and analyzing data to make better competitive decisions.

5 Explain **market segmentation.**

Consumer markets can be divided according to four criteria:

- Geographical factors
- Demographic characteristics, such as age and family size
- Psychographic variables, which involve behavioral and lifestyle profiles
- Product-related variables, such as the benefits consumers seek when buying a product or the degree of brand loyalty they feel toward it.

market segmentation process of dividing a total market into several relatively homogeneous groups.

geographic segmentation dividing a market into homogeneous groups on the basis of their location.

demographic segmentation distinguishes markets on the basis of various demographic or socioeconomic characteristics.

psychographic segmentation dividing consumer markets into groups with similar psychological characteristics, values, and lifestyles.

product-related segmentation dividing consumer markets into groups based on buyers' relationships to the good or service.

 List **the steps in building a marketing strategy.**

All organizations develop marketing strategies to reach customers. This process involves analyzing the overall market, selecting a target market, and developing a marketing mix that blends elements related to product, distribution, promotion, and pricing decisions.

consumer (B2C) product   good or service that is purchased by end users.

business (B2B) product   good or service purchased to be used, either directly or indirectly, in the production of other goods for resale.

target market   group of people toward whom an organization markets its goods, services, or ideas with a strategy designed to satisfy their specific needs and preferences.

marketing mix   blending of the four elements of marketing strategy—product, distribution, promotion, and pricing—to fit the needs and preferences of a specific target market.

 Discuss relationship marketing.

Relationship marketing is an organization's attempt to develop long-term, cost-effective links with individual customers for mutual benefit. Good relationships with customers can be a vital strategic weapon for a firm. By identifying current purchasers and maintaining a positive relationship with them, an organization can efficiently target its best customers, fulfill their needs, and create loyalty. Information technologies, frequency and affinity programs, and one-on-one efforts all help build relationships with customers.

relationship marketing   developing and maintaining long-term, cost-effective exchange relationships with partners.

lifetime value of a customer   revenues and intangible benefits (referrals and customer feedback) from a customer over the life of the relationship, minus the amount the company must spend to acquire and serve that customer.

frequency marketing   marketing initiative that rewards frequent purchases with cash, rebates, merchandise, or other premiums.

affinity program   marketing effort sponsored by an organization that solicits involvement by individuals who share common interests and activities.

>>> Quick Review >>

LO1

1 What is utility?

2 Identify some ways in which marketing creates utility.

LO2

1 Name the five eras in the history of marketing.

2 What is the marketing concept?

3 How is the marketing concept tied to the relationship and social eras of marketing?

LO3

1 What is consumer behavior?

2 What are some influences on consumer behavior?

3 Name the steps in the consumer behavior process.

LO4

1 Give examples of internal data and external data. How are they gathered?

2 Differentiate between primary and secondary data.

3 What is data mining, and how is it useful to marketers?

LO5

1 Name the most common form of market segmentation.

2 What are the three most popular approaches to product-related segmentation?

LO6

1 Identify the two steps in building a marketing strategy and describe what is involved.

2 Distinguish between a consumer product and a business product.

3 What are the elements of a marketing mix?

LO7

1 What is the lifetime value of a customer, and why is this concept important to marketers?

2 Identify some tools for nurturing customer relationships.

© fatihhoca/iStockphoto

chapter twelve

12

Product and Distribution Strategies

Learning Objectives

1 **Explain** product strategy.

2 **Describe** the four stages of the product life cycle.

3 **Discuss** product identification.

4 **Outline** the major components of an effective distribution strategy.

5 **Explain** wholesaling.

6 **Describe** retailing.

7 **Identify** distribution channel decisions and logistics.

Panama Canal's Expansion Is a Game Changer

Life has changed in many ways since the 1960s, but here's one way you might not have thought about. Back then, every commercial ship afloat could pass through the Panama Canal. Today, about 15 percent of shipping that could go through the 100-year-old passage between the Atlantic and Pacific Oceans must travel a different route instead, because the ships are too wide or too deep.

Rising fuel prices have driven shipping companies to build ever-larger ships that can carry more cargo in fewer trips. When ships can't travel through the canal, goods from Asia must travel over land by truck and rail, which is more expensive, to reach consumers on the East Coast, where about two-thirds of the U.S. population lives.

A $5.25 billion expansion project is under way to widen and deepen the canal, allowing larger, "post-Panama"-sized ships to pass through the all-water route from Asia to the U.S. Atlantic coast. The expansion doubles the amount of freight that can go through the canal and will have a significant impact on distribution.

By reducing shipping costs, the canal's expansion will reward shipping companies, manufacturers, and retailers with higher profit margins and consumers with lower prices, although goods will take a bit longer to arrive. Still, the trade-off is considered worthwhile. The largest ships passing through the canal today can carry about 4,000 20-foot containers; after the expansion is complete, ships carrying 12,600—triple the amount—will sail through.

Exactly where these ships will dock is still an open question. Currently they can put in only at Norfolk, Virginia, but ports in New York, New Jersey, Maryland, and Florida are among those racing to prepare for the arrival of the larger ships.

With new access to and from Asia through the canal, even railroads expect things in the transportation and distribution business to change. Whenever new capacity is built in a global transportation system, people find a way to use it.[1]

Overview > > >

This chapter focuses on the first two elements of the marketing mix: product and distribution. Its discussion of product strategy begins by describing the classifications of goods and services; customer service; product lines and the product mix; and the product life cycle. It also discusses product identification through brand name and distinctive packaging, and how companies foster customer loyalty to their brands. Distribution focuses on moving goods and services from producer to wholesaler to retailer to buyers and concludes with a look at the logistics of moving information, goods, and services to final consumers.

1 Products and Services

Most people respond to the question "What is a product?" by listing its physical features. In contrast, marketers take a broader view. To them, a **product** is a bundle of physical, service, and symbolic characteristics designed to satisfy consumer wants. The chief executive officer of a major tool manufacturer once startled his stockholders with this statement: "Last year our customers bought over 1 million quarter-inch drill bits, and none of them wanted to buy the product. They all wanted quarter-inch holes." Product strategy involves considerably more than just producing a good or service; instead, it focuses on benefits. The marketing conception of a product includes decisions about package design, brand name, trademarks, warranties, product image, new product development, and customer service.

CLASSIFYING CONSUMER GOODS AND SERVICES

The classification that marketers typically use for products that consumers buy for their own use and enjoyment and not for resale is based on consumer buying habits. *Convenience products* are items the consumer seeks to purchase frequently, immediately, and with little effort. Items stocked in gas station markets, vending machines, and local newsstands are usually convenience products—for example, newspapers, snacks, candy, coffee, and bread. *Shopping products* are those typically purchased only after the buyer has compared

product bundle of physical, service, and symbolic characteristics designed to satisfy consumer wants.

∧ Buying a *specialty product* takes extra effort. If the car you want to buy is a Lexus, you'll make the trip to the Lexus dealership even if it's not close.

competing products in competing stores. A person intent on buying a new sofa or dining room table may visit many stores, examine perhaps dozens of pieces of furniture, and spend days making the final decision. *Specialty products* are those that a purchaser is willing to make a special effort to obtain. The purchaser is already familiar with the item and considers it to have no reasonable substitute. The nearest Lexus dealer may be 75 miles away, but if you have decided you want one, you will make the trip.

The interrelationship of marketing mix factors is shown in **FIGURE 12.1**. By knowing the appropriate classification for a specific product, the marketing decision maker knows quite a bit about how the other mix variables will adapt to create a profitable, customer-driven marketing strategy.

CLASSIFYING BUSINESS GOODS

Business products are goods and services used in operating an organization. They can be as simple as paper towels and coffee filters for the break room to machinery, tools, raw materials, components, and buildings. Consumer products are classified by buying habits, and business products are classified based on how they are used and by their basic characteristics. Products that are long-lived and relatively expensive are called *capital items*. Less costly products that are consumed within a year are referred to as *expense items*.

CLASSIFYING SERVICES

Services can be classified as intended for the consumer market or the business market. Child- and elder-care centers and auto detail shops provide services for consumers; the Pinkerton security patrols at a local factory and Kelly Services' temporary office workers are examples of business services. In some cases, a service can accommodate both consumer and business markets. For example, ServiceMaster may clean the upholstery in a home or spruce up the painting system and robots in a manufacturing plant.

Like tangible goods, services can also be considered "convenience," "shopping," or "specialty," depending on customers' buying patterns. However, services are distinguished from goods in several ways. First, unlike goods, services are intangible. In addition, they are perishable because firms cannot stockpile them in inventory. Services are also difficult to standardize because they must meet individual customers' needs. Finally, from a buyer's perspective, the service provider *is* the service; the two are inseparable in the buyer's mind.

FIGURE 12.1 Marketing Impacts of Consumer Product Classification

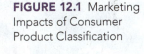

Marketing Strategy Factor	Convenience Product	Shopping Product	Specialty Product
· Purchase Frequency	· Frequent	· Relatively infrequent	· Infrequent
· Store Image	· Unimportant	· Very important	· Important
· Price	· Low	· Relatively high	· High
· Promotion	· By manufacturer	· By manufacturer and retailers	· By manufacturer and retailers
· Distribution Channel	· Many wholesalers and retailers	· Relatively few wholesalers and retailers	· Very few wholesalers and retailers
· Number of Retail Outlets	· Many	· Few	· Very few, often one per market area

PRODUCT LINES AND PRODUCT MIX

Few firms operate with a single product. If their initial entry is successful, they often try to increase their profit and growth chances by adding new offerings. A company's **product line** is a group of related products marked by physical similarities or intended for a similar market. A **product mix** is the assortment of product lines and individual goods and services that a firm offers to consumers and business users. The Coca-Cola Company and PepsiCo both have product lines that include old standards—Coke Classic and Diet Coke, Pepsi and Diet Pepsi. But recently, PepsiCo announced it would start distributing Tampico Plus in selected states. Unlike other products from Tampico Beverages, Tampico Plus drinks contain vitamins A, C, and E. They also have half as much sugar as regular Tampico drinks. Thus, they meet the guidelines for beverages that can be sold in U.S. high schools, which want to limit the amount of sugar in drinks available to students.[2]

Marketers must assess their product mix continually to ensure company growth, to satisfy changing consumer needs and wants, and to adjust to competitors' offerings. To remain competitive, marketers look for gaps in their product lines and fill

product line group of related products marked by physical similarities or intended for a similar market.

product mix the assortment of product lines and individual goods and services that a firm offers to consumers and business users.

182

∨ A *product line* includes several related products designed to have the same appearance, like these PepsiCo products.

Teri Stratford

them with new offerings or modified versions of existing ones. A helpful tool frequently used in making product decisions is the product life cycle.

>>> **Quick Review**

1 Describe the differences among convenience, shopping, and specialty products.

2 How do consumer products differ from business products?

3 How do marketers classify services?

2 Product Life Cycle

Once a product is on the market, it typically goes through four stages known as the **product life cycle**: introduction, growth, maturity, and decline. As **FIGURE 12.2** shows, industry sales and profits vary depending on the life cycle stage of an item.

product life cycle four basic stages—introduction, growth, maturity, and decline—through which a successful product progresses.

Product life cycles are not set in stone; not all products follow this pattern precisely, and different products may spend different periods of time in each stage. However, the concept helps marketers anticipate developments throughout the various stages of a product's life. Profits assume a predictable pattern through the stages, and promotional emphasis shifts from dispensing product information in the early stages to heavy brand promotion in the later ones.

STAGES OF THE PRODUCT LIFE CYCLE

In the *introduction stage,* the firm tries to stimulate demand for its new offering; inform the market about it, give free samples, and explain its features, uses, and benefits. Sales are limited in this phase, and new product development costs and extensive introductory promotions are expensive and commonly lead to losses in the introductory stage. Figure 12.2 shows an introduction phase of smoothly increasing sales, but this is not always the case. Sometimes an introduction begins well but quickly runs out of steam as product pricing or production issues restrict the number of buyers. Plasma televisions, Apple's Maps app, and Google Buzz are all examples of products that didn't quite make it through the introduction stages as planned.

During the *growth stage,* sales climb quickly as new customers join early users who now are repurchasing the item. Word-of-mouth referrals and continued advertising and other special promotions by the firm induce others to make trial purchases. At this point, the company begins to earn profits on the new product. This success may encourage competitors to enter the field with similar offerings, and if a number of new competitors come into the market, price competition develops. After its initial success

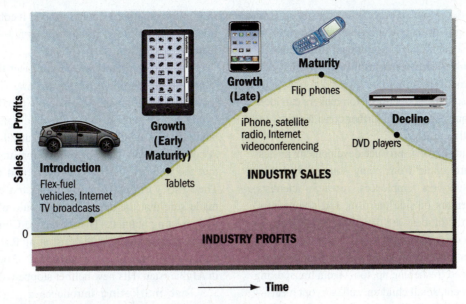

FIGURE 12.2 Stages in the Product Life Cycle

with the Kindle, Amazon faced competition from Barnes & Noble's Nook. In the evolving market for e-readers and tablets, a move by one of the market players elicits a response by the others. After Amazon rushed to launch its Kindle for the iPad, Barnes & Noble countered with its popular Nook Color. These two competitors plus Apple, Google, and others continue to release new models with additional features.[3]

In the *maturity stage,* industry sales at first increase but eventually reach a saturation level at which further expansion is difficult. Competition also intensifies, increasing product availability. Firms concentrate market share, trying to capture their competitors' customers, often by dropping prices to increase the appeal of their product. Manufacturers of mature products look to product line extension to redesign their products to appeal to smaller and smaller groups of customers. Soft drink and beer producers are constantly bringing out new products: low calorie, no-calorie, colored, uncolored, flavors, and more. Cell phones are also in the maturity stage: companies compete not only on price but also on features such as calendars, e-mail and attachments, messaging capability, full-color screens, keyboards, and fax and word-processing functions. Sales volume fades late in the maturity stage, and weaker competitors may leave the market.

Sales continue to fall in the *decline stage.* Profits decline and may become losses as further price cutting occurs in the reduced overall market for the item. Competitors gradually exit, making some profits possible for the remaining firms in the shrinking market. The decline stage usually is caused by a product innovation or a shift in consumer preferences. Sometimes technology change can hasten the decline stage for a product. For example, although more than 90 percent of U.S. homes contain at least one DVD player, DVDs have now been superseded by Blu-ray technology and online streaming sites. Carbon paper, film cameras, CDs, and newspaper want ads are examples of products that have declined because of changes in technology.

STAGES IN NEW PRODUCT DEVELOPMENT

So, what does it take to develop a successful new product? Most of today's newly developed items are aimed at satisfying specific consumer demands. New product development is becoming increasingly efficient and cost effective because marketers use a systematic approach to developing new products. As **FIGURE 12.3**

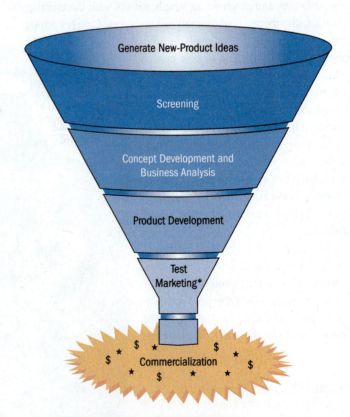

Generate New-Product Ideas

Screening

Concept Development and Business Analysis

Product Development

Test Marketing*

Commercialization

* Some firms skip this step and move directly from product development to commercialization.

FIGURE 12.3 Process for Developing New Goods and Services

shows, the new product development process has six stages. Each stage requires a "go/no-go" decision by management before the idea can move to a subsequent stage. Significant investments of time and money are involved in products as they go through each development stage—sometimes only to be rejected at one of the final stages. For this reason, the sooner decision makers can identify a marginal product and drop it from further consideration, the less time and money will be wasted.

The starting point in the new product development process is generating ideas. Ideas come from many sources, including customer suggestions, suppliers, employees, research scientists, marketing research, inventors outside the firm, and competitors' products. The most successful ideas are directly related to satisfying customer needs. Procter & Gamble's Febreze eliminates odors in the home and leaves a fresh scent. When P&G researchers discovered that cars often need freshening up, too—from transporting well-used athletic equipment, small children, and carryout meals—the company added Febreze CAR Vent Clips to the product line. The clip attaches to a car's air vent and comes in five scents.[4]

In the second stage, screening eliminates ideas that do not mesh with overall company objectives or that cannot be developed, given the company's resources. Some firms hold open discussions of new product ideas with specialists who work in different functional areas in the organization.

Further screening occurs during the concept development and business analysis phase. The analysis involves assessing the new product's potential sales, profits, growth rate, and competitive strengths and determining whether it fits with the company's product, distribution, and promotional resources. *Concept testing*—marketing research designed to solicit initial consumer reaction to new product ideas—may be used at this stage. For example, potential consumers might be asked about proposed brand names and other methods of product identification. *Focus groups* are sessions in which consumers meet with marketers to discuss what they like or dislike about current products and perhaps test or sample a new offering to provide some immediate feedback.

Next, an actual product is developed, subjected to a series of tests, and revised. Functioning prototypes or detailed descriptions of the product may be created. These designs are the joint responsibility of the firm's development

staff and its marketers, who provide feedback on consumer reactions to the proposed product design, color, and other physical features.

Sometimes prototypes do not meet the stated requirements. When the U.S. military began looking for an improved helmet, it asked four companies to submit prototypes for helmets that would be 35 percent more effective against fragmentation and handgun and small-arms bullets. But all four prototypes failed. A couple of years later, one firm submitted a prototype so strong that the military's test equipment could not penetrate the shell. The Army wasn't satisfied with the first series of prototypes and made sure that the new helmets would offer better performance than existing helmets. The Advanced Combat Helmet (ACH), as they are now known, is demonstrating this improved capability as an Iowa National Guard member found out while on deployment in Afghanistan. His new helmet stopped an AK-47 round.[5]

Test marketing introduces a new product supported by a complete marketing campaign to a selected city or TV coverage area. Marketers look for a location with a manageable size, where residents match their target market's demographic profile, to test their product. During the test-marketing stage, the item is sold in a limited area while the company examines both consumer responses to the new offering and the marketing effort used to support it. Test-market results can help managers determine the product's likely performance in a full-scale introduction. Some firms skip test marketing, however, because of concerns that the test could reveal their strategies to the competition. Also, the expense of doing limited production runs of complex products such as a new auto or refrigerator is sometimes so high that marketers skip the test-marketing stage and move directly to commercialization.

In the final stage, commercialization, the product is made available in the marketplace. Sometimes this stage is referred to as a product launch. Considerable planning goes into this stage because the firm's distribution, promotion, and pricing strategies must all be geared to support the new product offering. Video game maker Electronic Arts announced a new distribution strategy for future products. The company will release premium downloadable content for a game before releasing the complete, packaged version. The company will invite comments from reviewers and players and make changes to the final version prior to release.[6]

> **test marketing** introduction of a new product supported by a complete marketing campaign to a selected city or TV coverage area.

> After Procter & Gamble scored a success with its Febreze air freshener, adding CAR Vent Clips to the product line was a natural.

Mary Ann Price

3 Product Identification

A major aspect of developing a successful new product involves methods for identifying a product and distinguishing it from competing offerings. Both tangible goods and intangible services are identified by brands, brand names, and trademarks. A **brand** is a name, term, sign, symbol, design, or some combination that identifies the products of one firm and differentiates them from competitors' offerings. Tropicana, Pepsi, and Gatorade are all made by PepsiCo, but a unique combination of name, symbol, and package design distinguishes each brand from the others.

A **brand name** is that part of the brand consisting of words or letters included in a name used to identify and distinguish the firm's offerings from those of competitors. The brand name is the part of the brand that can be vocalized. Many brand names, such as Coca-Cola, McDonald's, American Express, Google, and Nike, are famous around the world. Likewise, the "golden arches" brand mark of McDonald's also is widely recognized.

A **trademark** is a brand that has been given legal protection. The protection is granted solely to the brand's owner. Trademark protection includes not only the brand name but also design logos, slogans, packaging elements, and product features such as color and shape. A well-designed trademark, such as the Nike "swoosh," can make a difference in how positively consumers perceive a brand.

brand a name, term, sign, symbol, design, or some combination that identifies the products of one firm and differentiates them from competitors' offerings.

brand name part of the brand consisting of words or letters included in a name used to identify and distinguish the firm's offerings from those of competitors.

trademark brand that has been given legal protection.

BRAND CATEGORIES, LOYALTY, AND EQUITY

A brand offered and promoted by a manufacturer is known as a *manufacturer's* (or *national*) *brand*. Examples are Tide, Cheerios, Windex, Fossil, and Nike. But not all brand names belong to manufacturers; some are the property of retailers or distributors. A *private* (or *store*) *brand* identifies a product that is not linked to the manufacturer but instead carries a wholesaler's or retailer's label. Sears's Craftsman tools and Walmart's Ol' Roy dog food are examples.

Marketers measure brand loyalty in three stages: brand recognition, brand preference, and brand insistence. *Brand recognition* is brand acceptance strong enough that the consumer is aware of the brand but not strong enough to cause a preference over other brands. *Brand preference* occurs when a consumer chooses one firm's brand over a competitor's if the favored brand is available. *Brand insistence* is the ultimate degree of brand loyalty, in which the consumer will look for it at another outlet, special-order it from a dealer, order by mail, or search the Internet for it.

Brand loyalty is at the heart of **brand equity**, the added value that a respected and successful name gives to a product. This value results from a combination of factors, including awareness, loyalty, and perceived quality, as well as any feelings or images the customer associates with the brand. High brand equity offers financial advantages to a firm because the product commands a relatively large market share and sometimes reduces price sensitivity, generating higher profits. **FIGURE 12.4** shows the world's ten most valuable brands and their estimated worth.

brand equity added value that a respected and successful name gives to a product.

PACKAGES AND LABELS

Packaging and labels are important in product identification. They also play an important role in a firm's overall product strategy. Packaging affects the durability, image, and convenience of an item and is the biggest cost in many consumer products. Due

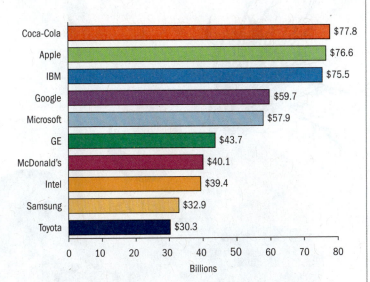

Brand	Value
Coca-Cola	$77.8
Apple	$76.6
IBM	$75.5
Google	$59.7
Microsoft	$57.9
GE	$43.7
McDonald's	$40.1
Intel	$39.4
Samsung	$32.9
Toyota	$30.3

Billions

FIGURE 12.4 The World's Ten Most Valuable Brands (billions)

SOURCE: Interbrand, Best Global Brands 2012, "Interactive Charts: Best Global Brands," http://www.interbrand.com, accessed May 30, 2013.

to a growing demand to produce smaller, more environmentally friendly packages, box manufacturers and chemical companies are now working harder to create packaging that uses less material, is made from renewable sources, and is recyclable.

Choosing the right package is especially crucial in international marketing because marketers must be aware of such factors as language variations and cultural preferences. Package size can vary according to a country's purchasing patterns and market conditions. In countries with small refrigerators, people may want to buy their beverages one at a time rather than in six-packs. Package weight is another important issue because shipping costs are often based on weight.

Labeling is an integral part of the packaging process. In the United States, federal law requires companies to provide enough information on labels to allow consumers to make value comparisons among competing products. In the case of food packaging, labels must also provide nutrition information. Companies who ship products to other countries must comply with labeling requirements in those nations.

Another important aspect of packaging and labeling is the *Universal Product Code (UPC),* the bar code read by optical scanners that print the name of the item and the price on a receipt. For many stores, these identifiers are useful not just for packaging and labeling but also for simplifying and speeding retail transactions and for evaluating customer purchases and controlling inventory. Industry observers believe that radio-frequency identification technology—embedded chips that can broadcast their product information to receivers—may ultimately replace UPC bar codes.

A relatively new technology akin to bar codes, Quick Response codes used in product packaging allow companies to create electronic paths directly to a company's Web site, providing consumers with information about the product or company.

4 Distribution Strategy

The next element of the marketing mix, **distribution**, deals with the marketing activities and institutions involved in getting the right good or service to the firm's customers. Distribution decisions involve modes of transportation, warehousing, inventory control, order processing, and selection of marketing channels. Marketing channels typically are made up of intermediaries such as retailers and wholesalers that move a product from producer to final purchaser.

The two major components of an organization's distribution are distribution channels and physical distribution. **Distribution channels** are the paths that products—and legal ownership of them—follow from producer to consumer or business user. They are the means by which all organizations distribute their goods and services. **Physical distribution** is the actual movement of products from producer to consumers or business users. Physical distribution covers a broad range of activities, including customer service, transportation, inventory control, materials handling, order processing, and warehousing.

distribution deals with the marketing activities and institutions involved in getting the right good or service to the firm's customers.

distribution channels path that products—and legal ownership of them—follow from producer to consumers or business user.

physical distribution actual movement of products from producer to consumers or business users.

< Due to the growing demand for eco-friendly packaging, consumer products companies are utilizing packaging that relies on renewable resources such as polylactic acid, a plastic substitute made from fermented plant starch.

Handout/MCT/Newscom

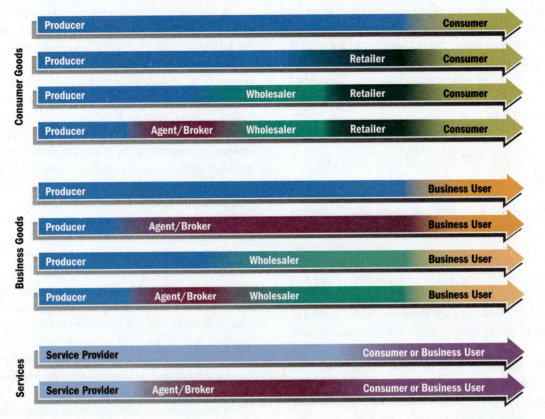

FIGURE 12.5 Alternative Distribution Channels

DISTRIBUTION CHANNELS

In their first decision for distribution channel selection, marketers choose which type of channel will best meet both their firm's marketing objectives and customers' needs. As shown in **FIGURE 12.5**, marketers can choose either a *direct distribution channel*, which carries goods directly from producer to consumer or business user, or distribution channels that involve several different marketing intermediaries. A *marketing intermediary* (also called a *middleman*) is a business firm that moves goods between producers and consumers or business users. Marketing intermediaries perform various functions that help the distribution channel operate smoothly, such as buying, selling, storing, and transporting products; sorting and grading bulky items; and providing information to other channel members. The two main categories of marketing intermediaries are wholesalers and retailers.

- **Direct Distribution** The shortest and simplest means of connecting producers and customers is direct contact between the two parties. Consumers who buy fresh fruits and vegetables at rural roadside stands or farmers markets use direct distribution, as do services ranging from banking and 10-minute oil changes to ear piercing and Mary Kay Cosmetics.

- **Using Marketing Intermediaries** Although direct channels allow simple and straightforward connections between producers and their customers, the list of channel alternatives in Figure 12.5 suggests that direct distribution is not the best

choice in every instance. Some products sell in small quantities for relatively low prices to thousands of widely scattered consumers. Makers of such products cannot cost effectively contact each of their customers, so they distribute products through specialized intermediaries called *wholesalers* and *retailers*.

>>> **Quick Review**

1 What are distribution channels? Why is channel choice an important decision for marketers?

2 What is a marketing intermediary?

5 Wholesaling

How do retailers get the products that fill their shelves? A **wholesaler** is the distribution channel member that sells primarily to retailers, other wholesalers, or business users. For instance, Sysco is a wholesaler that buys food products from producers and then resells them to restaurants, hotels, and other institutions across North America.

wholesaler distribution channel member that sells primarily to retailers, other wholesalers, or business users.

Wholesaling is a crucial part of the distribution channel for many products, particularly consumer goods and business supplies. Wholesaling intermediaries can be classified on the basis of ownership; some are owned by manufacturers, some are owned by retailers, and others are independently owned. The United States has about 486,000 wholesalers, two-thirds of which have fewer than 20 employees.[7]

MANUFACTURER-OWNED WHOLESALING INTERMEDIARIES

A manufacturer may decide to distribute goods directly through company-owned facilities to control distribution or customer service. Firms operate two main types of manufacturer-owned wholesaling intermediaries: sales branches and sales offices.

A *sales branch* stocks the products it distributes and fills orders from its inventory. It also provides offices for sales representatives. Sales branches are common in the chemical, petroleum products, motor vehicle, and machine and equipment industries.

A *sales office* is exactly what its name implies: an office for a producer's salespeople. Manufacturers set up sales offices in various regions to support local selling efforts and improve customer service. Some kitchen and bath fixture manufacturers maintain showrooms to display their products. Builders and decorators can visit these showrooms to see how the items would look in place. Unlike sales branches, however, sales offices do not store any inventory. When a customer orders from a showroom or other sales office, the merchandise is delivered from a separate warehouse.

INDEPENDENT WHOLESALING INTERMEDIARIES

An independent wholesaling intermediary is a business that represents a number of different manufacturers and makes sales calls on retailers, manufacturers, and other business accounts. Independent wholesalers are classified as either merchant wholesalers or agents and brokers, depending on whether they take title to the products they handle.

A *merchant wholesaler*, like apparel wholesaler WholesaleSarong.com, is an independently owned wholesaling intermediary that takes title to the goods it handles. Within this category, a *full-function merchant wholesaler* provides a complete assortment of services for retailers or industrial buyers, such as warehousing, shipping, and even financing. A subtype of full-function merchant is a *rack jobber,* such as Choice Books, which handles distribution of inspirational books to retail stores. This type of firm stocks, displays, and services particular retail products, such as calendars, books, and note cards, in drug stores and gift shops. Usually, the retailer receives a commission based on actual sales as payment for providing merchandise space to a rack jobber.

A *limited-function merchant wholesaler* also takes legal title to the products it handles, but it provides fewer services to the retailers to which it sells. Some limited-function merchant wholesalers only warehouse products but do not offer delivery service. Others warehouse and deliver products but provide no financing. One type of limited-function merchant wholesaler is a *drop shipper* such as Kate Aspen, a wholesaler of wedding favors. Drop shippers also operate in such industries as coal and lumber, characterized by bulky products for which no single producer can provide a complete assortment. They give access to many related goods by contacting numerous producers and negotiating the best possible prices. Cost considerations call for producers to ship such products directly to the drop shipper's customers.

Another category of independent wholesaling intermediaries consists of *agents* and *brokers*. They may or may not take possession of the goods they handle, but they never take title, working mainly to bring buyers and sellers together. Stockbrokers such as Charles Schwab and real estate agents such as RE/MAX perform functions similar to those of agents and brokers, but at the retail level. They do not take title to the sellers' property; instead, they create time and ownership utility for both buyer and seller by helping carry out transactions.

A *manufacturers' rep* acts as an independent sales force by representing the manufacturers of related but noncompeting products. This agent intermediary, sometimes referred to as a *manufacturers' agent,* receives commissions based on a percentage of sales.

RETAILER-OWNED COOPERATIVES AND BUYING OFFICES

Retailers sometimes band together to form their own wholesaling organizations. Such organizations can take the form of either a buying group or a cooperative. Participating retailers set up the new operation to reduce costs or to provide some special service that is not readily available in the marketplace. To achieve cost savings through quantity purchases, independent retailers may form a buying group that negotiates bulk sales with manufacturers. Ace Hardware is a retailer-owned cooperative. The independent owners of it 4,600 stores have access to bulk merchandise purchases that save them—and their customers—money.[8] In a cooperative, an independent group of retailers may decide to band together to share functions such as shipping or warehousing.

> > > **Quick Review**

1 What is wholesaling?

2 Describe the difference between a merchant wholesaler and an agent or broker in terms of title to the goods.

⑥ Retailing

The **retailer** is the distribution channel member that sells goods and services to individuals for their own use rather than for resale. Consumers usually buy their food, clothing, shampoo, furniture, and appliances from some type of retailer. The supermarket where you buy your groceries may have bought some of its items from a wholesaler such as Unified Grocers and then resold them to you. Retailers are a critical element—the so-called "last three feet"—in the distribution channel. Because retailers are often the only channel member that deals directly with consumers, manufacturers rely heavily on them to get their products into the hands of consumers.

> **retailer** distribution channel members that sell goods and services to individuals for their own use rather than for resale.

Retailers can be classified in two categories: nonstore and store.

NONSTORE RETAILERS

As **FIGURE 12.6** shows, nonstore retailing includes four forms: direct-response retailing, Internet retailing, automatic merchandising, and direct selling. *Direct-response retailing* reaches prospective customers through catalogs, telemarketing, and even magazine, newspaper, and television ads. *Internet retailing,* another form of nonstore retailing, has grown rapidly. Tens of thousands of retailers have set up shop online, with sales growing at a rate of about 15 percent a year (as compared to total retail sales growing at about 3.7 percent per year). Today, online sales account for about 5.5 percent of total retail sales.[9]

Automatic merchandising provides retailing convenience through vending machines. As banks find new ways to compete for customers, their ATMs will operate more like vending machines. Already some ATMs offer extra services, cashing checks and selling stamps, road maps, and even concert tickets. Future ATMs will be able to connect wirelessly to cell phones to allow customers to download and pay for games and music. *Direct selling* includes direct-to-consumer sales by Pampered Chef kitchen consultants and salespeople for Silpada sterling silver jewelry through party-plan selling methods. Both are forms of direct selling.

▲ This Zoom Shop kiosk dispenses Proactiv acne treatments automatically, just as an ATM dispenses cash. Automatic merchandising is a form of nonstore retailing.

©Jae C. Hong/AP Photos

STORE RETAILERS

In-store sales still outpace nonstore retailing methods like direct-response retailing and Internet selling. Store retailers range in size from tiny newsstands to multi-story department stores and multi-acre warehouse-like retailers such as Sam's Club. TABLE 12.1 lists different types of store retailers.

CHOOSING A LOCATION

A good location often marks the difference between success and failure in retailing. The location decision depends on the retailer's size, financial resources, product offerings, competition, and, of course, its target market. Traffic patterns, parking, the visibility of the store's signage, and the location of complementary stores also influence the choice of a retail location.

A *planned shopping center* is a group of retail stores planned, coordinated, and marketed as a unit to shoppers in a geographical trade area. By providing convenient locations with free parking, shopping centers have replaced downtown shopping in many urban areas. But time-pressed consumers are increasingly looking for more efficient ways to shop, including catalogs, Internet retailers,

FIGURE 12.6 Types of Nonstore Retailing

Nonstore Retailers

Direct-Response Retailing — **Examples:** sales through catalogs, telemarketing, and magazine, newspaper, and television ads

Internet Retailing — **Examples:** sales through virtual storefronts, Web-based sellers, and the Web sites of brick-and-mortar retailers

Direct Selling — **Examples:** direct manufacturer-to-consumer sales through party plans and direct contact by Amway, Home & Garden Party decorations, and Electrolux vacuum cleaner salespeople

Automatic Merchandising — **Examples:** sales of such consumer products as candy, soft drinks, ice, chewing gum, sandwiches, and soup through vending machines

TABLE 12.1 Can you describe different types of retail stores?

Store Type	Description	Example
Specialty store	Offers complete selection in a narrow line of merchandise	Bass Pro Shops, Dick's Sporting Goods, Williams-Sonoma
Convenience store	Offers staple convenience goods, easily accessible locations, extended store hours, and rapid checkouts	7-Eleven, Mobil Mart, QuikTrip
Discount store	Offers wide selection of merchandise at low prices; off-price discounters offer designer or brand-name merchandise	Target, Walmart, Nordstrom Rack, Marshalls
Warehouse club	Large, warehouse-style store selling food and general merchandise at discount prices to membership cardholders	Costco, Sam's Club, BJ's
Factory outlet	Manufacturer-owned store selling seconds, production overruns, or discontinued lines	Adidas, Coach, Pottery Barn, Ralph Lauren
Supermarket	Large, self-service retailer offering a wide selection of food and nonfood merchandise	Safeway, Whole Foods Market, Kroger
Supercenter	Giant store offering food and general merchandise at discount prices	Walmart Supercenter, Super Target, Meijer
Department store	Offers a wide variety of merchandise selections (cosmetics, housewares, clothing) and many customer services	Macy's, Nordstrom, Neiman Marcus, Dillard's

and one-stop shopping at large free-standing stores such as Walmart Supercenters. To lure more customers, shopping centers are recasting themselves as entertainment destinations, with movie theaters, restaurants, art displays, carousel rides, and musical entertainment. The giant Mall of America in Bloomington, Minnesota, features a seven-acre amusement park and an aquarium.

Large regional malls have witnessed a shift in shopping center traffic to smaller strip centers, name-brand outlet centers, and *lifestyle centers,* open-air complexes containing retailers that often focus on specific shopper segments and product interests.[10]

CREATING A STORE ATMOSPHERE

A successful retailer closely aligns its merchandising, pricing, and promotion strategies with *store atmospherics,* the physical characteristics of a store and its amenities, to influence consumers' perceptions of the shopping experience. Atmospherics begin with the store's exterior, which may use eye-catching architectural elements and signage to attract customer attention and interest. Interior atmospheric elements include store layout, merchandise presentation, lighting, color, sound, and cleanliness. A high-end store such as Nordstrom, for instance, features high ceilings in selling areas that spotlight tasteful and meticulously cared-for displays of carefully chosen items of obvious quality. Dick's Sporting Goods, on the other hand, carries an ever-changing array of moderately priced clothing and gear in its warehouse-like settings furnished with industrial-style display hardware.

> **>>> Quick Review**
>
> **1** What is a retailer?
>
> **2** Name the elements of a retailer's marketing strategy.

7 Distribution Channel Decisions and Logistics

A firm's choice of distribution channels creates the final link in the supply chain, the complete sequence of suppliers that contribute to creating a good or service and delivering it to business users and final consumers. The supply chain begins when the raw materials used in production are delivered to the producer and continues with the actual production activities that create finished goods. Finally, the finished goods move through the producer's distribution channels to end customers.

The process of coordinating the flow of goods, services, and information among members of the supply chain is called logistics. The term originally referred to strategic movements of military troops and supplies. Today, however, it describes all of the business activities involved in the supply chain, with the ultimate goal of getting finished goods to customers.

supply chain complete sequence of suppliers that contribute to creating a good or service and delivering it to business users and final consumers.

logistics process of coordinating the flow of goods, services, and information among members of the supply chain.

PHYSICAL DISTRIBUTION

A major focus of logistics management—identified earlier in the chapter as one of the two basic dimensions of distribution strategy—is *physical distribution,* the activities aimed at efficiently moving finished goods from the production line to the consumer or business buyer. As **FIGURE 12.7** shows, physical distribution is a broad concept that includes transportation and numerous other elements that help link buyers and sellers. An effectively managed physical distribution system can

Physical Distribution

Marketer — Customer Service · Transportation · Warehousing · Materials Handling · Inventory Control · Order Processing → Customers

FIGURE 12.7 Elements of a Physical Distribution System

increase customer satisfaction by ensuring reliable movements of products through the supply chain. Walmart studies the speed at which goods can be shelved once they arrive at the store because strategies that look efficient at the warehouse—such as completely filling pallets with goods—may actually be time-consuming or costly in the aisles.

The form of transportation used to ship products depends primarily on the kind of product, the distance involved, and the cost. The logistics manager can choose from a number of companies and modes of transportation. As TABLE 12.2 shows, the five major transport modes are—in order of total expenditures—trucks (with about 75 percent of total expenditures), railroads (approximately 12 percent), water carriers (6 percent), air freight (4 percent), and pipelines (3 percent). The faster methods typically cost more than the slower ones. Speed, reliable delivery, shipment frequency, location availability, handling flexibility, and cost are all important considerations when choosing the most appropriate mode of transportation.

About 15.5 million trucks operate in the United States, carrying most finished goods all or part of the way to the consumer. Nearly 2 million of these are tractor trailers.[11] But railroads, which compete with many truck routes, despite their recent loss of market share, are a major mode of transportation. The 567 freight railroads in the United States operate across nearly 168,000 miles of track and employed more than 175,000 people.[12]

Warehousing is the physical distribution activity that involves the storage of products. *Materials handling* is moving items within factories, warehouses, transportation terminals, and stores. *Inventory control* involves managing inventory

costs, such as storage facilities, insurance, taxes, and handling. The physical distribution activity of *order processing* includes preparing orders for shipment and receiving orders when shipments arrive.

Radio-frequency identification (RFID) technology relies on a computer chip implanted somewhere on a product or its packaging that emits a low-frequency radio signal identifying the item. The radio signal doesn't require a line of sight to register on the store's computers the way a bar code does, so a handheld RFID reader can scan crates and cartons before they are unloaded. Because the chip can store information about the product's progress through the distribution channel, retailers can efficiently manage inventories, maintain stock levels, reduce losses, track stolen goods, and cut costs.

The wide use of electronic data interchange (EDI) and the constant pressure on suppliers to improve their response time have led to *vendor-managed inventory*, in which the producer and the retailer agree that the producer (or the wholesaler) will determine how much of a product a buyer needs and automatically ship new supplies when needed.

> > > **Quick Review**

1. What is a supply chain?

2. Compare and contrast the five modes of transportation.

3. What factors must a marketer consider when making transportation decisions?

TABLE 12.2 What are the five major transport modes?

Mode	Speed	Dependability in Meeting Schedules	Frequency of Shipments	Availability in Different Locations	Flexibility in Handling	Cost
Truck	Fast	High	High	Very extensive	Average	High
Rail	Average	Average	Low	Low	High	Average
Water	Very slow	Average	Very low	Limited	Very high	Very low
Air	Very fast	High	Average	Average	Low	Very high
Pipeline	Slow	High	High	Very limited	Very low	Low

This chapter covered two of the elements of the marketing mix: product and distribution. It introduced the key marketing tasks of developing, marketing, and packaging of want-satisfying goods and services. It also focused on the three major components of an organization's distribution strategy: the design of efficient distribution channels; wholesalers and retailers who make up many distribution channels; and logistics and physical distribution. The next chapter discusses the remaining two elements of the marketing mix—promotion and pricing.

Weekly Updates spark classroom debate around current events that apply to your business course topics.
http://www.wileybusinessupdates.com

192

NOTES

1. Organization Web site, "Expansion Program," http://www.pancanal.com, accessed June 6, 2013; Theodore Prince, "Panama Canal Expansion: Game Changer, or More of the Same?" *CSCMP's Supply Chain Quarterly*, Quarter 1 2012, http://www.supplychainquarterly.com; Alex Leff, "Panama Canal Expansion a 'Game Changer,'" TicoTimes.net, June 17, 2011, http://www.ticotimes.net.

2. "Pepsi Beverages Company and Tampico Beverages Announce Distribution Agreement," *Bloomberg*, http://www.bloomberg.com, accessed May 8, 2013.

3. John Falcone, "Kindle vs. Nook vs. iPad: Which E-book Reader Should You Buy?" *CNET*, December 17, 2012, accessed September 18, 2013. http://news.cnet.com.

4. Company Web site, http://www.febreeze.com, accessed June 6, 2013; company Web site, "Drive Away Odors and Experience Freshness with Febreze CAR Vent Clips," press release, January 10, 2012, http://news.pg.com.

5. James Plafke, "Advanced Combat Helmet Stops an AK-47 Head Shot," *GEEK*, January 22, 2013, http://www.geek.com.

6. Company Web site, http://www.ea.com, accessed May 8, 2013; Zacks Equity Research, "EA to Release Amalur's Second DLC," *Yahoo Finance*, April 5, 2012, http://www.finance.yahoo.com.

7. Bureau of Labor Statistics, *Occupational Outlook Handbook, 2012–2013 Edition*, http://www.bls.gov, accessed May 8, 2013; U.S. Census Bureau, *"County Business Patterns,"* http://www.census.gov, accessed May 8, 2013.

8. Company Web site, http://www.acehardware.com, accessed May 8, 2013.

9. U.S. Census Bureau, "Quarterly Retail E-Commerce Sales, 1st Quarter 2013," May 15, 2013, http://www.census.gov.

10. John Coleman and David T. Whitaker, "Is There Life after Malls?" *Smart Growth Maryland*, Maryland Department of Planning, March 25, 2013, http://smartgrowthmd.wordpress.com.

11. Association Web site, "Trucking Statistics," http://www.truckinfo.net, accessed May 8, 2013.

12. Association Web site, "U.S. Freight Railroad Statistics," http://www.aar.org, accessed May 8, 2013.

Summary of Learning Objectives

 Explain product strategy.

A product is a bundle of physical, service, and symbolic attributes designed to satisfy consumer wants. The marketing conception of a product includes the brand, product image, warranty, service attributes, packaging, and labeling in addition to the physical or functional characteristics of the good or service.

Goods and services can be classified as either consumer or business. Consumer goods and services are purchased by ultimate consumers for their own use. Consumer goods can be convenience products, shopping products, or specialty products, depending on consumer habits in buying them. Business products and services are purchased for use either directly or indirectly in the production of other goods and services for resale. This classification is based on how the items are used and product characteristics.

A product mix is the assortment of goods and services a firm offers to individual consumers and business users. A product line is a series of related products.

product bundle of physical, service, and symbolic characteristics designed to satisfy consumer wants.

product line group of related products marked by physical similarities or intended for a similar market.

product mix the assortment of product lines and individual goods and services that a firm offers to consumers and business users.

 Describe the four stages of the product life cycle.

Every successful new product passes through four stages in its product life cycle: introduction, growth, maturity, and decline. In the introduction stage, the firm attempts to elicit demand for the new product. In the product's growth stage, sales climb and the company earns its initial profits. In the maturity stage, sales reach a saturation level. In the decline stage, both sales and profits decline. Marketers sometimes employ strategies to extend the product life cycle, including increasing the frequency of use, adding new users, finding new uses for the product, and changing package size, labeling, or product quality.

The new product development process for most products has six stages: idea generation, screening, concept development and business analysis, product development, test marketing, and commercialization. At each stage, marketers must decide whether to continue to the next stage, modify the new product, or discontinue the development process. Some new products skip the test marketing stage due to the desire to quickly introduce a new product with excellent potential, a desire not to reveal new product strategies to competitors, and the high costs involved in limited production runs.

product life cycle four basic stages—introduction, growth, maturity, and decline—through which a successful product progresses.

test marketing introduction of a new product supported by a complete marketing campaign to a selected city or TV coverage area.

 Discuss product identification.

Products are identified by brands, brand names, and trademarks, which are important elements of product images. Effective brand names are easy to pronounce, recognize, and remember, and they project the right images to buyers. Brand names cannot contain generic words. Under certain circumstances, a company loses exclusive rights to its brand name if common use makes it a generic term for product categories. Some brand names belong to retailers or distributors rather than to manufacturers. Some marketers use family brands to identify several related items in a product line. Others employ individual branding strategies by giving each product within a line a different brand name.

Brand loyalty is at the heart of brand equity and is measured in three degrees: brand recognition, brand preference, and brand insistence.

brand a name, term, sign, symbol, design, or some combination that identifies the products of one firm and differentiates them from competitors' offerings.

brand name part of the brand consisting of words or letters included in a name used to identify and distinguish the firm's offerings from those of competitors.

trademark brand that has been given legal protection.

brand equity added value that a respected and successful name gives to a product.

 Outline the major components of an effective distribution strategy.

A firm must consider whether to move products through direct or indirect distribution. Once the decision is made, the company needs to identify the types of marketing intermediaries, if any, through which it will distribute its goods and services. The Internet has made direct distribution an attractive option for many retail companies.

Another component is distribution intensity. The business must decide on the amount of market coverage—intensive, selective, or exclusive—needed to achieve its marketing strategies. For greatest effectiveness, marketers must carefully manage the distribution channel.

distribution deals with the marketing activities and institutions involved in getting the right good or service to the firm's customers.

distribution channels path that products—and legal ownership of them—follow from producer to consumers or business user.

physical distribution actual movement of products from producer to consumers or business users.

5 Explain wholesaling.

Wholesaling is a crucial part of the distribution channel for many products, particularly consumer goods and business supplies. Wholesaling intermediaries can be classified on the basis of ownership; some are owned by manufacturers, some are owned by retailers, and others are independently owned. Firms operate two main types of manufacturer-owned wholesaling intermediaries: sales branches and sales offices.

An independent wholesaling intermediary is a business that represents a number of different manufacturers and makes sales calls on retailers, manufacturers, and other business accounts. Independent wholesalers are classified as either merchant wholesalers or agents and brokers, depending on whether they take title to the products they handle.

Retailers sometimes band together to form their own wholesaling organizations. Such organizations can take the form of either a buying group or a cooperative.

wholesaler distribution channel member that sells primarily to retailers, other wholesalers, or business users.

6 Describe retailing.

Retailers sell goods and services to individuals for their own use rather than for resale. Nonstore retailing includes four forms: direct-response retailing, Internet retailing, automatic merchandising, and direct selling. Store retailers range in size from tiny newsstands to multi-story department stores and warehouse-like retailers such as Sam's Club.

A good location often marks the difference between success and failure in retailing. A successful retailer closely aligns its merchandising, pricing, and promotion strategies with store atmospherics, the physical characteristics of a store and its amenities, to influence consumers' perceptions of the shopping experience. Customer service is an important element of a retailer's product and distribution strategies.

retailer distribution channel member that sells goods and services to individuals for their own use rather than for resale.

7 Identify distribution channel decisions and logistics.

Marketers must make decisions about the supply chain—that is, the means of getting their product to the end user. They can choose to distribute their product directly or use intermediaries to navigate the path from producer to consumer. Ideally, the choice of a distribution channel should support a firm's overall marketing strategy. Before selecting distribution channels, firms must consider their target markets, the types of goods being distributed, their own internal systems and concerns, and competitive factors.

supply chain complete sequence of suppliers that contribute to creating a good or service and delivering it to business users and final consumers.

logistics process of coordinating the flow of goods, services, and information among members of the supply chain.

>>> Quick Review >>>

LO1

1 Describe the differences among convenience, shopping, and specialty products.

2 How do consumer products differ from business products?

3 How do marketers classify services?

LO2

1 Name the stages in the product life cycle.

2 What are the marketing implications of each stage in the product life cycle?

3 Describe the stages in the new product development process.

LO3

1 Describe a brand, a brand name, and a trademark. How are they different?

2 What is brand equity and why is it important to a company?

LO4

1 What are distribution channels? Why is channel choice an important decision for marketers?

2 What is a marketing intermediary?

LO5

1 What is wholesaling?

2 Describe the difference between a merchant wholesaler and an agent or broker in terms of title to the goods.

LO6

1 What is a retailer?

2 Name the elements of a retailer's marketing strategy.

LO7

1 What is a supply chain?

2 Compare and contrast the five modes of transportation.

3 What factors must a marketer consider when making transportation decisions?

13

Promotion and Pricing Strategies

Learning Objectives

1 **Discuss** integrated marketing communications (IMC).

2 **Describe** the different types of advertising.

3 **Outline** the tasks in personal selling.

4 **Name** and describe sales promotion activities.

5 **Discuss** publicity as a promotional tool.

6 **Discuss** pricing objectives and strategies.

Pfizer Faces the Impact of Generic Drug Pricing

What product has earned as much revenue in a year as Major League Baseball, or all the commercial films released in the United States?

The answer is Lipitor, the cholesterol-reducing drug taken by almost 9 million Americans. The most successful, most widely prescribed drug in the United States, for years Lipitor's patent protected it from competition, giving Pfizer the exclusive right to manufacture and market the drug. At one point Pfizer was earning almost $13 billion a year in sales, just from Lipitor.

Pfizer's patent on Lipitor has now expired, and competitors sell inexpensive generic versions of the drug, called atorvastatin. During the first six months, generic competition was limited by law to the first few companies that applied to the U.S. Food and Drug Administration, but after that any approved company could sell atorvastatin. At this point in a prescription drug's life, prices and revenues to the company that produced the drug typically plummet. Lipitor is no exception, as Pfizer's revenues from Lipitor went down 59 percent to $3.95 billion in 2012, its first full year of competition from generic drugs.

While patients and health care systems may directly benefit from the lower prices of generic drugs, there may be a downside. So many drugs are coming off patents in the next few years that some manufacturers have reduced their research and development budgets in anticipation of lower revenues. Without active research and development programs, drugs like Lipitor that improve the lives of millions of people may not be discovered as rapidly.[1]

Overview > > >

This chapter focuses on the last two elements of the marketing mix, promotion and pricing. **Promotion**—informing, persuading, and influencing a purchase decision—is the first of these elements. The chapter takes a broad view of promotion as an integrated part of an organization's communication strategy. It examines the components of the promotional mix—advertising, sales promotion, personal selling, and public relations—and the importance of promotional planning.

The final element of the marketing mix is **price**, the exchange value of a good or service. Since consumers have limited amounts of money and many ways to spend it, often price becomes the major factor in consumer buying decisions. This chapter addresses a variety of pricing strategies for goods and services.

promotion informing, persuading, and influencing a purchase decision.

price the exchange value of a good or service.

1 Integrated Marketing Communications

integrated marketing communications (IMC) coordination of all promotional activities—media advertising, direct mail, personal selling, sales promotion, and public relations—to produce a unified, customer-focused promotional strategy.

Marketers choose from among many promotional options to communicate with potential customers. Each marketing message a buyer receives—whether through a television or radio commercial, a newspaper or magazine ad, a Web site, a direct-mail flyer, or a sales call—reflects the product, place, person, cause, or organization promoted in the content. Through **integrated marketing communications (IMC)**, marketers coordinate all promotional activities—media advertising, direct mail, personal selling, sales promotion, and public relations—to produce a unified, customer-focused promotional strategy. This coordination is designed to avoid confusing the consumer and to focus positive attention on the promotional message.

PROMOTIONAL OBJECTIVES

Promotional objectives vary by organization. Some use promotion to expand their markets; others, to defend their current position. As **FIGURE 13.1** illustrates, common objectives include providing information, differentiating a product, increasing sales, stabilizing sales, and accentuating a product's value.

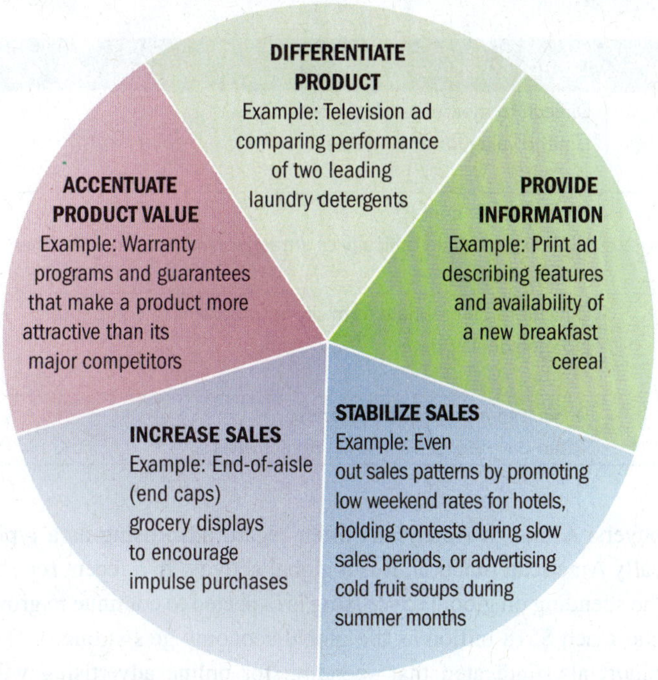

DIFFERENTIATE PRODUCT
Example: Television ad comparing performance of two leading laundry detergents

ACCENTUATE PRODUCT VALUE
Example: Warranty programs and guarantees that make a product more attractive than its major competitors

PROVIDE INFORMATION
Example: Print ad describing features and availability of a new breakfast cereal

INCREASE SALES
Example: End-of-aisle (end caps) grocery displays to encourage impulse purchases

STABILIZE SALES
Example: Even out sales patterns by promoting low weekend rates for hotels, holding contests during slow sales periods, or advertising cold fruit soups during summer months

FIGURE 13.1 Five Major Promotional Objectives

● **Provide Information** A major portion of U.S. advertising is information oriented. Credit card ads provide information about benefits and rates. Ads for hair care products include information about benefits such as shine and volume. Ads for breakfast cereals often contain nutritional information. Television ads for prescription drugs, a nearly $2 billion industry, are sometimes criticized for relying on emotional appeals rather than providing information about the causes, risk factors, and especially the prevention of disease.[2]

positioning the act of establishing a product in the minds of customers by communicating meaningful distinctions about the attributes, price, quality, or use of a good or service.

● **Differentiate a Product** Promotion can differentiate a firm's offerings from the competition. Applying a concept called **positioning**, marketers attempt to establish their products in the minds of customers. The idea is to communicate to buyers meaningful distinctions about the attributes, price, quality, or use of a good or service.

● **Increase Sales** Increasing sales volume is the most common objective of a promotional strategy. Naturalizer became the third-largest seller of women's dress shoes by appealing to Baby Boomers. But as these women age, they buy fewer pairs of shoes. To keep these customers but also attract younger ones, Naturalizer developed a new line of trendy shoes. The promotional strategy included ads in *Elle* and *Marie Claire*—magazines read by younger women—featuring models in beach attire and Naturalizer shoes. The ads yielded a substantial increase in department store sales.

● **Stabilize Sales** Firms can stabilize sales during slack periods through sales contests that motivate salespeople with such prizes as vacations, TVs, smart phones, and cash to those who meet certain goals. Companies attempt to stimulate sales during the off-season by distributing sales promotion materials such as calendars, pens, and notepads to customers. Jiffy Lube puts that little sticker on your windshield to remind you when to schedule your car's next oil change; regular visits help stabilize Jiffy Lube sales. A stable sales pattern brings several advantages. It evens out the production cycle, reduces some management and production costs, and simplifies financial, purchasing, and marketing planning. An effective promotional strategy can contribute to these goals.

● **Accentuate the Product's Value** Explaining the hidden benefits of ownership can enhance a product's value. Carmakers offer long-term warranty programs; life insurance companies promote certain policies as investments. The creation of brand awareness and brand loyalty also enhances a product's image and increases its desirability. Advertising with luxurious images supports the reputation of premium brands like Jaguar, Tiffany, and Rolex.

PUSHING AND PULLING STRATEGIES

Before developing its promotional plan, a firm's marketers need to consider two general promotional strategies: a pushing strategy or a pulling strategy. A **pushing strategy** relies on personal selling to market an item to wholesalers and retailers in a company's distribution channels. So companies promote the product to members of the marketing channel, not to end users. Sales personnel explain to marketing intermediaries why they should carry particular merchandise, usually supported by offers of special discounts and promotional materials. All of these strategies are designed to motivate wholesalers and retailers to "push" the good or service to their own customers.

pushing strategy personal selling to market an item to wholesalers and retailers in a company's distribution channels.

A **pulling strategy** attempts to promote a product by generating consumer demand for it, traditionally through advertising and sales promotions and more recently through Internet searches, social media, video-sharing sites, blogs, and other business directory/review services. From these sources, potential buyers develop favorable impressions of the product and then request that suppliers—retailers or local distributors—carry the product, thereby "pulling" it through the distribution channel. Given the success of the iRobot Roomba® robotic vacuum cleaner, many consumers wondered why they can't use similar technology to mow the grass. In response to this consumer demand (market pull), a number of leading lawn equipment manufacturers created automatic lawn mowers. Robotic mowers are projected to be among the most-demanded U.S. outdoor tools in

pulling strategy promoting a product by generating consumer demand for it, primarily through advertising and sales promotion appeals.

TABLE 13.1 How would you compare the components of promotion?

Component	Advantages	Disadvantages
Advertising	Reaches large consumer audience at low cost per contact Allows strong control of the message Message can be modified to match different audiences	Difficult to measure effectiveness Limited value for closing sales
Personal selling	Message can be tailored for each customer Produces immediate buyer response Effectiveness is easily measured	High cost per contact High expense and difficulty of attracting and retaining effective salespeople
Sales promotion	Attracts attention and creates awareness Effectiveness is easily measured Produces short-term sales increases	Difficult to differentiate from similar programs of competitors Nonpersonal appeal
Public relations	Enhances product or firm credibility Creates a positive attitude about the product or company	Difficult to measure effectiveness Often devoted to nonmarketing activities

the near future, according to Research and Markets, an international market research and data firm. A spokesman for Kyodo America Industries Co., the Atlanta-based manufacturer of LawnBott robotic mowers, stated, "In this next one- to three-year period, the market for robotic mowing in the United States is going to just explode."[3]

THE PROMOTIONAL MIX

Once the objectives and strategy are set, marketers create a **promotional mix** that blends various facets of promotion into a cohesive plan. This mix consists of two broad components—personal and nonpersonal selling. Marketers combine elements of both personal and nonpersonal selling to effectively communicate their message to targeted customers.

promotional mix combination of personal and nonpersonal selling activities designed to meet the needs of a firm's target customers.

Each component in the promotional mix has its own advantages and disadvantages, as described in TABLE 13.1

>>> Quick Review

1 What is the objective of an integrated marketing communications program?

2 Name the five most common objectives of promotional strategy.

2 Different Types of Advertising

According to one survey, consumers receive from 3,000 to 20,000 marketing messages each day, many of them in the form of advertising.[4] Advertising is the most visible form of nonpersonal promotion—and the most effective for many firms. **Advertising** is paid nonpersonal communication usually targeted at large numbers of potential

advertising paid nonpersonal communication, usually targeted at large numbers of potential buyers.

buyers. Although Americans often regard advertising as a typically American function, it is a global activity. In a recent report, the spending on global advertising is expected to continue to grow and reach $518 billion as the global economy gets stronger. The report also indicated that spending for online advertising will overtake spending on print advertising in just a few years.[5]

Advertising expenditures vary among industries, companies, and media. The top five categories for global advertisers are consumer goods, entertainment, industry and services, health care, and automotive. The categories recently showing the greatest percent change were telecommunications and consumer goods. Because advertising expenditures are so great and because consumers around the world are bombarded with messages, advertisers need to be increasingly creative and efficient at attracting consumers' attention.[6]

TYPES OF ADVERTISING

The two basic types of ads are product and institutional advertisements. **Product advertising** consists of messages designed to sell a particular good or service. Advertisements for Nantucket Nectars juices, iPods, and Capital One credit cards are examples of product advertising. One relatively recent form of product advertising is the practice of **product placement**. A growing number of marketers pay placement fees to have their products showcased in various media, ranging from newspapers and magazines to television and movies. Coca-Cola gets prominent placement on *American Idol*, which features as many as 102 product placements in a single month.

Institutional advertising involves messages that promote concepts, ideas, philosophies, or goodwill

product advertising messages designed to sell a particular good or service.

product placement form of promotion in which marketers pay placement fees to have their products showcased in various media, ranging from newspapers and magazines to television and movies.

institutional advertising involves messages that promote concepts, ideas, philosophies, or goodwill for industries, companies, organizations, or government entities.

Business Wire/Getty Images, Inc.

< Product advertising consists of messages designed to sell a particular good or service.

for industries, companies, organizations, or government entities. Each year, the Juvenile Diabetes Research Foundation promotes its "Walk for the Cure" fund-raising event, and your college may place advertisements in local papers or news shows to promote its activities.

cause advertising
form of institutional advertising that promotes a specific viewpoint on a public issue as a way to influence public opinion and the legislative process.

A form of institutional advertising that is growing in importance, **cause advertising**, promotes a specific viewpoint on a public issue as a way to influence public opinion and the legislative process about issues such as literacy, hunger and poverty, and alternative energy sources.

ADVERTISING AND THE PRODUCT LIFE CYCLE

Both product and institutional advertising fall into one of three categories based on whether the ads are intended to inform, persuade, or remind.

- *Informative advertising* builds initial demand for a product in the introductory phase of the product life cycle. Highly publicized new product entries attract the interest of potential buyers who seek information about the advantages of the new products over existing ones, warranties provided, prices, and places that offer the new products.

- *Persuasive advertising* attempts to improve the competitive status of a product, institution, or concept, usually in the late growth and maturity stages of the product life cycle. One of the most popular types of persuasive product advertising, *comparative advertising,* compares products directly with their competitors—either by name or by inference.

- *Reminder-oriented advertising* often appears in the late maturity or decline stages of the product life cycle to maintain awareness of the importance and usefulness of a product, concept, or institution.

ADVERTISING MEDIA

Marketers must choose how to allocate their advertising budget among various media. All media offer advantages and disadvantages. Cost is an important consideration in media selection, but marketers must also choose the media best suited for communicating their message. As **FIGURE 13.2** indicates, the three leading media outlets for advertising are television, the Internet, and newspapers.

- **Television** Television is still one of America's leading national advertising media. Television advertising can be classified as network, national, local, or cable. The four major national networks—ABC, CBS, NBC, and Fox—broadcast almost one-fifth of all television ads. Despite a decline in audience share and growing competition from cable TV, network television remains the easiest way for advertisers to reach large numbers of viewers—10 million to 20 million with a single commercial. Automakers, fast food restaurants, and food manufacturers are heavy users of network TV advertising.

- **Internet Advertising** Online and interactive media have already changed the nature of advertising. Starting with simple banner ads, Internet advertising has become much more complex and sophisticated. Miniature television screen images, called widgets or gadgets, can carry marketing messages only a few inches high on a Web site, blog, or desktop display. Another example is viral advertising, which creates a message that is novel or entertaining enough for consumers to forward it to others, spreading it like a virus. The great advantage is that spreading the word online, which often relies on social networking sites like Facebook, YouTube, and Twitter, costs advertisers little or nothing.

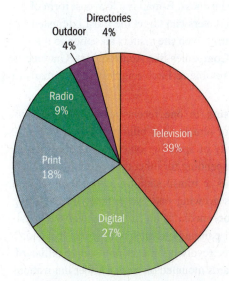

FIGURE 13.2
Projected 2014 Advertising Media Spend

NOTE: Percentages do not total to 100% due to rounding. Direct mail was not included in these data.

SOURCES: Data from, "U.S. Total Media Ad Spend Inches Up, Pushed by Digital," eMarketer, August 22, 2013, http://www.emarketer.com.

Newspapers Daily and weekly newspapers continue to dominate local advertising. Marketers can easily tailor newspaper advertising to local tastes and preferences. Advertisers can also coordinate advertisements with other promotional efforts such as discount coupons from supermarkets and one-day sales at department stores. One disadvantage is the relatively short lifespan of daily newspapers; people usually discard them soon after reading. Retailers and automobile dealers rank first among newspaper advertisers. Most newspapers now maintain Web sites, some of which offer separate material and features to complement their print editions.

Radio Despite the proliferation of other media, the average U.S. household owns five radios—including those in cars—a market penetration that makes radio an important advertising medium. Advertisers like the captive audience of listeners as they commute to and from work. As a result, morning and evening drive-time shows command top ad rates. In major markets, many stations serve different demographic groups with targeted programming. Internet radio programming also offers opportunities for yet more focused targeting.

Magazines Magazines include consumer publications and business trade journals. *Time, Reader's Digest,* and *Sports Illustrated* are consumer magazines, whereas *Advertising Age* and *Oil & Gas Journal* fall into the trade category. Magazines are a natural choice for targeted advertising. Media buyers study the demographics of subscribers and select magazines that attract the desired readers. American Express advertises in *Fortune* and *Bloomberg Businessweek* to reach business-people, while PacSun clothes and Clearasil skin medications are advertised in *Teen Vogue.*

Direct Mail The average U.S. household receives about 550 pieces of direct mail each year, including 100 catalogs. The huge growth in the variety of direct-mail offerings combined with the convenience they offer today's busy, time-pressed shoppers has made direct-mail advertising a multibillion-dollar business. E-mail is a low-cost form of direct marketing. Marketers can target the most interested Internet users by offering Web site visitors an option to register to receive e-mail. Companies like Amazon.com, Gardener's Supply, and Abercrombie & Fitch routinely send e-mails to regular customers.

Outdoor Advertising In one recent year, outdoor advertising accounted for almost $6.4 billion in advertising revenues.[7] The majority of spending on outdoor advertising is for billboards, but spending for other types of outdoor advertising, such as signs in transit stations, stores, airports, and sports stadiums, is growing fast. Advertisers are exploring new forms of outdoor media, many of which involve technology: computerized paintings; digital billboards; "trivision," which displays three revolving images on a single billboard; and moving billboards mounted on trucks. Other innovations

∧ Technology plays an important role in advertising, especially for outdoor media.

include ads displayed on the Goodyear blimp, using an electronic system that offers animation and video.

Sponsorship One of the hottest trends in promotion offers marketers the ability to integrate several elements of the promotional mix. *Sponsorship* involves providing funds for a sporting or cultural event in exchange for a direct association with the event. NASCAR, the biggest spectator sport in the United States, thrives on sponsorships. Sponsorships can run in the tens of millions. Hendricks Motorsports, currently the wealthiest and most successful NASCAR team, has more than $115 million in sponsorships from firms such as PepsiCo, DuPont, Lowes, and Farmers Insurance Group.[8]

> > > **Quick Review**

1 What are the two main types of advertising? Into what three categories do they fall?

2 What is the leading advertising medium in the United States?

3 In what two major ways do firms benefit from sponsorships?

③ Tasks in Personal Selling

Many companies consider **personal selling**—a person-to-person promotional presentation to a potential buyer—the key to marketing effectiveness. Unless a seller matches a firm's goods or services to the needs of a particular client or customer, none of the firm's other activities produces any benefits. Today, sales and sales-related jobs employ about 13.8 million U.S. workers.[9] Businesses often spend five to ten times more on personal selling than on advertising. Given the significant cost of hiring, training, benefits, and

personal selling
a direct person-to-person promotional presentation to a potential buyer.

200

salaries, businesses are very concerned with the effectiveness of their sales personnel.

How do marketers decide whether to make personal selling the primary component of their firm's marketing mix? In general, firms are likely to emphasize personal selling rather than advertising for sales promotion under four conditions:

1. Customers are relatively few in number and are geographically concentrated.
2. The product is technically complex, involves trade-ins, or requires special handling.
3. The product carries a relatively high price.
4. The product moves through direct-distribution channels.

Selling luxury items such as the Porsche 918 Spyder hybrid ($630,000) or a John Lennon–themed Steinway piano ($90,000) would require a personal touch. Then there's the $35,000 home theater device offered by Prima Cinema, which automatically sends Hollywood films to customers' home systems the same day they premiere. Installation, including instructions on how to use the system, would require personal selling.[10]

Personal selling can occur in several environments, each of which can involve business-to-business or business-to-consumer selling. Sales representatives who make sales calls on prospective customers at their businesses are involved in *field selling*. Companies that sell major industrial equipment typically rely heavily on field selling. *Over-the-counter selling* describes sales activities in retailing and some wholesale locations, where customers visit the seller's facility to purchase items. *Telemarketing* sales representatives make their presentations over the phone. A later section reviews telemarketing in more detail.

SALES TASKS

All sales activities involve assisting customers in some manner. Although a salesperson's work can vary significantly from one company or situation to another, it usually includes a mix of three basic tasks: order processing, creative selling, and missionary selling.

- **Order Processing** Although both field selling and telemarketing involve this activity, **order processing** is most often related to retail and wholesale firms. The salesperson identifies customer needs, points out merchandise to meet them, and processes the order. Route sales personnel process orders for such consumer goods as bread, milk, soft drinks, and snack foods. They check each store's stock, report inventory needs to the store manager, and complete the sale. Most of these jobs include at least minor order-processing functions.

order processing
form of selling, mostly at the wholesale and retail levels, that involves identifying customer needs, pointing them out to customers, and completing orders.

- **Creative Selling** Sales representatives for most business products and some consumer items perform **creative selling**, a persuasive type of promotional presentation. Creative selling promotes a good or service whose benefits are not readily apparent or whose purchase decision requires a close analysis of alternatives. Sales of intangible products such as insurance rely heavily on creative selling, but sales of tangible goods benefit as well.

creative selling
persuasive type of promotional presentation.

Most retail salespeople just process orders, but many consumers are looking for more in the form of customer service, which is where creative selling comes in. Personal shoppers at upscale Topshop help customers create entire looks from three floors of clothing. They also offer customers refreshments and the option to ring up purchases at a special cash register without waiting in line.

- **Missionary Selling** Sales work also includes **missionary selling**, an indirect form of selling in which the representative promotes goodwill for a company or provides technical or operational assistance to the customer. Many businesses that sell technical equipment, such as Oracle and Fujitsu, provide systems specialists who act as consultants to customers. These salespeople work to solve problems and sometimes help their clients with questions not directly related to their employers' products.

missionary selling
indirect form of selling in which the representative promotes goodwill for a company or provides technical or operational assistance to the customer.

TELEMARKETING

Personal selling conducted by telephone, known as **telemarketing**, provides a firm with a high return on its marketing expenditures, an immediate response, and an opportunity for personalized, two-way conversation. Many firms use telemarketing because expense or other obstacles prevent salespeople from meeting many potential customers in person. Telemarketers can use databases to target prospects based on demographic data. Telemarketing takes two forms. A sales representative who calls you is practicing *outbound telemarketing*. And outbound telemarketers must abide by the Federal Trade Commission's 1996 Telemarketing Sales Rule. Congress enacted another law in 2003 that created the National Do Not Call registry, intended to help consumers block unwanted telemarketing calls. On the other hand, *inbound telemarketing* occurs when you call a toll-free phone number to get product information or place an order.

telemarketing
personal selling conducted entirely by telephone, which provides a firm's marketers with a high return on their expenditures, an immediate response, and an opportunity for personalized two-way conversation.

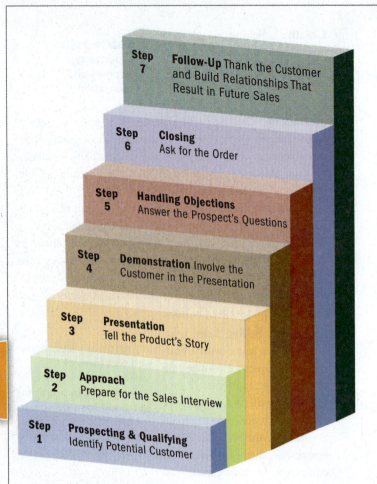

Step 7 **Follow-Up** Thank the Customer and Build Relationships That Result in Future Sales

Step 6 **Closing** Ask for the Order

Step 5 **Handling Objections** Answer the Prospect's Questions

Step 4 **Demonstration** Involve the Customer in the Presentation

Step 3 **Presentation** Tell the Product's Story

Step 2 **Approach** Prepare for the Sales Interview

Step 1 **Prospecting & Qualifying** Identify Potential Customer

FIGURE 13.3 Seven Steps in the Sales Process

THE SALES PROCESS

The sales process typically follows the seven-step sequence shown in **FIGURE 13.3**: prospecting and qualifying, the approach, presentation, the demonstration, handling objections, closing, and the follow-up. Remember the importance of flexibility, though; a good salesperson is not afraid to vary the sales process based on a customer's responses and needs. The process of selling to a potential customer who is unfamiliar with a company's products differs from the process of serving a long-time customer.

PROSPECTING, QUALIFYING, AND APPROACHING

At the prospecting stage, salespeople identify potential customers. They may seek leads for prospective sales from such sources as business associates, existing customers, friends, and family. The qualifying process identifies potential customers who have the financial ability and authority to buy.

Companies use different tactics to identify and qualify prospects. Some companies rely on business development teams, passing responses from direct mail along to their sales reps. Others believe in personal visits. Many firms are now using social media, which costs little or nothing, to boost sales. Online newsletters, virtual trade shows, podcasts, Webinars, and blogs are good examples. Experts advise developing a clear strategy in order to be successful with social media.[11]

Successful salespeople make careful preparations, analyzing available data about a prospective customer's product lines and other pertinent information before making the initial contact. They realize the importance of a first impression in influencing a customer's future attitudes toward the seller and its products.

PRESENTATION AND DEMONSTRATION

At the presentation stage, salespeople communicate promotional messages. They may describe the major features of their products, highlight the advantages, and cite examples of satisfied consumers. A demonstration helps reinforce the message that the salesperson has been communicating—a critical step in the sales process. Department store shoppers can get a free makeover at the cosmetics counter. Anyone looking to buy a car will take it for a test drive before deciding whether to purchase it.

HANDLING OBJECTIONS

Some salespeople fear potential customers' objections because they view the questions as criticism. But a good salesperson can use objections as an opportunity to answer questions and explain how the product will benefit the customer. Responding to a customer's objection that a product's price is too high, a salesperson might remind the individual that the product is exclusive and that a high price prevents the product from being widely available to everyone.

V At the makeup counter, salespeople provide a free makeup demonstration to reinforce the message of how their cosmetics can enhance your look.

Robert Nystrom/iStockphoto

CLOSING

The critical point in the sales process—the time at which the salesperson actually asks the prospect to buy—is the closing. If the presentation effectively matches product benefits to customer needs, the closing should be a natural conclusion. If there are more bumps in the process, the salesperson can try some different techniques, such as offering alternative products, offering a special incentive for purchase, or restating the product benefits. Closing the sale—and beginning a relationship in which the customer builds loyalty to the brand or product—is the ideal outcome of this interaction. But even if the sale is not made at this time, the salesperson should regard the interaction as the beginning of a potential relationship anyway. The prospect might very well become a customer in the future.

FOLLOW-UP

A salesperson's post-sale actions may determine whether the customer will make another purchase. Follow-up is an important part of building a long-lasting relationship. After closing, the salesperson should process the order efficiently. By calling soon after a purchase, the salesperson provides reassurance about the customer's decision to buy and creates an opportunity to correct any problems.

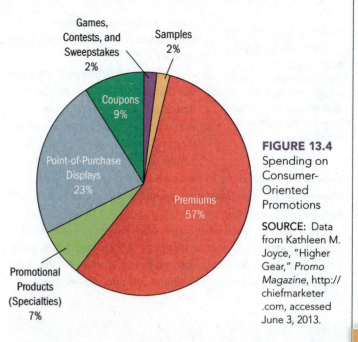

FIGURE 13.4
Spending on Consumer-Oriented Promotions

SOURCE: Data from Kathleen M. Joyce, "Higher Gear," *Promo Magazine,* http://chiefmarketer.com, accessed June 3, 2013.

> ## >>> Quick Review
>
> **1** Under what four conditions is a firm more likely to use personal selling rather than advertising or sales promotion?
>
> **2** Name the three basic tasks of personal selling.
>
> **3** What are the seven steps in the sales process?

④ Sales Promotion Activities

Traditionally viewed as a supplement to a firm's sales or advertising efforts, sales promotion has emerged as an integral part of the promotional mix. **Sales promotion** consists of activities that support advertising and personal selling.

sales promotion activities that support advertising and personal selling.

Both retailers and manufacturers use sales promotions to offer consumers extra incentives to buy. Examples include samples, coupons, contests, displays, trade shows, and dealer incentives. Beyond the short-term advantage of increased sales, sales promotions can also help marketers build brand equity and enhance customer relationships.

CONSUMER-ORIENTED PROMOTIONS

The goal of a consumer-oriented sales promotion is to get new and existing customers to try or buy products. In addition, marketers want to encourage repeat purchases by rewarding current users,

increase sales of complementary products, and boost impulse purchases. **FIGURE 13.4** shows how marketers allocate their consumer-oriented spending among the categories of promotions.

PREMIUMS, COUPONS, REBATES, AND SAMPLES

Nearly six of every ten sales promotion dollars are spent on *premiums*—items given free or at a reduced price with the purchase of another product. Cosmetics companies such as Clinique often offer sample kits with purchases of their products. Customers redeem *coupons* for small price discounts when they purchase the promoted products. Such offers may persuade a customer to try a new or different product. *Rebates* offer cash back to consumers who mail in required proofs of purchase. Rebates help packaged-goods manufacturers increase purchase rates, promote multiple purchases, and reward product users. A *sample* is a gift of a product distributed by mail, door to door, in a demonstration, or inside packages of another product.

TRADE-ORIENTED PROMOTIONS

Sales promotion techniques can also contribute to campaigns directed to retailers and wholesalers. **Trade promotion** is sales promotion geared to marketing intermediaries rather than to consumers. Marketers use trade promotion to encourage retailers to stock new products, continue carrying existing ones, and promote both new and existing products effectively to consumers. Successful trade promotions offer financial incentives. They require careful timing, attention to costs, and easy implementation for intermediaries. These promotions should bring quick results and improve retail sales. Major

trade promotion sales promotion geared to marketing intermediaries rather than to final consumers.

trade promotions include point-of-purchase advertising and trade shows.

Point-of-purchase (POP) advertising consists of displays or demonstrations that promote products when and where consumers buy them, such as in retail stores. Marketing research has shown that consumers are more likely to purchase certain products when such displays are present. Sunscreen, painting supplies, and snacks are typically displayed this way.

Manufacturers and other sellers often exhibit at *trade shows* to promote goods or services to members of their distribution channels. These shows are often organized by industry trade associations and attract large numbers of exhibitors and attendees each year.

>>> Quick Review

1. Why do retailers and manufacturers use sales promotion tactics?

2. Differentiate between consumer-oriented and trade-oriented promotions.

5 Publicity as a Promotional Tool

A final element of the promotional mix, public relations (PR)—including publicity—supports advertising, personal selling, and sales promotion, usually by pursuing broader objectives. Through PR, companies attempt to improve their prestige and image with the public by distributing specific messages or ideas to target audiences. Cause-related promotional activities are often supported by PR and publicity campaigns. In addition, PR helps a firm establish awareness of goods and services and then builds a positive image of them.

Public relations refers to an organization's communications and relationships with its various public audiences, such as customers, vendors, news media, employees, stockholders, the government, and the general public. Many of these communication efforts serve marketing purposes. Public relations is an efficient, indirect communications channel for promoting products. It can publicize items and help create and maintain a positive image of the company.

The public relations department links a firm with the media. It provides the media with news releases and video and audio clips, as well as holding news conferences to announce new products, the formation of strategic alliances, management changes, financial results, and similar developments. Publications issued by the department include newsletters, brochures, and reports.

PUBLICITY

The type of public relations that is tied most closely to promoting a company's products is **publicity**—nonpersonal stimulation of demand for a good, service, place, idea, event, person, or organization by unpaid placement of information in print or broadcast media. Press releases generate publicity, as does news or TV coverage. Publicity can even help find investors to grow a business. Shawn Davis appeared on the reality TV show *Shark Tank* recently hoping to have the show's entrepreneurs invest in his company. The investors didn't bite, but when the episode aired Davis received calls from other interested parties. He negotiated a deal and is moving forward with his plans to grow his food business.[12]

Not-for-profit organizations benefit from publicity when they receive coverage of events such as the Susan G. Komen Race for the Cure, which raises money for breast cancer research, community health outreach, advocacy, and programs. When a for-profit firm teams up with a not-for-profit firm in a fund-raising effort, the move usually generates good publicity for both organizations.

>>> Quick Review

1. How does public relations serve a marketing purpose?

2. How does a firm use publicity to enhance their image?

6 Pricing Objectives and Strategies

Price, the last element of the marketing mix, can best be thought of as the sum of all the other parts. If a firm has a unique product, creates a world class distribution strategy, or has an inventive promotional campaign, they become a *price setter* such as Apple. On the other hand, if a firm sells an undifferentiated product, with no distribution or promotional advantages, they are most likely a *price taker*. While firms have the freedom to set their prices at any level they choose, their success will be determined by how the firm's competitors and customers react to their prices. For example, if a firm sets prices too high relative to the perceived value of the product, customers will not purchase the product and the firm will generate little revenue. Alternately, if they set their prices too low, the firm may sell all their products but not make needed profits.

In making pricing decisions, businesspeople seek to accomplish certain objectives. Pricing objectives vary from firm to firm, and many companies pursue multiple pricing objectives at the same time. Some try to improve profits by setting higher prices, while others set lower prices to attract new business. Whatever a company's objectives, determination of price generally falls into two areas, those based on external market issues and those based on a firm's production costs. The following sections detail both approaches, identifying the pricing objective and the strategies that support the objective.

MARKET-BASED PRICING

Economic theory assumes that a market price will be set at the point at which the amount of a product demanded and the amount supplied are equal. Recall the supply and demand discussion from Chapter 3. In many lines of business, this holds true, as firms in any particular industry set their prices to match those of established leaders. In these markets, price becomes a nonissue and consumers will make their purchase decisions based on other attributes of the product or firm. Gas stations are a good example of this type of pricing. However, once a firm knows the equilibrium market price, the *competitive price*, they can choose to price their products at that price or move higher or lower to achieve specific business objectives. The following section describes pricing objectives that cause a firm to deviate from the equilibrium price.

VOLUME OBJECTIVE

Marketers attempting to build market share may use price to achieve their goal. The **volume objective** makes pricing decisions based on market share, the percentage of a market controlled by a certain company or product. One firm may seek to achieve a 25 percent market share in a certain product category, and another may want to maintain or expand its market share for particular products.

volume objective
pricing strategy that bases a pricing decision on the attainment of market share.

Family Dollar Stores relies on volume sales to make a profit, and these types of retailers typically price products lower than their competition to build sales. The nationwide chain of stores, which sells everything from ice cube trays to holiday decorations—for a dollar each—must find ways to attract as much traffic and sell as much product as possible on a given day.

PRESTIGE PRICING

On the other end of the spectrum, **prestige pricing** establishes a relatively high price to develop and maintain an image of quality and exclusiveness. Marketers set such objectives because they recognize the role of price in communicating an overall image for the firm and its products. People expect to pay more for a Mercedes, Christian Louboutin shoes, or a vacation on St. Barts in the Caribbean. Much of the value that consumers place on

prestige pricing
strategies that establish relatively high prices to develop and maintain an image of quality and exclusiveness.

⋀ Prestige pricing sets a relatively high price to develop and maintain an image of quality and exclusiveness. People expect to pay more for cars adorned with the Mercedes hood ornament known as "the star."

these types of products comes from the fact that they are expensive. A Rolex would not be a Rolex without a hefty price tag.

EVERYDAY LOW PRICING AND DISCOUNT PRICING

Everyday low pricing (EDLP) is a strategy devoted to maintaining continuous low prices rather than relying on short-term price-cutting tactics such as cents-off coupons, rebates, and special sales. This strategy has been used successfully by retailers such as Walmart and Lowes to consistently offer low prices to consumers; manufacturers also use EDLP to set stable prices for retailers and create the impression among consumers that they do not need to shop the "sales" to find a good deal at these stores.

everyday low pricing (EDLP)
strategy devoted to maintaining continuous low prices rather than relying on short-term price-cutting tactics such as cents-off coupons, rebates, and special sales.

▽ Some retailers such as Lowes use an everyday low-pricing strategy that maintains continuous low prices rather than relying on short-term price-cutting tactics.

206

SKIMMING PRICING

A shorter-term strategy, **skimming pricing**, sets an intentionally high price relative to the prices of competing products. The term comes from the expression "skimming the cream." This pricing strategy often works for the introduction of a distinctive good or service with little or no competition, although it can be used at other stages of the product life cycle as well. A skimming strategy can help marketers set a price that distinguishes a firm's high-end product from those of competitors. It can also help a firm recover its product development costs before competitors enter the field. This is often the case with prescription drugs.

skimming pricing strategy that sets an intentionally high price relative to the prices of competing products.

PENETRATION PRICING

penetration pricing strategy that sets a low price to enter competitive markets.

Another shorter-term approach and a variant of volume pricing is **penetration pricing**, a strategy that sets a low price in an effort to enter competitive markets. When using penetration pricing, businesses may price new products noticeably lower than competing offerings of competing brands. These firms may even price their products below their cost to gain market share. Once the new product achieves some market recognition through consumer trial purchases stimulated by its low price, marketers may increase the price to the level of competing products. However, stiff competition might prevent the price increase.

COST-BASED PRICING

Economic theory might lead to the best pricing decisions, but businesses may not have all the information they need to make those decisions. Additionally, many well-crafted pricing strategies end up costing the firm significant profits. So, firms almost always review their market-based strategies against their product costs using **cost-based pricing** formulas. Approaching pricing this way allows a firm to determine how much investment they will have to make to complete their strategy.

cost-based pricing strategy in which an organization calculates total costs per unit and then adds markups to cover overhead costs and generate profits.

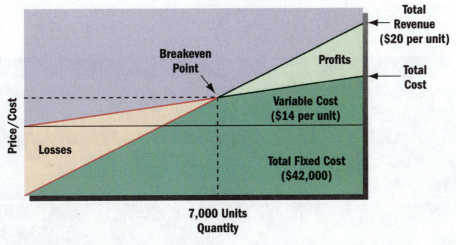

FIGURE 13.5 Breakeven Analysis

BREAKEVEN ANALYSIS

Businesses often conduct a **breakeven analysis** to determine the minimum sales volume a product must generate at a certain price level to cover all costs. This method involves a consideration of various costs and total revenues. *Total cost* is the sum of total variable costs and total fixed costs. *Variable costs* change with the level of production, as labor and raw materials do, while *fixed costs* such as insurance premiums and utility rates charged by water, natural gas, and electric power suppliers remain stable regardless of the production level. *Total revenue* is determined by multiplying price by the number of units sold.

> **breakeven analysis**
> pricing technique used to determine the minimum sales volume a product must generate at a certain price level to cover all costs.

FINDING THE BREAKEVEN POINT

The level of sales that will generate enough revenue to cover all of the company's fixed and variable costs is called the *breakeven point*. It is the point at which total revenue just equals total costs. Sales beyond the breakeven point will generate profits; sales volume below the breakeven point will result in losses. The following formulas give the breakeven point in units and dollars:

$$\text{Breakeven Point (in units)} = \frac{\text{Total fixed costs}}{\text{Contribution to fixed costs per unit}}$$

$$\text{Breakeven Point (in dollars)} = \frac{\text{Total fixed costs}}{1 - \text{Variable cost per unit/Price}}$$

A product selling for $20 with a variable cost of $14 per unit produces a $6 per-unit contribution to fixed costs. If the firm has total fixed costs of $42,000, it must sell 7,000 units to break even on the product, as shown in **FIGURE 13.5**. The calculation of the breakeven point in units and dollars is as follows:

$$\text{Breakeven Point (in units)} = \frac{\$42,000}{\$20 - \$14} = \frac{\$42,000}{\$6} = 7,000 \; units$$

$$\text{Breakeven Point (in dollars)} = \frac{\$42,000}{1 - \$14/\$20}$$

$$= \frac{\$42,000}{1 - 0.7} = \frac{\$42,000}{0.3} = \$140,000$$

Marketers use breakeven analysis to determine the profits or losses that would result from several different proposed prices. Because different prices produce different breakeven points, marketers could compare their calculations of required sales to break even with sales estimates from marketing research studies. This comparison can identify the best price—one that would attract enough customers to exceed the breakeven point and earn profits for the firm.

> >>> **Quick Review**
>
> **1** Why do marketers use breakeven analysis in pricing their good or service?
>
> **2** What is cost-based pricing?

What's Ahead? > > >

The previous few chapters have explained the main principles underlying marketing management and described how each fits a firm's overall business strategy. The next set of chapters will help you understand how companies manage the technology and information that are available to businesses to create value for their customers and enhance their competitiveness in the marketplace. You'll also learn how firms manage their financial resources.

Weekly Updates spark classroom debate around current events that apply to your business course topics. http://www.wileybusinessupdates.com

NOTES

1. Renee Williams, "Pfizer's Earnings Receive Boost from Joint Venture with China (NYSE:PFE)," *University Chronicle*, May 22, 2013, http://www.ssuchronicle.com; Associated Press, "Joint Venture with China Lifts Pfizer's Earnings," *New York Times*, April 30, 2013, http://www.nytimes.com; Larry Huston, "Generic Atorvastatin Hits the Market," *Forbes*, November 30, 2011, http://www.forbes.com; Matthew Herper, "Why There Will Never Be Another Drug like Lipitor," *Forbes*, November 30, 2011, http://www.forbes.com.

2. Jackie Judd, "FDA Calls Prescription Drug Ads Misleading," *ABC News*, January 3, 2013, http://abcnews.go.com.

3. Dave Larson, "Robotic Lawn Mowers See Growing Demand," *Dayton Daily News*, March 16, 2013, http://www.daytondailynews.com.

4. David Lamoureux, "How Many Marketing Messages Do We See in a Day?" *Fluid Drive Media*, February 23, 2012, http://www.fluiddrivemedia.com.

5. Dasha Afanasieva, "Economic Growth to Boost Global Advertising: Report," *Reuters*, April 29, 2013, http://www.reuters.com.

6. "Ad Spend by Sector: Consumer Goods and Telecom Take the Cake in 2012," Nielsen, April 25, 2013, http://www.nielsen.com.

7. Kantar Media, "2012 January-December Outdoor Advertising Expenditures," *Outdoor Advertising Association of America*, February 2013, http://www.oaaa.org.

8. Company Web site, http://www.hendrickmotorsports.com, accessed May 9, 2013; "Top NASCAR Team Helps Marketing for Lowes, Pepsi, DuPont and GoDaddy,"

Quarterly Retail Review, March 27, 2011, http://www.quarterlyretailreview.com.

9. U.S. Department of Labor, "Occupational Employment and Wages, May 2012," *Occupational Employment Statistics*, Bureau of Labor Statistics, June 12, 2013, http://www.bls.gov.

10. John Sciacca, "Prima Cinema Brings in-the-Theater Movies Home for $500 Each . . . and It's Worth It," *Digital Trends*, April 1, 2013, http://www.digitaltrends.com.

11. Eydie Stumpf, "Five Tips for Retailers to Drive Sales Using Social Media," *The Press Enterprise*, April 26, 2013, http://www.pe.com.

12. Carol Tice, "How One Entrepreneur Used the Law of Publicity to Get Investors," *Entrepreneur*, accessed September 20, 2013, http://www.entrepreneur.com.

Summary of Learning Objectives

 Discuss integrated marketing communications (IMC).

In practicing IMC, a firm coordinates promotional activities to produce a unified, customer-focused message. IMC identifies consumer needs and shows how a company's products meet them. Marketers select the promotional media that best target and reach customers. Teamwork and careful promotional planning to coordinate IMC strategy components are important elements of these programs.

A company's promotional mix integrates two components: personal selling and nonpersonal selling, which includes advertising, sales promotion, and public relations. By selecting the appropriate combination of promotional mix elements, marketers attempt to achieve the firm's five major promotional objectives: provide information, differentiate a product, increase demand, stabilize sales, and accentuate the product's value.

A pushing strategy relies on personal selling to market a product to wholesalers and retailers in a company's distribution channels. A pulling strategy promotes the product by generating consumer demand for it, through advertising and sales promotion.

promotion informing, persuading, and influencing a purchase decision.

price exchange value of a good or service.

integrated marketing communications (IMC) coordination of all promotional activities—media advertising, direct mail, personal selling, sales promotion, and public relations—to produce a unified, customer-focused promotional strategy.

positioning the act of establishing a product in the minds of customers by communicating meaningful distinctions about the attributes, price, quality, or use of a product or service.

pushing strategy personal selling to market an item to wholesalers and retailers in a company's distribution channels.

pulling strategy promoting a product by generating consumer demand for it, primarily through advertising and sales promotion appeals.

promotional mix combination of personal and nonpersonal selling activities designed to meet the needs of a firm's target customers.

 Describe the different types of advertising.

Advertising, the most visible form of nonpersonal promotion, is designed to inform, persuade, or remind. Product advertising promotes a good or service, while institutional advertising promotes a concept, idea, organization, or philosophy. Television, newspapers, and magazines are the largest advertising media categories. Others include

direct mail, radio, and outdoor advertising. Interactive advertising directly involves the consumer, who controls the flow of information.

advertising paid nonpersonal communication, usually targeted at large numbers of potential buyers.

product advertising messages designed to sell a particular good or service.

product placement form of promotion in which marketers pay placement fees to have their products showcased in various media, ranging from newspapers and magazines to television and movies.

institutional advertising involves messages that promote concepts, ideas, philosophies, or goodwill for industries, companies, organizations, or government entities.

cause advertising form of institutional advertising that promotes a specific viewpoint on a public issue as a way to influence public opinion and the legislative process.

 Outline the tasks in personal selling.

The three main tasks in personal selling are order processing, creative selling, and missionary selling.

● Order processing involves identifying customer needs, pointing them out to customers, and taking the order.

● Creative selling is a type of persuasive presentation.

● Missionary selling is an indirect form of selling in which the sales representative generates goodwill for a company or provides technical or operational assistance to customers.

personal selling a direct person-to-person promotional presentation to a potential buyer.

order processing form of selling, mostly at the wholesale and retail levels, that involves identifying customer needs, pointing them out to customers, and completing orders.

creative selling persuasive type of promotional presentation.

missionary selling indirect form of selling in which the representative promotes goodwill for a company or provides technical or operational assistance to the customer.

telemarketing personal selling conducted entirely by telephone, which provides a firm's marketers with a high return on their expenditures, an immediate response, and an opportunity for personalized two-way conversation.

④ Name and describe sales promotion activities.

Sales promotion accounts for greater expenditures than advertising. Consumer-oriented sales promotions such as coupons, games, rebates, samples, premiums, contests, sweepstakes, and promotional products offer an extra incentive to buy a product. Point-of-purchase advertising displays and trade shows are sales promotions directed to the trade markets. Personal selling involves face-to-face interactions between seller and buyer. The primary sales tasks are order processing, creative selling, and missionary selling. Public relations is non-paid promotion that seeks to enhance a companys public image.

sales promotion   activities that support advertising and personal selling.

trade promotion   sales promotion geared to marketing intermediaries rather than to final consumers.

point-of-purchase (POP) advertising   displays or demonstrations that promote products when and where consumers buy them, such as in retail stores.

5 Discuss **publicity as a promotional tool.**

Public relations—including publicity—is a final element of the promotional mix. It supports advertising, personal selling, and sales promotion usually by pursuing broader objectives.

public relations   organization's communications and relationships with its various public audiences.

publicity   nonpersonal stimulation of demand for a good, service, place, idea, event, person, or organization by unpaid placement of information in print or broadcast media.

6 Discuss **pricing objectives and strategies.**

Pricing objectives can be classified as profitability, volume, meeting competition, and prestige. Profitability objectives are the most common. Volume objectives base pricing decisions on

market share. Meeting competitors' prices makes price a nonissue in competition. Prestige pricing establishes a high price to develop and maintain an image of quality or exclusiveness.

Although economic theory determines prices by the law of demand and supply, most firms use cost-based pricing, which adds a markup after costs. By conducting a breakeven analysis, marketers can determine the minimum sales volume a product must generate at a certain price to cover costs.

The four alternative pricing strategies are skimming, penetration, everyday low pricing and discounting, and competitive pricing.

volume objective   pricing strategy that bases a pricing decision on the attainment of market share.

prestige pricing   strategy that establishes relatively high prices to develop and maintain an image of quality and exclusiveness.

everyday low pricing (EDLP)   strategy devoted to maintaining continuous low prices rather than relying on short-term price-cutting tactics such as cents-off coupons, rebates, and special sales.

skimming pricing   strategy that sets an intentionally high price relative to the prices of competing products.

penetration pricing   strategy that sets a low price as a way to enter competitive markets.

cost-based pricing   strategy in which an organization calculates total costs per unit and then adds markups to cover overhead costs and generate profits.

breakeven analysis   pricing technique used to determine the minimum sales volume a product must generate at a certain price level to cover all costs.

>>> Quick Review >>>

LO1

1 What is the objective of an integrated marketing communications program?

2 Name the five most common objectives of promotional strategy.

LO2

1 What are the two main types of advertising? Into what three categories do they fall?

2 What is the leading advertising medium in the United States?

3 In what two major ways do firms benefit from sponsorships?

LO3

1 Under what four conditions is a firm more likely to use personal selling rather than advertising or sales promotion?

2 Name the three basic tasks of personal selling.

3 What are the seven steps in the sales process?

LO4

1 Why do retailers and manufacturers use sales promotion tactics?

2 Differentiate between consumer-oriented and trade-oriented promotions.

LO5

1 How does public relations serve a marketing purpose?

2 How does a firm use publicity to enhance their image?

LO6

1 Why do marketers use breakeven analysis in pricing their good or service?

2 What is cost-based pricing?

Using Technology to Manage Information

Learning Objectives

1. **Distinguish** between data and information, and discuss information systems.

2. **List** the components and types of information systems.

3. **Discuss** computer hardware and software.

4. **Describe** computer networks.

5. **Discuss** the security and ethical issues affecting information systems.

6. **Explain** disaster recovery and backup.

7. **Review** information systems trends.

Evernote Raises Note Taking to a Profitable Art

If you've ever forgotten something—a deadline, the name of a restaurant, an idea—and worse, couldn't remember how to retrieve it, a software start-up called Evernote has a solution for you.

Evernote is a software app for desktops, laptops, and smart phones that lets users store "notes"— typed or handwritten jottings, Web clips, voice memos, receipts, photos, and other data and images—and easily find them. Evernote stores each user's data in the cloud, but in searchable (and rigorously backed-up) storage that lets you find whatever you've forgotten, using any Internet-connected device, by looking up information associated with it, like when and where you were when you recorded it, who you were with, what you were eating, or any other tag you've attached to it. You can create separate "notebooks" to file your data, and—although the platform isn't intended as a social network—you can also share your notes with others.

Evernote of the future may even help you "remember" things you might not have even known, like your grandmother's birthday, or sense your mood and suggest a restaurant when you appear to be hungry. To do this will require a whole new computing approach, and as the CEO says, "A computer should at least anticipate what you want, when you're happy or unhappy with something or you're frustrated. . . . That's incredibly difficult—but it's fun to work on."[1]

Overview > > >

Today, virtually all business functions—from human resources to production to supply chain management—rely on information systems. This chapter explores how organizations use technology to manage an important resource: information. The chapter begins by differentiating between information and data and then defines an information system. The components of information systems are presented, and two major types of information systems are described. Because of their importance to organizations, the chapter discusses databases, the heart of all information systems. Then the chapter looks at the computer hardware and software that drive information systems. Today, specialized networks make information access and transmission function smoothly, so the chapter examines different types of telecommunications and computer networks to see how start-ups like Evernote are applying them for competitive advantage. The chapter then turns to a discussion of the ethical and security issues affecting information systems, followed by a description of how organizations plan for, and recover from, information system disasters. A review of the current trends in information systems concludes the chapter.

212

1 Data, Information, and Information Systems

Daily, in organizations around the world, businesspeople ask themselves questions like these:

- How is our product doing in Dallas? Are sales to our target audience growing, declining, or staying static?
- Is the rising price of gas affecting our distribution costs?
- Are we winning the battle for market share?

data raw facts and figures that may or may not be relevant to a business decision.

An effective information system can help answer these and many other questions. **Data** refers to raw facts and figures that may or may not be relevant to a business decision. For example, the U.S. Census might report the average home price in a particular neighborhood. And while this datum might be interesting, it is probably not very useful to someone living across the country. On the other hand, data on home prices in your own neighborhood are clearly more valuable. **Information**—the knowledge gained from processing the facts and figures of raw data about home prices—would be useful for would-be buyers and sellers of these properties. So, although businesspeople need to gather data about the demographics of a target market or the specifications of a certain product, the data are useless unless they are transformed into relevant information that can be used to make a competitive decision.

information knowledge gained from processing data.

information system
organized method for collecting, storing, and communicating past, present, and projected information on internal operations and external intelligence.

chief information officer (CIO)
executive responsible for managing a firm's information system and related computer technologies.

An **information system** is an organized method for collecting, storing, and communicating past, present, and projected business information. Most information systems today use computer and telecommunications technology to handle the enormous volumes of information generated by large companies. A large organization typically assigns responsibility for directing its information systems and related operations to an executive called the **chief information officer (CIO)**. Often, the CIO reports directly to the firm's chief executive officer (CEO). An effective CIO will understand and harness technology so that the company can communicate internally and externally in one seamless operation. But small companies rely just as much on information systems as do large ones, even if they do not employ a manager assigned to this area on a full-time basis.

Information systems can be tailored to assist many business functions and departments—from marketing and manufacturing to finance and accounting. They can manage the overwhelming flood of information by organizing data in a logical and accessible manner. Through the system, a company can monitor all components of its operations and business strategy, identifying problems and opportunities. Information systems gather data from inside and outside the organization, then process the data to produce information that is relevant to all aspects of the organization. Processing steps could involve storing data for later use, classifying and analyzing them, and retrieving them easily when needed.

Today, however, when businesspeople think about an information system, they are most likely thinking about a **computer-based information system**. Such systems rely on computer and related technologies to store information electronically in an organized, accessible manner. So, instead of card catalogs, your college library uses a computerized information system that allows users to search through library holdings much faster and easier.

Computer-based information systems consist of four components and technologies:

- computer hardware
- computer software
- telecommunications and computer networks
- data resource management.

Computer hardware consists of machines that range from supercomputers to smart phones. It also includes the input, output, and storage devices needed to support computing

computer-based information system
information system that relies on computer and related technologies to store information electronically in an organized, accessible manner.

213

> ❯❯❯ **Quick Review**
>
> **1** What is the difference between data and information?
>
> **2** What is an information system?

2 Components and Types of Information Systems

The definition of *information system* in the previous section does not specifically mention the use of computers or technology. In fact, information systems have been around since the beginning of civilization but, by today's standards, they were very low tech. Think about your college or university's library. At one time the library probably had card catalog files to help you find information. Those files were information systems because they stored data about books and periodicals on 3- by 5-inch index cards.

∨ Libraries typically use a *computer-based information system* made up of computer hardware linked to the library's network and a database containing information on the books in the library. Specialized software allows users to access the database.

Purestock/Getty Images, Inc.

machines. Software includes operating systems, such as Microsoft's Windows 8 or Linux, and applications programs, such as Adobe Acrobat or Oracle's PeopleSoft Enterprise applications. Telecommunications and computer networks encompass the hardware and software needed to provide wired or wireless voice and data communications. This includes support for external networks such as the Internet and private internal networks. Data resource management involves developing and maintaining an organization's databases so that decision makers are able to access the information they need in a timely manner.

In the case of your institution's library, the computer-based information system is generally made up of computer hardware, such as monitors and keyboards, which are linked to the library's network and a database containing information on the library's holdings. Specialized software allows users to access the database. In addition, the library's network is likely also connected to a larger private network and the Internet. This connection gives users remote access to the library's database, as well as access to other computerized databases such as LexisNexis.

214

DATABASES

The heart of any information system is its **database**, a centralized integrated collection of data resources. A company designs

> **database** centralized integrated collection of data resources.

its databases to meet particular information processing and retrieval needs of its workforce. Businesses obtain databases in many ways. They can hire a staff person to build them on site, hire an outside source to do so, or buy packaged database programs from specialized vendors, such as Oracle. A database serves as an electronic filing cabinet, capable of storing massive amounts of data and retrieving it within seconds.

Decision makers can also look up online data. Online systems give access to enormous amounts of government data, such as economic data from the Bureau of Labor Statistics and the Department of Commerce. One of the largest online databases is that of the U.S. Census Bureau. The census of population, conducted every ten years, collects data on more than 120 million households across the United States. Another source of free information is company Web sites. Interested parties can visit firms' home pages to look for information about customers, suppliers, and competitors. Trade associations and academic institutions also maintain Web sites with information on topics of interest.

TYPES OF INFORMATION SYSTEMS

Many different types of information systems exist. In general, however, information systems fall into two broad categories: operational support systems and management support systems.

- An **operational support system** is designed to produce a variety of information on an organization's activities for both internal and external users. Examples of operational support systems include transaction processing systems and process control systems.

- A **transaction processing system** records and processes data from business transactions. For example, major retailers use point-of-sale systems, which link electronic cash registers to the retailer's computer centers. Sales data are transmitted from cash registers to the computer center either immediately or at regular intervals.

- A **process control system** monitors and controls physical processes. A steel mill, for instance, may have electronic sensors linked to a computer system monitoring the entire production process. The system makes necessary changes and alerts operators to potential problems.

> **operational support system** information system designed to produce a variety of information on an organization's activities for both internal and external users.

> **transaction processing system** operational support system that records and processes data from business transactions.

> **process control system** operational support system designed to monitor and control physical processes.

v The complex process of airline maintenance is critical to passenger safety.

Clay Petway, American Airlines Aviation Maintenance Technician and TWU member

PR NewsFoto/American Airlines, Inc.; The Transport Workers Union/NewsCom

MANAGEMENT SUPPORT SYSTEMS

An information system designed to provide support for effective decision making is classified as a **management support system**. Several different types of management support systems are available. A **management information system (MIS)** is designed to produce reports for managers and other personnel.

A **decision support system (DSS)** gives direct support to businesspeople during the decision-making process. For instance, a marketing manager might use a decision support system to analyze the impact on sales and profits of a product price change.

An **executive support system (ESS)** lets senior executives access the firm's primary databases, often by touching the computer screen, pointing and clicking a mouse, or using voice recognition. The typical ESS allows users to choose from many kinds of data, such as the firm's financial statements and sales figures for the company or industry. If they wish, managers can start by looking at summaries and then access more detailed information when needed.

Finally, an **expert system** is a computer program that imitates human thinking through complicated sets of "if-then" rules. The system applies human knowledge in a specific subject area to solve a problem. Expert systems are used for a variety of business purposes: determining credit limits for credit card applicants, monitoring machinery in a plant to predict potential problems or breakdowns, making mortgage loans, and determining optimal plant layouts. They are typically developed by capturing the knowledge of recognized experts in a field, whether within a business itself or outside it.

management support system information system designed to provide support for effective decision making.

management information system (MIS) information system designed to produce reports for managers and other personnel.

decision support system (DSS) system that provides direct support to businesspeople during the decision-making process.

executive support system (ESS) system that allows senior executives to access the firm's primary databases, often by touching the computer screen, pointing and clicking a mouse, or using voice recognition.

expert system computer program that imitates human thinking through complicated sets of "if-then" rules.

>>> Quick Review

1. List the four components of a computer-based information system.

2. What is a database?

3. Name the two general types of information systems and give an example of each.

3 Computer Hardware and Software

It may be hard to believe, but only a few decades ago computers were considered exotic curiosities, used only for very specialized applications and understood by only a few people. The first commercial computer, UNIVAC I, was sold to the U.S. Census Bureau in the early 1950s. It cost $1 million, took up most of a room, and could perform about 2,000 calculations per second.[2] The invention of transistors and then integrated circuits (microchips) quickly led to smaller and more powerful devices. By the 1980s, computers could routinely perform several million calculations per second. Now, computers perform billions of calculations per second, and some fit in the palm of your hand.

When the first personal computers were introduced in the late 1970s and early 1980s, the idea of a computer on every desk, or in every home, seemed farfetched. Today they have become indispensable to both businesses and households. Not only have computers become much more powerful and faster over the past 25 years, they are less expensive as well. IBM's first personal computer (PC), introduced in 1981, cost well over $5,000 fully configured. Today, the typical PC sells for under $800.

TYPES OF COMPUTER HARDWARE

Hardware consists of all tangible elements of a computer system—the input devices, the components that store and process data and perform required calculations, and the output devices that present the results to information users. Input devices allow users to enter data and commands for processing, storage, and output. The most common input devices are the keyboard and mouse. Storage and processing components consist of the hard drive as well as various other storage components, including DVD drives and flash memory devices. Flash memory devices are becoming increasingly popular because they are small and can hold large amounts of data. Some, called thumb drives, can even fit on a keychain. To gain access to the data they hold, users just plug them into an unused USB (universal serial bus) port, standard on today's computers. Output devices, such as monitors and printers, are the hardware elements that transmit or display documents and other results of a computer system's work.

hardware all tangible elements of a computer system.

Different types of computers incorporate widely varying memory capacities and processing speeds. These differences define four broad classifications: mainframe computers, midrange systems, personal computers, and handheld devices. A mainframe computer is the largest type of computer system with the most extensive storage capacity and the fastest processing speeds. Especially powerful mainframes called *supercomputers* can handle extremely rapid, complex calculations involving thousands of variables, such as weather modeling and forecasting.[3]

∧ The TITAN Supercomputer at Oak Ridge National Laboratory is the fastest computer on earth, performing 20,000 trillion calculations per second.

Midrange systems consist of high-end network servers and other types of computers that can handle large-scale processing needs. They are less powerful than mainframe computers but more powerful than most personal computers. A **server** is a dedicated computer that provides services to other computers on a network. Many Internet-related functions at organizations are handled by servers. File servers, gaming servers, print servers, and database servers are but a few of the applications of these types of computers. They are also commonly employed in process control systems, computer-aided manufacturing (CAM), and computer-aided design (CAD).

server a dedicated computer that provides services to other computers on a network.

Personal computers are everywhere today—in homes, businesses, schools, nonprofit organizations, and government agencies. According to recent estimates of PC ownership, more than two-thirds of American households have at least one personal computer. Personal computers have earned increasing popularity because of their ever-expanding capability to handle many of the functions that large mainframes performed only a few decades ago. Most desktop computers are linked to networks, such as the Internet.

Desktop computers were once the standard PC seen in offices and homes. And while millions of people still use desktop computers, laptop computers (including notebooks and netbooks) now account for more than half of all PCs sold. The increasing popularity of these computers can be explained by their improved displays, faster processing speeds, the ability to handle more intense graphics, larger storage capacities, and more durable designs. Their most obvious advantage is portability. Laptops are thinner and lighter than ever before. Business owners, managers, salespeople, and students all benefit from the constant innovation of the laptop.

Handheld devices such as smart phones are even smaller. Smart phones like the iPhone, Android, and BlackJack combine a phone with the Internet. Because of their ever-increasing capacity to surf the Internet, open and edit documents, send and receive messages, make calls, and more, sales of smart phones are rapidly outpacing traditional cell phones.

Two other devices—tablets and e-readers—are also making inroads in business. Besides Apple, Dell, Hewlett Packard, Motorola, and Samsung have all entered the tablet market with serious intentions and constant innovations designed to make them standard business tools. E-readers such as the Amazon Kindle and the Barnes & Noble Nook continue to expand their capacities as well—and will likely find their way into the business market before long.[4]

In addition to smart phones, specialized handheld devices are used in a variety of businesses for different applications. Some restaurants, for example, have small wireless devices that allow servers to swipe a credit card and print out a receipt right at the customer's table. Drivers for UPS and FedEx use special handheld scanning devices to track package deliveries and accept delivery signatures. The driver scans each package as it is delivered, and the information is transmitted to the delivery firm's network. Within a few seconds, using an Internet connection, a sender can obtain the delivery information and even see a facsimile of the recipient's signature.

COMPUTER SOFTWARE

Software includes all of the programs, routines, and computer languages that control a computer and tell it how to operate. The software that controls the basic workings of a computer system is its *operating*

software all the programs, routines, and computer languages that control a computer and tell it how to operate.

< Although smart phones can boost productivity, some people overuse or even misuse them.

© Neustockimages/iStockphoto

TABLE 14.1 Can you describe some common types of application software?

Type	Description	Examples
Word processing	Programs that input, store, retrieve, edit, and print various types of documents.	Microsoft Word, Pages (Apple)
Spreadsheets	Programs that prepare and analyze financial statements, sales forecasts, budgets, and similar numerical and statistical data.	Microsoft Excel, Numbers (Apple)
Presentation software	Programs that create presentations. Users can create bulleted lists, charts, graphs, pictures, audio, and even short video clips.	Microsoft PowerPoint, Keynote (Apple)
Desktop publishing	Software that combines high-quality type, graphics, and layout tools to create output that can look as attractive as documents produced by professional publishers and printers.	Adobe Acrobat, Microsoft Publisher
Financial software	Programs that compile accounting and financial data to create financial statements, reports, and budgets; they perform basic financial management tasks such as balancing a checkbook.	Quicken, QuickBooks
Database programs	Software that searches and retrieves data from a database; it can sort data based on various criteria.	Microsoft Access, Approach
Personal information managers	Specialized database programs that allow people to track communications with personal and business contacts; some combine e-mail capability.	Microsoft Outlook, Lotus Organizer
Enterprise resource planning	Integrated cross-functional software that controls many business activities, including distribution, finance, and human resources.	SAP Enterprise Resource Planning

system. More than 80 percent of personal computers use a version of Microsoft's popular Windows operating system. Personal computers made by Apple use the Mac operating system. Most handheld devices use other operating systems, such as Garnet or Windows Phone. The Droid and iPhone models have their own operating systems. Other operating systems include Unix, which runs on many midrange computer systems, and Linux, which runs on both PCs and midrange systems.

A program that performs the specific tasks that the user wants to carry out—such as writing a letter or looking up data—is called *application software*. Examples of application software include Adobe Acrobat, Microsoft PowerPoint, and Quicken. TABLE 14.1 lists the major categories of application software. Most application programs are currently stored on individual computers. The future of applications software is constantly changing. Some believe much of it will eventually become Web-based, with the programs themselves stored in the "cloud," on Internet-connected servers. Others disagree, arguing that most computer users will not want to rely on an Internet connection to perform tasks such as preparing a spreadsheet using Microsoft Excel.

 Computer Networks

As mentioned earlier, virtually all computers today are linked to networks. In fact, if your computer has Internet access, you're linked to a network. Local area networks and wide area networks allow businesses to communicate, transmit and print documents, and share data. These networks, however, require businesses to install special equipment and connections between office sites. But Internet technology has also been applied to internal company communications and business tasks, tapping a ready-made network. Among these new Internet-based applications are intranets, virtual private networks (VPNs), and voice over Internet protocol (VoIP). Each has contributed to the effectiveness and speed of business processes, so we discuss them next.

LOCAL AREA NETWORKS AND WIDE AREA NETWORKS

Most organizations connect their offices and buildings by creating a **local area network (LAN)**, a computer network that connects machines within limited areas, such as a building or several nearby buildings. LANs are useful because they link computers and allow them to share printers, documents, and information and provide access to the Internet. **FIGURE 14.1** shows what a small business computer network might look like.

> **local area network (LAN)** computer network that connects machines within limited areas, such as a building or several nearby buildings.

> > > **Quick Review**

1. List two input and two output devices.

2. What accounts for the increasing popularity of notebook computers?

3. What is software? List the two categories of software.

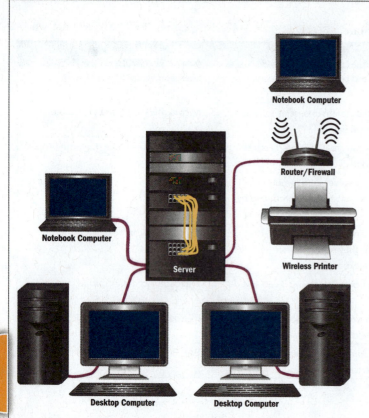

FIGURE 14.1 A Local Area Network

libraries, and coffee shops. Examples include Panera Bread's 1,500 bakery-cafes in the United States and Kansai International Airport in Osaka, Japan. Some locations provide free access, while others charge a fee.

Many believe that the successor to WiFi will be *Wi-Max*. Unlike WiFi's relatively limited geographic coverage area—generally around 300 feet—a single Wi-Max access point can provide coverage over many miles. In addition, cell phone service providers, such as Sprint Nextel and AT&T, offer broadband network cards for notebook PCs. These devices allow users to access the provider's mobile broadband network from virtually any location where cell phone reception is available.

INTRANETS

A broad approach to sharing information in an organization is to establish a company network patterned after the Internet. Such a network is called an **intranet**. Intranets are similar to the Internet, but they limit access to employees or other authorized users. An intranet blocks outsiders without valid passwords from entering its network by incorporating both software and hardware known as a **firewall**. Firewalls limit data transfers to certain locations and log system use so that managers can identify attempts to log on with invalid passwords and other threats to a system's security. Highly sophisticated packages immediately

intranet computer network that is similar to the Internet but limits access to authorized users.

firewall limits data transfers to certain locations and logs system use so that managers can identify attempts to log on with invalid passwords and other threats to a system's security.

wide area network (WAN) ties larger geographical regions together by using telephone lines and microwave and satellite transmission.

A **wide area network (WAN)** ties larger geographical regions together by using telephone lines and microwave and satellite transmission. One familiar WAN is long-distance telephone service. Companies such as AT&T and Verizon provide WAN services to businesses and consumers. Firms also use WANs to conduct their own operations. Typically, companies link their own network systems to outside communications equipment and services for transmission across long distances.

WIRELESS LOCAL NETWORKS

A wireless network allows computers, printers, and other devices to be connected without the hassle of stringing cables in traditional office settings. The current standard for wireless networks is called WiFi. **WiFi**—short for *wireless fidelity*—is a wireless network that connects various devices and allows them to communicate with one another through radio waves.

Any PC with a WiFi receptor can connect with the Internet at so-called hot spots—locations with a wireless router and a high-speed Internet modem. Hundreds of thousands of hot spots exist worldwide today, in such places as airports,

WiFi wireless network that connects various devices and allows them to communicate with one another through radio waves.

▲ WiFi connections are often called *hot spots*—locations with a wireless router and a high-speed Internet modem. Hundreds of thousands of hot spots worldwide are found airports, libraries, and restaurants.

Floresco Productions/Getty Images, Inc.

alert system administrators about suspicious activities and permit authorized personnel to use smart cards to connect from remote terminals.

Intranets solve the problem of linking different types of computers. Like the Internet, intranets can integrate computers running all kinds of operating systems. In addition, intranets are relatively easy and inexpensive to set up because most businesses already have some of the required hardware and software. For instance, a small business can simply purchase a DSL router and a few cables and create an intranet using phone jacks and internal phone lines. All the business's computers will be linked with each other and with the Internet.

VIRTUAL PRIVATE NETWORKS

To gain increased security for Internet communications, companies often turn to a **virtual private network (VPN)**, a secure connection between two points on the Internet. VPNs use firewalls and programs that encapsulate data to make them more secure during transit. Loosely defined, a VPN can include a range of networking technologies, from secure Internet connections to private networks from service providers like IBM. A VPN is cheaper for a company to use than leasing several of its own lines. It can also take months to install a leased line in some parts of the world, but a new user can be added to a VPN in a day. Because a VPN uses the Internet, it can be wired, wireless, or a combination of the two.

virtual private network (VPN) secure connection between two points on the Internet.

Advanced Systems Group (ASG) is a provider of data storage and management services. As the company expanded and opened branch offices, its own security became a concern. ASG turned to Check Point, which created a secure VPN connecting ASG's home office and five branch offices. The VPN allows ASG to add new sites and new remote users automatically.[5]

VoIP

VoIP—which stands for *Voice over Internet Protocol*—is an alternative to traditional telecommunication services. The VoIP telephone is not connected to a traditional phone jack but rather to a personal computer with any type of broadband connection. Special software transmits phone conversations over the Internet rather than through telephone lines. A VoIP user dials the phone as usual, and can make and receive calls to and from those with traditional telephone connections (landline or wireless).

VoIP alternative version of telecommunication service using the Internet.

A growing number of consumers and businesses have embraced VoIP, mainly due to its cost savings and extra features. As technology continues to advance, demand for the service has increased. Several wireless companies, including AT&T, Verizon, and Vonage, permit VoIP on smart phones. Google integrates its Google Voice over VoIP. The various VoIP providers are working together with the goal of creating VoIP standards that would, among other things, permit seamless roaming worldwide, 911 calls, and ensure communications in natural disasters.[6]

> > > **Quick Review**

1 What is a LAN?

2 Explain the differences between an intranet and a VPN.

3 How does VoIP work?

5 Security and Ethical Issues Affecting Information Systems

Numerous security and ethical issues affect information systems. As information systems become increasingly important business assets, they also become progressively harder and more expensive to replace. Damage to information systems or theft of data can have disastrous consequences. When computers are connected to a network, a problem at any individual computer can affect the entire network. Two of the major security threats are e-crime and so-called malware.

E-CRIME

Computers provide efficient ways for employees to share information, but they may also allow people with more malicious intentions to access information. Or they may allow pranksters—who have no motive other than to see whether they can hack into a system—to gain access to private information. Common e-crimes involve stealing or altering data in several ways:

- Employees or outsiders may change or invent data to produce inaccurate or misleading information.

- Employees or outsiders may modify computer programs to create false information or illegal transactions or to insert viruses.

- Unauthorized people can access computer systems for their own benefit or knowledge or just to see if they can get in.

Information system administrators implement two basic protections against computer crime: they try to prevent access to their systems by unauthorized users and the viewing of data by unauthorized system users. The simplest method of preventing access requires authorized users to enter passwords. The company may also install firewalls, described earlier. To prevent system users from reading sensitive information, the company may use encryption software, which encodes, or scrambles, messages. To read encrypted messages, users must use an electronic key to convert them to regular text. But as fast as software developers invent new and more elaborate protective measures, hackers seem to break through their defenses. Thus, security is an ongoing battle.

Consumers with credit cards are particularly at risk from hackers. Recently Global Payments, a payments processing company used by major credit card companies, announced that consumer credit and debit card information may have been compromised.[7] When a customer swipes a credit or debit card, the data are sent to a payment processor like Global Payments, which then forwards the transaction information to credit card companies like Visa and MasterCard.

As the size of computer hardware diminishes, it becomes increasingly vulnerable to theft. Handheld devices, for instance, can easily vanish with a pickpocket or purse snatcher. Many notebook computers and handheld devices contain special security software or passwords that make it difficult for a thief or any unauthorized person to access the data stored in the computer's memory. Notebook users should consider having such safeguards on their computers.

∧ Like their biological counterparts, computer viruses can infect their hosts, replicate quickly, and go on to infect many more computers.

Sergey Nivens/Shutterstock

COMPUTER VIRUSES, WORMS, TROJAN HORSES, AND SPYWARE

Viruses, worms, Trojan horses, and spyware, collectively referred to as **malware**, are malicious software programs designed to infect computer systems. These programs can destroy data, steal sensitive information, and even render information systems inoperable. Recently, malware was discovered in advertisements on major sites such as Yahoo, Fox, and Google as well as the *New York Times* and WhitePages.com. Malware attacks cost consumers and businesses billions of dollars annually. And malware is proliferating: according to a recent estimate, malware occurrences have exceeded 75 million.[8]

malware any malicious software program designed to infect computer systems.

Computer **viruses** are programs that secretly attach themselves to other programs (called *hosts*) and change them or destroy data. Viruses can be programmed to become active immediately or to remain dormant for a period of time, after which the infections suddenly activate themselves and cause problems. A virus can reproduce by copying itself onto other programs stored in the same drive. It spreads as users install infected software on their systems or exchange files with others, usually by exchanging e-mail, accessing electronic bulletin boards, trading disks, or downloading programs or data from unknown sources on the Internet.

virus program that secretly attaches itself to other programs (called *hosts*) and changes them or destroys data.

A **worm** is a small piece of software that exploits a security hole in a network to replicate itself. A copy of the worm scans the network for another machine that has a specific security hole. It copies itself to the new machine using the security hole and then starts replicating from there as well. Unlike viruses, worms don't need host programs to damage computer systems.

worm small piece of software that exploits a security hole in a network to replicate itself.

A **botnet** is a network of PCs that have been infected with one or more data-stealing viruses. Computer criminals tie the infected computers into a network, often without the owners being aware of it, and sell the botnet on the black market. They or others use the botnet to commit identity theft, sell fake pharmaceuticals, buy blocks of concert tickets for scalping, and attack the Internet itself. Thousands of botnets are active today, creating huge profits for the botnet creators.

botnet a network of PCs that have been infected with one or more data-stealing viruses.

Grum is an interesting case in point. At one time, Grum was thought to be responsible for about 17 percent of the world's e-mail spam. In mid-2012, a consortium of computer security companies working with Internet service providers around the world, removed the Grum computer servers from the Internet. For a time it appeared that Grum was out of business. However, computer security experts have seen some recent e-mail traffic, suggesting that Grum might not be so "dead" after all.[9]

220

Trojan horse program that claims to do one thing but in reality does something else, usually something malicious.

spyware software that secretly gathers user information through the user's Internet connection without his or her knowledge, usually for advertising purposes.

A **Trojan horse** is a program that claims to do one thing but in reality does something else, usually something malicious. For example, a Trojan horse might claim, and even appear, to be a game. When an unsuspecting user clicks on the Trojan horse to launch it, the program might erase the hard drive or steal any personal data stored on the computer.

Spyware is software that secretly gathers user information through the user's Internet connection without his or her knowledge, usually for advertising purposes. Spyware applications are typically bundled with other programs downloaded from the Internet. Once installed, the spyware monitors user activity on the Internet and transmits that information in the background to someone else.

Attacks by malware are not limited to computers and computer networks. Users of smart phones have reported a sharp increase in viruses, worms, and other forms of malware. Recently, a Trojan horse known as Nickispy, masquerading as a Google+ app, managed to infiltrate smart phones. By reverse-engineering the malware, technology experts were able to unravel how it ended up on smart phones and eliminate the threat.[10]

As viruses, worms, botnets, and Trojan horses become more complex, the technology to fight them must increase in sophistication as well. The simplest way to protect against computer viruses is to install one of the many available antivirus software programs, such as Norton AntiVirus and McAfee VirusScan. These programs, which also protect against worms and some Trojan horses, continuously monitor systems for viruses and automatically eliminate any they spot. Users should regularly update them by downloading the latest virus definitions. In addition, computer users should also install and regularly update antispyware programs because many Trojan horses are forms of spyware.

INFORMATION SYSTEMS AND ETHICS

Not surprisingly, the scope and power of today's information systems raise a number of ethical issues and concerns. These affect both employees and organizations. For instance, it is not uncommon for organizations to have specific ethical standards and policies regarding the use of information systems by employees and vendors. These standards include obligations to protect system security and the privacy and confidentiality of data. Policies also may cover the personal use of computers and related technologies, both hardware and software, by employees.

Ethical issues also involve organizational use of information systems. Organizations have an obligation to protect the privacy and confidentiality of data about employees and customers.

Employment records contain sensitive personal information, such as bank account numbers, which, if not protected, could lead to identity theft. Another ethical issue is the use of computer technology to monitor employees while they are working.

> > > **Quick Review**

1 Explain computer hacking.

2 What is malware?

3 How does a computer virus operate?

6 Disaster Recovery and Backup

Natural disasters, power failures, equipment malfunctions, software glitches, human error, and terrorist attacks can disrupt even the most sophisticated computer information systems. While these problems can cost businesses and other organizations billions of dollars, even more serious consequences can occur. For example, one study found that 93 percent of firms that lost their data centers for ten days or more went bankrupt within one year.[11]

FalconStor provides data backup applications and sophisticated disaster recovery solutions for businesses worldwide. The firm's services extend well beyond data replication because organizations that have suffered a major loss have needs well beyond replicating their data. FalconStor's software solutions permit them to access their applications, restart operations, and return to serving customers.[12]

Disaster recovery planning—deciding how to prevent system failures and continue operations if computer systems fail—is a critical function of all organizations. Disaster prevention programs can avoid some of these costly problems. The most basic precaution is routinely backing up software and data—at the organizational and individual levels. However, the organization's data center cannot be the sole repository of critical data because a single location is vulnerable to threats from both natural and human-caused disasters. Consequently, off-site data backup is a necessity, whether in a separate physical location or online. Companies that perform online backups store the encrypted data in secure facilities that in turn have their own backups. The initial backup may take a day or more, but subsequent ones take far less time because they involve only new or modified files.

> > > **Quick Review**

1 To what types of disasters are information systems vulnerable?

2 What is disaster recovery planning, and how does it work?

7 Information System Trends

Computer information systems are constantly—and rapidly—evolving. To keep their information systems up to date, firms must continually keep abreast of changes in technology. Some of the most significant trends in information systems today include the changing face of the workforce, the increased use of application service providers, on-demand computing, and cloud and grid computing.

THE DISTRIBUTED WORKFORCE

As discussed in earlier chapters, many companies rely more and more on a *distributed workforce*—employees who no longer work in traditional offices but rather in what are called *virtual offices*, including at home. Information technology makes a distributed workforce possible. Computers, networks, and other components of information systems allow workers to do their jobs effectively almost anywhere. For instance, none of JetBlue's reservations agents work in offices; they all work at home, connected to the airline's information system. Today, most employers have a policy regarding employees' remote access to their firm's network.

APPLICATION SERVICE PROVIDERS

As with other business functions, many firms find it makes sense to outsource at least some of their information technology function. Because of the increasing cost and complexity of obtaining and maintaining information systems, many firms

V Recent technological advances in data storage and cloud computing allow people to work on their laptops, tablets, or smart phones from anywhere in the world.

Cavan Images/Getty Images, Inc.

hire an **application service provider (ASP)**, an outside supplier that provides both the computers and the application support for managing an information system. An ASP can simplify complex software for its customers so that it is easier for them to manage and use. When an ASP relationship is successful, the buyer can then devote more time and resources to its core businesses instead of struggling to manage its information systems. Other benefits include stretching the firm's technology dollar farther and giving smaller companies more competitive information power. Even large companies turn to ASPs to manage some or all of their information systems. Microsoft outsourced much of its internal information technology services to Infosys Technology to save money and streamline, simplify, and support its services.[13]

A company that decides to use an ASP should check the background and references of a firm before hiring it to manage critical systems. In addition, customers should try to ensure that the service provider has strong security measures to block computer hackers or other unauthorized access to the data, that its data centers are running reliably, and that adequate data and applications backups are maintained.

> **application service provider (ASP)** outside supplier that provides both the computers and the application support for managing an information system.

ON-DEMAND, CLOUD, AND GRID COMPUTING

Another recent trend is **on-demand computing**, also called *utility computing*. Instead of purchasing and maintaining expensive software, firms essentially rent the software time from application providers and pay only for software usage, similar to purchasing electricity from a utility.

Cloud computing uses powerful servers to store applications software and databases. Users access the software and databases via the Web using anything from a PC to a smart phone. The software as a service (SaaS) movement is an example of cloud computing.

> **on-demand computing** an organization's rental of software time from application providers, paying only for software usage.

> **cloud computing** a type of information delivery under which powerful servers store applications software and databases for users to access on the Web.

> \>\>\> **Quick Review**
>
> **1** What is an application service provider?
>
> **2** Explain on-demand computing.

What's Ahead? > > >

This is the first of two chapters devoted to managing technology and information. The next chapter, "Understanding Accounting and Financial Statements," focuses on accounting, financial information, and financing reporting. Accounting is the process of measuring, interpreting, and communicating financial information to enable people inside and outside the firm to make informed decisions. The chapter describes the functions of accounting and role of accountants; the steps in the accounting cycle; the types, functions, and components of financial statements; and the role of budgets in an organization.

Weekly Updates spark classroom debate around current events that apply to your business course topics. http://www.wileybusinessupdates.com

NOTES

1. Company Web site, http://evernote.com, accessed May 15, 2013; Mary Branscombe, "Good Software Should Be at Least as Smart as Your Dog," *Techradar*, May 1, 2013, http://www.techradar.com; Neil McIntosh, "At Le Web, Visions of Not-So-Social Future," TechEurope blog, December 8, 2011, http://blogs.wsj.com.

2. Museum Web site, "Timeline of Computer History," http://www.computerhistory.org, accessed May 15, 2013.

3. Isha Suri, "Meet the Titan Super Computer and the World's Fastest Storage System," *Silicon Angle*, April 19, 2013, http://siliconangle.com.

4. Paul Lamkin, "Top 10 Tablets for Business," *Techradar*, accessed January 20, 2013, http://www.techradar.com.

5. Company Web site, http://www.virtual.com, accessed May 15, 2013.

6. Paul Barbagallo, "Views Vary on FCC Role as Regulator in All0-IP World," *Bloomberg BNA*, January 30, 2013, http://www.bna.com; Leena Rao, "Google Voice Founder Sets His Sights on VoIP Once Again," *Techcrunch*, March 7, 2012, http://techcrunch.com; Charles Schelle, "Update: Verizon VoIP Phone Outage Resolved," *SarasotaPatch*, February 25, 2012, http://sarasota.patch.com.

7. Julianne Pepitone and Leigh Remizowski, "'Massive' Credit Card Data Breach Involves All Major Brands," *CNNMoney*, March 31, 2012, http://money.cnn.com.

8. Kelly Jackson Higgins, "Mobile Malware on the Move, McAfee Report Says," *Dark Reading*, February 21, 2012, http://www.darkreading.com.

9. "Avast Says Grum Botnet Is Back from the Dead," *IT Security Pro*, May 24, 2013, http://itsecuritypro.co.uk; Brian Krebs, "Who's behind the World's Largest Spam Botnet?" *Krebs on Security*, February 1, 2012, http://krebsonsecurity.com.

10. Ken Dilanian, "Chinese Nickispy Malware Targets Smartphones," *Sydney Morning Herald*, February 26, 2012, http://www.smh.com.au.

11. Company Web site, "Data Loss Statistics," http://www.bostoncomputing.net, accessed May 15, 2013.

12. Company Web site, "FalconStor Provides Data Migration Technology for Dell Services Offering," press release, March 6, 2012, http://www.falconstor.com.

13. Company Web site, http://www.infosys.com, accessed May 15, 2013.

Summary of Learning Objectives

1 Distinguish between data and information, and discuss information systems.

It is important for businesspeople to know the difference between data and information. Data are raw facts and figures that may or may not be relevant to a business decision. Information is knowledge gained from processing those facts and figures. An information system is an organized method for collecting, storing, and communicating past, present, and projected information on internal operations and external intelligence. Most information systems today use computer and telecommunications technology.

data   raw facts and figures that may or may not be relevant to a business decision.

information   knowledge gained from processing data.

information system   organized method for collecting, storing, and communicating past, present, and projected information on internal operations and external intelligence.

chief information officer (CIO)   executive responsible for managing a firm's information system and related computer technologies.

2 List the components and types of information systems.

When people think about information systems today, they're generally thinking about computer-based systems, which rely on computers and related technologies. Computer-based information systems have four components:

1. Computer hardware
2. Software
3. Telecommunications and computer networks
4. Data resource management

The heart of an information system is its database, a centralized integrated collection of data resources. Information systems fall into two broad categories: operational support systems and management support systems.

● Operational support systems are designed to produce a variety of information for users. Examples include transaction processing systems and process control systems.

● Management support systems are those designed to support effective decision making. They include management information systems, decision support systems, executive support systems, and expert systems.

computer-based information system   information system that relies on computer and related technologies to store information electronically in an organized, accessible manner.

database   centralized integrated collection of data resources.

operational support system   information system designed to produce a variety of information on an organizations activities for both internal and external users.

transaction processing system   operational support system that records and processes data from business transactions.

process control system   operational support system designed to monitor and control physical processes.

management support system   information system designed to provide support for effective decision making.

management information system (MIS)   information system designed to produce reports for managers and other personnel.

decision support system (DSS)   system that provides direct support to businesspeople during the decision-making process.

executive support system (ESS)   system that allows senior executives to access the firm's primary databases, often by touching the computer screen, pointing and clicking a mouse, or using voice recognition.

expert system   computer program that imitates human thinking through complicated sets of "if-then" rules.

3 Discuss computer hardware and software.

Hardware consists of all tangible elements of a computer system, including input and output devices. Major categories of computers include mainframes, supercomputers, midrange systems, personal computers (PCs), and handheld devices.

Computer software provides the instructions that tell the hardware what to do. The software that controls the basic workings of the computer is its operating system. Other programs, called application software, perform specific tasks that users want to complete.

hardware   all tangible elements of a computer system.

server   a dedicated computer that provides services to other computers on a network.

software all the programs, routines, and computer languages that control a computer and tell it how to operate.

 Describe computer networks.

Local area networks connect computers within a limited area. Wide area networks tie together larger geographical regions by using telephone lines, microwave, or satellite transmission. A wireless network allows computers to communicate through radio waves. Intranets allow employees to share information on a ready-made company network. Access to an intranet is restricted to authorized users and is protected by a firewall. A virtual private networks (VPN) provides a secure Internet connection between two or more points. VoIP—voice over Internet protocol—uses a personal computer running special software and a broadband Internet connection to make and receive telephone calls over the Internet rather than over traditional telephone networks.

local area network (LAN) computer network that connects machines within limited areas, such as a building or several nearby buildings.

wide area network (WAN) ties larger geographical regions together by using telephone lines and microwave and satellite transmission.

WiFi wireless network that connects various devices and allows them to communicate with one another through radio waves.

intranet computer network that is similar to the Internet but limits access to authorized users.

firewall limits data transfers to certain locations and logs system use so that managers can identify attempts to log on with invalid passwords and other threats to a system's security.

virtual private network (VPN) secure connection between two points on the Internet.

VoIP alternative version of telecommunication service using the Internet.

 Discuss the security and ethical issues affecting information systems.

Numerous security and ethical issues affect information systems. Two of the main security threats are e-crime and malware. E-crimes range from hacking—unauthorized penetration of an information system—to the theft of hardware. Malware is any malicious software program designed to infect computer systems. Examples include viruses, worms, botnets, Trojan horses, and spyware.

Ethical issues affecting information systems include the proper use of the systems by authorized users. Organizations also have an obligation to employees, vendors, and customers to protect the security and confidentiality of the data stored in information systems.

malware any malicious software program designed to infect computer systems.

virus program that secretly attaches itself to other programs (called *hosts*) and changes them or destroys data.

worm small piece of software that exploits a security hole in a network to replicate itself.

botnet a network of PCs that has been infected with one or more data-stealing viruses.

Trojan horse program that claims to do one thing but in reality does something else, usually something malicious.

spyware software that secretly gathers user information through the user's Internet connection without his or her knowledge, usually for advertising purposes.

 Explain disaster recovery and backup.

Information system disasters, whether through human error or due to natural causes, can cost businesses billions of dollars. The consequences of a disaster can be minimized by routinely backing up software and data, both at an organizational level and at an individual level. Organizations should back up critical data at an off-site location. Some firms may also want to invest in extra hardware and software sites, which can be accessed during emergencies.

 Review information systems trends.

Information systems are continually and rapidly evolving. Some of the most significant trends are the increasing demands of the distributed workforce, the increased use of application service providers, on-demand computing, and grid computing. Many people now work in virtual offices, including at home; information technology makes this possible. Application service providers allow organizations to outsource most of their IT functions. Rather than buying and maintaining expensive software, on-demand computing offers users the option of renting software time from outside vendors and paying only for their usage. Grid computing consists of a network of smaller computers running special software creating a virtual mainframe or even supercomputer.

application service provider (ASP) outside supplier that provides both the computers and the application support for managing an information system.

on-demand computing an organization's rental of software time from application providers, paying only for software usage.

cloud computing a type of information delivery under which powerful servers store applications software and databases for users to access on the Web.

>>> Quick Review >>

LO1

1. What is the difference between data and information?
2. What is an information system?

LO2

1. List the four components of a computer-based information system.
2. What is a database?
3. Name the two general types of information systems and give an example of each.

LO3

1. List two input and two output devices.
2. What accounts for the increasing popularity of notebook computers?
3. What is software? List the two categories of software.

LO4

1. What is a LAN?
2. Explain the differences between an intranet and a VPN.
3. How does VoIP work?

LO5

1. Explain computer hacking.
2. What is malware?
3. How does a computer virus operate?

LO6

1. To what types of disasters are information systems vulnerable?
2. What is disaster recovery planning, and how does it work?

LO7

1. What is an application service provider?
2. Explain on-demand computing.

chapter fifteen

Understanding Accounting and Financial Statements

Learning Objectives

1 **Discuss** the users of accounting information.

2 **Describe** accounting professionals.

3 **Identify** the foundation of the accounting system.

4 **Outline** the steps in the accounting cycle.

5 **Explain** financial statements.

6 **Discuss** financial ratio analysis.

7 **Describe** the role of budgeting.

8 **Outline** international accounting practices.

BKD LLP: An Accounting Firm for the 21st Century

If you are thinking about a career in accounting, you would do well to consider BKD LLP, one of the top ten CPA and advisory firms in the United States. The 90-year-old firm reports more than $400 million a year in revenue, serving businesses and individuals in 30 offices in the South and Southwest.

BKD provides a wide range of accounting and audit services. It helps its corporate clients with mergers and acquisitions, sales, risk management, employee benefit plans, management buyouts, IPOs, and other financing operations. It advises individual clients on wealth planning, investments, estate planning, and insurance, and it also operates the BKD Foundation. The BKD Foundation, the firm's charitable arm, empowers partners and employees to contribute through a combination of sponsorships, grants, and volunteerism. Donations made through the foundation totaled nearly $1 million in a recent year. Outside of the foundation, BKD partners and employees contributed nearly $1 million to the United Way and also volunteered for a variety of groups, including Court Appointed Special Advocates (CASA), Salvation Army, Toys for Tots, Alzheimer's Association, March of Dimes, and the American Cancer Society. "I think every person in our firm believes it's their responsibility to give back to their communities. They are givers and not takers. It's in our cultural DNA," said the BKD CEO.[1]

Overview > > >

Accounting professionals prepare the financial information that organizations present in their annual reports. Whether you begin your career by working for a company or by starting your own firm, you need to understand what accountants do and why their work is so important in contemporary business.

Accounting is the process of measuring, interpreting, and communicating financial information to enable people inside and outside the firm to make informed decisions. In many ways, accounting is the language of business. Accountants gather, record, report, and interpret financial information in a way that describes the status and operation of an organization and aids in decision making.

> **accounting**
> process of measuring, interpreting, and communicating financial information to enable people inside and outside the firm to make informed decisions.

Millions of men and women throughout the world describe their occupation as an accountant. In the United States alone, more than 1.2 million people work as accountants. According to the U.S. Bureau of Labor Statistics, the number of accounting-related jobs is expected to increase by around 16 percent between now and 2020.[2] The availability of jobs and relatively high starting salaries for talented graduates have made accounting one of the most in-demand majors on college campuses.[3]

This chapter begins by describing who uses accounting information. It discusses business activities involving accounting statements: financing, investing, and operations. It explains the accounting process, defines double-entry bookkeeping, and presents the accounting equation. We then discuss the development of financial statements from information about financial transactions. The methods of interpreting these statements and the roles of budgeting in planning and controlling a business are described next. The chapter concludes with a discussion of the development and implementation schedule of a uniform set of accounting rules for global business.

1 Users of Accounting Information

People both inside and outside an organization rely on accounting information to help them make business decisions. **FIGURE 15.1** lists the users of accounting information and the applications they find for that information. Firms like Deloitte Consulting provide such information and help their customers make the best use of it.

Managers with a business, government agency, or not-for-profit organization are the major users of accounting information because it helps them plan and control daily and long-range operations. Business owners and boards of directors of not-for-profit groups also rely on accounting data to determine how well managers are operating the organizations. Union officials use accounting data in contract negotiations, and employees refer to it as they monitor their firms' productivity and profitability performance.

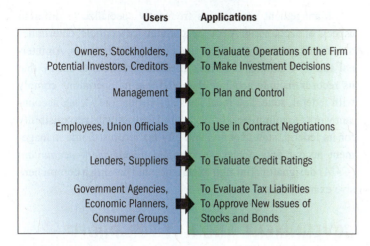

Users	Applications
Owners, Stockholders, Potential Investors, Creditors	To Evaluate Operations of the Firm — To Make Investment Decisions
Management	To Plan and Control
Employees, Union Officials	To Use in Contract Negotiations
Lenders, Suppliers	To Evaluate Credit Ratings
Government Agencies, Economic Planners, Consumer Groups	To Evaluate Tax Liabilities — To Approve New Issues of Stocks and Bonds

FIGURE 15.1 Users of Accounting Information

To help employees understand how their work affects the bottom line, many companies share sensitive financial information with their employees and teach them how to understand and use financial statements. Proponents of what is often referred to as *open book management* believe that allowing employees to view financial information helps them better understand how their work contributes to the company's success, which in turn benefits them.

Outside a firm, potential investors evaluate accounting information to help them decide whether to buy a firm's stock. As will be discussed in more detail later in the chapter, any company whose stock is traded publicly is required to report its financial results on a regular basis. So anyone can find out, for example, what Costco's sales were last year or how much money Intel made during the last quarter. Bankers and other lenders use accounting information to evaluate a potential borrower's financial soundness. The Internal Revenue Service (IRS) and state tax officials use it to determine a company's tax liability. Citizens' groups and government agencies use such information in assessing the efficiency of operations such as Massachusetts General Hospital; the Topeka, Kansas, school system; Community College of Denver; and the Art Institute of Chicago.

▼ Accountants play a key role in organizations by providing services to businesses, individuals, government agencies, and not-for-profit organizations.

Sawayasu Tsuji/iStockphoto

Accountants play fundamental roles not only in business but also in other aspects of society. Their work influences each of the business environments discussed earlier in this book. They clearly contribute important information to help managers deal with the competitive and economic environments.

Less obvious contributions help others understand, predict, and react to the technological, regulatory, and social and cultural environments. For instance, thousands of people volunteer each year to help people with their taxes. One of the largest organized programs is Tax-Aide, sponsored by AARP (formally known as the American Association of Retired Persons). For more than 40 years this volunteer program has assisted about 50 million low- and middle-income Americans—especially people age 60 and older—with their income tax preparation.[4]

BUSINESS ACTIVITIES INVOLVING ACCOUNTING

The natural progression of a business begins with financing. Subsequent steps, including investing, lead to operating the business. All organizations, profit oriented and not-for-profit, perform these three basic activities, and accounting plays a key role in each one:

- Financing activities provide necessary funds to start a business and expand it after it begins operating.
- Investing activities provide valuable assets required to run a business.
- Operating activities focus on selling goods and services, but they also consider expenses as important elements of sound financial management.

> >> **Quick Review**

1. Define *accounting*.
2. Who uses accounting information?
3. What three business activities involve accounting?

2 Accounting Professionals

Accounting professionals work in a variety of areas in and for business firms, government agencies, and not-for-profit organizations. They can be classified as public, management, government, and not-for-profit accountants.

PUBLIC ACCOUNTANTS

A **public accountant** provides accounting services to individuals or business firms for a fee. Most public

public accountant accountant who provides accounting services to individuals or business firms for a fee.

accounting firms provide three basic services to clients: (1) auditing, or examining, financial records; (2) tax preparation, planning, and related services; and (3) management consulting. Because public accountants are not employees of a client firm, they can provide unbiased advice about the firm's financial condition.

Although there are hundreds of public accounting firms in the United States, a handful of firms dominate the industry. The four largest public accounting firms—Deloitte & Touche, PricewaterhouseCoopers (PwC), Ernst & Young, and KPMG—bill well over $36 billion annually. In contrast, McGladrey & Pullen, the nation's fifth-largest accounting firm, has annual revenue of approximately $1.3 billion.[5]

Some years ago, public accounting firms came under sharp criticism for providing management consulting services to many of the same firms they audited. Critics argued that when a public accounting firm does both—auditing and management consulting—an inherent conflict of interest is created. In addition, this conflict of interest may undermine confidence in the quality of the financial statements that accounting firms audit. The bankruptcies of some high-profile firms increased pressure on public accounting firms to end this practice. Legislation also established strict limits on the types of consulting services auditors can provide.

A growing number of public accountants are also certified as *forensic accountants*, and some smaller public accounting firms actually specialize in forensic accounting. These professionals, and the firms that employ them, focus on uncovering potential fraud in a variety of organizations.

Certified public accountants (CPAs) demonstrate their accounting knowledge by meeting state requirements for education and experience and successfully completing a number of rigorous tests in accounting theory and practice, auditing, law, and taxes. Other accountants who meet specified educational and experience requirements and pass certification exams carry the title *certified management accountant, certified internal auditor,* or *certified fraud examiner.*

MANAGEMENT ACCOUNTANTS

An accountant employed by a business other than a public accounting firm is called a *management accountant*. Such a person collects and records financial transactions and prepares financial statements used by the firm's managers in decision making. Management accountants provide timely, relevant, accurate, and concise information that executives can use to operate their firms more effectively and more profitably than they could without this input. In addition to preparing financial statements, a management accountant plays a major role in interpreting them. A management accountant should provide answers to many important questions:

- Where is the company going?
- What opportunities await it?
- Do certain situations expose the company to excessive risk?
- Does the firm's information system provide detailed and timely information to all levels of management?

Management accountants frequently specialize in different aspects of accounting. A cost accountant, for example, determines the cost of goods and services and helps set their prices. An internal auditor examines the firm's financial practices to ensure that its records include accurate data and that its operations comply with federal, state, and local laws and regulations. A tax accountant works to minimize a firm's tax bill and assumes responsibility for its federal, state, county, and city tax returns. Some management accountants achieve a *certified management accountant (CMA)* designation through experience and passing a comprehensive examination.

GOVERNMENT AND NOT-FOR-PROFIT ACCOUNTANTS

Federal, state, and local governments also require accounting services. Government accountants and those who work for not-for-profit organizations perform professional services similar to those of management accountants. Accountants in these sectors concern themselves primarily with determining how efficiently the organizations accomplish their objectives.

Not-for-profit organizations, such as churches, labor unions, charities, schools, hospitals, and universities, also hire accountants. In fact, the not-for-profit sector is one of the fastest growing segments of accounting practice. An increasing number of not-for-profits publish financial information because contributors want more accountability from these organizations and are interested in knowing how the groups spend the money that they raise.

> ### >>> Quick Review
>
> **1** List the three services offered by public accounting firms.
>
> **2** What tasks do management accountants perform?

3 The Foundation of the Accounting System

To provide reliable, consistent, and unbiased information to decision makers, accountants follow guidelines, or standards, known as **generally accepted accounting principles (GAAP)**. These principles encompass the conventions, rules, and procedures for determining acceptable accounting and financial reporting practices.

All GAAP standards are based on four basic principles: consistency, relevance, reliability, and comparability. Consistency means that all

generally accepted accounting principles (GAAP) guidelines on the conventions, rules, and procedures for determining acceptable accounting and financial reporting practices.

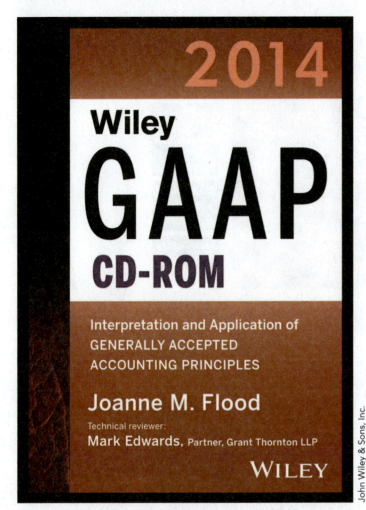

∧ Accountants and other financial professionals use GAAP to assure their customers that the statements they provide conform to well-established accounting practices.

data should be collected and presented in the same manner across all periods. Any change in the way in which specific data are collected or presented must be noted and explained. Relevance states that all information being reported should be appropriate and assist users in evaluating that information. Reliability implies that the accounting data presented in financial statements are reliable and can be verified by an independent party such as an outside auditor. Comparability ensures that one firm's financial statements can be compared with those of similar businesses.

In the United States, the **Financial Accounting Standards Board (FASB)** is primarily responsible for evaluating, setting, or modifying GAAP. The U.S. Securities and Exchange Commission (SEC), the chief federal regulator of the financial markets and accounting industry, actually has the statutory authority to establish financial accounting and reporting standards for publicly held companies.

Financial Accounting Standards Board (FASB) an organization responsible for evaluating, setting, or modifying GAAP in the United States.

The FASB carefully monitors changing business conditions, enacting new rules and modifying existing rules when necessary. It also considers input and requests from all segments of its diverse constituency, including corporations and the SEC. One major change in accounting rules recently dealt with executive and employee stock options. Stock options give the holder the right to buy stock at a fixed price. The FASB now requires firms that give employees stock options to calculate the cost of the options and treat the cost as an expense, similar to salaries.

In response to well-known cases of accounting fraud and questions about the independence of auditors, the Sarbanes-Oxley Act—commonly known as SOX—created the Public Accounting Oversight Board. The five-member board has the power to set audit standards and to investigate and sanction accounting firms that certify the books of publicly traded firms. Members of the Public Accounting Oversight Board are appointed by the SEC. No more than two of the five members of the board can be certified public accountants.

In addition to creating the Public Accounting Oversight Board, SOX also added to the reporting requirements for publicly traded companies. For example, senior executives including the CEO and chief financial officer (CFO) must personally certify that the financial information reported by the company is correct. As noted earlier, these requirements have increased the demand for accounting professionals, especially managerial accountants. One result of this increased demand has been higher salaries.

The **Foreign Corrupt Practices Act** is a federal law that prohibits U.S. citizens and companies from bribing foreign officials in order to win or continue business. This law was later extended to make foreign officials subject to penalties if they in any way cause similar corrupt practices to occur within the United States or its territories.

Foreign Corrupt Practices Act federal law that prohibits U.S. citizens and companies from bribing foreign officials in order to win or continue business.

>>> **Quick Review**

1 Define *GAAP*.

2 Name the four basic requirements to which all accounting rules must adhere.

1 What role does the FASB play?

④ The Accounting Cycle

Accounting deals with financial transactions between a firm and its employees, customers, suppliers, and owners; bankers; and various government agencies. For example, payroll checks result in a cash outflow to compensate employees. A payment to a vendor results in receipt of needed materials for the production process. Cash, check, and credit purchases by customers generate

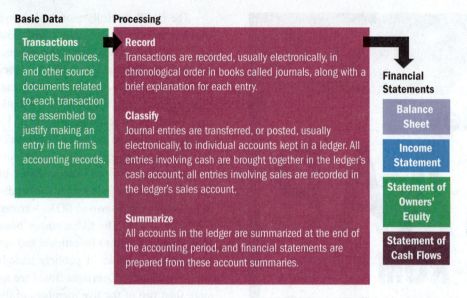

Basic Data	Processing	Financial Statements

Transactions
Receipts, invoices, and other source documents related to each transaction are assembled to justify making an entry in the firm's accounting records.

Record
Transactions are recorded, usually electronically, in chronological order in books called journals, along with a brief explanation for each entry.

Classify
Journal entries are transferred, or posted, usually electronically, to individual accounts kept in a ledger. All entries involving cash are brought together in the ledger's cash account; all entries involving sales are recorded in the ledger's sales account.

Summarize
All accounts in the ledger are summarized at the end of the accounting period, and financial statements are prepared from these account summaries.

Financial Statements
- Balance Sheet
- Income Statement
- Statement of Owners' Equity
- Statement of Cash Flows

FIGURE 15.2 The Accounting Cycle

funds to cover the costs of operations and to earn a profit. Prompt payment of bills preserves the firm's credit rating and its future ability to earn a profit. The procedure by which accountants convert data about individual transactions to financial statements is called the accounting cycle.

accounting cycle set of activities involved in converting information and individual transactions into financial statements.

FIGURE 15.2 illustrates the activities involved in the accounting cycle: recording, classifying, and summarizing transactions. Initially, any transaction that has a financial impact on the business, such as wages or payments to suppliers, should be documented. All these transactions are recorded in journals, which list transactions in chronological order. Journal listings are then posted to ledgers. A ledger shows increases or decreases in specific accounts such as cash or wages. Ledgers are used to prepare the financial statements, which summarize financial transactions. Management and other interested parties use the resulting financial statements for a variety of purposes.

THE ACCOUNTING EQUATION

Three fundamental terms appear in the accounting equation: assets, liabilities, and owners' equity. An **asset** is anything of value owned or leased by a business. Assets include land, buildings, supplies, cash, accounts receivable (amounts owed to the business as payment for credit sales), and marketable securities.

asset anything of value owned or leased by a business.

Although most assets are tangible assets, such as equipment, buildings, and inventories, intangible possessions such as patents and trademarks are often some of a firm's most important assets. This kind of asset is especially essential for many companies, including computer software firms, biotechnology companies, and pharmaceutical companies. For instance, Johnson & Johnson—which has both

biotechnology and pharmaceutical operations—reported more than $51 billion in intangible assets (including goodwill) in one recent year, out of a total of almost $121 billion in assets.[6]

Two groups have claims against the assets of a firm: creditors and owners. A **liability** of a business is anything owed to creditors—that is, the claims of a firm's creditors. When a firm borrows money to purchase inventory, land, or machinery, the claims of creditors are shown as accounts payable, notes payable, or long-term debt. Wages and salaries owed to employees also are liabilities (known as *wages payable* or *accrued wages*).

Owners' equity is the owner's initial investment in the business plus profits that were not paid out to owners over time in the form

liability anything owed to creditors—the claims of a firm's creditors.

owners' equity the owner's initial investment in the business plus profits that were not paid out to owners over time in the form of cash dividends.

V Although tangible assets like buildings, equipment, and inventories may look impressive, they are sometimes less important to a company than intangible assets, such as patents and trademarks.

Nikada/iStockphoto

232

accounting equation formula that states that assets must equal liabilities plus owners' equity.

of cash dividends. A strong owners' equity position often is used as evidence of a firm's financial strength and stability.

The **accounting equation** (also referred to as the *accounting identity*) states that assets must equal liabilities plus owners' equity. This equation reflects the financial position of a firm at any point in time:

$$\text{Assets} = \text{Liabilities} + \text{Owners' Equity}$$

Because financing comes from either creditors or owners, the right side of the accounting equation also represents the business's financial structure.

The accounting equation also illustrates **double-entry bookkeeping**—the process by which accounting transactions are recorded. Because assets must always equal liabilities plus equity, each transaction must have an offsetting transaction. For example, if a company increases an asset, either another asset must decrease, a liability must increase, or owners' equity must increase. So if a company uses cash to purchase inventory, one asset (inventory) is increased while another (cash) is decreased by the same amount. Similarly, a decrease in an asset must be offset by either an increase in another asset, a decrease in a liability, or a decrease in owners' equity. If a company uses cash to repay a bank loan, both an asset (cash) and a liability (bank loans) decrease, and by the same amount.

double-entry bookkeeping process by which accounting transactions are recorded; each transaction must have an offsetting transaction.

The relationship expressed by the accounting equation underlies development of the firm's financial statements. Three financial statements form the foundation of the financial statements: the balance sheet, the income statement, and the statement of owners' equity. The information found in these statements is calculated using the double-entry bookkeeping system and reflects the basic accounting equation. A fourth statement, the statement of cash flows, is also prepared to focus specifically on the sources and uses of cash for a firm from its operating, investing, and financing activities.

THE IMPACT OF COMPUTERS AND THE INTERNET ON THE ACCOUNTING PROCESS

For hundreds of years, bookkeepers recorded, or posted, accounting transactions as manual entries in journals. They then transferred the information, or posted it, to individual accounts listed in ledgers. Computers have streamlined the process, making it both faster and easier. For instance, point-of-sale terminals in retail stores perform a number of functions each time they record a sale. These terminals not only recall prices from computer system memory and maintain constant inventory counts of individual items in stock but also automatically perform accounting data entry functions.

Because the accounting needs of entrepreneurs and small businesses differ from those of larger firms, accounting software makers have designed programs that meet specific user needs. Some examples of accounting software programs designed for entrepreneurs and small businesses, and designed to run on personal computers, include QuickBooks, Peachtree, and BusinessWorks. Software programs designed for larger firms, often requiring more sophisticated computer systems, include products from Oracle and SAP.

For firms that conduct business worldwide, software producers have introduced new accounting programs that handle all of a company's accounting information for every country in which it operates. The software handles different languages and currencies as well as the financial, legal, and tax requirements of each nation in which the firm conducts business.

The Internet also influences the accounting process. Several software producers offer Web-based accounting products designed for small and medium-sized businesses. Among other benefits, these products allow users to access their complete accounting systems from anywhere using a standard Web browser.

>>> **Quick Review**

1. List the steps in the accounting cycle.

2. What is the accounting equation?

3. Explain how double-entry bookkeeping works.

5 Financial Statements

Financial statements provide managers with essential information they need to evaluate the liquidity position of an organization—its ability to meet current obligations and needs by converting assets into cash; the firm's profitability; and its overall financial health. The balance sheet, income statement, statement of owners' equity, and statement of cash flows provide a foundation on which managers can base their decisions. By interpreting the data provided in these statements, managers can communicate the appropriate information to internal decision makers and to interested parties outside the organization.

Of the four financial statements, only the balance sheet is considered to be a permanent statement; its amounts are carried over from year to year. The income statement, statement of owners' equity, and statement of cash flows are considered temporary because they are closed out at the end of each year.

Public companies are required to report their financial statements at the end of each three-month period as well as at the end of each fiscal year. Annual statements must be examined and verified by the firm's outside auditors. These financial statements are public information available to anyone. A fiscal year need not coincide

The balance sheet shows the firm's financial position on a particular date and its amounts are carried over from year to year.

with the calendar year, and companies set different fiscal years. For instance, Starbucks' fiscal year runs from October 1 to September 30 of the following year. Nike's fiscal year consists of the 12 months between June 1 and May 31. By contrast, GE's fiscal year is the same as the calendar year, running from January 1 to December 31.

THE BALANCE SHEET

A firm's **balance sheet** shows its financial position on a particular date. It is similar to a photograph of the firm's assets together with its liabilities and owners' equity at a specific moment in time. Balance sheets must be prepared at regular intervals because a firm's managers and other internal parties often request this information every day, every week, or at least every month. On the other hand, external users, such as stockholders or industry analysts, may use this information less frequently, perhaps every quarter or once a year.

balance sheet statement of a firm's financial position on a particular date.

The balance sheet follows the accounting equation. On the left side of the balance sheet are the firm's assets—what it owns. These assets, shown in descending order of liquidity (in other words, convertibility to cash), represent the uses that management has made of available funds. Cash is always listed first on the asset side of the balance sheet.

On the right side of the equation are the claims against the firm's assets. Liabilities and shareholders' equity indicate the sources of the firm's assets and are listed in the order in which they are due. Liabilities reflect the claims of creditors—financial institutions or bondholders that have loaned the firm money; suppliers that have provided goods and services on credit; and others to be paid, such as federal, state, and local tax authorities. Shareholders' equity represents the owners' claims (those of stockholders, in the case of a corporation) against the firm's assets. It also amounts to the excess of all assets over liabilities.

FIGURE 15.3 shows the balance sheet for Belle's Fine Coffees, a small coffee wholesaler. The accounting equation is illustrated by the three classifications of assets, liabilities, and shareholders'

equity on the company's balance sheet. Remember, total assets must always equal the sum of liabilities and shareholders' equity. In other words, the balance sheet must always balance.

THE INCOME STATEMENT

Whereas the balance sheet reflects a firm's financial situation at a specific point in time, the **income statement** indicates the flow of resources that reveals the performance of the organization over a specific time period. Resembling a video rather than a photograph, the income statement is a financial record summarizing a firm's financial performance in terms of revenues, expenses, and profits over a given time period, say, a quarter or a year.

income statement financial record summarizing a firm's financial performance in terms of revenues, expenses, and profits over a given time period, such as a quarter or a year.

In addition to reporting the firm's profit or loss results, the income statement helps decision makers focus on overall revenues and the costs involved in generating these revenues. Managers of a not-for-profit organization use this statement to determine whether its revenues from contributions, grants, and investments will cover its operating costs. Finally, the income statement provides much of the basic data needed to calculate the financial ratios managers use in planning and controlling activities. **FIGURE 15.4** shows the income statement for Belle's Fine Coffees.

An income statement (some times called *a profit-and-loss, or P&L, statement*) begins with total sales or revenues generated during a month, a quarter, or a year. Subsequent lines then deduct all of the costs related to producing the revenues. Typical categories of costs include those involved in producing the firm's goods or services, operating expenses, interest, and taxes. After all of them have been subtracted, the remaining net income may be distributed to the firm's owners (stockholders, proprietors, or partners) or reinvested in the company as retained earnings. The final figure on the income statement—net income after taxes—is literally the *bottom line.*

Keeping costs under control is an important part of running a business. Too often, however, companies concentrate more on increasing revenue than on controlling costs. Regardless of how much money a company collects in revenues, it won't stay in business for long unless it eventually earns a profit.

STATEMENT OF OWNERS' EQUITY

The **statement of owners'**, or shareholders', **equity** is designed to show the components of the change in equity from the end of one fiscal year to the end of the next. It uses information from both the balance sheet and income statement. A somewhat simplified example is shown in **FIGURE 15.5** for Belle's Fine Coffees.

statement of owners' equity record of the change in owners' equity from the end of one fiscal period to the end of the next.

1 Current Assets:
Cash and other liquid assets that can or will be converted to cash within one year.

2 Plant, Property, and Equipment (net):
Physical assets expected to last for more than one year; shown net of accumulated depreciation—the cumulative value that plant, property, and equipment have been expensed (depreciated).

3
Value of assets such as patents and trademarks.

4 Current Liabilities:
Claims of creditors that are to be repaid within one year; accruals are expenses, such as wages, that have been incurred but not yet paid.

5 Long-Term Debt:
Debts that come due one year or longer after the date on the balance sheet.

6 Owners' (or Shareholders') Equity:
Claims of the owners against the assets of the firm; the difference between total assets and total liabilities.

CHAPTER 15

235

Understanding Accounting and Financial Statements

Belle's Fine Coffees

Balance Sheet

($ thousands)	2014	2013
Assets		
1 Current Assets		
Cash	$ 800	$ 600
Short-term investments	1,250	940
Accounts receivable	990	775
Inventory	2,200	1,850
Total current assets	5,240	4,165
2 Plant, property, and equipment (net)	3,300	2,890
3 Goodwill and other intangible assets	250	250
Total Assets	8,790	7,305
Liabilities and Shareholders' Equity		
4 Current Liabilities		
Accruals	$ 350	$ 450
Accounts payable	980	900
Notes payable	700	500
Total current liabilities	2,030	1,850
5 Long-term debt	1,100	1,000
Total liabilities	3,130	2,850
6 Shareholders' equity	5,660	4,455
Total Liabilities and Equity	8,790	7,305

FIGURE 15.3 Belle's Fine Coffees Balance Sheet (Fiscal Year Ending December 31)

Note that the statement begins with the amount of equity shown on the balance sheet at the end of the prior year. Net income is added, and cash dividends paid to owners are subtracted (both are found on the income statement for the current year). If owners contributed any additional capital, say, through the sale of new shares, this amount is added to equity. On the other hand, if owners withdrew capital, for example, through the repurchase of existing shares, equity declines. All of the additions and subtractions, taken together, equal the change in owners' equity from the end of the last fiscal year to the end of the current one. The new amount of owners' equity is then reported on the balance sheet for the current year.

1 **Sales:**
Funds received from the sale of goods and services over a specified period of time.

2 **Cost of Goods Sold:**
Cost of merchandise or services that generate the firm's sales.

3 **Operating Expenses:**
Salaries and other operational expenses not directly related to the acquisition, production, or sale of the firm's output.

4 **Depreciation:**
Noncash expenses that reflect the systematic reduction in the value of the firm's plant, property, and equipment.

5 **Net Income:**
Sales minus total expenses; profit after taxes.

Belle's Fine Coffees
Income Statement

($ thousands)	2014	2013
1 Sales	$17,300	$14,200
2 Cost of goods sold	10,380	8,804
Gross profit	6,920	5,396
3 Operating expenses	3,550	2,950
Operating profit	3,370	2,446
4 Depreciation	350	300
Interest expense (net)	98	75
Earnings before taxes	2,922	2,071
Income taxes	1,005	650
5 Net income	1,917	1,421

FIGURE 15.4 Belle's Fine Coffees Income Statement (Fiscal Year Ending December 31)

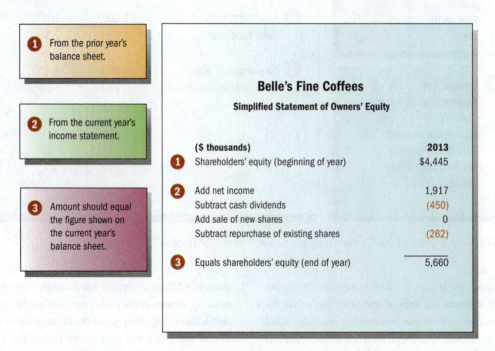

1 From the prior year's balance sheet.

2 From the current year's income statement.

3 Amount should equal the figure shown on the current year's balance sheet.

Belle's Fine Coffees
Simplified Statement of Owners' Equity

($ thousands)	2013
1 Shareholders' equity (beginning of year)	$4,445
2 Add net income	1,917
Subtract cash dividends	(450)
Add sale of new shares	0
Subtract repurchase of existing shares	(262)
3 Equals shareholders' equity (end of year)	5,660

FIGURE 15.5 Belle's Fine Coffees Simplified Statement of Owners' Equity (Fiscal Year Ending December 31)

THE STATEMENT OF CASH FLOWS

statement of cash flows statement showing the sources and uses of cash during a period of time.

In addition to the statement of owners' equity, the income statement, and the balance sheet, most firms prepare a fourth accounting statement—the **statement of cash flows**. Public companies are required to prepare and publish a statement of cash flows. In addition, commercial lenders often require a borrower to submit a statement of cash flows. The statement of cash flows provides investors and creditors with relevant information about a firm's cash receipts and cash payments for its operations, investments, and financing during an accounting period. **FIGURE 15.6** shows the statement of cash flows for Belle's Fine Coffees.

1 Operating Activities: The nuts and bolts of day-to-day activities of a company carrying out its regular business; increases in accounts receivable and inventory are uses of cash, while increases in accruals and accounts payables are sources of cash; in financially healthy firms, net cash flow from operating activities should be positive.

2 Investing Activities: Transactions to accumulate or use cash in ways that affect operating activities in the future; often a use of cash.

3 Financing Activities: Ways to transfer cash to or from creditors and to or from owners; can be either positive or negative.

4 Net Cash Flow: The sum of cash flow from operating, investing, and financing activities, a reconcilement of cash from the beginning to the end of the accounting period (one year in this example).

Belle's Fine Coffees
Statement of Cash Flows

($ thousands)	2013
1 Cash Flow from Operating Activities	
Net income	$1,917
Depreciation	350
Change in accounts receivable	(215)
Change in inventory	(350)
Change in accruals	(100)
Change in accounts payable	80
Total cash flow from operating activities	1,682
2 Cash Flow from Investing Activities	
Capital expenditures	(760)
Change in short-term investments	(310)
Total cash flow from investing activities	(1,070)
3 Cash Flow from Financing Activities	
Cash dividends	(450)
Sale/repurchase of shares	(262)
Change in notes payable	200
Change in long-term debt	100
Total cash flow from financing activities	(412)
4 Net Cash Flow	200
Cash (beginning of year)	600
Cash (end of year)	800

FIGURE 15.6 Belle's Fine Coffees Statement of Cash Flows (Fiscal Year Ending December 31)

Companies prepare a statement of cash flows due to the widespread use of accrual accounting. **Accrual accounting** recognizes revenues and costs when they occur, not when actual cash changes hands. As a result, there can be differences between what is reported as sales, expenses, and profits, and the amount of cash that actually flows into and out of the business during a period of time. An example is depreciation. Companies depreciate fixed assets—such as machinery and buildings—over a specified period of time, meaning that they systematically reduce the value of the asset. Depreciation is reported as an expense on the firm's income statement (see Figure 15.4) but does not involve any actual cash. The fact that depreciation is a noncash expense means that what a firm reports as net income (profits after tax) for a particular period actually understates the amount of cash the firm took in, less expenses, during that period of time. Consequently, depreciation is added back to net income when calculating cash flow.

238

The fact that *cash flow* is the lifeblood of every organization is evidenced by the business failure rate. Many owners of failed firms blame inadequate cash flow for their company's demise. Those who value the statement of cash flow maintain that its preparation and scrutiny by various parties can prevent financial distress for otherwise profitable firms, too many of which are forced into bankruptcy due to a lack of cash needed to continue day-to-day operations.

Even for firms for which bankruptcy is not an issue, the statement of cash flows can provide investors and other interested parties with vital information. For instance, assume that a firm's income statement reports rising earnings. At the same time, however, the statement of cash flows shows that the firm's inventory is rising faster than sales—often a signal that demand for the firm's products is softening, which may in turn be a sign of impending financial trouble.

> ### >>> Quick Review
>
> **1** List the four financial statements.
>
> **2** How is a balance sheet organized?
>
> **3** Define *accrual accounting*.

6 Financial Ratio Analysis

Accounting professionals fulfill important responsibilities beyond preparing financial statements. In a more critical role, they help managers interpret the statements by comparing data about the firm's current activities to those for previous periods and to results posted by other companies in the industry. *Ratio analysis* is one of the most commonly used tools for measuring a firm's liquidity, profitability, and reliance on debt financing, as well as the effectiveness of management's resource utilization. This analysis also allows comparisons with other firms and with the firm's own past performance.

LIQUIDITY RATIOS

A firm's ability to meet its short-term obligations when they must be paid is measured by *liquidity ratios*. Increasing liquidity reduces the likelihood that a firm will face emergencies caused by the need to raise funds to repay loans. On the other hand, firms with low liquidity may be forced to choose between default and borrowing from high-cost lending sources to meet their maturing obligations.

Two commonly used liquidity ratios are the current ratio and the acid-test, or quick, ratio. The current ratio compares current assets to current liabilities, giving executives information about the firm's ability to pay its current debts as they mature. The current ratio of Belle's Fine Coffees can be computed as follows (unless indicated, all amounts from the balance sheet or income statement are in thousands of dollars):

$$\text{Current Ratio} = \frac{\text{Current Assets}}{\text{Current Liabilities}} = \frac{5,240}{2,030} = 2.58$$

In other words, Belle's Fine Coffees has $2.58 of current assets for every $1.00 of current liabilities. In general, a current ratio of 2:1 is considered satisfactory liquidity. This rule of thumb must be considered along with other factors, such as the nature of the business, the season, and the quality of the company's management team. Belle's Fine Coffees' management and other interested parties are likely to evaluate this ratio of 2.58:1 by comparing it with ratios for previous operating periods and with industry averages.

The acid-test (or quick) ratio measures the ability of a firm to meet its debt payments on short notice. This ratio compares quick assets—the most liquid current assets—against current liabilities. Quick assets generally consist of cash and equivalents, short-term investments, and accounts receivable. So, generally quick assets equal total current assets minus inventory.

Belle's Fine Coffees' current balance sheet lists total current assets of $5.24 million and inventory of $2.2 million. Therefore, its quick ratio is as follows:

$$\text{Acid-Test Ratio} = \frac{\text{Current Assets} - \text{Inventory}}{\text{Current Liabilities}}$$

$$= \frac{(5,240 - 2,200)}{2,030} = 1.50$$

Because the traditional rule of thumb for an adequate acid-test ratio is around 1:1, Belle's Fine Coffees appears to have a strong level of liquidity. However, the same cautions apply here as for the current ratio. The ratio should be compared with industry averages and data from previous operating periods to determine whether it is adequate for the firm.

ACTIVITY RATIOS

Activity ratios measure the effectiveness of management's use of the firm's resources. One of the most frequently used activity ratios, the inventory turnover ratio, indicates the number of times merchandise moves through a business:

$$\text{Inventory Turnover} = \frac{\text{Cost of Goods Sold}}{\text{Average Inventory}}$$

$$= \frac{10,380}{[(2,200 + 1,850)/2]} = 5.13$$

Average inventory for Belle's Fine Coffees is determined by adding the inventory as of December 31 of the current year ($2.2 million) with the inventory as of December 31 of the previous year ($1.85 million) and dividing it by 2. Comparing the 5.13 inventory turnover ratio with industry standards gives a measure of efficiency. It is important to note, however, that inventory turnover can vary substantially, depending on the products a company sells and the industry in which it operates.

If a company makes a substantial portion of its sales on credit, measuring receivables turnover can provide useful information. Receivables turnover can be calculated as follows:

$$\text{Receivables Turnover} = \frac{\text{Credit Sales}}{\text{Average Accounts Receivable}}$$

Because Belle's Fine Coffees is a wholesaler, let's assume that all of its sales are credit sales. Average receivables equals the simple average of current year's receivables and previous year's receivables. The ratio for the company is:

$$\text{Receivables Turnover} = \frac{17,300}{[(990 + 775)/2]} = 19.60$$

Dividing 365 by the figure for receivables turnover, 19.6, equals the average age of receivables, 18.62 days. Assume Belle's Fine Coffees expects its retail customers to pay outstanding bills within 30 days of the date of purchase. Given that the average age of its receivables is less than 30 days, Belle's Fine Coffees appears to be doing a good job collecting its credit sales.

Another measure of efficiency is total asset turnover. It measures how much in sales each dollar invested in assets generates:

$$\text{Total Asset Turnover} = \frac{\text{Sales}}{\text{Average Total Assets}}$$

$$= \frac{17,300}{[(8,790 + 7,305)/2]} = 2.15$$

Average total assets for Belle's Fine Coffees equals total assets as of December 31 of the current year ($8.79 million) plus total assets as of December 31 of the previous year ($7.305 million) divided by 2.

Belle's Fine Coffees generates about $2.15 in sales for each dollar invested in assets. Although a higher ratio generally indicates that a firm is operating more efficiently, care must be taken when comparing firms that operate in different industries. Some industries simply require higher investment in assets than do other industries.

PROFITABILITY RATIOS

Some ratios measure the organization's overall financial performance by evaluating its ability to generate revenues in excess of operating costs and other expenses. These measures are called *profitability ratios*. To compute these ratios, accountants compare the firm's earnings with total sales or investments. Over a period of time, profitability ratios may reveal the effectiveness of management in operating the business. Three important profitability ratios are gross profit margin, net profit margin, and return on equity:

$$\text{Gross Profit Margin} = \frac{\text{Gross Profit}}{\text{Sales}} = \frac{6,920}{17,300} = 40.0\%$$

$$\text{Net Profit Margin} = \frac{\text{Net Income}}{\text{Sales}} = \frac{1,917}{17,300} = 11.1\%$$

$$\text{Return on Equity} = \frac{\text{Net Income}}{\text{Average Equity}}$$

$$= \frac{1,1917}{[(5,660 + 4,455)/2]} = 37.9\%$$

All of these ratios indicate positive evaluations of the current operations of Belle's Fine Coffees. For example, the net profit margin indicates that the firm realizes a profit of slightly more than 11 cents on each dollar of merchandise it sells. Although this ratio varies widely among business firms, Belle's Fine Coffees compares favorably with wholesalers in general,

ˇ Starbucks chairman and CEO Howard Schultz walks on stage to address Starbucks shareholders at a recent meeting and to discuss various topics. *Return on equity* may be one such topic.

Elaine Thompson/AP Wide World Photos

which have an average net profit margin of around 5 percent. However, like other profitability ratios, this ratio should be evaluated in relation to profit forecasts, past performance, or more specific industry averages to enhance the interpretation of results. Similarly, although the firm's return on equity of almost 38 percent appears outstanding, the degree of risk in the industry also must be considered.

LEVERAGE RATIOS

Leverage ratios measure the extent to which a firm relies on debt financing. They provide particularly interesting information to potential investors and lenders. If management has assumed too much debt in financing the firm's operations, problems may arise in meeting future interest payments and repaying outstanding loans. As Chapter 17 points out, borrowing money does have advantages. However, relying too heavily on debt financing may lead to bankruptcy. More generally, both investors and lenders may prefer to deal with firms whose owners have invested enough of their own money to avoid overreliance on borrowing. The debt ratio and long-term debt to equity ratio help interested parties evaluate a firm's leverage:

$$\text{Debt Ratio} = \frac{\text{Total Liabilities}}{\text{Total Assets}} = \frac{3,130}{8,790} = 35.6\%$$

$$\text{Long-Term Debt to Equity} = \frac{\text{Long-Term Debt}}{\text{Owners' Equity}} = \frac{1,100}{5,660} = 19.64\%$$

A total liabilities to total assets ratio greater than 50 percent indicates that a firm is relying more on borrowed money than on owners' equity. Because Belle's Fine Coffees' total liabilities to total assets ratio is 35.6 percent, the firm's owners have invested considerably more than the total amount of liabilities shown on the firm's balance sheet. Moreover, the firm's long-term debt to equity ratio is only 19.64 percent, indicating that Belle's Fine Coffees has only about 19.6 cents in long-term debt to every dollar in equity. The long-term debt to equity ratio also indicates that Belle's Fine Coffees hasn't relied very heavily on borrowed money.

The four categories of financial ratios relate balance sheet and income statement data to one another, help management pinpoint a firm's strengths and weaknesses, and indicate areas in need of further investigation. Large multiproduct firms that operate in diverse markets use their information systems to update their financial ratios every day or even every hour. Each company's management must decide on an appropriate review schedule to avoid the costly and time-consuming mistake of overmonitoring.

In addition to calculating financial ratios, managers, investors, and lenders should pay close attention to how accountants apply a number of accounting rules when preparing financial statements. GAAP gives accountants leeway in reporting certain revenues and expenses. Public companies are required to disclose, in footnotes to the financial statements, how the various accounting rules were applied.

>>> **Quick Review**

1. List the four categories of financial ratios.

2. Define the following ratios: *current ratio, inventory turnover, net profit margin,* and *debt ratio.*

7 Budgeting

Although the financial statements discussed in this chapter focus on past business activities, they also provide the basis for planning in the future. A **budget** is a planning and controlling tool that reflects the firm's expected sales revenues, operating expenses, and cash receipts and outlays. It quantifies the firm's plans for a specified future period. Because it reflects management estimates of expected sales, cash inflows and outflows, and costs, the budget is a financial blueprint and can be thought of as a short-term financial plan. It becomes the standard for comparison against actual performance.

budget a planning and controlling tool that reflects the firm's expected sales revenues, operating expenses, and cash receipts and outlays.

Budget preparation is frequently a time-consuming task that involves many people from various departments within the organization. The complexity of the budgeting process varies with the size and complexity of the organization. Large corporations such as United Technologies, Paramount Pictures, and Verizon maintain complex and sophisticated budgeting systems. Besides being planning and controlling tools, their budgets help managers integrate their numerous divisions. But budgeting in both large and small firms is similar to household budgeting in its purpose: to match income and expenses in a way that accomplishes objectives and correctly times cash inflows and outflows.

Because the accounting department is an organization's financial nerve center, it provides many of the data for budget development. The overall master, or operating, budget is actually a composite of many individual budgets for separate units of the firm. These individual budgets typically include the production budget, the cash budget, the capital expenditures budget, the advertising budget, the sales budget, and the travel budget. When you travel for business, you are responsible for keeping track of and recording your own financial transactions for the purpose of preparing your expense report.

Technology has improved the efficiency of the budgeting process. The accounting software products discussed earlier—such as QuickBooks—all include budgeting features. Moreover, modules designed for specific businesses are often available from third parties. Many banks now offer their customers personal financial management tools (PFMs) developed by software companies. Whether or not your bank offers PFM, there are many providers

Birchwood Paper Company
Four-Month Cash Budget

($ thousands)	May	June	July	August
Gross sales	$1,200.0	$3,200.0	$5,500.0	$4,500.0
Cash sales	300.0	800.0	1,375.0	1,125.0
One month prior	600.0	600.0	1,600.0	2,750.0
Two months prior	300.0	300.0	300.0	800.0
Total cash inflows	1,200.0	1,700.0	3,275.0	4,675.0
Purchases				
Cash purchases	1,040.0	1,787.5	1,462.5	390.0
One month prior	390.0	1,040.0	1,787.5	1,462.5
Wages and salaries	250.0	250.0	250.0	250.0
Office rent	75.0	75.0	75.0	75.0
Marketing and other expenses	150.0	150.0	150.0	150.0
Taxes		300.0		
Total cash outflows	1,905.0	3,602.5	3,725.0	2,327.5
Net cash flow				
(Inflows − Outflows)	(705.0)	(1,902.5)	(450.0)	2,347.5
Beginnning cash balance	250.0	150.0	150.0	150.0
Net cash flow	(705.0)	(1,902.5)	(450.0)	2,347.5
Ending cash balance	(455.0)	(1,752.5)	(300.0)	2,497.5
Target cash balance	150.0	150.0	150.0	150.0
Surplus (deficit)	(605.0)	(1,902.5)	(450.0)	2,347.5
Cumulative surplus (deficit)	(605.0)	(2,507.5)	(2,957.5)	610.0

FIGURE 15.7 Four-Month Cash Budget for Birchwood Paper Company

offering low or no cost software to help individuals and businesses keep track of their finances. Many of these software solutions integrate with smart phones and tablets allowing consumers to manage their finances remotely.[7]

One of the most important budgets prepared by firms is the *cash budget*. The cash budget, usually prepared monthly, tracks the firm's cash inflows and outflows. **FIGURE 15.7** illustrates a sample cash budget for Birchwood Paper, a small paper products company. The company has set a $150,000 target cash balance. The cash budget indicates months in which the firm will need temporary loans—May, June, and July—and how much it will need (close to $3 million). The document also indicates that Birchwood will generate a cash surplus in August and can begin repaying the short-term loan. Finally, the cash budget produces a tangible standard against which to compare actual cash inflows and outflows.

>>> Quick Review

1 What is a budget?

2 How is a cash budget organized?

8 International Accounting

Today, accounting procedures and practices must be adapted to accommodate an international business environment. The Coca-Cola Company and McDonald's both generate more than half their annual revenues from sales outside the United States. Nestlé, the giant chocolate and food products firm, operates throughout the world. It derives 98 percent of its revenues from outside Switzerland, its home country. International accounting practices for global firms must reliably translate the financial statements of the firm's international affiliates, branches, and subsidiaries and convert data about foreign currency transactions to dollars. Also, foreign currencies and exchange rates influence the accounting and financial reporting processes of firms operating internationally.

INTERNATIONAL ACCOUNTING STANDARDS

The International Accounting Standards Committee (IASC) was established in 1973 to promote worldwide consistency in financial reporting practices and soon developed its first set of accounting standards and interpretations. In 2001, the IASC became

International Accounting Standards Board (IASB) organization established in 1973 to promote worldwide consistency in financial reporting practices.

International Financial Reporting Standards (IFRS) standards and interpretations adopted by the IASB.

the **International Accounting Standards Board (IASB). International Financial Reporting Standards (IFRS)** are the standards and interpretations adopted by the IASB. The IASB operates in much the same manner as the FASB does in the United States, interpreting and modifying IFRS.

Because of the boom in worldwide trade, there is a real need for comparability of and uniformity in international accounting rules. Trade agreements such as NAFTA and the expansion of the European Union have only heightened interest in creating a uniform set of global accounting rules. In addition, an increasing number of investors are buying shares in foreign multinational corporations, and they need a practical way to evaluate firms in other countries. To assist global investors, more and more firms are beginning to report their financial information according to international accounting standards. This practice helps investors make informed decisions.

How does IFRS differ from GAAP? Although many similarities exist, they have some important differences. For example, under GAAP plant, property, and equipment are reported on the balance sheet at the historical cost minus depreciation. Under IFRS, on the other hand, plant, property, and equipment are shown on the balance sheet at current market value. This gives a better picture of the real value of a firm's assets. Many accounting experts believe IFRS is less complicated than GAAP overall and more transparent.[8]

> > > **Quick Review**

1 What is the IASB and what is its purpose?

2 Why is uniformity in international accounting rules important?

What's Ahead? > > >

This chapter describes the role of accounting in an organization. The next two chapters discuss the finance function of an organization: the planning, obtaining, and managing of an organization's funds to accomplish its objectives efficiently and effectively. Chapter 16 outlines the financial system, the system by which funds are transferred from savers to borrowers. Chapter 17 discusses the role of finance and the financial manager in an organization.

Weekly Updates spark classroom debate around current events that apply to your business course topics. http://www.wileybusinessupdates.com

NOTES

1. Jason Bramwell, "Community Service Is a Responsibility BKD Takes Full Throttle," *AccountingWeb*, June 3, 2013, http://www.accountingweb.com; company Web site, www.bkd.com, accessed May 20, 2013.

2. Bureau of Labor Statistics, *Occupational Outlook Handbook, 2012–2013*, http://data.bls.gov, accessed May 20, 2013.

3. National Association of Colleges and Employers, *Job Outlook 2013*, http://www.naceweb.org, accessed June 10, 2013.

4. AARP Foundation Tax-Aide Locator, http://www.aarp.org, accessed May 20, 2013.

5. "2013 *Accounting Today* Top 100 Firms & Regional Leaders," March 11, 2013, http://digital.accountingtoday.com.

6. Company Web site, Johnson & Johnson, "2012 Historical Financial Review," http://www.investor.jnj.com, accessed June 10, 2013.

7. Jill Duffy, "The Best Personal Finance Software," PCMag.com, May 16, 2013, http://www.pcmag.com.

8. Ra'id Marie, "IFRS vs. GAAP—What Does This Have to Do with the Financial Crisis?" *Meirc Training and Consulting*, http://www.meirc.com, accessed May 20, 2013; Michael Cohn, "Investors Predict U.S. Will Adopt IFRS," *Accounting Today*, November 16, 2012, http://www.accountingtoday.com.

Summary of Learning Objectives

 Discuss the users of accounting information.

Accountants measure, interpret, and communicate financial information to parties inside and outside the firm to support improved decision making. Accountants gather, record, and interpret financial information for management. They also provide financial information on the status and operations of the firm for evaluation by outside parties, such as government agencies, stockholders, potential investors, and lenders. Accounting plays key roles in financing activities, which help start and expand an organization; investing activities, which provide the assets it needs to continue operating; and operating activities, which focus on selling goods and services and paying expenses incurred in regular operations.

accounting process of measuring, interpreting, and communicating financial information to enable people inside and outside the firm to make informed decisions.

 Describe accounting professionals.

Public accountants provide accounting services to other firms or individuals for a fee. They are involved in such activities as auditing, tax return preparation, management consulting, and accounting system design. Management accountants collect and record financial transactions, prepare financial statements, and interpret them for managers in their own firms. Government and not-for-profit accountants perform many of the same functions as management accountants, but they analyze how effectively the organization or agency is operating, rather than its profits and losses.

public accountant one who provides accounting services to individuals or business firms for a fee.

 Identify the foundation of the accounting system.

The foundation of the accounting system in the United States is GAAP (generally accepted accounting principles), a set of guidelines or standards that accountants follow. There are four basic requirements to which all accounting rules should adhere: consistency, relevance, reliability, and comparability. The Financial Accounting Standards Board (FASB), an independent body made up of accounting professionals, is primarily responsible for evaluating, setting, and modifying GAAP. The U.S. Securities and Exchange Commission (SEC) also plays a role in establishing and modifying accounting standards for public companies, firms whose shares are traded in the financial markets.

generally accepted accounting principles (GAAP) guidelines on the conventions, rules, and procedures for determining acceptable accounting and financial reporting practices.

Financial Accounting Standards Board (FASB) an organization responsible for evaluating, setting, or modifying GAAP in the United States.

Foreign Corrupt Practices Act federal law that prohibits U.S. citizens and companies from bribing foreign officials in order to win or continue business.

4 **Outline the steps in the accounting cycle.**

The accounting process involves recording, classifying, and summarizing data about transactions and then using this information to produce financial statements for the firm's managers and other interested parties. Transactions are recorded chronologically in journals, posted in ledgers, and then summarized in accounting statements. Today, much of this activity takes place electronically. The basic accounting equation states that assets (what a firm owns) must always equal liabilities (what a firm owes creditors) plus owners' equity. This equation also illustrates double-entry bookkeeping, the process by which accounting transactions are recorded. Under double-entry bookkeeping, each individual transaction must have an offsetting transaction.

accounting cycle set of activities involved in converting information and individual transactions into financial statements.

asset anything of value owned or leased by a business.

liability anything owed to creditors—the claims of a firm's creditors.

owners' equity the owner's initial investment in the business plus profits that were not paid out to owners over time in the form of cash dividends.

accounting equation formula that states that assets must equal liabilities plus owners' equity.

$$Assets = Liabilities + Owners' Equity$$

double-entry bookkeeping process by which accounting transactions are recorded; each transaction must have an offsetting transaction.

5 Explain financial statements.

- The *balance sheet* shows the financial position of a company on a particular date. The three major classifications of balance sheet data are the components of the accounting equation: assets, liabilities, and owners' equity.

- The *income statement* shows the results of a firm's operations over a specific period. It focuses on the firm's activities—its revenues and expenditures—and the resulting profit or loss during the period. The major components of the income statement are revenues, cost of goods sold, expenses, and profit or loss.

- The *statement of owners' equity* shows the components of the change in owners' equity from the end of the prior year to the end of the current year.

- The *statement of cash flows* records a firm's cash receipts and cash payments during an accounting period. It outlines the sources and uses of cash in the basic business activities of operating, investing, and financing.

balance sheet statement of a firm's financial position on a particular date.

income statement financial record summarizing a firm's financial performance in terms of revenues, expenses, and profits over a given time period, such as a quarter or a year.

statement of owners' equity record of the change in owners' equity from the end of one fiscal period to the end of the next.

statement of cash flows statement showing the sources and uses of cash during a period of time.

accrual accounting method that records revenues and expenses when they occur, not necessarily when cash actually changes hands.

6 Discuss financial ratio analysis.

Financial ratios help managers and outside evaluators compare a firm's current financial information with that of previous years and with results for other firms in the same industry.

- *Liquidity ratios* measure a firm's ability to meet short-term obligations. Examples are the current ratio and the quick, or acid-test, ratio.

- *Activity ratios*—such as the inventory turnover ratio, accounts receivable turnover ratio, and the total asset turnover ratio—measure how effectively a firm uses its resources.

- *Profitability ratios* assess the overall financial performance of the business. The gross profit margin, net profit margin, and return on owners' equity are examples of profitability ratios.

- *Leverage ratios*, such as the total liabilities to total assets ratio and the long-term debt to equity ratio, measure the extent to which the firm relies on debt to finance its operations.

7 Describe the role of budgeting.

Budgets are financial guidelines for future periods and reflect expected sales revenues, operating expenses, and cash receipts and outlays. They reflect management expectations for future occurrences and are based on plans that have been made. Budgets are important planning and controlling tools because they provide standards against which actual performance can be measured. One important type of budget is the cash budget, which estimates cash inflows and outflows over a period of time.

budget a planning and controlling tool that reflects the firm's expected sales revenues, operating expenses, and cash receipts and outlays.

8 Outline international accounting practices.

The International Accounting Standards Board (IASB) was established to provide worldwide consistency in financial reporting practices and comparability of and uniformity in international accounting standards. It has developed International Financial Reporting Standards (IFRS). Many countries have already adopted IFRS, and the United States is in the process of making the transition to it.

International Accounting Standards Board (IASB) organization established in 1973 to promote worldwide consistency in financial reporting practices.

International Financial Reporting Standards (IFRS) standards and interpretations adopted by the IASB.

>>> Quick Review >>

LO1

1 Define *accounting*.

2 Who uses accounting information?

3 What three business activities involve accounting?

LO2

1 List the three services offered by public accounting firms.

2 What tasks do management accountants perform?

LO3

1 Define GAAP.

2 Name the four basic requirements to which all accounting rules must adhere.

3 What role does the FASB play?

LO4

1 List the steps in the accounting cycle.

2 What is the accounting equation?

3 Explain how double-entry bookkeeping works.

LO5

1 List the four financial statements.

2 How is a balance sheet organized?

3 Define *accrual accounting*.

LO6

1 List the four categories of financial ratios.

2 Define the following ratios: *current ratio*, *inventory turnover*, *net profit margin*, and *debt ratio*.

LO7

1 What is a budget?

2 How is a cash budget organized?

LO8

1 What is the IASB and what is its purpose?

2 Why is uniformity in international accounting rules important?

16

The Financial System

Learning Objectives

1. **Understand** the financial system.
2. **List** the various types of securities.
3. **Discuss** financial markets.
4. **Understand** the stock markets.
5. **Evaluate** financial institutions.
6. **Explain** the role of the Federal Reserve System.
7. **Describe** the regulation of the financial system.
8. **Discuss** the global perspective of the financial system.

Community Banks Team Up to Fight the Megabanks

Here's what one customer recently had to say about her relationship with a major U.S. bank: "I'm sick of their fees. I'm sick of not knowing where my money goes."

Does that sound familiar? Millions of bank customers who feel the same are finding smaller community banks and credit unions more appealing alternatives than megabanks, with their multiplying fees and impersonal service. But smaller institutions have been woefully lacking in competitive clout and product offerings compared to major banks like Bank of America and Citibank—until now.

Almost 130 banks and credit unions in 35 states have joined forces under a new national brand called Kasasa, pooling their resources to offer banking products that compete with the big names. BancVue is the parent company of Kasasa; it provides staff training to member institutions and does their marketing and promotion. Member banks pay Kasasa a fee based on their size and contribute some marketing funds. The small-bank alliance expects to double its membership soon, hoping to reach 1,000 members within a few years.

And how does the Kasasa bank alliance pay off for bank customers? How about a checking account that earns 4 percent interest with no fees and no minimum. Sound good? You are not alone. Consumers are moving their accounts, and Kasasa member banks have seen increases in checking and savings deposits between 15 and 25 percent.[1]

Overview > > >

Businesses, governments, and individuals often need to raise capital. Assume the owner of a small business either forecasts a sharp increase or drop in sales; one might require more inventory and the other reduced production in order to survive. The owner might turn to a major bank or a nontraditional lender like a Kasasa member bank for a loan that would provide the needed cash for either situation. On the other hand, some individuals and businesses have incomes that are greater than their current expenditures and wish to earn a rate of return on the excess funds.

The two transactions just described are small parts of what is known as the **financial system**, the process by which money flows from savers to users. Virtually all businesses, governments, and individuals participate in the financial system, and a well-functioning one is vital to a nation's economic well-being. The financial system is the topic of this chapter.

financial system process by which money flows from savers to users.

The chapter begins by describing the financial system and its components in more detail. Then, the major types of financial instruments, such as stocks and bonds, are outlined. Next the chapter discusses financial markets, where financial instruments are bought and sold, and describes the world's major stock markets, such as the New York Stock Exchange.

Next, banks and other financial institutions are described in depth. The structure and responsibilities of the U.S. Federal Reserve System, along with the tools the Fed uses to control the supply of money and credit, are detailed. The chapter concludes with an overview of the major laws and regulations affecting the financial system and a discussion of today's global financial system.

1 Understanding the Financial System

Households, businesses, government, financial institutions, and financial markets together form what is known as the financial system. A simple diagram of the financial system is shown in **FIGURE 16.1**.

On the left are savers—those with excess funds. For a variety of reasons, savers choose not to spend all of their current income, so they have a surplus of funds. Users are the opposite of savers;

their spending needs exceed their current income, so they have a deficit. They need to obtain additional funds to make up the difference. Savings are provided by some households, businesses, and the government, but other households, businesses, and the government are also borrowers. Households may need money to buy automobiles or homes. Businesses may need money to purchase inventory or build new production facilities. Governments may need money to build highways and courthouses.

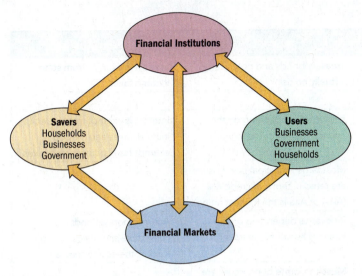

FIGURE 16.1 Overview of the Financial System and Its Components

Generally, in the United States, households are net savers—meaning that as a whole they save more funds than they use—whereas businesses and governments are net users—meaning that they use more funds than they save. The fact that most of the net savings in the U.S. financial system are provided by households may be a bit of a surprise initially because Americans do not have a reputation for being thrifty. Yet even though the savings rate of American households is low compared with those of other countries, American households still save hundreds of billions of dollars each year.

Funds can be transferred between savers and users in two ways: directly and indirectly. A direct transfer means that the user raises the needed funds directly from savers. While direct transfers occur, the vast majority of funds flow through either financial markets or financial institutions. For example, assume a local school district needs to build a new high school. The district doesn't have enough cash on hand to pay for the school construction costs, so it sells bonds to investors (savers) in the financial market. The district uses the proceeds from the sale to pay for the new school and in return pays bond investors interest each year for the use of their money.

The other way in which funds can be transferred indirectly is through financial institutions—for example, commercial banks like Fifth Third Bank or Regions Bank. The bank pools customer deposits and uses the funds to make loans to businesses and households. These borrowers pay the bank interest, and it in turn pays depositors interest for the use of their money.

>>> Quick Review

1 What is the financial system?

2 In the financial system, who are the borrowers and who are the savers?

3 Name the two most common ways funds are transferred between borrowers and savers.

2 Types of Securities

For the funds they borrow from savers, businesses and governments provide different types of guarantees for repayment. **Securities**, also called *financial instruments*, represent obligations on the part of the issuers—businesses and governments—to provide the purchasers with expected or stated returns on the funds invested or loaned. Securities can be grouped into three categories: money market instruments, bonds, and stock. Money market instruments and bonds are both debt securities. Stocks are units of ownership in corporations like General Electric, McDonald's, Apple, and PepsiCo.

> **securities** financial instruments that represent obligations on the part of the issuers to provide the purchasers with expected stated returns on the funds invested or loaned.

MONEY MARKET INSTRUMENTS

Money market instruments are short-term debt securities issued by governments, financial institutions, and corporations. Money market instruments are generally low-risk securities and are purchased by investors when they have surplus cash. Examples of money market instruments include U.S. Treasury bills, commercial paper, and bank certificates of deposit.

Treasury bills are short-term securities issued by the U.S. Treasury and backed by the full faith and credit of the U.S. government. Treasury bills are sold with a maturity of 30, 90, 180, or 360 days and have a minimum denomination of $1,000. They are considered virtually risk-free and easy to resell. *Commercial paper* is securities sold by corporations, such as Raytheon, that mature in from 1 to 270 days from the date of issue. Although slightly riskier than Treasury bills, commercial paper is still generally considered a very low risk security.

A *certificate of deposit (CD)* is a time deposit at a financial institution, such as a commercial bank, savings bank, or credit union. The sizes and maturity dates of CDs vary considerably and can often be tailored to meet the needs of purchasers. CDs in denominations of $250,000 or less per depositor are federally insured.

BONDS

Bondholders are creditors of a corporation or government body. Bonds are issued in various denominations, or face values, usually between $1,000 and $25,000. Each issue indicates a rate of interest to be paid to the bondholder—stated as a percentage of the bond's face value—as well as a maturity date on which the bondholder is paid the bond's full face value. Because bondholders are creditors, they have a claim on the firm's assets that must be satisfied before any claims of stockholders in the event of the firm's bankruptcy, reorganization, or liquidation.

A prospective bond investor can choose among a variety of bonds. The major types of bonds are summarized in TABLE 16.1. *Government bonds* are bonds sold by the U.S. Department of the

TABLE 16.1 What are the major types of bonds?

Issuer	Types of Securities	Risk	Special Features
U.S. Treasury (government bonds)	Notes: Mature in 10 years or less from date of issue.	Treasury bonds and notes carry virtually no risk.	Interest is exempt from state income taxes.
	Bonds: Mature in 30 years from date of issue.		
State and local governments (municipal bonds)	General obligation: Issued by state or local governmental units with taxing authority; backed by the full faith and credit of the state where issued.	Risk varies, depending on the financial health of the issuer.	Interest is exempt from federal income taxes and may be exempt from state income taxes.
	Revenue: Issued to pay for projects that generate revenue, such as water systems or toll roads; revenue from project used to pay principal and interest.	Most large municipal bond issues are rated in terms of credit risk (AAA or Aaa is the highest rating).	
Corporations	Secured bonds: Bonds are backed by specific assets.	Risk varies depending on the financial health of the issuer.	A few corporate bonds are convertible into shares of common stock of the issuing company.
	Unsecured bonds (debentures): Backed by the financial health and reputation of the issuer.	Most corporate bond issues are rated in terms of credit risk (AAA or Aaa is the highest rating).	
Financial institutions	Mortgage pass-through securities.	Generally very low risk.	They pay monthly income consisting of both interest and principal.

Treasury. Because government bonds are backed by the full faith and credit of the U.S. government, they are considered the least risky of all bonds. The Treasury sells bonds that mature in 2, 5, 10, and 30 years from the date of issue.

Municipal bonds are bonds issued by state or local governments. Two types of municipal bonds are available. A *revenue bond* is a bond issue whose proceeds will be used to pay for a project that will produce revenue, such as a toll road or bridge. The proceeds of a *general obligation bond* are to be used to pay for a project that will not produce any revenue,

Corporate bonds are a diverse group and often vary based on the collateral—the property pledged by the borrower—that backs the bond. For example, a *secured bond* is backed by a specific pledge of company assets. These assets are collateral, just like a home is collateral for a mortgage. However, many firms also issue unsecured bonds, called *debentures*. These bonds are backed only by the financial reputation of the issuing corporation.

Two factors determine the price of a bond: its risk and its interest rate. Bonds vary considerably in terms of risk. One tool that bond investors use to assess the risk of a bond is its *bond rating*. Several investment firms rate corporate and municipal bonds, the best known of which are Standard & Poor's (S&P), Moody's, and Fitch. TABLE 16.2 lists the S&P bond ratings. Moody's and Fitch use similar rating systems. Bonds with the lowest level of risk are rated AAA. As ratings descend, risk increases. Bonds with ratings of BBB and above are classified as *investment-grade bonds*. By contrast, bonds with ratings of BB and below are classified as *speculative* or *junk bonds*. Junk bonds attract investors by offering high interest rates in exchange for greater risk.

Another important influence on bond prices is the *market interest rate*. Because bonds pay fixed rates of interest, as market interest rates rise, bond prices fall, and vice versa. For instance,

the price of a ten-year bond, paying 5 percent per year, would fall by about 8 percent if market interest rates rose from 5 percent to 6 percent.

STOCK

The basic form of corporate ownership is embodied in **common stock**. Purchasers of common stock are the true owners of a corporation. Holders of common stock vote on major company decisions, such as purchasing another company or electing a board of directors. In return for the money they invest, they expect to receive some sort of return. This return can come in the form of dividend payments, expected price appreciation, or both. Dividends vary widely from

common stock basic form of corporate ownership.

TABLE 16.2 Can you list the Standard & Poor's bond ratings?

Highest	AAA	Investment grade
	AA	
	A	
	BBB	
	BB	Speculative grade
	B	
	CCC	
	CC	
Lowest	C	

NOTE: Standard & Poor's occasionally assigns a plus or minus following the letter rating. For instance, AA+ means the bond is higher quality than most AA bonds but hasn't quite met AAA standards. Ratings below C indicate that the bond may not be paying interest.

A certificate for General Motors' common stock.

❸ Financial Markets

Securities are issued and traded in **financial markets**. Although there are many different types of financial markets, one of the most important distinctions is between primary and secondary markets. In the **primary markets**, firms and governments issue securities and sell them initially to the general public. When a company needs capital to purchase inventory, expand a plant, make major investments, acquire another firm, or pursue other business goals, it may sell a bond or stock issue to the investing public.

financial markets
market in which securities are issued and traded.

primary markets
financial market in which firms and governments issue securities and sell them initially to the general public.

A stock offering gives investors the opportunity to purchase ownership shares in a firm and to participate in its future growth in exchange for providing current capital. When a company offers stock for sale to the general public for the first time, it is called an *initial public offering (IPO)*. Analysts predict IPOs from a number of American companies, notably Twitter and Box.[2]

Both profit-seeking corporations and government agencies also rely on primary markets to raise funds by issuing bonds. For example, the federal government sells Treasury bonds through an open auction to finance part of federal outlays such as interest on outstanding federal debt. State and local governments sell bonds to finance capital projects such as the construction of sewer systems, streets, and fire stations. Sales of most corporate and municipal securities are made via financial institutions such as Morgan Stanley. These institutions purchase the issue from the firm or government and then resell the issue to investors. This process is known as *underwriting*.

While the primary market is the way corporations and governments raise finds, most of the stock and bond trading that happens on a daily basis happens in the **secondary market**, a collection of financial markets in which previously issued securities are traded among investors. The corporations or governments that originally issued the securities being traded are not directly involved in the secondary market. They make no payments when securities are sold nor receive any of the proceeds when securities are purchased. The New York Stock Exchange (NYSE), for example, is a secondary market. In terms of the dollar value of securities bought and sold, the secondary market is four to five times as large as the primary market. Each day, more than 1.4 billion shares worth about $55 billion are traded on the NYSE.[3] The characteristics of the world's major stock exchanges are discussed in the next section.

secondary market
collection of financial markets in which previously issued securities are traded among investors.

firm to firm. As a general rule, faster-growing companies pay less in dividends because they need more funds to finance their growth. Consequently, investors expect stocks paying little or no cash dividends to show greater price appreciation compared with stocks paying more generous cash dividends.

Common stockholders benefit from company success, and they risk the loss of their investments if the company fails. If a firm dissolves, claims of creditors must be satisfied before stockholders receive anything. Because creditors have the first (or senior) claim to assets, holders of common stock are said to have a residual claim on company assets.

The market value of a stock is the price at which the stock is currently selling. For example, Facebook's stock price fluctuated between $17.55 and $45.00 per share during a recent year. What determines this market value is complicated; many variables cause stock prices to move up or down. However, in the long run, stock prices tend to follow a company's profits.

In addition to common stock, a few companies also issue *preferred stock*—stock whose holders receive preference in the payment of dividends. General Motors and Ford are examples of firms with preferred stock outstanding. Also, if a company is dissolved, holders of preferred stock have claims on the firm's assets that are ahead of the claims of common stockholders. On the other hand, preferred stockholders rarely have any voting rights, and the dividend they are paid is fixed, regardless of how profitable the firm becomes. Therefore, although preferred stock is legally classified as equity, many investors consider it to be more like a bond than common stock.

>>> Quick Review

1. Name the major types of securities.

2. What is a government bond? A municipal bond?

3. Why do investors buy common stock?

> > > **Quick Review**

1. What is a financial market?

2. Distinguish between a primary and a secondary financial market.

3. Briefly explain the role of financial institutions in the sale of securities.

4 Understanding Stock Markets

Stock markets, or **exchanges**, are probably the best known of the world's financial markets. In these markets, shares of stock are bought and sold by investors. The two largest stock markets in the world, the New York Stock Exchange (NYSE) and the NASDAQ stock market, are located in the United States. The Dow Jones Industrial Average (often referred to as the Dow) is a price-weighted average of the 30 most significant stocks traded on the NYSE and the NASDAQ.

stock markets (exchanges) market in which shares of stock are bought and sold by investors.

252

THE NEW YORK STOCK EXCHANGE

The New York Stock Exchange—sometimes referred to as the Big Board—is the most famous and one of the oldest stock markets in the world, having been founded in 1792. Today, the stocks of about 2,800 companies are listed on the NYSE. These stocks represent most of the largest, best-known companies in the United States and have a total market value exceeding $18 trillion. In terms of the total value of stock traded, the NYSE is the world's largest stock market.

THE NASDAQ STOCK MARKET

The world's second-largest stock market, NASDAQ, is very different from the NYSE. NASDAQ—which stands for National Association of Securities Dealers Automated Quotation—is actually a computerized communications network that links member investment firms. It is the world's largest intranet. All trading on NASDAQ takes place through its intranet rather than on a trading floor. More than 3,300 companies have their stocks listed on NASDAQ. While NASDAQ-listed corporations tend to be smaller firms and less well known than NYSE-listed ones, NASDAQ is also home to some of the largest U.S. companies and iconic brands—for example, Amgen, Cisco Systems, Dell, Intel, and Microsoft.

FOREIGN STOCK MARKETS

Stock markets exist throughout the world. Virtually all developed countries and many developing countries have stock exchanges.

∧ Often referred to as the Dow, the Dow Jones Industrial Average is a price-weighted average of the 30 most significant stocks traded on the NYSE and the NASDAQ.

Examples include Mumbai, Helsinki, Hong Kong, Mexico City, Paris, and Toronto. One of the largest stock exchanges outside the United States is the London Stock Exchange. Founded in the early 19th century, the London Stock Exchange lists approximately 3,000 stock and bond issues by companies from more than 70 countries around the world. Trading on the London Stock Exchange takes place using a NASDAQ-type computerized communications network.

The London Stock Exchange is the most international of all stock markets. Approximately two-thirds of all cross-border trading in the world—for example, the trading of stocks of American companies outside the United States—take place in London. It is

∨ Established in the 1800s, the London Stock Exchange is one of the largest stock markets outside of the United States. The Exchange uses a trading communications network similar to the one used at the NASDAQ.

not uncommon for institutional investors in the United States to trade NYSE- or NASDAQ-listed stocks in London.

INVESTOR PARTICIPATION IN THE STOCK MARKETS

Because most investors aren't members of the NYSE or any other stock market, they need to use the services of a brokerage firm to buy or sell stocks. Examples of brokerage firms include Edward Jones and TD Ameritrade. Investors establish an account with the brokerage firm and then enter orders to trade stocks. The most common type of order is called a *market order*. It instructs the broker to obtain the best possible price—the highest price when selling and the lowest price when buying. If the stock market is open, market orders are filled within seconds. Another popular type of order is called a *limit order*. It sets a price ceiling when buying or a price floor when selling. If the order cannot be executed when it is placed, the order is left with the exchange's market maker. It may be filed later if the price limits are met.

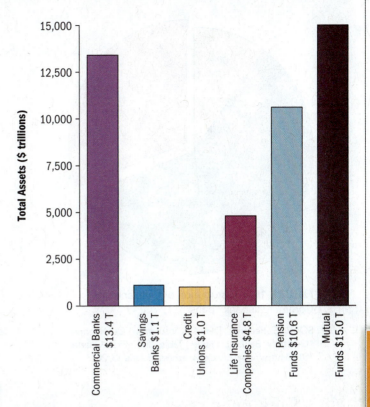

FIGURE 16.2 Assets of Major Financial Institutions

SOURCES: American Council of Life Insurers Web site, "Life Insurer Fact Book 2012," accessed June 16, 2013, http://www.acli.com; Federal Deposit Insurance Corporation, "Statistics at a Glance," http://www.fdic.gov, updated May 29, 2013; Warren S. Hearsch, "U.S. Mutual Fund Assets Set to Pass $15 Trillion," *LifeHealthPro*, February 13, 2013, http://www.lifehealthpro.com; Organization for Economic Co-Operation and Development Web site, "Pension Fund Assets Hit Record USD $20.1 T in 2011, but Investment Performance Weakens," September 2012, Issue 9, page 21, http://www.oecd.org; National Credit Union Association Web site, "Credit Union Industry Assets Top $1 Trillion," June 1, 2012, http://www.ncua.gov.

Quick Review

1. Name the world's two largest stock markets.

2. Why is the London Stock Exchange unique?

3. Explain the difference between a market order and a limit order.

5 Financial Institutions

One of the most important components of the financial system is **financial institutions**. They are an intermediary between savers and borrowers, collecting funds from savers and then lending the funds to individuals, businesses, and governments. Financial institutions greatly increase the efficiency and effectiveness of the transfer of funds from savers to users. Because of financial institutions, savers earn more and users pay less than they would without them. In fact, it is difficult to imagine how any modern economy could function without well-developed financial institutions. Think about how difficult it would be for a businessperson to obtain inventory financing or an individual to purchase a new home without financial institutions. Prospective borrowers would have to identify and negotiate terms with each saver individually.

Traditionally, financial institutions have been classified into depository institutions—institutions that accept deposits that customers can withdraw on demand—and nondepository institutions. Examples of depository institutions include commercial banks,

financial institutions intermediary between savers and borrowers, collecting funds from savers and then lending the funds to individuals, businesses, and governments.

such as US Bancorp and Sun Trust; savings banks, such as Acacia Federal Savings Bank and Ohio Savings Bank; and credit unions, such as the State Employees' Credit Union of North Carolina. Nondepository institutions include life insurance companies, such as Northwestern Mutual; pension funds, such as the Florida state employee pension fund; and mutual funds. In total, financial institutions have trillions of dollars in assets. **FIGURE 16.2** illustrates the size of the most prominent financial institutions.

COMMERCIAL BANKS

Commercial banks are the largest and probably most important financial institution in the United States, and in most other countries as well. In the United States, the approximately 6,000 commercial banks hold total assets of more than $13.3 trillion.[4] Commercial banks offer the most services of any financial institution. These services include a wide range of checking and savings deposit accounts, consumer loans, credit cards, home mortgage loans, business loans, and trust services. Commercial banks also sell other financial products, including securities and insurance.

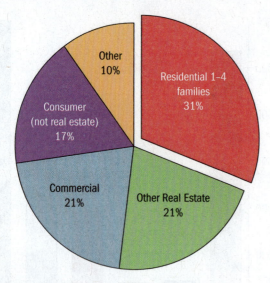

FIGURE 16.3 Distribution of Outstanding Commercial Bank Loans

SOURCE: Federal Deposit Insurance Corporation, "Quarterly Banking Profile: Table III-A, First Quarter 2013," http://www2.fdic.gov, accessed June 13, 2013.

HOW BANKS OPERATE

Banks raise funds by offering a variety of checking and savings deposits to customers. The banks then pool these deposits and lend most of them out in the form of consumer and business loans. Recently, banks held over $8.6 trillion in domestic deposits and had about $7.0 trillion in outstanding loans.[5] The distribution of outstanding loans is shown in **FIGURE 16.3**. As the figure shows, banks lend a great deal of money to both households and businesses for a variety of purposes. Commercial banks are an especially important source of funds for small businesses. When evaluating loan applications, banks consider the borrower's ability and willingness to repay the loan.

Banks make money primarily because the interest rate they charge borrowers is higher than the rate of interest they pay depositors. Banks also make money from other sources, such as fees they charge customers for checking accounts and using automated teller machines.

ELECTRONIC BANKING

More and more funds each year move through electronic funds transfer (EFT) systems, computerized systems for conducting financial transactions over electronic links. Millions of businesses and consumers now pay bills and receive payments electronically. Most employers, for example, directly deposit employee paychecks in their bank accounts rather than issue paper checks to employees. Today nearly all Social Security checks and other federal payments made each year arrive as electronic data rather than paper documents.

ONLINE BANKING

Today, many consumers do some or all of their banking on the Internet. Two types of online banks exist: Internet-only banks

(*direct banks*), such as ING Direct, and traditional brick-and-mortar banks with Web sites, such as JPMorgan Chase and PNC. It appears that direct banks are gaining in popularity. with a recent study showing market share gains for these types of banks compared with all other approaches.[6] Convenience is the primary reason people are attracted to online banking. Customers can transfer money, check account balances, and pay bills at any time. Plus with no branch offices to support, direct banks should be able to offer lower fees and better rates than their brick-and-mortar counterparts.

FEDERAL DEPOSIT INSURANCE

Most commercial bank deposits are insured by the **Federal Deposit Insurance Corporation (FDIC)**, a federal agency. Deposit insurance means that, in the event the bank fails, insured depositors are paid in full by the FDIC, up to $250,000. Federal deposit insurance was enacted by the Banking Act of 1933 as one of the measures designed to restore public confidence in the banking system. Before deposit insurance, so-called *runs* were common as people rushed to withdraw their money from a bank, often just on a rumor that the bank was in precarious financial condition. With more and more withdrawals in a short period, the bank was eventually unable to meet customer demands and closed its doors. Remaining depositors often lost most of the money they had in the bank. Deposit insurance shifts the risk of bank failures from individual depositors to the FDIC. Although banks still fail today, no insured depositor has ever lost any money on deposit up to the FDIC limit.

> **Federal Deposit Insurance Corporation (FDIC)** federal agency that insures deposits at commercial and savings banks.

SAVINGS BANKS AND CREDIT UNIONS

Commercial banks are by far the largest depository financial institution in the United States, but savings banks and credit unions also serve a significant segment of the financial community. Today, savings banks and credit unions offer many of the same services as commercial banks.

Previously, savings banks were called *savings and loan associations* or *thrift institutions*. They were originally established in the early 1800s to make home mortgage loans. Savings and loans raised funds by accepting only savings deposits and then lent these funds to consumers to buy homes. Today, around 971 savings banks operate in the United States, with total assets of about $1.062 trillion.[7] Although savings banks offer many of the same services as commercial banks, including checking accounts, they are not major lenders to businesses.

Credit unions are cooperative financial institutions that are owned by their depositors, all of whom are members. Around 92 million Americans belong to one of the nation's approximately 7,100 credit unions. Combined, credit unions have more than $962 billion in assets. By law, credit union members must share similar occupations, employers, or membership in certain organizations. This law effectively caps the size of credit unions. In fact, the nation's largest bank—JPMorgan Chase—holds more deposits than all the country's credit unions combined.[8]

NONDEPOSITORY FINANCIAL INSTITUTIONS

Nondepository financial institutions accept funds from businesses and households and invest it. Generally, these institutions do not offer checking accounts (demand deposits). Three examples of nondepository financial institutions are insurance companies, pension funds, and finance companies.

- **Insurance companies are organizations that** accept the risk from households and businesses in return for a series of payments, called *premiums. Underwriting* is the process insurance companies use to determine whom to insure and what to charge. During a typical year, insurance companies collect more in premiums than they pay in claims. After they pay operating expenses, they invest this difference. Life insurance companies alone have total assets of more than $4.8 trillion invested in everything from bonds and stocks to real estate.[9] Examples of life insurers include Prudential and New York Life.

- **Pension funds** provide retirement benefits to workers and their families. They are set up by employers and are funded by regular contributions made by employers and employees. Because pension funds have predictable long-term cash inflows and very predictable cash outflows, they invest heavily in assets, such as common stocks and real estate. U.S. private pension funds have more than $10.58 trillion in assets.[10]

- **Finance companies** offer short-term loans to borrowers. Commercial finance companies, such as Ford Credit, John Deere Capital Corporation, and Dollar Financial, supply short-term funds to businesses that pledge tangible assets such as inventory, accounts receivable, machinery, or property as collateral for the loan. A consumer finance company plays a similar role for consumers.

∨ Life insurance companies such as New York Life are a major source of financing for businesses. Considered a *nondepository financial institution,* insurance companies accept funds from consumers and businesses and invest most of the money.

John Crowe/Alamy Limited

MUTUAL FUNDS

One of the most significant types of financial institutions today is the mutual fund. *Mutual funds* are financial intermediaries that raise money from investors by selling shares. They then use the money to invest in securities that are consistent with the mutual fund's objectives, often hiring a professional manager to oversee the investments. Mutual funds have become extremely popular over the last few decades and currently have about $15 trillion in assets. [11]

6 The Role of the Federal Reserve System

Created in 1913, the **Federal Reserve System**, or the **Fed**, is the central bank of the United States and an important part of the nation's financial system. The Fed has four basic responsibilities: regulating commercial banks, performing banking-related activities for the U.S. Department of the Treasury, providing services for banks, and setting monetary policy.

Federal Reserve System (Fed) the central bank of the United States.

MONETARY POLICY

The Fed's most important function is monetary policy—that is, controlling the supply of money and credit. The Fed's job is to make sure the money supply grows at an appropriate rate, allowing the economy to expand and keeping inflation in check. If the money supply grows too slowly, economic growth will slow, unemployment will rise, and the risk of a recession will increase. If the money supply grows too rapidly, inflationary pressures will build. The Fed uses its policy to push interest rates up or down. By pushing the interest rates up, the growth rate of the money supply slows. By pushing the interest rates down, the growth rate of the money supply tends to rise.

The two common measures of the money supply are called M1 and M2. M1 consists of money in circulation and balances in bank checking accounts. M2 equals M1 plus balances in some savings accounts and money market mutual funds. The Fed has three major policy tools for controlling the growth in the supply of money and credit: reserve requirements, the discount rate, and open market operations.

The Fed requires banks to maintain reserves—defined as cash in their vaults plus deposits at district Federal Reserve banks or other banks—equal to a certain percentage of what the banks hold in deposits. For example, if the Fed sets the reserve requirement at 5 percent, a bank that receives a $500 deposit must reserve $25, so it has only $475 to invest or lend to individuals or businesses. By

TABLE 16.3 What three tools does the Fed use to regulate economic growth?

Tool	What It Is	How It Affects the Money Supply	How It Affects Interest Rates and the Economy	When the Fed Uses It
Reserve requirements	Change in the percentage of deposits banks hold in reserve	An increase slows the growth of the money supply	An increase pushes up interest rates and slows economic growth	Rarely
Discount rate	Change in the rate the Fed charges banks for loans	An increase slows the growth of the money supply	An increase pushes up interest rates and slows economic growth	Only in conjunction with open market operations
Open market operations	Buying and selling Treasury securities to increase or decrease bank reserves	Selling Treasury securities reduces bank reserves and slows the growth of the money supply	Selling Treasury securities pushes up interest rates and slows economic growth	Frequently

changing the reserve requirement, the Fed can affect the amount of money available for making loans. The higher the reserve requirement, the less banks can lend out to consumers and businesses. The lower the reserve requirement, the more banks can lend out. Because any change in the reserve requirement can have a sudden and dramatic impact on the money supply, the Fed rarely uses this tool.

Another policy tool is the so-called *discount rate,* the interest rate at which Federal Reserve banks make short-term loans to member banks. A bank may need a short-term loan if transactions leave it short of reserves. If the Fed wants to slow the growth rate in the money supply, it increases the discount rate. When this increase makes it more expensive for banks to borrow money, they in turn raise the interest rate they charge on loans to consumers and businesses. The end result is a slowdown in economic activity. Lowering the discount rate has the opposite effect.

The third policy tool, and the one most often used, is *open market operations,* the technique of controlling the money supply growth rate by buying or selling U.S. Treasury securities. If the Fed buys Treasury securities, the money it pays enters circulation, increasing the money supply and lowering interest rates. When the Fed sells Treasury securities, money is taken out of circulation and interest rates rise. When the Fed uses open market operations, it employs the so-called *federal funds rate*—the rate at which banks lend money to each other overnight—as its benchmark. TABLE 16.3 illustrates how the Federal Reserve uses tools to regulate the economy.

> >> Quick Review

1. What is the Federal Reserve System?

2. How is the Fed organized?

3. List the three tools the Fed uses to control the supply of money and credit.

7 Regulation of the Financial System

Given the importance of the financial system, it is probably not surprising that many components are subject to government regulation and oversight. In addition, industry self-regulation is commonplace.

BANK REGULATION

Banks are among the nation's most heavily regulated businesses—primarily to ensure public confidence in the safety and security of the banking system. Banks are critical to the overall functioning of the economy, and a collapse of the banking system can have disastrous results. Many believe one of the major causes of the Great Depression was the collapse of the banking system that started in the late 1920s.

Banks and credit unions are subject to periodic examination by state or federal regulators. Examinations ensure that the institution is following sound banking practices and is complying with all applicable regulations. These examinations include the review of detailed reports on the bank's operating and financial condition as well as on-site inspections. Regulators can impose penalties on institutions deemed not in compliance with sound banking practices, including forcing the delinquent financial institution into a merger with a healthier one.

GOVERNMENT REGULATION OF THE FINANCIAL MARKETS

Regulation of U.S. financial markets is primarily a function of the federal government, although states also regulate them. Federal regulation grew out of various trading abuses during the 1920s. To restore confidence and stability in the financial markets after the 1929 stock market crash, Congress passed a series of landmark legislative acts that have formed the basis of federal securities regulation ever since. Many other regulations have followed, including the Dodd-Frank Wall Street Reform and Consumer Protection Act, signed into law in 2010.

The U.S. Securities and Exchange Commission, created in 1934, is the principal federal regulatory overseer of the securities markets. The SEC's mission is to administer securities laws and protect investors in public securities transactions. The SEC has broad enforcement power. It can pursue civil actions against individuals and corporations, but actions requiring criminal proceedings are referred to the U.S. Justice Department.

The SEC requires virtually all new public issues of corporate securities to be registered. As part of the registration process for a new security issue, the issuer must prepare a *prospectus*. The typical prospectus gives a detailed description of

∧ The Securities and Exchange Commission is charged with regulating financial markets. Its Web site, shown here, is a good source of information for would-be investors.

8 The Financial System: A Global Perspective

Not surprisingly, the global financial system is becoming more and more integrated each year. With financial markets in existence throughout the world, shares of U.S. firms trade in other countries and shares of international companies trade in the United States. In fact, investors in China and Japan own more U.S. Treasury securities than do domestic investors.

Financial institutions have also become a global industry. Major U.S. banks—such as Wells Fargo and Bank of America—have extensive international operations where they maintain offices, lend money, and accept deposits from customers.

Although most Americans recognize large U.S. banks such as Citibank among the global financial giants, three of the world's 20 largest banks (measured by total assets) are U.S. institutions—JPMorgan Chase (ranked 12th), Bank of America (ranked 19th), and Citibank (ranked 20th). The other 17 are based in continental Europe, Great Britain, and Asia. The world's largest bank is Deutsche Bank AG, based in Germany, with $2.8 trillion in assets. These international banks operate worldwide, including locations in the United States.[12]

Like the United States, virtually all nations have some sort of a central bank. These banks play roles much

the company issuing the securities, including financial data, products, research and development projects, and pending litigation. It also describes the stock or bond issue and underwriting agreement in detail. The registration process seeks to guarantee full and fair disclosure. The SEC does not rule on the investment merits of a registered security. It is concerned only that an issuer gives investors enough information to make their own informed decisions.

insider trading use of material nonpublic information about a company to make investment profits.

One area to which the SEC pays particular attention is insider trading. **Insider trading** is defined as the use of material nonpublic information about a company to make investment profits. Examples of material nonpublic information include a pending merger or a major oil discovery, which could affect the firm's stock price.

> ### >>> Quick Review
>
> **1** Who regulates banks?
>
> **2** What is insider trading?

∨ In Frankfurt, Germany, a sculpture of the euro—the symbol for the European Union's currency—stands outside the headquarters of Europe's central bank. The 12 gold stars represent all the peoples of Europe.

like that of the Federal Reserve, controlling the money supply and regulating the banks. Policymakers at those banks often respond to changes in the U.S. financial system by making changes in their own system. For example, if the Fed lowers interest rates, the central bank in Japan may do the same. Such changes can influence events around the world.

>>> **Quick Review**

1 Where do U.S. banks rank compared with banks around the world?

2 How are foreign banks controlled?

What's Ahead? > > >

This chapter explored the financial system, a key component of the U.S. economy and something that affects many aspects of contemporary business. The financial system is the process by which funds are transferred between savers and borrowers and includes securities, financial markets, and financial institutions. The chapter also described the role of the Federal Reserve and discussed the global financial system. Chapter 17 discusses the finance function of a business, including the role of the financial managers, financial planning, asset management, and sources of short- and long-term funds.

Weekly Updates spark classroom debate around current events that apply to your business course topics. http://www.wileybusinessupdates.com

NOTES

1. Herb Welsbaum, "Better Checking: No Fee, No Minimum, 4% Interest," NBC News Business, February 11, 2013, http://www.nbcnews.com; Blake Ellis, "Community Banks Team Up to Fight the Megabanks," *CNN Money,* February 17, 2012, http://money.cnn.com; Jim Bruene, "Is BancVue's Kasasa to Checking What 'Intel Inside' Was to PCs?" *Net Banker,* January 11, 2012, http://www.netbanker.com; Eric Wilkinson, "Americans Urged to 'Break Up' with Big Banks Saturday," King5.com, November 4, 2011, http://www.king5.com.

2. Eric Markowitz, "All Signs Point to 2014 Twitter IPO," *Inc.,* May 21, 2013, http://www.inc.com; Douglas MacMillan & Mark Millan, "Box CEO Levie Targets 2014 IPO after Global Expansion," *Bloomberg,* January 16, 2013, http://www.bloomberg.com.

3. NYSE Euronext Web site, "NYSE Statistics Archive," May 2013, http://www.nyxdata.com.

4. Federal Deposit Insurance Corporation, "Statistics at a Glance," http://www.fdic.gov, updated May 29, 2013.

5. Ibid.

6. Maryalese LaPonsie, "Are Direct Banks the Future?" *MoneyRates.com,* March 15, 2013, http://www.money-rates.com.

7. Federal Deposit Insurance Corporation, "Statistics at a Glance," http://www.fdic.gov, updated May 29, 2013.

8. Jeff Blumenthal, "Which Local Banks Are among the 50 Largest?" *Philadelphia Business Journal,* June 4, 2013, http://www.bizjournals.com; Online Credit Union Data Analytics Systems, "1st Quarter 2013 Industry Trends Report," *CuData.com,* http://cudata.com.

9. American Council of Life Insurers Web site, "Life Insurer Fact Book 2012," http://www.acli.com, accessed June 16, 2013.

10. Organization for Economic Co-Operation and Development Web site, "Pension Fund Assets Hit Record USD $20.1 T in 2011, but Investment Performance Weakens," September 2012, Issue 9, page 21, http://www.oecd.org.

11. Warren S. Hearsch, "U.S. Mutual Fund Assets Set to Pass $15 Trillion," *LifeHealthPro,* February 13, 2013, http://www.lifehealthpro.com.

12. "Top Banks in the World," *Bankers Almanac,* February 18, 2013, http://www.bankersaccuity.com.

Summary of Learning Objectives

 Understand the financial system.

The financial system is the process by which funds are transferred between those having excess funds (savers) and those needing additional funds (users). Savers and users are individuals, businesses, and governments. Savers expect to earn a rate of return in exchange for the use of their funds. Financial markets, financial institutions, and financial instruments (securities) make up the financial system. Although direct transfers are possible, most funds flow from savers to users through the financial markets or financial institutions, such as commercial banks. A well-functioning financial system is critical to the overall health of a nation's economy.

financial system process by which money flows from savers to users.

2 List the various types of securities.

Securities, also called *financial instruments,* represent obligations on the part of issuers—businesses and governments—to provide purchasers with expected or stated returns on the funds invested or loaned. Securities can be classified into three categories: money market instruments, bonds, and stock.

- Money market instruments and bonds are debt instruments. Money market instruments are short-term debt securities and tend to be low-risk securities.

- Bonds are longer-term debt securities and pay a fixed amount of interest each year. Bonds are sold by the U.S. Department of the Treasury (government bonds), state and local governments (municipal bonds), and corporations. Mortgage pass-through securities are bonds backed by a pool of mortgage loans. Most municipal and corporate bonds have risk ratings.

- Common stock represents ownership in corporations. Common stockholders have voting rights and a residual claim on the firm's assets.

securities financial instruments that represent obligations on the part of the issuers to provide the purchasers with expected stated returns on the funds invested or loaned.

common stock basic form of corporate ownership.

3 Discuss financial markets.

A financial market is a market where securities are bought and sold. The primary market for securities serves businesses and governments that want to sell new security issues to raise funds. Securities are sold in the primary market either through an open auction or a process called *underwriting.* The secondary market handles transactions of previously issued securities between investors. The New York Stock Exchange is a secondary market.

The business or government that issued the security is not directly involved in secondary market transactions. In terms of the dollar value of trading volume, the secondary market is about four to five times larger than the primary market.

financial market market in which securities are issued and traded.

primary market financial market in which firms and governments issue securities and sell them initially to the general public.

secondary market collection of financial markets in which previously issued securities are traded among investors.

 Understand the stock markets.

The best-known financial markets are the stock exchanges. They exist throughout the world. The two largest—the New York Stock Exchange (NYSE) and NASDAQ—are located in the United States. Measured in terms of the total value of stock traded, the NYSE is bigger. Larger and better-known companies dominate the NYSE. Buy and sell orders are transmitted to the trading floor for execution. The NASDAQ stock market is an electronic market in which buy and sell orders are entered into a computerized communication system for execution. Most of the world's major stock markets today use similar electronic trading systems.

stock market (exchange) market in which shares of stock are bought and sold by investors.

 Evaluate financial institutions.

Financial institutions act as intermediaries between savers and users of funds.

- Depository institutions—commercial banks, savings banks, and credit unions—accept deposits from customers that can be redeemed on demand. Commercial banks are the largest and most important of the depository institutions and offer the widest range of services. Savings banks are a major source of home mortgage loans. Credit unions are not-for-profit institutions, offering financial services to consumers. Government agencies, most notably the Federal Deposit Insurance Corporation, insure deposits at these institutions.

- Nondepository institutions include pension funds and insurance companies. Nondepository institutions invest a large portion of their funds in stocks, bonds, and real estate. Mutual funds are another important financial institution. These companies sell shares to investors and in turn invest the proceeds in securities. Many individuals today invest a large portion of their retirement savings in mutual fund shares.

financial institution intermediary between savers and borrowers, collecting funds from savers and then lending the funds to individuals, businesses, and governments.

Federal Deposit Insurance Corporation (FDIC) federal agency that insures deposits at commercial and savings banks.

6 Explain the role of the Federal Reserve System.

The Federal Reserve System is the central bank of the United States. The Federal Reserve regulates banks, performs banking functions for the U.S. Department of the Treasury, and acts as the bankers' bank (clearing checks, lending money to banks, and replacing worn-out currency). It controls the supply of credit and money in the economy to promote growth and control inflation. The Federal Reserve's tools include reserve requirements, the discount rate, and open market operations. Selective credit controls and purchases and sales of foreign currencies also help the Federal Reserve manage the economy.

Federal Reserve System (Fed) the central bank of the United States.

7 Describe the regulation of the financial system.

Commercial banks, savings banks, and credit unions in the United States are heavily regulated by federal or state banking authorities. Banking regulators require institutions to follow sound banking practices and have the power to close noncompliant ones. In the United States, financial markets are regulated at both the federal and state levels. Markets are also heavily self-regulated by the financial markets and professional organizations. The chief regulatory body is the Securities and Exchange Commission. It sets the requirements for both primary and secondary market activity, prohibiting a number of practices, including insider trading. The SEC also requires public companies to disclose financial information regularly. Professional organizations and the securities markets also have rules and procedures that all members must follow.

insider trading use of material nonpublic information about a company to make investment profits.

8 Discuss the global perspective of the financial system.

Financial markets exist throughout the world and are increasingly interconnected. Investors in other countries purchase U.S. securities, and U.S. investors purchase foreign securities. Large U.S. banks and other financial institutions have a global presence. They accept deposits, make loans, and have branches throughout the world. Foreign banks also operate worldwide. The average European or Japanese bank is much larger than the average American bank. Virtually all nations have central banks that perform the same roles as the U.S. Federal Reserve System. Central bankers often act together, raising and lowering interest rates as economic conditions warrant.

>>> Quick Review >>>

LO1

1. What is the financial system?
2. In the financial system, who are the borrowers and who are the savers?
3. Name the two most common ways funds are transferred between borrowers and savers.

LO2

1. Name the major types of securities.
2. What is a government bond? A municipal bond?
3. Why do investors buy common stock?

LO3

1. What is a financial market?
2. Distinguish between a primary and a secondary financial market.
3. Briefly explain the role of financial institutions in the sale of securities.

LO4

1. Name the world's two largest stock markets.
2. Why is the London Stock Exchange unique?
3. Explain the difference between a market order and a limit order.

LO5

1. Name the two main types of financial institutions.
2. What are the primary differences between commercial banks and savings banks?
3. What is a mutual fund?

LO6

1. What is the Federal Reserve System?
2. How is the Fed organized?
3. List the three tools the Fed uses to control the supply of money and credit.

LO7

1. Who regulates banks?
2. What is insider trading?

LO8

1. Where do U.S. banks rank compared with banks around the world?
2. How are foreign banks controlled?

© UygarGeographic/iStockphoto

chapter seventeen

Financial Management

Learning Objectives

1 **Define** the role of the financial manager.

2 **Describe** financial planning.

3 **Outline** how organizations manage their assets.

4 **Discuss** the sources of funds and capital structure.

5 **Identify** short-term funding options.

6 **Discuss** sources of long-term financing.

7 **Describe** mergers, acquisitions, buyouts, and divestitures.

Raising Capital

Like other phone companies in Europe, Telecom Italia is struggling to fund improvements in its fixed and mobile networks. Raising capital for these projects is never easy, and given the economic conditions in Europe, this task is likely more difficult for company executives.

Recently, the company launched a plan to raise up to 3 billion euros ($4 billion) in a costly hybrid debt offering while halving its dividend to help fund its infrastructure spending. In raising new capital, Telecom Italia said it had opted for hybrid debt—which combines elements of both debt and equity—instead of a straightforward share issue because it did not want to upset its shareholding structure.

"Our shareholders have to be protected," Chairman Franco Bernabe said in a conference call. "We want to strengthen our infrastructure both in Italy and in Brazil and Argentina but at the same time we want to keep our deleveraging path."[1]

The chairman's comments mean that the company needs to walk a very fine line with its investors. Raising money solely by issuing stock dilutes the value of the existing shareholders' positions, causing the per-share price of the stock to decline. On the other hand, issuing bonds causes the company to become increasingly leveraged (that is, increasing debt),

resulting in higher interest payments and reduced earnings. Thus, Bernabe and his finance team settled on a hybrid approach, offering some debt and some equity to raise the necessary funds.

Organizations often use complicated financial transactions like this to meet their capital needs. And getting it right is a challenge, particularly for a telecommunications company that requires significant amounts of capital to build and maintain their networks.

Overview >>>

Previous chapters discuss two essential functions a business must perform: producing a good or service and marketing it to prospective customers. This chapter introduces a third, equally important, function: ensuring that an organization has enough money to perform its other tasks successfully, in both the present and the future, and that these funds are invested properly. Adequate funds must be available to buy materials, equipment, and other assets; pay bills; and compensate employees. This third business function is **finance**—planning, obtaining, and managing the company's funds in order to accomplish its objectives as effectively and efficiently as possible.

> **finance** planning, obtaining, and managing a company's funds to accomplish its objectives as effectively and efficiently as possible.

For an organization like Telecom Italia, financial objectives include not only meeting expenses and investing in assets but also maximizing overall worth, often determined by the value of the firm's common stock. Financial managers are responsible for meeting expenses, investing in assets, and increasing profits to shareholders. Solid financial management is critical to the success of a business.

This chapter focuses on the finance function of organizations. It begins by describing the role of financial managers, their place in the organizational hierarchy, and the increasing importance of finance. Next, the financial planning process and the components of a financial plan are outlined. Then the discussion focuses on how organizations manage assets as efficiently and effectively as possible. The two major sources of funds—debt and equity—are then compared, and the concept of leverage is introduced. The chapter also discusses major sources of short-term and long-term funding and concludes with a description of mergers, acquisitions, buyouts, and divestitures.

1 The Role of the Financial Manager

> **financial managers** executives who develop and implement the firm's financial plan and determine the most appropriate sources and uses of funds.

Because of the intense pressures they face today, organizations are increasingly measuring and reducing the costs of business operations as well as maximizing revenues and profits. As a result, **financial managers**—executives who develop and implement their firm's financial plan and determine the most appropriate sources and uses of funds—are among the most vital people on the corporate payroll.

FIGURE 17.1 shows what the finance function of a typical company might look like. At the top is the chief financial officer (CFO). The CFO usually reports directly to the company's chief executive officer (CEO) or chief operating officer (COO). In some companies, the CFO is also a member of the board of directors. In the case of the software maker Oracle,

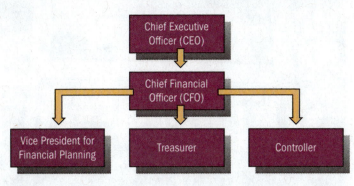

FIGURE 17.1 A Typical Finance Organization

both the current CFO and the former CFO serve on that company's board. Moreover, it's not uncommon for CFOs to serve as independent directors on other firms' boards, such as HP, Microsoft, and Target. As noted in Chapter 15, the CFO, along with the firm's CEO, must certify the accuracy of the firm's financial statements.

Reporting directly to the CFO are often three senior managers. Although titles can vary, these three executives are commonly called the *vice president for financial management* (or *planning*), the *treasurer,* and the *controller.* The vice president for financial management or planning is responsible for preparing financial forecasts and analyzing major investment decisions, such as new products, new production facilities, and acquisitions. The treasurer is responsible for all of the company's financing activities, including cash management, tax planning and preparation, and shareholder relations. The treasurer also works on the sale of new security issues to investors. The controller is the chief accounting manager. The controller's functions include keeping the company's books, preparing financial statements, and conducting internal audits.

In performing their jobs, financial professionals continually seek to balance risks with expected financial returns. Risk is the uncertainty of gain or loss; return is the gain or loss that results from an investment over a specified period of time. Financial managers strive to maximize the wealth of their firm's shareholders by striking the optimal balance between risk and return. This balance is called the **risk-return trade-off**. For example, relying heavily on borrowed funds may increase the return (in the form of cash) to shareholders, but the more money a firm borrows, the greater the risks to shareholders. An increase in a firm's cash on hand reduces the risk of being unable to meet unexpected cash needs. However, because cash in and of itself does not earn much, if any, return, failure to invest surplus funds in an income-earning asset—such as in securities—reduces a firm's potential return or profitability.

Every financial manager must perform this risk-return balancing act. For example, in the late 1990s, Airbus wrestled with

risk-return trade-off process of maximizing the wealth of a firm's shareholders by striking the optimal balance between risk and return.

a major decision: whether to begin development and production of the giant A380 jetliner. The development costs for the aircraft—the world's largest jetliner—were initially estimated at more than $10 billion. Before committing to such a huge investment, financial managers had to weigh the potential profits of the A380 against the risk that profits would not materialize. With its future on the line, Airbus decided to go ahead with the A380, spending more than $15 billion on research and development. The A380 entered commercial service a few years ago. Airbus currently has 262 confirmed orders for the A380 and so far has delivered 103 planes to such carriers as Emirates, China Southern Airlines, Air France, Lufthansa, Qantas Airways, and Singapore Airlines.[2]

Financial managers must also learn to adapt to changes in the financial system. The recent credit crisis has made it more difficult for some companies to borrow money from traditional lenders such as banks. This, in turn, has forced firms to scale back expansion plans or seek funding from other sources such as commercial financing companies. In addition, financial managers must adapt to internal changes as well.

>>> Quick Review

1. How is the finance function structured at the typical firm?

2. Explain the risk-return trade-off.

▼ Before committing to building the A380 jetliner, financial managers at Airbus had to weigh the potential profits for the company against the risk that the investment would not be profitable. The plane entered commercial service a few years ago, and the company currently has more than 262 confirmed orders.

Charly Diaz Azcue/LatinContent/Getty Images

2 Financial Planning

Financial managers develop their organization's **financial plan**, a document that specifies the funds needed by a firm for a given period of time, the timing of inflows and outflows, and the most

financial plan
document that specifies the funds needed by a firm for a period of time, the timing of inflows and outflows, and the most appropriate sources and uses of funds.

appropriate sources and uses of funds. Some financial plans, often called *operating plans,* are short term in nature, focusing on projections no more than a year or two in the future. Other financial plans, sometimes referred to as *strategic plans,* have a much longer time horizon, perhaps up to five or ten years.

Λ Costco has a lower *asset intensity* than a typical manufacturing business might have.

Regardless of the time period, a financial plan is based on forecasts of production costs, purchasing needs, plant and equipment expenditures, and expected sales activities for the period covered. Financial managers use forecasts to determine the specific amounts and timing of expenditures and receipts. They build a financial plan based on the answers to three questions:

- What funds will the firm require during the planning period?
- When will it need additional funds?
- Where will it obtain the necessary funds?

Some funds flow into the firm when it sells its goods or services, but funding needs vary. The financial plan must reflect both the amounts and timing of inflows and outflows of funds. Even a profitable firm may face a financial squeeze as a result of its need for funds when sales lag, when the volume of its credit sales increases, or when customers are slow in making payments.

In general, preparing a financial plan consists of three steps:

1. Forecast sales.
2. Determine longer-term profits.
3. Estimate what the firm will need to support projected sales.

The sales forecast is the key variable in any financial plan because without an accurate sales forecast, the firm will have difficulty accurately estimating other variables, such as production costs and purchasing needs. The best method of forecasting sales depends on the nature of the business. For instance, a retailer's CFO might begin with the current sales-per-store figure. Then he or she would look toward the near future, factoring in expected same-store sales growth, along with any planned store openings or closings, to come up with a forecast of sales for the next period. If the company sells merchandise through other channels, such as online, the forecast is adjusted to reflect those additional channels.

Next, the CFO uses the sales forecast to determine the expected level of profits for future periods. This longer-term projection involves estimating expenses such as purchases, employee compensation, and taxes. Many expenses are themselves functions of sales. For instance, the more a firm sells, generally the greater its purchases. Along with estimating future profits, the

CFO would also determine what portion of these profits will likely be paid to shareholders in the form of cash dividends.

Next, the CFO estimates how many additional assets the firm will need to support projected sales. Increased sales, for example, might mean the company needs additional inventory, stepped-up collections for accounts receivable, or even new plants and equipment. Depending on the nature of the industry, some businesses need more assets than do other companies to support the same amount of sales. The technical term for this requirement is *asset intensity.* For instance, DuPont has approximately $0.68 in assets for every dollar in sales. So for every $100 increase in sales, the firm would need about $68 of additional assets. Costco, by contrast, has roughly $0.34 in assets for every dollar in sales. It would require an additional $34 of assets for every $100 of additional sales. This difference is not surprising; manufacturing is a more asset-intensive business than retailing.

A simplified financial plan illustrates these steps. Assume a growing company forecasts that next year's sales will increase by $40 million to $140 million. After estimating expenses, the CFO believes that after-tax profits next year will be $12 million and the firm will pay nothing in dividends. The projected increase in sales next year will require the firm to invest another $20 million in assets, and because increases in assets are uses of funds, the company will need an additional $20 million in funds. The company's after-tax earnings will contribute $12 million, meaning that the other $8 million must come from outside sources. So the financial plan tells the CFO how much money will be needed and when it will be needed. Armed with this knowledge, and given that the firm has decided to borrow the needed funds, the CFO can then begin negotiations with banks and other lenders.

The cash inflows and outflows of a business are similar to those of a household. The members of a household depend on weekly or monthly paychecks for funds, but their expenditures vary greatly from one pay period to the next. The financial plan should indicate when the flows of funds entering and leaving the organization will occur and in what amounts. One of the most significant business expenses is employee compensation.

A good financial plan also includes financial control, a process of comparing actual revenues, costs, and expenses with forecasts. This comparison may reveal significant differences between projected and actual figures, so it is important to discover them early to take quick action.

> > > **Quick Review**

1 What three questions does a financial plan address?

2 List the steps involved in creating a financial plan.

③ Managing Assets

As we noted in Chapter 15, assets consist of what a firm owns. But assets also represent uses of funds. To grow and prosper, companies need to obtain additional assets. Sound financial management requires assets to be acquired and managed as effectively and efficiently as possible.

SHORT-TERM ASSETS

Short-term, or current, assets consist of cash and assets that can be (or are expected to be) converted into cash within a year. The major current assets are cash, marketable securities, accounts receivable, and inventory.

- **Cash and marketable securities** are used mainly to pay day-to-day expenses, much as when individuals maintain a balance in a checking account to pay bills or buy food and clothing. Most organizations also strive to maintain a minimum cash balance in order to have funds available in the event of unexpected expenses. As noted earlier, because cash earns little, if any, return, most firms invest excess cash in so-called *marketable securities*—low-risk securities that either have short maturities or can be easily sold in secondary markets. Money market instruments are popular choices for firms with excess cash.

- **Accounts receivable** are uncollected credit sales and can be a significant asset. The financial manager's job is to collect the funds owed the firm as quickly as possible while still offering sufficient credit to customers to generate increased sales. In general, a more liberal credit policy means higher sales but also increased collection expenses, higher levels of bad debt, and a higher investment in accounts receivable.

  Management of accounts receivable is composed of two functions: determining an overall credit policy and deciding which customers will be offered credit. Formulating a credit policy involves deciding whether the firm will offer credit and, if so, on what terms. Will a discount be offered to customers who pay in cash? Often, the overall credit policy is dictated by competitive pressures or general industry

practices. If all your competitors offer customers credit, your firm will likely have to as well. The other aspect of a credit policy is deciding which customers will be offered credit. Managers must consider the importance of the customer as well as its financial health and repayment history.

- **Inventory management** can be complicated because the cost of inventory includes more than just the acquisition cost. It also includes the cost of ordering, storing, insuring, and financing inventory as well as the cost of stockouts, or lost sales due to insufficient inventory. Financial managers try to minimize the cost of inventory, but production, marketing, and logistics also play important roles in determining proper inventory levels. Also, trends in the inventory turnover ratio can be early warning signs of impending trouble. For instance, if inventory turnover has been slowing for several consecutive quarters, it indicates that inventory is rising faster than sales. This may suggest that customer demand is softening and the firm needs to take action, such as reducing production or increasing promotional efforts.

ᐯ At Bed Bath & Beyond, inventory is the most valuable asset. Managing inventory can be a costly and highly complicated undertaking, especially for retailers.

Mark Peterson/Redux Pictures

CAPITAL INVESTMENT ANALYSIS

In addition to current assets, firms also invest in long-lived assets. Unlike current assets, long-lived assets are expected to produce economic benefits for more than one year. These investments often involve substantial amounts of money. For example, as noted earlier in the chapter, Airbus invested more than $15 billion in development of the A380. In another example, a few years ago, auto manufacturer BMW spent $750 million to expand its production facility in Spartanburg, South Carolina, bringing its total investment in the state to $4.6 billion.

The process by which decisions are made regarding investments in long-lived assets is called *capital investment analysis*. Firms make two basic types of capital investment decisions: expansion and replacement. The A380 and the BMW South Carolina plant investments are examples of expansion decisions. Replacement decisions involve upgrading assets by substituting new ones. A retailer might decide to replace an old store with a new Supercenter, as Walmart did in Oxford, Ohio.

Financial managers must estimate all of the costs and benefits of a proposed investment, which can be quite difficult, especially for very long-lived investments. Only those investments that offer an acceptable return—measured by the difference between benefits and costs—should be undertaken. BMW's financial managers believed that the benefits of expanding the South Carolina production facility outweighed the high cost. The expansion will allow BMW to produce three new models designed mainly for the North American market, so the expected profit from the sale of these models would be considered in the decision. Some other benefits cited by BMW include lower production costs, improved logistics, and expanded use of renewable energy. The expansion is paying off, with the Spartanburg facility producing a record 301,000 vehicles in a recent year.[3]

> ### >>> Quick Review
>
> **1** Why do firms often choose to invest excess cash in marketable securities?
>
> **2** Name the two aspects of accounts receivable management.
>
> **3** Explain the difference between an expansion decision and a replacement decision.

4 Sources of Funds and Capital Structure

The use of debt for financing can increase the potential for return as well as increase loss potential. Recall the accounting equation introduced in Chapter 15:

$$\text{Assets} = \text{Liabilities} + \text{Owners' Equity}$$

If you view this equation from a financial management perspective, it reveals that there are only two types of funding: debt and equity. *Debt capital* consists of funds obtained through borrowing. *Equity capital* consists of funds provided by the firm's owners when they reinvest earnings, make additional contributions, liquidate assets, issue stock to the general public, or raise capital from outside investors. The mix of a firm's debt and equity capital is known as its **capital structure**.

capital structure mix of a firm's debt and equity capital.

Companies often take very different approaches to choosing a capital structure. As more debt is used, the risk to the company increases since the firm is now obligated to make the interest payments on the money borrowed, regardless of the cash flows coming into the company. Choosing more debt increases the fixed costs a company must pay, which in turn makes a company more sensitive to changing sales revenues. Debt is frequently the least costly method of raising additional financing dollars, one of the reasons it is so frequently used.

Differing industries choose varying amounts of debt and equity to use when financing. Using the information provided by Datamonitor, we find that the automotive industry has debt ratios (the ratio of liabilities to assets) of over 60 percent for both Toyota and Honda and over 90 percent for Ford. These companies are primarily using debt to finance their asset expenditures. Food-service companies such as McDonald's and Starbucks use only 49 percent debt and 27 percent debt, respectively. The mixture of debt and equity a company uses is a major management decision.

LEVERAGE AND CAPITAL STRUCTURE DECISIONS

Raising needed cash by borrowing allows a firm to benefit from the principle of **leverage**, increasing the rate of return on funds invested by borrowing funds. The key to managing leverage is to ensure that a company's earnings remain larger than its interest payments, which increases the leverage on the rate of return on shareholders' investment. Of course, if the company earns less than its interest payments, shareholders lose money on their original investment.

leverage increasing the rate of return on funds invested by borrowing funds.

FIGURE 17.2 shows the relationship between earnings and shareholder returns for two identical hypothetical firms that choose to raise funds in different ways. Leverage Company obtains 50 percent of its funds from lenders who purchase company bonds. Leverage Company pays 10 percent interest on its bonds. Equity Company raises all of its funds through sales of company stock.

Notice that if earnings double—from, say, $10 million to $20 million—returns to shareholders of Equity Company also double, from 10 percent to 20 percent. But returns to shareholders of Leverage Company more than double, from 10 percent to 30 percent. However, leverage works in the opposite direction as well. If earnings fall from $10 million to $5 million—a decline of 50 percent—returns to shareholders of Equity Company also fall

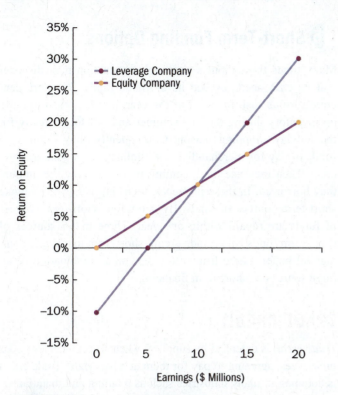

FIGURE 17.2 How Leverage Works

NOTE: The example assumes that both companies have $100 million in capital. Leverage Company consists of $50 million in equity and $50 million in bonds (with an interest rate of 10 percent). Equity Company consists of $100 million in equity and no bonds. This example also assumes no corporate taxes.

by 50 percent, from 10 percent to 5 percent. By contrast, returns to shareholders of Leverage Company fall from 10 percent to zero. Thus, leverage increases potential returns to shareholders but also increases risk.

A key component of the financial manager's job is to weigh the advantages and disadvantages of debt capital and equity capital, creating the most appropriate capital structure for the firm.

MIXING SHORT-TERM AND LONG-TERM FUNDS

Another decision financial managers face is determining the appropriate mix of short- and long-term funds. Short-term funds consist of current liabilities, and long-term funds consist of long-term debt and equity. Short-term funds are generally less expensive than long-term funds, but they also expose the firm to more risk. This is because short-term funds have to be renewed, or rolled over, frequently. Short-term interest rates can be volatile. During a recent 12-month period, for example, rates on commercial paper, a popular short-term financing option, ranged from a high of 0.22 percent (for 90-day loans) to a low of 0.04 percent (for 1-day loans).[4]

Because short-term rates move up and down frequently, interest expense on short-term funds can change substantially from year to year. For instance, if a firm borrows $50 million for ten years at 5 percent interest, its annual interest expense is fixed at $2.5 million for the entire ten years. On the other hand, if it

borrows $50 million for one year at a rate of 4 percent, its annual interest expense of $2 million is only fixed for that year. If interest rates increase the following year to 6 percent, $1 million will be added to the interest expense bill. Another potential risk of relying on short-term funds is availability. Even financially healthy firms can occasionally find it difficult to borrow money.

Because of the added risk of short-term funding, most firms choose to finance all of their long-term assets, and even a portion of their short-term assets, with long-term funds. Johnson & Johnson is typical of this choice. **FIGURE 17.3** shows a recent balance sheet broken down between short- and long-term assets and short- and long-term funds.

DIVIDEND POLICY

Along with decisions regarding capital structure and the mix of short- and long-term funds, financial managers also make decisions regarding a firm's dividend policy. *Dividends* are periodic

V Companies are under no legal obligation to pay dividends to shareholders of their common stock. However, some companies pay dividends every year, while others pay dividends sporadically. In 2012, Apple announced it would pay its first dividend in nearly 20 years.

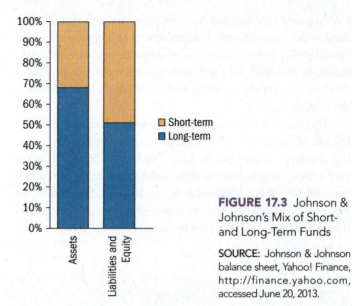

FIGURE 17.3 Johnson & Johnson's Mix of Short- and Long-Term Funds

SOURCE: Johnson & Johnson balance sheet, Yahoo! Finance, http://finance.yahoo.com, accessed June 20, 2013.

Kevork Djansezian/Getty Images, Inc.

cash payments to shareholders. The most common type of dividend is paid quarterly and is often labeled as a *regular dividend*. Occasionally, firms make one-time special or extra dividend payments, as Microsoft did some years ago. Earnings that are paid in dividends are not reinvested in the firm and don't contribute additional equity capital.

Firms are under no legal obligation to pay dividends to shareholders of common stock. Although some companies pay generous dividends, others pay nothing. Until 2010, Starbucks never paid a dividend to its shareholders, and Apple recently announced it would pay its first dividend in nearly 20 years. In contrast, 3M has paid dividends for 30-plus consecutive years, during which time the amount has more than quadrupled.

268

5 Short-Term Funding Options

Many times throughout a year, an organization may discover that its cash needs exceed its available funds. Retailers generate surplus cash for most of the year, but they need to build up inventory during the late summer and fall to get ready for the holiday shopping season. Consequently, they often need funds to pay for merchandise until holiday sales generate revenue. Then they use the incoming funds to repay the amount they borrowed. In these instances, financial managers evaluate short-term sources of funds. By definition, short-term sources of funds are repaid within one year. Three major sources of short-term funds exist: trade credit, short-term loans, and commercial paper. Large firms often rely on a combination of all three sources of short-term financing.

TRADE CREDIT

Trade credit is extended by suppliers when a firm receives goods or services, agreeing to pay for them at a later date. Trade credit is common in many industries such as retailing and manufacturing. Suppliers routinely ship billions of dollars of merchandise to retailers each day and are paid at a later date. Without trade

▼ Retailers like Target depend on trade credit to offer shoppers a broad array of merchandise.

DAWN VILLELLA/AP Images

credit, the retailing sector would probably look much different—with fewer selections. Under this system, the supplier records the transactions as an account receivable, and the retailer records it as an account payable. Retailer Target alone currently has more than $6.5 billion of accounts payable on its books. The main advantage of trade credit is its easy availability because credit sales are common in many industries. The main drawback to trade credit is that the amount a company can borrow is limited to the amount it purchases.

SHORT-TERM LOANS

Loans from commercial banks are a significant source of short-term financing for businesses. Often businesses use these loans to finance inventory and accounts receivable. For example, late fall and early winter is the period of highest sales for a small manufacturer of ski equipment. To meet this demand, it has to begin building inventory during the summer. The manufacturer also has to finance accounts receivable (credit sales to customers) during the fall and winter. So it takes out a bank loan during the summer. As the inventory is sold and accounts receivable collected, the firm repays the loan.

There are two types of short-term bank loans: lines of credit and revolving credit agreements. A line of credit specifies the maximum amount the firm can borrow over a period of time, usually a year. The bank is under no obligation actually to lend the money, however. It does so only if funds are available. Most lines of credit require the borrower to repay the original amount, plus interest, within one year. By contrast, a revolving credit agreement is essentially a guaranteed line of credit—the bank guarantees that the funds will be available when needed. Banks typically charge a fee, on top of interest, for revolving credit agreements.

Another form of short-term financing backed by accounts receivable is called *factoring*. The business sells its accounts receivable to either a bank or finance company—called a *factor*—at a discount. The size of the discount determines the cost of the transaction. Factoring allows the firm to convert its receivables into cash quickly without worrying about collections.

COMMERCIAL PAPER

Commercial paper is a short-term IOU sold by a company (this concept was briefly described in Chapter 16). Commercial paper is typically sold in multiples of $100,000 to $1 million and has a maturity that ranges from 1 to 270 days. Most commercial paper is unsecured. It is an attractive source of financing because large amounts of money can be raised at rates that are typically 1 to 2 percent less that those charged by banks. Recently, almost $1.04 trillion in commercial paper was outstanding.[5] Although commercial paper is an attractive short-term financing alternative, only a small percentage of businesses can issue it. That is because access to the

commercial paper market has traditionally been restricted to large, financially strong corporations.

>>> **Quick Review**

1. What are the three sources of short-term funding?

2. Explain trade credit.

3. Why is commercial paper an attractive short-term financing option?

6 Sources of Long-Term Financing

Funds from short-term sources can help a firm meet current needs for cash or inventory. However, a larger project or plan, such as acquiring another company or making a major investment in real estate or equipment, usually requires funds for a much longer period of time. Unlike short-term sources, long-term sources are repaid over many years.

Organizations acquire long-term funds from three sources. One is long-term loans obtained from financial institutions such as commercial banks, life insurance companies, and pension funds. A second source is bonds—certificates of indebtedness—sold to investors. A third source is equity financing that is acquired by selling stock in the firm or reinvesting company profits.

PUBLIC SALE OF STOCKS AND BONDS

Public sales of securities such as stocks and bonds are a major source of funds for corporations. Such sales provide cash inflows for the issuing firm and either a share in its ownership (for a stock purchaser) or a specified rate of interest and repayment at a stated time (for a bond purchaser). Because stock and bond issues of many corporations are traded in the secondary markets, stockholders and bondholders can easily sell these securities. When a recent European debt crisis seemed likely, it caused a massive slowdown in bond sales. But as fears of a crisis eased later in the year, bond sales reached their highest level since the same time the previous year. Through the middle of a recent year, U.S. corporations have sold bonds worth almost $690 billion.[6] Public sales of securities, however, can vary substantially from year to year, depending on conditions in the financial markets. Bond sales, for instance, tend to be higher when interest rates are lower.

Chapter 16 discussed the process by which most companies sell securities publicly—through investment bankers via a process called *underwriting*. Investment bankers purchase the securities from the issuer and then resell them to investors. The issuer pays a fee to the investment banker, called an *underwriting discount*.

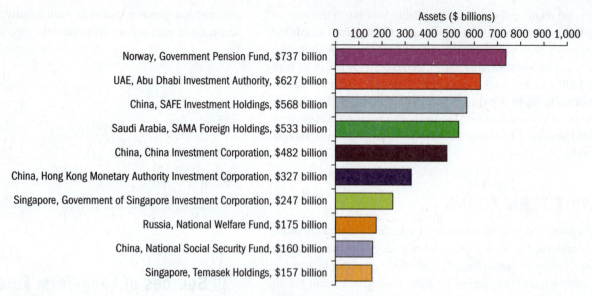

FIGURE 17.4 The World's Ten Largest Sovereign Wealth Funds

SOURCE: Sovereign Wealth Fund Institute, "Sovereign Wealth Fund Rankings," http://www.swfinstitute.org, accessed June 17, 2013.

PRIVATE PLACEMENTS

Some new stock or bond issues are not sold publicly but instead to a small group of major investors such as pension funds and insurance companies. Such a sale is referred to as a *private placement*. Companies will often raise funds with private placements as they are generally less expensive and quicker to complete than a public offering. Institutional investors such as insurance companies and pension funds buy private placements because they typically carry slightly higher interest rates than publicly issued bonds. In addition, the terms of the issue can be tailored to meet the specific needs of both the issuer and the institutional investors. Of course, the institutional investor gives up liquidity because privately placed securities do not trade in secondary markets.

PRIVATE EQUITY FUNDS

A *private equity fund* is an investment company that raises funds from wealthy individuals and institutional investors and uses those funds to make large investments in both public and privately held companies. Private equity funds invest in all types of businesses, including mature ones. For example, Cerberus Capital Management, a private equity fund, recently bought Supervalu's grocery chains, Albertsons, Acme, Jewel-Osco, Shaw's, and Star Market, for $3.3 billion.[7] Often, private equity funds invest in a leveraged buyout—a transaction that takes a public company private. In such transactions, discussed in more detail in the next section, a public company reverts to private status.

A variation of the private equity fund is the so-called *sovereign wealth fund*. This type of company is owned by a government

and invests in a variety of financial and real assets, such as real estate. Although sovereign wealth funds generally make investments based on the best risk-return trade-off, political, social, and strategic considerations also play a role in their investment decisions. The assets of the ten largest sovereign wealth funds are shown in **FIGURE 17.4**. Together, these ten funds have almost $4 trillion in assets.

HEDGE FUNDS

A *hedge fund* is a private investment company open only to qualified large investors. Operating much like a mutual fund, hedge funds raise capital from investors and then hire a manager to oversee investments matching the fund's stated goals. In recent years, hedge funds have become a significant presence in U.S. financial markets. Before the recent recession, some analysts estimated that hedge funds accounted for about 60 percent of all secondary bond market trading and around one-third of all activity on stock exchanges.

>>> **Quick Review**

1 Name the three sources of long-term funds for corporations.

2 Why might a firm engage in a private placement of its stock or bonds?

3 What is a hedge fund?

7 Mergers, Acquisitions, Buyouts, and Divestitures

Chapter 5 briefly described mergers and acquisitions. A merger is a transaction in which two or more firms combine into one company. In an acquisition, one firm buys the assets and assumes the obligations of another firm, such as Facebook's recent $1 billion acquisition of Instagram, a photo-sharing app for smart phones. Transactions like mergers, acquisitions, buyouts, and divestitures have financial implications.

Financial managers evaluate a proposed merger or acquisition in much the same way they would evaluate any large investment—by comparing the costs and benefits. Mergers are generally a transaction between two firms of roughly the same size. The merger between American Airlines Inc. and U.S. Airways Inc. is a good example of this type of merger. Unlike acquisitions, where the acquiring firm most often determines how the transaction will proceed, in mergers both firms have a significant stake in how the deal is structured. Who will be on the management team? Which corporate office will be the merged company headquarters? How much of the staff will be retained, doing what jobs, and in which locations? These and thousands of other questions must be discussed and resolved. To complete the American Airlines and U.S. Airways merger, the companies established 29 different committees, dealing with everything from in-flight service (will each customer receive a whole can of soda?) to who will be the new CEO (Doug Parker is currently the CEO and chairman of U.S. Airways).[8] Whatever the reason for the merger, the term often used to describe the benefits produced by a merger or acquisition is *synergy*—the notion that the combined firm is worth more than the companies are individually. The American Airlines and U.S. Airways merger will result in a combined company that is better able to compete with other U.S. carriers.

In a **leveraged buyout**, or **LBO**, the shareholders of a public company are bought out and the firm reverts to private status. The term *leverage* comes from the fact that many of these transactions are financed with high degrees of debt—often in excess of 75 percent. Private equity companies and hedge funds provide equity and debt financing for many LBOs. The firm's incumbent senior management is often part of the buyout group. LBO activity decreased sharply with the recent economic downturn, but as the economy began to recover, LBO activity increased again.

In a sense, a **divestiture** is the reverse of a merger—that is, a company sells an asset, such as a subsidiary, a product line, or a production facility. Two types of divestitures exist: sell-offs and spin-offs. In a *sell-off,* a firm sells an asset to another firm. After Verizon Wireless sold some of its assets to AT&T, AT&T announced plans to roll out 3G wireless service to about 1.6 million former Verizon subscribers in rural areas across 18 states.

The other type of divestiture is a *spin-off.* In this transaction, a new firm is formed by the sale of the assets. Shareholders of the divesting firm become shareholders of the new firm as well. For example, Motorola announced that it would split into two publicly traded firms. The parent company will handle its core business of mobile converged devices, digital home-entertainment devices, and video voice and data solutions. The spin-off firm will handle heavy-duty two-way radios, mobile computers, public security systems, wireless network infrastructure, and other business-oriented goods and services. Both entities will continue to use the Motorola brand name, with the parent company now named Motorola Solutions Inc. As part of the spin-off, Motorola shareholders received shares of the new company, Motorola Mobility Holdings, Inc.

divestiture sale of assets by a firm.

leveraged buyout (LBO) transaction in which public shareholders are bought out and the firm reverts to private status.

> > > **Quick Review**

1 Define *synergy*.

2 What is a leveraged buyout?

3 Name and describe the two types of divestitures.

NOTES

1. Danilo Masoni, "Telecom Italia Plots Hybrid Debt Issue, Cuts Dividend," *Reuters*, February 8, 2013, http://news.yahoo.com.

2. Company Web site, "Orders and Deliveries," http://www.airbus.com, accessed June 26, 2013.

3. Joel Hans, "BMW's SC Plant Hits Record Production," *Manufacturing.net*, January 10, 2013, http://www.manufacturing.net.

4. Federal Reserve Board, "Commercial Paper," Federal Reserve Release, http://federalreserve .gov, accessed June 17, 2013.

5. Federal Reserve Board, "Commercial Paper Outstanding," Federal Reserve Release, http://federalreserve.gov, accessed June 17, 2013.

6. Sarika Gangar, "Gross to Buffett, Omens Disregarded as Sales Soar: Credit Markets,"

Bloomberg, May 20, 2013, http://www .bloomberg.com.

7. Elliot Zwiebach and Mark Hamstra, "Supervalu Completes Sale of Chains to Cerberus," *Supermarket News*, March 21, 2013, http://supermarketnews.com.

8. Treey Maxon, "As American Airlines Merger Date Nears, Questions Abound," *Dallas News*, June 3, 2013, http://www.dallasnews.com.

REVIEW

Summary of Learning Objectives

1 Define the role of the financial manager.

Finance deals with planning, obtaining, and managing a company's funds to accomplish its objectives efficiently and effectively. The major responsibilities of financial managers are to develop and implement financial plans and determine the most appropriate sources and uses of funds. The chief financial officer (CFO) heads a firm's finance organization. Three senior executives reporting to the CFO are the vice president for financial management, the treasurer, and the controller. When making decisions, financial professionals continually seek to balance risks with expected financial returns.

finance planning, obtaining, and managing a company's funds to accomplish its objectives as effectively and efficiently as possible.

financial managers executives who develop and implement the firm's financial plan and determine the most appropriate sources and uses of funds.

risk-return trade-off process of maximizing the wealth of a firm's shareholders by striking the optimal balance between risk and return.

2 Describe financial planning.

A financial plan is a document that specifies the funds needed by a firm for a given period of time, the timing of inflows and outflows, and the most appropriate sources and uses of funds. The financial plan addresses three questions:

1. What funds will be required during the planning period?
2. When will funds be needed?
3. Where will funds be obtained?

Three steps are involved in the financial planning process:

1. Forecasting sales over a future period of time
2. Estimating the expected level of profits over the planning period
3. Determining the additional assets needed to support additional sales.

financial plan document that specifies the funds needed by a firm for a period of time, the timing of inflows and outflows, and the most appropriate sources and uses of funds.

3 Outline how organizations manage their assets.

Assets consist of what a firm owns and also comprise the uses of its funds. Sound financial management requires assets to be acquired and managed as effectively and efficiently as possible. The major current assets are cash, marketable securities, accounts receivable, and inventory. The goal of cash management is to have sufficient funds on hand to meet day-to-day transactions and pay

any unexpected expenses. Excess cash should be invested in marketable securities, which are low-risk securities with short maturities. Managing accounts receivable, which are uncollected credit sales, involves securing funds owed the firm as quickly as possible while offering sufficient credit to customers to generate increased sales. The main goal of inventory management is to minimize the overall cost of inventory. Production, marketing, and logistics also play roles in determining proper inventory levels. Capital investment analysis is the process by which financial managers make decisions on long-lived assets. This involves comparing the benefits and costs of a proposed investment. Managing international assets poses additional challenges for the financial manager, including the problem of fluctuating exchange rates.

4 Discuss the sources of funds and capital structure.

Businesses have two sources of funds: debt capital and equity capital. Debt capital consists of funds obtained through borrowing, and equity capital consists of funds provided by the firm's owners. The mix of debt and equity capital is known as the firm's capital structure, and the financial manager's job is to find the proper mix. Leverage is a technique of increasing the rate of return on funds invested by borrowing. However, leverage increases risk. Also, overreliance on borrowed funds may reduce management's flexibility in future financing decisions. Equity capital also has drawbacks. When additional equity capital is sold, the control of existing shareholders is diluted. In addition, equity capital is more expensive than debt capital. Financial managers are also faced with decisions concerning the appropriate mix of short- and long-term funds. Short-term funds are generally less expensive than long-term funds but expose firms to more risk. Another decision involving financial managers is determining the firm's dividend policy.

capital structure mix of a firm's debt and equity capital.

leverage increasing the rate of return on funds invested by borrowing funds.

5 Identify short-term funding options.

The three major short-term funding options are trade credit, short-term loans from banks and other financial institutions, and commercial paper.

- Trade credit is extended by suppliers when a firm receives goods or services, agreeing to pay for them at a later date. Trade credit is relatively easy to obtain and costs nothing unless a supplier offers a cash discount.

- Loans from commercial banks are a significant source of short-term financing and are often used to finance accounts receivable and inventory. Loans can be either unsecured or secured, with accounts receivable or inventory pledged as collateral.

- Commercial paper is a short-term IOU sold by a company. Although large amounts of money can be raised through the sale of commercial paper, usually at rates below those charged by banks, access to the commercial-paper market is limited to large, financially strong corporations.

6 Discuss sources of long-term financing.

Long-term funds are repaid over many years. There are three sources of long-term funds:

1. Long-term loans obtained from financial institutions

2. Bonds sold to investors

3. Equity financing

Public sales of securities represent a major source of funds for corporations. These securities can generally be traded in secondary markets. Public sales can vary substantially from year to year depending on the conditions in the financial markets. Private placements are securities sold to a small number of institutional investors. Most private placements involve debt securities. Private equity funds are investment companies that raise funds from wealthy individuals and institutional investors and use the funds to make investments in both public and private companies. Sovereign wealth funds are investment companies owned by governments.

7 Describe mergers, acquisitions, buyouts, and divestitures.

A merger is a combination of two or more firms into one company. An acquisition is a transaction in which one company buys another. Even in a merger, there is a buyer and a seller (called the *target*). The buyer offers cash, securities, or a combination of the two in return for the target's shares. Mergers and acquisitions should be evaluated as any large investment is, by comparing the costs with the benefits. *Synergy* is the term used to describe the benefits a merger or acquisition is expected to produce.

A leveraged buyout (LBO) is a transaction in which shares are purchased from public shareholders and the company reverts to private status. Usually LBOs are financed with substantial amounts of borrowed funds. Private equity companies are often major financers of LBOs.

Divestitures are the opposite of mergers, in which companies sell assets such as subsidiaries, product lines, or production facilities. A sell-off is a divestiture in which assets are sold to another firm. In a spin-off, a new firm is created from the assets divested. Shareholders of the divesting firm become shareholders of the new firm as well.

leveraged buyout (LBO) transaction in which public shareholders are bought out and the firm reverts to private status.

divestiture sale of assets by a firm.

>>> Quick Review >>

LO1

1 How is the finance function structured at the typical firm?

2 Explain the risk-return trade-off.

LO2

1 What three questions does a financial plan address?

2 List the steps involved in creating a financial plan.

LO3

1 Why do firms often choose to invest excess cash in marketable securities?

2 Name the two aspects of accounts receivable management.

3 Explain the difference between an expansion decision and a replacement decision.

LO4

1 Explain the concept of leverage.

2 Why do firms generally rely more on long-term funds than on short-term funds?

3 What is an important determinant of a firm's dividend policy?

LO5

1 What are the three sources of short-term funding?

2 Explain trade credit.

3 Why is commercial paper an attractive short-term financing option?

LO6

1 Name the three sources of long-term funds for corporations.

2 Why might a firm engage in a private placement of its stock or bonds?

3 What is a hedge fund?

LO7

1 Define *synergy*.

2 What is a leveraged buyout?

3 Name and describe the two types of divestitures.

absolute advantage the ability to produce more goods using fewer resources than other providers.

accounting process of measuring, interpreting, and communicating financial information to enable people inside and outside the firm to make informed decisions.

accounting cycle set of activities involved in converting information and individual transactions into financial statements.

accounting equation formula that states that assets must equal liabilities plus owners' equity.

accrual accounting accounting method that records revenues and expenses when they occur, not necessarily when cash actually changes hands.

acquisition agreement in which one firm purchases another.

advertising paid nonpersonal communication, usually targeted at large numbers of potential buyers.

affective conflict disagreement that focuses on individuals or personal issues.

affinity program marketing effort sponsored by an organization that solicits involvement by individuals who share common interests and activities.

angel investor a wealthy individual who invests money directly in new ventures in exchange for equity.

application service provider (ASP) outside supplier that provides both the computers and the application support for managing an information system.

asset anything of value owned or leased by a business.

balance of payments overall flow of money into or out of a country.

balance of trade difference between a nation's exports and imports.

balance sheet statement of a firm's financial position on a particular date.

balanced budget situation in which total revenues raised by taxes equal the total proposed spending for the year.

benchmarking determining how well other companies perform business functions or tasks.

board of directors governing body of a corporation.

botnet a network of PCs that have been infected with one or more data-stealing viruses.

brand name, term, sign, symbol, design, or some combination that identifies the products of one firm and differentiates them from competitors' offerings.

brand equity added value that a respected and successful name gives to a product.

brand name part of the brand consisting of words or letters included in a name used to identify and distinguish the firm's offerings from those of competitors.

branding process of creating an identity in consumers' minds for a good, service, or company; a major marketing tool in contemporary business.

breakeven analysis pricing technique used to determine the minimum sales volume a product must generate at a certain price level to cover all costs.

budget organization's plan for how it will raise and spend money during a given period of time; a planning and controlling tool that reflects the firm's expected sales revenues, operating expenses, and cash receipts and outlays.

budget deficit situation in which the government spends more than the amount of money it raises through taxes.

budget surplus excess funding that occurs when government spends less than the amount of funds raised through taxes and fees.

business all profit-seeking activities and enterprises that provide goods and services necessary to an economic system.

business (B2B) product good or service purchased to be used, either directly or indirectly, in the production of other goods for resale.

business ethics standards of conduct and moral values governing actions and decisions in the work environment.

business incubator a local program designed to provide low-cost shared business facilities to small start-up ventures.

business intelligence activities and technologies for gathering, storing, and analyzing data to make better competitive decisions.

business plan a written document that provides an orderly statement of a company's objectives, methods, and standards.

C corporation a form of legal organization with assets and liabilities separate from those of its owner(s).

capital an organization's technology, tools, information, and physical facilities.

capital structure mix of a firm's debt and equity capital.

capitalism economic system that rewards firms for their ability to perceive and serve the needs and demands of consumers; also called the private enterprise system.

cause advertising form of institutional advertising that promotes a specific viewpoint on a public issue as a way to influence public opinion and the legislative process.

Central America–Dominican Republic Free Trade Agreement (CAFTA-DR) agreement among the United States, Costa Rica, the Dominican Republic, El Salvador, Guatemala, Honduras, and Nicaragua to reduce tariffs and trade restrictions.

chief information officer (CIO) executive responsible for managing a firm's information system and related computer technologies.

classic entrepreneur a person who identifies a business opportunity and allocates available resources to tap that market.

cloud computing a type of information delivery under which powerful servers store applications software and databases for users to access on the Web.

code of conduct formal statement that defines how an organization expects its employees to resolve ethical questions.

cognitive conflict disagreement that focuses on problem- and issue-related differences of opinion.

collective bargaining process of negotiation between management and union representatives.

common stock shares that give owners voting rights but only residual claims to the firm's assets and income distributions; basic form of corporate ownership.

communication the meaningful exchange of information through messages.

communism economic system in which all property would be shared equally by the people of a community under the direction of a strong central government.

comparative advantage the ability to produce one good at a relatively lower opportunity cost than other goods.

compensation amount employees are paid in money and benefits.

competitive differentiation unique combination of organizational abilities, products, and approaches that sets a company apart from competitors in the minds of customers.

computer-aided design (CAD) process that allows engineers to design components as well as entire products on computer screens faster and with fewer mistakes than they could achieve by working with traditional drafting systems.

computer-aided manufacturing (CAM) computer tools to analyze CAD output and enable a manufacturer to analyze the steps that a machine must take to produce a needed product or part.

computer-based information system information system that relies on computer and related technologies to store information electronically in an organized, accessible manner.

conflict situation in which the needs of a person or group do not match those of another, and attempts may be made to block the opposing side's intentions or goals.

conflict of interest occurs when a businessperson is faced with a situation in which an action benefiting one person or group has the potential to harm another.

conglomerate merger agreement that combines unrelated firms, usually with the goal of diversification, spurring sales growth, or spending a cash surplus in order to avoid a takeover attempt.

consumer (B2C) product good or service that is purchased by end users.

consumer behavior actions of ultimate consumers directly involved in obtaining, consuming, and disposing of products and the decision processes that precede and follow these actions.

consumer orientation business philosophy that focuses first on determining unmet consumer wants and needs and then designing products to satisfy those needs.

Consumer Price Index (CPI) measurement of the monthly average change in prices of goods and services.

consumerism public demand that a business consider the wants and needs of its customers in making decisions.

controlling function of evaluating an organization's performance against its objectives.

core inflation rate inflation rate of an economy after energy and food prices are removed.

corporate culture an organization's system of principles, beliefs, and values.

corporate philanthropy an organization's effort to contribute to the communities in which it earns profits through cash contributions, donations of equipment and products, and supporting the volunteer efforts of company employees.

cost-based pricing strategy in which an organization calculates total costs per unit and then adds markups to cover overhead costs and generate profits.

creative selling persuasive type of promotional presentation.

creativity capacity to develop novel solutions to perceived organizational problems.

critical thinking ability to analyze and assess information to pinpoint problems or opportunities.

cross-functional team a working group of members from different functions, such as production, marketing, and finance.

crowd funding a source of financial support involving groups of individuals, often connected through the Internet, that pool small sums of money to support new businesses as well as philanthropic causes and artistic endeavors.

cyclical unemployment people who are out of work due to contraction in the economy.

data raw facts and figures that may or may not be relevant to a business decision.

data mining the task of using computer-based technology to evaluate data in a database and identify useful trends.

database centralized integrated collection of data resources.

debt financing borrowed funds that entrepreneurs must repay.

decision making process of recognizing a problem or opportunity, evaluating alternative solutions, selecting and implementing an alternative, and assessing the results.

decision support system (DSS) system that provides direct support to businesspeople during the decision-making process.

deflation opposite of inflation; occurs when prices continue to fall.

delegation managerial process of assigning work to employees.

demand willingness and ability of buyers to purchase goods and services at different prices.

demand curve graph of the amount of a product that buyers will purchase at different prices.

demographic segmentation distinguishes markets on the basis of various demographic or socioeconomic characteristics.

departmentalization process of dividing work activities into units within the organization.

depression prolonged recession or one that causes a significant drop in GDP.

devaluation drop in a currency's value relative to other currencies or to a fixed standard.

directing guiding and motivating employees to accomplish organizational objectives.

discrimination biased treatment of a job candidate or employee.

distribution deals with the marketing activities and institutions involved in getting the right good or service to the firm's customers.

distribution channels path that products—and legal ownership of them—follow from producer to consumers or business user.

diversity in a workforce, the blending of individuals of different genders, ethnic backgrounds, cultures, religions, ages, and physical and mental abilities.

divestiture sale of assets by a firm.

double-entry bookkeeping process by which accounting transactions are recorded; each transaction must have an offsetting transaction.

downsizing process of reducing the number of employees within a firm by eliminating jobs.

dumping selling products abroad at prices below production costs or below typical prices in the home market to capture market share from domestic competitors.

economics social science that analyzes the choices individuals, groups, and governments make in allocating scarce resources.

embargo total ban on importing specific products or a total halt to trading with a particular country.

employee benefits additional compensation such as vacation, retirement plans, profit-sharing, health insurance, gym memberships, child and elder care, and tuition reimbursement, offered by the employer.

employee ownership business arrangement in which workers buy shares of stock in the company that employs them.

employee separation broad term covering the loss of an employee for any reason, voluntary or involuntary.

empowerment in an organization, employees' shared authority, responsibility, and decision making with their manager; giving employees authority and responsibility to make decisions about their work.

entrepreneur a person who seeks a profitable opportunity and takes the necessary risks to set up and operate a business.

entrepreneurship ability to see an opportunity and take the risks inherent in creating and operating a business.

Equal Employment Opportunity Commission (EEOC) government commission created to increase job opportunities for women and minorities and to help end discrimination based on race, color, religion, disability, gender, or national origin in any personnel action.

equilibrium price prevailing market price at which you can buy an item.

equity financing funds invested in new ventures in exchange for part ownership.

equity theory an individual's perception of fair and equitable treatment.

European Union (EU) 28-nation European economic alliance.

everyday low pricing (EDLP) strategy devoted to maintaining continuous low prices rather than relying on short-term price-cutting tactics such as cents-off coupons, rebates, and special sales.

exchange process activity in which two or more parties give something of value to each other to satisfy perceived needs.

exchange rate the rate at which a nation's currency can be exchanged for the currencies of other nations.

executive support system (ESS) system that allows senior executives to access the firm's primary databases, often by touching the computer screen, pointing and clicking a mouse, or using voice recognition.

expansionary monetary policy government actions to increase the money supply in an effort to cut the cost of borrowing, which encourages business decision makers to make new investments, in turn stimulating employment and economic growth.

expert system computer program that imitates human thinking through complicated sets of "if-then" rules.

export domestically produced good or service sold in markets in other countries.

external communication meaningful exchange of information through messages transmitted between an organization and its major audiences.

factors of production four basic inputs: natural resources, capital, human resources, and entrepreneurship.

family leave unpaid leave of up to 12 weeks annually for any employee for the birth or adoption of a child; to become a foster parent; or to care for a seriously ill relative, spouse, or self in the event of a serious health condition or injury; prescribed for employers with 50 or more employees by the Family and Medical Leave Act of 1993.

Federal Deposit Insurance Corporation (FDIC) federal agency that insures deposits at commercial and savings banks.

Federal Reserve System (Fed) the central bank of the United States.

finance planning, obtaining, and managing a company's funds to accomplish its objectives as effectively and efficiently as possible.

Financial Accounting Standards Board (FASB) an organization responsible for evaluating, setting, or modifying GAAP in the United States.

financial institutions intermediary between savers and borrowers, collecting funds from savers and then lending the funds to individuals, businesses, and governments.

financial managers executives who develop and implement the firm's financial plan and determine the most appropriate sources and uses of funds.

financial markets market in which securities are issued and traded.

financial plan document that specifies the funds needed by a firm for a period of time, the timing of inflows and outflows, and the most appropriate sources and uses of funds.

financial system process by which money flows from savers to users.

firewall limit data transfers to certain locations and log system use so that managers can identify attempts to log on with invalid passwords and other threats to a system's security.

fiscal policy government spending and taxation decisions designed to control inflation, reduce unemployment, improve the general standard of living, and encourage economic growth.

Foreign Corrupt Practices Act federal law that prohibits U.S. citizens and companies from bribing foreign officials in order to win or continue business.

franchisee individual or business firm purchasing a franchise.

franchising contractual business arrangement between a manufacturer or other supplier and a dealer, such as a restaurant operator or retailer.

franchisor firm whose products are sold to customers by the franchisee.

frequency marketing marketing initiative that rewards frequent purchases with cash, rebates, merchandise, or other premiums.

frictional unemployment experienced by members of the workforce who are temporarily not working but are looking for jobs.

General Agreement on Tariffs and Trade (GATT) international trade accord that substantially reduced worldwide tariffs and other trade barriers.

generally accepted accounting principles (GAAP) guidelines on the conventions, rules, and procedures for determining acceptable accounting and financial reporting practices.

geographic segmentation dividing a market into homogeneous groups on the basis of their location.

goal-setting theory says that people will be motivated to the extent to which they accept specific, challenging goals and receive feedback that indicates their progress toward goal achievement.

grapevine internal information channel that transmits information from unofficial sources.

gross domestic product (GDP) sum of all goods and services produced within a country's boundaries.

hardware all tangible elements of a computer system.

horizontal merger agreement that joins firms in the same industry for the purpose of diversification, increasing customer bases, cutting costs, or expanding product lines.

human resource management the function of attracting, developing, and retaining employees who can perform the activities necessary to accomplish organizational objectives.

human resources in an organization, anyone who works, providing either the physical labor or intellectual inputs.

hyperinflation economic situation characterized by soaring prices.

import foreign-made product purchased by domestic consumers.

income statement financial record summarizing a firm's financial performance in terms of revenues, expenses, and profits over a given time period, such as a quarter or a year.

inflation economic situation characterized by rising prices caused by a combination of excess consumer demand and increases in the costs of raw materials, component parts, human resources, and other factors of production.

information knowledge gained from processing data.

information system organized method for collecting, storing, and communicating past, present, and projected information on internal operations and external intelligence.

insider trading use of material nonpublic information about a company to make investment profits.

institutional advertising involves messages that promote concepts, ideas, philosophies, or goodwill for industries, companies, organizations, or government entities.

integrated marketing communications (IMC) coordination of all promotional activities—media advertising, direct mail, personal selling, sales promotion, and public relations—to produce a unified, customer-focused promotional strategy.

integrity adhering to deeply felt ethical principles in business situations.

International Accounting Standards Board (IASB) organization established in 1973 to promote worldwide consistency in financial reporting practices.

International Financial Reporting Standards (IFRS) standards and interpretations adopted by the IASB.

International Monetary Fund (IMF) organization created to promote trade, eliminate barriers, and make short-term loans to member nations that are unable to meet their budgets.

intranet computer network that is similar to the Internet but limits access to authorized users.

intrapreneurship process of promoting innovation within the structure of an existing organization.

inventory control the act of balancing the need to keep stock on hand to meet demand against the costs of carrying inventory.

job requirements the minimum skills, education, and experience that a candidate must have to be considered for the position.

joint venture partnership between companies formed for a specific undertaking.

just-in-time (JIT) system broad management philosophy that reaches beyond the narrow activity of inventory control to influence the entire system of production and operations management.

labor union group of workers who have banded together to achieve common goals in the areas of wages, hours, and working conditions.

leadership ability to direct or inspire people to attain certain goals.

leverage increasing the rate of return on funds invested by borrowing funds.

leveraged buyout (LBO) transaction in which public shareholders are bought out and the firm reverts to private status.

liability anything owed to creditors—the claims of a firm's creditors.

lifetime value of a customer revenues and intangible benefits (referrals and customer feedback) from a customer over the life of the relationship, minus the amount the company must spend to acquire and serve that customer.

limited-liability company (LLC) a business entity that secures the corporate advantage of limited liability while avoiding the double taxation characteristic of a traditional corporation.

listening receiving a message and interpreting its intended meaning by grasping the facts and feelings it conveys.

local area network (LAN) computer network that connects machines within limited areas, such as a building or several nearby buildings.

logistics process of coordinating the flow of goods, services, and information among members of the supply chain.

macroeconomics study of a nation's overall economic issues, such as how an economy uses its resources and how national governmental policies affect people's standard of living.

make, buy, or lease decision choosing whether to manufacture a product or component in-house, purchase it from an outside supplier, or lease it.

malware any malicious software program designed to infect computer systems.

management process of achieving organizational objectives through people and other resources.

management by objectives systematic approach that allows managers to focus on attainable goals and to achieve the best results based on the organization's resources.

management information system (MIS) information system designed to produce reports for managers and other personnel.

management support system information system designed to provide support for effective decision making.

market segmentation process of dividing a total market into several relatively homogeneous groups.

marketing organizational function and set of processes for creating, communicating, and delivering value to customers and for managing customer relationships in ways that benefit the organization and its stakeholders.

marketing concept companywide consumer orientation to promote long-run success.

marketing mix blending of the four elements of marketing strategy—product, distribution, promotion, and pricing—to fit the needs and preferences of a specific target market.

marketing research collecting and evaluating information to help marketers make effective decisions.

Maslow's hierarchy of needs theory of motivation proposed by Abraham Maslow. According to the theory, people have five levels of needs that they seek to satisfy: physiological, safety, social, esteem, and self-actualization.

materials requirement planning (MRP) a computer-based production planning system that ensures a firm has all the parts and materials it needs to produce its output at the right time and place and in the right amounts.

merger agreement in which two or more firms combine to form one company.

microeconomics study of small economic units, such as individual consumers, families, and businesses.

microloan small-business loan often used to buy equipment or operate a business.

mission statement written explanation of an organization's business intentions and aims.

missionary selling indirect form of selling in which the representative promotes goodwill for a company or provides technical or operational assistance to the customer.

mixed market economy economic system that mixes both private enterprise systems and planned economies.

monetary policy government actions to increase or decrease the money supply and change banking requirements and interest rates to influence bankers' willingness to make loans.

monopolistic competition market structure in which large numbers of buyers and sellers exchange heterogeneous products so each participant has some control over price.

monopoly market situation in which a single seller dominates trade of a good or service for which buyers can find no close substitutes.

multinational corporation firm with significant operations and marketing activities outside its home country.

national debt money owed by government to individuals, businesses, and government agencies who purchase Treasury bills, Treasury notes, and Treasury bonds sold to cover expenditures.

natural resources all production inputs that are useful in their natural states, including agricultural land, building sites, forests, and mineral deposits.

nearshoring outsourcing production or services to locations near a firm's home base.

North American Free Trade Agreement (NAFTA) agreement among the United States, Canada, and Mexico to break down tariffs and trade restrictions.

not-for-profit corporation organization whose goals do not include pursuing a profit.

not-for-profit organization businesslike establishment that has primary objectives other than returning profits to owners.

objective quantitative (measurable) outcome by which managers define the organization's desired performance in such areas as new-product development, sales, customer service, growth, environmental and social responsibility, and employee satisfaction.

offshoring relocation of business processes to lower-cost locations overseas.

oligopoly market situation in which relatively few sellers compete and high start-up costs serve as barriers to new competitors.

on-demand computing an organization's rental of software time from application providers, paying only for software usage.

onshoring returning production to its original manufacturing location because of changes in costs or processes.

operational support system information system designed to produce a variety of information on an organization's activities for both internal and external users.

OPM money an entrepreneur raises from others to help start or expand a business.

opportunity cost the highest valued alternative forgone in the pursuit of an activity.

order processing form of selling, mostly at the wholesale and retail levels, that involves identifying customer needs, pointing them out to customers, and completing orders.

organization structured group of people working together to achieve common goals.

organizing process of blending human and material resources through a formal structure of tasks and authority: arranging work, dividing tasks among employees, and coordinating them to ensure implementation of plans and accomplishment of objectives.

outsourcing using outside vendors to produce goods or fulfill services and functions previously handled in-house or in-country; transferring jobs from inside a firm to outside the firm.

owners' equity the owner's initial investment in the business plus profits that were not paid out to owners over time in the form of cash dividends.

partnership association of two or more persons who operate a business as co-owners by voluntary legal agreement.

penetration pricing strategy that sets a low price to enter competitive markets.

performance appraisal evaluation of and feedback on an employee's job performance.

personal selling a direct person-to-person promotional presentation to a potential buyer.

physical distribution actual movement of products from producer to consumers or business users.

planned economy economic system in which government controls determine business ownership, profits, and resource allocation to accomplish government goals rather than those set by individual firms.

planning process of anticipating future events and conditions and determining courses of action for achieving organizational objectives.

point-of-purchase (POP) advertising displays or demonstrations that promote products when and where consumers buy them, such as in retail stores.

positioning the act of establishing a product in the minds of customers by communicating meaningful distinctions about the attributes, price, quality, or use of a good or service.

preferred stock shares that give owners limited voting rights, and the right to receive dividends or assets before owners of common stock.

prestige pricing strategies that establish relatively high prices to develop and maintain an image of quality and exclusiveness.

price the exchange value of a good or service.

primary markets financial market in which firms and governments issue securities and sell them initially to the general public.

private enterprise system economic system that rewards firms for their ability to identify and serve the needs and demands of customers.

private property most basic freedom under the private enterprise system; the right to own, use, buy, sell, and bequeath land, buildings, machinery, equipment, patents, individual possessions, and various intangible kinds of property.

privatization conversion of government-owned and -operated companies into privately held businesses.

problem-solving team temporary combination of workers who gather to solve a specific problem and then disband.

process control system operational support system designed to monitor and control physical processes.

product bundle of physical, service, and symbolic characteristics designed to satisfy consumer wants.

product advertising messages designed to sell a particular good or service.

product liability the responsibility of manufacturers for injuries and damages caused by their products.

product life cycle four basic stages—introduction, growth, maturity, and decline—through which a successful product progresses.

product line group of related products marked by physical similarities or intended for a similar market.

product mix the assortment of product lines and individual goods and services that a firm offers to consumers and business users.

product placement form of promotion in which marketers pay placement fees to have their products showcased in various media, ranging from newspapers and magazines to television and movies.

production use of resources, such as workers and machinery, to convert materials into finished goods and services.

production and operations management overseeing the production process by managing people and machinery in converting materials and resources into finished goods and services.

production control creates a well-defined set of procedures for coordinating people, materials, and machinery to provide maximum production efficiency.

productivity relationship between the goods and services produced in a nation each year and the inputs needed to produce them.

product-related segmentation dividing consumer markets into groups based on buyers' relationships to the good or service.

profits rewards earned by businesspeople who take the risks involved in blending people, technology, and information to create and market want-satisfying goods and services.

promotion informing, persuading, and influencing a purchase decision.

promotional mix combination of personal and nonpersonal selling activities designed to meet the needs of a firm's target customers.

psychographic segmentation dividing consumer markets into groups with similar psychological characteristics, values, and lifestyles.

public accountant accountant who provides accounting services to individuals or business firms for a fee.

public relations organization's communications and relationships with its various public audiences.

publicity nonpersonal stimulation of demand for a good, service, place, idea, event, person, or organization by unpaid placement of information in print or broadcast media.

pulling strategy promoting a product by generating consumer demand for it, primarily through advertising and sales promotion appeals.

pure competition market structure in which large numbers of buyers and sellers exchange homogeneous products and no single participant can significantly influence price.

pushing strategy personal selling to market an item to wholesalers and retailers in a company's distribution channels.

quality good or service that is free of deficiencies.

quality control involves measuring output against established quality standards.

quota limit set on the amounts of particular products that countries can import during specified time periods.

recession cyclical economic contraction that lasts for six months or longer.

recycling reprocessing of used materials for reuse.

regulated monopoly market situation in which local, state, or federal government grants exclusive rights in a certain market to a single firm.

relationship era business era in which firms seek ways to actively nurture customer loyalty by carefully managing their interactions with buyers.

relationship marketing developing and maintaining long-term, cost-effective exchange relationships with partners.

restrictive monetary policy government actions to reduce the money supply to curb rising prices, overexpansion, and concerns about overly rapid economic growth.

retailer distribution channel members that sell goods and services to individuals for their own use rather than for resale.

risk-return trade-off process of maximizing the wealth of a firm's shareholders by striking the optimal balance between risk and return.

S corporation a form of business organization in which the entity does not pay corporate taxes on profits; instead, profits are distributed to shareholders, who pay individual income taxes.

salary pay calculated on a periodic basis, such as weekly or monthly.

sales promotion activities that support advertising and personal selling.

Sarbanes-Oxley Act of 2002 federal legislation designed to deter and punish corporate and accounting fraud and corruption and to protect the interests of workers and shareholders through enhanced financial disclosures, criminal penalties on CEOs and CFOs who defraud investors, safeguards for whistle-blowers, and establishment of a new regulatory body for public accounting firms.

secondary market collection of financial markets in which previously issued securities are traded among investors.

securities financial instruments that represent obligations on the part of the issuers to provide the purchasers with expected stated returns on the funds invested or loaned.

seed capital initial funding used to launch a company.

self-managed team work group with authority to decide how its members complete their daily tasks.

serial entrepreneur person who starts one business, runs it, and then starts and runs additional businesses in succession.

server a dedicated computer that provides services to other computers on a network.

sexism discrimination against members of either sex, but primarily affecting women.

sexual harassment unwelcome and inappropriate actions of a sexual nature in the workplace.

skimming pricing strategy that sets an intentionally high price relative to the prices of competing products.

skunkworks project initiated by an employee who conceives an idea, convinces top management of its potential, and then recruits human and other resources from within the company to the idea into a commercial project.

small business an independent entity with fewer than 500 employees that is not dominant in its market.

Small Business Administration (SBA) principal government agency concerned with helping small U.S. firms.

social entrepreneur a person who recognizes societal problems and uses business principles to develop innovative solutions.

social responsibility management's acceptance of the role that ethics plays in their business and their obligation to consider consumer satisfaction, and societal well-being of equal value to profit in evaluating the firm's performance.

socialism economic system characterized by government ownership and operation of major industries such as communications.

software all the programs, routines, and computer languages that control a computer and tell it how to operate.

sole proprietorship business ownership in which there is no legal distinction between the sole proprietor's status as an individual and his or her status as a business owner.

spyware software that secretly gathers user information through the user's Internet connection without his or her knowledge, usually for advertising purposes.

stakeholders customers, investors, employees, and public affected by or with an interest in a company.

statement of cash flows statement showing the sources and uses of cash during a period of time.

statement of owners' equity record of the change in owners' equity from the end of one fiscal period to the end of the next.

stock markets (exchanges) market in which shares of stock are bought and sold by investors.

stockholder an owner of a corporation due to his or her purchase of stock in the corporation.

structural unemployment people who remain unemployed for long periods of time, often with little hope of finding a new job like their old one.

subcontracting international agreement that involves hiring local companies to produce, distribute, or sell goods or services in a specific country or geographical region.

supply amount of goods and services for sale at different prices.

supply chain complete sequence of suppliers that contribute to creating a good or service and delivering it to business users and final consumers.

supply curve graph that shows the relationship between different prices and the quantities that sellers will offer for sale, regardless of demand.

SWOT analysis SWOT is an acronym for *strengths, weaknesses, opportunities,* and *threats.* By systematically evaluating all four of these factors, a firm can then develop the best strategies for gaining a competitive advantage.

target market group of people toward whom an organization markets its goods, services, or ideas with a strategy designed to satisfy their specific needs and preferences.

tariff tax, surcharge, or duty on foreign products.

team group of people with certain skills who are committed to a common purpose, approach, and set of performance goals.

team cohesiveness extent to which team members feel attracted to the team and motivated to remain part of it.

team norm standard of conduct shared by team members that guides their behavior.

telemarketing personal selling conducted entirely by telephone, which provides a firm's marketers with a high return on their expenditures, an immediate response, and an opportunity for personalized two-way conversation.

test marketing introduction of a new product supported by a complete marketing campaign to a selected city or TV coverage area.

trade deficit the negative difference between what a country exports compared to what it imports.

trade promotion sales promotion geared to marketing intermediaries rather than to final consumers.

trade surplus the positive difference between what a country exports compared to what it imports.

trademark brand that has been given legal protection.

transaction management building and promoting products in the hope that enough customers will buy them to cover costs and earn profits.

transaction processing system operational support system that records and processes data from business transactions.

Trojan horse program that claims to do one thing but in reality does something else, usually something malicious.

unemployment rate percentage of the total workforce actively seeking work but who are currently unemployed.

utility a measure of the value of a good or service to a consumer; power of a good or service to satisfy a want or need.

venture capitalist a business organization or group of individuals that invests in early-stage, high-potential, and growth companies.

vertical merger agreement that combines firms operating at different levels in the production and marketing process.

virtual private network (VPN) secure connection between two points on the Internet.

virtual team a group of geographically or organizationally dispersed co-workers who use a combination of telecommunications and information technologies to accomplish an organizational task.

virus program that secretly attaches itself to other programs (called hosts) and changes them or destroys data.

vision the ability to perceive marketplace needs and what an organization must do to satisfy them; perception of marketplace needs and the ways a firm can satisfy them.

VoIP alternative version of telecommunication service using the Internet.

volume objective pricing strategy that bases a pricing decision on the attainment of market share.

wage pay based on an hourly rate or the amount of work accomplished.

whistle-blowing employee's disclosure to company officials, government authorities, or the media of illegal, immoral, or unethical practices committed by an organization.

wholesaler distribution channel member that sells primarily to retailers, other wholesalers, or business users.

wide area network (WAN) ties larger geographical regions together by using telephone lines and microwave and satellite transmission.

WiFi wireless network that connects various devices and allows them to communicate with one another through radio waves.

work team relatively permanent group of employees with complementary skills who perform the day-to-day work of organizations.

World Bank organization established by industrialized nations to lend money to less developed countries.

World Trade Organization (WTO) 153-member international institution that monitors GATT agreements and mediates international trade disputes.

worm small piece of software that exploits a security hole in a network to replicate itself.

Chapter 1

1. Company Web site, http://www.apple.com, accessed May 15, 2013; Katie Marsal, "Former Apple Product Manager Recounts How Jobs Motivated First iPhone Team," *Apple Insider*, February 3, 2012, www.appleinsider.com; Brian Caulfield, "The Steve Jobs Economy," *Forbes*, November 7, 2011, p. 16; Gianpiero Petriglieri, "How Steve Jobs Reinvented Leadership," *Forbes*, October 10, 2011, www.forbes.com; John Baldoni, "Learning from Steve Jobs: How to Lead with Purpose," *CNN Opinion*, October 14, 2011, www.cnn.com; John Markoff, "Apple's Visionary Redefined Digital Age," *New York Times*, October 5, 2011, www.nytimes.com; Joe Nocera, "What Makes Steve Jobs Great," *New York Times*, August 26, 2011, www.nytimes.com; David Pogue, "Steve Jobs Reshaped Industries," *New York Times*, blog post, August 25, 2011, www.nytimes.com.

2. National Center for Charitable Statistics, "Quick Facts about Nonprofits," http://nccs.urban.org/statistics, accessed April 24, 2013.

3. National Center for Charitable Statistics, "Quick Facts about Nonprofits," http://nccs.urban.org/statistics, accessed April 24, 2013; Foundation Center, Grant Space, http://grantspace.org/, accessed April 24, 2013; Bureau of Labor Statistics, *Career Guide to Industries, 2010–11 Edition*, http://www.bls.gov, accessed April 24, 2013.

4. "100 Best Companies to Work For (2013)," CNNMoney.com, http://money.cnn.com, accessed April 24, 2013.

5. Grace Austin, "inDinero: Helping Businesses Keep Tabs on Money," *Profiles in Diversity Journal*, July 16, 2012, http://www.diversityjournal.com/9603-indinero-helping -businesses-keep-tabs-on-money/.

6. Brad Reed, "Apple Loses Latest Round in Android Patent Fight," *Network World*, January 24, 2012, http://www .networkworld.com; Wayne Rash, "Apple, Microsoft, Oracle Lead Unholy Patent Alliance against Android," July 11, 2011, http:// www.eweek.com.

7. Government Web site, "Welcome to the Bureau of Competition," Federal Trade Commission, http://www.ftc.gov/bc, accessed May 15, 2013.

8. Company Web site, "History," http://www.steinway.com, accessed April 24, 2013.

9. "Best Global Brands 2012," *interbrand*, http://www.interbrand .com, accessed April 24, 2013.

10. Jennifer M. Ortman, "U.S. Population Projections: 2012 to 2060," U.S. Census Bureau, February 7, 2013, http://www .census.gov/population/projections.

11. "The 2013 DiversityInc Top 50 Companies for Diversity," DiversityInc, n.d., http://www.diversityinc.com, accessed April 24, 2013.

12. Company Web site, http://www.nobisengineering.com, accessed April 24, 2013; Matthew J. Mowry, "Celebrating Business Excellence," *Business NH Magazine*, May 2011, p. 54.

13. "World's Most Admired Companies 2013," *Fortune*, http://money.cnn.com, accessed April 24, 2013.

Chapter 2

1. Company website, http://www.panerabread.com, accessed April 21, 2013; Stuart Elliott, "Selling Products by Selling Shared Values," *New York Times*, February 13, 2013, http://www.nytimes.com; Kate Rogers, "Panera Opens Free-Food, Suggested-Donations-Only Cafes," *Fox Business*, January 23, 2013, http://smallbusiness.foxbusiness.com; S. W. Hartley, "Café of Sharing," July 2012, http://kerinmarketing.com.

2. Steve Strunsky, "Port Authority Manager Fired for Misrepresenting Academic Credentials," *Star-Ledger*, September 19, 2012, http://www.nj.com.

3. "Internet Abuse at Work," *Memory Spy*, January 15, 2012, http://memoryspy.com.

4. Robert N. Barger, "Summary of Lawrence Kohlberg's Stages of Moral Development," University of Notre Dame, www.library.spscc.ctc.edu, accessed January 23, 2013.

5. Company Web site, http://www.jnj.com, accessed September 13, 2013; Susan Todd, "Johnson & Johnson's New CEO Emphasizes Company Credo at Shareholder's Meeting," *The Star-Ledger*, April 27, 2012, http://blog.nj.com.

6. Walter Pavlo, "There Are No Nice Prosecutors When You Are a Defendant," Forbes, January 21, 2013, http://blogs.forbes.com.

7. Company Web site, http://www.cynthiacooper.com, accessed January 30, 2013.

8. Associated Press, "Indiana Hospital Fires 8 Workers Who Refused Flu Shot," Fox News, http://www.foxnews.com, January 1, 2013.

9. Organization Web site, Human Rights Campaign, http://www.hrc.org, accessed January 23, 2013.

10. "Conference Board Job Satisfaction Survey Finds Older Workers as Dissatisfied as Others," *Aging Workforce News*, http://www.agingworkforcenews.com, accessed January 23, 2013.

11. U.S. Equal Employment Opportunity Commission, "Sexual Harassment Charges EEOC & FEPAs Combined: FY 1997-FY 2011," http://www1.eeoc.gov, accessed January 23, 2013.

12. National Committee on Pay Equity, "Wage Gap Statistically Unchanged," http://www.pay-equity.org, accessed January 23, 2013.

13. "Many U.S. Kids Still Exposed to Smoke in Cars: Study," February 6, 2012, http://www.reuters.com.

14. Company Web site, http://www.subway.com, accessed January 23, 2013; Jared Foundation, http://www.jaredfoundation.org, accessed January 23, 2013.

15. Company Web site, http://www.pgscorecard.com, accessed March 31, 2013; Akhila Vijayaraghavan, "Kaiser Permanente Greens Its Supply Chain by Switching to Safer IV Equipment," *Triple Pundit*, January 20, 2012, http://www.triplepundit.com.

16. Company Web site, http://www.apple.com, accessed March 31, 2013.

17. Company Web site, http://www.bp.com, accessed January 21, 2013.

18. Company Web site, http://www.biodiesel.com, accessed April 23, 2013; Melanie Stephens, "Pono Biofuels Agriculture Plan for Maui Pacific Biodiesel: VP Kelly King Looks at the Possibilities," *Maui Weekly,* October 11, 2012.

19. Company Web site, "Brand Partnerships," http://www.generalmills.com, accessed January 23, 2013.

20. U.S. Food and Drug Administration, "Natura Pet Issues Voluntary Recall of Specialized Dry Pet Foods Due to Possible Health Risk," press release, March 18, 2013, http://www.fda.gov.

21. Company Web site, "Rules and Policies," http://pages.ebay.com, accessed January 23, 2013.

Chapter 3

1. Claudia Buck, "Lackluster Job Market Drives Thousands of Young Adults Back Home to Live with Parents," *The Sacramento Bee,* April 4, 2013, www.sacbee.com; Rebecca Trounson, "Boomerang Babies Don't Mind Return," *Chicago Tribune*, March 20, 2012.

2. Amy Chozick, "F.C.C Shift May Thwart a Murdoch Media Deal," *New York Times*, March 24, 2013, http://www.nytimes.com.

3. Company Web site, http://www.aircanada.com, accessed April 9, 2013.

4. *World Factbook*, Central Intelligence Agency, http://www.cia.gov, accessed April 9, 2013.

5. *Occupational Outlook Handbook 2012–2013 Edition*, U.S. Bureau of Labor Statistics, http://www.bls.gov, accessed April 9, 2013.

6. Emily Jane Fox, "Wal-Mart to Hire 100,000 Veterans," CNN Money, http://money.cnn.com, January 15, 2013.

7. U.S. National Debt Clock, http://www.brillig.com, accessed April 24, 2013.

Chapter 4

1. Chester Dawson, "Toyota Again World's Largest Autor Maker," *The Wall Street Journal*, January 28, 2013, http://online.wsj.com; Chris Isidore, "Toyota Motor Set to Reclaim 'Top Car Maker' Spot from GM," CNN Money, December 26, 2012, http://money.cnn.com.

2. *World Factbook*, "United States," https://www.cia.gov, accessed April 9, 2013.

3. Organization Web site, http://data.worldbank.org, accessed April 9, 2013.

4. Company Web site, http://walmartstores.com, "International," accessed April 9, 2013.

5. U.S. Census, "Top Ten Countries with Which the U.S. Trades, for the Month of December 2011," http://www.census.gov, accessed April 9, 2013.

6. U.S. Census, "Origin of Movement of U.S. Exports of Goods by State by NAICS-Based Product Code Groupings, Not Seasonally Adjusted, 2010," http://www.census.gov, accessed April 9, 2013.

7. U.S. Bureau of Economic Analysis, "U.S. International Trade in Goods and Services," press release, February 10, 2012, http://www.bea.gov.

8. Company Web site, http://en.shanghaidisneyresort.com.cn/en, accessed April 9, 2013; Shanghai Disney Resort, "First Steel Column of the Shanghai Disney Resort Project Administration Building Installed," press release, November 22, 2012, http://en.shanghaidisneyresort.com.cn.

9. Bank for International Settlements, http://www.bis.org, accessed April 9, 2013.

10. U.S. Department of Agriculture, Foreign Agriculture Service, "U.S. Sugar Import Program," http://www.fas.usda.gov, accessed April 9, 2013.

11. John Vidal, "Ethiopia Dam Project Is Devastating the Lives of Remote Indigenous Groups," *The Guardian*, February 6, 2013, http://www.guardian.co.uk; John Vidal, "Ethiopia Dam Project Rides Roughshod over Heritage of Local Tribespeople," *The Guardian*, February 23, 2012, http://www.guardian.co.uk.

12. Office of the United States Trade Representative, "CAFTA-DR," http://www.ustr.gov, accessed April 9, 2013.

13. European Union Web site, "Countries," http://europa.eu, accessed April 9, 2013; *World Factbook,* www.cia.gov, accessed April 9, 2013.

Chapter 5

1. Company Web site, www.snagajob.com, accessed April 18, 2013; John Reid Blackwell, "Snagajob Hires New CEO; Founder to Become Chairman," *Richmond Times-Dispatch*, March 7, 2013, http://www.timesdispatch.com; Pete Woody, "Corporate Wellness on the Menu at Active RVA Awards Luncheon," Sports Backers, February 14, 2013, http://www.sportsbackers.org.

2. U.S. Small Business Administration, "Advocacy Small Business Statistics and Research," http://web.sba.gov/faqs, accessed April 18, 2013.

3. Ibid.

4. U.S. Small Business Administration, "Guide to SBA's Definitions of Small Business," http://archive.sba.gov, "Table of Small Business Size Standards Matched to North American Industry Classification System Codes," http://www.sba.gov, accessed April 18, 2013.

5. Gwen Moran, "10 Hot Export Markets for Small Businesses," *Entrepreneur*, accessed September 17, 2013, http://www.entrepreneur.com.

6. U.S. Small Business Administration, "Frequently Asked Questions," http://archive.sba.gov/advo/stats/sbfaq.pdf, April 18, 2013.

7. U.S. Small Business Administration, "Small Business Jobs Act of 2010," http://www.sba.gov, accessed April 18, 2013; David Ferris, "Law Can Have Big Impact on Small Businesses," February 1, 2012, http://www.workforce.com.

8. U.S. Small Business Administration, Office for Advocacy "Frequently Asked Questions," http://www.sba.gov, accessed April 18, 2013.

9. Company Web site, http://www.newsroom.fb.com, accessed April 18, 2013.

10. U.S. Small Business Administration, Office of Advocacy, "Frequently Asked Questions: Advocacy Small Business Statistics and Research," http://www.sba.gov, accessed April 18, 2013.

11. Nick Reese, "10 Common Pitfalls of New Entrepreneurs—and How to Avoid Them," *Forbes*, July 13, 2012, http://www.forbes.com.

12. W. Mark Crain, "The Impact of Regulatory Costs on Small Firms," Office of Advocacy, U.S. Small Business Administration, http://www.sba.gov, accessed April 18, 2013.

13. U.S. Small Business Administration, "What We Do," http://www.sba.gov, accessed April 18, 2013.

14. U.S. Small Business Administration, "Mission Statement," http://www.sba.gov, accessed April 18, 2013.

15. U.S. Small Business Administration, "Loans and Grants," http://www.sba.gov, accessed April 18, 2013.

16. U.S. Small Business Administration, "Disaster Assistance," http://www.sba.gov, accessed April 18, 2013.

17. U.S. Small Business Administration, "Small Business Jobs Act of 2010," http://www.sba.gov, accessed April 18, 2013.

18. U.S. Small Business Administration, "Microloan Program," http://www.sba.gov, accessed April 18, 2013.

19. Small Business Investor Alliance, "SBIC Program History," http://www.sbia.org, accessed April 18, 2013.

20. Women Moving Millions, "Facts: Entrepreneurship & Small Business," http://www.womenmovingmillions.org, accessed April 18, 2013.

21. Associated Press, "BP Seeks to Block Payment of Business Claims under Gulf Spill Settlement," Fox News, March 15, 2013, http://www.foxnews.com.

22. Lewis Taub, "Maximizing the Benefits of the S Corporation in Turbulent Times," McGladrey, http://www.mcgladrey.com, accessed May 2, 2013.

23. Organization Web site, "About City Year," http://www.cityyear.org, accessed April 18, 2013.

24. Organization Web site, National Cooperative Business Association, http://usa2012.coop, accessed April 18, 2013.

25. Mary Schlangenstein, "US Airways Leads AMR Merger to Create Largest Airline," *Bloomberg*, February 14, 2013, http://www.bloomberg.com.

26. Rachel Landen, "Private-Equity Firm Buys EHR Subsidiary from GE," ModernHealthcare.com, March 7, 2013, http://www.modernhealthcare.com.

27. Richard Verrier, "Oriental DreamWorks and Chinese Partners Announce Tibet Movie," *Los Angeles Times*, April 20, 2013, http://www.latimes.com; Brookes Barnes, "DreamWorks Animation Forms Studio with Chinese Partners," *The New York Times*, February 17, 2012, http://mediacoder.blogs.nytimes.com; Brent Lang, "DreamWorks Animation Announces China Joint Venture," *The Wrap*, February 17, 2012, http://www.thewrap.com.

Chapter 6

1. Company Web site, www.marketingzen.com, accessed March 13, 2013; Claudia Chan, "Meet Shama Kabani," www.claudiachan.com, February 15, 2012; Matt Vilano, "From Grad Student to Social Media Millionaire," Entrepreneur.com, September 5, 2011, www.entrepreneur.com; Shama Kabani, "26 Lessons from a 26 Year Old CEO," Forbes.com, July 25, 2011, www.forbes.com.

2. Company Web site, http://investors.walmartstores.com, accessed March 13, 2013.

3. Company Web site, http://www.foxconn.com/companyintro.html, accessed March 13, 2013.

4. "Terry Gou," Forbes Profile, www.forbes.com, accessed September 9, 2013; Foxconn Technology, "Business Day," *New York Times*, September 24, 2012, http://topics.nytimes.com.

5. Mark Henricks, "Honor Roll," *Entrepreneur*, http://www.entrepreneur.com, accessed March 13, 2013.

6. Company Web site, http://www.dell.com, accessed March 10, 2013.

7. Company Web site, http://www.4food.com, accessed September 9, 2013; Amelia Levin, "4FOOD," Restaurant Development and Design, September 28, 2012, http://www.rddmag.com.

8. Company Web site, http://www.turningtechnologies.com, accessed March 13, 2013.

9. Organization Web site, http://www.keiretsuforum.com, accessed March 13, 2013.

10. Devin Thorpe, "Eight Crowdfunding Sites for Social Entrepreneurs," *Forbes*, September 10, 2012, http://www.forbes.com.

11. Organization Web site, "View Profile: Britta Riley, Windowfarms," http://socialcapitalmarkets.net, accessed March 13, 2013; company Web site, http://www.windowfarms.com, accessed March 13, 2013.

12. Association Web site, http://www.nbia.org, accessed March 13, 2013.

13. Organization Web site, http://www.nasa.gov, accessed March 13, 2013.

14. Science Daily Web site, "Ernest H. Volwiler Information," http://inventors.sciencedaily.com, accessed March 12, 2013.

15. Company Web site, "Peter Taunton video," http://www.snapfitness.com, accessed March 10, 2013.

16. Liz Welch, "John Vechey: Don't Waste Time with Mission Statements," *Inc.* magazine, http://www.inc.com, March 6, 2013.

17. Company website, http://www.fortheloveofdog.com, accessed April 9, 2013.

18. Personal Web site, http://elonmusk.com, accessed March 10, 2013.

19. Personal Web site, http://elonmusk.com, accessed March 10, 2013; Damon Poeter, "Is Elon Musk the Real-Life Tony Stark? Not So Fast," *PC Magazine*, May 23, 2012, http://www.pcmag.com.

20. Meg Cadoux Hirshberg, "The Full Story," http://www.stonyfield.com, accessed March 13, 2013.

21. Jone Johnson Lewis, "Oprah Winfrey Quotes," About Women's History, http://womenshistory.about.com, accessed April 10, 2013.

22. Hannah Seligson, "When the Work-Life Scales Are Unequal," *New York Times*, September 1, 2012, http://www.nytimes.com.

23. Deborah Gage, "The Venture Capital Secret: 3 Out of 4 Start-Ups Fail," *The Wall Street Journal Online*, September 19, 2012, http://online.wsj.com.

24. Association Web site, http://www.franchise.org, accessed March 13, 2013.

25. Company Web site, http://www.baskinrobbins.com, accessed March 13, 2013.

26. Company Web site, http://www.subway.com, accessed March 13, 2013.

27. Edward N. Levitt, "What's So Great about Franchising?" *FranchiseKnowHow*, http://www.franchiseknowhow.com, accessed March 13, 2013.

28. John Webb, "How Dreamworks, LinkedIn and Google Build Intrapreneurial Cultures," January 23, 2013, http://www.innovationexcellence.com.

29. Company Web site, http://www.3m.com, accessed March 13, 2013.

30. Company Web site, http://www.3m.com, accessed March 13, 2013.

Chapter 7

1. Fortune's "100 Best Companies to Work For" 2013, *CNNMoney*, http://money.cnn.com, accessed April 16, 2013; Emma Sapong "Wegmans Ranked among Best Places to Work for 16th Straight Year," *The Buffalo News,* January 16, 2013, http://www.buffalonews.com; "FMI Presents Robert B. Wegman Award to Danny Wegman," *Progressive Grocer,* January 30, 2012, http://www.progressivegrocer.com.

2. Brad Tuttle, "Apple, L.L. Bean—and Especially, Amazon—Score Big in Online Shopping Satisfaction," *Time*, May 14, 2012, http://business.time.com.

3. Company Web site, "Leadership," http://www.aboutmcdonalds.com, accessed May 3, 2013; Shaila Dewan, "McDonald's Says Its Chief Will Retire This Summer," *New York Times,* March 21, 2012, http://www.nytimes.com.

4. Company Web site, http://www.google.com, accessed May 3, 2013; Joseph Walker, "School's in Session at Google," *The Wall Street Journal*, July 5, 2012, http://onlinw.wsj.com.

5. Katie Couric, "The Man behind the Miracle on the Hudson: Captain Sully Sullenberger," *The Katie Show,* aired January 15, 2013, http://www.katiecouric.com.

6. Craig Chappelow, "5 Rules for Making Your Vision Stick," *Fast Company,* September 5, 2012, http://www.fastcompany.com/3000998/5-rules-making-your-vision-stick.

7. Company Web site, "Corporate Information," http://www.google.com, accessed March 13, 2013.

8. Bruce I. Jones, "People Management Lessons from Disney," http://www.trainingindustry.com, accessed April 16, 2013.

9. Gwen Moran, "Zappos' Secrets to Building an Empowering Company Culture," *Entrepreneur*, March 6, 2013, http://www.entrepreneur.com.

10. Company Web site, "Whole Foods Market's: Green Mission Report" http://www.wholefoodsmarket.com, accessed April 30, 2013.

11. Ibid.

12. Company Web site, http://www.starbucks.com, accessed April 16, 2013.

13. Ibid.

14. "Coolest College Startups 2013," *Inc.,* http://www.inc.com, accessed April 30, 2013.

15. Brandon Lamoncha, "Company Thrives on Empowering Employees," Interise, February 4, 2013, http://interise.org.

16. Company Web site, http://investor.activision.com, accessed April 16, 2013.

17. Company Web site, http://www.petswelcome.com, accessed April 16, 2013.

18. Company Web site, http://www.pg.com, accessed April 16, 2013.

19. Susan Schor, "10 Leadership Tips from Eileen Fisher," *Inc.,* http://www.inc.com, accessed April 16, 2013.

Chapter 8

1. Bureau of Labor Statistics, "Employment Situation of Veterans Summary," news release, March 20, 2013, http://www.bls.gov; "Disney to Hire 1,000 Vets, Launches PR Campaign," *West Orlando News,* March 13, 2012, http://westorlandonews.com; Halimah Abdullah, "Hiring Our Heroes: McChrystal on Hiring Veterans: We Need to Understand Where Soldiers Come From," *MSNBC*, March 26, 2012, http://hiringourheroes.today.com; company Web site, "Walmart U.S. CEO Bill Simon Calls on Veterans to Help Lead an 'American Renewal,'" press release, August 31, 2011, http://news.walmart.com.

2. Government Web site, "Fact Sheet on Employment Tests and Selection Procedures," http://eeoc.gov, accessed April 24, 2013.

3. "100 Best Companies to Work For (2013)," *CNN Money.com,* http://money.cnn.com, accessed April 24, 2013; "Nugget Market" in "100 Best Companies to Work For (2013)," *CNN Money.com,* http://money.cnn.com, accessed April 24, 2013; company Web site, "Nugget Markets Ranked in FORTUNE Magazine's '100 Best Companies to Work For' List for Seventh Consecutive Year," press release, January 20, 2012, http://www.nuggetmarket.com.

4. Tricia Phillips, "Job Focus: How to Get an Apprenticeship," *Mirror*, March 8, 2013, http://www.mirror.co.uk; company Web site, "McDonald's Puts Apprenticeships on the Menu," http://www.aboutmcdonalds.com, accessed April 24, 2013.

5. Victor Lipman, "4 Steps to Painless (and Effective) Performance Evaluations," *Forbes*, October 4, 2012, http://www.forbes.com.

6. Bureau of Labor Statistics, "Employer Costs for Employee Compensation," press release, March 12, 2013, http://www.bls.gov.

7. Company Web site, "Benefits Overview," http://www.qualcomm.com, accessed April 24, 2013; "100 Best Companies to Work For 2012: Best Benefits," *Fortune,* February 6, 2012, http://money.cnn.com.

8. Company Web site, "Careers," http://www.solipsys.com, accessed April 24, 2013.

9. "Abraham Maslow's Hierarchy of Needs," *Accel-Team.com,* http://www.accel-team.com, accessed April 24, 2013.

10. Bureau of Labor Statistics, "Union Membership News Release," January 23, 2013, http://www.bls.gov.

11. Organization Web site, http://www.afscme.org, accessed April 24, 2013; organization Web site, http://www.seiu.org, accessed April 24, 2013; organization Web site, http://www.teamster.org, accessed April 24, 2013; organization Web site, http://www.ufcw.org, accessed April 24, 2013; John C. Henry, "Largest Unions Pay Leaders Well, Give Extensively to Democrats," *Milwaukee Journal Sentinel,* March 3, 2011, http://www.jsonline.com.

12. Bureau of Labor Statistics, "Work Stoppages Summary," news release, February 8, 2013, http://www.bls.gov.

13. Steve Greenhouse, "4-Year Deals for Unions at Verizon," *New York Times*, September 19, 2012, http://www.nytimes.com.

14. "BA: United We Stand Campaign," http://archive.unitetheunion.org, accessed April 24, 2013; "BA Strike: Airline and Union

Agree to End Dispute," *BBC,* May 12, 2011, http://www.bbc .co.uk.

15. Associated Press, "Hostess Reopens Bakery for Twinkies, Ho Hos," *USA Today*, April 29, 2013, http://www.usatoday.com; Rachel Feintzeig, "New Twinkie Maker Shuns Union Labor," *Wall Street Journal*, April 23, 2013, http://online.wsj.com.

16. Organization Web site, "About the American Postal Workers Union," http://www.apwu.org, accessed April 24, 2013; Bureau of Labor Statistics, "Union Members—2012," news release, January 23, 2013, http://www.bls.gov.

Chapter 9

1. Company Web site, "Culture of Customer Service," http://www .aboutus.enterprise.com, accessed April 30, 2013; "Enterprise Rent-a-Car Ranked One of the 'Most Iconic Brands' of 2012," *KMOX News,* March 30, 2012, http://stlouis.cbslocal.com; "New Enterprise Plus Program Rewards Loyal Enterprise Rent-a-Car Customers," press release, March 13, 2012, http://www .finance.yahoo.com; Scott S. Smith, "The Car-Rental Enterprise of CEO Andy Taylor," *Investor's Business Daily,* January 24, 2012, http://news.investors.com; Christine M. Riordan, "Give the Holiday Gift of a Remarkable Customer Experience," *Forbes,* December 21, 2011, www.forbes.com; "Campaign Highlights Customer Service, Employee Empowerment, Family Heritage," *MarketWire,* February 28, 2011, www.marketwire.com.

2. Company Web site, http://www.andassoc.com, accessed April 30, 2013; Su Clauson-Wicker, "Warm Hearth CEO Ferne Moschella: Seeing the Trees & the Forest," *Ampersand* 24, no. 1, http://www.andassoc.com, accessed April 30, 2013.

3. Retirement Community Web site, http://www.lvbh.org, accessed May 15, 2013; David Farrell, "Empowerment Is Foundational to Success: Herzberg and the Green House Model," The Green House Project Blog, March 11, 2013, http://blog .thegreenhouse-project.org.

4. Organization Web site, http://www.nceo.org, accessed April 30, 2013.

5. Association Web site, http://www.esopassociation.org, accessed April 30, 2013.

6. Organization Web site, http://www.nceo.org, accessed April 30, 2013.

7. Organization Web site, "Employee Ownership as a Retirement Plan," http://www.nceo.org, accessed April 30, 2013.

8. Organization Web site, "Employee Stock Options Fact Sheet," http://www.nceo.org, accessed April 30, 2013.

9. Ibid.

10. Company Web site, https://secure.toyota.com/safety /smart-team/videos/rapid-response-smart-team.html, accessed April 30, 2013.

11. Company Web site, "Whole Foods Market's Core Values," http://www.wholefoodsmarket.com, accessed April 30, 2013.

12. Company Web site, http://ceochef.com, accessed April 30, 2013.

13. Tara Duggan, "Leadership vs. Conflict Resolution," *Chron.com,* http://smallbusiness.chron.com, accessed April 30, 2013.

14. Mike Ramsey, "Toyota in $1.1 Billion Gas-Pedal Settlement," *The Wall Street Journal*, December 27, 2012, http://online .wsj.com; Christopher Jensen, "Toyota Recalls Nearly 700,000 Vehicles for Potential Brake Light and Air-Bag Failures," *New York Times,* March 9, 2012, http://www.nytimescom.

15. Company Web site, "Why Outsource Email?" http://www .dakotapro.biz, accessed April 30, 2013.

16. "Expand Trust in Your Organization," *Peter Stark.com,* http:// www.peterstark.com, accessed April 30, 2013.

17. John Boe, "How to Read Your Prospect like a Book!" John Boe International, http://johnboe.com, accessed April 30, 2013.

Chapter 10

1. Company Web site, http://www.intel.com, accessed April 9, 2013; Esther Andrews, "What's behind the Products You Love?" Technology@Intel, January 22, 2012, http://blogs.intel .com; Chris Nuttall, "Intel's Chip Plans Bloom in Arizona Desert," *Financial Times,* January 22, 2012, http://www.ft.com; Jon Swartz, "Intel Bets Big on Manufacturing," *USA Today*, March 29, 2011, pp. 1B, 2B.

2. "How It's Made: Paintballs," Discovery Channel, http://www .youtube.com, accessed March 22, 2013.

3. Company Web site, "Operations Facilities," http://corporate .honda.com, accessed March 22, 2013.

4. Company Web site, http://www.shibuidesignsltd.com, accessed March 22, 2013.

5. Company Web site, "Chattanooga Plant," http://www .volkswagengroupamerica.com, accessed April 9, 2013; Dave Flessner, "VW Contractor Hiring More Workers in Chattanooga," *Chattanooga Times Free Press*, April 4, 2012, http://www .timesfreepress.com; "Volkswagen Chattanooga Earns LEED Platinum," press release, December 1, 2011, http://www .volkswagengroupamerica.com; Mike Ramsey, "VW Chops Labor Costs in U.S.," *Wall Street Journal*, May 23, 2011, http://online.wsj.com.

6. Company Web site, http://www.ariba.com, accessed March 22, 2013.

7. Company Web site, http://www.3dsystems.com/about-us, accessed March 21, 2013.

8. Katie Moisse, "Bumble Bee, Chicken of the Sea, Expand Tuna Recall," *ABC News*, March 8, 2013, http://www.abcnews .go.com.

9. Organization Web site, "What Is Six Sigma?" http://www .isixsigma.com, accessed March 22, 2013.

10. Organization Web site, http://www.iso.org, accessed March 22, 2013.

Chapter 11

1. Company Web site, "Here's What's Great for You," http://instoresnow.walmart.com, accessed May 13, 2013; Stephanie Strom, "Walmart to Label Healthy Foods," *New York Times*, February 7, 2012, http://www.nytimes.com; Jessica Wohl, "Walmart to Label Healthier Food as 'Great for You,'" *Reuters*, February 7, 2012, http://www.reuters.com.

2. Association Web site, "Definition of Marketing," http://www .marketingpower.com, accessed May 2, 2013.

3. Steve Carlotti and Jason Green, "Give the People What They Don't Know They Want," *The Washington Post*, May 14, 2012, http://articles.washingtonpost.com.

290

4. Reineke Reitsma, "Market Research That Goes beyond 'a Faster Horse,'" *RW Connect*, Septermber 27, 2012, http://rwconnect.esomar.org.

5. Kevin G. Hall, "Consumers Coming Back, but They May Not Run Up Credit Cards," *McClatchy Newspapers*, February 14, 2013, http://www.mcclatchydc.com.

6. Company Web site, http://www.pg.com, accessed May 13, 2013.

7. Stephanie Clifford, "Social Media Are Giving a Voice to Taste Buds," *New York Times*, July 30, 2012, http://www.nytimes.com.

8. Matthew Brown, "Understanding Gender and eCommerce," PFSweb blog, August 10, 2012, http://www.pfsweb.com.

9. U.S. Census Bureau, *2012 Statistical Abstract*, "Resident Population Projections by Sex and Age: 2010 to 2050," http://www.census.gov, accessed May 2, 2013.

10. Patricia Orsini, "Millennials in Aisle 2.0: Keeping Young Supermarket Shoppers Engaged with Brands," *eMarketer*, November 20, 2012, http://bx.businessweek.com.

11. Amy Morin, "How Much Money Do Parents Spend on Their Kids?," Mom.me, May 2013, http://mom.me.

12. Company Web site, "Forestry and Wood," http://www.ikea.com, accessed May 2, 2013.

13. Company Web site, http://www.takecarehealth.com, accessed May 2, 2013; "Take Care Clinics at Select Walgreens Offer Families Convenient and Affordable Option for Camp and Sports Physicals," press release, March 7, 2012, http://www.businesswire.com.

14. Company Web site, http://www.timberland.com, accessed May 2, 2013.

15. Company Web site, http://www.atlantis.com, accessed May 2, 2013.

16. Company Web site, http://www.netcall.com, accessed May 2, 2013.

Chapter 12

1. Organization Web site, "Expansion Program," http://www.pancanal.com, accessed June 6, 2013; Theodore Prince, "Panama Canal Expansion: Game Changer, or More of the Same?" *CSCMP's Supply Chain Quarterly*, Quarter 1 2012, http://www.supplychainquarterly.com; Alex Leff, "Panama Canal Expansion a 'Game Changer,'" TicoTimes.net, June 17, 2011, http://www.ticotimes.net.

2. "Pepsi Beverages Company and Tampico Beverages Announce Distribution Agreement," *Bloomberg*, http://www.bloomberg.com, accessed May 8, 2013.

3. John Falcone, "Kindle vs. Nook vs. iPad: Which E-book Reader Should You Buy?" *CNET*, December 17, 2012, accessed September 18, 2013. http://news.cnet.com.

4. Company Web site, http://www.febreeze.com, accessed June 6, 2013; company Web site, "Drive Away Odors and Experience Freshness with Febreze CAR Vent Clips," press release, January 10, 2012, http://news.pg.com.

5. James Plafke, "Advanced Combat Helmet Stops an AK-47 Head Shot," *GEEK*, January 22, 2013, http://www.geek.com.

6. Company Web site, http://www.ea.com, accessed May 8, 2013; Zacks Equity Research, "EA to Release Amalur's Second DLC," *Yahoo Finance*, April 5, 2012, http://www.finance.yahoo.com.

7. Bureau of Labor Statistics, *Occupational Outlook Handbook, 2012–2013 Edition*, http://www.bls.gov, accessed May 8, 2013; U.S. Census Bureau, "County Business Patterns," http://www.census.gov, accessed May 8, 2013.

8. Company Web site, http://www.acehardware.com, accessed May 8, 2013.

9. U.S. Census Bureau, "Quarterly Retail E-Commerce Sales, 1st Quarter 2013," May 15, 2013, http://www.census.gov.

10. John Coleman and David T. Whitaker, "Is There Life after Malls?" *Smart Growth Maryland*, Maryland Department of Planning, March 25, 2013, http://smartgrowthmd.wordpress.com.

11. Association Web site, "Trucking Statistics," http://www.truckinfo.net, accessed May 8, 2013.

12. Association Web site, "U.S. Freight Railroad Statistics," http://www.aar.org, accessed May 8, 2013.

Chapter 13

1. Renee Williams, "Pfizer's Earnings Receive Boost from Joint Venture with China (NYSE:PFE)," *University Chronicle*, May 22, 2013, http://www.ssuchronicle.com; Associated Press, "Joint Venture with China Lifts Pfizer's Earnings," *New York Times*, April 30, 2013, http://www.nytimes.com; Larry Huston, "Generic Atorvastatin Hits the Market," *Forbes,* November 30, 2011, http://www.forbes.com; Matthew Herper, "Why There Will Never Be Another Drug like Lipitor," *Forbes,* November 30, 2011, http://www.forbes.com.

2. Jackie Judd, "FDA Calls Prescription Drug Ads Misleading," *ABC News*, January 3, 2013, http://abcnews.go.com.

3. Dave Larson, "Robotic Lawn Mowers See Growing Demand," *Dayton Daily News*, March 16, 2013, http://www.daytondailynews.com.

4. David Lamoureux, "How Many Marketing Messages Do We See in a Day?" *Fluid Drive Media,* February 23, 2012, http://www.fluiddrivemedia.com.

5. Dasha Afanasieva, "Economic Growth to Boost Global Advertising: Report," *Reuters*, April 29, 2013, http://www.reuters.com.

6. "Ad Spend by Sector: Consumer Goods and Telecom Take the Cake in 2012," Nielsen, April 25, 2013, http://www.nielsen.com.

7. Kantar Media, "2012 January-December Outdoor Advertising Expenditures," *Outdoor Advertising Association of America*, February 2013, http://www.oaaa.org.

8. Company Web site, http://www.hendrickmotorsports.com, accessed May 9, 2013; "Top NASCAR Team Helps Marketing for Lowes, Pepsi, DuPont and GoDaddy," *Quarterly Retail Review*, March 27, 2011, http://www.quarterlyretailreview.com.

9. U.S. Department of Labor, "Occupational Employment and Wages, May 2012," *Occupational Employment Statistics,* Bureau of Labor Statistics, June 12, 2013, http://www.bls.gov.

10. John Sciacca, "Prima Cinema Brings in-the-Theater Movies Home for $500 Each . . . and It's Worth It," *Digital Trends*, April 1, 2013, http://www.digitaltrends.com.

11. Eydie Stumpf, "Five Tips for Retailers to Drive Sales Using Social Media," *The Press Enterprise*, April 26, 2013, http://www.pe.com.

12. Carol Tice, "How One Entrepreneur Used the Law of Publicity to Get Investors," *Entrepreneur*, accessed September 20, 2013, http://www.entrepreneur.com.

Chapter 14

1. Company Web site, http://evernote.com, accessed May 15, 2013; Mary Branscombe, "Good Software Should Be at Least as Smart as Your Dog," *Techradar*, May 1, 2013, http://www.techradar.com; Neil McIntosh, "At Le Web, Visions of Not-So-Social Future," TechEurope blog, December 8, 2011, http://blogs.wsj.com.

2. Museum Web site, "Timeline of Computer History," http://www.computerhistory.org, accessed May 15, 2013.

3. Isha Suri, "Meet the Titan Super Computer and the World's Fastest Storage System," *Silicon Angle*, April 19, 2013, http://siliconangle.com.

4. Paul Lamkin, "Top 10 Tablets for Business," *Techradar*, accessed January 20, 2013, http://www.techradar.com.

5. Company Web site, http://www.virtual.com, accessed May 15, 2013.

6. Paul Barbagallo, "Views Vary on FCC Role as Regulator in AllO-IP World," *Bloomberg BNA*, January 30, 2013, http://www.bna.com; Leena Rao, "Google Voice Founder Sets His Sights on VoIP Once Again," *Techcrunch*, March 7, 2012, http://techcrunch.com; Charles Schelle, "Update: Verizon VoIP Phone Outage Resolved," *SarasotaPatch*, February 25, 2012, http://sarasota.patch.com.

7. Julianne Pepitone and Leigh Remizowski, "'Massive' Credit Card Data Breach Involves All Major Brands," *CNNMoney*, March 31, 2012, http://money.cnn.com.

8. Kelly Jackson Higgins, "Mobile Malware on the Move, McAfee Report Says," *Dark Reading*, February 21, 2012, http://www.darkreading.com.

9. "Avast Says Grum Botnet Is Back from the Dead," *IT Security Pro*, May 24, 2013, http://itsecuritypro.co.uk; Brian Krebs, "Who's behind the World's Largest Spam Botnet?" *Krebs on Security*, February 1, 2012, http://krebsonsecurity.com.

10. Ken Dilanian, "Chinese Nickispy Malware Targets Smartphones," *Sydney Morning Herald*, February 26, 2012, http://www.smh.com.au.

11. Company Web site, "Data Loss Statistics," http://www.bostoncomputing.net, accessed May 15, 2013.

12. Company Web site, "FalconStor Provides Data Migration Technology for Dell Services Offering," press release, March 6, 2012, http://www.falconstor.com.

13. Company Web site, http://www.infosys.com, accessed May 15, 2013.

Chapter 15

1. Jason Bramwell, "Community Service Is a Responsibility BKD Takes Full Throttle," *AccountingWeb*, June 3, 2013, http://www.accountingweb.com; company Web site, www.bkd.com, accessed May 20, 2013.

2. Bureau of Labor Statistics, *Occupational Outlook Handbook, 2012–2013*, http://data.bls.gov, accessed May 20, 2013.

3. National Association of Colleges and Employers, *Job Outlook 2013*, http://www.naceweb.org, accessed June 10, 2013.

4. AARP Foundation Tax-Aide Locator, http://www.aarp.org, accessed May 20, 2013.

5. "2013 *Accounting Today* Top 100 Firms & Regional Leaders," March 11, 2013, http://digital.accountingtoday.com.

6. Company Web site, Johnson & Johnson, "2012 Historical Financial Review," http://www.investor.jnj.com, accessed June 10, 2013.

7. Jill Duffy, "The Best Personal Finance Software," PCMag.com, May 16, 2013, http://www.pcmag.com.

8. Ra'id Marie, "IFRS vs. GAAP—What Does This Have to Do with the Financial Crisis?" *Meirc Training and Consulting*, http://www.meirc.com, accessed May 20, 2013; Michael Cohn, "Investors Predict U.S. Will Adopt IFRS," *Accounting Today*, November 16, 2012, http://www.accountingtoday.com.

Chapter 16

1. Herb Welsbaum, "Better Checking: No Fee, No Minimum, 4% Interest," NBC News Business, February 11, 2013, http://www.nbcnews.com; Blake Ellis, "Community Banks Team Up to Fight the Megabanks," *CNN Money*, February 17, 2012, http://money.cnn.com; Jim Bruene, "Is BancVue's Kasasa to Checking What 'Intel Inside' Was to PCs?" *Net Banker*, January 11, 2012, http://www.netbanker.com; Eric Wilkinson, "Americans Urged to 'Break Up' with Big Banks Saturday," King5.com, November 4, 2011, http://www.king5.com.

2. Eric Markowitz, "All Signs Point to 2014 Twitter IPO," *Inc.*, May 21, 2013, http://www.inc.com; Douglas MacMillan & Mark Millan, "Box CEO Levie Targets 2014 IPO after Global Expansion," *Bloomberg*, January 16, 2013, http://www.bloomberg.com.

3. NYSE Euronext Web site, "NYSE Statistics Archive," May 2013, http://www.nyxdata.com.

4. Federal Deposit Insurance Corporation, "Statistics at a Glance," http://www.fdic.gov, updated May 29, 2013.

5. Ibid.

6. Maryalese LaPonsie, "Are Direct Banks the Future?" *MoneyRates.com*, March 15, 2013, http://www.money-rates.com.

7. Federal Deposit Insurance Corporation, "Statistics at a Glance," http://www.fdic.gov, updated May 29, 2013.

8. Jeff Blumenthal, "Which Local Banks Are among the 50 Largest?" *Philadelphia Business Journal*, June 4, 2013, http://www.bizjournals.com; Online Credit Union Data Analytics Systems, "1st Quarter 2013 Industry Trends Report," *CuData.com*, http://cudata.com.

9. American Council of Life Insurers Web site, "Life Insurer Fact Book 2012," http://www.acli.com, accessed June 16, 2013.

10. Organization for Economic Co-Operation and Development Web site, "Pension Fund Assets Hit Record USD $20.1 T in 2011, but Investment Performance Weakens," September 2012, Issue 9, page 21, http://www.oecd.org.

11. Warren S. Hearsch, "U.S. Mutual Fund Assets Set to Pass $15 Trillion," *LifeHealthPro*, February 13, 2013, http://www.lifehealthpro.com.

12. "Top Banks in the World," *Bankers Almanac*, February 18, 2013, http://www.bankersaccuity.com.

Chapter 17

1. Danilo Masoni, "Telecom Italia Plots Hybrid Debt Issue, Cuts Dividend," *Reuters*, February 8, 2013, http://news.yahoo.com.

2. Company Web site, "Orders and Deliveries," http://www.airbus.com, accessed June 26, 2013.

3. Joel Hans, "BMW's SC Plant Hits Record Production," *Manufacturing.net*, January 10, 2013, http://www.manufacturing.net.

4. Federal Reserve Board, "Commercial Paper," Federal Reserve Release, http://federalreserve.gov, accessed June 17, 2013.

5. Federal Reserve Board, "Commercial Paper Outstanding," Federal Reserve Release, http://federalreserve.gov, accessed June 17, 2013.

6. Sarika Gangar, "Gross to Buffett, Omens Disregarded as Sales Soar: Credit Markets," *Bloomberg*, May 20, 2013, http://www.bloomberg.com.

7. Elliot Zwiebach and Mark Hamstra, "Supervalu Completes Sale of Chains to Cerberus," *Supermarket News*, March 21, 2013, http://supermarketnews.com.

8. Treey Maxon, "As American Airlines Merger Date Nears, Questions Abound," *Dallas News*, June 3, 2013, http://www.dallasnews.com.

> > > Name Index

296

> > > Subject Index

*Entries in **bold** refer to key terms, which are listed at the end of each chapter.*

> > > International Index

*Entries in **bold** refer to key terms, which are listed at the end of each chapter.*

Learning Objectives

1 Define the term *business*.

2 Identify and describe the factors of production.

3 Describe the private enterprise system.

4 Identify the six eras in the history of business.

5 Explain how today's business workforce and the nature of work itself are changing.

6 Identify the skills and attributes needed for the 21st century manager.

7 Outline the characteristics that make a company admired.

Key Terms

business	branding
profits	brand
not-for-profit organization	transaction management
factors of production	relationship era
natural resources	diversity
capital	outsourcing
human resources	offshoring
entrepreneurship	nearshoring
private enterprise system	onshoring
capitalism	vision
competitive differentiation	critical thinking
private property	creativity
consumer orientation	

PROJECTS AND TEAMWORK APPLICATIONS

1. The entrepreneurial spirit fuels growth in the U.S. economy. Choose a company that interests you—one you have worked for or dealt with as a customer—and read about the company in the library or visit its Web site. Learn what you can about the company's early history. Who founded it and why? Is the founder still with the organization? In your opinion, does the company still embrace the founder's original vision? If not, how has the vision changed?

2. Brands distinguish one company's goods or services from those of its competitors. Each company you make purchases from hopes you will become loyal to its brand. Some well-known brands are Burger King, Coca-Cola, Hilton, and Old Navy. Choose a type of good or service you use regularly and identify the major brands associated with it. Are you loyal to a particular brand? Why or why not?

3. More and more businesses are forming strategic alliances to become more competitive. Sometimes, businesses pair up with not-for-profit organizations in a relationship that is beneficial to both. Choose a company whose goods or services interest you, such as Patagonia, FedEx, Kellogg, or Costco. On your own or with a classmate, research the firm on the Internet to learn about its alliances with not-for-profit organizations. Then describe one of the alliances, including goals and benefits to both parties. Create a presentation for your class.

4. This chapter describes how the nature of the workforce is changing: the population is aging, the labor pool is shrinking, the workforce is becoming more diverse, the nature of work is changing, the workplace is becoming more flexible and mobile, and employers are fostering innovation and collaboration among their employees. Form teams of two or three students; then select a company and research how that company is responding to changes in the workforce. After you have completed your research, prepare to present it to your class. Choose one of the following companies or select your own: State Farm, Archer Daniels Midland, Office Depot, Marriott, or Dell.

WEB ASSIGNMENTS

1. **Using search engines.** Gathering information is one of the most popular applications of the Web. Using two of the major search engines, such as Google and Firefox, search the Web for information pertaining to brand and relationship management. Sort through your results—you're likely to get thousands of hits—and identify the three most useful. What did you learn from this experience regarding the use of a search engine? http://www.google.com http://www.mozilla.org/en-US/firefox/new/

2. **Companies and not-for-profits.** In addition to companies, virtually all not-for-profit organizations have Web sites. Four

Web sites are listed below: two for companies (Alcoa and Sony) and two for not-for-profits (Cleveland Clinic and the Audubon Society). What is the purpose of each Web site? What type of information is available? How are the sites similar? How are they different? http://www.alcoa.com
http://www.sony.com
http://www.clevelandclinic.org
http://www.audubon.org

3. Characteristics of U.S. workforce. Visit the Web site listed below. It is the home page for the *Statistical Abstract of the United States,* published annually by the U.S. Bureau of the Census and a good source of basic demographic and economic data. Click on "Labor Force., Employment and Earnings." Use the relevant data tables to prepare a brief profile of the U.S. workforce (gender, age, educational level, and so forth). How is this profile expected to change over the next 10 to 20 years? http://www.census.gov/compendia/statab

Note: Internet Web addresses change frequently. If you don't find the exact sites listed, you may need to access the organization's home page and search from there or use a search engine.

CLASS ACTIVITIES

- Ask students to name businesses that used technology in their goods or services that transformed our lifestyles.

- Ask how many class members (or their family members) work in a company with fewer than 20 employees.

- Ask students to provide examples of people today who currently earn their income by making crafts.

- Lead a discussion to identify the oldest companies in the state or local area that are still in operation today.

- Ask students how many "frequent buyer" or loyalty cards they carry in their wallet or purse.

- Ask students what businesses might benefit or suffer from America's aging population.

- Solicit students' experiences working in diverse teams. What benefits and difficulties did teams encounter?

- Survey your class to see how many students work on a flexible or part-time basis.

- Lead a class brainstorming session to come up with a name for a new oil and lubrication business that also will sell coffee and snacks while customers wait in a comfortable lounge area.

LECTURE ENHANCERS

- Explain a possible objective of a not-for-profit organization.

- Name examples of private-sector, not-for-profit organizations.

- What possible risks do not-for-profits face if they choose to sell merchandise or to share advertising with a business in order to raise funds?

- Name a not-for-profit organization that sells merchandise or has a profit-generating arm.

- Name one factor of production and its method of payment. Think of a business in which this factor plays a major part.

- Provide an example of a business that recently upgraded or updated some form of its capital.

- Choose one of the four rights under the private enterprise system. Give an example of how this right allows freedom to a business.

- Give a hypothetical example of what government goals might be more easily achieved by limiting a citizen's freedom to choose his or her own employment.

- Why are smaller companies more likely to find innovative ways to use the factors of production?

- Compare the options available to buyers of a Ford automobile today compared with those during the production era.

- Name three brands of athletic shoes. How does each brand differentiate itself within the market?

- How has the shift in focus from production to customer relationships affected how innovation occurs within an industry?

- What unique skills might each generation bring to the workplace?

- Why might diverse workforces offer more innovative solutions to business problems than homogeneous workforces?

- In your opinion, have any factors or characteristics been left out of the most-admired list?

Learning Objectives

1 Explain **society's concern for ethical issues.**

2 Describe **the contemporary ethical environment.**

3 Discuss **how organizations shape ethical conduct.**

4 Describe **how businesses can act responsibly to satisfy society.**

5 Explain **the ethical responsibilities of businesses to the general public.**

6 Describe **the responsibilities to investors and the financial community.**

Key Terms

business ethics	Equal Employment Opportunity Commission (EEOC)
conflict of interest	
integrity	sexual harassment
stakeholders	sexism
code of conduct	social responsibility
whistle-blowing	recycling
Sarbanes-Oxley Act of 2002	corporate philanthropy
family leave	consumerism
discrimination	product liability

PROJECTS AND TEAMWORK APPLICATIONS

1. Write your own personal code of ethics. Create standards for your behavior at school, in personal relationships, and on the job. Then assess how well you meet your own standards and revise them if necessary.

2. On your own or with a classmate, visit the Web site of one of the following firms, or choose another that interests you. On the basis of what you can learn about the company

from the site, construct a chart or figure that illustrates examples of the firm's ethical awareness, ethical education, ethical actions, and ethical leadership. Present your findings to class.
   a. Sun Microsystems
   b. NFL, NHL, NBA, MLB, MLS (or any major professional sports league)
   c. Hewlett-Packard
   d. Aetna
   e. Irving Oil
   f. Costco
   g. IKEA

3. Now take the company you studied for Question 2 (or choose another one) and conduct a social audit of that firm. Do your findings match the firm's culture of ethics? If there are any differences, what are they and why might they occur?

4. As a consumer, you have come to expect a certain level of responsibility toward you on the part of companies with which you do business. Describe a situation in which you felt that a company did not recognize your rights as a consumer. How did you handle the situation? How did the company handle it? What was the final outcome?

WEB ASSIGNMENTS

1. **Ethical standards.** Go to the Web site listed below. It summarizes the ethical standards for all employees and suppliers of John Deere and Company. Review the material and then write a brief report relating Deere's ethical standards to the material on corporate ethics discussed in the chapter. In addition, consider how Deere's ethical standards are integrated with the firm's overall global citizenship efforts.
   http://www.deere.com/wps/dcom/en_US/corporate/our_company/citizenship/citizenship_landing.page

2. **Starting a career.** Each year *Businessweek* magazine rates the best companies to begin a career. Visit the *Businessweek* Web site and review the most recent list. What criteria did *Businessweek* use when building this list? What role do ethics and social responsibility play?
   http://www.businessweek.com

3. **Social responsibility.** Athletic footwear manufacturer New Balance is one of the few companies in its industry that still manufactures products in the United States. Go to the Web site listed below and learn more about the firm's commitment

to U.S. manufacturing. Prepare a report that relates this commitment to the firm's other core values.
http://www.newbalance.com/company/

Note: Internet Web addresses change frequently. If you don't find the exact sites listed, you may need to access the organization's home page and search from there or use a search engine.

CLASS ACTIVITIES

- Ask students if they think accepting Super Bowl tickets and trip expenses from a potential major supplier might affect their decision making as a buyer of that company's products.

- Obtain examples of workplace situations in which students struggled with whether their employer was misrepresenting important product information.

- Survey the class to see how many students work for companies that enforce a code of ethics.

- Ask students if they can think of any examples where an action may be legal but unethical.

- Ask students for examples of leaders who "walked the talk" and provided strong ethical leadership.

- Can students think of any examples of businesses that have portrayed or distorted their food products or beverages as "healthy" when, in fact, they are not?

- Survey the class to see if they have ever observed a workplace safety issue at work.

- Ask students to provide examples of older executives.

- Ask students to provide recent examples of cases of sexual harassment.

LECTURE ENHANCERS

- Can you think of a recent example where a company may have acted unethically?

- Share an example of a company that uses corporate philanthropy to highlight its social responsibility.

- How might one individual affect ethical behavior overall in the workplace?

- Have you ever been challenged by an ethical question as a student?

- Think of a hypothetical situation where the honesty and integrity of an employee might help to inspire a customer's trust in the company.

- Discuss whether students' employers have a policy in place to protect whistle-blowers and provide a clear pathway for reporting questionable incidents.

- Provide an example of a business in your local area that makes environmental concerns a priority.

- Discuss how students have disposed of their old computers or related equipment.

- What is one way a company could improve the quality of its workforce?

- What is a company ethically required to do if it discovers one of its products may not be safe?

- Can you think of a situation in which the needs of investors might be in conflict with the needs of customers?

Learning Objectives

1 **Discuss** microeconomics and explain the forces of demand and supply.

2 **Describe** macroeconomics and the issues for the entire economy.

3 **Identify** how to evaluate economic performance.

4 **Discuss** government's attempts to manage economic performance.

Key Terms

economics

microeconomics

macroeconomics

demand

supply

demand curve

supply curve

equilibrium price

pure competition

monopolistic competition

oligopoly

monopoly

regulated monopoly

planned economy

socialism

communism

mixed market economy

privatization

recession

depression

productivity

gross domestic product (GDP)

inflation

core inflation rate

hyperinflation

deflation

Consumer Price Index (CPI)

unemployment rate

frictional unemployment

cyclical unemployment

structural unemployment

monetary policy

expansionary monetary policy

restrictive monetary policy

fiscal policy

budget

budget deficit

national debt

budget surplus

balanced budget

PROJECTS AND TEAMWORK APPLICATIONS

1. Describe a situation in which you have had to make an economic choice in an attempt to balance your wants with limited means. What factors influenced your decision?

2. Choose one of the following products and describe the different factors that you think might affect its supply and demand.
   a. UGG boots
   b. Kindle
   c. Miles by Discover credit card
   d. newly introduced name-brand drug
   e. New England Patriots football tickets

3. Go online to research one of the following government agencies—its responsibilities, its budget, and the like. Then make the case for privatizing it:
   a. Veterans Administration
   b. Bureau of the Census
   c. Smithsonian Institution
   d. Transportation Security Administration
   e. Social Security

4. Some businesses automatically experience seasonal unemployment. More and more, however, owners of these businesses are making efforts to increase demand—and employment—during the off season. Choose a classmate to be your business partner, and together select one of the following businesses. Create a plan for developing business and keeping employees for a season during which your business does not customarily operate:
   a. children's summer camp
   b. ski lodge
   c. inn located near a beach resort
   d. house painting service
   e. greenhouse

5. On your own or with a classmate, go online to research the economy of one of the following countries. Learn what you can about the type of economy the country has, its major industries, and its competitive issues. (Note which industries or services are privatized and which are government owned.) Take notes on unemployment rates,

monetary policies, and fiscal policies. Present your findings to the class.

   a. China

   b. New Zealand

   c. India

   d. Denmark

   e. Mexico

   f. Canada

   g. Chile

WEB ASSIGNMENTS

1. Credit card regulations. Several new federal regulations governing credit cards went into effect recently. Visit the Web site listed here and click on "New Credit Card Rules." After reviewing these rules, prepare a brief report highlighting the most significant changes.
http://federalreserve.gov/creditcard/

2. Unemployment. In the United States, the Bureau of Labor Statistics (BLS) compiles and publishes data on unemployment. Go to the BLS Web site (http://www.bls.gov) and click on "Unemployment" (under "Subject Areas"). Read through the most recent report and answer the following questions:

   a. What is the current unemployment rate in the United States? How does it compare with those of other developed countries?

   b. Which state has the highest unemployment rate? Which state has the lowest unemployment rate?

   c. What is the U.S. underemployment rate?

3. Gross domestic product. Visit the Web site of the Bureau of Economic Analysis (http://www.bea.gov) and access the most recent statistics on the U.S. GDP. Prepare a brief report. What is the current GDP? What is the difference between real and nominal GDP? What are the individual components that make up GDP?

Note: Internet Web addresses change frequently. If you don't find the exact sites listed, you may need to access the organization's home page and search from there or use a search engine.

CLASS ACTIVITIES

- Lead a class discussion to obtain student examples of products that recently experienced sharp increases or decreases and why these changes may have occurred.

- Ask students how LeBron James's move from the Cleveland Cavaliers to the Miami Heat affected that team's ticket sales and prices.

- Discuss with the class how current economic weaknesses have affected their restaurant choices.

- Discuss with students how ticket prices could fluctuate depending on which teams are playing. For example, if your favorite team is playing the Yankees, ticket prices for those games could be higher than if your favorite team were playing the White Sox.

- Discuss how important incentives are to students, and whether they might leave their homes to pursue higher incentives elsewhere.

- Survey the class to see how many have purchased more store brand items rather than name-brand items at the grocery or drugstores where they shop as a result of softer economic conditions.

- Ask students which goods or services they think have risen and declined the most in the last few years.

LECTURE ENHANCERS

- How do microeconomic issues impact macroeconomics?

- In your opinion, which one of these factors has the most significant effect on a demand curve?

- How might a nation's cultural practices influence its economic system?

- How is a business rewarded in the private enterprise system?

- Share a specific example of each type of competition.

- Name an industry or business that has been a target for deregulation.

- What might be a likely drawback to contributing and distributing resources according to each person's needs and abilities?

- What are the key societal benefits of a mixed market economy?

- How can we determine which phase of the business cycle an economy is in at a certain time?

- How does inflation benefit wealthier individuals?

- Think of an example of each type of unemployment.

- Provide an example of a U.S. spending decision intended to encourage economic growth.

- Why must government spending policies be flexible and modifiable?

Learning Objectives

1 **Explain** why nations trade.

2 **Describe** how trade is measured between nations.

3 **Identify** the barriers to international trade.

4 **Discuss** reducing barriers to international trade.

5 **Explain** the decisions to go global.

Key Terms

export	General Agreement on Tariffs and Trade (GATT)
import	
absolute advantage	World Trade Organization (WTO)
comparative advantage	World Bank
opportunity cost	International Monetary Fund (IMF)
balance of trade	
trade surplus	North American Free Trade Agreement (NAFTA)
trade deficit	
balance of payments	Central America–Dominican Republic Free Trade Agreement (CAFTA-DR)
exchange rate	
devaluation	European Union (EU)
tariff	subcontracting
quota	joint venture
dumping	multinational corporation
embargo	

PROJECTS AND TEAMWORK APPLICATIONS

1. When Britain transferred Hong Kong to China in 1997, China agreed to grant Hong Kong a high degree of autonomy as a capitalist economy for 50 years. Do you think this agreement is holding up? Why or why not? Consider China's economy, population, infrastructure, and other factors in your answer.

2. The tremendous growth of online business has introduced new elements to the legal climate of international business. Patents, brand names, copyrights, and trademarks are difficult to monitor because of the boundaryless nature of the Internet. What steps could businesses take to protect their trademarks and brands in this environment? Come up with at least five suggestions, and compare your list with those of your classmates.

3. The WTO monitors GATT agreements, mediates disputes, and continues the effort to reduce trade barriers throughout the world. However, widespread concerns have been expressed that the WTO's focus on lowering trade barriers may encourage businesses to keep costs down through practices that may lead to pollution and human rights abuses. Others argue that human rights should not be linked to international business. Do you think environmental and human rights issues should be linked to trade? Why or why not?

4. Briefly describe the EU and its goals. What are the pros and cons of the EU? Do you predict that the European alliance will hold up over the next 20 years? Why or why not?

5. Use the most recent edition of "The *Fortune* Global 500," normally published in *Fortune* magazine in July, or go to *Fortune*'s online version at http://money.cnn.com/magazines/fortune/global500 to answer the following questions.
   a. On what is the Global 500 ranking based (e.g., profits, number of employees, revenues)?
   b. List the countries in which the world's ten largest corporations are based.
   c. Identify the top-ranked company, along with its Global 500 ranking and country, for the following industry classifications: Food and Drug Stores; Industrial and Farm Equipment; Petroleum Refining; Utilities: Gas and Electric; Telecommunications; Pharmaceuticals.

WEB ASSIGNMENTS

1. **WTO.** Visit the Web site of the World Trade Organization (http://www.wto.org). Research two current trade disputes. Which countries and products are involved? What, if anything, do the two disputes have in common? What procedures does the WTO follow in resolving trade disputes between member-countries?

2. **EU.** Europa.eu is the Web portal for the European Union. Go to the following Web site (http://europa.eu/index_en.htm) and answer the following questions:
   a. What are the steps a country must take to become a member of the EU?

b. How many EU members have adopted the euro? Which countries will be adopting the euro over the next few years?

c. What is the combined GDP of EU members? Which EU member has the largest GDP? The smallest GDP?

3. **Nestlé.** Nestlé is one of the world's largest global corporations. Visit the firm's Web site (http://www.nestle.com). Where is the company headquartered? What are some of its best-known brands? Are these brands sold in specific countries or are they sold worldwide? Make a list of three of four issues Nestle faces as a global corporation.

Note: Internet Web addresses change frequently. If you don't find the exact sites listed, you may need to access the organization's home page and search from there or use a search engine.

CLASS ACTIVITIES

- Ask students to provide examples of goods they have purchased that were made in other countries.

- Global companies are aggressively pursuing establishing new markets in the so-called BRIC countries (Brazil, Russia, India, and China). Ask students why this is occurring.

- Survey the class to see how many students have visited countries outside the United States.

- Ask students who are from other countries or who have traveled internationally about the differences they have seen in the way products of such companies as Coca-Cola or McDonald's are offered around the world.

- Lead a discussion of products sold within the United States that vary significantly by region and the reasons for this.

- Discuss the recent difficulties Google has faced doing business in China.

- Ask the class why a set of rules such as GATT is needed to provide a foundation for international trade.

- Lead a discussion of the factors contributing to the recent tension between the more prosperous European countries and the so-called "PIIGS" (Portugal, Italy, Ireland, Greece, Spain) members of the EU.

- What countries are likely attracting little international direct investment because of political instability, crime, war, or disease?

LECTURE ENHANCERS

- What are some risks associated with global economic interdependence?

- Choose a developing nation and discuss the goods and services that might be involved with U.S. trade.

- Choose one of the four barriers shown and discuss how it affects trade between the U.S. and another country.

- Can you think of a specific issue, tradition, or social norm within another culture that an American should be particularly sensitive to when doing business within that culture?

- Which countries seem to have the most corruption?

- What are some concerns that member countries might have regarding new countries joining the EU?

- Looking at Table 4.3, which site do you think would be the most objective?

Learning Objectives

1 **Discuss** why most businesses are small businesses.

2 **Determine** the contributions of small businesses to the economy.

3 **Discuss** why small businesses fail.

4 **Identify** the available assistance for small businesses.

5 **Outline** the forms of private business ownership.

6 **Describe** public and collective ownership of business.

7 **Discuss** organizing a corporation.

8 **Explain** what happens when businesses join forces.

Key Terms

small business

Small Business Administration (SBA)

microloan

sole proprietorship

partnership

C corporation

S corporation

limited-liability company (LLC)

employee ownership

not-for-profit corporation

stockholder

preferred stock

common stock

board of directors

merger

acquisition

vertical merger

horizontal merger

conglomerate merger

joint venture

PROJECTS AND TEAMWORK APPLICATIONS

1. Research a large firm to find out more about its beginnings as a small business. Who founded the company? Does the firm still produce its original offerings, or has it moved entirely away from them?

2. Brainstorm a small-business idea. Research the industry and major competition online. Draft a business plan. Include your decision on whether your firm will be a sole proprietorship or a partnership.

3. Identify an organization—such as AmeriCorps or the U.S. Postal Service—that is owned by a unit or agency of government. Imagine that you have been hired by that agency as a consultant to decide whether the organization should remain publicly owned. Research its successes and failures, and write a memo explaining your conclusion.

4. Identify a business and a not-for-profit organization that could form a joint venture beneficial to both. Draft a written proposal for this venture.

WEB ASSIGNMENTS

1. **Small-business successes.** Visit the *Entrepreneur* magazine Web site at http://www.entrepreneur.com/startingabusiness/successstories/index.html. Scroll through the titles of success stories and choose one that interests you. Read the feature and prepare a brief report answering these questions:
   a. What does the firm do?
   b. Where did the idea originate?
   c. What expertise does the owner have?
   d. How did the business begin?
   e. Who are its competitors?

2. **Great small workplaces.** Winning Workplaces is a not-for-profit organization committed to "helping small and midsize organizations create high-performance workplaces." Visit the organization's Web site at http://www.winningworkplaces.com and read at least two postings or articles there that interest you. Summarize the articles and explain how they help fulfill the Winning Workplaces' mission of helping small businesses succeed.

3. **Family-business tips for success.** Go to the Web site for Family Business Magazine at http://www.familybusinessmagazine.com and click on the feature article. Read the piece to learn about a particular family-owned business. Alternatively, choose a family-owned business such as S. C. Johnson (large) or Cider Hill Farm (small) and visit the firm's Web site to learn how the company has grown over the years and achieved success.

Note: Internet Web addresses change frequently. If you don't find the exact sites listed, you may need to access the organization's home page and search from there or use a search engine.

CLASS ACTIVITIES

- Ask students who work for larger corporations what services currently performed in-house might be the basis for a new company start-up.

- Restaurants are often characterized as a business with a high failure rate. Ask students what steps a restaurant owner might take to reduce the risk of failure.

- Ask students to imagine themselves as a potential investor in an idea that a friend or associate may present to them. What types of questions would they ask the friend/associate?

- Ask students how they might research a frozen yogurt franchise opportunity.

- Ask class members to offer a type of business (say, painting, landscaper, or pet grooming) and then ask them to provide examples of injuries, accidents, or damage that might occur in that business.

- Ask students to name the potential benefits and risks of employee ownership.

- Lead a class discussion about the pros and cons of working with and owning a business with family members.

- Ask students to share their ideas of benefits that might result from a merger of two large banks.

LECTURE ENHANCERS

- Poll the class to learn how many students work for small businesses. How many of those businesses are expanding?

- Do these statistics about small businesses surprise you?

- Why do you think the requirements to be considered a small business differ so much from industry to industry?

- Can you think of a local small business that provides customized personal services?

- Have you ever worked for a small business?

- Provide an example of a small business that was created as a result of innovation.

- Why might small-business managers be more prone to these shortcomings than those in larger companies?

- How might a smaller company that cannot offer a competitive salary or benefits package still attract and keep quality employees?

- Can you think of a woman-owned business?

- Can you think of a minority-owned business?

- Why do you think sole proprietorships are the most common type of business ownership?

- Why might a sole proprietorship or partnership firm want to become an LLC?

- Think of a family-owned business. What is your impression of the owner(s)?

- Can you think of an example of public ownership in your state?

Learning Objectives

1 **Define** what is an *entrepreneur*.

2 **Describe** the environment for entrepreneurs.

3 **Outline** the process of starting a new venture.

4 **Summarize** different ways to finance new ventures.

5 **Explain** why people choose entrepreneurship.

6 **Identify** the different categories of entrepreneurs.

7 **Describe** the franchising alternative.

8 **Explain** how organizations promote intrapreneurship.

Key Terms

entrepreneur	business incubator
business plan	classic entrepreneur
seed capital	serial entrepreneur
OPM	social entrepreneur
debt financing	franchising
equity financing	franchisee
venture capitalist	franchisor
angel investor	intrapreneurship
crowd funding	skunkworks

PROJECTS AND TEAMWORK APPLICATIONS

1. Interview an entrepreneur—you can do this in person, by e-mail, or on the phone. The person can be a local shop or restaurant owner, a hair salon owner, a pet groomer, a consultant—any field is fine. Find out why that person decided to become an entrepreneur. Ask whether his or her viewpoint has changed since starting a business. Decide whether the person is a classic, serial, or social entrepreneur. Present your findings to the class.

2. Certain demographic trends can represent opportunities for entrepreneurs—the aging of the U.S. population, the increasing diversity of the U.S. population, the growth in population of some states, and the predominance of two-income families, to name a few. On your own or with a classmate, choose a demographic trend and brainstorm for business ideas that could capitalize on the trend. Create a poster or PowerPoint presentation to present your idea—and its relationship to the trend—to your class.

3. Review the characteristics of successful entrepreneurs. Which characteristics do you possess? Do you think you would be a good entrepreneur? Why or why not? Create an outline of the traits you believe are your strengths—and those that might be your weaknesses.

4. Many entrepreneurs turn a hobby or area of interest into a business idea. Others get their ideas from situations or daily problems for which they believe they have a solution—or a better solution than those already offered. Think about an area of personal interest—or a problem you think you could solve with a new good or service—and create the first part of a potential business plan, the introduction to your new company and its offerings. Then outline briefly what kind of financing you think would work best for your business and what steps you would take to secure the funds.

5. Enterprise zones are designed to revitalize economically distressed areas. Choose an area with which you are familiar—it may be as close as a local neighborhood or as far away as a city in which you might like to live someday. Do some online research about the area. Then outline your own plan for an enterprise zone—including businesses that you think would do well in the area, jobs that might be created, and other factors.

6. Go to the Web site Entrepreneur.com and research information on franchises. Choose one that interests you and evaluate the information about its start-up requirements. Would you consider a partnership in your franchise with someone you know? Why or why not? Present your findings in class.

WEB ASSIGNMENTS

1. **Tools for entrepreneurs.** American Express has established something it calls "Open Forum" to allow entrepreneurs and small business owners to communicate with one another and share ideas. Visit the Open Forum Web site and

review the available material. Prepare a short report on how Open Forum could help an entrepreneur start and grow a business. **http://www.openforum.com/**

2. **Venture capitalists.** Venture capital firms are an important source of financing for entrepreneurs. Most actively solicit funding proposals. Go to the Web site shown here to learn more about venture capital. What are some famous businesses that were originally financed by venture capitalists? **http://www.nvca.org/**

3. **Getting started.** Visit the Web site of *Entrepreneur* magazine and click on "Startups". How should you go about researching a business idea? What are the steps involved in getting a product to market?

Note: Internet Web addresses change frequently. If you don't find the exact sites listed, you may need to access the organization's home page and search from there or use a search engine.

CLASS ACTIVITIES

- Ask students to share examples of friends or family members who operate their own businesses.

- Discuss the unique stresses and challenges being your own boss might present.

- Use the Web site www.alibaba.com and lead a discussion of the opportunity it offers entrepreneurs for the global marketing and purchasing of an incredible array of goods and parts for almost any imaginable business.

- Survey the class to see how many students have taken at least one specialized course focusing on entrepreneurship.

- Ask students why optimism is an important trait for potential entrepreneurs.

- Ask students to think about a basic product or service needed in their immediate community. Then obtain their comments and discuss their ideas.

- Discuss the benefits of developing a business plan, even if funds are already available.

- Lead a discussion of possible pitfalls of having friends or family invest in your business.

LECTURE ENHANCERS

- How do entrepreneurs view risk differently than managers in a large company?

- Think of a hypothetical example for each type of entrepreneur.

- Why do many people choose entrepreneurship when considering job security?

- What factors may have contributed to the increased globalization of entrepreneurship?

- What role does education play in encouraging students to start new businesses?

- Share an example of a successful business that was started by a student.

- What are some personal-life issues that might hinder an entrepreneur's success?

- What type of ambiguity might an entrepreneur face in the fashion retail industry?

- Why is it important that both of these criteria be considered before starting a business?

- What are some possible disadvantages of buying an existing business?

- What are the drawbacks to depending upon debt financing to start a business?

- What are some advantages to starting a business in an enterprise zone?

- What is another possible reason companies support rather than discourage intrapreneurship among their employees?

- Why would venture capitalists have tougher requirements for a business plan than a bank?

- What might be the advantages for a franchise to expand into foreign markets?

- Are you a loyal customer of any franchise?

- As a customer, have you ever refused to shop at one franchise location due to poor service or quality of goods at another location?

Learning Objectives

1. **Define** *management.*

2. **Evaluate** managers as leaders.

3. **Discuss** leading by setting a vision.

4. **Describe** managers as decision makers.

5. **Summarize** the importance of planning.

6. **Describe** the strategic planning process.

7. **Discuss** organizational structures.

Key Terms

management	mission statement
leadership	SWOT analysis
empowerment	objective
vision	organizing
corporate culture	organization
decision making	departmentalization
delegation	directing
planning	controlling

PROJECTS AND TEAMWORK APPLICATIONS

1. Imagine that you've been hired as a supervisor by a bakery shop called Clare's Cakes that is beginning to grow. Clare—the founder—is looking for ways to increase production capacity, expand deliveries, and eventually open several more shops in the area. Create a job description for yourself, including the managerial functions and skills you believe you'll need for success.

2. On your own or with a classmate, create a mission statement for Clare's Cakes. Think about the type of company it is, the products it offers customers (cakes for special occasions or milestones), and the type of growth it is planning.

3. Contingency planning requires a combination of foresight and adaptability. Josh James, founder of Omniture, the Web analytics firm he sold to Adobe, recalls the importance of being able to adapt when his company seemed on the brink of disaster. "There were times when I lay down on the floor at night, close to crying. Then my wife would come over and kick me and say, 'Get up and figure it out.'" Research the news headlines for situations that could (or did) require contingency planning. Report to the class what the challenge was and how the managers involved handled it. Also state whether the planning was effective or successful.

4. Identify a good leader—it can be someone you know personally or a public figure. Describe the traits that make the person an effective leader. Would this person's leadership style work in situations other than his or her current position? Why or why not?

5. Research a firm whose goods or services you purchase or admire. Learn what you can about the organization's culture. Do you think you would be an effective manager in this culture? Why or why not? Share your findings with the class.

WEB ASSIGNMENTS

1. **Strategic planning.** Visit the following Web site listed. It summarizes Johnson & Johnson's strategic planning philosophy. Review several recent acquisitions by Johnson & Johnson and prepare a brief report discussing how the acquisitions resulted from the company's strategic planning process. http://www.investor.jnj.com/strategic.cfm

2. **Mission statements.** Go to the Web sites of two organizations, a for-profit firm and a not-for-profit organization. Print out both organizations' mission statements. Bring the material with you to class to participate in a discussion on mission statements.

3. **Management structure.** Visit the following Web site listed. Click on "corporate governance" and answer the following questions:
   a. How would you characterize Target's organizational structure?
   b. What is the composition of Target's board of directors? http://investors.target.com/phoenix.zhtml?c=65828&p=irol-IRHome

Note: Internet Web addresses change frequently. If you don't find the exact sites listed, you may need to access the organization's home page and search from there or use a search engine.

CLASS ACTIVITIES

- Discuss the varying types of stress at each level of management and the contributing factors.

- Lead a discussion on whether recently promoted supervisors can remain friends with employees they now supervise.

- Obtain ideas from students on how they can personally develop and improve their individual strategic planning skills.

- Lead a class discussion to develop a mission for a new business specializing in baking and selling cupcakes.

- Ask students to discuss and develop a SWOT list for the college.

LECTURE ENHANCERS

- How might the role of a manager in a not-for-profit differ from the role of a manager in a for-profit-seeking firm?

- Discuss some long-range plans that top managers might focus on.

- What might happen if a manager lacks technical skills?

- What might happen if a manager lacks human skills?

- What might happen if a manager lacks conceptual skills?

- Which of these functions do you consider to be the most important? Why?

- Discuss the difference between directing and controlling.

- What might happen if a company does not allow for flexibility in its vision?

- Which type of planning do you consider to be the most important? Why?

- What specific details must be considered in operational planning?

- What are some possible problems that a company may encounter if it does not engage in contingency planning?

- Discuss the difficulties a company might encounter in the process of developing its mission statement.

- How often do you think a company should conduct a SWOT analysis? Why?

- Discuss specific companies that have successfully differentiated themselves within their markets.

- Discuss the possible outcomes if a manager were to skip one or more of the steps in the strategic-planning process.

- Think of a situation in which inaccurate information could affect the outcome of a managerial decision.

- Are there additional traits that you feel should be listed here? Why?

- What might be the effects upon a leader's power if he or she lacks one of these factors?

- Provide a hypothetical example of a decision made with autocratic leadership.

- Provide a hypothetical example of a decision made with democratic leadership.

- Provide a hypothetical example of a decision made with free-rein leadership.

- Which leadership style would you prefer to work under? Why?

- Provide an example of a ceremony or ritual that a manager might use to strengthen corporate culture.

- What are some possible effects on employees if organizational changes lead to aspects of their corporate culture being discontinued?

- Are each of these elements equally important? Why or why not?

- What are some potential negative results when a company increases its size?

- What are some potential drawbacks for a company with very rigid departmentalization?

- Discuss the pros and cons of each type of departmentalization.

- What are the possible negative effects of increasing a manager's span of management?

- Why do you think a line-and-staff structure might be the most effective structure in a crisis?

- Provide an example of a committee, a decision it must make, and the methods it uses to make the decision.

- What are some potential pitfalls of a matrix structure?

Learning Objectives

1 **Explain** the role of human resources: the people behind the people.

2 **Describe** recruitment and selection.

3 **Discuss** orientation, training, and evaluation.

4 **Describe** compensation.

5 **Discuss** employee separation.

6 **Explain** the different methods for motivating employees.

7 **Discuss** labor–management relations.

Key Terms

human resource management	downsizing
job requirements	outsourcing
performance appraisal	Maslow's hierarchy of needs
compensation	equity theory
wage	goal-setting theory
salary	management by objectives (MBO)
employee benefits	labor union
employee separation	collective bargaining

PROJECTS AND TEAMWORK APPLICATIONS

1. On your own or with a classmate, research consulting firms that provide management training programs. Prepare a presentation about one of these firms, describing the approach it takes as well as some of the specific elements of the program.

2. Choose one of the following companies, or one that you think you might like to work for sometime in the future. Using the firm's Web site and one of the job Web sites such as Monster.com (if applicable), research the company's benefits.

Outline the firm's benefits and then determine if you still want to work for that company and why. Suggested firms:
   a. Timberland
   b. SAS
   c. IBM
   d. Kraft Foods
   e. FedEx

3. With a classmate, choose an on-campus job and outline how you would share that job. Create a schedule and division of tasks.

4. Choose what you think would be your dream job five years from now. Then create a chart according to Maslow's hierarchy of needs, and identify the ways in which you envision this job fulfilling each level of need.

5. Research one of the major labor laws outlined in the text to learn more about the circumstances that led to its proposal and passage. In what ways do you believe this law has (or has not) affected the working world that you expect to enter when you graduate?

WEB ASSIGNMENTS

1. **Human resources (HR) as a profession.** Go to the Web site listed here and review the material. Answer the following questions:
   a. How many people are employed in HR?
   b. What are the educational requirements to become an HR manager?
   c. How rapidly is the occupation expected to grow over the next decade?
   http://www.bls.gov/oco/ocos021.htm

2. **Performance reviews.** Visit the Web sites listed here. Each lists some tips for conducting employee performance reviews. Print out the material and bring it to class to participate in a class discussion on performance reviews.
   http://www.squidoo.com/employeeperformancereview
   http://articles.techrepublic.com.com/5100-10878_11-1049853.html
   http://smallbusiness.dnb.com/human-resources/workforce-management/1385-1.html

3. **Teamsters.** The Teamsters is one of the nation's largest and oldest labor unions. Go to the union's Web site (http://www.teamster.org) and review the material. When was the union founded? Originally, the union represented workers in what industry? How many members do the Teamsters currently

have? Other than the United States, in what other country does the union represent workers?

Note: Internet Web addresses change frequently. If you don't find the exact sites listed, you may need to access the organization's home page and search from there or use a search engine.

CLASS ACTIVITIES

- Lead a classroom discussion on whether there should be a limit or ceiling on compensation for executives and the pros and cons of such a limit.

- Discuss the benefits of a 401(k) plan and why employees should try to maximize their contributions.

- Ask students why flexible benefits are becoming more popular.

- Ask students to name some problems that might be created by extremely low employee turnover.

- What techniques might a manager use to appeal to an employee with a primary need in each of the model's five categories?

- Ask students to provide examples of specific goals.

- Discuss the benefits of job rotation from the employer's perspective.

LECTURE ENHANCERS

- How does a good HR manager find strong employees and keep them satisfied? How might this role vary?

- Which steps seem most important in the recruitment and selection process?

- Discuss the pros and cons of implementing apprenticeship training within a professional business environment.

- Discuss the pros and cons of computer-based training versus classroom training.

- Why might some executives be hesitant to train and mentor potential future managers?

- Which of these types of performance reviews would you prefer as an employee? Why?

- Do you think these factors are appropriate as a basis for compensation policy? Should organizations consider any additional factors?

- What are the pros and cons of each type of compensation?

- If you had a choice, which would you choose: a set group of paid days off or PTO? Why?

- Which kinds of flexible work plans would you prefer as an employee? Which would you prefer as a manager? Why?

- Provide some examples of jobs that typically use a compressed workweek. What are the potential drawbacks to a compressed workweek?

- Discuss some possible drawbacks to job sharing.

- What are some specific drawbacks to telecommuting?

- What are some potential legal pitfalls that a manager must avoid during an involuntary separation?

- What are some drawbacks to outsourcing, from a managerial point of view?

- Discuss examples of common rewards and punishments in the workplace.

- Why might MBO focus on the "contributions" an employee makes to the company rather than his or her job "responsibilities"?

- Discuss the fact that some jobs are typically union jobs, while others usually aren't. Why might this be?

- Why might unionization be more common in the public sector?

- What are some potential drawbacks to working under a union contract?

- Discuss the pros and cons of each tactic.

CHAPTER NINE

Learning Objectives

1 **Discuss** empowering employees.

2 **Name** and describe the five types of teams.

3 **Identify** the stages of team development.

4 **Evaluate** team cohesiveness and norms.

5 **Describe** team conflict.

6 **Explain** the importance of effective communication.

7 **Compare** the basic forms of communication.

Key Terms

empowerment	team norm
team	conflict
work team	cognitive conflict
problem-solving team	affective conflict
self-managed team	communication
cross-functional team	listening
virtual team	grapevine
team cohesiveness	external communication

PROJECTS AND TEAMWORK APPLICATIONS

1. Having the power and authority to make decisions about work is the essence of empowerment. For this project, the instructor steps back and gives the class free rein to plan and implement a day of classwork. The class might appoint a leader, divide into teams (to plan a lecture, come up with an assignment, plan a field trip, and the like). It's completely up to the students how to organize and conduct the one-day class. After the class, discuss the experience—including the upside and downside (if any) of empowerment.

2. Divide the class into teams of relatively equal size. Each team may select one of the following problems to solve or decide on one of its own: arranging for a guest speaker or expanding the menu in the school's cafe. Although it is not necessary to complete the entire problem-solving process, each team should go through the forming and norming stages of team development and outline a plan for accomplishing the group's task. Is each team cohesive? Why or why not?

3. Try this listening exercise with a partner. First, spend a few minutes writing a paragraph or two about the most important thing that happened to you this week. Second, read your paragraph to your partner. Next, have your partner read his or her paragraph. Finally, take turns summarizing the most important points in one another's stories. How well did you listen to each other?

4. On your own or with a classmate, visit the college library, mall, or anywhere else people gather. For 10 to 15 minutes, observe the nonverbal cues that people give each other: Does the librarian smile at students? What is the body language of students gathered in groups? When you leave the venue, jot down as many of your observations as you can. Notice things such as changes in nonverbal communication when someone joins a group or leaves it.

5. Choose a company you know about or whose products you use. Research the company's offerings as well as some of its social responsibility and sustainability initiatives (such as a goal to reduce its energy consumption). Create an advertisement that focuses on one of these initiatives as an example of positive external communication from the company.

WEB ASSIGNMENTS

1. **Team-building exercises.** The Web site Team-Building -Bonanza.com represents "the mother lode of corporate team-building ideas." Select a team-building exercise to help resolve conflicts. What are some of the suggested activities? http://www.team-building-bonanza.com

2. **Writing better business letters.** Assume you'd like to improve your business letter-writing ability. Using a search engine such as Google or Bing, search the Web for sites with tips and suggestions to improve letter-writing skills. (An example is shown here.) Select two of these sites and review the material. Prepare a brief summary. http://www.askoxford.com/betterwriting/letterwriting /?view=uk

3. **Employee stock ownership plans.** Visit the Web site of the ESOP Association (http://www.esopassociation.org). Click on "About ESOPs." Print out the materials (including the

submenus) and bring them to class to participate in a discussion on employee stock ownership plans.

Note: Internet Web addresses change frequently. If you don't find the exact sites listed, you may need to access the organization's home page and search from there or use a search engine.

CLASS ACTIVITIES

- Discuss with students the possible pitfalls of sharing detailed operating and financial information with all employees.

- Ask students to identify and discuss the pros and cons of stock options.

- Lead a discussion to identify work situations in which a team composed solely of members from the same function would be more effective than a cross-functional team.

- Ask students to describe the possible challenges of working on a diverse team.

- Ask students how noise in their households affects their ability to participate in a distance learning activity.

- Ask students how they would communicate with employees about an across-the-board 20 percent workforce reduction.

- Ask students for examples of organizations that communicated effectively about a crisis in which they were involved.

LECTURE ENHANCERS

- Ask if any students have ever had a job where teamwork was strongly emphasized, and have them describe their experience.

- Which of these rewards would you prefer? Why?

- Which type of team do you imagine would be the easiest to manage? Why?

- During which stage is the manager's role most important? Why?

- What might be the effect on a team if a manager skips the adjourning stage?

- What is likely to happen if team cohesiveness is low or nonexistent?

- Provide an example of a team norm you have experienced.

- Share an instance of team conflict you have experienced within the workplace.

- Which type of conflict would be the most difficult for a manager to resolve?

- Can you think of a manager who you feel is or was exceptionally good at communicating? What specific traits helped that manager to be a good communicator?

- What can happen to the communication process if this step is ignored?

- Can you think of some additional drawbacks to oral communication?

- Are there specific body language cues for each type of listening behavior? What are they?

- What are some possible drawbacks to written communication?

- Share some typical methods that companies use for downward formal communication.

- What are some other ways in which managers can use the grapevine?

- What meaning do you infer if someone is standing too close to you when you are conversing? What if someone is standing unusually far away?

- Share a recent example of a company that did not communicate effectively during a crisis. What were the consequences?

Learning Objectives

1️⃣ **Identify** and describe the four main types of production processes.

2️⃣ **Identify** and describe the three major production methods.

3️⃣ **Describe** the strategic decisions made by production and operations managers.

4️⃣ **Identify** the steps in the production control process.

5️⃣ **Discuss** the importance of quality control.

Key Terms

utility	materials requirement planning (MRP)
production	
production and operations management	production control
	computer-aided design (CAD)
make, buy, or lease decision	computer-aided manufacturing (CAM)
inventory control	quality
just-in-time (JIT) system	benchmarking

PROJECTS AND TEAMWORK APPLICATIONS

1. Imagine that you recently became the owner of a popular ice cream shop. You want to attract more customers and ultimately expand the business. Choose the type of production process—continuous or intermittent—you think would best fit your business. Then create a plan outlining specifically how you would use this process and why it would help you achieve your goal as a business owner.

2. On your own or with a classmate, imagine that you've been hired to help a business group design a shopping mall. Taking into account the factors listed in the chapter, come up with recommendations for where the mall should be located—and why. Present your plan to the class.

3. On your own or with a classmate, select one of the following businesses and sketch or describe the layout that you think would be best for attracting and serving customers:
   a. Mexican restaurant
   b. home furnishings store
   c. pet store
   d. motorcycle dealership
   e. attorney's office

4. Suppose you and your best friend decided to operate a house-painting service. Draft a production plan for your business, including the following decisions: (a) make, buy, or lease; (b) suppliers; and (c) inventory control.

5. Choose two firms for comparison (one firm should provide a good benchmarking opportunity for its production processes). Keep in mind that the benchmarking firm doesn't necessarily have to be in the same industry as the other selected firm. Present your decisions to the class and explain why you made both choices.

WEB ASSIGNMENTS

1. **Just-in-time inventory management systems.** Go to the Web sites listed here to learn more about just-in-time inventory management systems. Take notes on what you learned and bring them to class to participate in a class discussion.
   http://www.wisegeek.com/what-is-a-just-in-time-inventory.htm
   http://smallbusiness.dnb.com/manage/finances/12375503-1.html
   http://www.smcdata.com/software-choices/just-in-time-inventory-control-systems-1.html

2. **Plant location decision.** Using an Internet news service, such as Google news (http://news.google.com) or Yahoo! news (http://news.yahoo.com), search for information on a recent plant location decision. An example is Volkswagen's Chattanooga plant. Research the decision and then prepare a brief report outlining the factors that went into the firm's decision to locate the plant where it did.
   http://www.vw.com/vwbuzz/browse/en/us/detail/Volkswagen_Group_of_America_announces_it_will_produce_cars_in_Chattanooga/219.

3. **ISO certification.** Visit the Web site of the International Organization for Standardization (http://www.iso.org). Click on "standards development" and then "processes and

procedures." What are some of the products for which ISO standards are currently being developed?

Note: Internet Web addresses change frequently. If you don't find the exact sites listed, you may need to access the organization's home page and search from there or use a search engine.

CLASS ACTIVITIES

- Lead a class discussion on the inputs, transformation process, and outputs of a college.

- Ask students if they have ever performed highly specialized job duties on a recurring basis, and discuss their reactions to that experience.

- Ask students how the very high costs of a shutdown in a continuous production process might lead to poor or unethical decision making by management.

- Ask students what factors were likely significant causes for the automotive industry to have been located in Detroit during that industry's first few decades.

- Lead a discussion on the factors that exist in Silicon Valley that might explain why that area is attractive to so many technology companies.

- Ask students what personality traits and skills they think would be needed to be an effective production manager.

- Ask students what type of a layout the Apple stores utilize.

- Discuss the benefits and risks of long-term, multiple-year supplier contracts.

- Lead a class discussion to identify other costs associated with carrying excessive inventory, in addition to warehousing costs, taxes, insurance, and maintenance.

- Ask students how the types of companies that a hospital might benchmark could improve the patient check-in process.

LECTURE ENHANCERS

- Discuss the conversion process that occurs, and the resources needed, in a resort hotel.

- Describe the production process for the American Red Cross during a crisis.

- What companies do you think provide examples of mass production?

- What are the advantages and disadvantages of increasing the specialization of labor?

- Do you think Chipotle is an example of customer-driven production? Can you provide other examples?

- Is carbonated beverage production an analytic or synthetic production system?

- Is meat processing an analytic or synthetic production system?

- Name some industries where robots are used as part of the assembly line process.

- What are the advantages and disadvantages of robotic surgery in the medical field?

- What locations on streets do you think are most avoided by retailers and why?

- In your state, what labor skills might attract certain businesses?

- What is most important—to plan, determine, implement, or control? Why?

- Think of a local business and its layout. If the business adds new products, how might its layout change?

- Provide local examples of businesses that use fixed-position layouts.

- Identify some challenges in identifying alternative suppliers for organic produce markets.

- What are the advantages of JIT?

- What control steps can you see that McDonald's takes to provide uniform quality and control costs?

- How would an unexpected spike in product demand affect human resources?

- Can you think of any examples of companies that incurred additional costs because of product quality issues?

- How might the standards for cake quality vary between a traditional bakery and a bakery that specializes in wedding cakes?

- Have you ever participated in a customer survey on quality?

- What types of benefits would a global manufacturer obtain from using ISO-certified suppliers?

Learning Objectives

1 **Define** marketing.

2 **Discuss** the evolution of the marketing concept.

3 **Summarize** consumer behavior.

4 **Describe** marketing research.

5 **Explain** market segmentation.

6 **List** the steps in building a marketing strategy.

7 **Discuss** relationship marketing.

Key Terms

marketing	psychographic segmentation
exchange process	product-related segmentation
utility	consumer (B2C) product
marketing concept	business (B2B) product
consumer behavior	target market
marketing research	marketing mix
data mining	relationship marketing
business intelligence	lifetime value of a customer
market segmentation	frequency marketing
geographic segmentation	affinity program
demographic segmentation	

PROJECTS AND TEAMWORK APPLICATIONS

1. On your own or with a classmate, choose one of the following products and create an advertisement that illustrates how your firm creates time, place, and form utility in its delivery of the product to the customer.
   a. auto repair service
   b. hiking tours
   c. craft supply store
   d. pet-sitting service

2. As a marketer, if you can find ways to classify your firm's goods and services as both business and consumer products, most likely your company's sales will increase as you build relationships with a new category of customers. On your own or with a classmate, choose one of the following products and outline a marketing strategy for attracting the classification of customer that is *opposite* the one listed in parentheses.
   a. hybrid car (consumer)
   b. LCD TV (consumer)
   c. limousine service (business)
   d. office furniture (business)

3. Think of two situations in which you have been a customer: one in which you were satisfied with the merchandise you received and one in which you were not. Make a list of the reasons you were satisfied in the first case and a list of the reasons you were not satisfied in the second case. Would you say that the failure was the result of the seller's not understanding your needs?

4. Co-marketing and co-branding are techniques that organizations often use to market their own and each other's products, such as Nike running shoes and the Apple iPod. On your own or with a classmate, choose two firms with products you think would work well together for co-marketing separate products or co-branding a single product. Then create an advertisement for your co-marketing or co-branding effort.

WEB ASSIGNMENTS

1. **Demographic trends.** The *Statistical Abstract of the United States* is an excellent source of demographic and economic data about the United States. Visit the Web site listed here and click on "population." In terms of age and race, what does the U.S. population currently look like? What will the U.S. population look like in the decades to come? http://www.census.gov/compendia/statab/

2. **Market segmentation.** Go to the Web site of Canon USA and review the company's array of product offerings. Prepare a brief report on how Canon segments its markets. http://www.usa.canon.com/home

3. **Customer loyalty programs.** Airlines and hotel chains have extensive customer loyalty programs. Pick an airline and

hotel chain and print out information on the firm's customer loyalty program. (Two examples are listed here.) Bring the material to class to participate in a discussion on this topic.
http://www.southwest.com/rapid_rewards/
http://www.marriott.com/rewards/rewards-program.mi

Note: Internet Web addresses change frequently. If you don't find the exact sites listed, you may need to access the organization's home page and search from there or use a search engine.

CLASS ACTIVITIES

- Discuss how the success of e-book readers (such as the iPad, Nook, and Kindle) and iTunes has affected Barnes & Noble and Sony Records.

- What challenges does Starbucks face in entering and successfully selling coffee in China? Ask students to share their ideas for tactics to overcome these challenges.

- Lead a class discussion on how students might collect primary and secondary data to research a potential pet grooming service in the community.

- Discuss food preferences by geographic region of the United States.

- Ask students what type of businesses might segment goods or services using religion as a key segmentation criterion.

- Ask students how they would market dating services such as eHarmony.com.

- Lead a discussion of why fast food restaurants and medical offices would likely be treated as two distinct segments by furniture manufacturers.

- Ask students how the recent recession altered their shopping habits.

LECTURE ENHANCERS

- Can you think of a company that serves customers' needs particularly well?

- Which of these steps seems to be the most important? Why?

- Can you envision how marketing might further evolve in the 21st century?

- Can you think of an example where a firm created a need for its product?

- Which of these strategies seems to be the most crucial? What might happen if a firm were to ignore one of these strategies?

- Which type of data do you think is more reliable? Why?

- What are some potential problems with data obtained through a focus group?

- Provide some examples of typical methods used to mine data from consumers.

- Name some market segments that have newly emerged within the past 10 years.

- What are the advantages and disadvantages of each method of segmentation?

- Provide a specific example of a psychographic segment.

- What methods might companies use to obtain information about customer purchasing habits?

- Can you think of a situation in which a consumer might skip one or more of these steps? Why?

- Provide examples of how modern banking uses relationship marketing to gain customers.

- Provide examples of ways in which frequent customers are rewarded by different businesses.

Learning Objectives

1 Explain **product strategy.**

2 Describe **the four stages of the product life cycle.**

3 Discuss **product identification.**

4 Outline **the major components of an effective distribution strategy.**

5 Explain **wholesaling**

6 Describe **retailing.**

7 Identify **distribution channel decisions and logistics.**

Key Terms

product	brand equity
product line	distribution
product mix	distribution channels
product life cycle	physical distribution
test marketing	wholesaler
brand	retailer
brand name	supply chain
trademark	logistics

PROJECTS AND TEAMWORK APPLICATIONS

1. On your own or with a classmate, choose one of the following goods or services. Decide whether you want to market it as a consumer product or a business product. Now create a brand name and marketing strategy for your product.
   a. lawnmower repair service
   b. health foods store
   c. soft drink
   d. English-language class
   e. accounting firm

2. Choose one of the following products that is either in the maturity or decline stage of its life cycle (or select one of your own), and develop a marketing strategy for extending its life cycle.
   a. popcorn
   b. fast food restaurant chain
   c. newspaper
   d. music CDs
   e. paper stationery or notecards

3. Where do you do most of your shopping—in stores or online? Choose your favorite retailer and analyze why you like it. Outline your reasons for shopping there; then add two or three suggestions for improvement.

4. Choose one of the following products and select a distribution intensity for the product. Describe specifically where and how your product would be sold. Then describe the reasons for your strategy.
   a. line of furniture manufactured from recycled or reclaimed materials
   b. custom-designed jewelry
   c. house painting service
   d. handicraft supplies
   e. talk radio show

WEB ASSIGNMENTS

1. **Product classification.** Visit the Web site of Johnson & Johnson (**http://www.jnj.com**) and click on "Our Products." Review the material in the chapter on product classification and then classify Johnson & Johnson's vast array of products.

2. **Shopping centers.** The Mall of America in Minnesota is the nation's largest shopping center. Go to the Mall's Web site (**http://www.mallofamerica.com**) to learn more about it. Make a list of five interesting facts you learned about the Mall of America.

3. **Railroad statistics.** Visit the Web site of the American Association of Railroads (**http://www.aar.org**). Click on "Statistics and Publication" and then "Railroad Statistics." Review the material and answer the following questions:
   a. What is a so-called Class I railroad? How many are there?
   b. How many workers do these railroads employ?

c. How much freight did Class I railroads carry during the most recent year for which data are available?

Note: Internet Web addresses change frequently. If you don't find the exact sites listed, you may need to access the organization's home page and search from there or use a search engine.

CLASS ACTIVITIES

- Ask students what product attributes an apple orchard might emphasize in marketing the apples to a pie-filling processor.

- Ask students what ideas they might have for a hotel cleaning service company to market their intangible service.

- Ask students to identify examples of products that are in each stage of the product life cycle.

- Lead a discussion of the ways in which M&M candies has increased customers' frequency of use.

- Ask students which trademarks they think are most recognizable.

- Lead a discussion regarding which store brand products are equal to or better than their brand-name counterparts.

- Survey students for the labels they read most carefully and the reasons why.

- Discuss the compensation methods for real estate and stock brokers with the class.

- Ask students how they would determine what types of items to sell if they owned their own convenience store. Lead a discussion with students to obtain their thoughts on the differences between the target markets of Panera Bread and Burger King.

- Ask students if they can think of products for which high prices increase consumer attraction.

- What retail stores seem always to be clustered together in strip malls, and why?

- Ask if students can think of any examples of store music being integral to a store's atmosphere.

- Survey students for other examples of products with an intensive distribution strategy.

- Ask students for examples of businesses with excellent and inferior customer service quality.

LECTURE ENHANCERS

- Discuss the pros and cons of marketing products versus services.

- Why might it be a good idea for marketers to include customer input in the development of new products? Think of a product introduced in recent years. How did it pass from introduction to growth cycle?

- In what stage of the product life cycle is a latte from Starbucks?

- When does a popular movie enter the decline stage? Why?

- What are some other possible factors that have increased the efficiency of new product development?

- What outside factors might affect the success or failure of a new product?

- Choose a popular product. What is the brand, brand name, and trademark of the product?

- Share an example of a brand name you have encountered that is not easy to pronounce. How does this affect the marketing of the good or service?

- Discuss which brands of tissues students typically purchase. What factors influence their choices?

- What names can you think of that have very high brand equity?

- How does global distribution affect a brand? Choose one of the channels and identify products that might be moved by this intermediary.

- How do intermediaries reduce the number of contacts needed to deliver goods?

- What are some of the challenges a retailer might face when participating in a buying group?

- As a customer, which type of retailing do you prefer? Why? Think of an Internet retailer with a particularly user-friendly Web site. What details make shopping on that Web site particularly convenient?

- Discuss a retailer that is particularly adept at shaping its customer service strategy.

Learning Objectives

1 **Discuss** integrated marketing communications (IMC).

2 **Describe** the different types of advertising.

3 **Outline** the tasks in personal selling.

4 **Name** and describe sales promotion activities.

5 **Discuss** publicity as a promotional tool.

6 **Discuss** pricing objectives and strategies.

Key Terms

promotion	missionary selling
price	telemarketing
integrated marketing communications (IMC)	sales promotion
	trade promotion
positioning	point-of-purchase (POP) advertising
pushing strategy	
pulling strategy	public relations
promotional mix	publicity
advertising	volume objective
product advertising	prestige pricing
product placement	everyday low pricing (EDLP)
institutional advertising	skimming pricing
cause advertising	penetration pricing
personal selling	cost-based pricing
order processing	breakeven analysis
creative selling	

PROJECTS AND TEAMWORK APPLICATIONS

1. Choose a product that you purchased recently. Identify the various media that were used to promote the product and analyze the promotional mix. Do you agree with the company's marketing strategy? Or would you recommend changes to the mix? Why? Create your own print ad for the product you chose, using any business strategies or knowledge you have learned in this course so far.

2. Evaluate the price of the product you selected in the preceding exercise. What appears to be the pricing strategy that its manufacturer used? Do you think the price is fair? Why or why not? Choose a different strategy and develop a new price for the product based on your strategy. Poll your classmates to learn whether they would purchase the product at the new price—and why.

3. Some schools have received financial benefits by allowing companies to promote their goods and services to students. Others have decided against this practice, and some states have laws banning this type of promotion. Find some examples of corporate sponsors in public elementary and high schools and colleges. With your class, discuss the pros and cons of promotion in public schools and on college campuses. In your view, is there a distinction between a public elementary or high school and a college campus? Why or why not?

4. On your own or with a classmate, research a recent situation that has caused a business, a not-for-profit organization, or a government agency to suffer from bad publicity. Evaluate the situation; then create a program outlining steps the organization might take to build better public relations.

5. You are the marketing manager for a company introducing a new line of video games. What approach would you take for establishing prices?

WEB ASSIGNMENTS

1. **Top advertisers.** *Advertising Age* compiles data annually on the top national advertisers. Visit the Web site listed here and access the most recent year. Answer the following questions:
   a. Who were the top ten advertisers in that year?
   b. How much did they spend on advertising?
   c. What was the most advertised brand that year?
   http://adage.com/datacenter/article?article_id=106348

2. **Online coupon fraud.** Go to the Web sites listed below to learn about online coupon fraud. Prepare a brief report. Make sure to answer the following questions: How big a problem is online coupon fraud? What are some changes marketers have made in an attempt to reduce online coupon fraud?
   http://www.newser.com/story/35962/hackers-spread-coupon-scam.html
   http://online.wsj.com/article/SB10001424052748703862704575099971939458554.html

http://multichannelmerchant.com/retail/news
/0308-curtailing-online-coupon-fraud/

3. **Yield management.** Assume you're interested in flying between Baltimore and Chicago. Visit some travel sites. Search for fares, varying such factors as advance purchase, day, time of departure, and so forth. What did this exercise teach you about yield management?
http://www.expedia.com
http://www.kayak.com
http://www.travelocity.com

Note: Internet Web addresses change frequently. If you don't find the exact sites listed, you may need to access the organization's home page and search from there or use a search engine.

CLASS ACTIVITIES

- Lead a discussion to obtain student ideas of the personality traits and skills needed for a person to excel in personal selling.

- In viewing pharmaceutical television product ads, do students perceive the information provided regarding benefits and risks of the medicine as fair or biased?

- Ask students for their ideas on how a local CPA firm might attract more summer business.

- Lead a discussion regarding which comparative advertising campaigns have been most memorable with students.

- Ask students which television ads they think have been most effective during the Super Bowl.

- Discuss goods or services in the local community for which outdoor advertising might be most effective.

- Discuss what types of companies might sponsor a golf tournament and why.

- Ask students how a salesperson might follow up after selling a car to a customer.

- Discuss ways in which a company can lower the breakeven point.

LECTURE ENHANCERS

- What challenges do companies face in trying to reach consumers?

- How do you prefer that advertisers reach you? TV? Online? Other?

- Choose a marketing component and think of a product that has been marketed through this strategy.

- Does the number of marketing messages received on a daily basis surprise you? Why or why not? As a consumer, are you conscious of this bombardment of marketing messages?

- For each category, think of a good or service that uses that method of advertising and discuss why.

- Discuss the qualities that set TV ads apart from other media.

- What are the most common drawbacks to Internet ads, particularly pop-ups?

- What are some possible threats to the continued effectiveness of magazine sales?

- Discuss how accurate direct-mail profiles may be. Have you ever received direct mail that drastically differed from your interests?

- Discuss some additional drawbacks to outdoor advertising.

- Which is the most commonly used form of consumer-oriented promotion?

- What are some possible drawbacks or risks involved with relying on samples as a product's primary method of promotion?

- Have you ever encountered a promotional item that seemed to be inconsistent with the image of the advertiser?

- Think of some goods or services that may benefit significantly from telemarketing.

- Which step in the sales process do you feel is the most crucial? Why?

- Which of these two strategies—push or pull—do you believe is the most powerful? Why?

- When should a company cut the price of a new product?

- Can you think of a specific example of a product whose size or amount has been reduced in an effort to maintain a steady price?

- Share a recent example of how consumers have benefited from a price war.

- Provide an example of cost-based pricing for a fast food cheeseburger.

- Consider a lemonade stand. What are the fixed and variable costs?

- Can you think of a recent product that used skimming pricing?

- Identify retailers that use EDLP and those that primarily use discount pricing. What are some differences within the retail shopping environment of each?

Learning Objectives

1 **Distinguish** between data and information, and discuss information systems.

2 **List** the components and types of information systems.

3 **Discuss** computer hardware and software.

4 **Describe** computer networks.

5 **Discuss** the security and ethical issues affecting information systems.

6 **Explain** disaster recovery and backup.

7 **Review** information systems trends.

Key Terms

data	server
information	software
information system	local area network (LAN)
chief information officer (CIO)	wide area network (WAN)
computer-based information system	WiFi
	intranet
database	firewall
operational support system	virtual private network (VPN)
transaction processing system	VoIP
process control system	malware
management support system	virus
	worm
management information system (MIS)	botnet
decision support system (DSS)	Trojan horse
	spyware
executive support system (ESS)	application service provider (ASP)
expert system	on-demand computing
hardware	cloud computing

PROJECTS AND TEAMWORK APPLICATIONS

1. Suppose you've been hired to design an information system for a midsize retailer. Describe what that information system might look like, including the necessary components. Would the system be an operational support system, a management support system, or both?

2. Select a local company and contact the person in charge of its information system for a brief interview. Ask that individual to outline his or her company's information system. Also, ask the person what he or she likes most about the job. Did this interview make you more or less interested in a career in information systems?

3. Working with a partner, research the current status of Wi-Max. Prepare a short report on its growth, its current uses, and its future for business computing.

4. Your supervisor has asked your advice. She isn't sure the company's information system needs any elaborate safeguards because the company has little Web presence beyond a simple home page. However, employees use e-mail extensively to contact suppliers and customers. Make a list of the threats to which the company's information system is vulnerable. What types of safeguards would you suggest?

5. Has your computer ever been hacked or attacked by a virus? What steps did you take to recover lost files and data? How would you prevent something similar from happening again?

WEB ASSIGNMENTS

1. **Enterprise resource planning (ERP).** SAP is one of the world's largest enterprise resource planning software companies. Go to the firm's Web site (http://www.sap.com) and click on "Customer Testimonials." Choose one of the customers listed and read its testimonial. Prepare a brief summary and explain how this exercise improved your understanding of the business applications of ERP software.

2. **Computer security.** Visit the Web site listed below. Review the material and answer the following questions:
   a. What are two current malware threats? How serious are they?
   b. What is a potentially unwanted program (PUP)? What are two recent PUPs?
   http://www.mcafee.com/us/threat center/default.asp

3. **Cloud computing.** IBM is one of the largest providers of cloud computing. Visit the IBM Web site (http://www.ibm.com) and click on "solutions" and then "cloud computing." Print out the material and bring it to class to participate in a class discussion on the subject.

Note: Internet Web addresses change frequently. If you don't find the exact sites listed, you may need to access the organization's home page and search from there or use a search engine.

CLASS ACTIVITIES

- Survey students to see how many have smart phones; ask if any use the phone more for Internet access than to talk to someone.
- Ask students if they have ever received fraudulent e-mails asking for their bank account or Social Security number, often called "phishing."
- List some drawbacks to accessing the Internet via a WiFi hotspot.
- Discuss a recent film or television show that featured an act of e-crime. What were the effects of the crime for the firms or individuals involved? Why might an employee wish to produce inaccurate or misleading company information?
- Discuss if you have ever been the victim of equipment theft. What steps did you take to protect the information stored on the equipment, either before or after the theft?
- Have students discuss additional antivirus software programs with which they are familiar.

LECTURE ENHANCERS

- Think of a recent situation in which you needed to gather data on a subject. What method(s) did you use to do so?
- What process have you ever used to transform data you collected into useful information?

- What recent changes in the business environment might account for this change in a CIO's role?
- Can you think of an example of an information system that is not computer-based?
- Does the availability of so many different types of data surprise you? Why or why not?
- Identify an example of a company in which the operational support system is the most vital information system.
- Share an example of a company in which the management support system is the most vital information system.
- What specific details must a company take into consideration when deciding on hardware purchases?
- What are some drawbacks to using mainframe computer systems?
- Consider and discuss the advantages and disadvantages of each type of PC.
- What are some drawbacks to a wireless local network?
- Describe a situation in which a VPN would be particularly useful for two firms.
- Share examples of current VoIP providers.
- Discuss specific examples of viruses and malware and the possible effects these might have on a PC.
- Have you ever worked for a company that had policies regarding the use of its information system? If so, how did the policy affect your use of the system and its components?
- Does this recovery-backup statistic surprise you? Discuss what types of vital information might cause a business to go bankrupt if the information were lost.
- Discuss the advantages and disadvantages of virtual offices.
- Can you think of an example of an ASP?

Learning Objectives

1. **Discuss** the users of accounting information.

2. **Describe** accounting professionals.

3. **Identify** the foundation of the accounting system.

4. **Outline** the steps in the accounting cycle.

5. **Explain** financial statements.

6. **Discuss** financial ratio analysis.

7. **Describe** the role of budgeting.

8. **Outline** international accounting practices.

Key Terms

accounting	accounting equation
public accountant	double-entry bookkeeping
generally accepted accounting principles (GAAP)	balance sheet
	income statement
Financial Accounting Standards Board (FASB)	statement of owners' equity
	statement of cash flows
Foreign Corrupt Practices Act	accrual accounting
	budget
accounting cycle	International Accounting Standards Board (IASB)
asset	
liability	International Financial Reporting Standards (IFRS)
owners' equity	

PROJECTS AND TEAMWORK APPLICATIONS

1. Contact a local public accounting firm and set up an interview with one of the accountants. Ask the individual what his or her educational background is, what attracted the individual to the accounting profession, and what he or she does during a typical day. Prepare a brief report on your interview. Do you now want to learn more about the accounting profession? Are you more interested in possibly pursuing a career in accounting?

2. Suppose you work for a U.S. firm that has extensive European operations. You need to restate data from the various European currencies in U.S. dollars in order to prepare your firm's financial statements. Which financial statements and which components of these statements will be affected?

3. Identify two public companies operating in different industries. Collect at least three years' worth of financial statements for the firms. Calculate the financial ratios discussed in the chapter. Prepare an oral report summarizing your findings.

4. You've been appointed treasurer of a local not-for-profit organization. You would like to improve the quality of the organization's financial reporting to current and potential donors. Describe the kinds of financial statements you would like to see the organization's accountant prepare.

5. Adapting the format of Figure 15.7, prepare on a sheet of paper your personal cash budget for next month. Keep in mind the following suggestions as you prepare your budget:

   a. *Cash inflows.* Your sources of cash would include your payroll earnings, if any; gifts; scholarship monies; tax refunds; dividends and interest; and income from self-employment.

   b. *Cash outflows.* When estimating next month's cash outflows, include any of the following that may apply to your situation:

      i. Household expenses (rent or mortgage, utilities, maintenance, home furnishings, telephone/cell phone, cable TV, household supplies, groceries)

      ii. Education (tuition, fees, textbooks, supplies)

      iii. Work (lunches, clothing)

      iv. Clothing (purchases, cleaning, laundry)

      v. Automobile (auto payments, repairs) or other transportation (bus, train)

      vi. Gasoline expenses

      vii. Insurance premiums
      - Renters (or homeowners)
      - Auto
      - Health
      - Life

      viii. Taxes (income, Social Security, Medicare, real estate)

      ix. Savings and investments

      x. Entertainment/recreation (dining, movies, health club, vacation/travel)

      xi. Debt (credit cards, installment loans)

      xii. Miscellaneous (charitable contributions, child care, gifts, medical expenses)

   c. *Beginning cash balance.* This amount could be based on a minimum cash balance you keep in your checking account and should include only the cash available for your use; therefore, money such as that invested in retirement plans should not be included.

WEB ASSIGNMENTS

1. **International Accounting Standards Board (IASB).** The IASB is responsible for setting and modifying international accounting rules. Go to the IASB's Web site (http://www.iasb.org) and click on "about us." Print out the material and bring it to class to participate in a class discussion on the IASB.

2. **Certified management accountant (CMA).** As noted in the chapter, managerial accountants often seek CMA certification. Visit the Web site of the Institute of Management Accountants (http://www.imanet.org). Click on "CMA Certification" and then "Become a CMA." Once on the Become a CMA page, click on the subsection, "How to Get Started." What are the educational and experiential requirements for obtaining a CMA? How many exams does a CMA candidate have to pass? What do these exams cover?

3. **Financial reporting requirements.** This chapter discussed the financial reporting requirements of U.S, public companies. Public companies are those whose shares are traded on a stock exchange. Visit the Web site listed here. Type in the name of a public company and then click on "financials" to view the firm's current financial statements. Prepare a brief report comparing those statements to the ones shown in the chapter. http://www.google.com/finance

Note: Internet Web addresses change frequently. If you don't find the exact sites listed, you may need to access the organization's home page and search from there or use a search engine.

CLASS ACTIVITIES

- Ask students how accounting supports a company's investing activities.

- Discuss how students could pursue a career in cost accounting, including the types of courses they might take to acquire needed skills.

- Discuss what aspects of payroll accounting allowed this area to be outsourced earlier than most other accounting applications.

- Discuss Bernie Madoff's Ponzi scheme and the SEC whistle-blower's attempts to expose it, which were ignored.

- Which asset value do students think would be most difficult to accurately measure?

- Ask students if depreciation expense is a cash expense (reduction of cash).

- Which industries generally have the highest net income? Lowest?

- Why would a decline in inventory turnover ratio several years in a row raise concern?

- What types of companies might have very slow receivables turnover?

LECTURE ENHANCERS

- Why would accounting information be useful to a union in its negotiations?

- How might managers use accounting information to help control daily operations?

- What are some possible drawbacks to practicing open book management?

- What situation could result when an accounting firm also provides consulting services to a client?

- In what way might providing consulting services affect the auditing services of a public accounting firm?

- Compare and contrast the role of a management accountant with that of a public accountant.

- Why might financial information be particularly important to a not-for-profit as opposed to a for-profit firm?

- Are the GAAP standards sufficient? Why or why not?

- Why is it important that senior executives, and not simply a firm's accountants, verify this information themselves?

- Think about your everyday financial transactions. Can you record, classify, and summarize them?

- What are some additional examples of intangible assets?

- In what ways have computers simplified your tax preparation, filing, and paperwork?

- Why is it important that public companies release their statements frequently?

- What does the balance sheet show about the status of a firm? What does a balance sheet not tell about a firm?

- If the expenses of a company are increasing from year to year, what might that indicate?

- Provide examples of industries with low and high inventory turnover.

- Is a company with no debt leverage better than one with some leverage? Why or why not?

- What are some items that you could include in your personal budget?

- What problems do American accounting firms face doing business abroad?

Learning Objectives

① **Understand** the financial system.

② **List** the various types of securities.

③ **Discuss** financial markets.

④ **Understand** the stock markets.

⑤ **Evaluate** financial institutions.

⑥ **Explain** the role of the Federal Reserve System.

⑦ **Describe** the regulation of the financial system.

⑧ **Discuss** the global perspective of the financial system.

Key Terms

financial system	stock market (exchange)
securities	financial institution
common stock	Federal Deposit Insurance Corporation (FDIC)
financial market	
primary market	Federal Reserve System (Fed)
secondary market	insider trading

PROJECTS AND TEAMWORK APPLICATIONS

1. Collect current interest rates on the following types of bonds: U.S. Treasury bonds, AAA-rated municipal bonds, AAA-rated corporate bonds, and BBB-rated corporate bonds. Arrange the interest rates from lowest to highest. Explain the reasons for the ranking.

2. You've probably heard of U.S. savings bonds—you may even have received some bonds as a gift. What you may not know is that two different types of savings bonds exist. Do some research and compare and contrast the two types of savings bonds. What are their features? Their pros and cons? Assuming you were interested in buying savings bonds, which of the two do you find more attractive?

3. Working with a partner, assume you are considering buying shares of Lowe's or Home Depot. Describe how you would go about analyzing the two companies' stocks and deciding which, if either, you would buy.

4. Working in a small team, identify a large bank. Visit that bank's Web site and obtain its most recent financial statements. Compare the bank's financial statements to those of a nonfinancial company, such as a manufacturer or retailer. Report on your findings.

5 Assume you're investing money for retirement. Specify several investment criteria you believe are most important. Go to the MSN Money Web site (**http://moneycentral.msn.com**). Click "Fund Research" (under "Investing"), then choose either "Find top performers by category" or "Find using Easy Screener." Identify at least three mutual funds that most closely meet your criteria. Choose one of the funds and research it. Answer the following questions:

   a. What was the fund's average annual return for the past five years?

   b. How well did the fund perform relative to its peer group and relative to an index such as the Standard & Poor's 500?

   c. What are the fund's ten largest holdings?

WEB ASSIGNMENTS

1. **Online stock trading.** Visit the Web site of a brokerage firm that offers online trading, such as E*Trade (**www.etrade.com**) or Charles Schwab (**www.schwab.com**), to learn more about online trading. Most electronic brokerage firms also offer a trading demonstration. Use the demonstration to see how to obtain price information, company news, place buy or sell orders, and check account balances. Make some notes about your experience and bring them to class to participate in a class discussion.

2. **Banking statistics.** Visit the Web site listed here. Access the most recent year you can find and answer the following questions:

   a. How many commercial banks were in operation at the end of the year? How many savings banks (institutions) were in operation?

   b. What were the total assets of commercial banks and savings banks at the end of the year?

   c. How many commercial banks had assets in excess of $5 billion at the end of the year? How many commercial banks had assets of less than $500 million at the end of the year? **http://www2.fdic.gov/sdi/sob/**

3. **Federal Reserve System.** Go to the Web site of the Board of Governors of the Federal Reserve System (**www.federalreserve.gov**). Prepare a short report on the seven-member board.

Who are the current members? What are their backgrounds? When were they appointed? When do their terms expire?

Note: Internet Web addresses change frequently. If you don't find the exact sites listed, you may need to access the organization's home page and search from there or use a search engine.

CLASS ACTIVITIES

- Ask students why it is difficult for them to save money as compared to older people.

- Review the academic courses that an investment banker might take.

- Discuss with students the differences between institutional investors and individual investors.

- Ask students why an individual might invest in a mutual fund rather than investing his or her own money in individually selected stocks.

- Ask students to discuss how an event such as FDA approval or rejection of a new drug to treat cancer might affect the stock price of a company when the news is disclosed to the media.

- Ask students to provide examples of inside information that would be considered inappropriate to share within a company.

LECTURE ENHANCERS

- How are savers served by the components of the financial system? How do users benefit?

- What expenses typically decrease as you get older? Which ones might rise?

- What type of person would be more likely to invest in low-risk securities?

- Compare the risks and features of each type of bond. Why would a firm choose a certain type as an investment?

- Do you think unsecured bonds would pay higher or lower interest? Why?

- What are the advantages and disadvantages of a mutual fund to an investor?

- How do higher interest rates affect consumer spending?

- Did the Fed need to inject capital into the financial system during the recent economic crisis?

- How might a fast-growing company need and use more money than a slower-growing company?

- In a corporate bankruptcy, would you rather hold preferred stock or common stock? Why?

- Do you think investment banking would be an interesting career opportunity?

- How might you find a broker if you wanted to begin investing?

- Which type of institution has the largest assets? The second largest?

- What would make your finances more attractive to a lender?

- Does having a debit card increase the likelihood that you will spend more?

- What types of insurance premiums do you pay each year?

Learning Objectives

1 **Define** the role of the financial manager.

2 **Describe** financial planning.

3 **Outline** how organizations manage their assets.

4 **Discuss** the sources of funds and capital structure.

5 **Identify** short-term funding options.

6 **Discuss** sources of long-term financing.

7 **Describe** mergers, acquisitions, buyouts, and divestitures.

Key Terms

finance	capital structure
financial manager	leverage
risk-return trade-off	leveraged buyout (LBO)
financial plan	divestiture

PROJECTS AND TEAMWORK APPLICATIONS

1. Assume you are about to start a business. Put together a rough financial plan that addresses the three financial planning questions listed in the textbook.

2. Working with a partner, assume that a firm needs $10 million in additional long-term capital. It currently has no debt and $40 million in equity. The options are issuing a ten-year bond (with an interest rate of 7 percent) or selling $10 million in new equity. You expect next year's earnings before interest and taxes to be $5 million. (The firm's tax rate is 35 percent.) Prepare a memo outlining the advantages and disadvantages of debt and equity financing. Using the numbers provided, prepare a numerical illustration of leverage similar to the one shown in Figure 17.2.

3. Working in a small team, select three publicly traded companies. Visit each firm's Web site. Most have a section devoted to information for investors. Review each firm's dividend policy. Does the company pay dividends? If so, when did it begin paying dividends? Have dividends increased each year? Or have they fluctuated from year to year? Is the company currently repurchasing shares? Has it done so in the past? Prepare a report summarizing your findings.

4. As noted in the chapter, one of the most unfortunate mergers in corporate history involved Time Warner and America Online. Research this merger. Why did analysts expect it to be successful? Why did it fail? What has happened to AOL since then?

WEB ASSIGNMENTS

1. **Jobs in financial management.** Visit the Web site listed here to explore careers in finance. How many people currently work as financial managers? What is the projected increase in employment over the next 10 to 20 years? What is the average level of compensation?
http://www.bls.gov/oco/ocos010.htm

2. **Capital structure.** Go to the Web site listed here to access recent financial statements for the retailer Costco Wholesale Corporation. Click on "balance sheet." What is the firm's current capital structure (the breakdown between debt and equity)? Has it changed significantly over the past five years? Why would a firm such as Costco choose to become more or less levered?
http://moneycentral.msn.com/investor/invsub/results/statemnt.aspx?symbol=cost

3. **Mergers and acquisitions.** Using a news source like Google News (http://news.google.com) or Yahoo! News (http://news.yahoo.com), search for a recent merger or acquisition announcement. An example would be the joint acquisition of H. J. Heinz by Berkshire Hathaway and an investment fund. (A link is shown here.) Print out the articles and bring them to class.
http://news.heinz.com/press-release/finance/berkshire-hathaway-and-3g-capital-complete-acquisition-hj-heinz-company

Note: Internet Web addresses change frequently. If you don't find the exact sites listed, you may need to access the organization's home page and search from there or use a search engine.

CLASS ACTIVITIES

● Discuss with students which position—treasurer, vice president for planning, or controller—might best lead to becoming a chief financial officer.

- Discuss why a skilled financial manager needs to not only have strong skills in accounting and finance, but also a keen understanding of the other business functions.

- Ask students what actions a company might take to speed up collections and reduce accounts receivable.

- Discuss the impact of style changes, spoilage, and obsolescence on inventory values.

- Ask students why large companies might be more likely to obtain favorable trade credit as compared to smaller companies.

- Lead a class discussion on the risks in lending to a ski manufacturer.

LECTURE ENHANCERS

- How does finance differ from accounting?

- If you were asked to invest by lending money to a friend for his or her business, would you do so? If so, what interest rate would you charge and why?

- Why does having strong skills in software like Excel strengthen your chances of obtaining an accounting or finance position?

- If accounts receivable are increasing over time, is this a positive or negative indication for a business?

- Can a change in exchange rates ever benefit a company?

- Which type of funds (debt or equity) offers a firm a more flexible pay arrangement? Which offers more control?

- Provide an example of a company that recently failed because of excessive leverage.

- Why do you think older investors prefer stock in companies that provide dividend payments?

- Why would trade credit be limited to the amount of goods or services a company purchases?

- What are the risks of private equity funds?

- Give an example of a recent merger and discuss the potential benefits to both companies.

- Can you provide an example of a recent divestiture that resulted from an unsuccessful acquisition?